Instructor's Resource Manual

Instructor's Resource Manual
to accompany RONALD J. COMER'S

Abnormal Psychology
EIGHTH EDITION

Karen Clay Rhines
Northampton Community College

with additional materials by
Ronald J. Comer
Princeton University

Ann Brandt-Williams
Glendale Community College

Nicolas Greco
College of Lake County

WORTH PUBLISHERS

Instructor's Resource Manual
by Karen Clay Rhines
to accompany
Abnormal Psychology, Eighth Edition

ISBN 13: 978-1-4641-1065-8
ISBN 10: 1-4641-1065-4

First Printing 2012

Worth Publishers

41 Madison Avenue

New York, NY 10010

www.worthpublishers.com

Contents

Preface

This manual is intended to be a resource for instructors to either develop an abnormal psychology course or improve an existing course. Each chapter of this manual includes the following sections:

Topic Overview: An outline of the chapter is provided for instructors as a quick reference to the material covered in the text.

Lecture Outline: A detailed lecture outline of the chapter is provided for instructors to use in part or in whole when preparing class lectures.

Learning Objectives: To enable instructors to coordinate lectures with the text, a list of the chapter's learning objectives is provided. These might be shared with students at the beginning of each chapter or prior to exams. Learning objectives also are posted on the *Abnormal Psychology* companion web site.

Key Terms: The key terms from the chapter, most of which are either in bold or in italics, are provided.

Media Resources: Several interactive and media-related activities are included for instructor use. Among these are:

Abnormal Psychology Student Tool Kit Produced and edited by Ronald J. Comer, Princeton University and Gregory Comer, Princeton Academic Resources. Tied directly to the CyberStudy sections in the text, this Student Tool Kit offers 57 intriguing Video Cases running three to seven minutes each. The Video Cases focus on persons affected by disorders discussed in the text. Students first view the video and then answer a series of thought-provoking questions. Additionally, the Student Tool Kit contains multiple-choice practice test questions with built-in instructional feedback for every option.

Abnormal Psychology Web-based Case Studies by Elaine Cassel, Marymount University; Danae Hudson, Missouri State University; and Brook Whisenhunt, Missouri State University. Found on the com-

panion Web site, these studies provide sixteen cases which describe the individual's history and symptoms. Each case is accompanied by a set of guided questions which points to the precise DSM-IV-TR criteria for each disorder and allows the student to both identify the disorder and suggest a course of treatment. Students can be assigned the appropriate case study and questions as homework or for class discussion.

Overhead Transparencies: You can download and print as transparencies any of the images (figures, tables, or photographs) from this text. The companion Web site for this textbook (http://www.worth publishers.com/comer) contains the images as high-resolution JPEGs (ideal for printing) and as PowerPoint slides (ideal for projecting or displaying on screen).

DSM-IV-TR Masters: DSM-IV-TR masters from Appendix B are referenced for each of the specific disorders covered in the chapter.

Internet Sites: Relevant Internet sites from the comprehensive listing in Appendix A are referenced in each chapter.

Mainstream Films: A brief synopsis of mainstream and current films relevant to chapter topics is included. Instructors may choose to screen sections of the film in class or to assign the film to be viewed outside of class or for extra credit. (Please note that some of the films suggested may have graphic sexual or violent content due to the nature of certain subject matters.)

Comer Video Segments: Available as a supplement, this revised set of video disks contains short clips depicting various topics related to abnormal psychology. The accompanying Video Guide links specific clips to general topics and specific textbook material.

Recommendations for Purchase or Rental: The Comer Video Segments include excerpts from many superb clinical documentaries. While the segments alone are ideal for use in lectures, it is often useful to assign the entire documentary for special class screenings or library use by students. A list of videos and other media available for purchase or rental, and appropriate for use in class or for assignment outside of class, is provided.

Class Demonstrations and Activities: Numerous demonstrations and activities that might prove useful in communicating the chapter's content to students are provided. These are intended to encourage students to interact with the material, to help them think critically about the topic being presented, and to pique their interest in the facts relevant to the activity.

Suggested Topics for Discussion: Several topics and suggestions to stimulate appropriate and relevant class discussion are provided. These suggestions are designed to spur student thought about, and discussion of, class material and to be easily integrated into lecture material.

Assignments/Extra Credit Suggestions: Several out-of-class activities or written assignments specifically related to chapter material are included as homework or extra credit options. They are intended to supplement in-class learning of chapter material.

Also included in this manual are several appendices to further enhance classroom preparation and presentation:

Appendix A: **Internet sites** Relevant, active Internet sites have been amassed and presented according to general topic in this appendix. Sites relevant to specific chapters are also referenced here.

Appendix B: **DSM-IV-TR Masters** The DSM-IV-TR criteria for each disorder discussed in the textbook (as well as many not discussed in the text) are presented here.

Appendix C: **Crossword Puzzles** Suitable for photocopying and distributing to students, these crossword puzzles have been created with content related to each chapter. These crossword puzzles are also available on the Web at: www.worthpublishers.com/comer.

Appendix D: **Word Searches** Suitable for photocopying and distributing to students, these word searches have been created with content related to each chapter.

Appendix E: **Video Faculty Guide** Written by Ronald J. Comer, this guide accompanies *Video Segments for Abnormal Psychology*, Third Edition. The guide is organized by topic and offers detailed information on each segment in the series.

Supplements

The following ancillaries may be obtained by contacting your sales representative:

Clinical Video Case File for Abnormal Psychology and **Accompanying Video Guide** edited by Ronald J. Comer, Princeton University. Featuring contemporary, authentic patient interviews and therapy sessions, this video provides students with a tangible and critical window into the world of abnormal psychology and the people who suffer from the disorders.

Video Segments for Abnormal Psychology and **Accompanying Video Guide** edited by Ronald J. Comer, Princeton University. Designed to bring an added dimension to lectures, this completely revised set of three videotapes contains more than 100 one- to eight-minute clips that depict disorders, show historical footage, and illustrate clinical topics, pathologies, treatments, laboratory experiments, and clinical dilemmas. The accompanying Video Guide links clips to general topics and specific textbook material. Availale in DVD and CD-ROM.

Test Bank by John H. Hull, Bethany College, and Debra B. Hull, Wheeling Jesuit University. This test bank offers more than 2,500 multiple-choice, fill-in-the-blank, and essay questions. Each question is rated by difficulty, identified as factual or applied, and keyed to the topic and page in the text where the source information appears. The electronic version on a dual platform CD-ROM allows you to add, edit, and resequence questions. The CD is also the access point for online testing. With Diploma from WIMBA, instructors can create and administer secure exams over a network and over the Internet. The program allows you to restrict tests to specific computers or time blocks, and includes an impressive suite of gradebook and result-analysis features.

Student Workbook by Ronald J. Comer, Princeton University. The Student Workbook actively involves students in the text material, using a variety of engaging exercises. Students who complete the exercises can better organize and apply what they have studied.

Case Studies in Abnormal Psychology by Ethan E. Gorenstein and Ronald J. Comer. This casebook provides 17 case histories based on the authors' clinical experiences. Rich in detail and integrated in approach, each case goes beyond DSM-IV-TR diagnosis to describe patient symptoms and history, the formulation and implementation of a treatment plan, and the results. In a unique feature, each case also includes the perspective of a relative or friend. Three additional cases without diagnoses or treatment plans provide opportunities for students to identify disorders and suggest appropriate therapies.

The Scientific American Reader Drawn from *Scientific American*, this collection of classic and cutting-edge articles enhances coverage of important topics within the textbook. Keyed to specific chapters, the selections have been hand-picked by Ron Comer, who provides a preview and discussion questions for each article.

Abnormal Psychology Web Companion

http://www.worthpublishers.com/comer

This Web site offers an ever-expanding set of resources for both students and instructors. Features include flashcards for learning key vocabulary, multiple-choice practice tests for every chapter with built-in instructional feedback, Web links, research exercises and crossword puzzles. The Web site is also the access point for online quizzing. Instructors can easily and securely quiz students online using prewritten, multiple-choice questions for each text chapter (not from the test bank). Students receive instant feedback and can take the quizzes many times. Instructors can review results by quiz, student, or even question, and can get weekly results via e-mail.

REVISED! Comprehensive PowerPoint Presentation Slides by Karen Clay Rhines, Northampton Community College. Closely following each chapter of *Abnormal Psychology*, Eighth Edition, these customized slides focus on key text terms and themes, reflect the main points in significant detail, and feature tables, graphs, and figures. Each set of chapter slides is accompanied by supplemental student handouts. These handouts were created using the instructor slides as a base, with key points replaced as "fill-in" items. Answer keys and suggestions for use are also provided.

General Class Demonstrations and Activities

The following activities can be used either in class or as homework assignments. All require direct student participation, and most are short enough to be incorporated in lectures.

The activities are based on the following assumptions:

1. Few students have read the material prior to class or to the particular discussion. That is, most students will have little or no exposure to the material being discussed.

2. Most students will have an opinion about the topic, even given the first assumption.

3. Abnormal psychology is an ongoing science. There are few facts or absolute truths, and it is essential that professionals and students in the field be able to think critically about information (i.e., to distinguish opinion from evidence). Mastery of the process of the scientific method is essential.

You will notice several recurrent ideas among these activities. General suggestions for implementing these activities are described in detail below.

Critical Thinking

Instructors often report difficulty in teaching critical thinking skills. One model relies on five questions as a base, and students may benefit from a brief discussion of these ideas:

1. What am I being asked to accept?

2. What evidence is available to support the assertion?

3. Are there alternative ways of interpreting the evidence?

4. What additional evidence would help to evaluate the alternatives?

5. What conclusions are most reasonable?

Students can be challenged to use these skills with examples from everyday media (e.g., Will using certain personal hygiene products make a boring person more interesting?) and from topics specific to the course material (e.g., How do we know what happened in prehistoric cultures? Are there alternative explanations for the "trephination" holes seen in skulls?). These questions can be brought up during lecture as a reminder to students to think critically.

Open (Class) Discussion

Many instructors desire to have occasional or even frequent discussion during classes. Discussion gives students the opportunity to interact with the material, which promotes learning, and to clarify problems, questions, or misunderstandings. However, generating discussions can be difficult. The following suggestions are ideas for encouraging students to participate in class discussions.

1. Establish discussion as a norm. If you want discussion throughout the semester, you *must* establish it from the very first class. Thus, it is important to get a discussion going the first class. It does not have to be lengthy or detailed, but there should be some discussion.

2. Your role in class ("sage on the stage" or "guide on the side") will depend on your teaching philosophy. Be careful to establish it early and be consistent. It may be useful to initiate a discus-

sion activity about halfway into the class period, rather than to start with one.

3. Establish rules for discussion. The SOLER rules are a useful start for all interpersonal communications.
    a. S: Sit up straight and square to the other person.
    b. O: Sit openly; don't cross your arms or scowl.
    c. L: Lean in when speaking or being spoken to.
    d. E: Establish eye contact with the other person.
    e. R: Relax (smile, nod).
    f. Speak to each other respectfully; be aware of your tone and volume.
    g. Be aware of body language (e.g., grimaces, rolling eyes).
    h. Expect disagreement; listen to other people's ideas before forming an opinion.

4. In the first class of the semester, choose an example that cannot fail to create opinions and discussion.

    Example 1: It is likely that, before the first class, there will be a nationally publicized incident or example of mental illness (e.g., a murder by a mentally ill person or a celebrity's suicide or overdose). Ask students for some popular explanations, whether implicit or explicit, of what happened.

    Example 2: Describe a famous but perhaps unknown (to your students) example of the behavior of a mentally ill person (e.g., Charles Manson or John Hinckley). Ask students for ideas about the causes of such behavior.

Be careful when using a highly controversial example, as some students may become upset or feel attacked about their opinion. Also, never use a recent local example, because there may be students who are personally involved in the issue.

Group Work

Some students are often reluctant to talk, even if they have something to say, whereas others won't stop talking. An extremely effective way to involve all students—setting a norm or expectation that they will participate in the class—is to divide them into smaller groups of six to eight and give them a task to accomplish in eight minutes or so. Dividing the class into smaller groups and giving instructions to accomplish a task (e.g., creating a list of questions to ask a suicidal person) can help both types of students. The loquacious tendency of the talkative student will be easier to

detect in a smaller group, and he or she will feel pressure to not dominate the conversation (although he or she may lead the discussion). The reserved student also will be more noticeable and will likewise feel pressure to contribute. The latter student may find it easier to speak up in a smaller group.

Some classes are fairly large, whereas others are fairly small. There may be anywhere from two to twenty divided groups in a class. If there are fewer groups, have them give a brief (e.g., two-minute) report to the class on their "findings." Have each group designate a spokesperson to discuss the group's findings with the class. This person usually misses some detail. When this happens, other group members may feel compelled to supplement the report, and the result is that all members of the group have an opportunity to speak up in the larger class. When there are a large number of groups, you may want them to produce a half-page report to be handed in immediately or at the end of the period.

Do not allow group members to adopt their own position: Force them to defend or promote a position (randomly assign the position). Forcing a debate position is a good way to help students to think about both sides of an argument. As social psychologists have shown, allowing group members to adopt their already established position encourages defensiveness and inhibits one's capacity to listen to others' arguments. Moreover, allowing a group to "vote" on their position can lead to arguments.

This activity works well even if more than one group promotes the same position, as different groups of students will often come up with very different conclusions about the same position, or different arguments defending similar conclusions.

Brainstorming as the Start of Science: Don't Ask for Recitations of Fact

The class will review the findings uncovered by the scientific method. However, the scientific method always starts with an opinion or an idea (i.e., an hypothesis about the relationship between two variables or events). Students sometimes feel compelled to demonstrate that they know things. More commonly, students will be reluctant to talk if they are uncertain about the veracity of what they are saying. Encourage students to brainstorm to generate ideas. After generating ideas, the students will be more likely to attend to the presentation of research evaluating their opinions and ideas.

There are two elements of brainstorming: thinking and reporting. Essential thinking instruction is similar to psychoanalytic free-association instructions: Think freely, without editing your thoughts; no idea is bad.

The second aspect is sharing your thoughts with others and writing or recording the thoughts.

If students brainstorm, they frequently will stumble across ideas, theories, and sometimes facts about mental illness and psychopathology, as many of these concepts are fairly intuitive. For example, eating disorders are related to pressures to be thin; depression is related to activity level; not exposing oneself to feared objects or situations will maintain those fears, whereas confronting an object or situation will result, eventually, in a reduction of that fear.

"It's Debatable"

To help students understand the complexity of issues in the field of abnormal psychology, have students stage a debate on the suggested (or another) topic. Students should be assigned to one side of the argument and should conduct research outside of class to bolster their case. Faculty can stage "debate days" and present multiple issues (perhaps before each exam as a review of significant issues or toward the end of the semester as a summary lesson), or they can devote up to 30 minutes of class time for a single topic. Students should follow standard debate format:

- The debate will consist of 2 teams, affirmative and negative, of between 2 and 5 debaters each.
- Each debater will deliver a prepared constructive speech (no more than 5 minutes) and an extemporaneous rebuttal speech (no more than 3 minutes). [NOTE: If students are uncomfortable speaking in front of the class, faculty can choose to let them be researchers only and have other students present the arguments for the team.]
- There will be 5 minutes of joint preparation time for the teams between the constructive speeches and the rebuttals.
- After all the speeches are made, the remaining time can be allotted to the audience asking questions of the debaters.

Speaking Schedule:

#1 Affirmative Debater's Constructive Speech
#1 Negative Debater's Constructive Speech
#2 Affirmative Debater's Constructive Speech
#2 Negative Debater's Constructive Speech
CONTINUE ALTERNATING FOR EACH SET OF SPEAKERS

Brief preparation time

#1 Negative Debater's Rebuttal Speech
#1 Affirmative Debater's Rebuttal Speech
#2 Negative Debater's Rebuttal Speech
#2 Affirmative Debater's Rebuttal Speech

CONTINUE ALTERNATING FOR EACH SET OF SPEAKERS

Audience questions

Students should be prompted to prepare both constructive and rebuttal arguments by anticipating the opposing side's primary points. Students also should be cautioned against *ad hominem* attacks. Faculty can evaluate each student's debate performance and also can require students to submit written documentation of their arguments.

Panel Discussion

Have students volunteer (or assign them) to portray "characters" with differing perspectives on a relevant topic. Depending on the faculty member's goals, each student could be assigned to research his/her perspective or to speak extemporaneously. Students also can be required to submit a paper or an outline of "talking points" either in advance or following the presentation. Students in the audience can ask questions of the panelists.

"Pretend, for a Moment, That You Are a . . ."

Activities and discussions work best when students recognize their relevance to their own lives. Most students can easily imagine themselves in the following careers, jobs, or situations:

- A manager or supervisor of a group of people (e.g., a McDonald's manager or a director of a group of salespeople)
- A business owner (e.g., "Pretend you are the CEO of Impact Airlines")
- A grade school or high school teacher, principal, or counselor
- A close relative (e.g., a parent having difficulty with a child, a spouse having difficulty with a mate, or an adult having difficulty with an elderly parent)
- A doctor or nurse
- A mental health professional, such as a therapist or counselor (this is particularly useful after viewing some of the Comer videos; e.g., "Suppose you were this person's therapist")
- A friend
- A consultant to attorneys, the U.S. Congress, schools, etc. (e.g., "Thanks to this class, you are now an expert on the topic of depression. You and I are going to testify before Congress on funding for more biological research on the causes of depression.")

The Anonymous Five-Minute Essay

A useful tool for evaluating what students understand is the five-minute essay. Ask students to tear a sheet of paper from their notebook. Instruct them that they are not to put their name on the sheet. Give them a topic, then ask them to start writing. After five minutes, collect the papers either to share with the class or, more likely, to evaluate between classes.

1. Essays can emphasize points, such as "Explain why high school principals and counselors should be concerned about alcohol abuse among students."

2. Essays can permit students to ask questions that they are hesitant to bring up either in class or to you in person, such as "Take five minutes and write down what you'd like to know about the sexual disorders that we haven't yet discussed."

3. Essays can allow instructors and students to evaluate students' understanding of key issues, such as "In as much detail as possible, explain the cognitive theory of depression." There are two advantages to this particular essay: To evaluate understanding and to evaluate (and improve) students' capacity to answer essay questions on exams.

After this particular type of essay, you either can ask immediately for questions (e.g., "Okay, who needs the theory reexplained?") or review the sheets between classes to gauge students' understanding and to clear up misconceptions.

This particular essay exercise is an excellent way to develop students' capacity to answer essay questions that may appear on exams. Many students complain that they understand what they are trying to write or communicate, but that they don't communicate it well, especially under time pressure (as with exams). A specific suggestion is to tell students to take their essay home and grade it as if they were the instructor. If they find that their essay is poor—that is, that it does not accurately reflect their understanding—then they should rewrite it. Then, they should compare their first essay with their revised essay.

"Here's $25,000 to Be Awarded to . . ."

Most academics can relate to the grant-seeking process. Students can relate to competition for money or awards as well. Present the students with a problem (e.g., the stigma associated with seeking mental health treatment), then ask for ideas on how it might be solved. Tell them that the best idea will be awarded $25,000 for implementation, but that only one idea gets the award.

This exercise encourages creative and critical thinking. Creative ideas get attention, but they won't get funded unless they are also practical (able to be completed). This exercise is best done in group work.

"Let's Write a Self-Help Bestseller"

This activity is an effective way to encourage students to integrate and organize the information presented to them on a particular topic or disorder. There are hundreds of self-help books on the market, and all tend to follow a simple outline:

I. Description of a common problem

II. Source of the problem

III. Possible solutions

These three points correspond to the themes of abnormal psychology courses (description, cause, and treatment). Students can write an outline of a self-help book or a draft of a chapter on the problem description (e.g., "How might this problem be influencing your life?"). Alternatively, they can generate self-help interventions to overcome the problem. Students should be encouraged to be as accurate as possible, that is, to have their work correspond to the descriptions and interventions presented in the textbook and lectures. Expressing this information in their own words is an excellent way to encourage students to assimilate the facts. This activity is especially helpful during discussions of disorders.

"Write a Pamphlet"

This activity is an excellent way to help students conceptualize material and effectively present it to an audience. With the use of a software program like Microsoft Publisher or simply paper and markers, students can create a pamphlet (similar to what they'd expect to see in the waiting room of a hospital or clinic) on a specific topic. Students should be encouraged to be as accurate and up-to-date as possible and also to present all sides of the issue (e.g., alternate treatment approaches or theories). The reading level and audience for the pamphlet can be changed to suit the purpose of the assignment—parents of a child diagnosed with ADD, patients newly diagnosed with depression, clients seeking treatment for anxiety, etc. The pamphlet format gives a built-in page limit and forces students to be clear and concise in their writing.

Keep a Journal

In addition to helping students synthesize material, this activity is helpful in developing writing skills.

Have students keep a journal of their thoughts on course material through the semester. This can be done in the first or last five minutes of class or as an out-of-class assignment. Faculty generally should have students submit their journals for review on an on-going basis as students can have the tendency to delay writing until the end of the semester. Some suggestions for journal topics include: reactions to the case examples; strengths and weaknesses of prevailing theoretical explanations; hypothetical conversations with sufferers of specific disorders, etc.

Case Study Evaluations

To complement the Comer and Gorenstein supplemental case study text, case study evaluations have been created. The relevant case studies are referenced in each chapter of these Instructor's Resources and the evaluations can be found on the companion Web site at www.worthpublishers.com/Comer.

Crossword Puzzles and Word Searches

As an inventive way for students to emphasize key chapter vocabulary, both crossword puzzles and word searches have been created for each chapter of the textbook. Students may complete the searches as homework or for extra credit. Grouped in their entirety in Appendices C and D, the specific chapter-relevant puzzles and word searches are referenced in each chapter.

Study Habits

Students often come to instructors, especially after the first exam has been returned, wondering why their grades do not reflect their intense effort. Many times, of course, inquiry into their "intense" effort reveals obvious problems, such as not reading all of the chapters, reading the chapters the night before the exam, or not coming to class. Other times inquiry reveals that the student simply has poor study habits.

The following are recommendations that can be made to students, either individually or to the entire class, for improving study habits. Because studying is indeed a habit (a repetitive behavior that is over-learned to the point that active self-observation about performance is inhibited), these suggestions can be presented within the context of behavioral or cognitive models (see Chapter 3). These suggestions also are posted on the *Abnormal Psychology* companion Web site.

The Essentials of Good Study Habits

1. Set up a regular and practical schedule.
   - Study at a specific time at a specific place.
   - Don't try to study every day if that is impractical (which it usually is). Be wary of setting yourself up for failure.
   - Stick to your schedule, especially early in the semester. (Establish the habit.)
2. Find a place where you can concentrate.
3. Reward yourself for studying (operant conditioning).
   - Use specific rewards for specific achievements (e.g., after finishing the first half of a chapter, reward yourself with ice cream; after finishing reading the chapter, reward yourself with a CD).
   - Remember the Premack principle: David Premack demonstrated an extremely important principle of behaviorism. Activities that people enjoy are effective reinforcers for engaging in activities that people do not enjoy doing. In other words, rewards for studying do not have to be material. To use the principle to reinforce studying, students should write an extensive list of activities they enjoy doing. This list can be generated, according to Premack, by simply observing what they spend a lot of free time doing. The principle maintains that they should engage in a specific enjoyable activity only after they have completed a less enjoyable task. A simple example, to which most students can relate, is studying their least favorite subject first (e.g., physics) and their most favorite subject last (e.g., psychology).

   NOTE: It is important that students establish realistic and attainable goals for themselves and that they reward themselves after they achieve even the smallest goal. Rewarding themselves only after finishing a chapter will lead to infrequent rewards and, thus, an ineffective reinforcement schedule.

Improving Reading: The SQ3R Technique

SQ3R is a proven, five-step technique for improving the effectiveness of reading.

1. Survey: Preview the material. This is best done section by section (rather than an entire chapter).
2. Question: After you have a sense of what the reading will be about, ask yourself some questions about the topic.

3. Read: Read with an eye toward answering the questions you asked.

4. Recite: After finishing that particular section, recite to yourself, aloud, the answers to the questions, including supporting evidence based on research.

5. Review: After you have read the section, go back and review.

Test-Taking Strategies

1. It is a myth that one's initial hunch is likely to be correct. A research study of answer changes has shown that answer changes from wrong to correct are more common than answer changes from correct to wrong.

2. Use test time efficiently. First, preview the test and its various sections (e.g., the multiple-choice section, the short-answer section, the essay section). Anticipate how long each section will take to complete, especially the essay sections. During the test, keep track of the remaining time and where you are in the test. (Most instructors announce the remaining time at regular intervals.)

3. Don't spend too much time on a particular question if you are uncertain of the answer. It is better either to guess at the answer or to mark the question and come back to it. "Incubation" research has shown that spending extended time on a problem is less likely to generate the correct solution than leaving the problem (letting it incubate), then coming back to it.

4. Don't assume that questions are more difficult than they are. Most instructors are not trying to trick you. Most write a question with one best answer in mind.

5. Improving performance on multiple-choice questions can be achieved by following these strategies.

   a. Read the question, then try to anticipate the answer before reviewing the choices; if your answer is one of the choices, you are probably correct.

   b. Read the question completely. Be sure you understand it; reread it if necessary. Ask for clarification if you do not understand the question (if instructors didn't want you to do this, they wouldn't bother coming to class during testing time).

   c. Eliminate choices that you know are incorrect.

   d. Options that present broad, sweeping generalizations (e.g., "always" and "never") are usually incorrect.

   e. Options that are carefully qualified are often correct.

6. Improving performance on essay questions can only be accomplished if you know the answer. Improving performance when you definitely know the right answer depends on your ability to communicate your answer. This skill can be improved by practice.

7. Review the test if you have time.

Karen Clay Rhines
Northampton Community College

Abnormal Psychology: Past and Present

LECTURE OUTLINE

I. **WHAT IS ABNORMAL PSYCHOLOGY?**
   A. Abnormal psychology is the field devoted to the scientific study of abnormal behavior in an effort to describe, predict, explain, and change abnormal patterns of functioning
   B. Workers in the field may be clinical scientists (researchers who gather information systematically so that they may describe, predict, and explain the phenomena they study) or clinical practitioners (therapists whose role is to detect, assess, and treat abnormal patterns of functioning)

II. **WHAT IS PSYCHOLOGICAL ABNORMALITY?**
   A. Many definitions have been proposed, yet none has won total acceptance
   B. Most definitions have certain features in common:
      1. Called "The Four Ds," this definition provides a useful starting point, but it has key limitations
      2. The key features of the definition include:
         a. Deviance—Different, extreme, unusual, perhaps even bizarre
            (a) From behaviors, thoughts, and emotions considered normal in a specific place and time and by specific people
            (b) From social norms, which are stated and unstated rules for proper conduct in a given society or culture
            (c) Judgments of abnormality vary from society to society as norms grow from a particular culture
               (i) They also depend on specific circumstances
         b. Distress—Unpleasant and upsetting to the person
            (a) According to many clinical theorists, behavior, ideas, or emotions have to cause distress before they can be labeled abnormal; this is not always the case
         c. Dysfunction—Interfering with the person's ability to conduct daily activities in a constructive way
            (a) Abnormal behavior tends to be dysfunctional—it interferes with daily functioning
            (b) Here again culture plays a role in the definition of abnormality
            (c) The presence of dysfunction alone does not necessarily indicate psychological abnormality
         d. Danger—Posing risk of harm
            (a) Abnormal behavior may become dangerous to oneself or others
               (i) Behavior may be careless, hostile, or confused
            (b) Although often cited as a feature of psychological abnormality, research suggests that dangerousness is the exception rather than the rule
   C. The elusive nature of abnormality
      1. Ultimately, a society selects general criteria for defining abnormality and then uses those criteria to judge particular cases
      2. Thomas Szasz places such emphasis on society's role that he finds the whole concept of mental illness to be invalid, a myth of sorts
         a. Deviations in functioning called "abnormal" are described by Szasz as "problems of living"
         b. He argues that societies invent the concept of mental illness to better control or change people whose unusual patterns of functioning upset or threaten the social order
      3. Even if we assume that psychological abnormality is a valid concept and that it can indeed be defined, we may be unable to apply our definition consistently. For example:
         a. Diagnosis of alcohol problems in colleges—some drinking is okay even though it is technically illegal

          b.   Issue of abnormality versus eccentricity [see PsychWatch, p. 6]
    4.   In short, while we may agree to define psychological abnormalities as patterns of functioning that are deviant, distressful, dysfunctional, and sometimes dangerous, we should be clear that these criteria are often vague and subjective
    5.   Few of the current categories of abnormality are as clear-cut as they seem, and most continue to be debated by clinicians

III. WHAT IS TREATMENT?
  A.   Once clinicians decide that a person is suffering from some form of psychological abnormality, they seek to treat it
  B.   Treatment (or therapy) is a procedure designed to change abnormal behavior into more normal behavior
    1.   It, too, requires careful definition
    2.   According to Jerome Frank, all forms of therapy have three essential features:
        a.   A sufferer who seeks relief from the healer
        b.   A trained, socially accepted healer, whose expertise is accepted by the sufferer and his or her social group
        c.   A series of contacts between the healer and the sufferer, through which the healer . . . tries to produce certain changes in the sufferer's emotional state, attitudes, and behavior
  C.   Despite this straightforward definition, clinical treatment is surrounded by conflict and confusion:
    1.   There is a lack of agreement of goals or aims
        a.   There is a lack of agreement about successful outcome
        b.   There is a lack of agreement about failure
    2.   Are clinicians seeking to cure? To teach?
    3.   Are sufferers "patients" (implying illness) or "clients" (suggesting they have problems in living)?
  D.   Despite their differences, most clinicians agree that large numbers of people need therapy of one kind or another, and research indicates that therapy often is helpful

IV. HOW WAS ABNORMALITY VIEWED AND TREATED IN THE PAST?
  A.   In any given year in the United States, 30 percent of adults and 19 percent of children and adolescents display serious psychological disturbances and are in need of clinical treatment
    1.   Furthermore, most people have difficulty coping at various times in their lives
  B.   It is tempting to conclude that something about the modern world is responsible, but it is hardly the primary cause
    1.   Every society, past and present, has witnessed psychological abnormality and had its own form of treatment
    2.   Many present-day ideas and treatments have roots in the past
  C.   Ancient views and treatment
    1.   Most historians believe that prehistoric societies regarded abnormal behavior as the work of evil spirits
        a.   May have begun as far back as the Stone Age, a half-million years ago
    2.   The treatment for severe abnormality was to force demons from the body through trephination or exorcism
  D.   Greek and Roman views and treatments; 500 B.C. to 500 A.D.
    1.   Philosophers and physicians offered different explanations and treatments for abnormal behaviors
    2.   Hippocrates, the father of modern medicine, believed that abnormality had natural causes and resulted from internal physical problems
        a.   He looked to an unbalance of the four fluids, or humors—yellow bile, black bile, blood, and phlegm
        b.   His suggested treatments attempted to "rebalance" using warm baths, massage, and blood letting
  E.   Europe in the Middle Ages: Demonology returns; 500–1350 A.D.

1. With the decline of Rome, demonological views and practices became popular once again, and a growing distrust of science spread through Europe
2. Abnormality again was seen as a conflict between good and evil, with deviant behavior seen as evidence of Satan's influence
3. Abnormal behavior apparently increased greatly, and outbreaks of mass madness occurred
4. Some of the earlier treatments, like exorcism, reemerged
5. At the close of the Middle Ages, demonology and its methods again began to lose favor

F. The Renaissance and the rise of asylums; 1400–1700
   1. German physician Johann Weyer believed that the mind was susceptible to sickness, just like the body
      a. He is considered the founder of modern study of psychopathology
   2. The care of people with mental disorders continued to improve in this atmosphere
      a. Across Europe, religious shrines were devoted to the humane, and loving treatment of people with mental disorders, and one shrine at Gheel, became a community mental health program of sorts
   3. Unfortunately, this time also saw a rise of asylums—institutions whose primary purpose was care of the mentally ill
      a. The intention was good care, but with overcrowding they became virtual prisons

G. The nineteenth century: Reform and moral treatment
   1. As 1800 approached, treatment improved once again
   2. Pinel (France) and Tuke (England) advocated moral treatment—care that emphasized humane and respectful treatment
      a. In the United States, the moral treatment model was furthered by Benjamin Rush (father of American psychiatry) and Dorothea Dix (Boston schoolteacher)
   3. By the end of the nineteenth century, there was a reversal of the moral treatment movement due to several factors:
      a. Money and staff shortages
      b. Declining recovery rates
      c. Overcrowding
      d. Emergence of prejudice against people with mental disorders
   4. By the early years of the twentieth century, the moral treatment movement had ground to a halt; long-term hospitalization became the rule once again

H. The early twentieth century: Dual perspectives
   1. As the moral movement was declining in the late 1800s, two opposing perspectives emerged:
      a. The Somatogenic Perspective: Abnormal functioning has physical causes
      b. The Psychogenic Perspective: Abnormal functioning has psychological causes
   2. The early twentieth century: The somatogenic perspective
      a. Two factors responsible for re-emergence:
         (a) Emil Kraepelin's textbook (1883) argued that physical factors (such as fatigue) are responsible for mental dysfunction
         (b) New biological discoveries were made, such as the link between untreated syphilis and general paresis
      b. Despite the general optimism, biological approaches yielded mostly disappointing results throughout the first half of the twentieth century, when a number of effective medications were finally discovered
   3. The early twentieth century: The psychogenic perspective
      a. The rise in popularity of this model was based on work with hypnotism:
         (a) Friedrich Mesmer and hysterical disorders
         (b) Sigmund Freud, the father of psychoanalysis, who argued that largely unconscious processes are at the root of abnormal functioning
      b. Freud and his followers offered treatment primarily to patients who did not require hospitalization—now known as outpatient therapy
      c. By the early twentieth century, psychoanalytic theory and treatment were widely accepted

V. CURRENT TRENDS

A. It would hardly be accurate to say that we now live in a period of great enlightenment about or dependable treatment of mental disorders
   1. 43 percent of people interviewed believe that people bring mental health disorders on themselves
   2. 35 percent consider mental health disorders to be caused by sinful behavior
   3. Nevertheless, the past 50 years have brought major changes in the ways clinicians understand and treat abnormal functioning

B. How are people with severe disturbances cared for?
   1. In the 1950s, researchers discovered a number of new psychotropic medications:
      a. Antipsychotic drugs
      b. Antidepressant drugs
      c. Antianxiety drugs
   2. These discoveries led to deinstitutionalization and a rise in outpatient care
      a. This change in care was not without problems
   3. Outpatient care is now the primary mode of treatment
      a. When patients do need greater care, they usually are given short-term hospitalizations and then, ideally, outpatient psychotherapy and medication in community settings
      b. The approach has been helpful for many patients, but there are too few community programs available in the Unites States; only 40 to 60 percent of those with severe disturbances receive treatment of any kind

C. How are people with less severe disturbances treated?
   1. Since the 1950s, outpatient care has continued to be the preferred mode of treatment for those with moderate disturbances
   2. While once this type of care was exclusively private psychotherapy, now most health insurance plans cover it, and now it includes various settings as well as specialty care
   3. Surveys suggest that nearly one in six adults in the Unites States receives treatment for psychological disorders in the course of a year, the majority for fewer than five sessions
   4. Yet another change in outpatient care has been the development of programs devoted exclusively to one kind of psychological problem

D. A growing emphasis on preventing disorders and promoting mental health
   1. The community mental health approach has given rise to the prevention movement
   2. Many of today's programs are trying to:
      a. Correct the social conditions that underlie psychological problems
      b. Help individuals at risk for developing emotional problems
   3. Prevention programs have been further energized by the growing interest in positive psychology, the study and promotion of positive feelings, traits, and abilities

E. Multicultural Psychology
   1. In response to the growing diversity in the United States, this new area of study has emerged
      a. Multicultural psychologists seek to understand how culture, race, ethnicity, and gender affect behavior and thought and how people of different cultures, races, and genders may differ psychologically

F. The growing influence of insurance coverage
   1. Today the dominant form of insurance coverage for mental health care is the managed care program—a program in which the insurance company determines key care issues
   2. At least 75 percent of all privately insured persons in the United States are enrolled in managed care programs
   3. A key problem is that reimbursements for mental disorders tend to be lower than those for medical disorders
      a. In 2011, a federal parity law went into effect, directing insurance companies to provide equal coverage for mental and medical problems

G. What are today's leading theories and professions?
   1. One important development in the field of abnormal psychology is the growth of theoretical perspectives (orientations), including:

      a.   Psychoanalytic
      b.   Biological
      c.   Behavioral
      d.   Cognitive
      e.   Humanistic-existential
      f.   Sociocultural

2. At present, no single perspective dominates the clinical field
3. In addition to multiple perspectives, a variety of professionals now offer help to people with psychological problems [See Table 1-2; p. 20]
4. One final key development in the study and treatment of mental disorders is a growing appreciation for the need for effective research
   a. Clinical researchers have tried to determine which concepts best explain and predict abnormal behavior, which treatments are most effective, and what kinds of changes may be required

LEARNING OBJECTIVES

1. Discuss some of the difficulties of defining a person's behavior as abnormal.

2. Describe the different ways of defining abnormality from the perspectives of deviance, distress, dysfunction, and danger.

3. Discuss what is meant by the "elusive nature of abnormality".

4. Describe the ways that ancient peoples, Greeks, Romans, and persons in the age of the Renaissance viewed and treated abnormal behavior.

5. Describe moral treatment.

6. Describe the somatogenic and psychogenic perspectives of the early 1900s.

7. Describe the current treatment of severely disturbed individuals. Contrast this to the current treatment of less severely disturbed individuals.

8. Discuss the impact of deinstitutionalization on the care and treatment of the severely mentally ill.

9. Discuss the development and foci of (a) prevention programs and (b) positive psychology. How are they related to the community mental health approach?

10. What is multicultural psychology? How does it enhance the clinical practice?

11. Describe the influence of managed care programs on the treatment of psychological abnormality. What is parity?

12. Compare and contrast the current dominant theories in abnormal psychology.

13. Compare and contrast the professions that study and treat abnormal behavior.

KEY TERMS

abnormal psychology	danger	eccentricity
asylum	deinstitutionalization	exorcism
clinical practitioners	demonology	humors
clinical psychologists	deviance	hypnotism
clinical scientists	distress	managed care program
culture	dysfunction	moral treatment

multicultural psychology
norms
parity
positive psychology
prevention

private psychotherapy
psychiatrists
psychoanalysis
psychogenic perspective
psychotropic medications

somatogenic perspective
state hospitals
therapy
treatment
trephination

MEDIA RESOURCES

Abnormal Psychology Student Tool Kit

Produced and edited by Ronald J. Comer, Princeton University and Gregory Comer, Princeton Academic Resources. Tied directly to the CyberStudy sections in the text, this Student Tool Kit offers 57 intriguing Video Cases running 3 to 7 minutes each. The Video Cases focus on persons affected by disorders discussed in the text. Students first view the video and then answer a series of thought-provoking questions. Additionally, the Student Tool Kit contains multiple-choice practice test questions with built-in instructional feedback for every option.

Video Cases and Discussions:

- What did past hospital treatments for severe mental disorders look like?
- Observe the predecessors of modern electroconvulsive therapy.
- Are the early treatments behind us?

Practical, Research, and Decision-Making Exercises:

- Comparing today's treatments to those of the past
- Tracing abnormality through the arts

PowerPoint Slides

Available at the Instructor's site on the companion Web site are comprehensive PowerPoint slide presentations and supplemental student handouts for Chapter 1. The slide files reflect the main points of the chapter in significant detail. Student handouts were created using the instructor slides as a base, with key points replaced as "fill-in" items. Answer keys and suggestions for use also are provided.

Internet Sites

Please see Appendix A for full and comprehensive references.
   Sites relevant to Chapter 1 material are:

http://www3.niu.edu/acad/psych/Millis/History/2002/mainsheet.htm
Abnormal Psychology Time Machine—This site details various theories to explain psychological disturbances over time.

http://elvers.us/hop/welcome.asp
The History of Psychology Web site, provided as a "gateway for teachers and students to over 1,000 World Wide Web resources related to the history of psychology."

Mainstream Films

Films relevant to Chapter 1 material are listed and summarized below:

Key to Film Listings:
P = psychopathology focus
T = treatment focus
E = ethical issues raised

Please note that some of the films suggested may have graphic sexual or violent content due to the nature of certain subject matters.

An Angel at My Table
This 1990 film by Jane Campion recounts the autobiographical tale of New Zealand poet Janet Frame, who was misdiagnosed with schizophrenia and spent eight years in a psychiatric hospital. **P, T, E, serious film**

Bedlam
This release from 1946 (starring Boris Karloff) gives a glimpse into the history of psychiatric hospitals, set in 18th century London. **P, T, E, historical, serious film**

David and Lisa
This film, made in 1962, follows the developing relationship between two mentally disturbed teens in a psychiatric hospital. **P, T, serious film**

Fear Strikes Out
This film is a 1950s biopic about baseball player Jimmy Piersall, who suffers a mental breakdown and is treated with ECT. **P, T, E, serious film**

A Fine Madness
From 1966, this film stars a young Sean Connery as Samson Shillito, an eccentric poet who is hospitalized and undergoes a lobotomy. **P, T, E, serious film**

Frances
From 1982, a staggering biopic on Frances Farmer, which covers her alcoholism, institutionalization, and eventual lobotomy. **P, T, E, serious film**

Freud
This pseudo-biographical movie filmed in 1962 depicts five years, beginning in 1885, in the life of the Viennese psychologist Sigmund Freud (1856–1939). **P, T, E, historical, serious film**

Girl, Interrupted
Based on an autobiographical novel by Susanna Kaysen, this film details the experiences of several women as patients in a psychiatric hospital in the 1960s. The 1999 film challenges the diagnosis of mental illness and the relationship between diagnosis and social norm violations. **P, T, serious film**

Good Will Hunting
This Academy Award winning film from 1997 stars Matt Damon, Ben Affleck, and Robin Williams and addresses a somewhat unconventional therapy program for a gifted yet troubled young man. **T, E, serious film**

Inside/Out
From 1997, this Rob Tregenza film profiles life in a psychiatric hospital. **P, T, E, serious film**

King of Hearts
From 1966, this "must-see" film is about a Scottish soldier who discovers a town abandoned by everyone except the inmates of an insane asylum. **P, T, E, serious film**

The Madness of King George
From 1994, this film is based on the real episode of dementia experienced by George III [now suspected to be a victim of porphyria, a blood disorder]. It showcases treatment practices in the later 1700s. **P, T, serious film**

One Flew Over the Cuckoo's Nest
From 1975, this film tells the story of Randall P. McMurphy (Jack Nicholson), a convict sent to a northwestern psychiatric hospital for evaluation and treatment. While there, McMurphy experiences first hand the use of electroconvulsive therapy. **P, T, E, serious film**

Pressure Point
This film from the 1960s, starts Sidney Potier as a psychiatrist treating a racist patient (played by Bobby Darin). **T, E, serious film**

Snake Pit
Based on an autobiography, this film, made in 1948, is one of the first and best about mental illness and the treatment of patients in asylums and hospitals. Olivia de Haviland portrays a woman suffering from a nervous breakdown. **P, T, E, serious film**

Titucut Follies
From 1967, this documentary covers the treatment of inmates/patients at a correctional institution in Massachusetts. **T, E, documentary**

West 47th Street
This 2001 film is a feature-length theatrical documentary following the lives of four people with serious mental illness, over three years. **P, T, E, documentary**

Other Films:

The Exorcism of Emily Rose (2005) addresses exorcism as a treatment for demonic possession. **P, T, E, commercial horror film**
The Exorcist (1973) addresses past views and treatments. **P, T, commercial horror film**

Comer Video Segments

Available as a supplement, this revised set of videotapes contains short clips depicting various topics related to abnormal psychology. Please see the accompanying Video Guide for specific clips linked to Chapter 1.

Recommendations for Purchase or Rental

The Comer Video Segments include excerpts from many superb clinical documentaries. While the segments alone are ideal for use in lectures, it often is useful to assign the entire documentary for special class screenings or library use by students.

Films on Demand is a Web-based digital delivery service that has impressive psychology holdings. Their catalog can be accessed here: http://ffh.films.com/digitallanding.aspx

In addition, the following videos and other media may be of particular interest and are available for purchase or rental and appropriate for use in class or for assignment outside of class.

Madness by Jonathan Miller (five 1-hour programs)
Lionheart Television International, Inc.
630 Fifth Avenue, Suite 2220
New York, NY 10111
(212) 373-4100

Available through: National Library of Medicine
History of Medicine Division
National Institutes of Health
8600 Rockville Pike
Bethesda, Maryland
(800) 272-4787

"Treatments in Mental Disorders," 1949
"Recent Modification of Convulsive Shock Therapy," 1941

"Metrazol, Electric, and Insulin Treatment of the Functional Psychoses," 1934
"Prefrontal Lobotomy in the Treatment of Mental Disorders," 1942
"Prefrontal Lobotomy in Chronic Schizophrenia," 1944
"Case Study of Multiple Personality," 1923

CLASS DEMONSTRATIONS AND ACTIVITIES

Panel Discussion

Have students volunteer (or assign them) to portray in a panel discussion of mental health "workers" from different historical times. Each student should present the prevailing theory of his or her time period (demonology, somatogenic, psychogenic, etc.) and the appropriate treatments. Students in the audience can ask questions of the panelists. Additionally, other students can role-play patients suffering from particular disorders ("eco anxiety," mass madness) and have the panelists attempt to diagnose, based on their orientation.

"It's Debatable: Somatogenic or Psychogenic?" (see Preface instructions for conducting this activity)

Have students volunteer (or assign them) in teams to opposite sides of the debate topic. Have students present their cases in class following standard debate guidelines.

The Pervasive Problem of Abnormality

To illustrate the prevalence of mental health disorders in the United States, ask students to participate in a brief class activity. Prior to class, from a stack of 100 index cards, create separate cards reflecting the following statistics: It is estimated that up to 18 of every 100 adults have a significant anxiety disorder, 10 suffer from profound depression, 5 display a personality disorder, 1 has schizophrenia, 1 experiences Alzheimer's disease, and 11 abuse alcohol or other drugs. To reduce stigma and increase the "surprise" of the activity, use different colors (rather than the diagnostic terms) to indicate the different diagnoses. Proportionally reduce the number of cards to reflect the number of students present in class (i.e., with 50 students, reduce the numbers by half; with 33 students, reduce by two-thirds, etc.). Randomly pass cards out to each student and ask

them to stand if they have a "pink" card (anxiety)—announce to the class that this group is experiencing anxiety symptoms severe enough to warrant treatment. Have them sit down and have "purple" stand next, etc., until all the disorders have been seen and seated. Then have everyone with a colored card stand so that the only ones left seated are the "normals." Points for discussion include the feelings of stigma at having to stand and be identified and the large number of people affected by these disorders.

Distress, Dysfunction, Danger, and Deviance

Maintain a file of newspaper clippings that depict the four criteria of abnormality: distress, dysfunction, danger, and deviance. You can use this file throughout the semester when attempting to make diagnoses of disorders.

Factors in Deinstitutionalization

A variety of factors led to the deinstitutionalization movement, including rising criticism of the inhumane treatment of mental patients and the discovery of powerful antipsychotic drugs. You can describe the dramatic reduction in the census of state mental hospitals in the United States from more than 500,000 in 1950 to about 100,000 in 1990. Ask students for their opinions on the pros and cons of this movement.

Defining Normal

Ask students to define "normal," then ask how they personally determine when someone's behavior is abnormal and solicit relevant examples. Ask students to discuss how they arrived at their definitions. Use an overhead transparency to keep track of the different definitions. Compare the specific criteria for abnormality discussed in the text to formulate a class definition.

Distinguishing Between Normal and Abnormal

Identify examples from literature or real life that exemplify the difficulty encountered when trying to draw clear distinctions between normal and abnormal behavior.

Example: Sometimes the distinction is obvious. A 32-year-old man complains that his thoughts are being repeated in public and on television and that he is being tortured by invisible rays. He claims that people living in the apartment above him are transmitting abusive messages through the heating system. At times he stares into the mirror, grimacing horribly. He often shouts nonsense words and phrases, seemingly from nowhere, and laughs loudly for no apparent reason. He screams at people walking by him on the street. His family takes him to the hospital after he begins pounding on the walls of his apartment, screaming nonstop.

Example: Joseph Heller's novel *Catch-22* tells the story of a bomber navigator (Yossarian) during World War II. His situation sounds unusual, at first: He is a 34-year-old flier who is terrified of flying. He has frequent nightmares and behavioral outbursts. He is known to threaten people and to drink too much. He begs to be let out of his current situation because he feels he is crazy. (The U.S. Army won't release him for reasons of insanity, however, because he obviously is sane if he wants to be released; if he were insane, he wouldn't ask to be released: "a perfect catch, Catch-22.") After explaining that he is terrified of being shot at, his drinking and other behavior suddenly seem "normal."

Example: Kurt Cobain, the lead singer for the alternative rock group Nirvana, had such chronic stomach problems that he had trouble eating. He awoke every morning starving and wanting food, but every time he ate, he would throw up and end up weeping. Doctors were unable to determine the cause of the problem. He despaired and became suicidal. Instead of committing suicide, he turned to drugs, becoming a heroin junkie. Is this normal? Was his drug use pathologic, even if it was understandable? (Cobain eventually did die by suicide.)

SUGGESTED TOPICS FOR DISCUSSION

Rosenhan's "On Being Sane in Insane Places"

To discuss the problem of "sticky" diagnostic labels and the manner in which they influence others' perceptions, describe Rosenhan's study, "On Being Sane in Insane Places" (*Science*, 1973, pp. 250–257). In this study, eight mentally healthy people, several of them psychologists and psychiatrists, complained of hearing voices that repeated "Empty," "Dull," and "Thud," and were admitted to mental hospitals. Once inside, they acted normally for the remainder of their stay. One of the pseudopatients was a professional artist, and the staff interpreted her work in terms of her illness and recovery. As the pseudopatients took notes about their experiences, staff members referred to the note-taking as schizophrenic writing. Ask students for any other types of behavior that they can think of that would be misinterpreted in this situation. Ask students for other examples, which they have encountered or could imagine occurring, where a psychiatric label (such as depression, anxiety, or eating disorder) might "stick" and influence others' perceptions.

When discussing this study and students' reactions to it, it might be worthwhile to discuss criticisms of the study. For example, it will be important to emphasize that auditory hallucinations (such as those supposedly heard by the pseudopatients) are extremely rare and pathognomonic (indicates severe pathology), and that it might have been entirely appropriate for these persons to be hospitalized immediately. Also, the "patients" were discharged with the diagnosis "in remission," which means "without signs of the illness," a very rare diagnosis. Regarding the use of the study to criticize psychiatric diagnoses as unreliable or invalid, one author responded: "If I were to drink a quart of blood and, concealing what I had done, come to the emergency room of any hospital vomiting blood, the behavior of the staff would be quite predictable. If they labeled and treated me as having a bleeding peptic ulcer, I doubt that I could argue convincingly that medical science does not know how to diagnose that condition" (Kety, 1974, p. 959).

Group Work: Positive and Negative Labeling

Ask small groups to develop lists of words used to label normal and abnormal behavior and persons. Typically, you should find that more words are listed for abnormal persons than for normal ones. Ask the class to explain the difference in the lengths of the lists. Discuss the positive and negative connotations of the lists.

Group Work *or* the Anonymous Five-Minute Essay *or* Open Discussion: This Place Makes Me Crazy

This can be done either in small groups, as a short essay, or as an open discussion. The general theme is that not only individuals but also families, workplaces, occupations, and neighborhoods can be dysfunctional. (1) Ask small groups to come up with examples of workplaces or occupations that fit this description. (2) Ask for anonymous essays of dysfunctional groups that students are personally familiar with (e.g., "I once worked in a job where . . . "). (3) Lead a general discussion on this topic. Ask students to describe the features that were dysfunctional (e.g., vindictive personnel, chaotic management, rules that kept changing, confusion, blaming, unethical practices). Many students will be able to identify with these examples of how environment and stress can affect individual behavior.

Rocks in My Head

Lead a discussion on material dealing with the Middle Ages, and ask students where they think the phrase "rocks in your head" originated. Explain that street vendors (quacks) performed pseudosurgery during the Middle Ages. A person troubled by negative emotions or other symptoms of mental illness could go to the vendor, who would make a minor incision in the scalp; an assistant would sneak the "surgeon" a few small stones, and the surgeon would pretend to have taken them from the patient's head. The stones, he claimed, were the cause of the person's problems and the patient was now "cured." Ask students for any modern-day examples of miracle cures. This is a useful way to discuss the concept of the placebo effect—that is, the effectiveness of treatment is often due to the patient's belief that it will work.

Institutional Treatment of the Mentally Ill

Lead a discussion that points out that asylums in the early twentieth century grew so fast and were so underfunded and understaffed that they became filthy, degrading human warehouses. Although there are more well-trained professionals today, mental health care and research are still greatly underfunded. One result is that a significant number of the homeless in the United States are mentally ill and are not getting the help they need. Another is that, in many states, mentally ill persons are being housed in jails even though they have not committed crimes. Discuss these consequences.

Why Should Students Care About Psychopathology? What Relevance Does It Have?

Discuss the relevance of mental illness and abnormal psychology. Beginning the course with this discussion is a useful way to set the "norm" for the rest of the semester (see the Preface).

Discuss the potential relevance of mental illness to those who work with the public (e.g., small business owners, salespeople, doctors, teachers, and lawyers). Emphasize that the issue of prevalence of psychological disorders is really a question of whether it would be beneficial to someone, in any of these situations, to be familiar with the existence and presentation of mental illnesses (e.g., to recognize depression or alcohol abuse). Frame the discussion by saying, "Pretend, for a moment, that you are a business owner (school principal, etc.). In any year, what impact will mental illness have on your business (school, etc.)?"

The ECA study conducted standardized household interviews of a random sample of 18,000 adults asking, among other things, about psychological symptoms and help-seeking behavior. Researchers found that, in any one-month period, 16 percent of persons are experiencing or suffering from a mental illness. This indicates an annual prevalence of over 25 percent and a lifetime prevalence of over 30 percent. (Only 28.5 percent of the diagnosable mentally ill in the study sought any treatment.)

Group Work *or* Open Discussion: What Are the Risk Factors for Mental Illness?

Ask students to generate a list of what they presume are some of the risk factors for mental illness. Inform them that risk factors are associated with an increased likelihood of a mental illness being present or developing. This activity can lead to a discussion of assumptions (or myths) about mental illness and/or a discussion of the scientific study of mental illness.

The following are risk factors:

- Age: Young people have higher rates of mental illness than older people.
- Marital status: Separated, divorced, and never married individuals have higher rates of mental illness than married or widowed people.
- Education: Less educated individuals have higher rates of mental illness.
- Personal income: The lower the income, the higher the rate.
- Employment: Unemployed people have higher rates of mental illness.
- Contact with friends: Isolation is a risk factor; fewer contacts are associated with higher rates of mental illness.

- Satisfaction with relationships: Greater satisfaction is associated with lower rates.
- Marital happiness: Greater happiness is associated with lower rates.

The following are not risk factors:

- Sex: It used to be thought that women had higher rates of mental illness.
- Ethnicity or race
- Intelligence: Measured intelligence (e.g., IQ) doesn't prevent mental illness, although there is some evidence that more intelligent people have more difficulty admitting that they have a mental illness.

How Do We Define "Abnormal Behavior"?

Discuss the limitations of each criterion for abnormal behavior if it were used as the sole criterion. This is an effective instructional technique to emphasize the complexity of the field and the danger of dismissing "incomplete" information. Follow this discussion with the DSM-IV-TR.

- Social norms or social deviancy: Social norms change; what is deviant in one era may not be in another. Ask students whether their parents think their musical taste is "normal," then instruct them to ask their parents about their tastes when they were younger.
- Danger criteria: Most mentally ill people are not dangerous to others.
- Maladaptiveness criterion: This criterion can be highly subjective and can change from situation to situation. For example, adaptive behavior on a Friday night at a fraternity party is not necessarily appropriate in a work situation.
- Personal distress criterion: Some mentally ill persons feel little distress.

Changing Explanations of Abnormal Behavior

Students often struggle with the changing explanations, over the years, of abnormal behavior. Lead a discussion of "the state of the world" as a way to understand these explanations. Explanations and ways of treating or controlling abnormal behavior are the result of the prevailing models or theories of humanity and human beings' relation to the world. Explanations also reflect the limits or the extent of knowledge. To understand how various historical cultures have viewed abnormal behavior, it is useful to examine what their world was like and what were the prevailing ideas for understanding that world.

- The Greeks explained insanity as the work of the gods. Treatment involved taking the afflicted to the temple of the god Asclepius, the god of healing.
- The Middle Ages (sixth to fourteenth centuries) were characterized by nearly constant warfare, the bubonic plague, and the ascendancy of the church, which rejected science and emphasized the activity of the devil. The mentally ill were "treated" for demonic possession.
- The Renaissance, the Enlightenment, and the Age of Reason marked the rise of science and the decline of demonology. The sixteenth-century German physician, Johann Weyer, concluded that many so-called witches were simply mentally imbalanced, and he argued successfully that the mentally ill needed to be cared for by the community and by the family.
- In the nineteenth and twentieth centuries, the discovery of biological causes of insanity led to the belief that mental illness is incurable (persuading some to commit patients permanently to state mental hospitals). The discovery of antipsychotics led to deinstitutionalization.

ASSIGNMENTS/EXTRA CREDIT SUGGESTIONS

"Write a Pamphlet"

With the use of a software program like Microsoft Publisher or simply paper and markers, students can create a pamphlet on mental health care in a particular period. For example, students can create a promotional brochure for Bethlehem Hospital (a.k.a. Bedlam) or a treatment brochure for one of the "modern problems" listed in Psych Watch on text p. 8. Students should be encouraged to be as accurate and up-to-date as possible and to present all sides of the issue (e.g., alternate treatment approaches or theories).

Mental Health and the Media

Ask students to find newspaper and magazine articles that deal with mental illness. They also can find videotapes of talk-show guests, television programs, and/or films with the same theme. Have them evaluate the quality of the coverage, the accuracy or inaccuracy of the information presented, and the assumptions made about mental illness. You can adapt this discussion as a written or extra-credit assignment.

Perceptions Portrayed by Self-Help Books

Ask students to visit local bookstores or libraries to examine self-help books. Have them evaluate the quantity and the quality of the books. Ask them to bring in examples of books that seem to be useful. You can facilitate this discussion during class.

Abnormal Psychology Tool Kit Video Questions

As a homework assignment, have students watch a video clip and answer the accompanying questions. Students can answer the questions directly into the online assessment feature. The results of these quizzes report to the site's built-in grade book.

Web Site Quiz

For homework or extra credit, have students complete the quizzes for Chapter 1 located on the companion Web site. Students can complete an online test of the key chapter material (using questions NOT from the test bank) and have their scores e-mailed directly to the course instructor.

Essay Topics

For homework or extra credit, have students write an essay addressing one (or more) of the following topics:

(1) Compare and contrast the Psychogenic and the Somatogenic perspectives of psychological abnormality.

(2) Detail alternative explanations for trephination (using the critical thinking model outlined in the Preface).

(3) Compare and contrast "eccentric" and "abnormal" behavior. [See PsychWatch on p. 6] Who decides the "diagnosis"?

(4) What behaviors might fit the criteria of deviant, distressful, dysfunctional, or dangerous but would not be considered abnormal by most people?

Research Topics

For homework or extra credit, have students write a research report addressing one (or more) of the following topics:

(1) Conduct a biographical search on one of the famous "eccentrics" discussed in PsychWatch: Marching to a Different Drummer: Eccentrics. (text p. 6).

(2) Research and report on one of the "Modern Pressures" discussed in PsychWatch (text p. 8).

(3) Research and report on the connection between the moon and the mind (see Between the Lines: Lunar Myths, text p. 13).

(4) Research and report on the study of Positive Psychology (see PsychWatch, text p. 18).

(5) Conduct a "Psych Info" search and write an annotated bibliography of five studies of "modern" treatments for psychopathology.

Film Review

To earn extra credit, have students watch one (or more) of the mainstream films listed earlier in this chapter and write a brief (3–5) page report. Students should summarize the plot of the film in sufficient detail to demonstrate familiarity, but should focus their papers on the depiction of psychological abnormality. What errors or liberties did the filmmaker make or take? What is the message (implicit or explicit) concerning the mentally ill?

Book Review

To earn extra credit, have students read a mental-health based autobiography or memoir and write a brief (3–5) page report. Students should summarize the text but should focus on the psychological disorder discussed by the author. How does the author conceptualize his or her illness? What type of treatment (if any) did he or she receive? Were the Four Ds of abnormality present in the symptom descriptions?

Crossword Puzzles

As a homework assignment or for extra credit, have students complete and submit Crossword Puzzle #1.

Word Searches

As a homework assignment or for extra credit, have students complete and submit Word Search #1.

CHAPTER :2

Research in Abnormal Psychology

TOPIC OVERVIEW

LECTURE OUTLINE

I. **RESEARCH IN ABNORMAL PSYCHOLOGY**
   A. Research is the systematic search for facts through the use of careful observations and investigations
      1. It is the key to accuracy in all fields, but it is particularly important (and challenging) in the field of abnormal psychology
         a. Theories and treatments that seem reasonable and effective in individual instances may prove disastrous when widely applied
      2. Only by fully testing a theory or technique on representative groups of individuals can clinicians evaluate the accuracy, effectiveness, and safety of their ideas and techniques
   B. Clinical researchers face certain challenges that make their work very difficult
      1. Measuring unconscious motives
      2. Assessing private thoughts
      3. Monitoring mood changes
      4. Calculating human potential
   C. In addition, they must consider different cultural background, races, and genders of the people they study
   D. They also must always ensure that the rights of their research participants, both human and animal, are not violated

II. **WHAT DO CLINICAL RESEARCHERS DO?**
   A. Clinical researchers try to discover universal laws, or principles, of abnormal psychological functioning
      1. They search for general, or nomothetic, truths about the nature, causes, and treatments of abnormality
      2. Typically they do not assess, diagnose, or treat individual clients
      3. They rely on the scientific method to pinpoint and explain relationships between variables
         a. They utilize three main methods of investigation to form and test hypotheses and to draw broad conclusions:
            (a) The Case Study
            (b) The Correlational Method
            (c) The Experimental Method

III. **THE CASE STUDY**
   A. The case study provides a detailed description of a person's life and psychological problems
      1. Case studies are helpful:
         a. They can serve as a source of new ideas about behavior
            (a) For example, Freud's theories were based mainly on case studies
         b. They may offer tentative support for a theory
         c. They may challenge a theory's assumptions
         d. They may inspire new therapeutic techniques
         e. They may offer opportunities to study unusual problems
      2. Case studies also are limited:
         a. Observers are biased
         b. Data collection relies on subjective evidence (i.e., low internal validity)
         c. They provide little basis for generalization (i.e., low external validity)
      3. The limitations associated with this model are addressed by the two other methods of investigation—the correlational method and the experimental method
         a. Neither method offers richness of detail
         b. Both methods allow researchers to draw broad conclusions
         c. Thus, they are the preferred methods of clinical investigation
            (a) Both typically involve the observation of many individuals
            (b) Both models require the uniform application of study procedures

(i)   As a result, studies can be replicated
(c)   Both methods use statistical tests to analyze results

IV.   **THE CORRELATIONAL METHOD**
   A.   Correlation is the degree to which events or characteristics vary with each other
      1.   The correlational method is a research procedure used to determine the "co-relationship" between variables
   B.   The people chosen for a study are its subjects or participants, collectively called a sample
      1.   The sample must be representative of the larger population [See Table 2-2 on p. 36]
   C.   Correlational data can be graphed and a "line of best fit" drawn [See Figures 2-1 through 2-3 on pp. 32 and 33 of the text]
      1.   Positive correlation = variables change in the same direction
      2.   Negative correlation = variables change in the opposite direction
      3.   Unrelated = no consistent relationship
   D.   The magnitude (strength) of a correlation also is important [See Figure 2-4 on p. 33 of the text]
      1.   High magnitude = variables that vary closely together; fall close to the line of best fit
      2.   Low magnitude = variables that do not vary as closely together; loosely scattered around the line of best fit
      3.   Direction and magnitude of a correlation often are calculated numerically
         a.   This statistic is called the "correlation coefficient" and is symbolized by the letter "r"
         b.   The correlation coefficient can vary from +1.00 (perfect positive correlation) to −1.00 (perfect negative correlation)
         c.   Sign (+ or −) indicates direction
         d.   Number (from 0.00 to 1.00) indicates magnitude
            (a)   0.00 = no consistent relationship
      4.   Most correlations found in psychological research fall far short of "perfect"
   E.   Correlations can be trusted based on a statistical analysis of probability
      1.   "Statistical significance" means that the finding is unlikely to have occurred by chance
      2.   By convention, if there is less than a 5 percent probability that findings are due to chance ($p < .05$), results are considered "statistically significant" and are thought to reflect the larger population
      3.   Generally, confidence increases with the size of the sample and the magnitude of the correlation
   F.   What are the merits of the correlational method? [See Table 2-1, text p. 34]
      1.   These studies have high external validity; therefore, clinical researchers can generalize findings
      2.   Using this model, clinical researchers can repeat (replicate) studies on other samples
   G.   What are the difficulties with correlational studies?
      1.   These studies lack internal validity
      2.   Results describe but do not *explain* relationships; in other words, results say nothing about causation
   H.   There are two special forms of correlational study:
      1.   Epidemiological studies—these studies reveal the incidence and prevalence of a disorder in a particular population
         a.   Incidence = Number of new cases that emerge in a given period of time
         b.   Prevalence = Total number of cases in a given period of time
      2.   Longitudinal studies—in this design, researchers observe the same individuals on many occasions over a long period of time

V.   **THE EXPERIMENTAL METHOD**
   A.   An experiment is a research procedure in which a variable is manipulated and the manipulation's effect on another variable is observed
      1.   Manipulated variable = independent variable
      2.   Variable being observed = dependent variable

B. This model allows researchers to ask such questions as: Does a particular therapy relieve the symptoms of a particular disorder?
   1. Questions about relationships can only be answered by an experiment [See Table 2-2 on p. 36 of the text]
C. Statistics and research design are very important
   1. Researchers must try to eliminate all confounds from their studies—variables other than the independent variable that may also be affecting the dependent variable
   2. Three features are included in experiments to guard against confounds:
      a. The control group
         (a) A control group is a group of participants who are not exposed to the independent variable, but whose experience is similar to that of the experimental group
         (b) By comparing the two groups, researchers can better determine the effect of the independent variable
         (c) Rules of statistical significance are applied
         (d) In addition, clinicians may evaluate clinical significance—whether the amount of improvement is meaningful in the individual's life
      b. Random assignment
         (a) Researchers must watch out for preexisting differences between the experimental and control groups
            (i) To do so, researchers use random assignment—any selection procedure that ensures that every participant in the experiment is as likely to be placed in one group as another
               1. Examples: coin flip; picking names out of a hat
      c. Blind design
         (a) A final confound problem is bias
            (i) To avoid bias by the participant, experimenters employ a "blind design"—participants are kept from knowing which assigned group (experimental or control) they are in
               1. One strategy for this is providing a placebo—something that looks or tastes like real therapy but has none of its key ingredients
            (ii) To avoid bias by the experimenter, experimenters employ a "double-blind design," in which the experimenters and the participants are kept from knowing which condition of the study that the participants are in
               1. Often used in medication trials

VI. ALTERNATIVE EXPERIMENTAL DESIGNS
   A. It is not easy to devise an experiment that is both well controlled and enlightening
   B. Clinical researchers often must settle for designs that are less than ideal and include:
      1. Quasi-experimental designs
         a. In quasi-experimental, or mixed, designs, investigators do not randomly assign participants to groups, but make use of groups that already exist
            (a) Example: children with a history of child abuse
         b. To address the problem of confounds, researchers use matched control groups
            (a) These groups are "matched" to the experimental group based on demographic and other variables
      2. Natural experiments
         a. In natural experiments, nature manipulates the independent variable and the experimenter observes the effects
            (a) Example: psychological impact of flooding
         b. Natural experiments cannot be replicated at will
         c. Broad generalizations cannot be made
      3. Analogue experiments
         a. Analogue experiments allow investigators to freely manipulate independent variables while avoiding ethical and practical limitations
         b. They induce laboratory subjects to behave in ways that seem to resemble real life

        (a)   Example: animal subjects

    c.   The major limitation of all analogue research is that experimenters can never be certain that the phenomena observed in the lab are the same as the psychological disorders being investigated

4.   Single-subject experiments

    a.   In a single-subject experiment, a single participant is observed both before and after manipulation of an independent variable

        (a)   Baseline data is gathered to set a standard for comparison

    b.   An experimental design is the ABAB, or reversal, design

        (a)   In an ABAB (reversal) design, a participant's reactions are measured during a baseline period (A), after the introduction of the independent variable (B), after the removal of the independent variable (A), and after reintroduction of the independent variable (B)

            (i)   The participant is, essentially, compared against himself or herself rather than against control subjects

    c.   Single-subject experiments are similar to individual case studies:

        (a)   Both focus on one subject only

        (b)   Both have low external validity

        (c)   However, the single-subject experiment has higher internal validity than the case study, given the manipulation of an independent variable

LEARNING OBJECTIVES

1.   Describe the role of clinical researchers in the field of abnormal psychology.

2.   Describe the case study, including its uses and limitations (strengths and weaknesses).

3.   Describe the correlational method. What is a positive versus a negative versus a null correlation? What are the uses and limitations of correlational research?

4.   Describe the experiment. What are the uses and limitations of experimental research? Describe the reasons that experimenters use control groups, random assignment, and blind design.

5.   Describe the following alternative experimental designs: quasi-experimental design; natural experiments; analogue experiments; single-subject experiments.

KEY TERMS

ABAB design
analogue experiment
blind design
case study
clinical significance
confound
control group
correlation
correlation coefficient
correlational method
dependent variable
double-blind design
epidemiological study

experiment
experimental group
external validity
hypothesis
incidence
independent variable
internal validity
line of best fit
longitudinal study
magnitude of correlation
natural experiment
negative correlation
no (zero) correlation

nomothetic understanding
placebo therapy
positive correlation
prevalence
quasi-experiment
random assignment
sample
scientific method
single-subject experimental
   design
statistical significance
variable

MEDIA RESOURCES

Abnormal Psychology Student Tool Kit

Produced and edited by Ronald J. Comer, Princeton University and Gregory Comer, Princeton Academic Resources. Tied directly to the CyberStudy sections in the text, this Student Tool Kit offers 57 intriguing Video Cases running 3 to 7 minutes each. The Video Cases focus on persons affected by disorders discussed in the text. Students first view the video and then answer a series of thought-provoking questions. Additionally, the Student Tool Kit contains multiple-choice practice test questions with built-in instructional feedback for every option.

Video Cases and Discussions:

- How do researchers measure psychopathology?
- Observe the power of bias and expectations in research.

Practical, Research, and Decision-Making Exercises:

- Misusing anecdotal evidence
- Testing clinical hypotheses

PowerPoint Slides

Available at the Instructor's site on the companion Web site are comprehensive PowerPoint slide presentations and supplemental student handouts for Chapter 2. The slide files reflect the main points of the chapter in significant detail. Student handouts were created using the instructor slides as a base, with key points replaced as "fill-in" items. Answer keys and suggestions for use also are provided.

Internet Sites

Please see Appendix A for full and comprehensive references.
  Sites relevant to Chapter 2 material are:

http://www.med.nyu.edu/bhp/
This Web site provides an overview of the behavioral health programs offered at NYU Medical Center, including clinical research and current studies. It also provides links to general psychological research, hospital and patient care information, and education.

http://www.nimh.nih.gov
National Institute of Mental Health–NIMH
The homepage of NIMH, a component of NIH. NIMH is the federal agency that conducts and supports (funds) research on mental illness and mental health.

Mainstream Films

Films relevant to Chapter 2 material are listed and summarized below.

Key to Film Listings:
P = psychopathology focus
T = treatment focus
E = ethical issues raised

Please note that some of the films suggested may have graphic sexual or violent content due to the nature of certain subject matters.

Charly
From the award-winning book *Flowers for Algernon*, this 1968 film portrays Charly, an adult suffering from mental retardation. The film details Charly's experiences with doctors attempting to "cure" him, leading up to his participation in an experimental treatment that raises his IQ to genius levels but not his emotional maturity. Issues of informed consent and the responsibilities that accompany science are handled well. **P, T, E, serious film**

Kinsey
From 2004, this biopic details the life story of Alfred Kinsey, author of the controversial *Sexual Behavior in the Human Male*. **P, E, serious film**

Trading Places
This 1983 film loosely addresses issues related to correlational and experimental research design. Dan Akroyd and Eddie Murphy play a privileged but priggish broker and a street hustler who are experimentally manipulated (without informed consent) into trading places. **E, comedy**

Wrong Answer
From 2005, this short film follows a participant in a psychology study of the effects of mild electric shocks on recall. Based on the classic Milgram obedience study. **E, serious film**

Other Films:

Brain Candy (1996) Plot involves a drug company's research into and development of a drug to treat depression. **P, T, comedy**

The Nutty Professor (1996 remake) research. **P, T, comedy**

The Royal Tennenbaums (2001) One character is conducting research on the brain functions of a boy and makes his living publishing pseudo-scientific results. **P, comedy/serious film**

Comer Video Segments

Available as a supplement, this revised set of videotapes contains short clips depicting various topics related to abnormal psychology. Please see the accompanying Video Guide for specific clips linked to Chapter 2.

CLASS DEMONSTRATIONS AND ACTIVITIES

"It's Debatable: Is it ethical to use animals in psychological research?" (see Preface instructions for conducting this activity)

Have students volunteer (or assign them) in teams to opposite sides of the debate topic (see PsychWatch, text p. 27 for more information). Have students present their cases in class, following standard debate guidelines.

The Double-Blind Study

To illustrate the risks and benefits of the double-blind procedure, have students break up into small groups. Pass out index cards (one patient, several "blind" doctors, several "un-blind" doctors per group) and a treatment scenario (e.g., a patient in an antidepressant medication trial complaining of sexual side effects). How does being blind/un-blind influence your questioning of the patient?

Case Study

Present a case study to the class. Some of Freud's cases (e.g., Little Hans [excerpt in the text], Dora, the Rat Man, and/or the case of the "Genain" sisters) are especially interesting.

Correlational Study

Discuss a situation in which a correlational design is required, that is, where it is either practically or ethically impossible to conduct an experiment. Examples include the association between smoking and heart disease, sexual abuse and eating disorders, alcohol abuse and work problems, and high levels of expressed emotion and schizophrenia.

Autism and Emotionally Frigid Parenting: The Dangers of Concluding Causation from Correlation

Present the case of clinicians concluding that autism is due to parenting practices. Children with autism were taken by their parents to Leo Kanner, a child psychiatrist at Johns Hopkins University. Kanner observed the behavior exchanges between children and parents and found that these parents appeared to be less warm than other parents. He concluded that these parents were "emotional refrigerators" and that their detached, emotionally vacant child-rearing practices caused the autism; the children responded to this rejection by becoming defensive and rejecting themselves. Psychoanalyst Bruno Bettelheim reached the same conclusion, but he argued that their hostility was unconscious and unintended. Nonetheless, Bettelheim advocated placing the children in residential settings with more loving caregivers so that the children could learn to trust and to let down their defenses. Discuss the fact that Kanner and Bettelheim were sincere in their efforts to help, but that they had concluded causation based on correlation (the observation that two events—autism and emotional detachment—coincided). Discuss the effect such conclusions might have had on parents. Point out that the axiom "Correlation does not imply causation," if not followed, can cause serious problems.

Facilitated Communication: Strict Experimental Controls Debunk a Useless Intervention

Facilitated communication (FC) is a method for providing assistance to a nonverbal person—such as a child with autism—by using a keyboard to type messages and thus communicate with others. The procedure involves the "facilitator" or assistant supporting the patient's hand, making it easier for the patient to strike the keys he or she wishes to strike. Proponents of FC have asserted that previously uncommunicative persons, such as those with autism or profound mental retardation, can now communicate with others and, in fact, that many such patients have been found to be highly intelligent. In one study of FC, patients were asked how they felt. With the facilitator's help, patients described themselves, revealing their personalities. Patients exhibited unique spellings, or typographical errors, or unique word usages. They occasionally reported, via FC, that they had been sexually abused. A number of questions were raised about FC. The most important was whether the facilitators were unwittingly selecting the keys that spelled out the messages. What was needed was a controlled experiment. An article in *American Psychologist* summarized the findings as follows:

> Relevant controlled, peer-reviewed published studies repeatedly show that, under circumstances when access to information by facilitators is systematically and tightly manipulated, the ability to produce communication through FC varies predictably and in a manner that demonstrates that the content of the communication is being determined by the facilitator. (Jacobson, Mulick, and Schwartz, 1995, p. 754)

The following is from an abstract of a 1998 article in the journal *Focus on Autism and Other Developmental Disabilities*:

> The first author, a certified speech-language pathologist (SLP), served as the facilitator for two students with autism to assess pointing control during facilitated communication. The teacher instructed the students during typical classroom activities, and two classroom assistants collected data. We used a counterbalanced alternating treatments design with the SLP/facilitator being either blind or sighted. She wore sunglasses throughout the investigation with a cardboard cutout inserted for the blind condition. The alternating treatments data reveal that the students responded more accurately when the SLP/facilitator could see in spite of the fact that she did not think she was influencing their responding and did not intentionally do so.

Science and Society

The previous example clearly illustrates the sometimes dramatic tension between concrete experimental evidence and the human desire to believe certain things. In the FC example, there is great desire to help persons with autism, which can be a profoundly disabling disorder.

SUGGESTED TOPICS FOR DISCUSSION

Double-Blind Research

Discuss the ethical dilemmas involved in the use of control groups in research. Double-blind research requires that both the subject and the experimenter not know who receives treatment and who is given a placebo. Discuss whether there is an ethical obligation to halt the research if it becomes clear that treatment subjects are benefiting significantly from the treatment that is not being received by control subjects.

Research Ethics I

Discuss the ethical dilemmas related to informed consent (see PsychWatch, text p. 37). Why is this procedure so important? What should the penalty be for investigators who fail to obtain such documentation?

Research Ethics II

Discuss the necessity and importance of selecting representative samples. Why is this procedure so critical? What are the implications if a study sample is NOT representative? Can any sample ever truly be representative?

Research Ethics III

Discuss the ethical issues involved in the widespread (yet unvalidated) early use of lobotomy. The memoir, *My Lobotomy*, [See p. 26 of the text] details one man's experience.

Research Design

Using the "Most Investigated Questions in Clinical Research" from text p. 36, ask students to select a variable for study and discuss the potential design problems and hypothesize outcomes/conclusions.

ASSIGNMENTS/EXTRA CREDIT SUGGESTIONS

Abnormal Psychology Tool Kit Video Questions

As a homework assignment, have students watch a video clip and answer the accompanying questions. Students can answer the questions directly into the online assessment feature. The results of these quizzes report to the site's built-in grade book.

Web Site Quiz

For homework or extra credit, have students complete the quizzes for Chapter 2 located on the companion Web site. Students can complete an on line test of the key chapter material (using questions NOT from the test bank) and have their scores e-mailed directly to the course instructor.

Essay Topics

For homework or extra credit, have students write an essay addressing one (or more) of the following topics:

(1) Compare and contrast the Case Study, the Correlational Method, and the Experimental Method.

(2) Design a detailed correlational study or experiment addressing one of the questions listed on text p. 36.

(3) The correlation found between life stress and depression does not necessarily indicate that stressors *cause* depression. Discuss other possible factors to explain this finding and other correlations in life that are often interpreted as causal but that may actually reflect a different relationship between the variables.

Research Topics

For homework or extra credit, have students write a research report addressing one (or more) of the following topics:

(1) Research and report on the clinical practice of Sigmund Freud (see Between the Lines, text p. 28). What interesting case studies did he write? How could he have conducted experimental research? What limitations did he face?

(2) Research and report on the case of the "Genain" sisters—identical quadruplets who all developed schizophrenia in their twenties (text p. 30).

(3) Conduct a "Psych Info" search and write an annotated bibliography on double-blind experiments.

(4) Conduct a "Psych Info" search and write an annotated bibliography on violations of research ethics.

(5) Conduct a "Psych Info" search and write an annotated bibliography on research conducted through Facebook or other social media platforms [See MediaSpeak, text p. 31].

Film Review

To earn extra credit, have students watch one (or more) of the mainstream films listed earlier in this chapter and write a brief (3–5 pages) report. Students should summarize the plot of the film in sufficient detail to demonstrate familiarity, but yet should focus their papers on the depiction of psychological abnormality. What errors or liberties did the filmmaker take? What is the message (implicit or explicit) concerning the mentally ill?

Crossword Puzzles

As a homework assignment or for extra credit, have students complete and submit Crossword Puzzle #2.

Word Searches

As a homework assignment or for extra credit, have students complete and submit Word Search #2.

Models of Abnormality

TOPIC OVERVIEW

LECTURE OUTLINE

I. MODELS OF ABNORMALITY

A. In science, the perspectives used to explain events are known as models or paradigms
   1. Each model spells out basic assumptions, gives order to the field under study, and sets guidelines for investigation
   2. Models influence what investigators observe, the questions they ask, the information they seek, and how they interpret this information

B. Until recently, clinical scientists of a given time and place tended to agree on a single model of abnormality—a model greatly influenced by the beliefs of their cultures

C. Today, several models are used to explain and treat abnormal functioning
   1. Sometimes in conflict, each model focuses on one aspect of human functioning and no single model can explain all aspects of abnormality

II. THE BIOLOGICAL MODEL

A. This model adopts a medical perspective

B. The main focus is that psychological abnormality is an illness brought about by malfunctioning parts of the organism—typically point to problems in brain anatomy or brain chemistry

C. How do biological theorists explain abnormal behavior?
   1. The first area of examination is brain anatomy
      a. The brain is composed of approximately 100 billion nerve cells (called neurons) and thousands of billions of support cells (called glia)
      b. Within the brain, large groups of neurons form distinct areas called brain regions
      c. Clinical researchers have discovered connections between certain psychological disorders and problems in specific brain areas
         (a) Example: Huntington's disease and the basal ganglia (forebrain)
   2. A second avenue of examination is brain chemistry
      a. Information is communicated throughout the brain in the form of electrical impulses that travel from one neuron to one or more others
      b. An impulse first is received at a neuron's dendrites, travels down the axon, and is transmitted through the nerve endings to other neurons [See Figure 3-2, text p. 49]
      c. Neurons don't actually touch—they are separated by a space (the synapse) across which a message moves
      d. When an electrical impulse reaches a nerve ending, the ending is stimulated to release a chemical (a neurotransmitter or "NT") that travels across the synaptic space to receptors on the dendrites of neighboring neurons
         (a) Some NTs tell receiving neurons to "fire"; other NTs tell receiving neurons to stop firing
         (b) Researchers have identified dozens of NTs
            (i) Examples: serotonin, dopamine, GABA
      e. Studies indicate that abnormal activity in certain NTs can lead to specific mental disorders
         (a) For example: Depression has been linked to low activity in serotonin and norepinephrine
      f. Additionally, researchers have learned that mental disorders are sometimes related to abnormal chemical activity in the endocrine system
         (a) Endocrine glands release hormones that propel body organs into action
         (b) Abnormal secretions have been linked to psychological disorders
            (i) Example: Cortisol release is related to anxiety and mood disorders
   3. A third area of investigation is genetic abnormalities
      a. Abnormalities in brain anatomy or chemistry are sometimes the result of genetic inheritance

b.   Each cell in the human body contains 23 pairs of chromosomes, each with numerous genes that control the characteristics and traits a person inherits

c.   Studies suggest that inheritance plays a part in mood disorders, schizophrenia, and other mental disorders

    (a)   It appears that in most cases, several genes combine to produce our actions and reactions

4.   A fourth area of focus is on biological abnormalities passed on through evolution

a.   Genes that contribute to mental disorders are viewed as unfortunate occurrences:

    (a)   Such genes may be mutations

    (b)   Such genes may be inherited after a mutation in the family line

    (c)   Such genes may be the result of normal evolutionary principles

b.   Evolutionary theorists argue that human reactions and the genes responsible for them have survived over the course of time because they have helped individuals thrive and adapt

    (a)   One example of this is the fear response

c.   In today's world, however, those genes and reactions may not be so adaptive

d.   This model has been criticized and remains controversial, yet it receives considerable attention

5.   The fifth avenue of research examines biological abnormalities as a result of viral infections

a.   Viral infection provides another possible source of abnormal brain structure or biochemical dysfunction

    (a)   Example: schizophrenia and prenatal viral exposure

b.   The scientific interest in viral explanations of psychological disorders has been growing in the past decade

    (a)   Example: anxiety and mood disorders

D.   Biological treatments

1.   Biological practitioners attempt to pinpoint the physical source of dysfunction to determine the course of treatment

2.   There are three general types of biological treatment:

a.   Drug therapy

    (a)   The 1950s heralded the advent of psychotropic medications and changed the fairly bleak outlook for a number of mental disorders, yet the revolution has produced some major problems

    (b)   Four groups:

        (i)   Antianxiety drugs (anxiolytics; minor tranquilizers)

        (ii)   Antidepressant drugs

        (iii)   Antibipolar drugs (mood stabilizers)

        (iv)   Antipsychotic drugs

b.   Electroconvulsive therapy (ECT)

    (a)   Its use is indicated for severe depression, particularly when drugs and other therapies have failed

    (b)   This treatment is used on tens of thousands of depressed persons annually

c.   Psychosurgery (or neurosurgery)

    (a)   Psychosurgery finds its historical roots in trephination

    (b)   The first lobotomy was performed in the 1930s

    (c)   The procedure now is much more precise than in the past, but is considered experimental and used only in extreme cases

E.   Assessing the biological model

1.   Model strengths:

a.   The biological model earns considerable respect in the field

b.   It constantly produces valuable new information

c.   Biological treatments often bring great relief

2.   Weaknesses of the model:
   a.   The biological model can limit rather than enhance our understanding
       (a)   It is criticized as being too simplistic
   b.   Biological treatments produce significant undesirable (negative) effects

III.   THE PSYCHODYNAMIC MODEL

A.   The psychodynamic model is the oldest and most famous psychological model

B.   It is based on the belief that a person's behavior (whether normal or abnormal) is determined largely by underlying dynamic—that is, interacting—psychological forces of which he or she is not aware
   1.   Abnormal symptoms are the result of conflict among these forces

C.   The father of psychodynamic theory and psychoanalytic therapy was Sigmund Freud (1856–1939)

D.   How did Freud explain normal and abnormal functioning?
   1.   Freud argued that all behavior was caused by three UNCONSCIOUS forces:
       a.   The Id, guided by the Pleasure Principle, is comprised of instinctual needs, drives, and impulses; it is sexual and fueled by libido (sexual energy)
       b.   The Ego is governed by the Reality Principle; it seeks gratification but guides us to know when we can and can't get and express our wishes
           (a)   Ego defense mechanisms protect us from anxiety
           (b)   These defenses include repression, repression, denial, projection, rationalization, displacement, intellectualization, and regression [See Table 3-1, text p. 54]
       c.   The Superego is considered the moral center of the psyche and is guided by the Morality Principle; it is also called a "conscience" and unconsciously is adopted from our parents
   2.   According to Freud, these three parts of the personality are often in some degree of conflict
       a.   A healthy personality is one in which an effective working relationship, an acceptable compromise, has formed among the three forces
       b.   If the id, ego, and superego are in excessive conflict, the person's behavior may show signs of dysfunction
   3.   Freud proposed that humans must negotiate five stages of psychosexual development in their journeys to adulthood
       a.   These stages include:
           (a)   Oral (0 to 18 months of age)
           (b)   Anal (18 months to 3 years of age)
           (c)   Phallic (3 to 5 years of age)
           (d)   Latent (5 to 12 years of age)
           (e)   Genital (12 years of age to adulthood)
       b.   Freud believed that at each stage of development, new events and pressures require adjustment in the id, ego, and superego
           (a)   If one is successful negotiating these stages, he or she will achieve personal growth
           (b)   If one is unsuccessful, fixation will occur at the developmental stage and will lead to psychological abnormality
               (i)   Because parents are the key environmental figures in early life, they often are seen as the cause of improper development

E.   How do other psychodynamic explanations differ from Freud's?
   1.   Although new theories depart from Freud's ideas in important ways, each retains the belief that human functioning is shaped by dynamic (interacting) forces:
       a.   Ego theorists emphasize the role of the ego and consider it independent and more powerful than did Freud
       b.   Self theorists emphasize the unified personality over any one component
       c.   Object relations theorists emphasize the human need for (healthy) interpersonal relationships, especially between children and caregivers

F. Psychodynamic therapies
1. These therapies range from Freudian psychoanalysis to more modern therapies
2. All psychodynamic therapies seek to uncover past trauma and inner conflicts and believe that an understanding of early life experience is critically important
3. The therapist acts as a "subtle guide"
4. Psychodynamic therapists utilize various techniques, including:
    a. Free association—A technique in which the patient describes any thought, feeling, or image that comes to mind, even if it seems unimportant or irrelevant
    b. Therapist interpretation, including addressing issues such as:
        (a) Resistance—An unconscious refusal to participate fully in therapy
        (b) Transference—A process that occurs during therapy, in which patients act toward the therapist as they did or do toward important figures in their lives
        (c) Dream interpretation—A process in which the therapist examines the manifest and latent content of a patient's dream
    c. Catharsis—The reliving of past repressed feelings in order to settle internal conflicts and overcome problems
    d. Working through—The process of facing conflicts, reinterpreting feelings, and overcoming one's problems
    e. Contemporary psychodynamic therapists also may use short-term dynamic or relational psychoanalytic approaches to therapy rather than more traditional but longer/intense psychoanalysis
G. Assessing the psychodynamic model
1. Strengths of the model:
    a. The psychodynamic model was the first to recognize the importance of psychological theories and treatment
    b. This model described abnormal functioning as rooted in the same processes as normal functioning
    c. Proponents of this model were the first to apply theory and techniques systematically to treatment, a practice that had a monumental impact on the field
2. Weaknesses of the model:
    a. The ideas proposed by the model largely are unsupported and difficult or impossible to research
        (a) The model addresses components of functioning that are nonobservable and inaccessible to human subjects (unconscious)

IV. THE BEHAVIORAL MODEL
A. Like the psychoanalytic perspective, behaviorism also is deterministic, based on the idea that our actions are determined largely by our life experiences
B. The model concentrates wholly on behaviors and environmental factors.
C. Behavioral theorists base their explanations and treatments on principles of learning, the process by which these behaviors change in response to the environment
D. The historical beginnings of behaviorism is in laboratories where conditioning studies were conducted
E. How do behaviorists explain abnormal functioning?
1. There are several forms of conditioning addressed by this model, all of which may produce normal or abnormal behavior:
    a. Operant conditioning
        (a) According to this conditioning paradigm, humans and animals learn to behave in certain ways as a result of receiving *rewards* whenever they do so
    b. Modeling
        (a) In a modeling paradigm, individuals learn responses simply by observing and repeating behavior
    c. Classical conditioning
        (a) Classical conditioning is learning by temporal association

            (i)   When two events repeatedly occur close together in time, they become fused in a person's mind and, before long, the person responds in the same way to both events

        (b)   The father of classical conditioning was Russian physiologist Ivan Pavlov (1849–1936)

            (i)   In his classic study, Pavlov examined the effects of hearing a bell on a dog's salivation response

            (ii)   Relevant components of the model are the unconditioned stimulus (US), the unconditioned response (UR), the conditioned stimulus (CS), and the conditioned response (CR)

               1.   If, after conditioning, the CS repeatedly is presented alone, it will eventually stop eliciting the CR, a process called extinction

        (c)   This model explains many familiar behaviors (both normal and abnormal)

F.   Behavioral therapies

    1.   The aim of behavioral therapy is to identify the behaviors that are causing problems and replace them with more appropriate ones

    2.   Behavioral therapists may use classical conditioning, operant conditioning, or modeling approaches

        a.   In this model, the therapist is a "teacher" rather than a "healer"

    3.   Classical conditioning treatments may be used to change abnormal reactions to particular stimuli

        a.   Example: step-by-step systematic desensitization for phobia

            (a)   Learn relaxation skills

            (b)   Construct a fear hierarchy

            (c)   Confront feared situations (covertly or in vivo)

G.   Strengths of the behavioral model:

    1.   This model has become a powerful force in the field

    2.   It can be tested in the laboratory

        a.   The behaviorists' basic concepts can be observed and measured

    3.   There has been significant research support for behavioral therapies

H.   Weaknesses of the model:

    1.   There is still no indisputable evidence that most people with psychological disorders are victims of improper conditioning

    2.   Behavioral therapies have limitations

    3.   This model has been criticized as being too simplistic

        a.   There is a new focus on self-efficacy and cognitive-behavioral theories

V.   THE COGNITIVE MODEL

A.   This model proposes that we can best understand abnormal functioning by looking at cognitive processes—the center of behaviors, thoughts, and emotions

    1.   Proponents of the model argue that clinicians must ask questions about assumptions, attitudes, and thoughts of a client

B.   How do cognitive theorists explain abnormal functioning?

    1.   According to cognitive theorists, abnormal functioning can result from several kinds of cognitive problems

    2.   Theorists have identified several kinds of faulty thinking, including:

        a.   Faulty assumptions and attitudes

        b.   Illogical thinking processes

            (a)   Example: overgeneralization

C.   Cognitive therapies

    1.   According to cognitive therapists, people with psychological disorders can overcome their problems by developing new, more functional ways of thinking

    2.   The main therapy model is Aaron Beck's Cognitive Therapy

        a.   The goal of this therapy is to help clients recognize and restructure their thinking

        b.   Therapists also guide clients to challenge their dysfunctional thoughts, try out new interpretations, and apply new ways of thinking into their daily lives

(a) This form of treatment is widely used in treating depression
D. Assessing the cognitive model
   1. Strengths of the cognitive model:
      a. This model has very broad appeal
      b. It has been shown to be clinically useful and effective
         (a) There is a demonstrated correlation between symptoms and maladaptive cognition
         (b) Therapies have been found effective in treating several disorders, especially depression
      c. The focus of the model is on a uniquely human process
      d. Treatments adapt well to technology
      e. The model and treatment are research-based
   2. Weaknesses of the cognitive model:
      a. The precise role of cognition in abnormality has yet to be determined.
      b. While effective for many disorders and clients, the model does not help everyone
      c. Some changes may not be possible to achieve
         (a) In response, a new wave of therapies has emerged, including Acceptance and Commitment Therapy and mindfulness-based techniques

VI. THE HUMANISTIC-EXISTENTIAL MODEL
A. This is a combination model, uniting the humanist and existential views.
   1. The Humanist Model emphasizes people as friendly, cooperative, and constructive; focus is on the drive to self-actualization through honest recognition of strengths and weaknesses.
   2. The Existentialist Model places an emphasis on self-determination, choice, and individual responsibility; focus is on authenticity
B. The primary theory and therapy associated with the humanistic component of the model is Rogers' Humanistic Theory and Therapy
   1. Rogers argued that there is a basic human need for *unconditional positive regard*
      a. If this is received, it leads to unconditional self-regard
      b. If this is not received, it leads to "conditions of worth"
         (a) Example: "I only have worth if I earn straight As"
         (b) People who do not have unconditional self-regard are, according to Rogers, incapable of self-actualization because of internal distortion—they don't know what they really need, etc.
   2. Rogers' therapy is termed "client-centered"
      a. In it, the therapist provides the client unconditional positive regard, through accurate and genuine empathy and reflective listening
         (a) To date, there has been little research support for this model, but it has had a positive impact on clinical practice
C. Another primary theory in the humanistic model is gestalt theory and its associated therapy
   1. Developed by Fritz Perls, the goal is to achieve client self-recognition through patient-challenging techniques, including:
      a. Skillful frustration
      b. Role-playing
      c. Therapy rules, including "Here and Now" and "I" language
   2. There has been little research support for this model
D. For most of the twentieth century, clinical scientists viewed religion as a negative—or at best neutral—factor in mental health
   1. This historical alienation seems to be ending
   2. Researchers have learned that spirituality can, in fact, be of psychological benefit to people
   3. Many therapists now make a point of including spiritual issues when they treat religious clients

E. More general theoretical and therapeutic models represent the existential half of the combined model

1. Like humanists, existentialists believe that psychological dysfunction is caused by self-deception: People hide from life's responsibilities and fail to recognize that it is up to them to give meaning to their lives

2. Therapy is focused on patient acceptance of personal responsibility for their problems and recognition of freedom of action

3. For these therapists, the goals of treatment are more important than the use of any specific technique. These therapists tend to be eclectic in their use of therapy tools

4. There is a great emphasis placed on the client-therapist relationship

5. Existential therapists do not believe that experimental methods can adequately test the effectiveness of their treatments; as a result, little controlled research has been conducted

F. Assessing the humanistic-existential model

1. Strengths of the model:

a. H-E emphasizes the individual and taps into domains missing from other theories

(a) This is a nondeterministic model and, as such, is more optimistic than most models seen in abnormal psychology

b. The emphasis of this model is on health rather than illness

2. Weaknesses of the model:

a. H-E focuses on abstract issues and has been criticized for not dealing with "serious" mental health problems

b. The model has not had much influence on the field, due, in part, to its disapproval of the scientific approach, but this is changing somewhat

VII. THE SOCIOCULTURAL MODEL: THE FAMILY-SOCIAL AND MULTICULTURAL PERSPECTIVES

A. According to two sociocultural perspectives—the family-social perspective and the multicultural perspective—abnormal behavior is best understood in light of the broad forces that influence an individual; as such, they address the norms of, and people's roles in, society.

B. This model is comprised of two major perspectives: the family-social perspective and the multicultural perspective

C. How do family-social theorists explain abnormal functioning?

1. Proponents of this model argue that theorists should concentrate on forces that operate directly on an individual, including:

a. The role of social labels and roles

(a) Diagnostic labels (e.g., Rosenhan study)

b. The role of social connections and support

c. Family structure and communication

(a) Grounded in family systems theory

(i) Abnormal functioning within a family leads to abnormal behavior in its members (i.e., an insane environment causes insane behavior)

(ii) Example: enmeshed, disengaged structures

D. Family-social treatments

1. Treatments based on this model may include traditional individual therapy, but the model has been credited with broadening therapy to include:

a. Group therapy—A therapy format in which people with similar problems meet together with a therapist to work on those problems

(a) May include "self-help" (or mutual help) groups comprised of people with similar problems who help and support each other without the direct leadership of a therapist

b. Family therapy—A therapy format in which the therapist meets with all members of a family and helps them change in therapeutic ways

c. Couple therapy—A therapy format in which the therapist works with two people who share a long-term relationship

             (a)   May follow the principles of any of the major therapy orientations, for example, cognitive-behavioral couple therapy

             (b)   May include integrative couple therapy

        d.   Community treatment—A treatment approach that emphasizes community care, such as agencies, group homes, and community mental health centers (CMHCs)

             (a)   May include primary, secondary, and/or tertiary prevention work

E.   How do multicultural theorists explain abnormal functioning?

    1.   The role of culture

        a.   Set of values, attitudes, beliefs, history, and behaviors shared by a group of people and communicated from one generation to the next

        b.   Multicultural, or culturally diverse, psychology is a growing field of study

        c.   Multicultural psychologists seek to understand how culture, race, ethnicity, gender, and similar factors affect behavior and thought and how people of different cultures, races, and genders differ psychologically

        d.   The model holds that an individual's behavior is best understood when examined in the light of that individual's unique cultural context

    2.   The impact of poverty

        a.   Researchers have learned that psychological abnormality is more common among poorer people than among wealthier people

    3.   The role of prejudice and discrimination

F.   Multicultural treatments

    1.   Studies have found that members of ethnic and racial minority groups tend to show less improvement in clinical treatment than members of majority groups

    2.   Two features of treatment can increase a therapist's effectiveness with minority clients:

        a.   Greater sensitivity to cultural issues

        b.   Inclusion of cultural models in treatment, especially in therapies for children and adolescents

    3.   Given such findings, some clinicians have developed culture-sensitive therapies as well as gender-sensitive, or feminist, therapies

G.   Assessing the sociocultural model

    1.   Strengths of the sociocultural model:

        a.   This model has added greatly to the clinical understanding and treatment of abnormality

            (a)   This model has increased awareness of clinical and social roles

        b.   Practitioners have demonstrated clinical success with this model when other treatments have failed

    2.   Weaknesses of the sociocultural model:

        a.   Research is difficult to interpret due to the overwhelming number of possible confounds and the difficulty in designing true experiments

            (a)   Research findings also are limited by the correlational design of most sociocultural research

        b.   While the model can successfully explain abnormality within and across cultures, it is unable to predict abnormality in specific individuals

VIII. INTEGRATION OF THE MODELS

A.   Today's leading models vary widely, and none of the models has proved consistently superior [See Table 3-4, text p. 79]

B.   A growing number of clinicians favor explanations of abnormal behavior that consider more than one cause at a time

    1.   Many theorists, clinicians, and practitioners adhere to a *biopsychosocial* model, which asserts that abnormality results from the interaction of genetic, biological, developmental, emotional, behavioral, cognitive, social, and societal influences

C.   Some biopsychosocial theorists favor a diathesis-stress approach

1. This approach asserts that a biological, psychological, or social predisposition to a disorder (the diathesis) is triggered by environmental stressor, resulting in abnormality

D. Integrative therapists are often called "eclectic"—taking the strengths from each model and using them in combination [See Figure 3-5, text p. 61]

LEARNING OBJECTIVES

1. Define and describe the basic biological terminology, including parts of neurons, the brain, and types of neurotransmitters. Discuss the various therapies used by the biological model, including a discussion of drugs, electroconvulsive therapy, and psychosurgery.

2. Summarize the origins of Freud's theory. Describe Freud's explanation of abnormal functioning, including descriptions of the id, ego, superego, ego defense mechanisms, and psychosexual stages.

3. Summarize the behavioral model of abnormal functioning, including the main features of classical conditioning and operant conditioning and how they are used to explain abnormal behavior.

4. Summarize the cognitive model. Give examples of typical maladaptive assumptions, specific upsetting thoughts, and illogical thinking processes. Describe cognitive therapy.

5. Summarize Rogers' theory and therapy, including definitions of unconditional positive regard, unconditional self-regard, and conditions of worth. Describe Gestalt theory and therapy. Describe existential theories and therapies.

6. Summarize the sociocultural models. Describe the various sociocultural-based therapies.

7. Compare and contrast the various models of abnormal functioning. Describe the different ways of defining abnormality from the perspectives of deviance, distress, dysfunction, and danger.

KEY TERMS

antianxiety drugs
antibipolar drugs
antidepressant drugs
antipsychotic drugs
anxiolytics
biopsychosocial theories
catharsis
classical conditioning
client-centered therapy
cognitive therapy
cognitive-behavioral
    therapies
community mental health
    treatment
conditioned response
conditioned stimulus
conditioning

conditions of worth
conscience
couple therapy
culture-sensitive therapies
deterministic
diathesis-stress
dream
ego
ego defense mechanisms
ego theory
electroconvulsive therapy
    (ECT)
existential therapy
family systems theory
family therapy
fear hierarchy
fixation

free association
gender-sensitive therapies
gene
gestalt therapy
group therapy
hormones
id
libido
lobotomy
model
modeling
multicultural perspective
neuron
neurosurgery
neurotransmitter
object relations theory
operant conditioning

paradigm
pleasure principle
prevention
psychosurgery
psychotropic medications
reality principle
receptor
relational psychoanalytic
   therapy

resistance
self theory
self-actualization
self-efficacy
self-help group
superego
synapse
systematic desensitization
transference

unconditional positive regard
unconditional self-regard
unconditioned response
unconditioned stimulus
unconscious
working through

MEDIA RESOURCES

Abnormal Psychology Student Tool Kit

Produced and edited by Ronald J. Comer, Princeton University and Gregory Comer, Princeton Academic Resources. Tied directly to the CyberStudy sections in the text, this Student Tool Kit offers 57 intriguing Video Cases running 3 to 7 minutes each. The Video Cases focus on persons affected by disorders discussed in the text. Students first view the video and then answer a series of thought-provoking questions. Additionally, the Student Tool Kit contains multiple-choice practice test questions with built-in instructional feedback for every option.

Video Cases and Discussions:

- Observe the biological, psychodynamic, and sociocultural models in operation.
- How do treatments vary?
- Are dreams the "royal road to the unconscious?"

Practical, Research, and Decision-Making Exercises:

- Detecting past models in today's theories
- Sorting out today's models
- Recognizing Freud's wide-ranging influence

PowerPoint Slides

Available at the Instructor's site on the companion Web site are comprehensive PowerPoint slide presentations and supplemental student handouts for Chapter 3. The slide files reflect the main points of the chapter in significant detail. Student handouts were created using the instructor slides as a base, with key points replaced as "fill-in" items. Answer keys and suggestions for use also are provided.

Internet Sites

Please see Appendix A for full and comprehensive references.
  Sites relevant to Chapter 3 material are:

http://www.med.harvard.edu/AANLIB/home.html
The Whole Brain Atlas offers information, images, and QuickTime movies all related to the brain. Included is a discussion on the pathology of Alzheimer's disease. A complete reference to the brain.

http://www.nlm.nih.gov/research/visible/visible_human.html
The Visible Human Project is creating a complete, anatomically detailed, three-dimensional representation of both the male and female human bodies.

http://faculty.washington.edu/chudler/ehceduc.html
Extremely detailed site that consists of links for neuroscience education. This site is large enough to spend several days exploring.

http://www.4therapy.com/
A general therapy site, this listing is full of good information on many types of psychological models and associated therapies but is geared toward provider referral.

http://easyweb.easynet.co.uk/simplepsych/204.html
This site offers general information on psychodynamic therapy—what it is, duration of treatment, training, etc.

http://www.abct.org
This site is the home page for the Association for Behavioral and Cognitive Therapies, a "professional, interdisciplinary organization which is committed to the advancement of a scientific approach to the understanding and amelioration of problems of the human condition."

http://www.rebt.org
A form of cognitive-behavior therapy created in 1955 by Dr. Albert Ellis, Rational Emotive Behavior Therapy (REBT) is an action-oriented approach that stimulates emotional growth by teaching people to replace their self-defeating thoughts, feelings, and actions with new and more effective ones.

http://www.ahpweb.org
The Association for Humanistic Psychology is "the voice of ordinary people with an extraordinary vision for a more conscious and humane global society."

Mainstream Films

Films relevant to Chapter 3 material are listed and summarized below:

Key to Film Listings:
P = psychopathology focus
T = treatment focus
E = ethical issues raised

Please note that some of the films suggested may have graphic sexual or violent content due to the nature of certain subject matters.

A Clockwork Orange
In this 1971 film by Stanley Kubrick, Alex (Malcolm McDowell), a member of a brutal teenage gang, is imprisoned and agrees to aversion therapy. **P, T, E, serious film**

Analyze This/Analyze That
Made in 1999 with a sequel in 2002, this film details the therapeutic relationship between a Mafioso (Robert DeNiro) and his psychiatrist (Billy Crystal). **T, comedy**

Anger Management
In this Adam Sandler comedy, a mild-mannered man is ordered to attend unorthodox anger management sessions. **T, E, commercial comedy**

The Caretakers
This movie, filmed in 1963, chronicles the trials of the mentally ill and their caregivers in an overcrowded hospital ward. Robert Stack portrays a new, optimistic doctor who attempts to start an outpatient program for the women in the ward. His nonpunishing treatment method is met with resistance by the head nurse, played by Joan Crawford. During treatment, the phobias and illnesses of the various women in the test group are explored. **P, T, serious/commercial film**

Don Juan DeMarco
A young man (Johnny Depp) claiming to be the legendary Don Juan, comes to New York in search of his lost love. Dr. Mickler (Marlon Brando) is a near-to-retirement psychiatrist who helps the young man come to his senses. **P, T commercial film**

The Dream Team
This amusing film follows the exploits of four mental patients "loose" in New York City when their group therapist gets waylaid. **P, T, commercial comedy**

Equus
In this 1977 film, psychiatrist Richard Burton treats a young boy (Peter Firth) who has blinded horses, seemingly for no reason. **P, T, E, serious film**

Freud
This pseudo-biographical movie filmed in 1962 depicts 5 years, beginning in 1885, in the life of the Viennese psychologist Sigmund Freud (1856-1939). **P, T, E, historical, serious film**

Good Will Hunting
This Oscar-winning film (1997) stars Robin Williams as a troubled psychologist providing treatment for the main character (Matt Damon), a mathematical prodigy. The film also depicts (with humor) various treatment failures. **T, E, serious film**

I Never Promised You a Rose Garden
From 1977, this gripping drama recounts a schizophrenic teenager's struggle to cope with her mental illness with the help of a caring psychiatrist. **P, T, E, serious film**

Ordinary People
This 1980 film examines the treatment of a teenager suffering from depression, anxiety, and PTSD in the aftermath of his brother's death. **P, T, serious film**

Prince of Tides
In this 1991 film, an adaptation of a Pat Conroy novel, Nick Nolte plays a football coach who is estranged from his wife and who enters into an affair with the psychiatrist (Barbra Streisand) of his suicidal sister. **P, T, E, serious/commercial film**

The Sixth Sense
In this 1999 film by M. Night Shyamalan, Bruce Willis plays a child psychologist attempting to treat a young boy (Haley Joel Osment) who "sees dead people." **P, T, commercial/suspense/paranormal film**

Spellbound
From 1945, this Hitchcock film (with scenery by Salvador Dali) stars Ingrid Bergman as a psychiatrist and Gregory Peck as a patient involved in a manhunt. **P, T, E, commercial thriller/romance**

What About Bob?
From 1991, this comedy stars Bill Murray as a neurotic, insecure new patient attempting to see a preeminent psychiatrist (played by Richard Dreyfuss). Failing that, Murray stalks Dreyfuss and his family while they vacation. **P, T, E, comedy/commercial film**

Other Films:

Captain Newman, MD (1963) treatment. **P, T, serious film**
A Fine Madness (1966) personality disorders, lobotomy. **P, T, serious/comedy film**
High Anxiety (1977) anxiety, treatment. **T, comedy/ commercial film**
I'm Dancing As Fast As I Can (1982) substance dependence. **P, T, serious film**
The Royal Tennenbaums (2001) family dysfunctioning. **P, comedy/serious film**
Serial (1980) therapy. **P, T, comedy**
Tender Is the Night (1962) therapy. **P, T, E, commercial/serious film**
They Might Be Giants (1971) schizophrenia, treatment. **P, T, E, commercial/serious/comedy film**
A Woman Under the Influence (1974) institutionalization and ECT. **P, T, E, serious film**

Comer Video Segments

Available as a supplement, this revised set of videotapes contains short clips depicting various topics related to abnormal psychology. Please see the accompanying Video Guide for specific clips linked to Chapter 3.

Recommendations for Purchase or Rental

The Comer Video Segments include excerpts from many superb clinical documentaries. While the segments alone are ideal for use in lectures, it often is useful to assign the entire documentary for special class screenings or library use by students.

Films on Demand is a Web-based digital delivery service that has impressive psychology holdings. Their catalog can be accessed here: http://ffh.films.com/digitallanding.aspx

In addition, the following videos and other media may be of particular interest, and are available for purchase or rental and appropriate for use in class or for assignment outside of class.

Demonstration of the Cognitive Therapy of Depression
Aaron T. Beck, M.D., Director
The Beck Institute for Cognitive Therapy and Research

GSB Building, Suite 700
1 Belmont Avenue
Bala Cynwyd, PA 19004-1610
(610) 664-3020

The Royal Road—Psychoanalytic Approaches to the Dream
Menninger Video
Box 829
Topeka, KS 66601-0829
(913) 273-7500

Clinical Choice Points
Arnold Lazarus
56 Herrontown Circle
Princeton, NJ 08540

Multimodal Therapy Conducted by Arnold A. Lazarus, Ph.D.
APA Psychotherapy Videotape Series
American Psychological Association
(This videotape is part of the 12-program "APA Psychotherapy Videotape Series," produced by the American Psychological Association. Information about the APA Psychotherapy Videotape Series can be obtained from the APA Order Department: (800) 374-2721.)

Client-Centered Therapy: Part II—Therapy in Process: The 32nd Interview (Carl Rogers and Reuben H. Segel)
Distributor: Penn State Audio-Visual Services
University Division of Media and Learning Resources
The Pennsylvania State University
University Park, PA 16802
(800) 826-0132

Three Approaches to Psychotherapy I, II, and III
Showcasing various renowned therapists working with actual clients, the originals of this series are the infamous "Gloria films" with Drs. Rogers, Perls, and Ellis.
Psychological & Educational Films
3334 East Coast Highway, #252
Corona Del Mar, CA 92625
(949) 640-4029; Toll-Free in USA (888) 750-4029
Email: psychedfilms@earthlink.net

An impressive number of therapy demonstration films worth examining can be found through:

Psychological & Educational Films
3334 East Coast Highway, #252
Corona Del Mar, CA 92625
(949) 640-4029; Toll-Free in USA (888) 750-4029
Email: psychedfilms@earthlink.net

CLASS DEMONSTRATIONS AND ACTIVITIES

Panel Discussion I

Invite local therapists from varying theoretical orientations into your classroom to speak. It may be helpful to provide them in advance with a list of questions or topics to address, including: how their orientation impacts their assessment, diagnosis, and treatment of clients, therapy techniques they use based on their orientation, typical disorders they see in clients and their explanation for these disorders, the type of training they received, etc.

Panel Discussion II

Have students volunteer (or assign them) to portray therapists or theorists with differing theoretical orientations. Each student should present the prevailing theory and the related treatments/techniques. Students in the audience can ask questions of the panelists.

"It's Debatable: Do Children Model the Violence They See in the Media?" (see Preface instructions for conducting this activity)

Have students volunteer (or assign them) in teams to opposite sides of the debate topic. Have students present their cases in class following standard debate guidelines. See the box on p. 62 of the textbook.

Drug Treatment and the Revolving-Door Syndrome

Discuss the pros and cons of drug treatment with your students; list these on an overhead transparency, chalk or white board, or SMART Board. For which types of patients and mental disorders is drug treatment the most cost-efficient approach? Next, discuss the revolving-door syndrome in mental hospital admissions. The release of patients into the community without adequate support services has resulted in an increase in admissions to mental hospitals, with patients experiencing a greater frequency of admissions, though with shorter stays than in the past. A possible contributing factor is the use of drugs as a major outpatient treatment method. Individuals are admitted, stabilized with drugs and other therapy, then released with drug therapy. The symptoms diminish or disappear, the patient stops the drug treatment, the symptoms return, and the patient is readmitted.

Role-Playing

Using the sociocultural perspective, the techniques of role-playing can be demonstrated to the class. Have the class form small groups, and then ask one of the students in each group to assume the role of a patient and another the role of a therapist. You can suggest the disorders and perspectives that each group should use, or let the students develop their own. The students then can attempt to role-play the respective parts. Observe the groups as they role-play. Select the best example and have them continue in front of the class.

Overview of Models of Abnormality I

Write the names of the various models (psychodynamic, behavioral, cognitive, humanistic-existential) on an overhead transparency, chalk or white board, or SMART Board. Then ask students to list words, ideas, and names that they associate with each of the models. This activity will reintroduce the concepts of these models to the students and help them realize how much they already know about these models.

Overview of Models of Abnormality II

Divide the class into six sections, and then have each section adopt one of the theoretical perspectives described in this chapter. Using a case from the text, or one from your own experience, have each group attempt to explain the "client's" behavior from their theoretical model. After each group has presented its perspective, continue with a discussion of how each model explains some behaviors better than other behaviors.

Overview of Models of Abnormality III

Asking students how they might react to someone's mental illness is an interesting and useful way to reveal to them their "working model" of the causes and treatments of mental illness.

Present the following or a similar scenario: A friend comes to you depressed and talks about how "lousy" a person she is. Your friend has a very negative view of herself. You've noticed that for the last several weeks she hasn't exercised, which she usually does, and hasn't gone out with friends. Your friend describes difficulty sleeping and studying and generally feels physically unwell. You also know that she has had a great deal of difficulty with her family, and you suspect she may have been emotionally abused. She tells you she's going nowhere, that she can't do anything, that she has no future, and that no one will ever love her.

What do you say to your friend?

Of the following list of issues, which is the most important?

- How your friend *thinks* about herself and her future (cognitive perspective)
- What she *does* and doesn't do (i.e., she is isolated and is not getting any exercise) (behavioral perspective)
- She might have a neurochemical imbalance or *physical* disorder of the brain (biological perspective)
- Her problem might stem from her *past* and perhaps she is not even aware of it (psychodynamic perspective)
- She should realize what a good person she is and that she has the *potential* to be anything (humanistic perspective)

Based on your perspective, what do you tell her to do?

Classical Conditioning: Taste Aversion

Discuss conditioned taste aversions within the context of classical conditioning. Present the pictorial classical conditioning model to the class for discussion. For example, discuss taste aversions associated with food poisoning or the flu. You can also describe Garcia's research on coyotes that avoided sheep after eating lithium-treated mutton. Ask students for other examples.

"Here's $25,000 to Be Awarded to . . . ": Operant Conditioning and Classrooms

Present small groups with the challenge of using operant conditioning to manage unruly groups, such as schoolchildren. Ask the groups to come up with creative and nonaversive and practical solutions. Have the groups present their ideas, and then have the class vote on which group receives the grant to implement their idea.

Cognitive Model

An excellent way to introduce cognitive theory and the idea of irrational ideas and cognitive errors is to generate a list of common cognitive mistakes that college students make. Develop a handout with these types of examples: "An A is the only grade worth earning" or "The teachers are out to fail us." You can use the following list from Freeman and DeWolf's *Woulda, Coulda, Shoulda* to help students develop relevant examples of incorrect thinking.

- All-or-nothing thinking: believing the world is all good or all bad, all gain or all loss.
- Catastrophizing: exaggerating the negative aspects of an event.
- Comparing: judging by others' rather than by one's own performance, feelings, and values.
- Emotion reasoning: letting emotions overwhelm common sense.
- Fortune-telling: being disappointed with oneself for not being able to predict the future.
- Mind reading: jumping to conclusions about what others think or what they think you are thinking.
- Overgeneralization: thinking that if something has happened once, it will always happen.
- Perfectionism: requiring oneself to perform flawlessly.
- Unquestioning acceptance of critics: letting others define one's self-worth.

Categories of Irrational Thinking or Cognitive Errors

Write a list of categories of irrational thinking on an overhead transparency or on the board. Give examples of statements that a person might make to himself or herself, and then ask students to categorize each statement. Discuss what kind of effects these thoughts might have on a person.

Example Statements

- "He didn't say 'Hi' when I passed him in the hall. He must be mad at me." (Could lead to social phobia.)
- "He doesn't seem to like me. Nobody likes me." (Could lead to depression.)
- "She made critical remarks about my favorite singer. I need to reconsider my musical taste." (Could lead to intense self-doubt and relying on opinions of others.)
- "She got upset when I asked about her family. I should have known she was going to react like that." (Could lead to fear of conversing with others.)
- "I look heavier than her. I need to lose weight." (Could lead to eating disorders.)
- "I did poorly on this test. I will do poorly in this class." (Could lead to intense exam anxiety.)

Role-Playing a Therapist

Assign small groups of students a theoretical model. Have some students role-play the client, while others interview the client from the assigned perspective. Psychoanalytic and behavioral therapists are good choices.

SUGGESTED TOPICS FOR DISCUSSION

Modeling

Have students give examples of modeling from their experiences, the media, etc.

Cybertherapy

Lead students in a discussion of the Internet as a portal for therapy [see Psych Watch, text p. 69]. Faculty could conduct a survey of Internet usage, student attitudes about the Internet in general, its use for therapy, their own willingness to use it in that way, etc.

Spontaneous Remission

An area of debate in therapy outcome research concerns the percentage of patients who improve over time without treatment. Eysenck suggested that the figure is about two out of three, the same as those who improve with psychotherapy. How can therapists continue to provide therapy when many patients will spontaneously remit symptoms? Ask students to discuss this question.

Genetic Testing for Huntington's Disease

Discuss specific tests now available for genetic disorders, using Huntington's disease as an example. With Huntington's, all individuals with the genetic marker develop this fatal degenerative disease in middle age; those who test free of the genetic marker never develop this disease. If a person does not undergo such testing and has a parent with Huntington's disease, he or she has a 50 percent chance of having the disease (i.e., testing takes the odds to 100 percent or to 0 percent). Family members can be tested before they make reproductive decisions to find out if they might pass this dominant-gene disease onto offspring. Discuss the human genome project and the likelihood that, in the future, the genetic markers of many such diseases (including mental disorders) will be identified. Have students discuss the pros and cons of having a genetic test done. Would the students want to be tested for these disorders? If not, why not?

Developing a Personal Perspective

Discuss how the theoretical model of behavior that a student adopts has an impact not just on the student's view of psychology but also on the student's view of himself or herself. Ask students if they think of their own behaviors as being caused by unconscious processes, by biological forces, by learning experiences, or by their environment. Lead a discussion on individual understanding of psychology based on the

perspective. Ask students to identify their model and explain why they are influenced by this model.

Sociocultural Perspective

When addressing the sociocultural explanations of abnormal behavior, point out some of the major factors that are associated with this perspective, such as poverty, family structure and communications, societal stress, and class. Then ask students, if they were mental health professionals, what kinds of clients they would like to serve. Where would they like to practice: a private practice or an inner-city agency for homeless individuals? Continue this discussion with input from the students on the best methods available to mediate sociocultural factors.

Classical Conditioning: Childhood (and Adult) Fears

Simple examples of classical conditioning abound, such as the child who is afraid of dogs after being bitten, or the student who is afraid of school after being bullied. Ask for examples of common fears and how they might develop.

Operant Conditioning: Maintaining Fears

A useful way to introduce the idea of operant conditioning is to ask students how they might help someone overcome a serious fear. This will almost always generate suggestions about exposure, such as, "Have the fearful child sit on your lap while someone else pets the dog." This is a useful way to introduce ideas related to operant conditioning.

The Biological Model

Lead a discussion of the following topic. A tremendous amount of research on neurotransmitters in abnormal behavior has been conducted over the last 10 years. Although the exact causal relationships have not been determined, there is mounting evidence that neurotransmitters play a significant role in various abnormal behaviors. Some research areas have emphasized deficiencies of dopamine and its link to Parkinson's disease. Other findings have shown that excesses in dopamine reactivity are found in schizophrenia. Antipsychotic drugs are thought to alleviate the symptoms of schizophrenia by blocking or masking the action of dopamine. Many of the disorders that were best explained by other models are now being better explained by the biological model. Ask students for their input and examples.

Evil As the Cause of Mental Illness

Joan Houghton spent 5 weeks in a hospital following a psychotic episode. She recovered completely and took a job at the National Institute of Mental Health. In 1980, she wrote about her experiences, including her return home after being hospitalized:

> One Sunday I went to church alone after being absent for several weeks. The minister (who knew of my history, faith, and strong belief in God) began his sermon with reference to the devil. He said, "If you ever want to be convinced of the existence of the devil, you should visit a mental institution." To illustrate his point, he described people who had lost control of their bodily functions, who screamed out obscenities. I . . . drove home vowing to never return . . . but maybe I had misunderstood. [I invited the minister to my home.] His visit was our last encounter. Not only did he see evil in mental illness, but he conveyed an unforgiving attitude to those who have the misfortune of residing in mental hospitals.

Discuss how some people believe that mental illness is God's punishment or the result of evil. Ask students what they think of that belief. Be sensitive to the diverse religious views likely present (and largely unspoken) in the class.

Paradise Lost?

In *Paradise Lost*, Milton wrote, "The mind . . . can make a heaven of hell, a hell of heaven." Which model(s) of abnormality would agree?

An Integrative Model?

Lead a discussion on the strengths and weaknesses of an integrated approach to research and therapy. Often, young psychologists self-identify as "eclectic" and are told this is a "cop-out." Ask students why senior faculty are likely to have this reaction. Is it fair? Do they agree? What are the benefits of adopting a single theoretical model?

ASSIGNMENTS/EXTRA CREDIT SUGGESTIONS

Abnormal Psychology Tool Kit Video Questions

As a homework assignment, have students watch a video clip and answer the accompanying questions. Students can answer the questions directly into the online assessment feature. The results of these quizzes report to the site's built-in grade book.

Web Site Quiz

For homework or extra credit, have students complete the quizzes for Chapter 3 located on the companion Web site. Students can complete an online test of the key chapter material (using questions NOT from the test bank) and have their scores e-mailed directly to their instructor.

Essay Topics

For homework or extra credit, have students write an essay addressing one (or more) of the following topics:

(1) Research and report on the similarities seen in identical twins (see p. 50 of the text for an example).

(2) Which of the defense mechanisms listed in Table 3-1 (p. 54 of the text) have you seen in action? Do you agree with the underlying psychodynamic explanations? Are there alternative explanations?

(3) Compare and contrast the major theoretical models described in the chapter. Based on the information presented, which model is most appealing personally?

(4) What might the enormous popularity of psychotropic drugs suggest about the needs and coping styles of individuals today and about problem-solving in our technological society?

Research Topics

For homework or extra credit, have students write a research report addressing one (or more) of the following topics:

(1) Have students research the self-help groups in the local area. Most counties or states maintain a self-help clearinghouse of information. Some groups are "open" to nonsufferers attending, while others are "closed." Have students attend a few open meetings and report on their observations.

(2) Conduct a "Psych Info" search and write an annotated bibliography on two different theoretical perspectives and their research support.

(3) Do some research into Clinical Research Trials for medications. [See Figure 3-3 on p. 52] in the text for some guidance. What new drugs are coming "down the pipeline"?

(4) Conduct a "Psych Info" search on biological treatments for mental health disorders. Is psychosurgery still conducted?

(5) Conduct some Internet research into cybertherapy offerings for various disorders. [See Psychwatch on p. 69] of your text to get started. What do you think of these types of clinical offerings? Should they really be considered "therapy?"

Film Review

To earn extra credit, have students watch one (or more) of the mainstream films listed earlier in this chapter and write a brief (3–5 pages) report. Students should summarize the plot of the film in sufficient detail to demonstrate familiarity, but should focus their papers on the depiction of psychological abnormality. What errors or liberties did the filmmaker take? What is the message (implicit or explicit) concerning the mentally ill?

Crossword Puzzles

As a homework assignment or for extra credit, have students complete and submit Crossword Puzzle #3.

Word Searches

As a homework assignment or for extra credit, have students complete and submit Word Search #3.

Clinical Assessment, Diagnosis, and Treatment

LECTURE OUTLINE

I. **CLINICAL ASSESSMENT: HOW AND WHY DOES THE CLIENT BEHAVE ABNORMALLY?**
   A. Assessment is the collecting of relevant information in an effort to reach a conclusion
      1. Clinical assessment is used to determine how and why a person is behaving abnormally and how that person may be helped
      2. The focus of assessment is idiographic, that is, on an individual person

3.   Assessments also may be used to evaluate treatment progress

    B.   The specific tools used in an assessment depend on a clinician's theoretical orientation

    C.   Hundreds of clinical assessment tools have been developed and fall into three categories:

        1.   Clinical interviews

        2.   Tests

        3.   Observations

II.   CHARACTERISTICS OF ASSESSMENT TOOLS

    A.   To be useful, assessment tools must be standardized and have clear reliability and validity

    B.   To standardize a technique is to set up common steps to be followed whenever it is administered

        1.   One must standardize administration, scoring, and interpretation

    C.   Reliability refers to the consistency of an assessment measure; a good tool will always yield the same results in the same situation

        1.   There are two main types of reliability:

            a.   Test-retest reliability

                (a)   To test for this type of reliability, participants are tested on two occasions and the scores are correlated

                (b)   Because a good tool will yield the same results in the same situation, the higher the correlation, the greater the test's reliability

            b.   Interrater reliability

                (a)   Different judges independently agree on how to score and interpret a particular tool

    D.   Validity refers to the accuracy of a test's results

        1.   A good assessment tool must accurately measure what it is supposed to measure

        2.   There are three specific types of validity:

            a.   Face validity—a tool appears to measure what it is supposed to measure; does not necessarily indicate true validity

            b.   Predictive validity—a tool accurately predicts future characteristics or behavior

            c.   Concurrent validity—a tool's results agree with independent measures assessing similar characteristics or behavior

III.   CLINICAL INTERVIEWS

    A.   Interviews are face-to-face encounters and often are the first contact between a client and a clinician/assessor

        1.   They are used to collect detailed information, especially personal history, about a client

        2.   They are useful because they allow the interviewer to focus on whatever topics he or she considers most important

    B.   The focus of an interview depends on the interviewer's theoretical orientation

        1.   Interviews can be either unstructured or structured

            a.   In unstructured interviews, clinicians ask open-ended questions

            b.   In structured interviews, clinicians ask prepared questions, often from a published interview schedule

                (a)   These types of interviews also may include a mental status exam—a systematic assessment of the client's awareness, orientation to time and place, attention span, memory, judgment and insight, thought content and processes, mood, and appearance

    C.   What are the limitations of clinical interviews?

        1.   Interviews may lack validity or accuracy; individuals may be intentionally misleading

        2.   Interviewers may be biased or may make mistakes in judgment

        3.   Interviews, particularly unstructured ones, may lack reliability

IV.   CLINICAL TESTS

    A.   Clinical tests are devices for gathering information about specific topics from which broader information can be inferred

B. There are more than 500 different tests in use, falling into six categories:
1. Projective tests
   a. These tests require that subjects interpret vague and ambiguous stimuli or follow open-ended instructions
   b. They are used mainly by psychodynamic practitioners
   c. The most popular are the Rorschach test, Thematic Apperception Test, Sentence Completion, and Drawings
   d. What are the merits of projective tests?
      (a) They are helpful for providing "supplementary" information
      (b) They rarely have demonstrated much reliability or validity
      (c) They may be biased against minority ethnic groups
2. Personality inventories
   a. Usually self-response, these tests are designed to measure broad personality characteristics and focus on behaviors, beliefs, and feelings
   b. The most widely used is the Minnesota Multiphasic Personality Inventory (MMPI)—For adults, there is the original 1945 version or the 1989 revision (MMPI-2); there also is a special version (the MMPI-A) available for adolescents
      (a) The MMPI consists of more than 500 self-statements describing physical concerns; mood; morale; attitudes toward religion, sex, and social activities; and psychological symptoms that can be answered "true," "false," or "cannot say"
      (b) The MMPI has items to assess both careless responding and lying
      (c) It derives 10 clinical scales:
         (i) Hypochondriasis (HS): Items showing abnormal concern with bodily functions
         (ii) Depression (D): Items showing extreme pessimism and hopelessness
         (iii) Conversion hysteria (Hy): Items suggesting that the person may use physical or mental symptoms as a way of unconsciously avoiding conflicts and responsibilities
         (iv) Psychopathic deviate (PD): Items showing a repeated and gross disregard for social customs and an emotional shallowness
         (v) Masculinity-femininity (Mf): Items that are thought to distinguish male and female respondents
         (vi) Paranoia (Pa): Items that show abnormal suspiciousness and delusions of grandeur or persecution
         (vii) Psychathenia (Pt): Items that show obsessions, compulsions, abnormal fears, and guilt and indecisiveness
         (viii) Schizophrenia (Sc): Items that show bizarre or unusual thoughts or behavior, including extreme withdrawal, delusions, or hallucinations
         (ix) Hypomania (Ma): Items that show emotional excitement, overactivity, and flight of ideas
         (x) Social introversion (Si): Items that show shyness, little interest in people, and insecurity
      (d) Scores on the MMPI range from 0–120; Scores above 70 are considered deviant
      (e) Scores are graphed to create a "profile"
   c. What are the merits of personality inventories?
      (a) They are easier, cheaper, and faster to administer than projective tests
      (b) They are objectively scored and standardized
      (c) They appear to have greater validity than projective tests
         (i) However, they cannot be considered highly valid—measured traits often cannot be directly examined. How can we really know the assessment is correct?
      (d) Tests fail to allow for cultural differences in responses
3. Response inventories

      a.   Response inventories usually are self-response measures that focus on one specific area of functioning:

         (a) Affective inventories: measure the severity of such emotions as anxiety, depression, and anger

            (i)   One of the most widely used affective inventories is the Beck Depression Inventory (BDI)

         (b) Social skill inventories: ask respondents to indicate how they would respond in a variety of social situations

            (i)   These inventories usually are used by behavioral and sociocultural clinicians

         (c) Cognitive inventories: reveal a person's typical thoughts and assumptions

            (i)   These inventories usually are used by cognitive clinicians and researchers

      b.   What are the merits of response inventories?

         (a) Response inventories have strong face validity

         (b) Few (BDI is one exception) have been subjected to careful standardization, reliability, and/or validity procedures

4.   Psychophysiological tests

      a.   Psychophysiological tests measure physiological response as an indication of psychological problems

         (a) This includes measurement of heart rate, blood pressure, body temperature, galvanic skin response, and muscle contraction

      b.   The most popular psychophysiological test is the polygraph (lie detector)

      c.   What are the merits of psychophysiological tests?

         (a) These tests require expensive equipment that must be tuned and maintained

         (b) They also can be inaccurate and unreliable

            (i)   This weakness is described in more detail in *PsychWatch* on p. 95 of the text

5.   Neurological and neuropsychological tests

      a.   Neurological tests *directly* assess brain function by assessing brain structure and activity

         (a) Examples: EEG, PET scans, CAT scans, MRI, fMRI

      b.   Neuropsychological tests *indirectly* assess brain function by measuring cognitive, perceptual, and motor functioning on certain tasks

         (a) The most widely used neuropsychological test is the Bender Visual-Motor Gestalt Test

      c.   What are the merits of neurological and neuropsychological tests?

         (a) These types of tests can be very accurate

         (b) These tests are, at best, only rough and general screening devices

            (i)   They are best when used in a battery of tests, each targeting a specific skill area

6.   Intelligence tests

      a.   Intelligence tests are designed to indirectly measure intellectual ability and are typically comprised of a series of tests assessing both verbal and nonverbal skills

         (a) They generate an intelligence quotient—the ratio of a person's "mental" age relative to his or her "chronological" age

      b.   What are the merits of intelligence tests?

         (a) These are among the most carefully produced of all clinical tests

         (b) They are highly standardized on large groups of subjects, and, as such, have very high reliability and validity

         (c) Performance can be influenced by nonintelligence factors (e.g., motivation, anxiety, test-taking experience)

         (d) Tests may contain cultural biases in language or tasks

         (e) Members of minority groups may have less experience and be less comfortable with these types of tests, influencing their results

V. CLINICAL OBSERVATIONS
  A. Clinical observations are systematic observations of behavior
  B. There are several different kinds:
   1. Naturalistic and Analog
    a. Naturalistic observations occur in everyday environments, including homes, schools, institutions (hospitals and prisons), and community settings
    b. Most focus on parent-child, sibling-child, or teacher-child interactions
    c. Observations generally are made by "participant observers" and reported to a clinician
    d. If naturalistic observation is impractical, analog observations are used and occur in an artificial setting
    e. What are the merits of naturalistic and analog observations?
     (a) Reliability is a concern as different observers may focus on different aspects of behavior
     (b) Validity is a concern
      (i) There is a risk of "overload," "observer drift," and observer bias
      (ii) Client reactivity also may limit validity
      (iii) Observations may lack cross-situational validity
   2. Self-monitoring
    a. People observe themselves and carefully record the frequency of certain behaviors, feelings, or cognitions as they occur over time
    b. What are the merits of self-monitoring?
     (a) Self-monitoring is useful in assessing both infrequent behaviors and overly frequent behaviors
     (b) It provides a means of measuring private thoughts or perceptions
     (c) Validity often is a problem:
      (i) Clients may not record information accurately
      (ii) When people monitor themselves, they often change their behavior

VI. DIAGNOSIS: DOES THE CLIENT'S SYNDROME MATCH A KNOWN DISORDER?
  A. Using all available information, clinicians attempt to paint a "clinical picture"
   1. This picture is influenced by their theoretical orientation
  B. Using assessment data and the clinical picture, clinicians attempt to make a *diagnosis*—a determination that a person's psychological problems constitute a particular disorder
   1. This diagnosis is based on an existing classification system
  C. Classification systems are lists of categories, disorders, and symptom descriptions, with guidelines for assignment, focusing on clusters of symptoms (syndromes)
  D. In current use in the United States is the DSM-IV-TR: Diagnostic and Statistical Manual of Mental Disorders (4th edition, Text Revision)
   1. The DSM-IV was published in 1994 and revised slightly in 2000 (TR); it lists approximately 400 disorders [See Figure 4-3, text p. 99]
   2. The DSM describes criteria for diagnosis, key clinical features, and related features that are often, but not always, present
   3. The DSM is multi-axial, that is, it uses five axes (branches of information) to develop a full clinical picture
    a. People usually receive a diagnosis on either Axis I or Axis II, but they may receive diagnoses on both
     (a) Axis I: Most frequently diagnosed disorders, except personality disorders and mental retardation
     (b) Axis II: Personality disorders and mental retardation
      (i) Long-standing problems
     (c) Axis III: Relevant general medical conditions
     (d) Axis IV: Psychosocial and environmental problems
     (e) Axis V: Global assessment of psychological, social, and occupational functioning (GAF)
      (i) Currently and in the past year
      (ii) 0–100 Scale

E. Is DSM-IV-TR an effective classification system?
  1. A classification system, like an assessment method, is judged by its reliability and validity
  2. Reliability in this context means that different clinicians are likly to agree on a diagnosis using the system to diagnose the same client
      a. DSM-IV-TR appears to have greater reliability than any previous editions due to the extensive use of field trials
      b. However, reliability still is a concern
  3. Validity in this context means an accuracy of the information that its diagnostic categories provide; predictive validity is of the most use clinically
      a. DSM-IV-TR has greater validity than any previous editions due to extensive literature reviews and field studies
      b. However, validity still is a concern
  4. Beyond concerns about reliability and validity, a growing number of theorists believe that two fundamental problems weaken the DSM-IV-TR:
      a. The basic assumption that disorders are *qualitatively* different from normal behavior
      b. The reliance on *discrete* diagnostic categories
F. Call for change: DSM-5
  1. Given such concerns about DSM-IV-TR, it's no surprise that a new and improved DSM has been in the works for decades.
  2. A Task Force and numerous work groups have been at work since 2006
  3. A first draft was released online in 2010, with a request for suggestions, and a revised draft was released in 2011
  4. Some proposed changes include additions to and removals of diagnostic categories, reorganization of categories, and changes in terminology [See p. 104 in the text for a partial list of proposed changes]
  5. The publication of DSM-5 currently is set for 2013
G. Can diagnosis and labeling cause harm?
  1. Misdiagnosis is always a concern because of the reliance on clinical judgment
  2. Also present is the issue of labeling and stigma; for some, diagnosis may be a self-fulfilling prophecy
  3. Because of these problems, some clinicians would like to do away with the practice of diagnosis

VII. **TREATMENT: HOW MIGHT THE CLIENT BE HELPED?**
  A. Treatment decisions
    1. Treatment decisions begin with assessment information and diagnostic decisions to determine a treatment plan
        a. Clinicians use a combination of idiographic and nomothetic information
        b. Other factors important for determining a treatment plan are:
            (a) Therapist theoretical orientation
            (b) Current research
            (c) General state of clinical knowledge—currently focusing on empirically supported, evidence-based treatment
  B. The effectiveness of treatment
    1. There are over 400 forms of therapy in practice, but is therapy effective?
        a. This is a difficult question to answer:
            (a) How do you define success?
            (b) How do you measure improvement?
            (c) How do you compare treatments—people differ in their problems, personal styles, and motivations for therapy; therapists differ in skill, knowledge, orientation, and personality; and therapies differ in theory, format, and setting
    2. Therapy outcome studies typically assess one of the following questions:
        a. Is therapy in *general* effective?

        (a)   Research suggests that therapy is generally more helpful than no treatment or a placebo

        (b)   In one major study using meta-analysis, the average person who received treatment was better off than 75 percent of the untreated subjects [See Figure 4-4, text p. 107].

        (c)   Some clinicians are concerned with a related question: Can therapy be harmful?

            (i)   Therapy does have the potential to be harmful

            (ii)   Studies suggest that 5–10 percent of clients get worse with treatment

    b.   Are *particular* therapies generally effective?

        (a)   Generally, treatment outcome studies lump all therapies together to consider their general effectiveness

            (i)   One critic has called this the "uniformity myth"

        (b)   It is argued that scientists must look at the effectiveness of particular therapies

            (i)   There is a movement ("rapprochement") to look at commonalities among therapies, regardless of clinician orientation

    c.   Are *particular* therapies effective for *particular* problems?

        (a)   Studies now are being conducted to examine the effectiveness of specific treatments for specific disorders:

            (i)   "*What* specific treatment, by *whom*, is the most effective for *this* individual with *that* specific problem, and under *which* set of circumstances?"

        (b)   Recent studies focus on the effectiveness of combined approaches—drug therapy combined with certain forms of psychotherapy—to treat certain disorders

LEARNING OBJECTIVES

1.   Define clinical assessment and discuss the roles of the clinical interview, tests, and observations.

2.   Summarize the axis approach of the DSM series, and describe the general features of DSM-IV-TR.

3.   List the major classification of disorders from Axis I of the DSM-IV-TR.

4.   Explain some of the proposed changes to DSM-5.

5.   Discuss the dangers of diagnosing and labeling in classifying mental disorders.

6.   Discuss types and effectiveness of treatments for mental disorders.

KEY TERMS

analog observation	clinical interview	face validity
assessment	comorbidity	field trial
battery	concurrent validity	fMRI
Bender Visual-Motor Gestalt Test	diagnosis	idiographic understanding
	Draw-a-Person (DAP) Test	intelligence quotient (IQ)
CAT scan	DSM-IV	intelligence test
classification system	EEG	interrater reliability

mental status exam
Minnesota Multiphasic
   Personality Inventory
   (MMPI)
MRI
naturalistic observation
neuroimaging techniques
neurological test
neuropsychological
   test
observer bias
observer drift
observer overload

participant observer
personality inventory
PET scan
predictive validity
projective test
psychopharmacologist
psychophysiological test
rapprochement movement
reactivity
reliability
response inventories
Rorschach test
self-monitoring

sentence-completion test
standardization
structured interview
syndrome
test
test–retest reliability
Thematic Apperception Test
   (TAT)
therapy outcome study
uniformity myth
unstructured interview
validity

MEDIA RESOURCES

Abnormal Psychology Student Tool Kit

Produced and edited by Ronald J. Comer, Princeton University and Gregory Comer, Princeton Academic Resources. Tied directly to the CyberStudy sections in the text, this Student Tool Kit offers 57 intriguing Video Cases running 3 to 7 minutes each. The Video Cases focus on persons affected by disorders discussed in the text. Students first view the video and then answer a series of thought-provoking questions. Additionally, the Student Tool Kit contains multiple-choice practice test questions with built-in instructional feedback for every option.

Video Cases and Discussions:

- How do clinicians arrive at a diagnosis?
- See neuroimaging in action.
- What causes aggression and violence?

Practical, Research, and Decision-Making Exercises:

- Assessing and labeling in everyday life
- Uncovering the effects of expectations on observations

PowerPoint Slides

Available at the Instructor's site on the companion Web site are comprehensive PowerPoint slide presentations and supplemental student handouts for Chapter 4. The slide files reflect the main points of the chapter in significant detail. Student handouts were created using the instructor slides as a base, with key points re-

placed as "fill-in" items. Answer keys and suggestions for use also are provided.

DSM-IV-TR Masters

B-3, B-4 What's New in DSM-IV-TR?
B-5, B-6 Axis I Disorders in DSM-IV-TR
B-7, B-8 Global Assessment of Functioning (GAF) Scale

Internet Sites

Please see Appendix A for full and comprehensive references.

   Sites relevant to Chapter 4 material are:

http://www.apa.org/science/programs/testing/index.aspx
Created by the American Psychological Association's Science Directorate, this site offers information on the process of psychological testing and assessment.

http://www.guidetopsychology.com/testing.htm
http://www.guidetopsychology.com/diagnos.htm
These Web sites, part of the main site—A Guide to Psychology and its Practice—are maintained by Dr. Raymond Lloyd Richmond and cover the process of psychological testing and diagnosis clearly.

http://www.queendom.com
http://www.psychtests.com
These two sites, run by the same parent company, offer many versions of different psychological tests. Some tests mirror more famous (and expensive) assessments and tout solid psychometrics, while others are strictly

for fun. There is a fee to use some of the more detailed measures.

Mainstream Films

Films relevant to Chapter 4 material are listed and summarized below.

Key to Film Listings:
P = psychopathology focus
T = treatment focus
E = ethical issues raised

Please note that some of the films suggested may have graphic sexual or violent content due to the nature of certain subject matters.

An Angel at My Table
This 1990 film by Jane Campion recounts the autobiographical tale of New Zealand poet Janet Frame who was misdiagnosed with schizophrenia and spent 8 years in a mental hospital. **P, T, E, serious film**

Nuts
This 1987 film stars Barbra Streisand as a prostitute charged with murder facing not incarceration but commitment to an institution. **P, T, E, serious/commercial film**

Other Films:

Captain Newman, MD (1963) treatment. **P, T, serious film**
A Fine Madness (1966) personality disorders, lobotomy. **P, T, serious/comedy film**
The Exorcist (1973) clinical assessment, diagnosis, and treatment. **P, T, commercial/serious film**
Igby Goes Down (2002) dysfunctional family. **P, serious film**
Serial (1980) therapy. **P, T, comedy**
Tender Is the Night (1962) therapy. **P, T, E, commercial/serious film**
They Might Be Giants (1971) schizophrenia, treatment. **P, T, E, commercial/serious/comedy film**
A Woman Under the Influence (1974) institutionalization and ECT. **P, T, E, serious film**

Comer Video Segments

Available as a supplement, this revised set of videotapes contains short clips depicting various topics related to abnormal psychology. Please see the accompanying Video Guide for specific clips linked to Chapter 4.

Recommendations for Purchase or Rental

The Comer Video Segments include excerpts from many superb clinical documentaries. While the segments alone are ideal for use in lectures, it often is useful to assign the entire documentary for special class screenings or library use by students.

Films on Demand is a Web-based digital delivery service that has impressive psychology holdings. The catalog can be accessed here: http://ffh.films.com/digitallanding.aspx

In addition, the following videos and other media may be of particular interest, and are available for purchase or rental and appropriate for use in class or for assignment outside of class.

Hillcrest Family: Studies in Human Communication—Assessment Interviews 1–4
This is a series of films consisting of four separate interviews of the Hillcrest family by four psychiatrists.
Educational Media Collection
Box 353090
University of Washington
Seattle, WA 98195-3090
Scheduling: (206) 543-9909
Preview: (206) 543-9908
Reference: (206) 543-9907

Psychiatric Interview #18: Evaluation for Diagnosis
Psychiatric Interview #21: Evaluation for Diagnosis
Educational Media Collection
Box 353090
University of Washington
Seattle, WA 98195-3090
Scheduling: (206) 543-9909
Preview: (206) 543-9908
Reference: (206) 543-9907

CLASS DEMONSTRATIONS AND ACTIVITIES

Personality Inventories

Bring to class examples of personality inventories, projective tests, and intelligence tests. Discuss the most important aspects of each test. Try to include items from the tests mentioned in this chapter, such as the MMPI, Rorschach Inkblot, and TAT. Elicit student reactions to the content of the tests. Ask the question: Are these tests valid today? Request suggestions from the class on how to improve these specific examples you have presented.

Mental Status Exam

Solicit a volunteer from class as a participant in a mental status exam [Note: Choose carefully!] Demonstrate the technique of establishing rapport and the systematic evaluation of client awareness, orientation, etc. Alternatively, a video presentation of such an interview can be shown.

Projective Testing

Bring in, display, and discuss the "results" seen in fake Rorschach inkblots. Some manufactured board games include such cards, and some popular press books are projective in nature. As discussed in the text [See MediaSpeak, text p. 89], the 10 original Rorschach inkblots and common answers are available on Wikipedia. Whether faculty choose to show these images in class is worthy of a discussion of ethics and in of itself.

"Pretend, for a moment, that you are a . . . ": DSM-IV Multi-axial Assessment

Multi-axial assessment can be confusing to students who do not understand its relevance. Students can realize the importance of multiple axes when discovering for themselves the importance of Axes III and IV in particular. Present yourself as a patient seeking psychotherapy for depression or anxiety. Tell students that you recently have had medical problems and that you have experienced some stressful life events. Present fairly severe instances of both, and ask which is more relevant to the treatment being planned by them. A disagreement will likely ensue about which is more important, leading to a general consensus that both are important. Discuss Axes III and IV within this context.

Role-Playing an Interviewer

Divide students into small groups and tell them to role-play as counselors. Each student is to develop a list of things he or she would most want to know about a client at the end of the first session together. Next, have the students share their lists and develop one master list. Discuss what their impressions of the important information are and why.

The Importance of Standardization

All tests must be standardized if a person's score is to be compared to others. This means giving the same test in the same fashion to all who take it; it also means comparing a person's scores to an appropriate comparison group. The importance of these can be demonstrated easily.

Ask for four volunteers to do the following. Hand each of them a sheet with several multiplication problems (e.g., 325 × 27). The numbers should be the same, but some should be presented in a row and others in column format (the manner in which they need to be written to do the problem). Ask each student to do the problems. Collect the sheet after 15 seconds for the first student, after 30 seconds for the second, and after completion for the other two students. Compare the results and ask the first two for their reaction (they will complain that they weren't given as much time). With the latter two, state this: "You [point to student] did very well when compared to a group of fifth-grade kids I gave these problems to; you are very smart" [give student a "Very Smart" certificate]. "You [point to other student] did not do so well. The advanced college math students down the hall did much better" [don't give student a "Very Smart" certificate]. Ask for their reactions.

This activity can be used to introduce the standardization of administration necessary for the WAIS, the Rorschach, and the MMPI.

Neuropsychological Testing

A growing area of assessment in the past two decades is neuropsychological testing. Several simple neuropsych tests can be brought to class (or created), such as the Trail-Making Tests (two tests: in the first, the patient draws lines through a series of numbers in circles in consecutive order; in the second, numbers and letters are alternated, i.e., 1-A-2-B-, etc.). The Finger-Tapping Test is also easy to demonstrate (i.e., how many times can a person tap his or her index finger in a set amount of time, usually 1 minute). Simple tests such as these, when administered to many people, can reveal whether the parts of the brain are working well together (e.g., the part of the brain that alternates numbers and letters). Persons with neurological problems (such as injuries) may have difficulty with these tasks, depending on whether that part of the brain is being tested.

Evaluating the DSM Series

Compile and show the lists of disorders from DSM, DSM-II, DSM-III, DSM-III-R, DSM-IV, and DSM-IV-TR. The increase in material since the DSM-I is quite dramatic and worth discussing. Ask students to discuss why each edition has more material than the prior editions. One explanation is that our society is becoming more disordered. An alternative explanation is that the mental health profession has become more specific and inclusive of true problems. A third is that the profession "wants" more problems to increase business. An interesting disorder to trace through the series is schizophrenia. NOTE: This activity can be further enhanced by a discussion of the likely changes to DSM-5. See p. 104 in the text for a partial list.

SUGGESTED TOPICS FOR DISCUSSION

Validity

Ask students for examples of each of the following kinds of validity they have experienced in college: face validity, predictive validity, content validity, and construct validity. Ask them to provide examples of situations in which proper validity standards were not met.

Reliability and Ratings

Ask students to cite examples of ratings used in the media or everyday life (e.g., television's *American Idol, Dancing with the Stars, The Bachelor;* movie ratings, interpersonal ratings of attractiveness, etc.). Discuss the reliability (or lack thereof) of such scores.

Projective Testing

Have students discuss types of "projective" tests they have seen or taken. Some common examples include looking for shapes in the clouds, looking at abstract art, and some magazine, book, and Internet tests. One could stretch the topic to include reactions to films with ambiguous endings (e.g., *Unfaithful*).

Multicultural Psychology

Using Table 4-1 (text p. 91) as a guide, have students discuss the importance of sensitivity to, and awareness of, multicultural "hotspots."

Diagnostic Categories: Criticisms and Advantages

It is useful to have a discussion of the rationale and criticisms of diagnoses. This activity works best by starting with criticisms of diagnoses, which are easier for students to generate. After generating criticisms, point out that diagnostic labels are necessary, and request guesses as to why.

Criticisms

- Diagnoses can give scientists and clinicians a false sense of having explained behavior. For example, a clinician might claim that his patient is highly suspicious because he has a paranoid disorder, but this tells us nothing about why the patient is paranoid. Likewise, to say that a patient is suicidal because of her depression does

not aid in either understanding or helping the patient.
- Diagnoses can be used to rationalize or excuse certain undesirable behaviors.
- Diagnoses can and sometimes do stigmatize persons, creating an "us versus them" sense, that is, by promoting the idea that there is a clear-cut distinction between normal and abnormal behavior.
- Diagnoses may be "sticky," influencing others' perceptions of subsequent behavior, as exemplified in the Rosenhan study.

Advantages

- Scientific: Science relies upon a common language and categorization. Agreed-upon categories or names for illnesses are necessary to facilitate research into their etiology and treatment. Agreeing on findings from studies of depression or schizophrenia would be very difficult if scientists did not agree on what these disorders are and are not.
- Clinical: The presence of an illness is indicated by giving someone a diagnosis. If there is no diagnosis, then the person has no illness. Thus, diagnoses tell clinicians when to initiate treatment and when treatment should be terminated (because the person is better). Likewise, diagnoses can tell us what treatment might be effective.
- Legal significance: Defining abnormal behavior helps us determine when a person is responsible for his or her behavior. On March 30, 1981, John Hinckley Jr. shot and seriously wounded President Ronald Reagan outside a hotel in Washington, D.C. In May 1982, a jury declared Hinckley innocent by reason of insanity.

Personality Tests and Job Screening

A trend that appears to be increasing in recent years is the tendency of companies to use personality tests in the application screening process for prospective hires. Ask students to share such experiences. Explore the types of questions asked and what the students thought of the tests. Ask the class to discuss the pros and cons of using personality tests in this situation.

ASSIGNMENTS/EXTRA CREDIT SUGGESTIONS

Media and Personality Testing

Have students collect questionnaires from popular magazines or self-help books (definitely give a deadline, and consider giving extra credit). Compare these items with the more standardized, classical personality inventories, such as the MMPI.

Abnormal Psychology Student Tool Kit Video Questions

As a homework assignment, have students watch a video clip and answer the accompanying questions. Students can answer the questions directly into the online assessment feature. The results of these quizzes report to the site's built-in grade book.

Clinical Observations

Have students conduct two different types of clinical observation: naturalistic and self-monitoring. Behaviors to monitor must be preapproved by the instructor.

Web Site Quiz

For homework or extra credit, have students complete the quiz for Chapter 4 located on the companion Web site. Students can complete an on line test of the key chapter material (using questions NOT from the test bank) and have their scores e-mailed directly to the course instructor.

Essay Topics

For homework or extra credit, have students write an essay addressing one (or more) of the following topics:

(1) Design a research study using clinical observation as the means of data collection. Address the issues associated with clinical observation and be sure to specify naturalistic or analog with support for your decision.

(2) Visit the Queendom.com or Psychtests.com Web site and complete two clinical tests. Compare and contrast the two in terms of reliability and validity. Do you feel confident in the results of the assessment? Why or why not?

(3) How would you grade the tests you take in school? That is, how reliable and valid are they? What about tests you see in newspapers or magazines? Attach some examples.

Research Topics

For homework or extra credit, have students write a research report addressing one (or more) of the following topics:

(1) Research the MMPI and report on its validity, reliability, and utility in different populations.

(2) Conduct a "Psych Info" search and write an annotated bibliography on new assessment tools for a particular diagnosis (e.g., alcohol dependence, anorexia nervosa)

(3) Research and report on Culture-Bound Abnormality [See PsychWatch, text p. 101 for an example].

(4) Conduct a Web site review of some sites similar to those listed in PsychWatch on p. 108 in the text. Compare the information to more objective and science-based sites on the same topics (see Appendix A for suggestions).

Film Review

To earn extra credit, have students watch one (or more) of the mainstream films listed earlier in this chapter and write a brief (3–5 pages) report. Students should summarize the plot of the film in sufficient detail to demonstrate familiarity, but should focus their papers on the depiction of psychological abnormality. What errors or liberties did the filmmaker make or take? What is the message (implicit or explicit) concerning the mentally ill?

Crossword Puzzles

As a homework assignment or for extra credit, have students complete and submit Crossword Puzzle #4.

Word Searches

As a homework assignment or for extra credit, have students complete and submit Word Search #4.

CHAPTER **5**

Anxiety Disorders

LECTURE OUTLINE

I. **ANXIETY**
   A. What distinguishes fear from anxiety?
      1. Fear is a state of immediate alarm in response to a serious threat to one's well-being

2. Anxiety is a state of alarm in response to a vague sense of being in danger
3. Both fear and anxiety have the same physiological features: increase in respiration, perspiration, muscle tension, etc.

B. Although unpleasant, experiences of fear/anxiety are useful
1. They prepare us for action—for "fight or flight"—when danger threatens
2. However, for some people, the discomfort is too severe or too frequent, lasts too long, or is triggered too easily
   a. These people are said to have an anxiety or related disorder

II. ANXIETY DISORDERS

A. Anxiety disorders are the most common mental disorders in the United States
B. In any given year, 18 percent of the adult population suffer from one or another of the six DSM-IV-TR anxiety disorders; close to 29 percent develop one of the disorders at some point in their lives
C. Only around one-fifth of these individuals seek treament
D. Anxiety disorders cost $42 billion each year in health care, lost wages, and lost productivity
E. There are six disorders characterized as anxiety disorders:
1. Generalized anxiety disorder (GAD)
2. Phobia
3. Panic disorder
4. Obsessive-compulsive disorder (OCD)
5. Acute stress disorder
6. Posttraumatic stress disorder (PTSD)
F. Most individuals with one anxiety disorder suffer from a second as well
1. In addition, many individuals with an anxiety disorder also experience depression

III. GENERALIZED ANXIETY DISORDER (GAD)

A. This disorder is characterized by excessive anxiety under most circumstances and worry about practically anything
1. GAD often is called "free-floating" anxiety
2. The "danger" of the situation is not a factor
B. Symptoms include restlessness, easy fatigue, irritability, muscle tension, and/or sleep disturbance and last at least six months
C. The disorder is common in Western society
1. As many as 4 percent of the U.S. population have symptoms of the disorder in any given year and about 6 percent at some time during their lives
D. It usually first appears in childhood or adolescence
E. Women are diagnosed more than men by 2:1
F. Around one-quarter are currently in treatment
G. Various theories have been offered to explain development of the disorder:
1. The sociocultural perspective: societal and multicultural factors
   a. GAD is most likely to develop in people faced with social conditions that truly are dangerous
      (a) Research supports this theory (e.g., nuclear disaster at Three Mile Island (TMI) in 1979, Hurricane Katrina in 2005, Haiti earthquake in 2010)
   b. One of most powerful forms of societal stress is poverty
      (a) Why? Less equality, less power, and greater vulnerability; run-down communities, higher crime rates, fewer educational and job opportunities, and greater risk for health problems
   c. As would be predicted by the model, rates of GAD are higher in lower SES groups
   d. Because race is closely tied to stress in the United States, it also is tied to the prevalence of GAD
      (a) In any given year, African Americans are 30 percent more likely than white Americans to suffer from GAD
      (b) African American women have the highest rates (6.6 percent)

- (c) If, however, income and job opportunity are held steady across races, this racial difference disappears
- (d) Multicultural researchers have not consistently found a heightened rate of GAD among Hispanics in the United States, although they do note the prevalence of *nervios* in that population
  - e. Although poverty and other social pressures may create a climate for GAD, other factors clearly are at work
    - (a) Most people living in dangerous environments do not develop GAD
    - (b) Other models attempt to explain why some develop the disorder and others do not
2. The psychodynamic perspective
   - a. Freud believed all children experience anxiety and use ego defense mechanims to help control it
     - (a) *Realistic anxiety* results from actual danger
     - (b) *Neurotic anxiety* results when children are prevented from expressing id impulses
     - (c) *Moral anxiety* results when children are punished for expressing id impulses
     - (d) Some children experience particularly high levels of anxiety, or their defense mechanisms are particularly inadequate, and they may develop GAD
   - b. Today's psychodynamic theorists often disagree with specific aspects of Freud's explanation, but most continue to believe the disorder can be traced to inadequate parent–child relationships
   - c. Some researchers have found some support for the psychodynamic perspective:
     - (a) People with GAD are particularly likely to use defense mechanisms (especially repression)
     - (b) Children who were severely punished for expressing id impulses have higher levels of anxiety later in life
   - d. Some scientists question whether these studies show what they claim to show, for example
     - (a) Discomfort with painful memories or "forgetting" in therapy is not necessarily defensive
   - e. Psychodynamic therapies
     - (a) Use the same general techniques for treating all dysfunction:
       - (i) Free association
       - (ii) Therapist interpretation of transference, resistance, and dreams
     - (b) Specific treatment for GAD:
       - (i) Freudians focus less on fear and more on control of id
       - (ii) Object-relations therapists attempt to help patients identify and settle early relationship conflicts
     - (c) Overall, controlled research has not typically shown psychodynamic approaches to be helpful in treating cases of GAD
     - (d) Short-term dynamic therapy may be the exception to this trend
3. The humanistic perspective
   - a. Theorists propose that GAD, like other psychological disorders, arises when people stop looking at themselves honestly and acceptingly
   - b. This view is best illustrated by Carl Rogers' explanation:
     - (a) Lack of "unconditional positive regard" in childhood leads to harsh self-standards, known as "conditions of worth"
     - (b) These threatening self-judgments break through and cause anxiety, setting the stage for GAD to develop
   - c. Practitioners of Rogers' treatment approach, "client-centered" therapy, focus on the creation of an accepting environment where they can show positive regard and empathize with clients

(a)   Although case reports have been positive, controlled studies have only sometimes found client-centered therapy to be more effective than placebo or no therapy

(b)   Further, only limited support has been found for Rogers' explanation of causal factors

4.   The cognitive perspective

a.   Followers of this model suggest that psychological problems are caused by dysfunctional ways of thinking

b.   Because GAD is characterized by excessive worry (a cognitive symptom), these theorists have had much to say

c.   Initially, cognitive theorists suggested that GAD is caused primarily by *maladaptive assumptions*

d.   Albert Ellis proposed that the presence of basic irrational assumptions lead people to act in inappropriate ways, for example:

(a)   It is a necessity for humans to be loved by everyone

(b)   It is catastrophic when things are not as I want them

(c)   If something is fearful, I should be terribly concerned and dwell on the possibility of its occurrence

(d)   I should be competent in all domains to be a worthwhile person

(e)   When these assumptions are applied to everyday life, GAD may develop

e.   Similarly, another theorist is Aaron Beck, who argued that those with GAD hold unrealistic silent assumptions implying imminent danger:

(a)   Any strange situation is dangerous

(b)   A situation/person is unsafe until proven safe

f.   Research supports the presence of both of these types of assumptions in GAD, particularly about dangerousness

g.   New wave cognitive explanations

(a)   In recent years, three new explanations have emerged:

(i)   Metacognitive theory developed by Wells; holds that people with GAD implicitly hold both positive and negative beliefs about worrying

(ii)   Certain individuals consider it unacceptable that negative events may occur, even if the possibility is very small; they worry in an effort to find "correct" solutions

(iii)   Avoidance theory developed by Borkovec; holds that worrying serves a "positive" function for those with GAD by reducing unusually high levels of bodily arousal

(b)   Both theories have received considerable research support

h.   There are two kinds of cognitive approaches

(a)   Changing maladaptive assumptions—based on the work of Ellis & Beck:

(i)   Ellis's rational-emotive therapy (RET):

1.   Point out irrational assumptions

2.   Suggest more appropriate assumptions

3.   Assign related homework

4.   This model has limited research, but findings are positive

(b)   Helping clients understand the special role that worrying plays and changing their views about it

(i)   Breaking down worrying

1.   Therapists begin with psychoeducation about worrying and GAD

2.   Assign self-monitoring of bodily arousal and cognitive responses

3.   As therapy progresses, clients become increasingly skilled at identifying their worrying and their misguided attempts to control their lives by worrying

        4. With continued practice, clients are expected to see the world as less threatening; to adopt more constructive ways of coping; and to worry less

    (ii) Research has begun to indicate that a concentrated focus on worrying is a helpful addition to traditional cognitive therapy

5. The biological perspective

    a. Biological theorists hold that GAD is caused chiefly by biological factors

    b. This model is supported by family pedigree studies

        (a) Biological relatives more likely to have GAD (~15 percent) compared to the general population (~6 percent); the closer the relative, the greater the likelihood

            (i) There is, however, the competing explanation of shared upbringing

    c. One biological factor that has been examined is GABA inactivity

        (a) In the 1950s, researchers determined that benzodiazepines (Valium, Xanax) reduced anxiety—Why?

            (i) Neurons have specific receptors (like a lock and key)

            (ii) Benzodiazepine receptors ordinarily receive gamma-aminobutyric acid (GABA, a common NT in the brain)

            (iii) GABA is an inhibitory messenger; when received, it causes a neuron to STOP firing

        (b) In the normal fear reaction:

            (i) Key neurons fire more rapidly creating a general state of excitability experienced as fear/anxiety

            (ii) Continuous firing triggers a feedback system; brain and body activities work to reduce the level of excitability

            (iii) Some neurons release GABA to inhibit neuron firing, thereby reducing the experience of fear/anxiety

            (iv) Problems with the feedback system are theorized to cause GAD

                1. It may be: GABA too low, too few receptors, ineffective receptors

        (c) Promising (but problematic) explanation:

            (i) Other NTs also bind to GABA receptors

            (ii) Research conducted on lab animals—is fear in animals really like anxiety in humans? [See sidebar box on text p. 123]

            (iii) Issue of causal relationships—do physiological events *cause* anxiety? How can we know? What are alternative explanations?

    d. Biological treatments

        (a) Antianxiety drugs

            (i) Pre-1950s treatments were barbiturates (sedative-hypnotics)

            (ii) Post-1950s treatments were benzodiazepines:

                1. Benzodiazepines provide temporary, modest relief but can cause rebound anxiety with withdrawal and cessation of use

                2. Physical dependence is possible

                3. Benzodiazepines also have undesirable effects (drowsiness, etc.)

                4. Benzodiazepines also multiply the effects of other drugs (especially alcohol)

            (iii) In recent decades, still other drugs have become available

                1. In particular, it has been discovered that a number of antidepressant and antipsychotic medications are helpful in the treatment of GAD

        (b) Relaxation training

            (i) Theory: Physical relaxation leads to psychological relaxation

            (ii) Research indicates that relaxation training is more effective than placebo or no treatment

            (iii) Best when used in combination with cognitive therapy or biofeedback

(c) Biofeedback
  (i) Uses electrical signals from the body to train people to control physiological processes
  (ii) Most widely used = electromyograph (EMG); provides feedback about muscle tension
  (iii) Found to have a modest effect but has its greatest impact when used in combination for the treatment of certain medical problems (e.g., headache, back pain, etc.)

IV. **PHOBIAS**
  A. From the Greek word for "fear," phobias are defined as persistent and unreasonable fears of particular objects, activities, or situations
    1. Formal names also are often from Greek words [See PsychWatch, text p. 129]
  B. People with phobias often avoid the object or situation as well as thoughts about it
  C. All of us have our areas of special fear—it is a normal and common experience
    1. How do these "normal" experiences differ from phobias?
      a. More intense and persistent fear
      b. Greater desire to avoid the feared object/situation
      c. Distress that interferes with functioning
    2. Most phobias technically are categorized as "specific"; there also are two broader kinds: social phobia and agoraphobia (discussed later)
  D. Specific phobias
    1. Specific phobias are defined as persistent fears of specific objects or situations
    2. When exposed to the object or situation, sufferers experience immediate fear
    3. The most common specific phobias are of specific animals or insects, heights, enclosed spaces, thunderstorms, and blood
    4. Specific phobias affect about 9 percent of the U.S. population in any given year and about 12 percent at some point in their lives
      a. Many sufferers have more than one phobia at a time
      b. Women outnumber men at least 2:1
      c. The prevalence of the disorder differs across racial and ethnic minority groups; the reason is unclear
      d. The vast majority of sufferers *do not* seek treatment
  E. What causes specific phobias?
    1. Each model offers explanations, but evidence tends to support the behavioral explanations:
      a. Phobias develop through classical conditioning
        (a) Once fears are acquired, they are continued because feared objects are avoided
      b. Phobias develop through modeling, that is, through observation and imitation
      c. Phobias may develop into GAD when large numbers are acquired through the process of stimulus generalization: responses to one stimulus also are produced by similar stimuli
      d. Behavioral explanations have received some empirical support:
        (a) Classical conditioning studies with Little Albert
        (b) Modeling studies by Bandura including confederates, buzz, and shock
      e. The research conclusion is that phobias *can* be acquired in these ways, but there is no evidence that the disorder is *ordinarily* acquired in this way
    2. Another promising model is the behavioral-biological explanation
      a. Theorists argue that there is a species-specific biological *predisposition* to develop certain fears
        (a) Called "preparedness," this theory posits that humans are more "prepared" to acquire phobias around certain objects or situations and not others
        (b) The model explains why some phobias (snakes, heights) are more common than others (grass, meat)
        (c) It is unknown if these predispositions are due to evolutionary or environmental factors

F. How are specific phobias treated?
    1. Surveys reveal that 19 percent of those with specific phobia currently are in treatment
    2. All models offer treatment approaches
    3. Behavioral techniques (exposure treatments) are the most widely used
        a. These models include desensitization, flooding, and modeling:
            (a) Systematic desensitization, a technique developed by Joseph Wolpe
                (i)   Teach relaxation skills
                (ii) Create fear hierarchy
                (iii) Pair relaxation with feared object or situations
                    1. Since relaxation is incompatible with fear, the relaxation response is thought to substitute for the fear response
                (iv) Two types:
                    1. In vivo desensitization—Live
                    2. Covert desensitization—Imagined
            (b) Flooding
                (i)   Forced nongradual exposure to feared objects or situations
            (c) Modeling
                (i)   Therapist confronts the feared object while the fearful person observes
        b. Clinical research supports these treatments
        c. The key to success is *actual* contact with the feared object or situation
        d. A growing number of therapists are using virtual reality as a useful exposure tool
G. Social phobia
    1. Social phobias are defined as severe, persistent, and irrational fears of social or performance situations in which embarrassment may occur
        a. They may be *narrow*—talking, performing, eating, or writing in public
        b. They may be *broad*—general fear of functioning inadequately in front of others
        c. In *both* forms, people judge themselves as performing less competently than they actually did
    2. Given its broad scope, this disorder is also known as *social anxiety disorder*
    3. Social phobias can greatly interfere with functioning and often are kept secret
    4. Social phobias affect about 7.1 percent of U.S. population in any given year
        a. Women outnumber men 3:2
    5. The disorders often begin in childhood and may persist for many years
    6. Research finds the poor people are 50 percent more likely than wealthier people to experience social phobia
    7. There are some indications that social phobias may be more common among African Americans and Asian Americans than white Americans
    8. What causes social phobia?
        a. The leading explanation for social phobia has been proposed by cognitive theorists and researchers
        b. They contend that people with this disorder hold a group of social beliefs and expectations that consistently work against them, including:
            (a) Unrealistically high social standards
            (b) Views of themselves as unattractive and socially unskilled
        c. Cognitive theorists hold that, because of these beliefs, people with social phobia anticipate that social disasters will occur, and they perform "avoidance" and "safety" behaviors to prevent them
        d. In addition, after a social event, they review the details and overestimate how poorly things went or what negative results will occur
    9. Treatments for social phobia
        a. Only in the past 15 years have clinicians been able to treat social phobia successfully
        b. Two components must be addressed:
            (a) Overwhelming social fear—address behaviorally with exposure

(b) Lack of social skills—social skills and assertiveness trainings have proved helpful

   c. Unlike specific phobias, social phobias respond well to medication (particularly antidepressant drugs)

   d. Several types of psychotherapy have proved at least as effective as medication

      (a) People treated with psychotherapy are less likely to relapse than people treated with medication alone

      (b) One psychological approach is exposure therapy, either in an individual or group setting

      (c) Cognitive therapies also have been widely used

   e. Another treatment option is social skills training, a combination of several behavioral techniques to help people improve their social skills

      (a) Therapist provides feedback and reinforcement

      (b) In addition, social skills training groups and assertiveness training groups allow clients to practice their skills with other group members

V. PANIC DISORDER

  A. Panic, an extreme anxiety reaction, can affect anyone when a real threat suddenly emerges; the experience of "panic attacks," however, is different

  B. Panic attacks are periodic, short bouts of panic that occur suddenly, reach a peak, and pass

    1. Sufferers often fear they will die, go crazy, or lose control, in the presence of no *real* threat

  C. More than one-quarter of all people have one or more panic attacks at some point in their lives, but some people have panic attacks *repeatedly* and *unexpectedly* and *without apparent reason*

    1. They may be suffering from panic disorder

    2. Sufferers also experience dysfunctional changes in thinking and behavior as a result of the attacks (i.e., worry persistently about having an attack; plan)

  D. Panic disorder is often (but not always) accompanied by agoraphobia

    1. Those with panic disorder and agoraphobia are afraid to leave home and travel to locations from where escape might be difficult or help unavailable

      a. The intensity of the disorder may fluctuate

    2. There has only recently been a recognition of the link between agoraphobia and panic attacks (or panic-like symptoms)

    3. There are two related diagnoses: panic disorder with (or without) agoraphobia

  E. Panic disorder affects about 2.8 percent of U.S. population per given year and close to 5 percent of U.S. population in their lifetimes

    1. The disorder is likely to develop in late adolescence and early adulthood

    2. The ratio of women to men is 2:1

    3. Poor people are 50 percent more likely than wealthier people to experience these disorders

    4. The prevalence of the disorder is the same across various cultural and racial groups in the United States and seems to occur in equal numbers in cultures across the world

    5. Around 35 percent of those with panic disorder are in treatment

  F. The biological perspective

    1. In the 1960s, it was recognized that people with panic disorder were helped more by antidepressants than by the benzodiazepines used for treating anxiety

    2. Researchers worked backward from their understanding of antidepressant drugs

      a. What biological factors contribute to panic disorder?

        (a) NT at work is norepinephrine—it is irregular in folks with panic attacks

        (b) Research suggests that panic reactions are related to changes in norepinephrine activity in the locus ceruleus

        (c) While norepinephrine clearly is linked to panic disorder, recent research indicates that the root of panic attacks is more complicated; they tie the experience to brain circuits, especially including the amygdala

        (d)   It also is unclear as to why some people have such biological abnormalities:
               (i)   An inherited biological predisposition is possible
               (ii)   If so, prevalence should be (and is) greater among close relatives:
                       1.   Among monozygotic (MZ or identical) twins, the rate is as high as 31 percent
                       2.   Among dizygotic (DZ or fraternal) twins, the rate is only 11 percent

    3.   Drug therapies
        a.   Antidepressants are effective at preventing or reducing panic attacks, whether or not the panic disorder is accompanied by depressive symptoms
        b.   These drugs restore proper activity of norepinephrine in the locus ceruleus and other parts of the panic brain circuit
        c.   They bring at least some improvement to 80 percent of patients with panic disorder
            (a)   Improvements can last indefinitely, as long as the drugs are continued
        d.   Some benzodiazepines (especially Xanax (alprazolam)) also have proved helpful

G.   The cognitive perspective
    1.   Cognitive theorists have come to recognize that biological factors are only part of the cause of panic attacks
    2.   In their view, full panic reactions are experienced only by people who *misinterpret* physiological events occurring within the body
    3.   Cognitive treatment is aimed at changing such misinterpretations
    4.   Panic-prone people may be very sensitive to certain bodily sensations and may misinterpret them as signs of a medical catastrophe (leading to panic)
    5.   In biological challenge tests, researchers produce hyperventilation or other biological sensations by administering drugs or by instructing clinical research participants to breathe, exercise, or simply think in certain ways
        a.   Participants with panic disorder experience greater upset than those without the disorder
    6.   Why might some people be prone to such misinterpretations?
        a.   Experience more frequent or intense bodily sensations
        b.   Have experienced more trauma-filled events over the course of their lives
    7.   Whatever the precise causes, panic-prone people generally have a high degree of "anxiety sensitivity"
        a.   They focus on bodily sensations much of the time, are unable to assess them logically, and interpret them as potentially harmful
    8.   Cognitive therapy
        a.   Cognitive therapists try to correct people's misinterpretations of their bodily sensations:
            (a)   Step 1: Educate clients:
                 (i)   About the general nature of panic attacks
                 (ii)   About the actual causes of bodily sensations
                 (iii)   About their tendency of misinterpretation
            (b)   Step 2: Teach the application of more accurate interpretations (especially when stressed)
            (c)   Step 3: Teach anxiety coping skills, for example, relaxation, breathing
        b.   May also use "biological challenge" procedures to induce panic sensations so that clients can apply their new skills under watchful supervision
            (a)   Induce physical sensations that cause feelings of panic:
                 (i)   Jump up and down
                 (ii)   Run up a flight of steps
        c.   According to research, cognitive therapy often is helpful in panic disorder:
            (a)   Around 80 percent panic-free for 2 years vs. 13 percent for controls
            (b)   Such treatments also are helpful for treating panic with agoraphobia; in those cases, therapists often add exposure techniques to the cognitive aspects of treatment

          (c)   Cognitive therapy is at least as helpful as antidepressants

          (d)   Combination therapy may be most effective and is still under investigation

VI. OBSESSIVE-COMPULSIVE DISORDER

  A.   Obsessive-compulsive disorder is comprised of two components:

      1.   Obsessions—persistent thoughts, ideas, impulses, or images that seem to invade a person's consciousness

      2.   Compulsions—repetitive and rigid behaviors or mental acts that people feel they must perform in order to prevent or reduce anxiety

  B.   This diagnosis is called for when symptoms:

      1.   Feel excessive or unreasonable

      2.   Cause great distress

      3.   Take up much time

      4.   Interfere with daily functions

  C.   This disorder is classified as an anxiety disorder because obsessions cause intense anxiety, while compulsions are aimed at preventing or reducing anxiety

      1.   Anxiety rises if obsessions or compulsions are resisted

  D.   Between 1 and 2 percent of people throughout the world suffer from OCD in a given year, as many as 3 percent at some point during their lifetimes

      1.   It is equally common in men and women and among different racial and ethnic groups

  E.   It is estimated that more than 40 percent of these individuals will OCD seek treatment

  F.   What are the features of obsessions and compulsions?

      1.   Obsessions are thoughts that feel intrusive and foreign; attempts to ignore or resist them trigger anxiety

          a.   They take various forms: wishes, impulses, images, ideas, or doubts

          b.   They have common themes: dirt/contamination, violence/aggression, orderliness, religion, sexuality

      2.   Compulsions are "voluntary" behaviors or mental acts that feel mandatory/unstoppable

          a.   Many indiviuals recognize that their behaviors are unreasonable, but they believe, though, that without them, something terrible will happen

          b.   Performing the behaviors reduces anxiety but ONLY FOR A SHORT while

          c.   Behaviors often develop into detailed *rituals*

          d.   Compulsions also have common forms/themes: cleaning, checking, order or balance, touching, verbal, and/or counting

  G.   Are obsessions and compulsions related?

      1.   Most people with OCD experience both

          a.   Compulsive acts are often a response to obsessive thoughts

          b.   Compulsions seem to represent a *yielding* to obsessions

          c.   Also, compulsions sometimes serve to help *control* obsessions

      2.   Many with OCD worry that they will act on their obsessions, but most of these concerns are unfounded

          a.   Compulsions usually do not lead to violence or "immoral" conduct

  H.   OCD was once among the least understood of the psychological disorders

      1.   In recent decades, however, researchers have begun to learn more about it

      2.   The most influential explanations are from the psychodynamic, behavioral, cognitive, and biological models:

          a.   The psychodynamic perspective

             (a)   Anxiety disorders develop when children come to fear their id impulses and use ego defense mechanisms to lessen the anxiety

             (b)   OCD differs in that the "battle" is not unconscious—it is played out in unreasonable thoughts and actions

                (i)   Id impulses = obsessive thoughts

                (ii)   Ego defenses = counter-thoughts or compulsive actions

             (c)   According to psychodynamic theorists, three ego defense mechanisms are particularly common:

           (i)   Isolation—Disown disturbing thoughts
           (ii)   Undoing—Perform acts to "cancel out" thoughts
           (iii) Reaction formation—Take on a lifestyle in contrast to unacceptable impulses

    (d)   Freud traced OCD to the anal stage of development
           (i)   Not all psychodynamic theorists agree

    (e)   Psychodynamic therapies
           (i)   Therapy goals are to uncover and overcome underlying conflicts and defenses
           (ii)   The main techniques are free association and interpretation
           (iii) Research has offered little evidence; some therapists now prefer to treat these patients with short-term psychodynamic therapies

b.   Behaviorists have concentrated on explaining and treating compulsions rather than obsessions
    (a)   The model focuses on learning by chance; people happen on compulsions randomly:
           (i)   In a fearful situation, they coincidentally perform a particular act (washing hands)
           (ii)   When the threat lifts, they link the improvement with the random act
           (iii) After repeated associations, they believe the compulsion is changing the situation—bringing luck, warding away evil, etc.
           (iv) The act becomes a key method of avoiding or reducing anxiety

    (b)   The key investigator is Stanley Rachman
           (i)   Compulsions do appear to be rewarded by an eventual decrease in anxiety

    (c)   Behavioral therapy: exposure and response prevention (ERP)
           (i)   Clients repeatedly are exposed to anxiety-provoking stimuli and told to resist responding with compulsions
           (ii)   Therapists often model the behavior while the client watches
           (iii) Homework is an important component
           (iv) Between 55 and 85 percent of clients have been found to improve considerably with ERP, and improvements often continue indefinitely
           (v)   However, as many as 25 percent fail to improve at all, and the approach is of limited help to those with obsessions but no compulsions

c.   The cognitive perspective
    (a)   Cognitive theorists point out that everyone has repetitive, unwanted, and intrusive thoughts
    (b)   Those with OCD, however, blame themselves for such thoughts and expect that terrible things will happen as a result
    (c)   To avoid such negative outcomes, they try to neutralize their thoughts with actions (or other thoughts)
           (i)   Neutralizing thoughts/actions may include:
                1.   Seeking reassurance
                2.   Thinking "good" thoughts
                3.   Washing
                4.   Checking
           (ii)   When a neutralizing action reduces anxiety, it is reinforced
           (iii) The client becomes more convinced that the thoughts are dangerous
           (iv) As fear of thoughts increases, the number of thoughts increases

    (d)   In support of this explanation, studies have found that people with OCD experience intrusive thoughts more often than other people. If everyone has intrusive thoughts, why do only some people develop OCD?
           (i)   According to this model, people with OCD tend:
                1.   To be more depressed than others
                2.   To have exceptionally high standards of conduct and morality

3. To believe thoughts are equivalent to actions and are capable of bringing harm

4. To believe that they should have perfect control over their thoughts and behaviors

(e) Cognitive therapists focus on the cognitive processes that help to produce and maintain obsessive thoughts and compulsive acts and may include:

(i) Psychoeducation

(ii) Guiding the client to identify, challenge, and change distorted cognitions

(f) Research suggests that a combination of the cognitive and behavioral models (CBT) often is more effective than either intervention alone

d. The biological perspective

(a) Family pedigree studies provided the earliest clues that OCD may be linked in part to biological factors

(i) Studies of twins found a 53 percent concordance rate in identical twins versus 23 percent in fraternal twins

(b) In recent years, two additional lines of research have uncovered more direct evidence:

(i) Abnormal serotonin activity

1. Evidence that serotonin-based antidepressants reduce OCD symptoms

2. Recent studies have suggested that other NTs may also play important roles in OCD

(ii) Abnormal functioning in key regions of the brain

1. OCD linked to orbitofrontal cortex and caudate nuclei, which compose the brain circuit that converts sensory information into thoughts and actions

2. Either area may be too active, letting through troublesome thoughts and actions

(iii) Some research support evidence that these two lines may be connected:

1. Serotonin plays a key role in the operation of the orbitofrontal cortex and the caudate nuclei

2. Abnormal NT activity might interfere with the proper functioning of those brain parts

(c) Biological therapies include serotonin-based antidepressants, including Anafranil (clomipramine), Prozac (fluoxetine), Luvox (fluvoxamine)

(i) These medications bring improvement to 50 to 80 percent of those with OCD

(ii) Relapse occurs if medication is stopped

(d) Research suggests that combination therapy (medication + cognitive behavioral therapy approaches) may be most effective

VII. CALL FOR CHANGE: DSM-5

A. The DSM-5 Task Force has proposed several changes that would affect the anxiety disorders:

1. Regrouping several disorders:

a. *Acute stress disorder* and *posttraumatic stress disorder* (discussed in Chapter 6) should be listed under "Trauma and Stressor Related Disorders"

b. *Obsessive-compulsive disorder* should be listed under "Obsessive-Compulsive and Related Disorders"

(a) May be joined by *hoarding disorder, hair pulling disorder,* and *skin picking disorder*

2. Replace the term *social phobia* with *social anxiety disorder*

3. List *agoraphobia* as a distinct category

4. Create a new category called *mixed anxiety/depression*

LEARNING OBJECTIVES

1. Distinguish between fear and anxiety.

2. Describe each of the anxiety disorders and how common these disorders are.

3. Discuss the major theories and treatments for generalized anxiety disorder.

4. Define phobia; then distinguish between specific phobias and social phobia; discuss the major theories and treatments for each type

5. Describe the features of panic disorder, with or without agoraphobia, and discuss the biological and cognitive explanations and therapies of this disorder.

6. Distinguish between obsessions and compulsions. Discuss the major theories and treatments for obsessive-compulsive disorder.

7. Discuss the changes for these disorders proposed by the DSM-5 Task Force.

KEY TERMS

agoraphobia
alprazolam
amygdala
anal stage
antianxiety drug
antidepressant drugs
anxiety
anxiety disorder
anxiety sensitivity
assertiveness training
avoidance theory
basic irrational assumptions
benzodiazepines
biofeedback
biological challenge test
buspirone
caudate nuclei
classical conditioning
client-centered therapy
clomipramine
cognitive therapy
compulsion
conditioned response
conditioned stimulus
conditions of worth
covert desensitization
diathesis-stress
dreams
diazepam
electromyograph (EMG)
exposure and response
   prevention

exposure treatments
family pedigree study
fear
fear hierarchy
flooding
fluoxetine
fluvoxamine
free association
free-floating anxiety
gamma-aminobutyric acid
   (GABA)
generalized anxiety
   disorder
intolerance of uncertainty
   theory
in vivo desensitization
isolation
locus ceruleus
lorazepam
maladaptive assumptions
metacognitive theory
metaworries
modeling
moral anxiety
neuromodulator
neurotic anxiety
neutralizing
new wave cognitive
   explanations
norepinephrine
obsession

obsessive-compulsive
   disorder
orbitofrontal cortex
panic attacks
panic disorder
panic disorder with
   agoraphobia
participant modeling
phobia
preparedness
rational-emotive therapy
reaction formation
realistic anxiety
relaxation training
resistance
sedative-hypnotic drugs
serotonin
social phobia
social skills training
specific phobia
stimulus generalization
systematic desensitization
transference
unconditional positive
   regard
unconditioned response
unconditioned stimulus
undoing
unpredictable negative
   events
virtual reality

MEDIA RESOURCES

Abnormal Psychology Student Tool Kit

Produced and edited by Ronald J. Comer, Princeton University and Gregory Comer, Princeton Academic Resources. Tied directly to the CyberStudy sections in the text, this Student Tool Kit offers 57 intriguing Video Cases running 3 to 7 minutes each. The Video Cases focus on persons affected by disorders discussed in the text. Students first view the video and then answer a series of thought-provoking questions. Additionally, the Student Tool Kit contains multiple-choice practice test questions with built-in instructional feedback for every option.

Video Cases and Discussions:

- How does worrying affect psychological functioning?
- How disruptive are obsessions and compulsions?
- Observe treatments for anxiety disorders.

Practical, Research, and Decision-Making Exercises:

- Identifying and correcting irrational assumptions
- Distinguishing bothersome fears from phobias
- Detecting superstitions and habits in everyday life

PowerPoint Slides

Available at the Instructor's site on the companion Web site are comprehensive PowerPoint slide presentations and supplemental student handouts for Chapter 5. The slide files reflect the main points of the chapter in significant detail. Student handouts were created using the instructor slides as a base, with key points replaced as "fill-in" items. Answer keys and suggestions for use also are provided.

DSM-IV-TR Masters

B-9 DSM-IV-TR Diagnostic Criteria for Generalized Anxiety Disorder
B-10 DSM-IV-TR Diagnostic Criteria for Specific Phobia
B-11 DSM-IV-TR Diagnostic Criteria for Social Phobia
B-12 Criteria for Panic Attack
B-13 Criteria for Agoraphobia
B-14 DSM-IV-TR Diagnostic Criteria for Panic Disorder Without Agoraphobia
B-15 DSM-IV-TR Diagnostic Criteria for Obsessive-Compulsive Disorder

Internet Sites

Please see Appendix A for full and comprehensive references.

Sites relevant to Chapter 5 material are:

http://www.ocfoundation.org
This comprehensive site, homepage of the Obsessive Compulsive Foundation, details both research and treatment of obsessive-compulsive disorder.

http://www.anxietynetwork.com/gahome.html
This site is the Anxiety Network International's Generalized Anxiety Home Page, filled with information about the disorder.

http://www.socialphobia.org/
This site is the home page of the Social Phobia/Social Anxiety Association.

http://www.nimh.nih.gov/health/topics/anxiety-disorders/index.shtml
This site provided by the National Institute of Mental Health supplies downloadable links to PDF files and booklets on a variety of mental health topics, including anxiety disorders.

http://www.adaa.org/
Homepage of the Anxiety Disorders Association of America, this site is dedicated to the research, education, and treatment of anxiety disorders. It includes helpful links to finding a therapist, the different types of anxiety disorders, support groups, and other resources.

http://www.npadnews.com/
This Web site is concerned with anxiety, panic attacks, and other phobias. It offers links to different forms of anxiety disorders including social anxiety disorder, posttraumatic stress disorder, and obsessive-compulsive disorder. It also has current articles on the topic.

http://www.mentalhealth.com/dis/p20-an03.html
This is the "Internet Mental Health Site" page for social phobia and includes an assessment measure.

http://www.apa.org/topics/anxiety/panic-disorder.aspx
Created by the APA, this Fact Sheet is home to very good information on panic disorder and its treatments.

Mainstream Films

Films relevant to Chapter 5 material are listed and summarized below.

Key to Film Listings:
P = psychopathology focus
T = treatment focus
E = ethical issues raised

Please note that some of the films suggested may have graphic sexual or violent content due to the nature of certain subject matters.

As Good As It Gets
From 1997, this Academy award–winning film details the trials and tribulations of a writer (Jack Nicholson) dealing with obsessive-compulsive disorder. **P, comedy**

The Aviator
From 2004, this biopic stars Leonardo DiCaprio as the obsessive Howard Hughes. **P, serious film**

Copycat
This 1996 film stars Sigourney Weaver as a forensic psychologist who develops agoraphobia as the result of an assault. Her help is needed to capture a psychopath who is copying the crimes of renowned serial killers. **P, T, serious/commercial film**

Matchstick Men
From 2003, this Nicholas Cage film follows Roy, a grifter with obsessive-compulsive tendencies. **P, commercial film**

Unstrung Heroes
This comedy-drama follows a boy who moves in with his "crazy" uncles. **P, commercial film**

Vertigo
This Hitchcock classic from 1958 stars Jimmy Stewart as a police detective overcome with a severe case of acrophobia—a deep fear of heights. **P, serious/commercial film**

What About Bob?
From 1991, this comedy stars Bill Murray as a neurotic, insecure new patient attempting to see a pre-eminent psychiatrist (played by Richard Dreyfuss). Failing that, Murray stalks Dreyfuss and his family while they vacation. **P, T, E, comedy/commercial film**

Other Films:

Annie Hall (1977) anxiety disorder. **P, comedy**
Compulsion (1959) compulsion. **P, serious film**
Fear Strikes Out (1957) anxiety disorder and depression. **P, T, serious film**
High Anxiety (1977) anxiety, treatment. **T, comedy/commercial film**
Punch-Drunk Love (2002) social phobia, Type A personality pattern. **P, commercial/serious film**

Comer Video Segments

Available as a supplement, this revised set of videotapes contains short clips depicting various topics related to abnormal psychology. Please see the accompanying Video Guide for specific clips linked to Chapter 5.

Recommendations for Purchase or Rental

The Comer Video Segments include excerpts from many superb clinical documentaries. While the segments alone are ideal for use in lectures, it often is useful to assign the entire documentary for special class screenings or library use by students.

In addition, the following videos and other media are available for purchase or rental and appropriate for use in class or for assignment outside of class.

Phobias: Overcoming the Fear
Filmmakers Library, Inc.
122 E. 58th Street, Suite 703A
New York, NY 10022
Phone: 212-889-3820

Anxiety Disorders: Psychology of Abnormal Behavior
Magic Lantern Communications
1075 North Service Road West, Suite 27
Oakville, ON L6M 2G2 Canada
Phone: 905-827-2755
Fax: 905-827-2655
TOLL-FREE:
Phone: 800-263-1717
Fax: 866-852-2755
www.magiclantern.ca

Fight or Flight?: Overcoming Panic and Agoraphobia
Guilford Publications, Inc.
72 Spring Street
New York, NY 10012
Phone: (800) 365-7006
or (212) 431-9800
Fax: (212) 966-6708
(800) 365-7006
www.guilford.com

I Think They Think . . . : Overcoming Social Phobia
Guilford Publications, Inc.
72 Spring Street
New York, NY 10012
Phone: (800) 365-7006
or (212) 431-9800
Fax: (212) 966-6708
(800) 365-7006
www.guilford.com

Additional titles available through:
Films for the Humanities and Sciences
P.O. Box 2053
Princeton, NJ 08543-2053

Phone: 800-257-5126
Fax: 609-275-3767
E-mail: custserv@films.com
ffh.films.com

CLASS DEMONSTRATIONS AND ACTIVITIES

Case Study

Present a case study to the class.

Relaxation Training

Invite students to participate in a mini-session of relaxation training. Students who choose not to participate should be encouraged to sit quietly. Lead the class in a 15-minute session of progressive muscle relaxation, meditation, or autogenic training. Several excellent books are available for such activities.

Panel Discussion

Have students volunteer (or assign them) to portray mental health "workers" from different theoretical perspectives in a panel discussion. Each student should present the main explanation and treatment for the anxiety disorders from his or her theoretical background. Students in the audience can ask questions of the panelists. Additionally, other students can role-play patients suffering from particular anxiety disorders. [NOTE: A brief reminder about sensitivity and professionalism is worthwhile here.] Have the panelists or audience members attempt to make a diagnosis.

"It's Debatable: Psychotherapy or Psychopharmacology?" (see Preface instructions for conducting this activity)

Have students volunteer (or assign them) in teams to opposite sides of the debate topic. Have students present their cases in class following standard debate guidelines.

Group Work: Rational and Irrational Fears (Phobias)

Phobia was the Greek god of fear. The scary face of Phobia was painted on the shields of Greek warriors to strike fear into the hearts of their opponents. Ask different groups of students to generate lists of rational and irrational fears. A comparison of the lists will generate disagreement. Inevitably, an irrational fear on one list will appear on the rational fear list of

another group. Discuss how mental health professionals distinguish irrational from rational fears, given that there is no easy agreement. Phobias evoke intense anxiety and avoidant behaviors that interfere greatly with everyday living and usually require professional treatment.

Group Work: Common Student Phobias

Before dividing into groups, ask the whole class to generate a list of typical situations that make students anxious. Next, divide the class into small groups, then ask each group to develop a strategy for coping with one of the situations. This is a good method to create a discussion and solicit suggestions to change behaviors without embarrassing students.

A complementary exercise is to tally the fears of class members (you can ask students to write them down to preserve anonymity), then discuss the most common fears. If the class is typical of the American population, public speaking will rank very high. It is beneficial to have the class determine which of the fears are specific and which are social phobias. Sometimes this is easy (e.g., fear of storms, fear of spiders, fear of bats), but social phobias may be mislabeled as specific (e.g., fear of eating in restaurants, fear of blushing).

Diathesis-Stress Model

Direct genetic causation of illness and abnormal behavior is rare. Recent research has indicated that many illnesses are now understood in terms of the interaction of hereditary and environmental factors, the diathesis-stress model. According to this theory, certain genes or hereditary vulnerability give rise to a diathesis or a constitutional predisposition. When an individual's predisposition is then combined with certain kinds of environmental stress, illness may result. With diseases like heart disease, high blood pressure, and cancer, both hereditary and environmental factors play a role. A major effort in abnormal research and clinical practice is to identify specific risk factors in a given individual, including both family history and personal lifestyle, then predict the onset of a mental disorder.

Howard Hughes and Obsessive-Compulsive Disorder

The following list provides an interesting look at Howard Hughes's obsessive-compulsive behavior. You can display this information about his odd behavior in the form of an overhead transparency. Use this list to start a discussion of any relative's or friend's behaviors that might also be considered obsessive-compulsive. Be certain the students do not become too personal in their discussions.

- Hughes would not touch any object unless he first picked up a tissue (which he called "insulation"), so that he would never directly touch an object that might expose him to germs.
- Hughes saved his own urine in mason jars; hundreds of them were stored in his apartment. From time to time, a staff member would covertly empty some of the filled jars.
- Hughes saved his newspapers in high stacks—so many of them that visitors sometimes had to weave carefully through a room to avoid toppling them.
- Hughes sometimes watched one film (his favorite was *Ice Station Zero*) more than 100 times before switching to another. Similarly, he might have gone for days eating the same food (e.g., chicken noodle soup and one flavor of Baskin-Robbins ice cream) and no others.
- Hughes used heroin and other drugs.

"Pretend, for a moment, that you just had a panic attack . . ."

On an overhead or slide, show the symptoms of panic attacks. Ask students to pretend that they have just experienced one (be aware that some have actually had panic attacks). Ask students what their reaction to these symptoms might be. Students likely will suggest that they would go to a hospital emergency room or assume that there was something seriously wrong. Encourage them to imagine that the panic attack was the worst experience of their lives. Lead them to see that they would be intensely fearful of another panic attack. Using the process of questioning, help them to see how panic disorder (fear of more panic attacks, leading to misinterpretation of otherwise benign somatic experiences) can lead to more panic attacks.

"Here's $25,000 to be awarded to . . ."

Divide students into groups, then ask each group to propose a method to reduce the occurrence of one of the causes of heart disease, such as smoking, drinking, and being overweight. Have the groups present their ideas, then have a class vote to see which group receives the grant to implement the group's idea.

Let's Write a Self-Help Best-Seller (see Preface instructions for conducting this activity)

Ask students for ideas on how to write a self-help manual on overcoming severe shyness (which might be diagnosable as social phobia), a traumatic experience (such as childhood abuse), or panic. Ideas for self-help interventions should include a rationale for why they might work.

SUGGESTED TOPICS FOR DISCUSSION

Open Discussion: How Fears Change with Age

Lead a discussion of how an individual's fears change with age. Many fears increase or decrease during certain stages of life. Cite examples such as the young child's fear of the dark and the college student's fear of academic failure. What are some major fears of college students? Discuss how certain fears increase with age, whereas other fears decrease.

Open Discussion: Student Phobias

Make an overhead transparency or slide of Psych-Watch, p. 129 in the text and discuss the list. State that students should mention only phobias that "friends" have. Have students speculate on why phobias were given such technical and complicated labels. One clever explanation is that when professionals can't treat and understand something, they give it an unpronounceable name so that the patient can understand why progress is slow. Until behavioral therapy techniques proved successful, phobias were resistant to change.

Brainstorming Session: Reducing Stress

Ask students to volunteer something that students could do to alleviate stress. This generally evokes a wide variety of suggestions, illustrating how personal the experience of stress can be.

Psychology and Medical Health

The major causes of morbidity (illness) and mortality (death) have changed in the last century. In the early 1900s, viruses and bacteria were the leading causes of death. Ask students what happened to change this. (Medical and scientific advances such as antibiotics, vaccinations, and improvements in sanitation helped stamp out these causes of death.) Presently, leading causes of death include heart disease (related to smoking, eating, not exercising, being overweight, drinking too much), cancer, motor vehicle accidents, and suicide. Ask students what these causes have in common (all are related to behavior). Psychology is thus becoming increasingly important in overall health care. In particular, the field of health psychology is emerging as an important area of the health care system.

ASSIGNMENTS/EXTRA CREDIT SUGGESTIONS

"Write a Pamphlet"

With the use of a software program like Microsoft Publisher or simply paper and markers, students can create a pamphlet on one or all of the anxiety disorders. Students should be encouraged to be as accurate and up-to-date as possible, and to present all sides of the disorder (e.g., alternate treatment approaches or theories).

Keep a Journal

In addition to helping students synthesize material, this activity also is helpful in developing writing skills. Have students keep a journal of their thoughts on course material throughout the semester. This can be done in the first or last 5 minutes of class or as an out-of-class assignment. Faculty generally should have students submit their journals for review on an ongoing basis as students can have the tendency to delay writing until the end of the semester. Some suggestions for journal topics include: reactions to the case examples; strengths and weaknesses of prevailing theoretical explanations; hypothetical conversations with sufferers of specific disorders, etc.

Anxiety Disorders on Television and in the Movies

To emphasize the idea that disorders have specific criteria, have students report on diagnosable mental illnesses they encounter on television or in the movies. Students should document the specific behaviors or experiences that a character is exhibiting, which fulfills the diagnostic criteria. This assignment helps emphasize the difference between the appearance of a disorder and meeting criteria for a disorder, that is, the difference between popular and professional conceptions of mental illness. If assignments are turned in before the lecture on particular disorders, you can use the information generated to enhance your lecture and to give these disorders a more personal touch.

Abnormal Psychology Student Tool Kit Video Questions

As a homework assignment, have students watch a video clip and answer the accompanying questions. Students can answer the questions directly into the online assessment feature. The results of these quizzes report to the site's built-in grade book.

Web Site Quiz

For homework or extra credit, have students complete the Web site quiz for Chapter 5 located on the companion Web site. Students can complete an online test of the key chapter material (using questions NOT from the test bank) and have their scores e-mailed directly to the course instructor.

Essay Topics

For homework or extra credit, have students write an essay addressing the following topic:

(1) Write an essay comparing and contrasting the various anxiety disorders. Do you agree with the diagnostic criteria? Is it too "easy" or "hard" to get a particular diagnosis?

(2) Discuss the existence of "Playlist Anxiety" (as described in the textbox on p. 121) as a real disorder. Do you think it should be included in the revision of DSM? Discuss other anxieties that have arisen as a result of modern technology.

Research Topics

For homework or extra credit, have students write a research report addressing one (or more) of the following topics:

(1) Conduct a "Psych Info" search and write an annotated bibliography on treatments for the various anxiety disorders. What model(s) are the current studies examining?

(2) Choose a popular press book on anxiety disorders/anxiety disorder treatment from the Self-Help section of your local bookstore. Read and review the text and critically evaluate the findings. What theoretical model does the text endorse? Do you agree with the author's presentation of the disorder/treatment?

(3) Write a research report on the various biological treatments for anxiety disorders.

(4) Conduct an Internet search on the various drugs listed in Table 5-4. What is their availability online? What is the popular press about them?

Film Review

To earn extra credit, have students watch one (or more) of the mainstream films listed earlier in this chapter and write a brief (3–5 pages) report. Students should summarize the plot of the film in sufficient detail to demonstrate familiarity, but should focus their papers on the depiction of psychological abnormality. What errors or liberties did the filmmaker take? What is the message (implicit or explicit) concerning the mentally ill?

Case Study Evaluations

To complement the Comer and Gorenstein supplemental case study text, case study evaluations have been created. Students can be assigned the appropriate case study and evaluation as homework or for class discussion. While case study evaluation questions are listed in their entirety on the companion Web site at www.worthpublishers.com/comer, the relevant case studies are referenced below.

Case Study 2: Panic Disorder

Case Study 3: Obsessive-Compulsive Disorder

Web-Based Case Study

Nine Web-based case studies have been created and posted on the companion Web site. These cases describe the individual's history and symptoms and are accompanied by a series of guided questions that point to the precise DSM-IV-TR criteria for each disorder. Students can both identify the disorder and suggest a course of treatment. Students can be assigned the appropriate case study and questions as homework or for class discussion. The cases relevant to Chapter 5 are referenced below.

The Case of Tina: Anxiety and Panic Disorders

The Case of Jake: Obsessive-Compulsive Disorder

The Case of Allison: Generalized Anxiety Disorder

Crossword Puzzles

As a homework assignment or for extra credit, have students complete and submit Crossword Puzzle #5.

Word Searches

As a homework assignment or for extra credit, have students complete and submit Word Search #5.

Stress Disorders

LECTURE OUTLINE

I. **STRESS, COPING, AND THE ANXIETY RESPONSE**
   A. The state of stress has two components:
      1. Stressor: Event creating demands
      2. Stress response: The person's reactions to the demands
         a. Our stress response is influenced by how we judge (a) the event, and (b) our capacity to react to the event effectively
         b. People who sense that they have the ability and resources to cope are more likely to take stressors in stride and respond well
      3. When we view a stressor as threatening, the natural reaction is arousal and a sense of fear.
         a. The fear response is a "package" of responses—physical, emotional, and cognitive
   B. Stress reactions, and the fear they produce, often are at play in psychological disorders

       1.   People who experience a large number of stressful events are particularly vulnerable to the onset of GAD, social phobia, panic disorder, and OCD, as well as other psychological problems

  C.   In addition, stress plays a more central role in certain psychological disorders, including:

       1.   Acute stress disorder

       2.   Posttraumatic stress disorder

       3.   Technically, DSM-IV-TR lists these patterns as anxiety disorders

  D.   And, it plays a role in certain physical disorders called *psychophysiological disorders*

       1.   These disorders are listed in the DSM-IV-TR under "psychological factors affecting medical condition"

  E.   The features of arousal and fear are set in motion by the hypothalamus

       1.   Two important systems are activated:

          a.   Autonomic nervous system (ANS)—an extensive network of nerve fibers that connect the central nervous system (the brain and spinal cord) to the body's other organs

          b.   Endocrine system—a network of glands throughout the body that release hormones

       2.   There are two pathways by which the ANS and the endocrine system produce arousal and fear reactions—the first pathway is the sympathetic nervous system [See Figure 6-1, text p. 155]

          a.   When we face a dangerous situation, the hypothalamus first activates the sympathetic nervous system, which stimulates key organs either directly or indirectly

          b.   When the perceived danger passes, the parasympathetic nervous system helps return bodily processes to normal

       3.   The second pathway is the hypothalamic-pituitary-adrenal (HPA) pathway [See Figure 6-2, text p. 156]

          a.   When we are faced with stressors, the hypothalamus also signals the pituitary gland, which signals the adrenal cortex to release corticosteroids—the stress hormones—into the bloodstream

  F.   The reactions on display in these two pathways are referred to as the fight-or-flight response [See Figure 6-3, text p. 156]

       1.   People differ in their particular patterns of autonomic and endocrine functioning and, therefore, in their particular ways of experiencing arousal and fear

       2.   The experience of fear/anxiety differs in two ways:

          a.   People differ in the general level of anxiety—called "trait anxiety"

             (a)   Some people always are tense, others always are relaxed

             (b)   Differences appear soon after birth

          b.   People also differ in their sense of threat—called "state anxiety"

             (a)   Situation-based (e.g., fear of flying)

II.   THE PSYCHOLOGICAL STRESS DISORDERS

  A.   During and immediately after trauma, many people become highly aroused, anxious, and depressed

       1.   For some, feelings will persist well after the upsetting situation is over

          a.   These people may be experiencing:

             (a)   Acute stress disorder

                (i)   Symptoms begin within four weeks of the traumatic event and last for less than a month

             (b)   Posttraumatic stress disorder (PTSD) [See Table 6-1, text p. 157]

                (i)   Symptoms can begin at any time following the event but must last for longer than one month

                (ii)   May develop from acute stress disorder (about 80 percent of all cases)

  B.   The situations that cause these disorders usually involves actual or threatened serious injury to self or others and would be traumatic to anyone (unlike other anxiety disorders)

  C.   Aside from differences in onset and duration, symptoms of acute and posttraumatic stress disorders (PTSDs) are almost identical:

       1.   Reexperiencing the traumatic event (flashbacks, nightmares)

        2.   Avoidance
        3.   Reduced responsiveness
        4.   Increased arousal, anxiety, and guilt

D.   These disorders can occur at any age and affect all aspects of life
        1.   They affect about 3.5 percent of U.S. population per year and about 7-9 percent of U.S. population per lifetime
        2.   Approximately two-thirds of sufferers seek treatment at some point
        3.   Women are twice as likely as men to develop stress disorders; after trauma, 20 percent of women vs. 8 percent of men develop disorders
        4.   In addition, people with low incomes are twice as likely as people with higher incomes to experience one of the stress disorders

E.   What triggers a psychological stress disorder?
        1.   Any traumatic event can trigger a stress disorder, however, some events are more likely to cause disorders than others, including combat, disasters, abuse, and victimization:
            a.   Combat and stress disorders
               (a)   For years, clincians have recognized that many soldiers experience distress *during* combat (called "shell shock," "combat fatigue")
               (b)   Post–Vietnam War clinicians discovered that soldiers also experienced distress *after* combat
               (c)   About 29 percent of Vietnam veterans suffered an acute or PTSD
                   (i)   An additional 22 percent had at least some symptoms
                   (ii)   About 10 percent are still experiencing problems
               (d)   A similar pattern is currently unfolding among veterans of the wars in Iraq and Afghanistan
            b.   Disasters and stress disorders
               (a)   Acute or posttraumatic stress disorders also may follow natural and accidental disasters such as earthquakes, tornadoes, fires, airplane crashes, and serious car accidents
               (b)   Civilian traumas have been implicated in stress disorders at least 10 times as often as combat trauma (because they occur more often)
            c.   Victimization and stress disorders
               (a)   People who have been abused or victimized often experience lingering stress symptoms
                   (i)   More than one-third of all victims of physical of sexual assault develop PTSD
                   (ii)   As many as half of those directly exposed to terrorism or torture may develop this disorder
               (b)   A common form of victimization is sexual assault
                   (i)   One study found 94 percent of rape survivors developed an acute stress disorder within 12 days after assault
               (c)   Ongoing victimization and abuse in the family also may lead to stress disorders
            d.   Terrorism and torture
               (a)   The experience of terrorism often leads to posttraumatic stress symptoms, as does the experience of torture
                   (i)   Unfortunately, these sources of traumatic stress are on the rise in our society

F.   Why do people develop a psychological stress disorder?
        1.   Clearly, extraordinary trauma can cause a stress disorder; however, the event alone may not be the entire explanation
        2.   To understand the development of these disorders, researchers have looked to the survivors' biological processes, personalities, childhood experiences, social support systems, and cultural backgrounds, as well as the severity of the traumas:
            a.   Biological and genetic factors
               (a)   Traumatic events trigger physical changes in the brain and body that may lead to severe stress reactions and, in some cases, to stress disorders

(b) Some research suggests abnormal neurotransmitter (NT) and hormone activity (especially norepinephrine and cortisol)

(c) Evidence suggests that once a stress disorder sets in, further biochemical arousal and damage may also occur (especially in the hippocampus and amygdala)

(d) There may be a biological/genetic predisposition to such reactions

b. Personality factors

(a) Some studies suggest that people with certain personalities, attitudes, and coping styles are more likely to develop stress disorders, including:

(i) Preexisting high anxiety

(ii) Negative worldview

(b) Alternatively, a set of positive attitudes (called *resiliency* or *hardiness*) is protective against developing stress disorders

c. Childhood experiences

(a) Researchers have found that certain childhood experiences increase risk for later stress disorders, including:

(i) An impoverished childhood

(ii) Psychological disorders in the family

(iii) The experience of assault, abuse, or catastrophe at an early age

(iv) Being younger than 10 years of age when parents separated or divorced

d. Social support

(a) People whose social support systems are weak are more likely to develop a stress disorder after a traumatic event

e. Multicultural factors

(a) There is a growing suspicion among clinical researchers that the rates of PTSD may differ among ethnic groups in the United States

(i) It seems that Hispanic Americans might be more vulnerable to PTSD than other cultural groups

(ii) Possible explanations include cultural belief systems about trauma and the cultural emphasis on social relationships and social support

f. Severity of the trauma

(a) Generally, the more severe trauma and the more direct one's exposure to it, the greater the likelihood of developing a stress disorder

(b) Especially risky: mutilation and severe injury; witnessing the injury or death of others

3. How do clinicians treat the psychological stress disorders?

a. About half of all cases of PTSD improve within six months; the remainder may persist for years

b. Treatment procedures vary depending on type of trauma

(a) General treatment goals include helping the client to:

(i) End lingering stress reactions

(ii) Gain perspective on the traumatic experience

(iii) Return to constructive living

d. Treatment for combat veterans

(a) Drug therapy

(i) Antianxiety and antidepressant medications are most common

(b) Behavioral exposure techniques

(i) Reduce specific symptoms, increase overall adjustment

(ii) Use of flooding and relaxation training

(iii) Use of eye movement desensitization and reprocessing (EMDR)

(c) Insight therapy

(i) Bring out deep-seated feelings, create acceptance, lessen guilt

(d) Often use couple, family, or group therapy formats such as rap groups

e. Psychological debriefing

(a) A form of crisis intervention that has victims of trauma talk extensively about their feelings and reactions within days of the critical incident

        (b)   Four-stage approach
- (i)   Normalize responses to the disaster
- (ii)   Encourage expressions of anxiety, anger, and frustration
- (iii)   Teach self-helping skills
- (iv)   Provide referrals

        (c)   The approach has come under careful scrutiny

        (d)   While many health professionals continue to believe in the approach despite unsupportive research findings, the current climate is moving away from outright acceptance
- (i)   It's possible that certain high-risk individuals may profit from debriefing programs, but that others shouldn't receive such interventions

III. THE PHYSICAL STRESS DISORDERS: PSYCHOPHYSIOLOGICAL DISORDERS

A. In addition to affecting psychological functioning, stress also can have great impact on physical functioning

B. The idea that stress and related psychosocial factors may contribute to physical illnesses has ancient roots—yet it had few supporters before the twentieth century

C. About 80 years ago, clinicians first identified a group of physical illnesses that seemed to result from an interaction of biological, psychological, and sociocultural factors

D. Early versions of the DSM labeled these illnesses psychophysiological, or psychosomatic, disorders
1. DSM-IV-TR labels them as psychological factors affecting medical condition [See Table 6-3, text p. 169]
2. It is important to recognize that these psychophysiological disorders bring about *actual* physical damage
   a. They are different from "apparent" physical illnesses like factitious disorders or somatoform disorders, which will be discussed in Chapter 7

E. Traditional psychophysiological disorders
1. Before the 1970s, the best known and most common of the psychophysiological disorders were ulcers, asthma, insomnia, chronic headaches, high blood pressure, and coronary heart disease
2. Recent research has shown that many other physical illnesses may be caused by an interaction of psychosocial and physical factors
3. The psychophysiological disorders include:
   a. Ulcers—lesions in the wall of the stomach resulting in burning sensations or pain, vomiting, and stomach bleeding
      - (a)   Experienced by over 25 million people at some point in their lives
      - (b)   Causal psychosocial factors: environmental pressures, intense feelings of anger or anxiety
      - (c)   Causal physiological factors: bacterial infection
   b. Asthma—a narrowing of the body's airways that makes breathing difficult
      - (a)   Affects up to 25 million people in the United States each year
      - (b)   Most victims are children at the time of first attack
      - (c)   Causal psychosocial factors: environmental pressures or anxiety
      - (d)   Causal physiological factors: allergies, a slow-acting sympathetic nervous system, weakened respiratory system
   c. Insomnia—difficulty falling asleep or maintaining sleep
      - (a)   Affects 10 percent of people in the United States each year
      - (b)   Causal psychosocial factors: high levels of anxiety or depression
      - (c)   Causal physiological factors: overactive arousal system, certain medical ailments
   d. Chronic headaches—frequent intense aches of the head or neck that are not caused by another physical disorder
      - (a)   Tension headaches affect 45 million Americans a year
      - (b)   Migraine headaches affect 23 million Americans a year
      - (c)   Causal psychosocial factors: environmental pressures, general feelings of helplessness, anger, anxiety, depression

          (d)   Causal physiological factors: abnormal serotonin activity, vascular problems, muscle weakness

     e.   Hypertension—chronic high blood pressure, usually producing no outward symptoms

          (a)   Affects 75 million Americans each year

          (b)   Causal psychosocial factors: constant stress, environmental danger, general feelings of anger or depression

          (c)   Causal physiological factors: obesity, smoking, poor kidney function, high proportion of collagen rather than elastic tissue in an individual's blood vessels

              (i)   10 percent caused by physiological factors alone

     f.   Coronary heart disease—caused by a blocking of the coronary arteries; the term refers to several problems, including myocardial infarction (heart attack)

          (a)   Nearly 18 million people in the United States suffer from some form of coronary heart disease

              (i)   It is the leading cause of death in men older than 35 years and women older than 40

          (b)   Causal psychosocial factors: job stress, high levels of anger or depression

          (c)   Causal physiological factors: high level of cholesterol, obesity, hypertension, the effects of smoking, lack of exercise

  4.   A number of factors contribute to the development of psychophysiological disorders, including:

     a.   Biological factors

          (a)   Defects in the autonomic nervous system (ANS) are believed to contribute to the development of psychophysiological disorders

          (b)   Other more specific biological problems also may contribute

               (i)   For example, a weak gastrointestinal system may create a predisposition to developing ulcers

     b.   Psychological factors

          (a)   According to many theorists, certain needs, attitudes, emotions, or coping styles may cause people to overreact repeatedly to stressors, thereby increasing their likelihood of developing a psychophysiological disorder

          (b)   Examples include a repressive coping style and the Type A personality style—particularly hostility and time urgency

     c.   Sociocultural factors

          (a)   Adverse social conditions may set the stage for psychophysiological disorders

               (i)   One of society's most adverse social conditions is poverty

              (ii)   Research also reveals that belonging to ethnic and cultural minority groups increases the risk of developing these disorders and other health problems

  5.   Clearly, biological, psychological, and sociocultural variables combine to produce psychophysiological disorders

     a.   In fact, the interaction of psychosocial and physical factors is now considered the rule of bodily function, not the exception

     b.   In recent years, more and more illnesses have been added to the list of psychophysiological disorders

F.   New psychophysiological disorders

  1.   Since the 1960s, researchers have found many links between psychosocial stress and a range of physical illnesses

  2.   Are physical illnesses related to stress?

     a.   The development of the Social Adjustment Rating Scale in 1967 enabled researchers to examine the relationship between life stress and the onset of illness [See Table 6-5, text p. 179]

     b.   Using this measure, studies have linked stresses of various kinds to a wide range of physical conditions

      c.   Overall, the greater the amount of life stress, the greater the likelihood of illness
          (a)   Researchers have even found a relationship between traumatic stress and death
      d.   One shortcoming of the Social Adjustment Rating Scale is that it does not take into consideration the particular stress reactions of specific populations
          (a)   For example, members of minority groups may respond to stress differently, and women and men have been shown to react differently to certain life changes measured by the scale

3.   Researchers have increasingly looked to the body's immune system as the key to the relationship between stress and infection
      a.   This area of study is called *psychoneuroimmunology*—the immune system is the body's network of activities and cells that identify and destroy antigens (foreign invaders, such as bacteria) and cancer cells
      b.   Among the most important cells in this system are the lymphocytes, white blood cells that circulate through the lymph system and bloodstream and attack invaders
      c.   Lymphocytes include helper T-cells, natural killer T-cells, and B-cells
      d.   Researchers now believe that stress can interfere with the activity of lymphocytes, slowing them down and increasing a person's susceptibility to viral and bacterial infections
      e.   Several factors influence whether stress will result in a slowdown of the system, including biochemical activity, behavioral changes, personality style, and degree of social support
          (a)   Biochemical activity
             (i)   Stress leads to increased activity of the sympathetic nervous system, including a release of norepinephrine
             (ii)   In addition to supporting nervous system activity, this chemical also appears to slow down the functioning of the immune system
             (iii)   Similarly, the body's endocrine glands reduce immune system functioning during periods of prolonged stress through the release of corticosteroids
             (iv)   In addition, corticosteroids also trigger increased cytokines, which lead to chronic inflammation
          (b)   Behavioral changes
             (i)   Stress may set into motion a series of behavioral changes—poor sleep patterns, poor eating, lack of exercise, increase in smoking, and/or drinking—that indirectly affect the immune system
          (c)   Personality style
             (i)   An individual's personality style, including his or her level of optimism, constructive coping strategies, and resilience, can help him or her to experience better immune system functioning and to be better prepared to fight off illness
          (d)   Social support
             (i)   People who have few social supports and feel lonely seem to display poorer immune functioning in the face of stress than people who do not feel lonely
             (ii)   Studies have shown that social support and affiliation with others may actually protect people from stress, poor immune system functioning, and subsequent illness, or help speed up recovery from illness or surgery

4.   As clinicians have discovered that stress and related psychosocial factors may contribute to physical disorders, they have applied psychological treatment to more and more medical problems
      a.   The most common of these interventions are relaxation training, biofeedback training, meditation, hypnosis, cognitive interventions, support groups, and therapies designed to increase awareness and expression of emotion

b.   The field of treatment that combines psychological and physical interventions to treat or prevent medical problems is known as *behavioral medicine*

(a)   Relaxation training

(i)   People can be trained to relax their muscles at will, a process that sometimes reduces feelings of anxiety

(ii)   Relaxation training can help prevent or treat medical illnesses that are related to stress

(iii) Relaxation training often is used in conjunction with medication in the treatment of high blood pressure

(iv) Relaxation training often is used alone to treat chronic headaches, insomnia, asthma, pain after surgery, certain vascular diseases, and the undesirable effects of cancer treatments

(b)   Biofeedback

(i)   Patients given biofeedback training are connected to machinery that gives them continuous readings about their involuntary bodily activities

(ii)   Somewhat helpful in the treatment of anxiety disorders, this procedure has been used successfully to treat headaches and muscular disabilities caused by stroke or accident

(iii) Some biofeedback training has been effective in the treatment of heartbeat irregularities, asthma, migraine headaches, high blood pressure, stuttering, and pain from burns

(c)   Meditation

(i)   Although meditation has been practiced since ancient times, Western health care professionals have only recently become aware of its effectiveness in relieving physical distress

(ii)   The technique involves turning one's concentration inward and achieving a slightly changed state of consciousness

(iii) Meditation has been used to manage pain, treat high blood pressure, heart problems, insomnia, and asthma

(d)   Hypnosis

(i)   Individuals who undergo hypnosis are guided into a sleeplike, suggestible state during which they can be directed to act in unusual ways, to remember unusual sensations, or to forget remembered events

(ii)   With training, hypnosis can be done without a hypnotist (self-hypnosis)

(iii) This technique seems to be particularly helpful in the control of pain and is now used to treat such problems as skin diseases, asthma, insomnia, high blood pressure, warts, and other forms of infection

(e)   Cognitive interventions

(i)   People with physical ailments have sometimes been taught new attitudes or cognitive responses as part of treatment

(ii)   One example is stress inoculation training, where patients are taught to rid themselves of negative self-statements and to replace them with coping self-statements

(f)   Emotion expression and support groups

(i)   If negative psychological symptoms (e.g., depression, anxiety) contribute to a person's physical ills, intervention to reduce these emotions should help reduce the ills

(ii)   These techniques have been used to treat a variety of illnesses including HIV, asthma, cancer, headache, and arthritis

(g)   Combination approaches

(i)   Studies have found that the various psychological interventions for physical problems tend to be equal in effectiveness

(ii)   Psychological treatments often are most effective when they are combined and used with medical treatment

(iii) With these combined approaches, today's practitioners are moving away from the mind-body dualism of centuries past

IV. **CALL FOR CHANGE: DSM-5**
   A. The DSM-5 Task Force recommended a number of changes that would affect these disorders
      1. For example, they proposed that the Stress Disorders be listed under a new grouping called "trauma and stressor related disorder"
      2. Also included in this new category would be adjustment disorder and a new disorder called posttraumatic stress disorder in preschool children
      3. The Task Force also recommended some changes in the diagnostic criteria for acute and posttraumatic stress disorders, namely to distinguish a "traumatic" event from one that is merely "distressing"
      4. Finally, the Task Force proposed that the psychophysiological disorders should be listed under a grouping called "Somatic Symptom Disorders"

LEARNING OBJECTIVES

1. Distinguish between fear and anxiety, and describe the fight-or-flight response.

2. Define stress disorder and posttraumatic stress disorder, list typical symptoms, and discuss treatments for these disorders.

3. Discuss triggers for the psychological stress disorders, including combat, disasters, and victimization.

4. Detail the various factors that put people at risk for developing a psychological stress disorder.

5. Describe the traditional psychophysiological disorders: ulcers, asthma, chronic headaches, hypertension, and coronary heart disease.

6. Discuss how perceptions of control, personality, mood, and social support affect immune system functioning.

7. Describe the field of psychoimmunology and the various factors that influence the impact of stress on the immune system.

8. Discuss typical psychological treatments for psychophysiological disorders.

9. Discuss the changes for these disorders proposed by the DSM-5 Task Force.

KEY TERMS

acute stress disorder
adrenal glands
antigen
arousal
asthma
autonomic nervous system (ANS)
behavioral medicine
biofeedback training
central nervous system
coronary heart disease
corticosteroids

critical incident stress debriefing
endocrine system
eye movement desensitization and reprocessing (EMDR)
fight-or-flight response
flashback
hormones
hypertension
hypnosis
hypothalamic-pituitary-adrenal (HPA) pathway

hypothalamus
immune system
insomnia
lymphocytes
meditation
migraine headache
mind-body dualism
muscle contraction headache
parasympathetic nervous system
pituitary gland
posttraumatic stress disorder

psychological debriefing	relaxation training	sympathetic nervous system
psychological factors affecting medical condition	resiliency or "hardiness"	torture
	self–hypnosis	trait anxiety
psychoneuroimmunology	self-instruction training	Type A personality style
psychophysiological disorders	situation ("state") anxiety	Type B personality style
rap group	stress response	ulcer
rape	stressor	

MEDIA RESOURCES

Abnormal Psychology Student Tool Kit

Produced and edited by Ronald J. Comer, Princeton University and Gregory Comer, Princeton Academic Resources. Tied directly to the CyberStudy sections in the text, this Student Tool Kit offers 57 intriguing Video Cases running 3 to 7 minutes each. The Video Cases focus on persons affected by disorders discussed in the text. Students first view the video and then answer a series of thought-provoking questions. Additionally, the Student Tool Kit contains multiple-choice practice test questions with built-in instructional feedback for every option.

Video Cases and Discussions:

- How might stress and anxiety affect performance?
- Observe "fight-or-flight" reactions in operation.
- How do physical, psychological, and sociocultural factors affect health?

Practical, Research, and Decision-Making Exercises:

- Linking modern-day pressures to psychological symptoms
- Examining the connection between life changes and health

PowerPoint Slides

Available at the Instructor's site on the companion Web site are comprehensive PowerPoint slide presentations and supplemental student handouts for Chapter 6. The slide files reflect the main points of the chapter in significant detail. Student handouts were created using the instructor slides as a base, with key points replaced as "fill-in" items. Answer keys and suggestions for use also are provided.

DSM-IV-TR Masters

B-16–17 DSM-IV-TR Diagnostic Criteria for Posttraumatic Stress Disorder

B-18 DSM-IV-TR Diagnostic Criteria for Acute Stress Disorder
B-19 DSM-IV-TR Criteria for Psychological Factors Affecting General Medical Condition

Internet Sites

Please see Appendix A for full and comprehensive references.

Sites relevant to Chapter 6 material are:

http://www.ptsd.va.gov/
This Web site of the National Center for PTSD is provided as an educational resource concerning PTSD and other enduring consequences of traumatic stress.

http://www.nimh.nih.gov/health/topics/
post-traumatic-stress-disorder-ptsd/index.shtml
This Web site, provided by the National Institute of Mental Health, supplies downloadable links to PDF files and booklets on a variety of mental health topics, including stress disorders.

Mainstream Films

Films relevant to Chapter 6 material are listed and summarized below:

Key to Film Listings:
P = psychopathology focus
T = treatment focus
E = ethical issues raised

Please note that some of the films suggested may have graphic sexual or violent content due to the nature of certain subject matters.

Born on the Fourth of July
This 1989 film stars Tom Cruise in the true story of Ron Kovic, a Marine wounded in Vietnam and a well-known antiwar activist. **P, serious film**

The Deer Hunter
From 1978 and starring a now-famous cast, this film details the relationship between friends and the impact

of the Vietnam War, including posttraumatic stress disorder. **P, serious film**

The Fisher King
This 1991 film follows Jack Lucas (Jeff Bridges), an irreverent radio talk show host who sinks into alcoholism after a tragedy. He is rescued by a delusional, homeless man (Robin Williams) on a quest for the Holy Grail. **P, serious film**

Full Metal Jacket
This 1987 film by Stanley Kubrick tackles the training of a squad of Marines and the climactic battle of the 1968 Tet Offensive (the turning point of the Vietnam War). **P, serious film**

Garden State
This independent film follows Andrew Largeman (Zach Braff), an underemployed actor returning home for his mother's funeral after being estranged from his family for a decade. **P, T, comedy-drama**

Gods and Monsters
From 1998, this film is the story of James Whale, the director of *Frankenstein* (1931) and *Bride of Frankenstein* (1935), in the period following the Korean War. **P, serious film**

Man in the Gray Flannel Suit
This 1956 drama stars Gregory Peck as a man struggling to realize the American Dream without sacrificing his family and his soul. While Tom Rath seems a typical, solid business and family man, he suffers from posttraumatic stress disorder. **P, serious film**

Mystic River
From 2003, Clint Eastwood directed this dark film about three men who shared a childhood trauma. **P, serious film**

Ordinary People
This 1980 film examines the treatment of a teenager suffering from depression, anxiety, and posttraumatic stress disorder in the aftermath of his brother's death. **P, T, serious film**

The Pianist
This Oscar-winning film recounts the experiences of a Polish Jewish musician trying to survive the destruction of the Warsaw ghetto of World War II. **P, serious film**

Reign Over Me
This 2007 film stars Adam Sandler and Don Cheadle as they deal with post-9/11 losses. **P, serious film**

Shutter Island
This 2010 film stars Leonardo DiCaprio as a U.S. Marshall investigating a case at a mental institution. **P, T, E, serious film**

Speak
From 2004, this film stars Kristen Stewart as a teen coming to terms with a sexual assault by becoming selectively mute. **P, serious film**

Stop Loss
Starring Ryan Phillippe, this 2008 drama focuses on an Iraq war veteran called back up for duty. **P, serious film**

The War
This 1994 film explores the summer of 1970, when a returning soldier (Kevin Costner) struggles with his emotional and psychological scars, including posttraumatic stress disorder. **P, serious film**

Other Films:
Apocalypse Now (1979) posttraumatic stress disorder. **P, serious film**
The Bell Jar (1979) anxiety and depression. **P, T, serious film**
Crash (1996) posttraumatic stress disorder. **P, serious film**
Fearless (1993) posttraumatic stress disorder. **P, T, serious film**
Platoon (1986) posttraumatic stress disorder. **P, serious film**
Punch-Drunk Love (2002) social phobia, Type A personality pattern. **P, commercial/serious film**
The Royal Tennenbaums (2001) posttraumatic stress disorder. **P, comedy/serious film**
Sleeping with the Enemy (1991) **P, serious film**
Sophie's Choice (1982) posttraumatic stress disorder. **P, serious film**
Tommy (1975) posttraumatic stress disorder. **P, T, rock musical**
An Unmarried Woman (1978) stress reaction. **P, T, serious film**

Comer Video Segments

Available as a supplement, this revised set of videotapes contains short clips depicting various topics related to abnormal psychology. Please see the accompanying Video Guide for specific clips linked to Chapter 6.

Recommendations for Purchase or Rental

The Comer Video Segments include excerpts from many superb clinical documentaries. While the segments alone are ideal for use in lectures, it often is useful to assign the entire documentary for special class screenings or library use by students.

Films on Demand is a Web-based digital delivery service that has impressive psychology holdings. The catalog can be accessed here: http://ffh.films.com/digitallanding.aspx

In addition, the following videos and other media may be of particular interest and are available for purchase or rental and appropriate for use in class or for assignment outside of class.

9/11: Ten Years Later
http://www.cbs.com/shows/ten_years_later

EMDR: A Closer Look
www.guilford.com

The Falling Man:
http://topdocumentaryfilms.com/911-falling-man/

Neurotic, Stress-Rleated, and Somatoform Disorders
ffh.films.com

Reserved to Fight: A Documentary
http://www.reservedtofight.com/reserved/

CLASS DEMONSTRATIONS AND ACTIVITIES

Case Study

Present a case study to the class.

Guest Speaker

Invite a medical doctor or practitioner who specializes in treatment of psychophysiological stress disorders. He or she can speak to the prevalence and impact as well as the biological, psychological, social causes, and interventions for such disorders.

Invite a mental health provider from the local Veteran's Hospital or Veteran's Affairs Units to come and speak to class about PTSD. Similarly, many college and universities have student groups focused on veterans who are returning to school post-service. That group might be a good source for a potential guest speaker.

Diathesis-Stress Model

Direct genetic causation of illness and abnormal behavior is rare. Recent research has indicated that many illnesses are now understood in terms of the interaction of hereditary and environmental factors, the diathesis-stress model. According to this theory, certain genes or hereditary vulnerability give rise to a diathesis or a constitutional predisposition. When an individual's predisposition is then combined with certain kinds of environmental stress, illness may result. With diseases like heart disease, high blood pressure, and cancer, both hereditary and environmental factors play a role. A major effort in abnormal research and clinical practice is to identify specific risk factors in a given individual, including both family history and personal lifestyle, then predict the onset of a mental disorder.

"Pretend, for a moment, that you are a victim of a terrible trauma"

The symptoms of PTSD are fairly well known and intuitively obvious to most people. To emphasize this, ask students to pretend that they went through some trauma, such as a motor vehicle accident in which someone died, or war combat, or being assaulted. Ask them to imagine what they would go through over the next few days and weeks. It is likely that students will generate the concepts of reexperiencing the trauma (e.g., dreams, intrusive recollections) and avoiding stimuli that might remind them of the trauma. It is unlikely that they will realize, intuitively, that there is a general numbing of responsiveness to the external world as well.

The Anonymous Five-Minute Essay: Type A Personality

Ask for anonymous descriptions of individuals with whom students are familiar that fit the description of the Type A personality. Likely examples will be Little League coaches, teachers, parents, and even some friends. Inform students that you may select their example for reading to the class.

(1) "Here's $25,000 to be awarded to . . ."

Type A personality styles are sometimes displayed by children. Researchers suggest that children as young as 3 can exhibit a marked pattern of impatience and restlessness, expectation of meeting high standards, and above-average competitiveness. Children may carry these personality styles, with their potential impact on health, with them into adulthood. Ask groups to develop a school-based program for encouraging these children to develop healthier personality patterns or styles. Have the groups present their ideas, then have the class vote on which group receives the grant to implement their idea.

(2) "Here's $25,000 to be awarded to . . ."

Discuss how optimism or fatalism affects the chances of eventually recovering from cancer. Recent research indicates that the state of mind concerning recovery is a powerful influence on the recovery rates of cancer patients. The more optimistic and positive the person is, the more likely he or she is to recover. Divide the class into groups, then have them create programs, to be used at hospitals or other sites, to encourage optimism in cancer patients. Have the groups present their ideas, then have the class vote on which group receives the grant to implement their idea.

(3) "Here's $25,000 to be awarded to . . ."

Divide students into groups, then ask each group to propose a method to reduce the occurrence of one of the causes of heart disease, such as smoking, drinking, and being overweight. Have the groups present their ideas, then have a class vote to see which group receives the grant to implement the group's idea.

SUGGESTED TOPICS FOR DISCUSSION

Brainstorming Session: Reducing Stress

Ask students to volunteer something that students could do to alleviate stress. This generally evokes a wide variety of suggestions, illustrating how personal the experience of stress can be.

Psychology and Medical Health

The major causes of morbidity (illness) and mortality (death) have changed in the last century. In the early 1900s, viruses and bacteria were the leading causes of death. Ask students what happened to change this. (Medical and scientific advances such as antibiotics, vaccinations, and improvements in sanitation helped stamp out these causes of death.) Presently, leading causes of death include heart disease (related to smoking, eating, not exercising, being overweight, drinking too much), cancer, motor vehicle accidents, and suicide. Ask students what these causes have in common (all are related to behavior). Psychology is thus becoming increasingly important in overall health care. In particular, the field of health psychology is emerging as an important area of the health care system.

Open Discussion: Stress and Appraisal

The Holmes and Rahe Social Readjustment Rating Scale attempted to quantify stressful events. Researchers have found a relationship between total score (adding up the events) and the likelihood of medical illness. The relationship is complex, however. Not everyone who is stressed gets sick, although being stressed clearly puts one at greater risk for being sick. An important issue is the person's appraisal of the event, which has two parts. During primary appraisal, the person decides whether the event is threatening or not (e.g., not all events are perceived as bad by everyone—a divorce might be a wonderful thing from a certain perspective). During secondary appraisal, the person decides whether he or she has the capacity to cope with the event. Discuss potentially stressful events in the lives of college students, such as midterm exams and term papers. Frame the events in terms of primary and secondary appraisal, then discuss what events are particularly stressful. Typically, these will be events that are both threatening (to good grades) and difficult to cope with (e.g., "impossible midterms," a confluence of deadlines).

Open Discussion: Coping with Stress and War

Currently, as noted in the text (p. 5), nearly 20 percent of U.S. troops returning from Iraq and Afghanistan now suffer PTSD. Fewer than half have sought treatment.

The Vietnam War is a useful vehicle for discussing PTSD. Walker and Cavenar (1982) found that 20 to 25 percent of those who served in Vietnam suffered from PTSD. In comparison, it has been estimated that about 1 in 10 World War II veterans suffered PTSD. The events of the war were traumatic and stressful, but World War II is a particularly good example of the effect of the absence of coping factors.

Seeking social support among one's peers is an excellent coping strategy.

- In Vietnam, soldiers were transported (put into and taken out of combat) via jet plane, sometimes overnight. In previous wars, groups of soldiers would be put in and taken out of combat together—ships took soldiers in and out of combat, and the return home would take months, during which experiences could be shared with other combat veterans, catharsis could occur, and a general adjustment could be made.
- During the Vietnam War, it was standard procedure to replace individual soldiers who were killed or wounded with new recruits—rookies who were shunned by more experienced soldiers because, as rookies, they were more likely to do something reckless or dangerous.
- Every soldier had his own DEROS (date of expected return from overseas), which also tended to discourage a sense of being in the war as a group, but rather encouraged an individual's attempts to keep himself alive.

Another effective way to cope with a traumatic incident is to reappraise it, that is, to reexamine one's initial perceptions of it and try to convert a negative appraisal to a positive one.

- In previous wars, soldiers came home—after having done terrible things—to parades and encouragement that they did what needed to be done.
- In contrast, soldiers in Vietnam came home to parades protesting the war and belittling those who served in it. It was just as honorable, in some people's eyes, to refuse to serve as it was to serve. The combat veterans may have felt they were doing the right thing, going to risk life and limb for one's country, but they came home and were told over and over again that the war was wrong and that they were wrong to go.
- Currently, as noted in the text (p. 5), nearly 20 percent of U.S. troops returning from Iraq and Afghanistan now suffer PTSD. Fewer than half of them have sought treatment.

Open Discussion: Social Adjustment Rating Scale

Hand out or display the Holmes and Rahe Scale. What are the most common and least common stressors experienced by students in the class? Alternatively, point to specific examples on the list and ask for a show of hands regarding whether such an event would be (or was) stressful. Discuss why or why not. This emphasizes the subjective nature of stress and the importance of appraisal.

Open Discussion: Student Health

Conduct a class discussion on the relationship between health and academic stress. Ask students whether health problems fit a semester pattern. Discuss students' beliefs about their own roles in health and sickness. Can they affect the course of a disease? Can they do things that prevent diseases? Is the patient to blame for being ill?

ASSIGNMENTS/EXTRA CREDIT SUGGESTIONS

"Write a Pamphlet"

With the use of a software program like Microsoft Publisher or simply paper and markers, students can create a pamphlet on the stress or psychophysiological disorders. Students should be encouraged to be as accurate and up-to-date as possible and to present all sides of the disorder (e.g., alternate treatment approaches or theories).

Keep a Journal

In addition to helping students synthesize material, this activity is helpful in developing writing skills. Have students keep a journal of their thoughts on course material through the semester. This can be done in the first or last five minutes of class or as an out-of-class assignment. Faculty generally should have students submit their journals for review on an ongoing basis because students can have the tendency to delay writing until the end of the semester. Some suggestions for journal topics include: reactions to the case examples; strengths and weaknesses of prevailing theoretical explanations; hypothetical conversations with sufferers of specific disorders, etc.

Abnormal Psychology Student Tool Kit Video Questions

As a homework assignment, have students watch a video clip and answer the accompanying questions.

Students can answer the questions directly into the online assessment feature. The results of these quizzes report to the site's built-in grade book.

Web Site Quiz

For homework or extra credit, have students complete the quizzes for Chapter 6 located on the companion Web site. Students can complete an on-line test of the key chapter material (using questions NOT from the test bank) and have their scores e-mailed directly to the course instructor.

Essay Topics

For homework or extra credit, have students write an essay addressing one (or more) of the following topics:

(1) MediaSpeaks (on p. 167 of the text) discusses the case of an Iraq combat veteran on trial for murder. How do you think PTSD and the experience of trauma should be weighed by the justice system when a crime has been committed?

(2) PsychWatch (on p. 161 in the text) focuses on the psychological aftermath of September 11, 2001. What was the experience like for you at the time? What (if any) stress symptoms did you experience? Where were you living? Did you talk to any-

one about your experiences or feelings? Should you talk to someone now?

(3) PsychWatch (on p. 163 in the text) addresses the diagnostic categories of adjustment disorder. Do you agree or disagree with the use of the diagnosis as a "catch-all?" Do you think people truly have difficulty adjusting to life circumstances? What type of evidence would you like to see?

(4) Using the box on page 185 in the text, write an essay on the "psychological danger of social networking." How might Facebook lead to increased experiences of stress?

Research Topics

For homework or extra credit, have students write a research report addressing one (or more) of the following topics:

(1) Conduct a "Psych Info" search and write an annotated bibliography on EMDR—a popular treatment for PTSD.

(2) Conduct a "Psych Info" search and write an annotated bibliography on the fight-or-flight response. What is the current biological research?

(3) Conduct a "Psych Info" search and write a brief literature review on "hardiness" or resiliency. Is this personality characteristic being actively researched? If so, what are the main findings?

(4) Using the PsychWatch box on p. 173 of the text as a platform, research one or more of the sleep disorders identified in DSM-IV-TR.

Film Review

To earn extra credit, have students watch one (or more) of the mainstream films listed earlier in this chapter and write a brief (3–5 pages) report. Students should summarize the plot of the film in sufficient detail to demonstrate familiarity, but should focus their papers on the depiction of psychological abnormality. What errors or liberties did the filmmaker take? What is the message (implicit or explicit) concerning the mentally ill?

Case Study Evaluations

To complement the Comer and Gorenstein supplemental case study text, case study evaluations have been created. Students can be assigned the appropriate case study and evaluation as homework or for class discussion. While case study evaluation questions are listed in their entirety on the companion Web site at www.worthpublishers.com/comer, the relevant case studies are referenced below.

Case Study 1: Posttraumatic Stress Disorder

Case Study 7: Psychological Factors Affecting Medical Condition: Type A Behavior Pattern

Case Study 8: Psychological Intervention for a Medical Problem: Cancer Treatment for a Child

Crossword Puzzles

As a homework assignment or for extra credit, have students complete and submit Crossword Puzzle #6.

Word Searches

As a homework assignment or for extra credit, have students complete and submit Word Search #6.

Somatoform
and Dissociative Disorders

LECTURE OUTLINE

I.   **SOMATOFORM AND DISSOCIATIVE DISORDERS**
    A.   In addition to disorders covered earlier, two other kinds of disorders are commonly linked to stress and anxiety—somatoform disorders and dissociative disorders
    B.   Somatoform disorders are problems that appear to be medical but are actually caused by psychosocial factors

1. Unlike psychophysiological disorders, in which psychosocial factors interact with genuine physical ailments, somatoform disorders are psychological disorders masquerading as physical problems
C. Dissociative disorders are patterns of memory loss and identity change that are caused almost entirely by psychosocial factors rather than physical ones
D. The somatoform and dissociative disorders have much in common:
   1. Both may occur in response to severe stress
   2. Both have traditionally been viewed as forms of escape from stress
   3. A number of individuals suffer from both a somatoform and a dissociative disorder
   4. Theorists and clinicians often explain and treat the two groups of disorders in similar ways

II. **SOMATOFORM DISORDERS**
   A. When a physical ailment has no apparent medical cause, doctors may suspect a somatoform disorder
   B. People with somatoform disorder do not consciously want or purposely produce their symptoms
      1. They believe their problems are genuinely medical
   C. There are two main types of somatoform disorders: hysterical and preoccupation

III. **WHAT ARE HYSTERICAL SOMATOFORM DISORDERS?**
   A. People with hysterical somatoform disorders suffer actual changes in their physical functioning
      1. These disorders are often hard to distinguish from genuine medical problems
   B. It is always a potential that a diagnosis of hysterical disorder is a mistake and the patient's problem has an undetected organic cause
   C. DSM-IV-TR lists three hysterical somatoform disorders [See Table 7-1, text p. 191]:
      1. Conversion disorder
         a. In this disorder, a psychosocial conflict or need is converted into dramatic physical symptoms that affect voluntary or sensory functioning
            (a) Symptoms often seem neurological, such as paralysis, blindness, or loss of feeling
         b. Most conversion disorders begin between late childhood and young adulthood
         c. They are diagnosed in women twice as often as in men
         d. They usually appear suddenly, at times of stress, and are thought to be rare
      2. Somatization disorder
         a. People with somatization disorder have many long-lasting physical ailments that have little or no organic basis
            (a) Also known as Briquet's syndrome
         b. To receive a diagnosis, a patient must have a range of ailments, including several pain symptoms, gastrointestinal symptoms, a sexual symptom, and a neurological symptom
            (a) Patients usually go from doctor to doctor in search of relief
            (b) Patients often describe their symptoms in dramatic and exaggerated terms
            (c) Most also feel anxious and depressed
         c. This disorder lasts much longer than a conversion disorder, typically for many years
         d. Symptoms may fluctuate over time but rarely disappear completely without therapy
         e. Between 0.2 and 2 percent of all women in the United States experience a somatization disorder in any given year (compared with less than 0.2 percent of men)
         f. The disorder often runs in families and begins between adolescence and young adulthood
      3. Pain disorder associated with psychological factors

a. Patients may receive this diagnosis when psychosocial factors play a central role in the onset, severity, or continuation of pain

b. Although the precise prevalence has not been determined, it appears to be fairly common

c. The disorder often develops after an accident or illness that has caused genuine pain

d. The disorder may begin at any age, and more women than men seem to experience it

D. Hysterical vs. medical symptoms

1. Because hysterical somatoform disorders are so similar to "genuine" medical ailments, physicians sometimes rely on oddities in the patient's medical picture to help distinguish the two

a. For example, hysterical symptoms may be at odds with the known functioning of the nervous system, as in cases of glove anesthesia [See Figure 7-1, text p. 193]

E. Hysterical vs. factitious symptoms

1. Hysterical somatoform disorders are different from patterns in which individuals are purposefully producing or faking medical symptoms

a. Patients may *malinger*, intentionally fake illness to achieve external gain (e.g., financial compensation, military deferment)

b. Patients may display a *factitious disorder*—intentionally producing or faking symptoms simply out of a wish to be a patient

2. Factitious disorder

a. People with factitious disorder often go to extremes to create the appearance of illness

b. Many secretly give themselves medications to produce symptoms

c. Patients often research their supposed ailments and are impressively knowledgeable about medicine

3. Psychotherapists and medical practitioners often become angry at people with a factitious disorder, feeling that they are wasting their time

a. People with the disorder, however, feel they have no control over their problems and often experience great distress

4. Munchausen syndrome is the extreme and long-term form of factitious disorder

a. In a related disorder, Munchausen syndrome by proxy, parents make up or produce physical illnesses in their children

IV. WHAT ARE PREOCCUPATION SOMATOFORM DISORDERS?

A. Preoccupation somatoform disorders include hypochondriasis and body dysmorphic disorder

B. People with these problems misinterpret and overreact to bodily symptoms or features

C. Although these disorders also cause great distress, their impact on one's life differs from that of hysterical disorders

D. There are two main disorders [See Table 7-2, text p. 196]:

1. Hypochondriasis

a. People with hypochondriasis unrealistically interpret bodily symptoms as signs of a serious illness

(a) Often their symptoms are merely normal bodily changes, such as occasional coughing, sores, or sweating

b. Although some patients recognize that their concerns are excessive, many do not

c. Although this disorder can begin at any age, it starts most often in early adulthood, among men and women in equal numbers

(a) Between 1 and 5 percent of all people experience the disorder

d. For most patients, symptoms rise and fall over the years

2. Body dysmorphic disorder (BDD)

a. People with this disorder, also known as dysmorphobia, become deeply concerned about some imagined or minor defect in their appearance

                (a)   Most often they focus on wrinkles, spots, facial hair, swelling, or mis-shapen facial features (nose, jaw, or eyebrows)

          b.   Most cases of the disorder begin in adolescence but are often not revealed until adulthood

          c.   Up to 5 percent of people in the United States experience BDD, and it appears to be equally common among women and men

V.   WHAT CAUSES SOMATOFORM DISORDERS?

   A.   Theorists typically explain the preoccupation somatoform disorders the same way as they explain the anxiety disorders:

      1.   Behaviorists = classical conditioning or modeling

      2.   Cognitive theorists = oversensitivity to bodily cues

   B.   In contrast, the hysterical somatoform disorders are widely considered unique and in need of special explanation

      1.   No explanation has received much research support, and the disorders are still poorly understood

   C.   The psychodynamic view

      1.   Freud believed that hysterical disorders represented a *conversion* of underlying emotional conflicts into physical symptoms

      2.   Because most of his patients were women, Freud centered his explanation on the psychosexual development of girls and focused on the phallic stage (ages 3–5)

         a.   During this stage, girls develop a pattern of sexual desires for their fathers (the Electra complex) while recognizing that they must compete with their mothers for their fathers' attention

         b.   Because of the mother's more powerful position, however, girls repress these sexual feelings

         c.   Freud believed that if parents overreacted to such feelings, the Electra complex would remain unresolved and the child would reexperience sexual anxiety through her life

         d.   Freud concluded that some women unconsciously hide their sexual feelings in adulthood by converting them into physical symptoms

      3.   Today's psychodynamic theorists take issue with Freud's explanation of the Electra conflict

         a.   They do continue to believe that sufferers of these disorders have unconscious conflicts carried from childhood

      4.   Psychodynamic theorists propose that two mechanisms are at work in hysterical disorders:

         a.   Primary gain—Hysterical symptoms keep internal conflicts out of conscious awareness

         b.   Secondary gain—Hysterical symptoms further enable people to avoid unpleasant activities or to receive sympathy from others

   D.   The behavioral view

      1.   Behavioral theorists propose that the physical symptoms of hysterical disorders bring *rewards* to sufferers

         a.   May remove individual from an unpleasant situation

         b.   May bring attention from other people

      2.   In response to such rewards, sufferers learn to display symptoms more and more prominently

      3.   This focus on rewards is similar to the psychodynamic idea of secondary gain, but behaviorists view them as the primary cause of the development of the disorder

   E.   The cognitive view

      1.   Some cognitive theorists propose that hysterical disorders are forms of *communication*, providing a means for people to express difficult emotions

         a.   Like psychodynamic theorists, cognitive theorists hold that emotions are being converted into physical symptoms

b. This conversion is not to defend against anxiety but to communicate extreme feelings

F. The multicultural view

1. Some theorists believe that Western clinicians hold a bias that considers somatic symptoms as an *inferior* way of dealing with emotions

a. The transformation of personal distress into somatic complaints is the norm in many non-Western cultures

b. As we saw in Chapter 6, reactions to life's stressors are often influenced by one's culture

G. A possible role for biology

1. The impact of biological processes on somatoform disorders can be understood through research on placebos and the placebo effect

a. Placebos are substances with no known medicinal value

b. Treatment with placebos has been shown to bring improvement to many—possibly through the power of suggestion but likely because expectation triggers the release of endogenous chemicals

c. Perhaps traumatic events and related concerns or needs can also trigger our "inner pharmacies" and set in motion the bodily symptoms of hypterical somatoform disorders

VI. HOW ARE SOMATOFORM DISORDERS TREATED?

A. People with somatoform disorders usually seek psychotherapy only as a last resort

B. Individuals with preoccupation disorders typically receive the kinds of treatments applied to anxiety disorders, particularly OCD:

1. Antidepressant medication, especially selective serotonin reuptake inhibitors (SSRIs)

2. Exposure and response prevention (ERP)

3. Cognitive-behavioral therapies of this kind are also applied

C. Treatments for hysterical disorders often focus on the cause of the disorder and apply the same kind of techniques used in cases of PTSD, particularly:

1. Insight—often psychodynamically oriented

2. Exposure—Client thinks about traumtic event(s) that triggered the physical symptoms

3. Drug Therapy—especially antidepressant medication

D. Other therapists try to address the physical symptoms of the hysterical disorders, applying techniques such as:

1. Suggestion—usually an offering of emotional support that may include hypnosis

2. Reinforcement—a behavioral attempt to change reward structures

3. Confrontation—an overt attempt to force patients out of the sick role

E. Researchers have not fully evaluated the effects of these particular approaches in hysterical disorders

VII. DISSOCIATIVE DISORDERS

A. The key to our identity—the sense of who we are and where we fit in our enviroment—is memory

B. Our recall of past experiences helps us to react to present events and guides us in making decisions about the future

C. People sometimes experience a major disruption of their memory:

1. They may not remember new information

2. They may not remember old information

D. When such changes in memory lack a clear physical cause, they are called "dissociative" disorders

1. In such disorders, one part of the person's memory typically seems *dissociated,* or separated, from the rest

2. These disorders often are memorably portrayed in books, movies, and television programming

3.   DSM-IV also lists depersonalization disorder as a dissociative disorder, but this listing is controversial

E.   One should keep in mind that dissociative symptoms often are found in cases of acute and posttraumatic stress disorders

    1.   When such symptoms occur as part of a stress disorder, they do not necessarily indicate a dissociative disorder—a pattern in which dissociative symptoms dominate

        a.   On the other hand, research suggests that people with one of these disorders also develop the other as well

F.   There are several kinds of dissociative disorders [See Table 7-4, text p. 204]:

    1.   Dissociative amnesia

        a.   People with dissociative amnesia are unable to recall important information, usually of an upsetting nature, about their lives

        b.   The loss of memory is much more extensive than normal forgetting and is not caused by physical factors

        c.   Often an episode of amnesia is directly triggered by a specific upsetting event

        d.   Dissociative amnesia may be:

            (a)   Localized—most common type; loss of all memory of events occurring within a limited period of time

            (b)   Selective—loss of memory for some, but not all, events occurring within a period of time

            (c)   Generalized—loss of memory, beginning with an event, but extending back in time; may lose sense of identity; may fail to recognize family and friends

            (d)   Continuous—forgetting into the future; quite rare in cases of dissociative amnesia

        e.   All forms of the disorder are similar in that the amnesia interferes mostly with a person's memory for personal material

            (a)   Memory for abstract or encyclopedic information usually remains intact

        f.   Clinicians do not know how common dissociative amnesia is, but many cases seem to begin during serious threats to health and safety

    2.   Dissociative fugue

        a.   People with dissociative fugue not only forget their personal identities and details of their past lives, but also flee to an entirely different location

            (a)   For some, the fugue is brief: a matter of hours or days—and ends suddenly

            (b)   For others, the fugue is more severe: people may travel far from home, take a new name and establish new relationships, and even a new line of work; some display new personality characteristics

        b.   Approximately 0.2 percent of the population experience dissociative fugue

        c.   It usually follows a severely stressful event

            (a)   Fugues tend to end abruptly

            (b)   When people are found before their fugue has ended, therapists may find it necessary to continually remind them of their own identity

        d.   The majority of people regain most or all of their memories and never have a recurrence

    3.   Dissociative identity disorder/multiple personality disorder

        a.   A personality with dissociative identity disorder (DID; formerly multiple personality disorder) develops two or more distinct personalities—subpersonalities—each with a unique set of memories, behaviors, thoughts, and emotions

        b.   At any given time, one of the subpersonalities dominates the person's functioning

            (a)   Usually one of these subpersonalities, called the primary, or host, personality, appears more often than the others

            (b)   The transition from one subpersonality to the next ("switching") is usually sudden and may be dramatic

        c.   Cases of this disorder were first reported almost three centuries ago

d. Many clinicians consider the disorder to be rare, but some reports suggest that it may be more common than once thought

e. Most cases are first diagnosed in late adolescence or early adulthood
   (a) Symptoms generally begin in childhood after episodes of abuse
   (b) Typical onset is prior to age five
   (c) Women receive the diagnosis three times as often as men

f. How do subpersonalities interact?
   (a) The relationship between or among subpersonalities varies from case to case
   (b) Generally there are three kinds of relationships:
       (i) Mutually amnesic relationships—subpersonalities have no awareness of one another
       (ii) Mutually cognizant patterns—each subpersonality is well aware of the rest
       (iii) One-way amnesic relationships—most common pattern—some personalities are aware of others, but the awareness is not mutual
            1. Those who are aware ("co-conscious subpersonalities") are "quiet observers"
   (c) Investigators used to believe that most cases of the disorder involved two or three subpersonalities
       (i) Studies now suggest that the average number per patient is much higher—15 for women, 8 for men
       (ii) There have been cases with over 100

g. How do subpersonalities differ?
   (a) Subpersonalities often exhibit dramatically different characteristics, including
       (i) Identifying features
            1. Subpersonalities may differ in features as basic as age, sex, race, and family history
       (ii) Abilities and preferences
            1. Although encyclopedic information is not usually affected by dissociative amnesia or fugue, in DID it is often disturbed
            2. It is not uncommon for different subpersonalities to have different abilities, including being able to drive, speak a foreign language, or play an instrument
       (iii) Physiological responses
            1. Researchers have discovered that subpersonalities may have physiological differences, such as differences in autonomic nervous system activity, blood pressure levels, and allergies

h. How common is dissociative identity disorder?
   (a) Traditionally, DID was believed to be rare
   (b) Some researchers even argue that many or all cases are *iatrogenic*, that is, unintentionally produced by practitioners
       (i) These arguments are supported by the fact that many cases of DID first come to attention only after a person is already in treatment
            1. This is not true of all cases
   (c) The number of people diagnosed with the disorder has been increasing
   (d) Although the disorder still is uncommon, thousands of cases have been documented in the United States and Canada alone
       (i) Two factors may account for this increase:
            1. A growing number of clinicians believe that the disorder does exist and are willing to diagnose it
            2. Diagnostic procedures have become more accurate
   (e) Despite changes, many clinicians continue to question the legitimacy of this category

i. How do theorists explain dissociative disorders?

(a) A variety of theories have been proposed to explain dissociative disorders
  (i) Older explanations have not received much investigation
  (ii) Newer viewpoints, which combine cognitive, behavioral, and biological principles, have captured the interest of clinical scientists
(b) The psychodynamic view
  (i) Psychodynamic theorists believe that dissociative disorders are caused by *repression*, the most basic ego defense mechanism
  (ii) People fight off anxiety by unconsciously preventing painful memories, thoughts, or impulses from reaching awareness
  (iii) In this view, dissociative amnesia and fugue are *single episodes* of massive repression
  (iv) DID is thought to result from a *lifetime* of excessive repression, motivated by very traumatic childhood events
  (v) Most of the support for this model is drawn from case histories, which report brutal childhood experiences
    1. Yet, some individuals with DID do not seem to have experiences of abuse
    2. Further, why might only a small fraction of abused children develop this disorder?
(c) The behavioral view
  (i) Behaviorists believe that dissociation grows from normal memory processes and is a response learned through operant conditioning
  (ii) Momentary forgetting of trauma leads to a drop in anxiety, which increases the likelihood of future forgetting
  (iii) Like psychodynamic theorists, behaviorists see dissociation as escape behavior
  (iv) Also, like psychodynamic theorists, much of the support for this model comes from case histories
  (v) Moreover, these explanations fail to explain all aspects of these disorders
(d) State-dependent learning
  (i) If people learn something when they are in a particular state of mind, they are likely to remember it best when they are in the same condition
  (ii) This link between state and recall is called state-dependent learning
  (iii) This model has been demonstrated with substances and mood, and may be linked to arousal levels
  (iv) People who are prone to develop dissociative disorders may have state-to-memory links that are unusually rigid and narrow—each thought, memory, and skill is tied *exclusively* to a particular state of arousal, so that they recall a given event only when they experience an arousal state almost identical to the state in which the memory was first acquired
(e) Self-hypnosis
  (i) While hypnosis can help people remember events that occurred and were forgotten years ago, it also can help people forget facts, events, and their personal identity
  (ii) Called "hypnotic anmesia," this phenomenon has been demonstrated in research studies with word lists
  (iii) The parallels between hypnotic amnesia and dissociative disorders are striking and have led researchers to conclude that dissociative disorders may be a form of self-hypnosis
j. How are dissociative disorders treated?
(a) People with dissociative amnesia and fugue often recover on their own
  (i) Only sometimes do their memory problems linger and require treatment

(b) In contrast, people with DID usually require treatment to regain their lost memories and develop an integrated personality

(c) Treatments for dissociative amnesia and fugue tends to be more successful than those for DID

(d) How do therapists help people with dissociative amnesia and fugue?

    (i) The leading treatments for these disorders are psychodynamic therapy, hypnotic therapy, and drug therapy

        1. Psychodynamic therapists guide patients to their unconscious and bring forgotten experiences into consciousness

        2. In hypnotic therapy, patients are hypnotized and guided to recall forgotten events

        3. Sometimes intravenous injections of barbiturates are used to help patients regain lost memories

            a. Often called "truth serums," the key to the drugs' success is their ability to calm people and free their inhibitions

(e) How do therapists help individuals with DID?

    (i) Unlike victims of dissociative amnesia or fugue, people with DID do not typically recover without treatment

    (ii) Treatment for this pattern, like the disorder itself, is complex and difficult

    (iii) Therapists usually try to help the client by:

        1. Recognizing the disorder

            a. Therapists typically try to bond with the primary personality and with each of the subpersonalities

            b. As bonds are forged, therapists try to educate the patients and help them recognize the nature of the disorder

            c. Some use hypnosis or video as a means of presenting other subpersonalities

            d. Many therapists recommend group or family therapy

        2. Recovering memories

            a. To help patients recover missing memories, therapists use many of the approaches applied in other dissociative disorders, including psychodynamic therapy, hypnotherapy, and drug treatment

            b. These techniques tend to work slowly in cases of DID

        3. Integrating the subpersonalities

            a. The final goal of therapy is to merge the different subpersonalities into a single, integrated identity

            b. Integration is a continuous process with fusion as the final merging

            c. Many patients distrust this final treatment goal, and their subpersonalities see integration as a form of death

            d. Once the subpersonalities are integrated, further therapy is typically needed to maintain the complete personality and to teach social and coping skills to prevent later dissociations

VIII. DEPERSONALIZATION DISORDER

A. DSM-IV-TR categorizes depersonalization disorder as a dissociative disorder, even though it is different from the other dissociative patterns

B. The central symptom is persistent and recurrent episodes of *depersonalization*—a change in one's experience of the self in which one's mental functioning or body feels unreal or foreign

C. People with depersonalization disorder feel as though they have become separated from their bodies and are observing themselves from outside

    1. This sense of unreality can extend to other sensory experiences and behavior

       2.   Depersonalization often is accompanied by *derealization*—the feeling that the external world, too, is unreal and strange

    D.   Depersonalization experiences alone do not indicate a depersonalization disorder

       1.   Transient depersonalization reactions are fairly common

       2.   The symptoms of a depersonalization are persistent or recurrent, cause considerable distress, and interfere with social relationships and job performance

    E.   The disorder occurs most frequently in adolescents and young adults, hardly ever in people over 40

    F.   The disorder comes on suddenly and tends to be long-lasting

    G.   Few theories have been offered to explain depersonalization disorder, and little research has been conducted on the problem

VIX. CALL FOR CHANGE: DSM-5

    A.   The DSM-5 task force proposed several changes to these disorders, particularly the somatoform disorders:

       1.   It was suggested that three disorders—somatization disorder, pain disorder, and certain kinds of hypochondriasis—be combined into one: complex somatic symptom disorder

       2.   The task force also proposed two new disorders: simple somatic symptom disorder, for milder cases, and illness anxiety disorder, for cases with trivial somatic symptoms but severe anxiety

       3.   It was suggested that the notion that symptoms must be "medically unexplained" should be dropped

       4.   The task force further suggested replacing the current "Somatoform Disorders" grouping with one called "Somatic Symptom Disorders" and reorganizing the categorization of some disorders

          a.   For example, Body Dysmorphic Disorder would be listed under "Obsessive-Compulsive and Related Disorders"

    B.   The proposed changes to the dissociative disorders are few, and the most prominent one suggests that dissociative fugue should be dropped and merged into dissociative amnesia

LEARNING OBJECTIVES

    1.   Define somatoform disorders, including conversion disorders, somatization disorders, and pain disorders.

    2.   Explain how physicians distinguish between hysterical somatoform disorders and true medical problems.

    3.   Describe the criteria for diagnosing factitious disorder; include in this discussion Munchausen syndrome and Munchausen syndrome by proxy.

    4.   Compare and contrast hypochondriasis and body dysmorphic disorders.

    5.   Compare and contrast the psychodynamic, cognitive, and behavioral views of somatoform disorders. Discuss the multicultural view and the possible role of biology.

    6.   Describe the general characteristics of the dissociative disorders: dissociative amnesia, dissociative fugue, and dissociative identity disorder.

    7.   Discuss the explanations of dissociative disorder to include psychodynamic explanations, behavioral explanations, state-dependent learning, and self-hypnosis.

    8.   Discuss treatment for the dissociative disorders.

    9.   Describe depersonalization disorder.

    10.   Discuss the changes for these disorders proposed by the DSM-5 Task Force.

KEY TERMS

alternate personalities
amnestic episode
body dysmorphic disorder
Briquet's syndrome
continuous amnesia
conversion disorder
depersonalization disorder
dissociative amnesia
dissociative disorders
dissociative fugue
dissociative identity disorder
dysmorphophobia
Electra complex
exposure and response
  prevention
factitious disorder
fusion
generalized amnesia

glove anesthesia
host personality
hypnotic therapy
hypochondriasis
hysterical somatoform
  disorders
iatrogenic disorder
identity
localized amnesia
malingering
memory
multiple personality disorder
Munchausen syndrome
Munchausen syndrome by
  proxy
mutually amnesic relationships
mutually cognizant patterns
one-way amnesic relationships

operant conditioning
pain disorder associated with
  psychological factors
phallic stage
placebo
placebo effect
preoccupation somatoform
  disorders
primary gain
repression
secondary gain
selective amnesia
self-hypnosis
somatization disorder
somatoform disorder
state-dependent learning
subpersonalities
switching

MEDIA RESOURCES

Abnormal Psychology Student Tool Kit

Produced and edited by Ronald J. Comer, Princeton University and Gregory Comer, Princeton Academic Resources. Tied directly to the CyberStudy sections in the text, this Student Tool Kit offers 57 intriguing Video Cases running 3 to 7 minutes each. The Video Cases focus on persons affected by disorders discussed in the text. Students first view the video and then answer a series of thought-provoking questions. Additionally, the Student Tool Kit contains multiple-choice practice test questions with built-in instructional feedback for every option.

Video Cases and Discussions:

- When do somatoform symptoms impair functioning and endanger sufferers?
- Why is it important to distinguish somatoform symptoms from factitious or true medical symptoms?
- Observe an individual with multiple personality disorder, and see "switches" from subpersonality to subpersonality.

Practical, Research, and Decision-Making Exercises:

- Observing and measuring the power of suggestion.
- Manufacturing memories.

PowerPoint Slides

Available at the Instructor's site on the companion Web site are comprehensive PowerPoint slide presentations and supplemental student handouts for Chapter 7. The slide files reflect the main points of the chapter in significant detail. Student handouts were created using the instructor slides as a base, with key points replaced as "fill-in" items. Answer keys and suggestions for use also are provided.

DSM-IV-TR Masters

B-20, DSM-IV-TR Diagnostic Criteria for Somatization Disorder

B-21, DSM-IV-TR Diagnostic Criteria for Conversion Disorder

B-22, DSM-IV-TR Diagnostic Criteria for Pain Disorder

B-22, DSM-IV-TR Diagnostic Criteria for Hypochondriasis

B-23, DSM-IV-TR Diagnostic Criteria for Body Dysmorphic Disorder

B-23, DSM-IV-TR Diagnostic Criteria for Factitious Disorder

B-24, DSM-IV-TR Diagnostic Criteria for Dissociative Amnesia

B-24, DSM-IV-TR Diagnostic Criteria for Dissociative Fugue

B-25, DSM-IV-TR Diagnostic Criteria for Dissociative Identity Disorder

B-25, DSM-IV-TR Diagnostic Criteria for Depersonalization Disorder

Internet Sites

Please see Appendix A for full and comprehensive references.

Sites relevant to Chapter 7 material are:

http://www.isst-d.org
This Web site is the International Society for the Study of Trauma and Dissociation and supplies copyrighted Guidelines for Treating Dissociative Identity Disorder in Adults, with links to each section of the guidelines. There are also links specified for general information, assisting professionals, and finding a therapist.

http://www.cdc.gov/cfs
A comprehensive page from the CDC that discusses the many factors associated with chronic fatigue syndrome.

http://allpsych.com/disorders/somatoform/
This site includes characteristics, etiology, symptoms, and treatment of somatoform disorders.

Mainstream Films

Films relevant to Chapter 7 material are listed and summarized below.

Key to Film Listings:
P = psychopathology focus
T = treatment focus
E = ethical issues raised

Please note that some of the films suggested may have graphic sexual or violent content due to the nature of certain subject matters.

Agnes of God
This 1985 film stars Jane Fonda as Dr. Livingston, a psychiatrist who is called in as part of the investigation when a dead infant is found at a convent. The child is found to belong to solemn, naive Sister Agnes (Meg Tilly), who offers little information about who the father is or why she committed the crime. **P, T, E, serious film**

The Butterfly Effect
Starring Ashton Kutcher, this 2004 suspense film follows a boy who blocks out painful memories of his life, only to recall them in an unusual way. **P, commercial/suspense film**

Hannah and Her Sisters
From 1986, this film chronicles the changing relationships among three sisters living in New York City. The film stars Woody Allen as a television writer who is divorced from Hannah and suffers from hypochondriasis. **P, T, comedy**

Identity
Released in 2003, this film seems to follow strangers from all different walks of life: a limo driver escorting a movie star, parents with a young son, a cop transporting a convict, a prostitute, a young couple, and a motel manager who are then brought together in a rainstorm. As they are killed off one by one, the connections between them become clearer. **P, T, commercial/suspense film**

Mulholland Drive
This 2001 Oscar-nominated David Lynch film is about a woman with amnesia lost in Los Angeles who is helped by an ingenue also new to the city. Everything is not, however, as it seems. **P, commercial/suspense film**

The Piano
This Oscar-winning film from 1993 stars Holly Hunter as Ada, a mute-by-choice nineteenth-century woman sent to New Zealand in an arranged marriage with a patriarchal landowner (Sam Neill). **P, serious film**

Primal Fear
From 1996, this film stars Edward Norton as an accused killer claiming dissociative identity disorder (multiple personality disorder) and Richard Gere as his attorney. The film is full of plot twists and turns. **P, T, E, serious/commercial film**

Psycho
This 1960 classic Hitchcock film (remade in 1998) follows Norman Bates, a lonely hotel clerk with a dissociative disorder. **P, horror/commercial film**

Secret Window
This 2004 film stars Johnny Depp as an author with dissociative identify disorder. **P, horror/commercial film**

Send Me No Flowers
From 1964, this film stars Rock Hudson as a sweet and hopeless man with hypochondriasis. **P, comedy**

The Sixth Sense
While not a major point of this 1999 film about a young boy who "sees dead people," a child victim of Munchausen syndrome by proxy is briefly profiled. **P, commercial/suspense/paranormal film**

Spellbound
From 1945, this Hitchcock film (with scenery by Salvador Dali) stars Ingrid Bergman as a psychiatrist and Gregory Peck as an amnestic patient involved in a manhunt. **P, T, E, commercial thriller/romance film**

Sybil
From 1976, Sally Field gives an award-winning performance as Sybil, a disturbed young woman who suffers from dissociative identity behavior. **P, serious film**

The Three Faces of Eve
This 1957 film is the true story of a Georgia housewife (played by Joanne Woodward in an award-winning performance) with three personalities. **P, T, serious film**

Vanilla Sky
This 2001 Cameron Crowe film stars Tom Cruise as a successful publisher who finds his life taking a turn for the surreal after a car accident. **P, commercial/suspense film**

Other Films:

Apocalypse Now (1979) dissociative disorder. **P, serious film**
Arsenic and Old Lace (1944) dissociative disorder. **P, comedy film**
The Boston Strangler (1968) multiple personality disorder. **P, serious film**
Captain Newman, MD (1963) dissociative disorder. **P, T, serious film**
Fight Club (1999) dissociative disorder. **P, serious film**
Hollywood Ending (2002) somatoform disorder (hysterical blindness). **P, comedy/commercial film**
The King of Comedy (1983) dissociative disorder. **P, serious/comedy film**
Nurse Betty (2000) dissociative disorder. **P, serious/comedy film**
Play It Again Sam (1972) hypochondriacs. **P, comedy film**
Raising Cain (1992) multiple personality disorder. **P, commercial/suspense film**
Sunset Boulevard (1950) dissociative disorder. **P, serious film**
Tommy (1975) somatoform disorder. **P, T, rock musical**

Comer Video Segments

Available as a supplement, this revised set of videotapes contains short clips depicting various topics related to abnormal psychology. Please see the accompanying Video Guide for specific clips linked to Chapter 7.

Recommendations for Purchase or Rental

The Comer Video Segments include excerpts from many superb clinical documentaries. While the segments alone are ideal for use in lectures, it often is useful to assign the entire documentary for special class screenings or library use by students.

Films on Demand is a Web-based digital delivery service that has impressive psychology holdings. Their catalog can be accessed here: http://ffh.films.com/digitallanding.aspx

In addition, the following videos and other media may be of particular interest and are available for purchase or rental and appropriate for use in class or for assignment outside of class.

Living with Amnesia
Lost in the Mirror: Women with Multiple Personalities
Neurotic, Stress-Related, and Somatoform Disorders
ffh.films.com
Films for the Humanities and Sciences
P.O. Box 2053
Princeton, NJ 08543-2053
Phone: 800-257-5126

The United States of Tara
www.sho.com
This television show is available from Showtime and stars Toni Collette as a suburban mom coping with DID.

CLASS DEMONSTRATIONS AND ACTIVITIES

Case Study

Present a case study to the class.

Panel Discussion

Have students volunteer (or assign them) to portray mental health "workers" from different theoretical perspectives in a panel discussion. Each student should present the main explanation and treatment for the anxiety disorders from his or her theoretical background. Students in the audience can ask questions of the panelists. Additionally, other students can role-play patients suffering from particular somatoform or dissociative disorders. [NOTE: A brief reminder about sensitivity and professionalism is worthwhile here.] Have the panelists or audience members attempt to make a diagnosis.

"It's Debatable I: Dissociative Identity Disorder is 'real' " (see Preface instructions for conducting this activity)

Have students volunteer (or assign them) in teams to opposite sides of the debate topic. Have students present their cases in class following standard debate guidelines.

"It's Debatable II: Repressed Childhood Memories or False Memory Syndrome? (see Preface instructions for conducting this activity and PsychWatch (text p. 206) for more information on the topic)

Have students volunteer (or assign them) in teams to opposite sides of the debate topic. Have students present their cases in class following standard debate guidelines.

The Anonymous Five-Minute Essay: "I can't go to school today"

An amusing exercise is to have students write down their most creative excuse for not attending school (re-lated to faking illness). It should be an episode "in which they probably could have qualified for some acting award, and of which, to this day, they are proud." Inform students that you may select their example for reading to the class.

Group Work: Dissociative Identity Disorder

Tell the class that you have been called as an expert witness at a trial of a person who is claiming, as his defense, that he has multiple personality disorder. You will be questioned as to the validity of the diagnostic category (which is still being debated among psychologists). Divide students into groups and assign them either the position that multiple personality disorder is or is not a valid disorder. Have groups present their arguments.

Distinguishing Disorders

The differences among factitious disorder, conversion disorder, somatization disorder, pain disorder, hypochondriasis, and body dysmorphic disorder can be difficult to understand. Pointing out the important distinction (such as the voluntary nature of symptoms in factitious disorder) is very helpful. Displaying the DSM criteria for these disorders simultaneously while leading a discussion of the differences also can be helpful.

SUGGESTED TOPICS FOR DISCUSSION

Munchausen Syndrome versus Munchausen Syndrome by Proxy

Lead a discussion of these disorders. Munchausen syndrome is an extreme and long-term form of factitious disorder in which a person feigns symptoms to gain admission to a hospital and receive treatment. Munchausen syndrome by proxy is a factitious disorder in which parents feign or produce physical illnesses in their children. In both instances, the motivation appears to be attention from doctors (either because one is sick or because one's child is sick). See PsychWatch on p. 195 of the text for more information.

Open Discussion: Too Healthy?

Ask students whether there should be a DSM category for people who are overly concerned with good health. They can be people who are overly concerned about eating habits or exercise. Should these types of behaviors be considered abnormal?

Development of Dissociative Disorders

Lead a discussion of why some people who are sexually abused as children develop dissociative identity disorder while most don't. Research indicates that individuals who develop dissociative disorders are much more susceptible to self-hypnosis and hypnotic suggestion than the average person. Additionally, why is this disorder more common among females than males? Are there regions of the country where this disorder is more prevalent?

ASSIGNMENTS/EXTRA CREDIT SUGGESTIONS

"Write a Pamphlet"

With the use of a software program like Microsoft Publisher or simply paper and markers, students can create a pamphlet on one or all of the somatoform and/or dissociative disorders. Students also could create a pamphlet on "How to Detect Malingering" or "A Guide to Factitious Disorders." Students should be encouraged to be as accurate and up-to-date as possible, and to present all sides of the disorder (e.g., alternate treatment approaches or theories).

Keep a Journal

In addition to helping students synthesize material, this activity also is helpful in developing writing skills. Have students keep a journal of their thoughts on course material throughout the semester. This can be done in the first or last five minutes of class or as an out-of-class assignment. Faculty generally should have students submit their journals for review on an ongoing basis as students can have the tendency to delay writing until the end of the semester. Some suggestions for journal topics include: reactions to the case examples; strengths and weaknesses of prevailing theoretical explanations; hypothetical conversations with sufferers of specific disorders, etc.

Presume You Are an Expert . . . (The Development of Dissociative Disorders)

Tell the students that you received a phone call from your senator last night. He or she recognizes that you are doing a fine job instructing students on the issue of childhood abuse. Your senator wants you and several students to come to Washington, D.C., to testify before a Senate subcommittee about the effects of the abuse on children. Ask students to prepare a five-minute presentation outlining a position on why some people who are sexually abused as children develop dissociative identity disorder while most don't. One position might be: "It is actually normal for dissociative disorder to develop following severe abuse." A second position is: "Only in unusual cases or examples does dissociative disorder develop as a result of childhood sexual abuse." Have groups present their discussions and positions.

Abnormal Psychology Student Tool Kit Video Questions

As a homework assignment, have students watch a video clip and answer the accompanying questions. Students can answer the questions directly into the on-line assessment feature. The results of these quizzes report to the site's built-in grade book.

Web Site Quiz

For homework or extra credit, have students complete the quizzes for Chapter 7 located on the companion Web site. Students can complete an online test of the key chapter material (using questions NOT from the test bank) and have their scores e-mailed directly to the course instructor.

Essay Topics

For homework or extra credit, have students write an essay addressing one (or more) of the following topics:

(1) Discuss your thoughts about the impact of sociocultural factors on (a) body image and (b) BDD. PsychWatch [See text p. 199] details perceptions of beauty in other cultures. What beauty aesthetics in Western culture would outsiders see as bizarre? To what extent do these perceptions impact the rates and types of cosmetic surgery seen in the world today [See text p. 196]?

(2) PsychWatch on p. 195 in the text discusses Munchausen syndrome by proxy, a disorder many find both bizarre and disturbing. What do you think is the explanation behind such a disorder? Do you think Munchausen syndrome by proxy should be considered a psychological disorder or a crime?

(3) Compare and contrast factitious disorders, malingering, and somatoform disorders. What are your reactions to each type of disorder? Do you think they are "legitimate" psychological disorders?

Research Topics

For homework or extra credit, have students write a research report addressing one (or more) of the following topics:

(1) Conduct a "Psych Info" search and write an annotated bibliography on treatments for factitious disorders and somatoform disorders. What theoretical model is being evaluated?

(2) Conduct a "Psych Info" search and write an annotated bibliography on the dissociative disorders, including depersonalization disorder. What research is being conducted on these disorders?

Are they being researched in the same ways? Does the classification of depersonalization as a dissociative disorder make sense diagnostically?

(3) Research the beauty standard in non-Western countries (as discussed on p. 199 in the text). Why are practices in other cultures considered "wrong," while analogous acts in one's own culture are "right?" Can you think of other examples from Western culture that support this argument?

(4) Conduct a Psych Info search on Repression and False Memory Syndrome and write a review [See PsychWatch, text p. 206]. Which side of the argument is most compelling to you?

(5) Research some of the "Pecularities of Memory" discussed in PsychWatch on p. 213 in the text. Should any of these be included as disorders in the DSM?

Film Review

To earn extra credit, have students watch one (or more) of the mainstream films listed earlier in this chapter and write a brief (3–5 pages) report. Students should summarize the plot of the film in sufficient detail to demonstrate familiarity, but should focus their papers on the depiction of psychological abnormality. What errors or liberties did the filmmaker take? What is the message (implicit or explicit) concerning the mentally ill?

Case Study Evaluations

To complement the Comer and Gorenstein supplemental case study text, case study evaluations have been created. Students can be assigned the appropriate case study and evaluation as homework or for class discussion. While case study evaluation questions are listed in their entirety on the companion Web site at www.worthpublishers.com/comer, the relevant case studies are referenced next.

Case Study 6: Hypochondriasis

Crossword Puzzles

As a homework assignment or for extra credit, have students complete and submit Crossword Puzzle #7.

Word Searches

As a homework assignment or for extra credit, have students complete and submit Word Search #7.

Mood Disorders

LECTURE OUTLINE

I. **DEPRESSION AND MANIA ARE THE KEY EMOTIONS IN MOOD DISORDERS:**
    A. Depression—a low, sad state in which life seems dark and its challenges overwhelming
    B. Mania—a state of breathless euphoria or frenzied energy
    C. Most people with a mood disorder experience only depression
        1. This pattern is called *unipolar depression*
        2. There is no history of mania
        3. Mood returns to normal when depression lifts
    D. Others experience periods of mania that alternate with periods of depression
        1. This pattern is called *bipolar disorder*
    E. One might logically expect a third pattern—unipolar mania, in which people suffer from mania only—but this pattern is uncommon
    F. Mood disorders have always captured people's interest

    G.   Mood problems have been shared by millions, and today the economic costs amount to more than $80 billion each year
        1.   The human suffering is beyond calculation

II.   **UNIPOLAR DEPRESSION**
    A.   The term *depression* is often used to describe general sadness or unhappiness
        1.   This loose use of the term confuses a normal mood swing with a clinical syndrome
        2.   Clinical depression can bring severe and long-lasting psychological pain that may intensify over time
    B.   How common is unipolar depression?
        1.   Almost 7 percent of adults in the United States suffer from severe unipolar depression in any given year
        2.   As many as 5 percent suffer mild forms
        3.   About 17 percent of all adults will experience unipolar depression in their lifetimes
        4.   The prevalence is similar in Canada, England, France, and many other countries
        5.   The risk of experiencing this problem has increased steadily since 1915
    C.   Women are at least twice as likely as men to experience episodes of severe unipolar depression
        1.   As many as 26 percent of women (as opposed to 12 percent men) may have an episode at some time in their lives
        2.   Among children, the prevalence is similar for boys and girls
        3.   These rates hold true across socioeconomic classes and ethnic groups
    D.   Approximately half of those with unipolar depression recover within six weeks, and 90 percent recover within a year, some without treatment
        1.   Most will experience another episode at some point
    E.   What are the symptoms of depression?
        1.   Symptoms may vary from person to person
        2.   Five main areas of functioning may be affected:
            a.   Emotional symptoms
            b.   Motivational symptoms
                (a)   Between 6 and 15 percent of those with severe depression commit suicide
            c.   Behavioral symptoms
            d.   Cognitive symptoms
            e.   Physical symptoms
    F.   Diagnosing unipolar depression
        1.   Criteria 1: Major depressive episode
            a.   Marked by five or more symptoms lasting two weeks or more
            b.   In extreme cases, symptoms are psychotic, including:
                (a)   Hallucinations
                (b)   Delusions
        2.   Criteria 2: No history of mania
        3.   Two diagnoses to consider:
            a.   Major depressive disorder
                (a)   Criteria 1 and 2 are met
            b.   Dysthymic disorder
                (a)   Symptoms are "mild but chronic"
                (b)   Experience longer-lasting but less disabling depression
                (c)   Consistent symptoms for greater than two years
                (d)   When dysthymic disorder leads to major depressive disorder, it is termed *double depression*

III. **WHAT CAUSES UNIPOLAR DEPRESSION?**
    A.   Stress may be a trigger for depression
        1.   People with depression experience a greater number of stressful life events during the month just before the onset of their symptoms than do others
        2.   Some clinicians distinguish reactive (exogenous) depression from endogenous depression, which seems to be a response to internal factors

3. Today's clinicians usually concentrate on recognizing both the situational *and* internal aspects of any given case

B. The current explanations of unipolar depression point to biological, psychological, and sociocultural factors

1. The biological view—Genetic factors
    a. Family pedigree, twin, adoption, and molecular biology gene studies suggest that some people inherit a biological predisposition to unipolar depression
    b. Researchers have found that as many as 20 percent of relatives of those with depression are themselves depressed, compared with fewer than 10 percent of the general population
    c. Twin studies demonstrate a strong genetic component:
        (a) Concordance rates for identical (MZ) twins are 46 percent
        (b) Concordance rates for fraternal (DZ) twins are 20 percent
    d. Adoption has implicated a genetic factor in cases of severe unipolar depression
    e. Using techniques from the field of molecular biology, researchers have found evidence that unipolar depression may be tied to specific genes

2. The biological view—Biochemical factors
    a. Low activity of two neurotransmitters—norepinephrine and serotonin—has been strongly linked to unipolar depression
        (a) In the 1950s, medications for high blood pressure were found to cause depression; some lowered serotonin, others lowered norepinephrine
        (b) The discovery of truly effective antidepressant medications, which relieved depression by increasing either serotonin or norepinephrine, confirmed the NT role.
            (i) In terms of NTs, it is likely not one or the other—a complex interaction is at work and other NTs may be involved
        (c) Biological researchers have also learned that the endocrine system may play a role
            (i) People with depression have been found to have abnormal levels of cortisol, which is released by the adrenal glands during times of stress
            (ii) People with depression have been found to have abnormal melatonin secretion
            (iii) Other researchers are investigating deficiencies of important proteins *within* neurons as tied to depression
    b. This model has produced much enthusiasm but has certain limitations
        (a) Relies on analogue studies: depression-like symptoms created in lab animals
            (i) Do these symptoms correlate with human emotions?
        (b) Measurement of brain activity has been difficult and indirect
            (i) Current studies with modern technology are attempting to address this issue

3. The biological view—Brain anatomy and brain circuits
    a. Biological researchers have determined that emotional reactions of various kinds are tied to brain circuits
        (a) These are networks of brain structures that work together, triggering each other into action and producing a particular kind of emotional reaction
        (b) It appears that one circuit is tied to GAD, another to panic disorder, and yet another to OCD
    b. Although research is far from complete, a circuit responsible for unipolar depression has begun to emerge
        (a) Likely brain areas in the circuit include: prefrontal cortex, hippocampus, amygdala, and Brodmann's Area 25

4. Psychological views
    a. There are three main psychological models:
        (a) Psychodynamic view—no strong research support
            (i) Developed by Freud and his student Abraham, this model links depression and grief

          1.   When a loved one dies, an unconscious process begins, and the mourner regresses to the oral stage and experiences introjection—a merging of his or her own identity with that of the lost person

          2.   For most people, introjection is temporary

          3.   If grief is severe and long-lasting, depression results

    (ii) At greater risk for developing depression are those with oral stage issues—either unmet or excessively met needs

   (iii) Some people experience "symbolic" (or imagined) loss

   (iv) Newer psychoanalysts (object relations theorists) propose that depression results when people's relationships leave them feeling unsafe and insecure

    (v) Strengths

          1.   Studies have offered general support for the psychodynamic idea that depression may be triggered by a major loss (e.g., anaclitic depression)

          2.   Research supports the theory that early losses set the stage for later depression

          3.   Research also suggests that people whose childhood needs were improperly met are more likely to become depressed after experiencing a loss

   (vi) Limitations

          1.   Early losses and inadequate parenting don't inevitably lead to depression and may not be *typically* responsible for development of depression

          2.   Many research findings are inconsistent

          3.   Certain features of the model are nearly impossible to test

  (b) Behavioral view—modest research support

     (i) Behaviorists believe that unipolar depression results from significant changes in rewards and punishments people receive

    (ii) Lewinsohn suggests that the positive rewards in life dwindle for some people, leading them to perform fewer and fewer constructive behaviors, and they spiral toward depression

   (iii) Research supports the relationship between the number of rewards received and presence of depression

          1.   Social rewards are especially important

    (iv) Strengths

          1.   Researchers have compiled significant data to support this theory

     (v) Limitations

          1.   Research has relied heavily on the self-reports of depressed subjects

          2.   Behavioral studies are largely correlational and do not establish that decreases in rewards are the initial cause of depression

  (c) Cognitive views (two main theories)—considerable research support

     (i) Negative thinking

          1.   Beck theorizes that four interrelated cognitive components combine to produce unipolar depression:

              (1) Maladaptive attitudes

                 i.   Self-defeating attitudes are developed during childhood

                ii.   Beck suggests that upsetting situations later in life can trigger an extended round of negative thinking

              (2) Negative thinking typically takes three forms called the cognitive triad:

                 i.   Individuals repeatedly interpret their (1) experiences, (2) themselves, and (3) their futures in negative ways that lead them to feel depressed

        (3)   Depressed people also make errors in their thinking, including:

            i.   Arbitrary inferences

            ii.   Minimization of the positive; magnification of the negative

        (4)   Depressed people experience automatic thoughts, a steady train of unpleasant thoughts suggesting inadequacy and hopelessness

    2.   Strengths

        a.   Many studies have produced evidence in support of Beck's explanation:

            i.   There is a high correlation between the level of depression and the number of maladaptive attitudes held

            ii.   Both the cognitive triad and errors in logic are seen in people with depression

            iii. Automatic thinking has been linked to depression

    3.   Limitations

        a.   Research fails to show that such cognitive patterns are the cause and core of unipolar depression

(ii)   Learned helplessness

    1.   This theory asserts that people become depressed when they think that:

        a.   They no longer have control over the reinforcements (rewards and punishments) in their lives

        b.   They themselves are responsible for this helpless state

    2.   The theory is based on Seligman's work with laboratory dogs

        a.   Dogs who were subjected to uncontrollable shock were later placed in a shuttle box

        b.   Even when presented with an opportunity to escape, dogs that had experienced uncontrollable shocks made no attempt to do so

        c.   Seligman theorized that the dogs had "learned" to be "helpless" to do anything to change negative situations and drew parallels to human depression

    3.   There has been significant research support for the model:

        a.   Human subjects who undergo helplessness training score higher on depression scales and demonstrate passivity in laboratory trials

        b.   Animal subjects lose interest in sex and social activities—a common symptom of human depression

        c.   In rats, uncontrollable negative events result in lower serotonin and norepinephrine levels in the brain

    4.   Recent versions of the theory focus on attributions

        a.   *Internal* attributions that are *global* and *stable* lead to greater feelings of helplessness and, possibly, depression; if they make other kinds of attributions, this reaction is unlikely

            i.   Example: "It's all my fault" [internal]; "I ruin everything I touch" [global] "and I always will" [stable]

            ii.   Example: "She never did know what she wanted" [external], but "The way I've behaved the past couple of weeks blew this relationship" [specific]; "I don't know what got into me—I don't usually act like that" [unstable]

        b.   Some theorists have refined the helplessness model yet again in recent years—they suggest that attributions are likely to cause depression only when they further produce a sense of hopelessness in an individual

    5.   Strengths

        a.   Hundreds of studies have supported the relationship among styles of attribution, helplessness, and depression

    6.   Limitations

        a.   Laboratory helplessness does not parallel depression in every way

        b.   Much of the research relies on animal subjects

        c.   The attributional component of the theory raises particularly difficult questions in terms of animal models of depression

4.   Sociocultural views

    a.   Sociocultural theorists propose that unipolar depression is greatly influenced by the social context that surrounds people

       (a)   This belief is supported by the finding that depression often is triggered by outside stressors

       (b)   There are two kinds of sociocultural views:

           (i)   The family-social perspective

           (ii)   The multicultural perspective

    b.   The family-social perspective

       (a)   The connection between declining social rewards and depression (as discussed by the behaviorists) is a two-way street

           (i)   Depressed people often display social deficits that make other people uncomfortable and may cause them to avoid the depressed individuals

           (ii)   This leads to decreased social contact and a further deterioration of social skills

       (b)   Consistent with these findings, depression has been tied repeatedly to the unavailability of social support such as that found in a happy marriage

           (i)   People who are separated or divorced display three times the depression rate of married or widowed persons and double the rate of people who have never been married

           (ii)   There also is a high correlation between level of marital conflict and degree of sadness that is particularly strong among those who are clinically depressed

       (c)   Finally, it appears that people whose lives are isolated and without intimacy are particularly likely to become depressed at times of stress

    c.   The multicultural perspective

       (a)   Two kinds of relationships have captured the interest of multicultural theorists:

       (b)   Gender and depression

           (i)   A strong link exists between gender and depression

           (ii)   Women cross-culturally are twice as likely as men to receive a diagnosis of unipolar depression

           (iii)   Women also appear to be younger, have more frequent and longer-lasting bouts, and to respond less successfully to treatment

           (iv)   Various theories have been offered:

               1.   The *artifact theory* holds that women and men are equally prone to depression but that clinicians often fail to detect depression in men

               2.   The *hormone explanation* holds that hormone changes trigger depression in many women

               3.   The *life stress theory* suggests that women in our society experience more stress than men

               4.   The *body dissatisfaction theory* states that females in Western society are taught, almost from birth, to seek a low body weight

and slender body shape—goals that are unreasonable, unhealthy, and often unattainable

5. The *lack-of-control theory* picks up on the learned helplessness research and argues that women may be more prone to depression because they feel less control than men over their lives

6. The *self-blame explanation* holds that women are more likely than men to blame their failures on lack of ability and to attribute their successes to luck—an attribution style that has been linked to depression

7. The *rumination theory* holds that people who ruminate when sad—keep focusing on their feelings and repeatedly consider the causes and consequences of their depression—are more likely to become depressed and stay depressed longer.

(v) Each explanation offers food for thought and has gathered just enough supporting evidence to make it interesting (and just enough contrary evidence to raise questions about its usefulness)

(c) Cultural background and depression

(i) Depression is a worldwide phenomenon, and certain symptoms seem to be constant across all countries, including sadness, joylessness, anxiety, tension, lack of energy, loss of interest, and thoughts of suicide

(ii) Beyond such core symptoms, research suggests that the precise picture of depression varies from country to country

1. Depressed people in non-Western countries are more likely to be troubled by physical symptoms of depression than by cognitive one.

2. As countries become more Westernized, depression seems to take on the more cognitive character it has in the West.

(iii) Within the United States, researchers have found few differences in depression symptoms among members of different ethnic or racial groups; however, sometimes striking differences exist in specific populations living under special circumstances

1. Rate of depression in Native American women is 37 percent, versus 17 percent of men and 28 percent overall

2. These findings are theorized to be the result of economic and social pressures

III. BIPOLAR DISORDERS

A. People with a bipolar disorder experience both the lows of depression and the highs of mania

    1. Many describe their lives as an emotional roller coaster

B. Unlike those experiencing depression, people in a state of mania typically experience dramatic and inappropriate rises in mood

    1. Five main areas of functioning may be affected:

        a. Emotional symptoms

        b. Motivational symptoms

        c. Behavioral symptoms

            (a) Flamboyance is not uncommon

        d. Cognitive symptoms

            (a) Especially prone to poor judgment and planning

        e. Physical symptoms

C. Diagnosing bipolar disorders

    1. Criteria 1: Manic episode

        a. Three or more symptoms of mania lasting one week or more

        b. In extreme cases, symptoms are psychotic

    2. Criteria 2: History of mania

        a. If currently experiencing hypomania or depression

    3. DSM-IV-TR distinguishes between two kinds of bipolar disorder:

a. Bipolar I disorder
  (a) This disorder requires full manic and major depressive episodes
  (b) Most sufferers experience an alteration of mood
  (c) Some experience mixed episodes
b. Bipolar II disorder
  (a) Hypomanic episodes and major depressive episodes
4. Without treatment, the mood episodes tend to recur for people with either type of bipolar disorder
  a. If people experience four or more episodes within a one-year period, their disorder is further classified as rapid cycling
  b. If their episodes vary with the seasons, their disorder is further classified as seasonal
5. Regardless of the particular pattern, individuals with bipolar disorder tend to experience depression more than mania over the years
  a. In most cases, depressive episodes occur three times as often as manic ones, and last longer
6. Between 1 and 2.6 percent of all adults suffer from a bipolar disorder at any given time, and as many as 4 percent over the course of their lives
  a. The disorders are equally common in women and men and among all socio-economic classes and ethnic groups
  b. Women may experience more depressive and fewer manic episodes than men, and rapid cycling is more common in women
7. Onset usually occurs between 15 and 44 years of age
  a. In most cases, the manic and depressive episodes eventually subside, only to recur at a later time
  b. Generally, when episodes recur, the intervening periods of normality grow shorter and shorter
8. A final diagnostic option:
  a. If a person experiences numerous episodes of hypomania and mild depressive symptoms, a diagnosis of cyclothymic disorder is appropriate
  (a) Mild symptoms for greater than two years, interrupted by periods of normal mood
  (b) Cyclothymia affects at least 0.4 percent of the population
  (c) May eventually blossom into Bipolar I or II
D. What causes bipolar disorders?
  1. Throughout the first half of the twentieth century, the search for the cause of bipolar disorders made little progress
  2. More recently, biological research has produced some promising clues
  3. These insights have come from research into NT activity, ion activity, brain structure, and genetic factors
    a. Neurotransmitters NTs
      (a) After finding a relationship between low norepinephrine and unipolar depression, early researchers expected to find a link between high norepinephrine and mania
      (b) This theory is supported by some research studies; bipolar disorders may be related to overactivity of norepinephrine
      (c) Because serotonin activity often parallels norepinephrine activity in unipolar depression, theorists expected that mania also would be related to high serotonin activity
      (d) While no relationship with *high* serotonin has been found, bipolar disorder may be linked to *low* serotonin activity, which seems contradictory
        (i) This apparent contradiction is addressed by the "permissive theory" of mood disorders
        (ii) It may be that low serotonin "opens the door" to a mood disorder and permits norepinephrine activity to define the particular form the disorder will take

1. Low serotonin + Low norepinephrine = Depression
2. Low serotonin + High norepinephrine = Mania
    b. Ion activity
        (a) Ions, necessary to send incoming messages to nerve endings, may be improperly transported through the cells
        (b) Some theorists believe that irregularities in the transport of these ions may cause neurons to fire too easily (mania) or to stubbornly resist firing (depression)
        (c) There is some research support for this theory
    c. Brain structure
        (a) Brain imaging and postmortem studies have identified a number of abnormal brain structures in people with bipolar disorder, in particular the basal ganglia and cerebellum, among others
        (b) It is not clear what role such structural abnormalities play
    d. Genetic factors
        (a) Many theorists believe that people inherit a biological predisposition to develop bipolar disorders
        (b) Findings from twin studies support this theory:
            (i) The rate of bipolar disorder among identical (MZ) twins is 40 percent
            (ii) The rate of bipolar disorder among fraternal (DZ) twins and siblings is 5 to 10 percent
            (iii) The rate of bipolar disorder among the general population is 1 to 2.6 percent
        (c) Recently, genetic linkage studies have examined the possibility of "faulty" genes
        (d) Other researchers are using techniques from molecular biology to further examine genetic patterns
        (e) Such wide-ranging findings suggest that a number of genetic abnormalities probably combine to help bring about bipolar disorders

IV. **CALL FOR CHANGE: DSM-V**
    A. The DSM-5 Task Force proposed a number of changes regarding mood disorders, including:
        1. Breaking the disorders into two separate groupings—"Depressive Disorders" and "Bipolar and Related Disorders"
        2. They further proposed adding "Substance-induced Bipolar Disorder" under the latter category
    B. Within the "Depressive Disorders" grouping, the Task Force proposed removing Dysthymic Disorder and creating a category called "Chronic Depressive Disorder"
        1. They also proposed adding three new categories—"Mixed Anxiety/Depression," "Premenstrual Dysphoric Disorder," and "Disruptive Mood Regulation Disorder"

LEARNING OBJECTIVES

1. Compare depression and mania while discussing the symptoms of each.

2. Contrast unipolar depression and bipolar disorder while discussing the symptoms of each.

3. Describe the biological, psychological, and sociocultural perspectives of depression.

4. Describe the possible roles of neurotransmitters in unipolar depression.

5. Distinguish among the three diagnostic options for bipolar disorder.

6. Discuss the biological theory of bipolar disorder.

KEY TERMS

adoption studies
anaclitic depression
analogue studies
arbitrary inference
automatic thoughts
bipolar disorder
bipolar I disorder
bipolar II disorder
brain circuits
cognitive triad
cortisol
cyclothymic disorder
delusion
depression
double depression
dysthymic disorder

endocrine system
endogenous depression
errors in thinking
family pedigree study
genetic linkage study
hallucination
hopelessness
hormones
hypomanic episode
imagined loss
introjection
learned helplessness
major depressive disorder
major depressive episode
maladaptive attitudes
mania

manic episode
melancholic
melatonin
molecular biology
negative thinking
norepinephrine
postpartum
reactive (exogenous)
    depression
recurrent rumination
serotonin
shuttle box
sodium ion
symbolic loss
twin study
unipolar depression

MEDIA RESOURCES

Abnormal Psychology Student Tool Kit

Produced and edited by Ronald J. Comer, Princeton University and Gregory Comer, Princeton Academic Resources. Tied directly to the CyberStudy sections in the text, this Student Tool Kit offers 57 intriguing Video Cases running 3 to 7 minutes each. The Video Cases focus on persons affected by disorders discussed in the text. Students first view the video and then answer a series of thought-provoking questions. Additionally, the Student Tool Kit contains multiple-choice practice test questions with built-in instructional feedback for every option.

PowerPoint Slides

Available at the Instructor's site on the companion Web site are comprehensive PowerPoint slide presentations and supplemental student handouts for Chapter 8. The slide files reflect the main points of the chapter in significant detail. Student handouts were created using the instructor slides as a base, with key points replaced as "fill-in" items. Answer keys and suggestions for use also are provided.

DSM-IV-TR Masters

B-26, DSM-IV-TR Criteria for Major Depressive Episode
B-27, DSM-IV-TR Criteria for Manic Episode

B-27, DSM-IV-TR Criteria for Mixed Episode
B-28, DSM-IV-TR Diagnostic Criteria for Hypomanic Episode
B-29, DSM-IV-TR Diagnostic Criteria for Major Depression Disorder, Single Episode
B-30, DSM-IV-TR Diagnostic Criteria for Dysthymic Disorder
B-31, DSM-IV-TR Diagnostic Criteria for Bipolar I Disorder, Single Manic Episode
B-31, DSM-IV-TR Diagnostic Criteria for Bipolar II Disorder
B-32, DSM-IV-TR Diagnostic Criteria for Cyclothymic Disorder

Internet Sites

Please see Appendix A for full and comprehensive references.

Sites relevant to Chapter 8 material are:

http://www.nimh.nih.gov/health/publications
This Web site, provided by the National Institute of Mental Health, supplies downloadable links to PDF files and booklets on a variety of mental health topics.

http://en.wikipedia.org/wiki/Mood_disorder
This free Internet encyclopedia offers a definition for mood disorders and links to the major types of disorders. In addition, there are links to other mood-related topics as well as to additional disorders related to mood disorders.

http://www.depression.com/
This site, developed and funded by GlaxoSmithKline, is devoted to the understanding and treatment of depression as well as to coping with living with depression day by day.

http://bipolar.mentalhelp.net/
A site that includes the symptoms, treatments, and online support groups for bipolar disorder.

http://sandbox.xerox.com/pair/cw/testing.html
This site includes the Clinical Depression Screening Test, a quick test of depressive symptoms, as well as some advice for individuals who score in the depressed range.

http://www.adolescent-mood-disorders.com/
This site reviews the difficulties in recognizing depression and other mood disorders among teenagers.

http://www.mdsg.org/
This is a comprehensive site of the mood disorder support group of New York City.

http://www.psycom.net/depression.central.html
Maintained by a private individual, this site is the Internet's central clearinghouse for information on all types of depressive disorders and on the most effective treatments for individuals suffering from major depression, manic-depression (bipolar disorder), cyclothymia, dysthymia, and other mood disorders.

Mainstream Films

Films relevant to Chapter 8 material are listed and summarized below.

Key to Film Listings:
P = psychopathology focus
T = treatment focus
E = ethical issues raised

Please note that some of the films suggested may have graphic sexual or violent content due to the nature of certain subject matters.

It's a Wonderful Life
This film from 1946 stars Jimmy Stewart as George Bailey, a small-town man whose life seems so desperate he contemplates suicide. **P, commercial film**

Leaving Las Vegas
This 1995 film stars Nicolas Cage as a Hollywood screenwriter who has become an alcoholic. After being fired, he takes his severance pay to Las Vegas, where he plans to drink himself to death. **P, serious film**

Mr. Jones
This 1993 Richard Gere film follows the relationship between a bipolar man, Mr. Jones, and the female doctor who takes more than a professional interest in his treatment. **P, T, E, commercial film**

Ordinary People
This 1980 film examines the treatment of a teenager suffering from depression, anxiety, and posttraumatic stress disorder in the aftermath of his brother's death. **P, T, serious film**

Spellbound
From 1945, this Hitchcock film (with scenery by Salvador Dali) stars Ingrid Bergman as a psychiatrist and Gregory Peck as an amnestic patient involved in a manhunt. **P, T, E, commercial thriller/romance film**

Other Films:

About a Boy (2002) depression and suicide. **P, commercial/serious film**
About Schmidt (2002) depression. **P, serious film**
The Accidental Tourist (1988) depression. **P, serious film**
The Bell Jar (1979) anxiety and depression. **P, T, serious film**
Fear Strikes Out (1957) depression. **P, T, serious film**
Love Liza (2002) depression. **P, serious/art film**
Magnolia (1999) depression. **P, serious film**
Sophie's Choice (1982) depression. **P, serious film**

Comer Video Segments

Available as a supplement, this revised set of videotapes contains short clips depicting various topics related to abnormal psychology. Please see the accompanying Video Guide for specific clips linked to Chapter 8.

Recommendations for Purchase or Rental

The Comer Video Segments include excerpts from many superb clinical documentaries. While the segments alone are ideal for use in lectures, it often is useful to assign the entire documentary for special class screenings or library use by students.

Films on Demand is a Web-based digital delivery service that has impressive psychology holdings. Their catalog can be accessed here: http://ffh.films.com/digitallanding.aspx

In addition, the following videos and other media may be of particular interest and are available for purchase or rental and appropriate for use in class or for assignment outside of class.

When the Brain Goes Wrong
Franklin Institute, Tulip Films
Fanlight Productions
(800) 937-4113
info@fanlight.com

CLASS DEMONSTRATIONS AND ACTIVITIES

Case Study

Present a case study to the class.

Panel Discussion

Have students volunteer (or assign them) to portray mental health "workers" of different theoretical perspectives in a panel discussion. Each student should present the main explanation and treatment for the mood disorders from his or her theoretical background. Students in the audience can ask questions of the panelists. Additionally, other students can role-play patients suffering from particular mood disorders. [NOTE: A brief reminder about sensitivity and professionalism is worthwhile here.] Have the panelists attempt to diagnose based on their orientation.

Depression Inventories

Bring in depression inventories. Discuss why these inventories are useful in both therapy and research. Ask students to suggest changes or modifications that could improve these instruments.

"Pretend, for a moment, that you are a ..."

Divide students into groups and assign each group a task similar to the following. Pretend they are business owners who are interested in alleviating the negative (and costly) effects of depression on workplace productivity. Ask them to come up with creative and practical solutions to identifying and intervening with workers suffering from mood disorders. Similar roles are a high school principal, a medical doctor, a fraternity or sorority president, a college instructor, and a baseball team manager.

The Anonymous Five-Minute Essay

It is useful to ask students to take five minutes to explain the biological model of depression. Reviewing these answers can alert instructors to misconceptions and poor communication of important ideas. This can be done for the cognitive, behavioral, and psychodynamic models as well.

SUGGESTED TOPICS FOR DISCUSSION

Women and Depression

Ask the class to brainstorm [See text pp. 261–262] why the rates of depression, even cross-culturally, are twice as high for women as for men.

Open Discussion: Manic Episodes

Discuss the idea that manic episodes can be extraordinarily pleasant. Encourage students to imagine aloud why such episodes might be enjoyable (more cheerful, more productive, more outgoing).

"Let's Write a Self-Help Best-Seller"

Discuss the stigma associated with mood disorders. Many persons implicitly (and sometimes explicitly) presume that mood disorders occur only in persons who are weak or who "enjoy being sad." Discuss the effect such attitudes might have on persons with mood disorders (reluctance to admit they have a problem or to seek help). Ask for ideas about how to educate the

public about causes of these disorders, thus alleviating the stigma associated with them.

Open Discussion: Learned Helplessness

Martin Seligman and his colleagues suggested that depression is the result of learned helplessness. They proposed that depression, like learned helplessness, is the result of inescapable trauma or negative situations. The person learns that he or she has no control over these negative events and stops trying to respond in an efficient, adaptive manner. The individual thus learns to be helpless. Ask students for examples of how such a model of depression might apply.

Open Discussion: Beck's Cognitive Theory

According to Aaron Beck and his colleagues, depression is caused by an individual's tendency to think or reason in a certain fashion. In particular, people become depressed because of their personal schema about themselves, their world, and their future. Introduce the notion of perceptual sets and bias, which influence the manner in which a person perceives things. Perceptual sets cause distortions and selective attention that support the negative schema. An interesting exercise is to provide such a set of assumptions (personal schema), and then present a series of experiences and ask students for "congruent" (with the schema) interpretations of the event. For example, a woman may

have a schema of herself as a terrible person. Her daughter is caught smoking at school. Another example: A young man believes that he is unlovable. His girlfriend breaks up with him. (These two people will take one event and distort it, then ignore or minimize contrary evidence, such as the fact that the daughter is a straight-A student or, in the case of the young man, that he acted in a way that encouraged his girlfriend to break up with him.)

ASSIGNMENTS/EXTRA CREDIT SUGGESTIONS

"Write a Pamphlet"

With the use of a software program like Microsoft Publisher or simply paper and markers, students can create a pamphlet on one or all of the mood disorders. Students should be encouraged to be as accurate and up-to-date as possible and to present all sides of the disorder (e.g., alternate treatment approaches or theories).

Keep a Journal

In addition to helping students synthesize material, this activity also is helpful in developing writing skills. Have students keep a journal of their thoughts on course material throughout the semester. This can be done in the first or last five minutes of class or as an out-of-class assignment. Faculty generally should have students submit their journals for review on an ongoing basis as students can have the tendency to delay writing until the end of the semester. Some suggestions for journal topics include: reactions to the case examples; strengths and weaknesses of prevailing theoretical explanations; hypothetical conversations with sufferers of specific disorders, etc.

Abnormal Psychology Student Tool Kit Video Questions

As a homework assignment, have students watch a video clip and answer the accompanying questions. Students can answer the questions directly into the online assessment feature. The results of these quizzes report to the site's built-in grade book.

Web Site Quiz

For homework or extra credit, have students complete the quiz for Chapter 8 located on the companion Web site. Students can complete an online test of the key

chapter material (using questions NOT from the test bank) and have their scores e-mailed directly to the course instructor.

Essay Topics

For homework or extra credit, have students write an essay addressing one (or more) of the following topics:

(1) Write an essay discussing the power and acceptability of male vs. female tears [See The Media Speaks, text p. 245]

(2) Discuss the Rhythms of Depression [See A Closer Look, text pp. 252–253], including the link between sleep and depression and the effectiveness of light therapy.

(3) Write an essay discussing postpartum depression [See Psych Watch, text p. 248]. Address various theories/factors, the 4 Ds of the experience, and the shame and stigma experienced by many women.

(4) Discuss the relationship between pet owners and their pets. What components of these types of relationships may help to explain the link between pet ownership and reduced depression? [See text p. 260]

Research Topics

For homework or extra credit, have students write a research report addressing one (or more) of the following topics:

(1) Conduct a "Psych Info" search and write a brief report on seasonal affective disorder, circadian rhythms [See text pp. 252–253], and depression. Compare and contrast.

(2) Conduct a "Psych Info" search and write an annotated bibliography on the various theories described on pp. 261–262 in the text to explain depression in women. Which of these models (if any) does the research most strongly support? With which of these models do you most agree?

(3) Conduct a literature review on abnormality and creativity (as discussed in Psych Watch, p. 268 in the text). Does research support the link between the two? Is this association simply anecdotal or have controlled studies examined the association? What famous examples can you find?

Film Review

To earn extra credit, have students watch one (or more) of the mainstream films listed earlier in this chapter and write a brief (3-5 pages) report. Students should summarize the plot of the film in sufficient detail to demonstrate familiarity, but should focus their papers on the depiction of psychological abnormality. What errors or liberties did the filmmaker take? What is the message (implicit or explicit) concerning the mentally ill?

Case Study Evaluations

To complement the Comer and Gorenstein supplemental case study text, case study evaluations have been created. Students can be assigned the appropriate case study and evaluation as homework or for class discussion. While case-study evaluation questions are listed in their entirety on the companion Web site at www.worthpublishers.com/comer, the relevant case studies are referenced next.

Case Study 4: Major Depressive Disorder

Case Study 5: Bipolar Disorder

Web-Based Case Studies

Nine Web-based case studies have been created and posted on the companion Web site. These cases describe the individual's history and symptoms and are accompanied by a series of guided questions that point to the precise DSM-IV-TR criteria for each disorder. Students can both identify the disorder and suggest a course of treatment. Students can be assigned the appropriate case study and questions as homework or for class discussion. The case relevant to Chapter 8 is referenced below.

The Case of Ellen: Depression and Suicidality

Crossword Puzzles

As a homework assignment or for extra credit, have students complete and submit Crossword Puzzle #8.

Word Searches

As a homework assignment or for extra credit, have students complete and submit Word Search #8.

CHAPTER :9

Treatments for Mood Disorders

Treatments for Unipolar Depression
    Psychological Approaches
    Sociocultural Approaches
    Biological Approaches
    How Do the Treatments for Unipolar Depression Compare?

Treatments for Bipolar Disorders
    Lithium and Other Mood Stabilizers
    Adjunctive Psychotherapy

Putting It Together: With Success Come New Questions

LECTURE OUTLINE

I. **TREATMENTS FOR MOOD DISORDERS**
    A. Mood disorders—as painful and disabling as they tend to be—respond more successfully to more kinds of treatments than do most other forms of psychological dysfunction
    B. This range of treatment options has been a source of reassurance and hope for the millions of people who desire to regain some measure of control over their moods

II. **TREATMENTS FOR UNIPOLAR DEPRESSION**
    A. Approximately one-half of persons with unipolar depression (major depressive or dysthymic disorder) receive treatment from a mental health professional each year
        1. In addition, many other people in therapy experience depressed feelings as part of another disorder—thus, much of the therapy being administered today is for unipolar depression
    B. A variety of treatment approaches are currently in widespread use and can be divided into psychological, sociocultural, and biological approaches

C. Psychological approaches
1. The psychological treatments used most often to combat unipolar depression come from three main models:
   a. Psychodynamic—Widely used despite no strong research evidence
      (a) Believing that unipolar depression results from unconscious grief over real or imagined losses, compounded by excessive dependence on other people, psychodynamic therapists seek to bring these issues into consciousness and work them through
      (b) Psychodynamic therapists use the same basic procedures for all psychological disorders:
         (i) Free association
         (ii) Therapist interpretation
         (iii) Review of past events and feelings
      (c) Despite successful case reports, researchers have found that long-term psychodynamic therapy is only occasionally helpful in cases of unipolar depression
      (d) Two features may be particularly limiting:
         (i) Depressed clients may be too passive or weary to fully participate in clinical discussions
         (ii) Depressed clients may become discouraged and end treatment too early when treatment is unable to provide quick relief
      (e) Short-term approaches have performed better than traditional approaches
   b. Behavioral—Primarily used for mild or moderate depression but practiced less than in past decades
      (a) Most behavioral treatment for unipolar depression is modeled after the interventions proposed by Lewinsohn:
         (i) Reintroduce clients to pleasurable activities and events, often using a weekly schedule
         (ii) Appropriately reinforce their depressive and nondepressive behaviors using a contingency management approach
         (iii) Help them improve their social skills
      (b) The behavioral techniques seem to be of only limited help when just one of them is applied
      (c) When two or more of the techniques are combined, behavioral treatment does seem to reduce depressive symptoms, particularly if mild
      (d) It is worth noting that Lewinsohn himself has combined behavior techniques with cognitive strategies in recent years
   c. Cognitive—Has performed so well in research that it has a large and growing clinical following
      (a) Beck viewed unipolar depression as resulting from a pattern of negative thinking that may be triggered by current upsetting situations
         (i) *Maladaptive attitudes* lead people to the *"cognitive triad:"*—repeatedly viewing oneself, the world, and the future in negative ways
         (ii) These biased views combine with *illogical thinking* to produce *automatic thoughts*
      (b) Beck's cognitive therapy—which includes a number of behavior techniques—is designed to help clients recognize and change their negative cognitive processes
         (i) This approach follows four phases and usually lasts less than 20 sessions:
            1. Increasing activities and elevating mood
            2. Challenging automatic thoughts
            3. Identifying negative thinking and biases
            4. Changing primary attitudes

        (c)   Over the past three decades, hundreds of studies have shown that Beck's therapy and similar cognitive and cognitive-behavioral approaches help with unipolar depression

            (i)   Approximately 50 to 60 percent of clients show a near-total elimination of symptoms

        (d)   It is worth noting that a growing number of today's cognitive-behavioral therapists disagree with Beck's proposition that individuals must fully discard negative cognitions

            (i)   These therapists guide clients to recognize and accept their negative cognitions

D. Sociocultural approaches

   1. Theorists trace the causes of unipolar depression to the broader social structure in which people live and the roles they are required to play

   2. Two groups of sociocultural treatments are now widely applied:

     a. Multicultural treatments

       (a)   Culture-sensitive approaches are increasingly being combined with traditional forms of psychotherapy to help maximize the likelihood of minority clients overcoming their disorders

       (b)   It also appears that the medication needs of many depressed minority clients are inadequately addressed

     b. Family-social treatments: Interpersonal Therapy (IPT)

       (a)   IPT holds that four interpersonal problems may lead to depression and must be addressed:

          (i)   Interpersonal loss

          (ii)   Interpersonal role dispute

         (iii)   Interpersonal role transition

         (iv)   Interpersonal deficits

       (b)   Studies suggest that IPT has a success rate similar to cognitive therapy for depression

     c. Family-social treatment: Couple Therapy

       (a)   The main type of couple therapy is behavioral marital therapy (BMT)

       (b)   The clinical focus is on developing specific communication and problem-solving skills

       (c)   If marriage is filled with conflict, BMT is as effective as other therapies

E. Biological approaches

   1. Biological treatments can bring great relief to people with unipolar depression

   2. Usually, biological treatment means antidepressant drugs, but for severely depressed individuals who do not respond to other forms of treatment, it sometimes includes electroconvulsive therapy or brain stimulation

     a. Electroconvulsive therapy (ECT)

       (a)   One of the most controversial forms of treatment

          (i)   It now is used frequently because it is an effective and fast-acting intervention

       (b)   The procedure consists of targeted electrical stimulation to cause brain seizure

       (c)   The usual course of treatment is 6 to 12 sessions spaced over 2 to 4 weeks

          (i)   Treatment may be bilateral or unilateral

       (d)   The discovery of ECT's effectiveness was accidental and based on a fallacious link between psychosis and epilepsy

       (e)   The procedure has been modified in recent years to reduce some of the negative effects

          (i)   For example, patients are given muscle relaxants and anesthetics before and during the procedure

         (ii)   Patients generally report some memory loss

       (f)   ECT is clearly effective in treating unipolar depression

          (i)   Studies find improvement in 60 to 80 percent of patients

    (g)   The procedure seems particularly effective in cases of severe depression with delusions, but it has been difficult to determine why ECT works so well

          (i)   Although effective, the use of ECT has declined since the 1950s, due to the memory loss caused by the procedure, the frightening nature of the procedure, and the emergence of effective antidepressant drugs

b.   Antidepressant drugs

    (a)   In the 1950s, two kinds of drugs were found to reduce the symptoms of depression [See Table 9-2, text p. 270]:

          (i)   Monoamine oxidase inhibitors (MAO-Is)

               1.   Originally used to treat TB, doctors noticed that the medication (iproniazid) seemed to make patients happier

               2.   The drug works biochemically by slowing down the body's production of MAO; MAO breaks down norepinephrine; MAO-inhibitors stop this breakdown from occurring

               3.   This leads to a rise in norepinephrine activity and a reduction in depressive symptoms; about half of patients who take these drugs are helped by them

               4.   MAO-inhibitors pose a potential danger

                    a.   People who take MAOIs experience a dangerous rise in blood pressure if they eat foods containing tyramine (cheese, bananas, wine)

               5.   In recent years, a new MAO inhibitor in the form of a skin patch has become available; dangerous food interactions do not appear to be as common a problem with this kind of MAO inhibitor

         (ii)   Tricyclics

               1.   In searching for medications for schizophrenia, it was discovered that imipramine lessened depressive symptoms

                    a.   These drugs are known as *tricyclics* because they share a three-ring molecular structure

               2.   Hundreds of studies have found that depressed patients taking tricyclics have improved much more than similar patients taking placebos

               3.   Drugs must be taken for at least 10 days before such improvement will be seen

                    a.   About 60 to 65 percent of patients will find symptom improvement

               4.   If drugs are stopped immediately upon relief of symptoms, most patients relapse within one year

               5.   If drugs are continued for five additional months ("continuation therapy"), the risk of relapse decreases significantly

                    a.   Other studies suggest that patients who take antidepressant drugs for three or more years after initial improvement ("maintenance therapy") may reduce the risk of relapse even more

               6.   Tricyclics are believed to reduce depression by affecting neurotransmitter (NT) "reuptake" mechanisms [See Figure 9-3, text p. 271]

                    a.   In order to prevent an NT from remaining in the synapse too long, a pumplike mechanism recaptures it and draws it back into the presynaptic neuron

                    b.   This reuptake process appears to be too efficient in some people, drawing in too much of the NT from the synapse

                    c.   This reduction is theorized to result in clinical depression

d. Tricyclics block this reuptake process, thus increasing NT activity in the synapse

7. There is growing evidence that when tricyclics are ingested, they initially slow down the activity of the neurons that use norepinephrine and serotonin

 a. After a week or two, the neurons adapt to the drugs and go back to releasing normal amounts of the NTs

8. Today, tricyclics are prescribed more often than MAOIs

 a. They do not require dietary restrictions

 b. Some patients show higher rates of improvement

(b) In the past few decades, these drugs have been joined by a third group, the "second-generation" antidepressants

1. Structurally different from the MAO-inhibitors and tricyclics is a third group of effective antidepressant drugs:

 a. Most of these are labeled selective serotonin reuptake inhibitors (SSRIs)

 b. These drugs increase serotonin activity specifically (no other NTs are affected)

 c. This class includes fluoxetine (Prozac), sertraline (Zoloft), and escitalopram (Lexapro)

2. Selective norepinephrine reuptake inhibitors and serotonin-norepinephrine reuptake inhibitors also are now available

3. The effectiveness and speed of action of these drugs is on par with the tricyclics, yet their sales have skyrocketed

 a. Clinicians often prefer these drugs because it is harder to overdose on them than the other kinds of antidepressants

 b. In addition, there are no dietary restrictions like with the MAO-inhibitors

 c. There are fewer side effects than the tricyclics

 i. These drugs may cause some undesired effects of their own, including a reduction in sex drive

c. As effective as antidepressant drugs are, it is important to recognize that they do not work for everyone

 (i) Even the most successful of them fails to help at least 35 percent of clients with depression

d. Brain stimulation

(a) In recent years, three additional biological approaches have been developed:

 (i) Vagus nerve stimulation

 1. Depression researchers surmised they might be able to stimulate the brain by electrically stimulating the vagus nerve through use of a pulse generator implanted under the skin of the chest

 2. Research has found that the procedure brings significant relief to as many as 40 percent of those with treatment-resistant depression

 3. As with ECT, researchers do not yet know precisely why this technique reduces depression

 (ii) Transcranial magnetic stimulation (TMS)

 1. Another technique designed to stimulate the brain without the undesired effects of ECT, TMS has been found to reduce depression when administered daily for two to four weeks

 2. It is not yet approved by the FDA

 (iii) Deep brain stimulation

 1. Theorizing a "depression switch" located deep within the brain, researchers have successfully experimented with electrode implantation in the brain's Brodman Area 25

(b)   While such positive initial findings have produced considerable enthusiasm in the clinical field, it is important to recognize and remember that in the past, certain promising brain interventions (e.g., lobotomy) later proved problematic and even dangerous upon closer inspection

F.   How do the treatments for unipolar depression compare?

1.   For most kinds of psychological disorders, no more than one or two treatments or combinations of treatments, if any, emerge as highly successful

a.   Unipolar depression seems to be an exception, responding to any of several approaches

2.   Findings from a number of research studies suggest that:

a.   Cognitive, cognitive-behavioral, interpersonal, and biological therapies are all highly effective treatments for unipolar depression, ranging in severity from mild to severe

b.   Although the cognitive, cognitive-behavioral, and interpersonal therapies may lower the likelihood of relapse, they are hardly relapse-proof

c.   When people with unipolar depression experience significant marital discord, couple therapy tends to be very helpful

d.   Depressed people who receive strictly behavioral therapy have shown less improvement than those who receive cognitive, cognitive-behavioral, interpersonal, or biological therapy

e.   Traditional psychodynamic therapies are less effective than these other therapies in treating all levels of unipolar depression

f.   A combination of psychotherapy and drug therapy is modestly more helpful to depressed people than either treatment alone

g.   These various trends do not always carry over to the treatment of depressed children and adolescents

h.   Among biological treatments, ECT appears to be somewhat more effective than antidepressant drugs, and ECT seems to act more quickly; in addition, the newly developed brain stimulation treatments seem helpful for some severely depressed individuals who have been repeatedly unresponsive to drug therapy, ECT, or psychotherapy

III.   TREATMENTS FOR BIPOLAR DISORDERS

A.   Until the latter part of the twentieth century, people with bipolar disorders were destined to spend their lives on an emotional roller coaster

1.   Psychotherapists reported almost no success

2.   Antidepressant drugs were of limited help

a.   These drugs sometimes triggered manic episodes

3.   ECT only occasionally relieved either the depressive or the manic episodes of bipolar disorder

B.   The use of lithium, an element naturally occurring as mineral salt, and other mood stabilizers, have dramatically changed this picture

1.   Lithium is extraordinarily effective in treating bipolar disorders and mania

2.   Determining the correct dosage for a given patient is a delicate process

a.   Too low = no effect

b.   Too high = lithium intoxication (poisoning)

3.   Given the effectiveness, approximately one-third of all persons with bipolar disorder seek treatment in a given year; another 15% are monitored by family physicians

4.   All manner of research has attested to the effectiveness of lithium and other mood stabilizers in treating manic episodes

a.   More than 60 percent of patients with mania improve on these medications

b.   Most individuals experience fewer new episodes while on the drug

c.   Findings suggest that the mood stabilizers are also prophylactic drugs, ones that actually help prevent symptoms from developing

d.   Mood stabilizers also helps those with bipolar disorder overcome their depressive episodes to a lesser degree

5. Researchers do not fully understand how mood stabilizing drugs operate
   a. They suspect that the drugs change synaptic activity in neurons, but in a different way from that of antidepressant drugs:
     (a) While antidepressant drugs affect a neuron's initial reception on NTs, mood stabilizers seem to affect a neuron's second messengers
   b. These drugs also increase the production of neuroprotective proteins, which may decrease bipolar symptoms
   c. Another theory is that mood stabilizers correct bipolar functioning by directly changing sodium and potassium ion activity in neurons

C. Adjunctive psychotherapy
  1. Psychotherapy alone rarely is helpful for persons with bipolar disorder
  2. Mood stabilizing drugs alone are not always sufficient either
   a. 30 percent or more of patients don't respond, may not receive the correct dose, and/or may relapse while taking it
   b. As a result, clinicians often use psychotherapy as an adjunct to lithium (or other medication-based) therapy
  3. Therapy focuses on medication management, social skills, and relationship issues
  4. Few controlled studies have tested the effectiveness of such adjunctive therapy
   a. Growing research suggests that it helps to reduce hospitalization, improves social functioning, and increases a client's ability to obtain and hold a job

LEARNING OBJECTIVES

1. Describe the major psychological approaches to treatment of unipolar depression. That is, compare and contrast the psychodynamic, behavioral, and cognitive/cognitive-behavioral approaches to treatment.

2. Describe the sociocultural approaches to treat unipolar depression.

3. What are the major biological approaches to unipolar depression? Describe ECT and the other techniques for brain stimulation. Compare and contrast early antidepressants to currently used antidepressants.

4. How do the various approaches to treating depression compare?

5. Describe mood stabilizer therapy for bipolar disorder, including issues related to their use and their mechanism of action.

6. Describe adjunctive psychotherapy for bipolar disorder. What is it and why is it important?

KEY TERMS

adjunctive psychotherapy
cognitive therapy
couple therapy
deep brain stimulation
electroconvulsive therapy (ECT)
interpersonal psychotherapy (IPT)

lithium
MAO inhibitor
monoamine oxidase
mood stabilizing drugs
second-generation antidepressant
second messengers

selective serotonin reuptake inhibitors (SSRIs)
transcranial magnetic stimulation
tricyclic
vagus nerve stimulation

MEDIA RESOURCES

Abnormal Psychology Student Tool Kit

Produced and edited by Ronald J. Comer, Princeton University and Gregory Comer, Princeton Academic Resources. Tied directly to the CyberStudy sections in the text, this Student Tool Kit offers 57 intriguing Video Cases running 3 to 7 minutes each. The Video Cases focus on persons affected by disorders discussed in the text. Students first view the video and then answer a series of thought-provoking questions. Additionally, the Student Tool Kit contains multiple-choice practice test questions with built-in instructional feedback for every option.

PowerPoint Slides

Available at the Instructor's site on the companion Web site are comprehensive PowerPoint slide presentations and supplemental student handouts for Chapter 9. The slide files reflect the main points of the chapter in significant detail. Student handouts were created using the instructor slides as a base, with key points replaced as "fill-in" items. Answer keys and suggestions for use also are provided.

Internet Sites

Please see Appendix A for full and comprehensive references.

Sites relevant to Chapter 9 material are:

http://www.nimh.nih.gov/health/publications
This Web site, provided by the National Institute of Mental Health, supplies downloadable links to PDF files and booklets on a variety of mental health topics.

http://en.wikipedia.org/wiki/Mood_disorder
This free Internet encyclopedia offers a definition for mood disorders and links to the major types of disorders. In addition, there are links to other mood-related topics as well as to additional disorders related to mood disorders.

http://www.depression.com/
This site, developed and funded by GlaxoSmithKline, is devoted to the understanding and treatment of depression as well as to coping with living with depression day by day.

http://bipolar.mentalhelp.net/
A site that includes the symptoms, treatments, and on-line support groups for bipolar disorder.

http://sandbox.xerox.com/pair/cw/testing.html
This site includes the Clinical Depression Screening Test, a quick test of depressive symptoms, as well as some advice for individuals who score in the depressed range.

http://www.adolescent-mood-disorders.com/
This site reviews the difficulties in recognizing depression and other mood disorders among teenagers.

http://www.mdsg.org/
This is a comprehensive site of the mood disorder support group of New York City.

http://www.psycom.net/depression.central.html
Maintained by a private individual, this site is the Internet's central clearinghouse for information on all types of depressive disorders and on the most effective treatments for individuals suffering from major depression, manic-depression (bipolar disorder), cyclothymia, dysthymia, and other mood disorders.

Mainstream Films

Films relevant to Chapter 9 material are listed and summarized below.

Key to Film Listings:
P = psychopathology focus
T = treatment focus
E = ethical issues raised

Please note that some of the films suggested may have graphic sexual or violent content due to the nature of certain subject matter.

One Flew Over the Cuckoo's Nest
This 1975 film tells the story of Randall P. McMurphy (Jack Nicholson), a convict sent to a northwestern psychiatric hospital for evaluation and treatment. While there, McMurphy experiences first-hand the use of electroconvulsive therapy. **P, T, E, serious film**

Ordinary People
This 1980 film examines the treatment of a teenager suffering from depression, anxiety, and posttraumatic stress disorder in the aftermath of his brother's death. **P, T, serious film**

Other Films:

The Bell Jar (1979) anxiety and depression. **P, T, serious film**

Brain Candy (1996) plot involves a drug company's research into and development of a drug to treat depression. **P, T, comedy**

Fear Strikes Out (1957) depression. **P, T, serious film**

It's Kind of a Funny Story (2010) depression. **T, comedy**

A Woman under the Influence (1974) institutionalization and ECT. **P, T, E, serious film**

Comer Video Segments

Available as a supplement, this revised set of videotapes contains short clips depicting various topics related to abnormal psychology. Please see the accompanying Video Guide for specific clips linked to Chapter 9.

Recommendations for Purchase or Rental

The Comer Video Segments include excerpts from many superb clinical documentaries. While the segments alone are ideal for use in lectures, it often is useful to assign the entire documentary for special class screenings or library use by students.

Films on Demand is a Web-based digital delivery service that has impressive psychology holdings. Their catalog can be accessed here: http://ffh.films.com/digitallanding.aspx

In addition, the following videos and other media may be of particular interest and are available for purchase or rental and appropriate for use in class or for assignment outside of class.

APA Cognitive-Behavior Therapy for Depression Video Series
American Psychological Association
1-800-374-2721
fax: 1-202-336-5502
E-mail: order@apa.org

Gender Differences in Depression: A Marital Therapy Approach
From The Ackerman Institute for the Family Series
Guilford Publications, Inc.
72 Spring Street
New York, NY 10012
tel: (800) 365-7006 or (212) 431-9800
fax: (212) 966-6708
www.guilford.com

Living Well with Bipolar Disorder: A New Look
Guilford Publications, Inc.
72 Spring Street
New York, NY 10012
tel: (800) 365-7006 or (212) 431-9800
fax: (212) 966-6708
www.guilford.com

Depression: Back from the Bottom
Beating Depression
Bellevue: Inside Out
Psychosurgery: Best Hope of False Hope?
Troubled Minds: The Lithium Revolution
Films for the Humanities and Sciences
P.O. Box 2053
Princeton, NJ 08543-2053
Phone: 800-257-5126
ffh.films.com

CLASS DEMONSTRATIONS AND ACTIVITIES

Beating Mild Depression

Ask students what they do to get rid of the "blues." Everyone has an occasional down day. Ask students to share the types of strategies that they use to alter their mood level. Everyone has something that makes them happier—playing golf, seeing a movie, swimming, or talking to a friend, for example. How successful are these strategies? Develop a list on an overhead transparency to see if there is a common thread.

Case Study

Present a case study to the class.

"It's Debatable: Psychotherapy or Psychopharmacology?" (see Preface instructions for conducting this activity)

Have students volunteer (or assign them) in teams to opposite sides of the debate topic. Have students present their case in class following standard debate guidelines.

Panel Discussion

Have students volunteer (or assign them) to portray mental health "workers" from different theoretical perspectives in a panel discussion. Each student should present the main explanation of and treatment for each mood disorder from his or her theoretical perspective. Students in the audience can ask questions of the panelists. Additionally, other students can role-play patients suffering from particular mood disorders. [NOTE: A brief reminder about sensitivity and professionalism may be useful here.] Have the panelists, based on their theoretical orientation, diagnose these "patients."

"Here's $25,000 to be awarded to . . . "

Discuss the idea that manic episodes (e.g., a husband's emptying the bank account to buy cuckoo clocks) can have devastating effects on the trust between spouses. Point out that many impulsive and perhaps silly decisions are made without the influence of a manic episode, but that couples (especially the nonbipolar spouse) have difficulty distinguishing them. The result is a profound lack of trust. Divide students into groups to compete for an award to be given by an organization interested in bipolar disorder research. The assignment is to design a contract or an agreement between a patient with bipolar disorder and his or her spouse that will enable them to distinguish correctly between "normal" impulsive and perhaps irrational decisions or ideas and the onset of another manic episode. Have the groups present their ideas, then have a class vote to see which group receives the grant to implement the idea.

"Pretend, for a moment, that you are a counselor."

Divide students into groups. Ask them to imagine that they are counselors seeing a patient with fairly severe depression. Ask them to assume a cognitive stance in therapy. How would they proceed? The groups likely will come up with ideas that are extremely similar to the manner in which Beck recommends that cognitive therapy proceed (e.g., "Ask the patient to write down his thoughts for the week."). Use this as a lead-in to a discussion of cognitive therapy.

The Anonymous Five-Minute Essay

Ask students to turn in an anonymous essay describing a personal experience they had with a friend or a loved one with a serious episode of depression. Some students will not have had such an experience, but most will have. Ask them to describe the situation and anything particularly memorable about it, such as talking to (or intervening with) a friend about suicide. You can expect that at least half the class will have had an experience with depression, which emphasizes the ubiquity of the disorder.

SUGGESTED TOPICS FOR DISCUSSION

"And Remember to Ask Your Doctor . . ."

Using PsychWatch (p. 277 in the text) as a platform, lead the class in a discussion about direct-to-consumer (DTC) drug advertising. What are the benefits and risks of such ad campaigns? Which can your class readily remember? Do the commercials and magazine ads create a balanced portrayal of benefits and risks? Students can bring in examples for extra credit.

The Grieving Process

As discussed MediaSpeaks on p. 260 in the text, student mental health issues are a growing concern on college campuses. Have your class break into groups to discuss the responsbility of colleges to safeguard the mental health of their students. What services and strategies should be available? You can also assign students to research the mental health care offered at your college.

The Relationship Between Exercise and Depression

Research has shown a link between regular physical exercise and the alleviation of depression. People who exercise regularly are less depressed. But could it be that people who are depressed just exercise less? Ask students to volunteer experiences when they or their friends used exercise as a way to feel better.

Electroconvulsive Therapy

Lead a discussion on the use of electroconvulsive therapy (ECT). What have students heard or seen about the procedure prior to class? Are there ethical concerns with this procedure? Can someone experiencing such severe depression to warrant ECT give informed consent for the procedure?

ASSIGNMENTS/EXTRA CREDIT SUGGESTIONS

Abnormal Psychology Student Tool Kit Video Questions

As a homework assignment, have students watch a video clip and answer the accompanying questions. Students can answer the questions directly into the online assessment feature. The results of these quizzes report to the site's built-in grade book.

"Write a Pamphlet"

With the use of a software program like Microsoft Publisher or simply paper and markers, students can create a pamphlet on one or all of the mood disorder treatments. Students should be encouraged to be as accurate and up-to-date as possible and also to present all sides of the disorder (e.g., alternate treatment approaches or theories).

Keep a Journal

In addition to helping students synthesize material, this activity is helpful in developing writing skills. Have students keep a journal of their thoughts on course material through the semester. This can be done in the first or last five minutes of class or as an out-of-class assignment. Faculty generally should have students submit their journals for review on an on-going basis, since students can tend to delay writing until the end of the semester. Some suggestions for journal topics include: reactions to the case examples; strengths and weaknesses of prevailing theoretical explanations; hypothetical conversations with sufferers of specific disorders, etc.

Web Site Quiz

For homework or extra credit, have students complete the quiz for Chapter 9 located on the companion Web site. Students can complete an online test of the key chapter material (using questions NOT from the test bank) and have their scores e-mailed directly to the course instructor.

Essay Topics

For homework or extra credit, have students write an essay addressing one (or more) of the following topics:

(1) Write a list of treatment recommendations, supported by the literature, for a client facing moderate depression. Be sure to include suggestions from both psychological and biological perspectives. For which would you advocate most strongly?

(2) Discuss the multicultural findings regarding the likelihood of being prescribed antidepressants. [See PsychWatch, text p. 272 for some information]

(3) Separately discuss the issues for a patient choosing among the various biological treatments for unipolar depression and bipolar disorder. What issues are common between the two disorders? What issues would be most troubling to resolve? Why do you think some patients refuse biological interventions?

(4) Discuss the current popular use of herbal supplements for better health [See PsychWatch, text p. 267]. What are the main disorders targeted by such treatments? Do you think such drugs should be regulated by the Food and Drug Administration (FDA)?

(5) Describe the mechanism of action of the tricyclic antidepressants.

Research Topics

For homework or extra credit, have students write a research report addressing one (or more) of the following topics:

(1) Research the growing use of "herbal" supplements and "natural" hormones to treat psychological problems. [See PsychWatch, text p. 267 for a good start]

(2) Conduct a "Psych Info" search and write an annotated bibliography on comparison studies of psychological approaches for unipolar depression. What sample populations are most common?

(3) Conduct a literature review on the history of treatments for unipolar depression, focusing on the induction of brain seizure.

Case Study Evaluations

To complement the Comer and Gorenstein supplemental case study text, case study evaluations have been created. Students can be assigned the appropriate case study and evaluation as homework or for class discussion. While case study evaluation questions are listed in their entirety on the companion Web site at www.worthpublishers.com/comer, the relevant case studies are referenced next.

Case Study 4: Major Depressive Disorder

Case Study 5: Bipolar Disorder

Web-Based Case Studies

Nine Web-based case studies have been created and posted on the companion Web site. These cases describe the individual's history and symptoms and are accompanied by a series of guided questions that point to the precise DSM-IV-TR criteria for each disorder. Students can both identify the disorder and suggest a course of treatment. Students can be assigned the appropriate case study and questions as homework or for class discussion. The case relevant to Chapter 9 is referenced below.

The Case of Ellen: Depression and Suicidality

Crossword Puzzles

As a homework assignment or for extra credit, have students complete and submit Crossword Puzzle #9.

Word Searches

As a homework assignment or for extra credit, have students complete and submit Word Search #9.

Suicide

TOPIC OVERVIEW

LECTURE OUTLINE

I. **SUICIDE IS ONE OF THE LEADING CAUSES OF DEATH IN THE WORLD**
   A. It has been estimated that 1 million people die of it each year, with more than 36,000 suicides per year in the United States alone

B. Many more (600,000 in the United States) make unsuccessful attempts
1. Such attempts are called "parasuicide"
C. It is difficult to obtain accurate figures on rates of suicide, and many investigators believe that estimates are often low
1. Many "accidents" may be intentional deaths
2. Since suicide is frowned upon in our society, relatives and friends often refuse to acknowledge that loved ones have taken their own lives
D. Suicide is not classified as a mental disorder in the DSM-IV-TR
1. Although suicide is frequently linked to depression, approximately half of all suicides result from other mental disorders or involve no clear mental disorder at all

II. **WHAT IS SUICIDE?**
A. Shneidman defines suicide as an intentioned death—a self-inflicted death in which one makes an intentional, direct, and conscious effort to end one's life
B. He characterizes four kinds of suicide seekers:
1. Death seekers—clearly intend to end their lives
2. Death initiators—intend to end their lives because they believe that the process of death already is underway
3. Death ignorers—do not believe that their self-inflicted death will mean the end of their existence
4. Death darers—have mixed (ambivalent) feelings about death and show this in the act itself
C. When individuals play indirect, covert, partial, or unconscious roles in their own deaths, Shneidman classifies them in a category called "subintentional death"
1. In recent years, another behavioral pattern, self-injury or self-mutilation, has been added to this list
2. The DSM-5 Task Force has recommended it be added as a category called non-suicidal self injury

III. **HOW IS SUICIDE STUDIED?**
A. Suicide researchers face a major obstacle—their subjects are no longer alive
B. Two different strategies are used to try to overcome this obstacle (with partial success):
1. Retrospective analysis—a kind of psychological autopsy
2. Studying people who survive their suicide attempts

IV. **PATTERNS AND STATISTICS**
A. Researchers have gathered statistics regarding the social contexts in which suicides take place
1. Suicide rates vary from country to country, with religious *devoutness* (not simply affiliation) helping to explain some of the difference
B. The suicide rates of men and women also differ:
1. Women have a higher attempt rate (3x men)
2. Men have a higher completion rate (4x women)
3. Why? Different methods have differing lethality
a. Men use more violent methods (shooting, stabbing, or hanging), compared to women (drug overdose)
b. Guns are used in nearly two-thirds of the male suicides in the United States, compared to 40 percent of the female suicides
C. Suicide also is related to social environment and marital status
1. One study found that half of the subjects who had committed suicide were found to have no close friends
2. Divorced people have a higher suicide rate than married or cohabiting individuals
D. In the United States, suicide also seems to vary according to race [See Figure 10-1, text p. 291]
1. The suicide rate of white Americans is almost twice as high as that of African Americans, Hispanic Americans, and Asian Americans

2. A major exception to this pattern is the very high suicide rate of Native Americans, which overall is 1.5 times the national average

V. WHAT TRIGGERS A SUICIDE?
A. Suicidal acts may be connected to recent events or current conditions in a person's life
1. Although such factors may not be the basic motivation for the suicide, they can precipitate it
B. Common triggers include stressful events, mood and thought changes, alcohol and other drug use, mental disorders, and modeling:
1. Stressful events and situations
a. Researchers have counted more stressful events in the lives of suicide attempters than in the lives of nonattempters
b. One stressor that has been consistently linked to suicide is combat stress
c. Both immediate stress and long-term stresses can be risk factors for suicide
(a) Immediate stresses can include the loss of a loved one, the loss of a job, or natural disaster
(b) Long-term stresses can include:
(i) Social isolation—individuals without social support are particularly vulnerable
(ii) Serious illness—especially illnesses that cause great pain or severe disability
(iii) Abusive environments—from which there is little or no hope of escape
(iv) Occupational stress—research has found particularly high rates of suicide among psychiatrists and psychologists, physicians, nurses, dentists, lawyers, police officers, farmers, and unskilled laborers
2. Mood and thought changes
a. Many suicide attempts are preceded by changes in mood
(a) These changes may not be enough to warrant a diagnosis of a mental disorder
(b) The most common change is a rise in sadness
(c) Also common are increases in feelings of anxiety, tension, frustration, anger, or shame
(d) Shneidman calls this "psychache"—a feeling of psychological pain that seems intolerable to the person
b. Suicide attempts also may be preceded by shifts in patterns of thinking
(a) Individuals may become preoccupied, lose perspective, and see suicide as the only effective solution to their difficulties
(b) They often develop a sense of hopelessness—a pessimistic belief that their present circumstances, problems, or mood will not change
(c) Some clinicians believe that a feeling of hopelessness is the single most likely indicator of suicidal intent
(d) People who attempt suicide fall victim to dichotomous thinking—viewing problems and solutions in rigid either/or terms
(i) The "four-letter word" in suicide is *only*, as in "suicide was the only thing I could do"
3. Alcohol and other drug use
a. Studies indicate that as many as 70 percent of the people who attempt suicide drink alcohol just prior to the act
b. Autopsies reveal that about one-fourth of these people are legally intoxicated
c. Research shows the use of other kinds of drugs may have similar ties to suicide, particularly in teens and young adults
4. Mental disorders
a. Attempting suicide does not necessarily indicate the presence of a psychological disorder

(a) Nevertheless, the majority of all suicide attempters do display such a disorder [See Table 10-2, text p. 295]

(b) At greatest risk are those with mood disorders, substance use disorders, and/or schizophrenia

5. Modeling: The contagion of suicide

a. It is not unusual for people, particularly teenagers, to try to commit suicide after observing or reading about someone who has done so

(a) One suicidal act appears to serve as a model for another

b. Suicides by family members and friends, celebrities, other highly publicized suicides, and ones by co-workers are particularly common triggers

c. Suicides with bizarre or unusual aspects often receive intense coverage by the news media, possibly leading to similar suicides

d. Even media programs clearly intended to educate and help viewers may have the paradoxical effect of spurring imitators

(a) Some clinicians argue that more responsible reporting and postvention could reduce this effect

VI. WHAT ARE THE UNDERLYING CAUSES OF SUICIDE?

A. Most people faced with difficult situations never try to kill themselves

B. In an effort to explain suicide-proneness, theorists have proposed more fundamental explanations for self-destructive actions

1. Leading theories come from the psychodynamic, sociocultural, and biological perspectives

2. These hypotheses have received limited research support and fail to address the full range of suicidal acts

C. The psychodynamic view

1. Theorists believe that suicide results from depression and from anger at others that is redirected toward oneself

2. Additionally, Freud proposed that humans have a basic death instinct ("Thanatos") that operates in opposition to the life instinct

a. While most people learn to direct their death instinct toward others, suicidal people direct it at themselves

D. Durkheim's sociocultural view

1. Durkheim argued that the probability of suicide is determined by how attached a person is to such social groups as the family, religious institutions, and community

a. The more thoroughly a person belongs, the lower the risk of suicide

2. He developed several categories of suicide, including egoistic, altruistic, and anomic suicide:

a. Egoistic suicides are committed by people over whom society has little or no control

b. Altruistic suicides are committed by people who are so well integrated into their society that they intentionally sacrifice their lives for its well-being

c. Anomic suicides are those committed by people whose social environment fails to provide stable structures to support and give meaning to life

(a) A major change in an individual's immediate surroundings also can lead to this type of suicide

3. Despite the influence of Durkheim's theory, it cannot by itself explain why some people who experience particular societal pressures commit suicide while the majority do not

E. The biological view

1. Family pedigree and twin studies support the position that biological factors contribute to suicidal behavior

a. For example, there are higher rates of suicide among the parents and close relatives of those who commit suicide than among nonsuicidal people

b. As always with this type of research, however, nonbiological factors, such as shared environment, also must be considered

2. In the past three decades, laboratory research has offered more direct support for a biological model of suicide
    a. Serotonin levels have been found to be low in people who commit suicide
        (a) There is a known link between low serotonin and depression
        (b) There is evidence, though, of low serotonin activity among suicidal subjects with no history of depression
        (c) One possibility is that low serotonin activity may contribute to aggressive and impulsive behaviors

VII. IS SUICIDE LINKED TO AGE?
    A. The likelihood of committing suicide increases with age, although people of all ages may try to kill themselves
    B. Although the general findings about suicide hold true across age groups, three age groups (children, adolescents, and the elderly) have been the focus of much study because of the unique issues that face them
      1. Children
        a. Suicide is infrequent among children
        b. Rates have been increasing over the past several decades
            (a) More than 6 percent of all deaths among children between the ages of 10 and 14 are caused by suicide
        c. Boys outnumber girls by as much as five to one
        d. Suicide attempts by the very young generally are preceded by such behavioral patterns as running away, accident-proneness, temper tantrums, self-criticism, social withdrawal, dark fantasies, and marked personality changes
        e. Despite common misconceptions, many child suicides appear to be based in a clear understanding of death and on a clear wish to die
      2. Adolescents
        a. Suicidal actions become much more common after the age of 14 than at any earlier age
        b. About 1,500 teens commit suicide in the United States each year
            (a) As many as 10% make suicide attempts, and 1 in 6 may think about suicide each year
        c. About half of teen suicides have been tied to clinical depression, low self-esteem, and feelings of hopelessness
            (a) Anger, impulsiveness, poor problem-solving, substance use, and stress also play a role
            (b) Some theorists believe that the period of adolescence itself produces a stressful climate in which suicidal actions are more likely
        d. Far more teens attempt suicide than succeed
            (a) The ratio may be as high as 200:1
            (b) Several explanations, most pointing to societal factors, have been proposed for the high rate of attempts among teenagers
        e. Teen suicide rates vary by ethnicity in the United States
            (a) Young white Americans are more suicide prone than African Americans or Hispanic Americans at this age
            (b) Rates are becoming closer
            (c) The highest suicide rates of all is displayed by Native Americans
      3. The elderly
        a. In Western society, the elderly are more likely to commit suicide than people in any other age group
        b. There are many contributory factors:
            (a) Illness
            (b) Loss of close friends and relatives
            (c) Loss of control over one's life
            (d) Loss of social status
        c. Elderly persons are typically more determined than younger persons in their decision to die, so their success rate is much higher

        d.   The suicide rate among the elderly is lower in some minority groups in the United States, especially Native Americans and African Americans

VIII. TREATMENT AND SUICIDE

A.   Treatment of suicidal persons falls into two categories:
1.   Treatment after suicide has been attempted
2.   Suicide prevention

B.   What treatments are used after suicide attempts?
1.   After a suicide attempt, most victims need medical care
2.   Psychotherapy or drug therapy may begin once a person is medically stable
    a.   Unfortunately, even after trying to kill themselves, many suicidal people fail to receive systematic follow-up care
3.   Therapy goals are to keep the patient alive, reduce psychological pain, help them achieve a nonsuicidal state of mind and a sense of hope, and guide them to develop better ways of handling stress
4.   Various therapies and techniques have been employed
5.   Cognitive and cognitive-behavioral therapies may be particularly helpful

C.   What is suicide prevention?
1.   During the past 50 years, emphasis worldwide has shifted from suicide treatment to suicide prevention
2.   There are hundreds of suicide prevention programs in the United States
3.   There also are hundreds of suicide hotlines, 24-hour-a-day telephone services
    a.   Hot lines predominantly are staffed by paraprofessionals—persons trained in counseling but without a formal degree
4.   Both suicide prevention programs and suicide hotlines provide crisis intervention
5.   The general approach includes:
    a.   Establishing a positive relationship
    b.   Understanding and clarifying the problem
    c.   Assessing suicide potential
    d.   Assessing and mobilizing the caller's resources
    e.   Formulating a plan
6.   Although crisis intervention may be sufficient treatment for some suicidal people, longer-term therapy is needed for most
7.   Another way to prevent suicide may be to limit the public's access to common means of suicide
    a.   Examples: gun control, safer medications, better bridge barriers, and car emissions controls
8.   Do suicide prevention programs work?
    a.   It is difficult to measure the effectiveness of suicide prevention programs
    b.   Prevention programs do seem to reduce the number of suicides among those high-risk people who do call
    c.   Many theorists have argued for more effective public education about suicide as the ultimate form of prevention

LEARNING OBJECTIVES

1.   Define suicide and know the current prevalence.

2.   Describe each of the four kinds of people who intentionally end their lives: death seekers, death initiators, death ignorers, and death darers. Also describe the category of subintentional death.

3.   Describe the effects of cultural factors, race, and sex on suicide rates.

4.   Discuss the common precipitating factors in suicide.

5.   Discuss how mood changes, hopelessness, and dichotomous thinking are related to suicide.

6.   Describe the common predictors of suicide.

7.   Detail the psychodynamic view for suicide, including the role of Thanatos.

8.   Explain the role of biological factors in suicide, including the role of serotonin.

9.   Explain the role of sociocultural factors while comparing and contrasting Durkheim's three categories of suicide: egoistic, altruistic, anomic.

10. Discuss the characteristics of suicide prevention programs.

KEY TERMS

altruistic suicide
anomic suicide
anomie
crisis intervention
death darer
death ignorer
death initiator

death seeker
dichotomous thinking
egoistic suicide
hopelessness
paraprofessional
parasuicide
postvention

retrospective analysis
subintentional death
suicide
suicide prevention program
Thanatos

MEDIA RESOURCES

Abnormal Psychology Student Tool Kit

Produced and edited by Ronald J. Comer, Princeton University and Gregory Comer, Princeton Academic Resources. Tied directly to the CyberStudy sections in the text, this Student Tool Kit offers 57 intriguing Video Cases running 3 to 7 minutes each. The Video Cases focus on persons affected by disorders discussed in the text. Students first view the video and then answer a series of thought-provoking questions. Additionally, the Student Tool Kit contains multiple-choice practice test questions with built-in instructional feedback for every option.

PowerPoint Slides

Available at the Instructor's site on the companion Web site are comprehensive PowerPoint slide presentations and supplemental student handouts for Chapter 10. The slide files reflect the main points of the chapter in significant detail. Student handouts were created using the instructor slides as a base, with key points replaced as "fill-in" items. Answer keys and suggestions for use also are provided.

Internet Sites

Please see Appendix A for full and comprehensive references.

Sites relevant to Chapter 10 material are:

http://www.nimh.nih.gov/health/topics/ suicide-prevention/index.shtml
This Web site, provided by the National Institute of Mental Health, supplies downloadable links to PDF files and booklets on a variety of mental health topics, including suicide prevention.

http://www.suicideinfo.ca
This Canadian site, the Centre for Suicide Prevention, is a library and resource center providing information on suicide and suicidal behavior.

http://www.cdc.gov/violenceprevention/suicide/ index.html
This is the Web site of the National Center for Injury Prevention and Control. It includes a suicide fact sheet, prevention strategies, and publications focused on the topic of suicide.

http://www.afsp.org/
This site is the home of the American Foundation for Suicide Prevention. It offers fundraisers and supports

for those who are suffering from suicidal thoughts or have had someone pass away. There is supporting research and education for professionals and survivors as well.

http://www.save.org/
Suicide awareness/voices of education Web site, which includes links and other information on suicide.

http://www.suicidology.org/
The Web site for the American Association of Suicidology, which is dedicated to the understanding and prevention of suicide.

http://www.hopeline.com
The Kristin Brooks Hope Center offers crisis support and information on suicide.

Mainstream Films

Films relevant to Chapter 10 material are listed and summarized below.

Key to Film Listings:
P = psychopathology focus
T = treatment focus
E = ethical issues raised

Please note that some of the films suggested may have graphic sexual or violent content due to the nature of certain subject matter.

The Bridge
A haunting documentary looking at the lives and deaths of 24 people who died at the Golden Gate bridge in 2004. **P, serious film**

Dead Poet's Society
This 1989 film stars Robin Williams as an unconventional teacher in a strict prep school. The suicide of one of his students is explored. **P, E, serious film**

Girl, Interrupted
Based on an autobiographical novel by Susanna Kaysen, this film details the experiences of several women as patients in a psychiatric hospital in the 1960s. The 1999 film challenges the diagnosis of mental illness and the relationship between diagnosis and social norm violations. **P, T, serious film**

The Hours
From 2003, this film stars Nicole Kidman as Virginia Woolf, Julianne Moore as a 1950s homemaker, and Meryl Streep as a NY socialite—one of the common links among them all is suicide. **P, T, serious film**

It's a Wonderful Life
This film from 1946 stars Jimmy Stewart as George Bailey, a small-town man whose life seems so desperate he contemplates suicide. **P, commercial film**

Leaving Las Vegas
This 1995 film stars Nicolas Cage as a Hollywood screenwriter who has become an alcoholic. After being fired, he takes his severance pay to Las Vegas, where he plans to drink himself to death. **P, serious film**

Ordinary People
This 1980 film examines the treatment of a teenager suffering from depression, anxiety, and posttraumatic stress disorder in the aftermath of his brother's death. **P, T, serious film**

Sylvia
This film stars Gwyneth Paltrow as the talented, troubled, and eventually suicidal poet Sylvia Plath. **P, serious film**

The Virgin Suicides
From 2000 and set in the 1970s, this adaptation of Jeffrey Eugenide's novel deals with sexual attraction and teen suicide. **P, T, E, serious film**

What Dreams May Come
This 1998 film stars Robin Williams as a husband distraught by the tragic death of his child. The later suicide of his wife is a significant component of the film. **P, serious film**

Whose Life Is It Anyway?
From 1981, this film follows Ken Harrison (Richard Dreyfuss), an artist paralyzed from his neck down in a car accident. He goes to court for the right to commit suicide. **P, E, serious film**

William Shakespeare's Romeo + Juliet
This 1996 Baz Luhrmann adaptation of the Shakespeare classic stars Leonardo DiCaprio and Claire Danes as star-crossed, teen-aged lovers whose ill-fated relationship ultimately ends in both their deaths. **P, serious film**

Other Films:

About a Boy (2002) depression and suicide. **P, commercial/serious film**
The Bell Jar (1979) anxiety and depression. **P, T, serious film**
The Deer Hunter (1978) **P, serious film**
Love Liza (2002) suicide. **P, serious/art film**
The Royal Tennenbaums (2001) suicide attempt. **P, comedy/serious film**
Sophie's Choice (1982) depression. **P, serious film**

Comer Video Segments

Available as a supplement, this revised set of videotapes contains short clips depicting various topics related to abnormal psychology. Please see the accompanying Video Guide for specific clips linked to Chapter 10.

Recommendations for Purchase or Rental

The Comer Video Segments include excerpts from many superb clinical documentaries. While the segments alone are ideal for use in lectures, it often is useful to assign the entire documentary for special class screenings or library use by students.

Films on Demand is a Web-based digital delivery service that has impressive psychology holdings. The catalog can be accessed here: http://ffh.films.com/digitallanding.aspx

In addition, the following videos and other media may be of particular interest and are available for pur-

chase or rental and appropriate for use in class or for assignment outside of class.

Don't Kill Yourself
Films for the Humanities & Sciences
Box 2053, Princeton, NJ 08543-2053
Phone 1-800-257-5126

Calling Dr. Kevorkhian: A Date with Dr. Death
Films for the Humanities & Sciences
Box 2053, Princeton, NJ 08543-2053
Phone 1-800-257-5126

Silent Epidemic: Teen Suicide
A Desperate Act: Suicide and the Elderly
Patrick's Story: Attempted Suicide, Attempting Life
Suicide: A Guide for Prevention
Films for the Humanities and Sciences
P.O. Box 2053
Princeton, NJ 08543-2053
Phone: 800-257-5126
ffh.films.com

CLASS DEMONSTRATIONS AND ACTIVITIES

Case Study

Present a case study to the class.

Guest Speaker

Invite a crisis intervention worker (from a suicide hotline or prevention center) into your class to discuss his or her work in the field.

"It's Debatable: Can Rock and Roll Inspire Suicide?" (see Preface instructions for conducting this activity)

Have students volunteer (or assign them) in teams to opposite sides of the debate topic [see PsychWatch, text p. 294 for more information]. Have students present their cases in class, following standard debate guidelines.

"It's Debatable: We Have the Right to Commit Suicide" (see Preface instructions for conducting this activity)

Have students volunteer (or assign them) in teams to opposite sides of the debate topic [see PsychWatch,

text p. 308 for more information]. Have students present their case in class, following standard debate guidelines.

Group Work: Examples of "Suicidal Messages"

Divide students into groups, then ask each group to come up with an example of either a popular song or a movie that might influence someone to commit suicide. Discuss the examples with the whole class. After several recognizable examples are generated, lead a discussion on whether this could actually happen and whether a music group or movie producer could be held responsible for a suicide.

Group Work: Who Decides?

Divide students into groups, then assign one of the following positions: (1) It should be legal (or illegal) for doctors to help patients kill themselves. (2) It is a personal decision about whether an individual chooses to die. (This can lead to heated opinions, so warn students about group work rules, such as respecting others' opinions and defending positions.)

SUGGESTED TOPICS FOR DISCUSSION

"The Right to Commit Suicide"

Using PsychWatch (p. 308 in the text) as a platform, lead a discussion into the myriad issues surrounding assisted suicide.

"The Role of Occupational Stress"

Discuss the dramatically increased rates of suicide among workers in certain occupations. Be sure to highlight psychologists and psychiatrists. Solicit theories to explain such findings. Students can also be encouraged (or assigned) to follow up the discussion with a research report (see the following).

Statistics and Suicide

Discuss the accuracy of statistics on suicide. For example, might some national statistics be adjusted to account for cultural beliefs and values? Ask students for cultural or religious examples. How often are deaths listed as accidents instead of suicides to spare mourners? May accidents sometimes be called intentional suicides?

Live Web Suicides

Using MediaSpeaks on p. 311 of the text as a platform, discuss the growing phenomenon of live Web suicide. Ask the class how common an occurrence they believe this to be and what social psychology factors might be at work here? In addition, what strategies do they think should be used to address this growing problem?

Women at Risk for Suicide

The chapter mentions that men are more likely than women to kill themselves, but that women make three to four times as many attempts. What factors are involved in the risk of suicide among women? Lead a discussion of the following factors related to suicide.

- A history of physical and/or sexual abuse
- Major depression
- Borderline personality disorder (all personality disorders increase the risk for men)
- Loss of the father through death or desertion before age 20 (this factor is found in 50 percent of women who commit suicide but in only 20 percent of other women)
- European ancestry (twice the suicide rate of African Americans and other ethnic groups)
- Age at the middle of the life span (youngest and oldest groups have the lowest rates)
- Unemployment
- Impulsiveness and emotionality, moodiness, unhappiness, and lack of self-confidence
- An IQ above 135 (the Terman Genetic Studies of Genius found that the rate of suicide among gifted women was nearly 250 times that of the general population of women)

Contrast the list to the following, which are *not* indicators:

- Any particular phase of the menstrual cycle
- Pregnancy (actually associated with lower risk)
- Loss of the mother through death or desertion before age 20
- Chronic stress in the family of origin, parental conflict, and conflict in a woman's relationship with her parents

Open Discussion: Suicide and the Media

Research suggests that suicide rates increase following depictions or descriptions of suicides in the media (e.g., in newscasts and movies). Many of these incidents have been well documented. Lead an open discussion on why this might happen. Alternatively, assign groups to take a position on whether there should be oversight (censorship) of such media accounts.

ASSIGNMENTS/EXTRA CREDIT SUGGESTIONS

"Field Experience Opportunity"

Students can volunteer as paraprofessionals at a crisis center or on a hotline for suicide prevention. Most centers offer significant training and provide an exceptional opportunity for hands-on (though intense) work with clients.

"Write a Pamphlet"

With the use of a software program like Microsoft Publisher or simply paper and markers, students can create a pamphlet targeting suicide prevention. Students can focus on a specific age group or be more general. Students should be encouraged to be as accurate and up-to-date as possible and to present all sides of the disorder (e.g., alternate treatment approaches or theories).

Abnormal Psychology Student Tool Kit Video Questions

As a homework assignment, have students watch a video clip and answer the accompanying questions. Students can answer the questions directly into the online assessment feature. The results of these quizzes report to the site's built-in grade book.

Web Site Quiz

For homework or extra credit, have students complete the quiz for Chapter 10 located on the companion Web site. Students can complete an online test of the key chapter material (using questions NOT from the test bank) and have their scores e-mailed directly to the course instructor.

Essay Topics

For homework or extra credit, have students write an essay addressing one (or more) of the following topics:

(1) Compare and contrast Shneidman's four types of suicide seekers. Use media examples of each.

(2) Discuss the right to commit suicide [See Psych Watch, text p. 308]. Do you agree or disagree? Are there any circumstances where ending one's life is acceptable or unacceptable?

(3) Discuss the "Black Box Controversy" as listed in PsychWatch (p. 304 in the text). Do antidepressants cause suicide?

(4) Discuss the growing phenomenon of self-cutting. [See MediaSpeaks, text p. 290] What factors do you think particularly influence this behavior?

Research Topics

For homework or extra credit, have students write a research report addressing one (or more) of the following topics:

(1) Research and report on cross-cultural views of suicide. What do theorists believe are the main determinants of the suicide rate?

(2) Research and report on the practice of mass suicide. What are common links seen among these groups? How did the media/culture react to the event?

(3) Conduct a "Psych Info" search and write an annotated bibliography on research into suicide prevention. What are the various strategies being investigated? What are the limitations of the research?

(4) Research has shown increased rates of suicide and suicide attempts among workers in different occupations, especially psychology and psychiatry. What theories have been posited to explain such findings?

(5) Research and report on the phenomenon of live Web suicides. [See MediaSpeaks, text p. 311 for some information] What strategies are being used to address this growing problem?

Web-Based Case Studies

Nine Web-based case studies have been created and posted on the companion Web site. These cases describe the individual's history and symptoms and are accompanied by a series of guided questions that point to the precise DSM-IV criteria for each disorder. Students can both identify the disorder and suggest a course of treatment. Students can be assigned the appropriate case study and questions as homework or for class discussion. The case relevant to Chapter 10 is referenced below.

The Case of Ellen: Depression and Suicidality

Crossword Puzzles

As a homework assignment or for extra credit, have students complete and submit Crossword Puzzle #10.

Word Searches

As a homework assignment or for extra credit, have students complete and submit Word Search #10.

Eating Disorders

LECTURE OUTLINE

I. **EATING DISORDERS**
    A. It has not always done so, but Western society today equates thinness with health and beauty
        1. Thinness has become a national obsession
    B. There has been a rise in eating disorders in the past three decades

C. The core issue is a morbid fear of weight gain
D. Two main diagnoses:
   1. Anorexia nervosa
   2. Bulimia nervosa

II. **ANOREXIA NERVOSA**
   A. The main symptoms of anorexia nervosa (see Table 11-1, text p. 318) are:
      1. A refusal to maintain more than 85 percent of normal body weight
      2. Intense fear of becoming overweight
      3. Distorted view of weight and shape
      4. Amenorrhea
   B. There are two main subtypes:
      1. Restricting type
         a. Lose weight by cutting out sweets and fattening snacks, eventually eliminating nearly all food
         b. Show almost no variability in diet
      2. Binge-eating/Purging type
         a. Lose weight by forcing themselves to vomit after meals or by abusing laxatives or diuretics
         b. Similar to bulimia nervosa, people with this subtype may engage in eating binges
   C. About 90 to 95 percent of cases occur in females
      1. The peak age of onset is between 14 to 18 years
      2. Between 0.5 and 3.5 percent of females in Western countries will develop the disorder in their lifetimes
         a. Many more display some symptoms
      3. Rates of anorexia nervosa are increasing in North America, Europe, and Japan
   D. The "typical" case:
      1. A normal to slightly overweight female has been on a diet
      2. The escalation toward anorexia nervosa may follow a stressful event:
         a. Separation of parents
         b. Move away from home
         c. Experience of personal failure
      3. Most patients recover
         a. However, about 2 to 6 percent become seriously ill and die as a result of medical complications or suicide
   E. The clinical picture
      1. The key goal for people with anorexia nervosa is becoming thin
      2. The driving motivation is fear:
         a. Of becoming obese
         b. Of giving in to the desire to eat
         c. Of losing control of body size and shape
      3. Despite their dietary restrictions, people with anorexia are preoccupied with food
         a. This includes thinking and reading about food and planning for meals
         b. This relationship is not necessarily causal:
            (a) It may be the *result* of food deprivation as evidenced by the famous 1940s "starvation study" with conscientious objectors
      4. Persons with anorexia nervosa also think in distorted ways:
         a. Usually have a low opinion of their body shape
         b. Tend to overestimate their actual proportions
            (a) Adjustable lens assessment technique
         c. Hold maladaptive attitudes and misperceptions:
            (a) "I must be perfect in every way"
            (b) "I will be a better person if I deprive myself"
            (c) "I can avoid guilt by not eating"
      5. People with anorexia also may display certain psychological problems:
         a. Depression (usually mild)
         b. Anxiety

    c. Low self-esteem
    d. Insomnia or other sleep disturbances
    e. Substance abuse
    f. Obsessive-compulsive patterns
    g. Perfectionism
   6. People with anorexia also are susceptible to certain medical problems caused by starvation:
    a. Amenorrhea
    b. Low body temperature
    c. Low blood pressure
    d. Body swelling
    e. Reduced bone density
    f. Slow heart rate
    g. Metabolic and electrolyte imbalance
    h. Dry skin, brittle nails
    i. Poor circulation
    j. Lanugo

III. BULIMIA NERVOSA

 A. Bulimia nervosa, also known as "binge-purge syndrome," is characterized by binges:
   1. Bouts of uncontrolled overeating during a limited period of time
    a. Eat objectively more than most people would eat in a similar period
   2. The disorder also is characterized by inappropriate compensatory behaviors, which designate the subtype of the condition (see Table 11-2, text p. 320):
    a. Purging-type bulimia nervosa
     (a) Forced vomiting
     (b) Misusing laxatives, diuretics, or enemas
    b. Nonpurging-type bulimia nervosa
     (a) Fasting
     (b) Exercising frantically
 B. Like anorexia nervosa, about 90 to 95 percent of bulimia nervosa cases are in females
   1. The peak age of onset is between 15 and 21 years
   2. Symptoms may last for several years with periodic letup
   3. Patients generally are of normal weight
    a. May be slightly overweight
    b. Often experience marked weight fluctuations
 C. A related diagnosis may be "binge eating disorder"
   1. Symptoms include a pattern of binge eating with *no* compensatory behaviors
   2. This pattern is not yet listed in the DSM-IV-TR
 D. Many teenagers and young adults go on occasional binges or experiment with vomiting or laxatives after hearing about these behaviors from friends or the media
   1. According to global studies, 25 to 50 percent of students report periodic binge eating or self-induced vomiting
 E. People with bulimia nervosa may have between 1 and 30 binge episodes per week
   1. Binges often are carried out in secret
   2. There is consumption of massive amounts of food very rapidly with little chewing
    a. Usually sweet high-calorie foods with soft texture
   3. Binge-eaters commonly consume between 1,000 and 10,000 calories per binge episode
   4. Binges usually are preceded by feelings of great tension and/or powerlessness
    a. Although the binge itself may be pleasurable, it usually is followed by feelings of extreme self-blame, guilt, depression, and fears of weight gain and being discovered
 F. After a binge, people with bulimia nervosa try to compensate for and "undo" the caloric effects
   1. The most common compensatory behaviors:
    a. Vomiting
     (a) Fails to prevent the absorption of only half the calories consumed during a binge

(b) Repeated vomiting affects the ability to feel satiated leading to greater hunger and frequent and intense bingeing

   b. Laxatives and diuretics

      (a) Also largely fails to reduce the number of calories consumed

  2. Compensatory behaviors may temporarily relieve the negative feelings attached to binge eating

  3. Over time, however, a cycle develops in which purging leads to bingeing, which leads to purging.

G. The "typical" case of bulimia nervosa:

  1. A normal to slightly overweight female has been on an intense diet

  2. Research suggests that, even among normal participants, bingeing often occurs after strict dieting

IV. BULIMIA NERVOSA VERSUS ANOREXIA NERVOSA

A. Similarities

  1. Begin after a period of dieting

  2. Fear of becoming obese

  3. Drive to become thin

  4. Preoccupation with food, weight, appearance

  5. Feelings of anxiety, depression, obsessiveness, perfectionism

  6. Heightened risk of suicide attempts

  7. Substance abuse

  8. Distorted body perception

  9. Disturbed attitudes toward eating

B. Differences

  1. People with bulimia are more concerned about pleasing others, being attractive to others, and having intimate relationships

  2. People with bulimia tend to be more sexually experienced and active

  3. People with bulimia are more likely to have histories of mood swings, low frustration tolerance, and poor coping

  4. More than one-third of people with bulimia are more likely to display characteristics of a personality disorder, particularly borderline personality disorder

  5. Different medical complications:

    a. Only half of women with bulimia experience amenorrhea vs. almost all women with anorexia

    b. People with bulimia suffer damage caused by purging—especially from vomiting and laxatives

V. WHAT CAUSES EATING DISORDERS?

A. Most theorists and researchers use a multidimensional risk perspective to explain eating disorders:

  1. Several key factors place individuals at risk

    a. More factors equals greater likelihood of developing an eating disorder

    b. Leading factors:

      (a) Psychological problems (ego, cognitive, and mood disturbances)

      (b) Biological factors

      (c) Sociocultural conditions (societal, family, and multicultural pressures)

B. Psychodynamic factors: Ego deficiencies

  1. Hilde Bruch developed a largely psychodynamic theory of eating disorders

  2. Bruch argued that eating disorders are the result of disturbed mother–child interactions, which lead to serious ego deficiencies in the child and to severe perceptual disturbances

  3. Bruch argues that parents may respond to their children either effectively or ineffectively:

    a. Effective parents accurately attend to a child's biological and emotional needs

    b. Ineffective parents fail to attend to child's needs; they feed when the child is anxious, comfort when he or she is tired, etc.

(a) Such children may grow up confused and unaware of their own internal needs and turn, instead, to external guides

4. Clinical reports and research have provided some empirical support for this theory

C. Cognitive factors

1. Bruch's theory also contains several cognitive factors, such as improper labeling of internal sensations and needs

a. According to cognitive theorists, these deficiencies contribute to a broad cognitive distortion that lies at the center of disordered eating

b. For example, people with anorexia and bulimia negatively judge themselves based on their body shape and weight

D. Mood disorders

1. Many people with eating disorders, particularly those with bulimia nervosa, experience symptoms of depression

2. Theorists believe mood disorders may "set the stage" for eating disorders

a. There is empirical support for this model:

(a) Many more people with an eating disorder qualify for a clinical diagnosis of major depressive disorder than do people in the general population

(b) Close relatives of those with eating disorders seem to have higher rates of mood disorders

(c) People with eating disorders, especially those with bulimia nervosa, have serotonin abnormalities

(d) Symptoms of eating disorders are helped by antidepressant medications

E. Biological factors

1. Biological theorists suspect certain genes may leave some people particularly susceptible to eating disorders

2. Consistent with this idea:

a. Relatives of people with eating disorders are up to six times more likely to develop the disorder themselves

b. Identical twins with anorexia = 70 percent; fraternal twins = 20 percent

c. Identical (MZ) twins with bulimia = 23 percent; fraternal twins = 9 percent

3. These findings may be related to low serotonin

4. Other theories are that eating disorders may be related to dysfunction of the hypothalamus

5. Researchers have identified two separate areas that control eating: the lateral hypothalamus (LH) and the ventromedial hypothalamus (VMH)

a. Some theorists believe that the hypothalamus, related brain areas, and chemicals together are responsible for weight set point—a "weight thermostat" of sorts

b. Set by genetic inheritance and early eating practices, this mechanism is responsible for keeping an individual at a particular weight level

(a) If weight falls below the set point, hunger increases while metabolic rate decreases, often leading to binges

(b) If weight rises above the set point, hunger decreases while metabolic rate increases

(c) Dieters end up in a battle against themselves to lose weight

F. Societal pressures

1. Many theorists believe that current Western standards of female attractiveness are partly responsible for the emergence of eating disorders

2. Western standards have changed throughout history toward a thinner ideal:

a. Miss America = <0.28 lbs/yr for contestant; 0.37 lbs/yr for winner

b. Playboy centerfolds have lower average weight, bust, and hip measurements than in the past

3. Members of certain subcultures are at greater risk from these pressures:

a. Models, actors, dancers, and certain athletes

(a) Of college athletes surveyed, 9 percent met full criteria for an eating disorder, while another 50 percent had symptoms

(b) 20 percent of gymnasts appear to have an eating disorder

4. Societal attitudes may explain economic and racial differences seen in prevalence rates
5. Historically, women of higher SES expressed greater concern about thinness and dieting and had higher rates of eating disorders compared with women of the lower socioeconomic classes
6. Recently, dieting and preoccupation with thinness, along with rates of eating disorders, are increasing in all groups
7. The socially accepted prejudice against overweight people also may add to the "fear" and preoccupation about weight
    a. About 50 percent of elementary and 61 percent of middle school girls currently are dieting
    b. A recent survey of adolescent girls tied eating disorders and body dissatisfaction to social networking, Internet activities, and television browsing
G. Family environment
1. Families may play an important role in the development of eating disorders
2. As many as half of the families of those with eating disorders have a long history of emphasizing thinness, appearance, and dieting
3. Mothers of those with eating disorders are more likely to be dieters and perfectionistic themselves
4. Abnormal interactions and forms of communication within a family also may set the stage for an eating disorder
    a. Influential family theorist Salvador Minuchin cites "enmeshed family patterns" as causal factors of eating disorders
        (a) These patterns include overinvolvement and overconcern in the details of family member's lives
H. Multicultural factors: Racial and ethnic differences
1. A widely publicized 1995 study found that eating behaviors and attitudes of young African American women were more positive than those of young white American women
    a. Specifically, nearly 90 percent of the white American respondents were dissatisfied with their weight and body shape, compared to approximately 70 percent of the African American teens
    b. The study also suggested the groups had different ideals of beauty
2. Unfortunately, research conducted over the past decade suggests that body image concerns, dysfunctional eating patterns, and eating disorders are on the rise among young African American women as well as among women of other minority groups
    a. The shift appears to be partly related to acculturation
3. Eating disorders among Hispanic American female adolescents are about equal to those of white American women
4. Eating disordeers also appear to be on the increase among young Asian American women and young women in several Asian countries
I. Multicultural factors: Gender differences
1. Males account for only 5 to 10 percent of all cases of eating disorders
2. The reasons for this striking difference are not entirely clear, but Western society's double standard for attractiveness is, at the very least, one reason
3. A second reason may be the different methods of weight loss favored
    a. Men are more likely to exercise
    b. Women more often diet
4. It seems that some men develop eating disorders as linked to the requirements and pressures of a job or sport
    a. The highest rates of male eating disorders have been found among:
        (a) Jockeys
        (b) Wrestlers
        (c) Distance runners
        (d) Body builders
        (e) Swimmers
5. For other men, body image appears to be a key factor

6. Last, some men seem to be caught up in a new kind of eating disorder–reverse anorexia nervosa or muscle dysmorphobia

VI. TREATMENTS FOR EATING DISORDERS

A. Eating disorders treatments have two main goals:
1. Correct dangerous eating patterns
2. Address broader psychological and situational factors that have led to and are maintaining the eating problem
    a. This often requires participation of family and friends

B. Treatments for anorexia nervosa
1. The immediate aims of treatment for anorexia nervosa are to:
    a. Regain lost weight
    b. Recover from malnourishment
    c. Eat normally again
2. In the past, treatment occurred in a hospital setting; it now is offered in day hospitals or outpatient settings
    a. In life-threatening cases, clinicians may need to force tube and intravenous feeding on the patient
        (a) This may breed distrust in the patient and create a power struggle
    b. In contrast, behavioral weight-restoration approaches have clinicians use rewards whenever patients eat properly or gain weight
    c. The most popular weight-restoration technique has been the combination of the use of supportive nursing care, nutritional counseling, and high-calorie diets
    d. Necessary weight gain often is achieved in 8 to 12 weeks
3. Researchers have found that people with anorexia must overcome their underlying psychological problems in order to achieve lasting improvement
    a. Therapists use a combination of therapy and education to achieve this broader goal, using a combination of individual, group, and family approaches; psychotropic drugs have been helpful in some cases
    b. In most treatment programs, a combination of behavioral and cognitive interventions are included
        (a) On the behavioral side, clients are required to monitor feelings, hunger levels, and food intake and the ties among those variables
        (b) On the cognitive side, they are taught to identify their "core pathology"
    c. Therapists help patients recognize their need for independence and control
    d. Therapists help patients recognize and trust their internal feelings
    e. A final focus of treatment is helping clients change their attitudes about eating and weight
    f. Using cognitive approaches, therapists will correct disturbed cognitions and educate about body distortions
    g. Family therapy is important for anorexia
        (a) The main issue often is separation/boundaries
4. The use of combined treatment approaches has greatly improved the outlook for people with anorexia nervosa
    a. Even with combined treatment, recovery is difficult
    b. The course and outcome of the disorder vary from person to person
5. Positives of treatment:
    a. Weight gain often is quickly restored
        (a) As many as 90 percent of patients still showed improvements after several years
    b. Menstruation often returns with return to normal weight
    c. The death rate from anorexia is declining
6. Negatives of treatment:
    a. As many as 20 percent of patients remain troubled for years
    b. Even when it occurs, recovery is not always permanent
        (a) Anorexic behavior recurs in at least one-third of recovered paients, usually triggered by new stresses

    c.   Many patients still express concerns about their weight and appearance

    d.   Lingering emotional problems are common

C. Treatments for bulimia nervosa

    1.   Treatment often is offered in eating disorder clinics

    2.   The immediate aims of treatment for bulimia nervosa are to:

        a.   Eliminate binge-purge patterns

        b.   Establish good eating habits

        c.   Eliminate the underlying cause of bulimic patterns

    4.   Programs emphasize education as much as therapy

    5.   Cognitive-behavioral therapy is particularly helpful:

        a.   Behavioral techniques

            (a)   Diaries often are a useful component of treatment

            (b)   Exposure and response prevention (ERP) is used to break the binge-purge cycle

        b.   Cognitive techniques

            (a)   Help clients recognize and change their maladaptive attitudes toward food, eating, weight, and shape

            (b)   Typically teach individuals to identify and challenge the negative thoughts that precede the urge to binge

    6.   Other forms of psychotherapy

        a.   If clients do not respond to cognitive-behavioral therapy, other approaches may be tried

        b.   A common alternative is interpersonal psychotherapy, the treatment that seeks to improve interpersonal functioning

        c.   Psychodynamic therapy has also been used

        d.   The various forms of psychotherapy are often supplemented by family therapy and may be offered in either individual or group therapy format

            (a)   Group formats provide an opportunity for patients to express their thoughts, concerns, and experiences with one another

            (b)   Group therapy is helpful in as many as 75 percent of cases

    7.   Antidepressant medications

        a.   During the past 15 years, all groups of antidepressant drugs have been used in bulimia treatment

        b.   Drugs help as many as 40 percent of patients

        c.   Medications are best when used in combination with other forms of therapy

    8.   Left untreated, bulimia can last for years

        a.   Treatment provides immediate, significant improvement in about 40 percent of cases

        b.   An additional 40 percent show moderate response

        c.   Follow-up studies suggest that 10 years posttreatment, about 75 percent of patients have recovered fully or partially

    9.   Relapse can be a significant problem, even among those who respond successfully to treatment

        a.   Relapses usually are triggered by stress

        b.   Relapse is more likely among persons with a longer history of symptoms, who vomited frequently, who had histories of substance use, and who have lingering interpersonal problems

VII. CALL FOR CHANGE: DSM-5

    A.   The DSM-5 Task Force proposed that the name of the grouping for eating disorders be changed to "Feeding and Eating Disorders," with the inclusion of three childhood feeding problems

    B.   In the proposal regarding anorexia, the Task Force recommended removal of the 85% standard and, instead, they suggested a body weight that is "significantly less than minimally-normal"

    A.   The Task Force also recommended inclusion of a new category: binge-eating disorder. This disorder is marked by recurrent binge episodes but not by the symptom of purging or other compensatory behaviors

LEARNING OBJECTIVES

1. List the central features of anorexia nervosa and bulimia, then discuss the age groups in which anorexia and bulimia are most common.

2. Compare and contrast the various behavioral patterns of anorexia and bulimia.

3. Compare and contrast ways in which those with anorexia and bulimia perceive their eating disorders.

4. Describe medical problems that can be caused by each of the major eating disorders.

5. Explain how each of the following factors can place a person at risk for an eating disorder: ego deficiencies, cognitive factors, mood disorders, biological factors, societal pressures, family environment, racial and ethnic differences, and gender differences.

6. Describe treatments for anorexia nervosa, including weight restoration and resumption of eating; then discuss broader psychological changes and the aftermath of this disorder.

7. Describe treatments for bulimia nervosa, including individual insight therapy, group therapy, behavioral therapy, and antidepressant drugs; then discuss the aftermath of this disorder.

8. Discuss the changes for these disorders proposed by the DSM-5 Task Force.

KEY TERMS

amenorrhea
anorexia nervosa
binge
binge-eating disorder
binge-purge syndrome
bulimia nervosa

compensatory behavior
enmeshed family pattern
exposure and response
   prevention
hypothalamus
lateral hypothalamus (LH)

multidimensional risk
   perspective
ventromedial
   hypothalamus (VMH)
weight set point

MEDIA RESOURCES

Abnormal Psychology Student Tool Kit

Produced and edited by Ronald J. Comer, Princeton University and Gregory Comer, Princeton Academic Resources. Tied directly to the CyberStudy sections in the text, this Student Tool Kit offers 57 intriguing Video Cases running 3 to 7 minutes each. The Video Cases focus on persons affected by disorders discussed in the text. Students first view the video and then answer a series of thought-provoking questions. Additionally, the Student Tool Kit contains multiple-choice practice

test questions with built-in instructional feedback for every option.

PowerPoint Slides

Available at the Instructor's site on the companion Web site are comprehensive PowerPoint slide presentations and supplemental student handouts for Chapter 11. The slide files reflect the main points of the chapter in significant detail. Student handouts were created using the instructor slides as a base, with key points replaced as "fill-in" items. Answer keys and suggestions for use also are provided.

DSM-IV-TR Masters

B-33, DSM-IV-TR Diagnostic Criteria for Anorexia Nervosa

B-34, DSM-IV-TR Diagnostic Criteria for Bulimia Nervosa

Internet Sites

Please see Appendix A for full and comprehensive references. Sites relevant to Chapter 11 material are:

http://www.nedic.ca/
The National Eating Disorders Information Centre of Canada provides information relevant to eating disorders, body image, and self-esteem, including definitions, treatment, prevention, and statistics. It also includes a resource library with different forms of information related to the topic.

http://www.nimh.nih.gov/topics/topic-page-eating-disorders.shtml
This Web site, provided by the National Institute of Mental Health, supplies downloadable links to PDF files and booklets on a variety of mental health topics, including eating disorders.

http://www.nimh.nih.gov/topics/topic-page-eating-disorders.shtml
The Web site for the National Eating Disorders Association, an excellent source of resource information and support

http://www.eating-disorder.com
This site contains discussion of symptoms, support groups, and links to other sites to explore the eating disorders.

http://www.something-fishy.org
A major site on all eating disorders including descriptions, diagnosis, and treatments.

Mainstream Films

Films relevant to Chapter 11 material are listed and summarized below.

Key to Film Listings:
P = psychopathology focus
T = treatment focus
E = ethical issues raised

Please note that some of the films suggested may have graphic sexual or violent content due to the nature of certain subject matter.

The Best Little Girl in the World
From 1986, this film poignantly portrays a young woman's struggle with anorexia nervosa. **P, T, serious film**

Girl, Interrupted
Based on an autobiographical novel by Susanna Kaysen, this film details the experiences of several women as patients in a psychiatric hospital in the 1960s. The 1999 film challenges the diagnosis of mental illness and the relationship between diagnosis and social norm violations. **P, T, serious film**

I Don't Buy Kisses Anymore
This 1991 film stars Jason Alexander as a store owner with a compulsive eating disorder. **P, comedy/serious film**

Requiem for a Dream
From 2000, this film addresses the multiple addictions of a boy, his girlfriend, his buddy, and his mother (including food and diet pills). **P, serious film**

Other Films:

The Nutty Professor (1996 remake) eating disorder. **P, T, comedy**

Comer Video Segments

Available as a supplement, this revised set of videotapes contains short clips depicting various topics related to abnormal psychology. Please see the accompanying Video Guide for specific clips linked to Chapter 11.

Recommendations for Purchase or Rental

The Comer Video Segments include excerpts from many superb clinical documentaries. While the segments alone are ideal for use in lectures, it often is useful to assign the entire documentary for special class screenings or library use by students. The following videos and other media are available for purchase or rental and appropriate for use in class or for assignment outside of class.

An Anorexic's Tale: The Brief Life of Catherine
Battling Eating Disorders
Eating Disorders: Mind, Body, and Society
Eating Disorders: New Approaches to Treatment
Eating Disorders: The Inner Voice
Films for the Humanities and Sciences
P.O. Box 2053, Princeton, NJ 08543
1-800-257-5126
ffh.films.com

Eating Disorders: When Food Hurts
I Don't Have to Hide
Inside Out: Stories of Bulimia
Shadows and Lies: The Unseen Battle of
Eating Disorders
Cut
Gorgeous
Made Over in America
Fanlight Productions
4196 Washington St., Suite 2
Boston, MA 02131
1-800-937-4113
http://www.fanlight.com/

Slender Existence
Filmakers Library
124 East 40th Street
New York, NY 10016
1-212-808-4980

Slim Hopes
Media Education Foundation
26 Center Street
Northampton, MA 01060
1-413-586-4170

CLASS DEMONSTRATIONS AND ACTIVITIES

Case Study

Present a case study to the class.

Panel Discussion

Have students volunteer (or assign them) to portray mental health "workers" from different theoretical perspectives in a panel discussion. Each student should present the main explanation and treatment for the eating disorders from his or her theoretical perspective. Students in the audience can ask questions of the panelists. Additionally, other students can role-play patients suffering from particular eating disorders. [NOTE: A brief reminder about sensitivity and professionalism is useful here.] Have the panelists attempt to diagnose, based on their theoretical orientation.

Group Work: Cultural Attitudes and Food

Have the class form small groups and develop an example of contradictory cultural or familial attitudes with respect to food and eating behavior. That is, ask groups to come up with extreme or dramatic differences in attitudes between two cultures or families. Have groups present their findings. Discuss how these may influence eating-disordered behavior.

Calculating BMI

The best way to determine whether weight is reasonable is to calculate the body mass index (BMI). BMI equals one's weight in kilograms divided by one's height in meters squared (kg/m^2). (There are several reliable BMI calculators available free of charge online.) Allow the students some time to calculate their own BMIs. It will be necessary to provide conversion formulas for pounds to kilograms and inches to meters. Write the following on the board:

BMI	Classification
17.5	cutoff for anorexia nervosa
<18	severely underweight
18–20	slightly underweight
20–25	optimal for health
25–27	slightly overweight
>30	obese

The typical reaction to these figures, which are based on scientific, longitudinal research, is skepticism. Students are often skeptical that a BMI can be considered healthy, given that the person "looks fat." This is an extremely useful way to jump-start a discussion on the attitudes of Americans toward weight; that is, Americans are more concerned about weight with respect to appearance than about weight with respect to health.

Ideal Female Body

To emphasize the changes in the ideal female body image, you can bring in pictures of women considered to embody the ideal in various eras. Good examples are a painting by Reubens; any screen idol of the 1950s (e.g., Marilyn Monroe), whose bust and hips swelled from a tiny waist; the emaciated model Twiggy of the 1960s; and Kate Moss today.

The Anonymous Five-Minute Essay

Ask students to develop a list of assumptions they make when they see a thin person or a fat person. What do the students assume about the person based solely on body type? Read some of these stereotypes and open the class to discussion. Be careful not to offend anyone in the class.

What Effect Does Dieting Have?

Dieting makes one hungry and predisposes one to binge-eat, which predisposes one to feel guilty and either try to purge the food (e.g., vomit) or expunge it through even more dieting, setting up a vicious cycle. In short, dieting declares war on food, a biological necessity, and encourages one to conclude that food is the enemy and must be avoided at all costs (e.g., anorexia nervosa) or that any admission of food into the body must be counteracted (e.g., purging). While leading a general discussion on the effects of dieting, bring up the following two studies. A sample of 15-year-old schoolgirls in London was divided into dieters and nondieters; of the dieters, 21 percent developed an eating disorder within the subsequent year, compared to about 3 percent of the nondieters. In a different study of 1,033 twins, researchers found that dieting status predicted subsequent diagnosis of bulimia nervosa over a 3-year follow-up period.

"Here's $25,000 to be awarded to . . ."

Related to the previous activity, divide the class into groups and have them create school-based programs to encourage girls to resist the messages they are exposed to every day that are pressuring them to be thin and to dislike their bodies. Have the groups present their ideas, then have a class vote to see which group receives the grant to implement their idea.

"Pretend, for a moment, that you are a counselor."

Divide students into groups. Ask them to imagine that they are counselors seeing patients with anorexia nervosa. Ask them to develop an effective therapy. How would they proceed? After five minutes or so, change the presenting problem to bulimia nervosa. Now how would they proceed? Do groups favor cognitive or behavioral approaches? Do the disorders require similar or different approaches? Why? Use this as a lead-in to a discussion of therapies and treatments for these disorders, pointing out that forced feeding is often necessary with anorexia nervosa; that is, reasoning with the person simply does not work.

SUGGESTED TOPICS FOR DISCUSSION

"Not for Women Only"

Using the chapter as a platform [See text p. 335], discuss the rising incidence of eating disorders in men. Which of the possible explanations strikes students as the most probable?

Open Discussion: Twin Studies and Weight

A research study analyzed weight and height records from a Swedish sample of 247 identical twin pairs and 426 fraternal twin pairs. The investigators found that identical twin siblings ended up with similar body weights whether or not they were raised in the same home, whereas childhood environment did not strongly affect body weight. Lead a discussion on the implications of this study. What does it say about dieting and trying to lose weight? Point out that many persons are well over their set weight and should attempt to lose weight, but that deciding what one's body should look like without regard to what one's body "wants" may set one up for extreme frustration and eating-disordered behavior.

Advertising

The message implicit in all advertising is "never be satisfied." If consumers can be convinced that the way they look or the way they are is inadequate, then they will be more likely to buy products that help them be the way they want to be. It has been estimated that the average person sees between 400 and 600 ads per day, and it is estimated that 1 in 11 ads include a direct message about beauty. Ask the class whether these might have anything to do with the finding that most young women in the United States are dissatisfied with their bodies (i.e., consider themselves overweight). Discuss the Dove "Campaign for Real Beauty" advertising.

Open Discussion: Why More Women Than Men?

Judith Rodin coined the term "normative discontent" to describe women's pervasive dissatisfaction with their bodies. Forty-five percent of U.S. households have someone currently on a diet; 55 percent of females between the ages of 25 and 54 are currently "dieting," and a study in California found that 80 percent of fourth-grade girls are currently dieting or have in the past dieted. Most (63 percent) females say their weight affects how they feel about themselves. Ask groups or the whole class to discuss why women are

particularly vulnerable to eating disorders (e.g., beauty ideals apply more to women than to men; boys are praised for doing and excelling, whereas girls are praised for how they look).

ASSIGNMENTS/EXTRA CREDIT SUGGESTIONS

"Write a Pamphlet"

With the use of a software program like Microsoft Publisher or simply paper and markers, students can create a pamphlet on one or all of the eating disorders (anorexia, bulimia, and/or binge-eating disorder). Students should be encouraged to be as accurate and up-to-date as possible and to present all sides of the disorder (e.g., alternate treatment approaches or theories).

Keep a Journal

In addition to helping students synthesize material, this activity is helpful in developing writing skills. Have students keep a journal of their thoughts on the course material throughout the semester. This can be done in the first or last five minutes of class or as an out-of-class assignment. Faculty generally should have students submit their journals for review on an on-going basis since students can tend to delay writing until the end of the semester. Some suggestions for journal topics include: reactions to the case examples; strengths and weaknesses of prevailing theoretical explanations; hypothetical conversations with sufferers of specific disorders, etc.

Food and the Media

In preparation for the next class, ask students to analyze messages (implicit and explicit) from television, popular magazines, newspapers, and tabloids about food. Some students can contrast food ads on prime-time TV and on children's TV shows. Others can evaluate whether food is sold as a biological necessity or as a reward, a status symbol, or as a way to fulfill a psychological need. Others can evaluate types of manipulations used to lure the potential customer into buying specific foods. Lead an open discussion on the findings during the next class.

Diets

Ask students to collect diet articles in popular magazines. Additionally, ask them to find some very old examples; these might be found in your school library. On an overhead transparency, analyze the advice, the quality, and the emotional tone of current and older diets. Ask students to discuss the differences between the two types as listed on the overhead. Do the students think the current approach is more effective?

Abnormal Psychology Student Tool Kit Video Questions

As a homework assignment, have students watch a video clip and answer the accompanying questions. Students can answer the questions directly into the online assessment feature. The results of these quizzes report to the site's built-in grade book.

Web Site Quiz

For homework or extra credit, have students complete the quiz for Chapter 11 located on the companion Web site. Students can complete an online test of the key chapter material (using questions NOT from the test bank) and have their scores e-mailed directly to the course instructor.

Essay Topics

For homework or extra credit, have students write an essay addressing one (or more) of the following topics:

(1) Compare and contrast anorexia nervosa and bulimia nervosa. What are the main similarities and differences? Do you think that either disorder is common on your campus?

(2) What are your thoughts and opinions on the Western beauty standard as described in the chapter (and PsychWatch, text p. 333)? Do you think the media are responsible for the increase in eating disorders? If so, what can be done to change the situation?

(3) Read Obesity: To Lose or Not to Lose in PsychWatch, p. 328 in the text, and discuss the obesity issue. What are the relevant factors.

Research Topics

For homework or extra credit, have students write a research report addressing one (or more) of the following topics:

(1) Conduct a "Psych Info" search and write an annotated bibliography on treatments for eating disorders. What are the major treatment variables that are compared? Are researchers studying different populations?

(2)   Research and report on famous examples of people with eating disorders. Aside from their eating disorders, what else did these people have in common?

(3)   Research and report on men with eating disorders. Are there any articles in the psychological literature that specifically deal with this population?

(4)   Research the proposals by the DSM-5 Task Force. What are the Feeding Disorders that they propose to include?

Case Study Evaluations

To complement the Comer and Gorenstein supplemental case study text, case study evaluations have been created. Students can be assigned the appropriate case study and evaluation as homework or for class discussion. While case study evaluation questions are listed in their entirety on the companion Web site at www.worthpublishers.com/comer, the relevant case studies follow.

Case Study 9: Bulimia Nervosa

Case Study—You Decide

The Comer and Gorenstein supplement case study text offers three cases in which patients are neither diagnosed nor treated. These cases provide students with the opportunity to identify disorders and suggest appropriate therapies. Throughout each case, students are asked to consider a number of issues and to arrive at various decisions, including diagnostic and treatment decisions. The case study relevant to Chapter 11 is referenced below.

You Decide: The Case of Julia, Excessive Weight Loss

Web-Based Case Study Evaluations

Nine Web-based case studies have been created and posted on the companion Web site. These cases describe each individual's history and symptoms and are accompanied by a series of guided questions that point to the precise DSM-IV-TR criteria for each disorder. Students can both identify the disorder and suggest a course of treatment. Students can be assigned the appropriate case study and questions as homework or for class discussion. The cases relevant to Chapter 11 follow.

The Case of Carrie: Anorexia Nervosa

The Case of Laura: Bulimia Nervosa

Crossword Puzzles

As a homework assignment or for extra credit, have students complete and submit Crossword Puzzle #11.

Word Searches

As a homework assignment or for extra credit, have students complete and submit Word Search #11.

Substance-Related Disorders

TOPIC OVERVIEW

LECTURE OUTLINE

I. **SUBSTANCE-RELATED DISORDERS**
    A. What is a drug?
        1. Any substance other than food that affects our bodies or minds
            a. Need not be a medicine or be illegal
    B. Current language uses the term *substance* rather than *drug* to overtly include alcohol, tobacco, and caffeine
    C. Substances may cause *temporary* changes in behavior, emotion, or thought
        1. May result in substance *intoxication* (literally, "poisoning"), a temporary state of poor judgment, mood changes, irritability, slurred speech, and poor coordination
        2. Some substances such as LSD may produce a particular form of intoxication, sometimes call *hallucinosis*, which consists of perceptual distortion and hallucinations
    D. Some substances also can produce *long-term* problems [See Table 12-1, text p.348]
        1. Substance abuse: A pattern of behavior where a person relies on a drug excessively and chronically, damaging relationships, affecting work functioning, and/or putting self or others in danger
        2. Substance dependence: A more advanced pattern of use where a person abuses a drug and centers his or her life around it
            a. Also called *addiction*
            b. May include *tolerance* (need increasing doses to get an effect) and *withdrawal* (unpleasant and dangerous symptoms when substance use is stopped or cut down)
    E. About 9 percent of all teens and adults in the United States display substance abuse or dependence
        1. The highest rates of substance abuse or dependence in the United States is found among Native Americans (15.5 percent), while the lowest is among Asian Americans (3.5 percent)
        2. White Americans, Hispanic Americans, and African Americans display rates between 9 and 10 percent
        3. Only 11 percent receive treatment from a mental health professional
    F. Many drugs are available in our society
        1. Some are harvested from nature, others derived from natural substances, and still others are produced in a laboratory
        2. Some require a physician's prescription for legal use; others, like alcohol and nicotine, are legally available to adults
        3. Still others, like heroin, are illegal under all circumstances
    G. Recent statistics suggest that drug use is a significant social problem
        1. Twenty two million people in the United States have used an illegal substance within the past month
        2. Almost 24 percent of all high school seniors have used an illegal drug within the past month
    H. There are several categories of substances under use and study:
        1. Depressants
        2. Stimulants
        3. Hallucinogens
        4. Cannabis
        5. Polydrug use

II. **DEPRESSANTS**
    A. Depressants slow the activity of the central nervous system (CNS)
        1. Reduce tension and inhibitions
        2. May interfere with judgment, motor activity, and concentration
    B. Three most widely used:
        1. Alcohol
        2. Sedative-hypnotic drugs

3. Opioids
C. Alcohol
   1. The World Health Organization estimates that 2 billion people worldwide consume alcohol
   2. In the United States, more than half of all residents drink alcoholic beverages from time to time
   3. When people consume five or more drinks in a single occasion, it is called a binge-drinking episode
      a. 24 percent of all people in the United States over age 11, most of them male, binge-drink each month
   4. Nearly 7 percent of people over age 11 binge-drink at least 5 times each month
      a. Considered heavy drinkers, males outnumber females by more than 2:1 (approximately 8 percent to 4 percent)
   5. All alcoholic beverages contain ethyl alcohol
      a. It is absorbed into the blood through stomach lining and takes effect in the bloodstream and CNS
         (a) Short-term, alcohol blocks messages between neurons—alcohol helps GABA (an inhibitory messenger) shut down neurons and relax the drinker
         (b) First brain area affected is that which controls judgment and inhibition
         (c) Next affected are additional areas in the cenral nervous system, leaving the drinker even less able to make sound judgments, speak clearly, and remember well
         (d) Motor difficulties increase as drinking continues, and reaction times slow
   6. The extent of the effect of ethyl alcohol is determined by its concentration (proportion) in the blood
      a. A given amount of alcohol will have less effect on a large person than on a small one
      b. Gender also affects blood alcohol concentration
         (a) Women have less alcohol dehydrogenase, an enzyme in the stomach, which metabolizes alcohol before it enters the blood
         (b) Women become more intoxicated than men on equal doses of alcohol
      c. Levels of impairment are closely tied to the concentration of ethyl alcohol in the blood:
         (a) BAC = 0.06: Relaxation and comfort
         (b) BAC = 0.09: Intoxication
         (c) BAC > 0.55: Death
            (i) Most people lose consciousness before they can drink this much
   7. The effects of alcohol subside only after alcohol is metabolized by the liver
      a. The average rate of this metabolism is 25 percent of an ounce per hour
         (a) You can't increase the speed of this process!
   8. Alcohol abuse and dependence
      a. Though legal, alcohol is one of the most dangerous recreational drugs
         (a) Its effects can extend across the life span
         (b) Alcohol use is a major problem in high school, college, and adulthood
         (c) In any given year, 6.6 percent of the world's population fall into a long-term pattern of abuse or dependence
            (i) 13.2 percent experience one of the patterns sometime during their lives
         (d) 7.4 percent of all adults in the U.S. display an alcohol use disorder over a one-year period, while over 13 percent display it at some point in their lives
            (i) Men outnumber women 2:1
         (e) The prevalence of alcoholism in a given year is about the same (7 to 9 percent) for white Americans, African Americans, and Hispanic Americans
            (i) The men in these groups show strikingly different age patterns
         (f) Generally, Asians have lower rates of alcohol disorders than people from other cultures
            (i) As many as one-half of these individuals have a deficiency of alcohol dehydrogenase, causing a negative reaction to even modest alcohol intake

9. Alcohol abuse
   a. In general, people who abuse alcohol drink large amounts regularly and rely on it to enable them to do things that would otherwise make them anxious
      (a) Eventually, the drinking interferes with social behavior and the ability to think and work
   b. Individuals, patterns of alcohol abuse vary
10. Alcohol dependence
    a. For many people, the pattern of alcohol misuse includes dependence
       (a) They build up a physiological tolerance and need to drink greater amounts to feel its effects
       (b) They may experience withdrawal when they stop drinking, including nausea and vomiting
       (c) A small percentage of alcohol-dependent people experience a dramatic and dangerous withdrawal syndrome known as delirium tremens ("the DTs"), which can be fatal
11. What is the personal and social impact of alcoholism?
    a. Alcoholism destroys families, social relationships, and careers
       (a) Losses to society total many billions of dollars annually
       (b) Alcohol plays a role in suicides, homicides, assaults, rapes, and accidents
       (c) Has serious effects on the children (some 30 million) of persons with this disorder
12. Long-term excessive drinking also can seriously damage physical health
    a. Especially damaged is the liver (cirrhosis)
    b. Long-term excessive drinking also can cause major nutritional problems
       (a) Example: Korsakoff's syndrome
13. Women who drink alcohol during pregnancy place their fetuses at risk from fetal alcohol syndrome (FAS) and increased risk of miscarriage

D. Sedative-hypnotic drugs
   1. Sedative-hypnotic (anxiolytic) drugs produce feelings of relaxation and drowsiness
      a. At low doses, they have a calming or sedative effect
      b. At high doses, they function as sleep inducers or hypnotics
      c. The sedative-hypnotic drugs include barbiturates and benzodiazepines
   2. Barbiturates
      a. First discovered more than 100 years ago, barbiturates were widely prescribed in the first half of the twentieth century to fight anxiety and to help people sleep
         (a) Although still prescribed, they have been largely replaced by benzodiazepines
         (b) They can cause many problems, not the least of which are abuse, dependence, and overdose
      b. Barbiturates usually are taken in pill or capsule form
         (a) At low doses, they reduce excitement in a manner similar to alcohol, by attaching to the GABA receptors and helping GABA operate
         (b) Also similar to alcohol, barbiturates are metabolized by the liver
      c. At too high a level, they can halt breathing, lower blood pressure, and can lead to coma and death
      d. Repeated use of barbiturates can quickly result in a pattern of abuse and/or dependence
      e. A great danger of barbiturate dependence is that the lethal dose of the drug remains the same, even while the body is building a tolerance for the sedative effects
      f. Barbiturate withdrawal is particularly dangerous because it can cause convulsions
   3. Benzodiazepines
      a. Benzodiazepines often are prescribed to relieve anxiety
         (a) They are the popular sedative-hypnotics available
         (b) The class includes Xanax, Ativan, and Valium
      b. These drugs have a depressant effect on the central nervous system by binding to GABA receptors and increasing GABA activity

        c.   Unlike barbiturates and alcohol, however, benzodiazepines relieve anxiety without causing drowsiness
            (a)   They are also less likely to slow breathing and lead to death by overdose
        d.   Once thought to be a safe alternative to other sedative-hypnotic drugs, benzodiazepine use can cause intoxication and lead to abuse and dependence
            (a)   As many as 1 percent of U.S. adults abuse or become physically dependent on benzodiazepines at some point in their lives

E.   Opioids
    1.   This class of drug includes both natural (opium, heroin, morphine, codeine) and synthetic (methadone) compounds and is known collectively as "narcotics"
    2.   Narcotics are smoked, inhaled, injected by needle just under the skin ("skin popped"), or injected directly into the bloodstream ("mainlined")
        a.   Injection seems to be the most common method of use, although other techniques have been increasing in recent years
        b.   An injection quickly brings on a "rush"—a spasm of warmth and ecstasy that sometimes is compared with orgasm
        c.   This spasm is followed by several hours of pleasurable feelings (called a "high" or "nod")
    3.   Opioids create these effects by depressing the CNS
        a.   These drugs attach to the receptors in the brain ordinarily receiving endorphins (neurotransmitters that naturally help relieve pain and decrease emotional tension)
        b.   When these sites receive opioids, they produce pleasurable and calming feelings just as endorphins do
        c.   In addition to reducing pain and tension, opioids can cause nausea, narrowing of the pupils, and constipation
    4.   Heroin abuse and dependence
        a.   Heroin use exemplifies the problems posed by opioids:
            (a)   After just a few weeks, users may become caught in a pattern of abuse (and often dependence)
            (b)   Users quickly build a tolerance for the drug and experience withdrawal when they stop taking it
            (c)   Early withdrawal symptoms include anxiety and restlessness; later symptoms include twitching, aches, fever, vomiting, diarrhea, and weight loss from dehydration
            (d)   People who are dependent on heroin soon need the drug just to avoid experiencing withdrawal, and they must continually increase their doses in order to achieve even that relief
            (e)   Many users must turn to criminal activity to support their "habit" and avoid withdrawal symptoms
        b.   Surveys suggest that close to 1 percent of adults in the United States become addicted to heroin or other opioids at some time in their lives
        c.   What are the dangers of heroin abuse?
            (a)   The most immediate danger is overdose
            (b)   The drug closes down the respiratory center in the brain, paralyzing breathing and causing death
                (i)   Death is particularly likely during sleep
            (c)   Ignorance of tolerance also is a problem
            (d)   About 2 percent of folks dependent on heroin and other opioids die under the influence of the drug per year
            (e)   Users run the risk of getting impure drug
            (f)   Opioids often are "cut" with noxious chemicals
            (g)   Dirty needles and other equipment can spread infection

III. STIMULANTS
    A.   Stimulants are substances that increase the activity of the central nervous system CNS
        1.   They cause an increase in blood pressure, heart rate, and alertness

2. They cause rapid behavior and thinking
3. The four most common stimulants are cocaine, amphetamines, caffeine, and nicotine

B. Cocaine
1. Derived from the leaves of the coca plant, cocaine is the most powerful natural stimulant known
   a. 28 million people in the United States have tried cocaine
      (a) 1.6 million people are using it currently
2. Cocaine produces a euphoric rush of well-being and confidence
   a. The drug seems to work by increasing dopamine at key receptors in the brain by preventing the neurons that release dopamine from reabsorbing it
      (a) It also appears to increase norepinephrine and serotonin
   b. High doses of cocaine can produce mania, paranoia, and impaired judgment, known as *cocaine intoxication*
      (a) Some people also experience hallucinations and/or delusions, a condition known as *cocaine-induced psychotic disorder*
   c. As the stimulant effects of the drug subside, the user experiences a depression-like letdown, popularly called "crashing"
3. Cocaine abuse and dependence
   a. Regular use may lead to a pattern of abuse in which the person remains under its effects much of the day each day and functions poorly in social relationships and at work
   b. Dependence on the drug also may develop
   c. Cocaine use historically was limited by the drug's cost:
      (a) Since 1984, cheaper, more powerful versions of the drug have become available, including:
         (i) A "freebase" form where the drug is heated and inhaled with a pipe
         (ii) "Crack," a powerful form of freebase that has been boiled down for smoking in a pipe
      (b) Currently, 0.5 percent of all people in the United States over the age of 11 manifest cocaine abuse or dependence in a given year
4. What are the dangers of cocaine?
   a. Aside from its behavioral effects, cocaine poses significant physical danger
   b. The greatest danger of use is the risk of overdose
      (a) Excessive doses depress the respiratory center of the brain and stop breathing
      (b) Cocaine use also can cause heart failure
      (c) Pregnant women who use cocaine have an increased likelihood of miscarriage and of having children with abnormalities

C. Amphetamines
1. Amphetamines are stimulant drugs that are manufactured in the laboratory
   a. Most often taken in pill or capsule form
   b. Some people inject the drugs intravenously or smoke them for a quicker, more powerful effect
2. Like cocaine, amphetamines:
   a. Increase energy and alertness and reduce when taken in small doses
   b. Produce a rush, intoxication, and psychosis in high doses
   c. Cause an emotional letdown as they leave the body
3. Also like cocaine, amphetamines stimulate the CNS by increasing dopamine, norepinephrine, and serotonin
4. Tolerance builds quickly so users are at great risk of becoming dependent
5. When people dependent on the drug stop taking it, serious depression and extended sleep follow
   a. Approximately 1.5 to 2 percent of Americans become dependent on amphetamines at some point in their lives
6. One kind of amphetamine, methamphetamine (meth), has had a major surge in popularity in recent years
   a. Almost 6 percent of all persons over the age of 11 in the United States have used this stimulant at least once

            b.   Most of the nonmedical meth is made in "stovetop laboratories"

            c.   Meth is about as likely to be used by women as men and has gained popularity as a "club drug"

    D.   Caffeine

        1.   Caffeine is the world's most widely used stimulant

            a.   Around 80 percent of the world's population consumes it daily

                (a)   Most is in the form of coffee; the rest is in the form of tea, cola, energy drinks, chocolate, and over-the-counter medications

            b.   Around 99 percent of ingested caffeine is absorbed by the body and reaches its peak concentration within an hour

                (a)   It acts as a stimulant in the CNS, producing a release of dopamine, serotonin, and norepinphrine in the brain

            c.   More than 2 to 3 cups of brewed coffee can lead to caffeine intoxication

                (a)   Seizures and respiratory failure can occur at doses greater than 10 grams of caffeine (about 100 cups of coffee)

        2.   Most people who suddenly stop or cut back their usual intake experience withdrawal symptoms, including headaches, depression, anxiety, and fatigue

            a.   Studies suggest correlations between high doses of caffeine and heart rhythm irregularities, high cholesterol levels, and risk of heart attacks

            b.   High doses during pregnancy also increase the risk of miscarriage

IV. HALLUCINOGENS, CANNABIS, AND COMBINATIONS OF SUBSTANCES

    A.   Other kinds of substances may also cause problems for users and for society:

        1.   Hallucinogens

            a.   Produce delusions, hallucinations, and other sensory changes

        2.   Cannabis substances

            a.   Produce sensory changes, but have both depressant and stimulant effects

        3.   Combinations of substances = Polysubstance use

    B.   Hallucinogens

        1.   Hallucinogens, also known as *psychedelics*, produce powerful changes in sensory perceptions (sometimes called "trips")

            a.   Include both natural hallucinogens:

                (a)   Mescaline

                (b)   Psilocybin

            b.   And laboratory-produced hallucinogens:

                (a)   Lysergic acid diethylamide (LSD)

                (b)   MDMA (Ecstasy)

        2.   LSD is one of the most famous and powerful hallucinogens

            a.   Within two hours of being swallowed, LSD brings on a state of hallucinogen intoxication (hallucinosis)

                (a)   Increased and altered sensory perception

                    (i)   Hallucinations may occur

                    (ii)   The drug may cause different senses to cross, an effect called *synesthia*

                (b)   May induce extremely strong emotions

                (c)   May have some physical effects

                (d)   Effects wear off in about six hours

        3.   LSD produces these symptoms by binding to serotonin receptors

            a.   These neurons help control visual information and emotions, thereby explaining the various effects of the drug on the user

        4.   More than 14 percent of Americans have used hallucinogens at some point in their lives

        5.   Tolerance and withdrawal are rare, but the drugs do pose dangers:

            a.   Users may experience a "bad trip"—the experience of enormous perceptual, emotional, and behavioral reactions

            b.   Another danger is the risk of "flashbacks"

                (a)   Can occur days or months after last drug use

    C.   Cannabis

        1.   The drugs produced from varieties of the hemp plant are, as a group, called *cannabis*

a. They include:
    (a) Hashish, the solidified resin of the cannabis plant
    (b) Marijuana, a mixture of buds, crushed leaves, and flowering tops
2. The major active ingredient in cannabis is tetrahydrocannabinol or THC
    a. The greater the THC content, the more powerful the drug
3. When smoked, cannabis produces a mixture of hallucinogenic, depressant, and stimulant effects
    a. At low doses, the user feels joy and relaxation
        (a) May become anxious, suspicious, or irritated
        (b) This overall "high" is technically called *cannabis intoxication*
    b. At high doses, cannabis produces odd visual experiences, changes in body image, and hallucinations
    c. Most of the effects of cannabis last two to six hours
        (a) Mood changes may continue longer
4. Marijuana abuse and dependence
    a. Once believed not to cause abuse or dependence, today many users are caught in a pattern of abuse
    b. Some users develop tolerance and withdrawal, experiencing flu-like symptoms, restlessness, and irritability when drug use is stopped
        (a) About 1.7 percent of people in the United States displayed marijuana abuse or dependence in the past year
        (b) Between 4 and 5 percent will fall into these patterns at some point in their lives
    c. One theory to explain the increase in abuse and dependence is the change in the drug itself
        (a) The marijuana available today is much more potent (by as many as four times) than the drug used in the early 1970s
5. Is marijuana dangerous?
    a. As the strength and use of the drug has increased, so have the risks of using it
        (a) Similar to hallucinosis, marijuana users may panic as a result of marijuana intoxication
        (b) Because of its sensorimotor effects, marijuana has been implicated in accidents
        (c) Marijuana use has been linked to poor concentration and impaired memory
    b. Long-term use poses additional dangers:
        (a) May cause respiratory problems and lung cancer
        (b) May affect reproduction:
            (i) In males, it may lower sperm count
            (ii) In women, abnormal ovulation has been found
6. Cannabis and Society: A rocky relationship
    a. For centuries, cannabis played a respected role in medicine, but its use fell out of favor and was criminalized
    b. In the late 1980s, several interest groups campaigned for the medical legalization of marijuana
    c. The U.S. federal government has continued to fight and punish the production and distribution of marijuana for medical purposes
        (a) However, in 2009, the U.S. Attorney General directed federal prosecutors to not pursue cases against medical marijuana users complying with state laws
        (b) Both the Netherlands and Canada permit its use
D. Combinations of substances
1. People often take more than one drug at a time, a pattern called *polysubstance use*
2. Researchers have studied the ways in which drugs interact with one another, focusing on cross-tolerance and synergistic effects
    a. Cross-tolerance
        (a) Sometimes, two or more drugs are so similar in their actions on the brain and body that as people build a tolerance for one drug, they are simultaneously developing a tolerance for the other (even if they have never taken it)

             (b)   Users who display this cross-tolerance can reduce the symptoms of withdrawal from one drug by taking the other
                 (i)   Examples: alcohol and benzodiazepines

       b.   Synergistic effects
             (a)   When different drugs are in the body at the same time, they may multiply or potentiate each other's effects
             (b)   This combined impact is called a *synergistic effect* and is often greater than the sum of the effects of each drug taken alone
             (c)   One kind of synergistic effect occurs when two or more drugs have similar actions
                 (i)   Examples: alcohol, barbiturates, benzodiazepines, and opioids
                     1.   All are depressants, and they may severely depress the CNS when mixed, leading to death
             (d)   A different kind of synergistic effect results when drugs have opposite (antagonistic) actions
                 (i)   Examples: stimulants or cocaine with barbiturates or alcohol
                     1.   May build up lethal levels of the drugs because of metabolic issues (stimulants impede the liver's processing of barbiturates and alcohol)

       c.   Each year, tens of thousands of people are admitted to hospitals because of polysubstance use
             (a)   May be accidental or intentional
             (b)   As many as 90 percent of people who use one illegal drug also are using another to some extent

V.   WHAT CAUSES SUBSTANCE-RELATED DISORDERS?
    A.   Clinical theorists have developed sociocultural, psychological, and biological explanations for substance abuse and dependence
       1.   No single explanation has gained broad support
       2.   The best explanation is *a combination* of factors
    B.   Sociocultural Views
       1.   A number of theorists propose that people are more likely to develop patterns of substance abuse or dependence when living in stressful socioeconomic conditions
           a.   Example: Higher rates of unemployment correlate with higher rates of alcohol use
           b.   Example: People of lower SES have higher rates of substance use in general
       2.   Other theorists propose that substance abuse and dependence are more likely to appear in families and social environments where substance use is valued or accepted
           a.   Example: Rates of alcohol use vary among cultures
    C.   Psychodynamic Views
       1.   Psychodynamic theorists believe that people who abuse substances have powerful dependency needs that can be traced to their early years
           a.   Caused by a lack of parental nurturing
           b.   Some people may develop a "substance abuse personality" as a result
       2.   Limited research does link early impulsivity to later substance use, but it is confounded, and researchers cannot presently conclude that any one personality trait or group of traits stands out in substance-related disorders
    D.   Cognitive-Behavioral Views
       1.   According to behaviorists, operant conditioning may play a key role in substance abuse
           a.   They argue that the temporary reduction of tension produced by a drug has a rewarding effect, thus increasing the likelihood that the user will seek this reaction again
           b.   Similarly, the rewarding effects also may lead users to try higher doses or more powerful methods of ingestion
       2.   Cognitive theorists further argue that such rewards eventually produce an expectancy that substances will be rewarding, and this expectation is sufficient to motivate individuals to increase drug use at times of tension

3.   In support of these views, studies have found that many subjects do in fact drink more alcohol or seek heroin when they feel tense
   a.   In a manner of speaking, this model is arguing a "self-medication" hypothesis
   b.   If true, one would expect higher rates of substance use among people with psychological symptoms
      (a)   In fact, more than 22 percent of all adults who suffer from psychological disorders have been dependent on or abused alcohol or other substances within the past year
   c.   Other behaviorists have proposed that classical conditioning may play a role in substance abuse and dependence
      (a)   Objects presented at the time drugs are taken may act as classically conditioned stimuli and come to produce some of the pleasure brought on by the actual drugs
      (b)   Although classical conditioning may be at work, it has not received widespread research support as the *key* factor in such patterns
E.   Biological Views
   1.   In recent years, researchers have come to suspect that drug misuse may have biological causes
   2.   Studies on genetic predisposition and specific biochemical processes have provided some support for this model
      a.   Genetic predisposition
         (a)   Research with "alcohol-preferring" animals has demonstrated that offspring have similar alcohol preferences
         (b)   Similarly, research with human twins has suggested that people may inherit a predisposition to abuse substances
            (i)   Concordance rates in identical (MZ) twins = 54 percent
            (ii)   Concordance rates in fraternal (DZ) twins = 28 percent
         (c)   Stronger support for a genetic model may come from adoption studies
            (i)   Studies compared adoptees whose biological parents were dependent on alcohol with adoptees whose biological parents were not dependent
            (ii)   By adulthood, those whose biological parents were dependent showed higher rates of alcohol use themselves
         (d)   Genetic linkage strategies and molecular biology techniques provide more direct evidence in support of this hypothesis
            (i)   An abnormal form of the dopamine-2 (D2) receptor gene was found in the majority of subjects with alcohol or other substance dependence but in less than 20 percent of nondependent subjects
      b.   Biochemical factors
         (a)   Over the past few decades, investigators have pieced together a general biological understanding of drug tolerance and withdrawal, based on neurotransmitter functioning in the brain
            (i)   The specific neurotransmitter(s) affected depends on which drug is used
         (b)   Recent brain imaging studies have suggested that many (perhaps all) drugs eventually activate a reward center or "pleasure pathway" in the brain
            (i)   The reward center apparently extends from the brain area called the *ventral tegmental area* to the nucleus accumbens and on to the frontal cortex
               1.   The key NT appears to be dopamine
               2.   When dopamine is activated at this center, a person experiences pleasure
            (ii)   Certain drugs stimulate the reward center directly
               1.   Examples: cocaine, amphetamines, caffeine
            (iii)   Other drugs stimulate the reward center in roundabout ways
               1.   Examples: alcohol, opioids, and marijuana
         (c)   A number of theorists believe that when substances repeatedly stimulate the reward center, the center develops a hypersensitivity to the substances
            (i)   This theory, called the incentive-sensitization theory, has received considerable support in animal studies

(d) Theorists believe that people who abuse substances suffer from a reward-deficiency syndrome
(i) Their reward center is not readily activated by "normal" life events so they turn to drugs to stimulate this pleasure pathway, particularly in times of stress
(ii) Defects in D2 receptors have been cited as a possible cause

VI. HOW ARE SUBSTANCE-RELATED DISORDERS TREATED?

A. Many approaches have been used to treat substance-related disorders, including psychodynamic, behavioral, cognitive-behavioral, and biological, along with several sociocultural therapies
1. Although these treatments sometimes meet with great success, more often they are only moderately helpful
2. Today, treatments are typically used in combination on both an inpatient and outpatient basis
3. The value of treatment for substance abuse or dependence can be difficult to determine
a. Different substance-related disorders pose different problems
b. Many people with substance abuse patterns drop out of treatment early
c. Some people recover without any intervention at all
d. Different criteria are used by different clinical researchers
B. Psychodynamic therapies
1. Psychodynamic therapists first guide clients to uncover and work through the underlying needs and conflicts that they believe led to the disorder, then try to help them change their styles of living
2. Research has not found this model to be very effective
3. The model tends to be of greater help when combined with other approaches in a multidimensional treatment program
C. Behavioral therapies
1. A widely used behavioral treatment is aversion therapy, an approach based on classical conditioning principles
a. Individuals repeatedly are presented with an unpleasant stimulus at the very moment they are taking a drug
b. After repeated pairings, they are expected to react negatively to the substance itself and to lose their craving for it
2. Aversion therapy is most commonly applied to alcohol abuse/dependence
a. In one version, drinking behavior is paired with drug-induced nausea and vomiting
b. Another version of this approach requires people with alcoholism to imagine extremely upsetting, repulsive, or frightening scenes while they are drinking
c. The pairing is expected to produce negative responses to liquor itself
3. A behavioral approach successful in the short-term treatment of people who abuse cocaine and some other drugs is contingency management
a. This procedure makes incentives contingent on the submission of drug-free urine specimens
4. Behavioral interventions have usually had only limited success when used alone
a. They are best when used in combination with either biological or cognitive approaches
D. Cognitive-behavioral therapies
1. Cognitive-behavioral treatments for substance-related disorders help clients identify and change the patterns and cognitions contributing to their patterns of use
2. The most prominent of these approaches is relapse-prevention training
a. The overall goal is for clients to gain control over their substance-related behaviors
b. Clients are taught to identify and plan ahead for high-risk situations and to learn from mistakes and lapses
c. This approach is used particularly to treat alcohol use; also used to treat cocaine and marijuana abuse

E. Biological treatments
 1. Biological approaches may be used to help people withdraw from substances, abstain from them, or simply maintain their level of use without further increases
    a. These approaches are of limited success long-term when used alone but can be helpful when combined with other approaches
 2. Detoxification
    a. Systematic and medically supervised withdrawal from a drug
       (a) Can be outpatient or inpatient
    b. Two strategies:
       (a) Gradual withdrawal by tapering doses of the substance
       (b) Induce withdrawal but give additional medication to block symptoms
    c. Detoxification programs seem to help motivated people withdraw from drugs
       (a) For people who fail to receive psychotherapy after withdrawal, however, relapse rates tend to be high
 3. Antagonist drugs
    a. As an aid to resist falling back into a pattern of substance abuse or dependence, antagonist drugs block or change the effects of the addictive substance
       (a) Example: disulfiram (Antabuse) for alcohol
       (b) Example: naloxone for narcotics, naltrexone for alcohol
 4. Drug maintenance therapy
    a. A drug-related lifestyle may be a greater problem than the drug's direct effects
       (a) Example: heroin addiction
    b. Methadone maintenance programs are designed to provide a safe substitute for heroin
    c. Methadone is a laboratory opioid with a long half-life, taken orally once a day
    d. Roundly criticized as "substituting addictions" but regaining in popularity since the spread of HIV/AIDS
F. Sociocultural therapies
 1. Three main sociocultural approaches have been applied to substance-related disorders:
    a. Self-help and residential treatment programs
       (a) Most common: Alcoholics Anonymous (AA)
           (i) Offers peer support along with moral and spiritual guidelines to help people overcome alcoholism
           (ii) It is worth noting that the abstinence goal of AA directly opposes the controlled-drinking goal of relapse prevention training and several other interventions for substance misuse—this issue has been debated for years
       (b) Many self-help programs have expanded into residential treatment centers or therapeutic communities
       (c) People formerly dependent on drugs live, work, and socialize in a drug-free environment while undergoing individual, group, and family therapies
    b. Culture- and gender-sensitive programs
       (a) A growing number of treatment programs try to be sensitive to the special sociocultural pressures and problems faced by drug abusers who are poor, homeless, or members of ethnic minority groups
       (b) Similarly, therapists have become more aware that women often require treatment methods different from those designed for men
    c. Community prevention programs
       (a) Perhaps the most effective approach to substance-related disorders is to prevent them
       (b) Some prevention programs argue for total abstinence from drugs, while others teach responsible use
       (c) Prevention programs may focus on the individual, the family, the peer group, the school, or the community at large
       (d) The most effective of these prevention efforts focus on multiple areas to provide a consistent message about drug use in all areas of life

VII. CALL FOR CHANGE: DSM-5
   A. The DSM-5 Task Force proposed two key changes regarding the substance-related disorders:
     1. Change the name of the overall grouping to "Substance Use and Addictive Disorders"
       a. This terminology includes behavioral addictions
     2. Eliminate the distinction between substance abuse and substance dependence in favor of a combined category called "substance use disorder"

LEARNING OBJECTIVES

1. Distinguish among substance intoxication, substance abuse, and substance dependence.

2. Explain the terms *tolerance* and *withdrawal* and give examples.

3. Name some commonly used depressants, including alcohol, and explain their effects on the central nervous system.

4. Distinguish between two major sedative-hypnotic drugs—antianxiety drugs and barbiturates—and explain why barbiturate abuse is especially dangerous.

5. Know which drugs are opioids and be able to explain the effects of these drugs, including heroin.

6. Describe the typical effects of cocaine and contrast these with the effects of the other major stimulant, amphetamines.

7. Describe the general effects of the hallucinogen LSD.

8. Describe the short-term and long-term effects of cannabis use.

9. Describe, compare, and contrast the psychodynamic, behavioral, cognitive, biological, and sociocultural explanations of substance abuse; then discuss the therapies of each view.

10. Discuss the changes for these disorders proposed by the DSM-5 Task Force.

KEY TERMS

addiction
alcohol
alcohol dehydrogenase
Alcoholics Anonymous (AA)
alcoholism
amphetamine
antagonist drugs
aversion therapy
barbiturate
benzodiazepines
caffeine
cannabis drugs
cirrhosis
classical conditioning
cocaine

community prevention program
crack
crashing
cross-tolerance
culture-sensitive program
delirium tremens (DTs)
depressant
detoxification
disulfiram (Antabuse)
dopamine
dopamine-2 (D2) receptor gene
drug
endorphins

ethyl alcohol
fetal alcohol syndrome
flashback
free-base
GABA
hallucinogen
hallucinosis
hashish
heroin
intoxication
Korsakoff's syndrome
LSD (lysergic acid diethylamide)
marijuana
methadone

methadone maintenance program	polysubstance use	stimulant
methamphetamine	psychedelic drugs	substance
morphine	relapse-prevention training	substance abuse
narcotic	residential treatment center	substance dependence
opioid	reward center	synergistic effect
opium	reward-deficiency syndrome	synesthesia
polysubstance-related disorder	rush	tetrahydrocannabinol (THC)
	sedative-hypnotic drug	tolerance
	serotonin	withdrawal

MEDIA RESOURCES

Abnormal Psychology Student Tool Kit

Produced and edited by Ronald J. Comer, Princeton University and Gregory Comer, Princeton Academic Resources. Tied directly to the CyberStudy sections in the text, this Student Tool Kit offers 57 intriguing Video Cases running 3 to 7 minutes each. The Video Cases focus on persons affected by disorders discussed in the text. Students first view the video and then answer a series of thought-provoking questions. Additionally, the Student Tool Kit contains multiple-choice practice test questions with built-in instructional feedback for every option.

PowerPoint Slides

Available at the Instructor's site on the companion Web site are comprehensive PowerPoint slide presentations and supplemental student handouts for Chapter 12. The slide files reflect the main points of the chapter in significant detail. Student handouts were created using the instructor slides as a base, with key points replaced as "fill-in" items. Answer keys and suggestions for use also are provided.

DSM-IV-TR Masters

B-35, DSM-IV-TR Diagnostic Criteria for Substance Intoxication

B-35, DSM-IV-TR Diagnostic Criteria for Substance Withdrawal

B-36, DSM-IV-TR Diagnostic Criteria for Substance Abuse

B-37, DSM-IV-TR Diagnostic Criteria for Substance Dependence

Internet Sites

Please see Appendix A for full and comprehensive references. Sites relevant to Chapter 12 material are:

http://www.aa.org
A large site containing the history of Alcoholics Anonymous (AA), meeting sites and regional meetings, online meetings, and other resources.

http://www.al-anon.alateen.org
AL-ANON (and ALATEEN for younger members) is a worldwide organization that offers a self-help recovery program for families and friends of alcoholics, whether or not the alcoholic seeks help or even recognizes the existence of a drinking problem.

http://www.ccsa.ca/
(Canadian Centre on Substance Abuse)
The Canadian Centre on Substance Abuse is a nonprofit organization working to minimize the harm associated with the use of alcohol, tobacco, and other drugs.

http://www.higheredcenter.org/
The National Clearinghouse for Alcohol and Drug Information (NCADI) is the information service of the Center for Substance Abuse Prevention of the U.S. Department of Health & Human Services. NCADI is the world's largest resource for current information and materials concerning substance-abuse prevention.

http://www.nida.nih.gov/nidahome.html
National Institute on Drug Abuse Web site featuring informational links for students, young adults, parents, teachers, researchers, and health professionals.

http://www.nimh.nih.gov/health/publications
This Web site, provided by the National Institute of Mental Health, supplies downloadable links to PDF

files and booklets on a variety of mental health topics, including substance-related disorders.

http://www.abovetheinfluence.com/
Informational resource from the Youth Anti-Drug Media Campaign on illegal substances including club drugs, hallucinogens, heroin, rohypnol, and methamphetamines geared toward writers and feature journalists.

Mainstream Films

Films relevant to Chapter 12 material are listed and summarized below.

Key to Film Listings:
P = psychopathology focus
T = treatment focus
E = ethical issues raised

Please note that some of the films suggested may have graphic sexual or violent content due to the nature of certain subject matter.

Arthur
This 1981 classic stars Dudley Moore as an alcoholic millionaire with no ambition or pretense. **P, comedy**

Barfly
In this 1987 film, Mickey Rourke plays Henry Chinaski, a poet and alcoholic. **P, comedy/drama**

Bird
Directed by Clint Eastwood, this 1988 film portrays the story of jazz great Charlie Parker, including his drug use and compulsive eating. **P, serious film**

The Boost
From 1989, this intense film stars James Woods as a investment broker addicted to cocaine. **P, serious film**

Clean and Sober
From 1988, this film stars Michael Keaton as an alcoholic executive realizing he's "hit bottom" and entering a drug rehabilitation center. **P, T, serious film**

Crazy/Beautiful
This 2001 film stars Kirsten Dunst as a troubled, rebellious rich girl who abuses drugs and alcohol and is medicated for depression. Her romance with a boy from the wrong side of the tracks helps her put her life back together. **P, serious film**

Days of Wine & Roses
This 1962 film stars Jack Lemmon and Lee Remick as a middle-class family dealing with alcohol dependence. **P, serious film**

The Doors
This 1991 film stars Val Kilmer as Jim Morrison, a drug-addled rock star of the 1960s. **P, serious film**

Drugstore Cowboy
Starring Matt Dillon and set in the 1960s, this troubling film from 1989 details the actions of a gang of drug users. **P, T, serious film**

The Fisher King
This 1991 film follows Jack Lucas (Jeff Bridges), an irreverent radio talk show host who sinks into alcoholism after a tragedy. He is rescued by a delusional, homeless man (Robin Williams) on a quest for the Holy Grail. **P, serious film**

Lady Sings the Blues
Starring Diana Ross, this 1972 film depicts the story of Billie Holiday, a jazz singer whose career was cut short by drug addiction. **P, serious biopic**

Leaving Las Vegas
This 1995 film stars Nicolas Cage as a Hollywood screenwriter who has become an alcoholic. After being fired, he takes his severance pay to Las Vegas, where he plans to drink himself to death. **P, serious film**

Less Than Zero
This disturbing 1987 film portrays the drug use among a postcollege crowd in Los Angeles. **P, serious film**

Metallica: Some Kind of Monster
From 2004, this documentary follows the band as they record their *St. Anger* album and see an on-call psychiatrist to help with the growing tensions between band members. **P, T, documentary**

Permanent Midnight
From 1998, this fact-based film details the story of Jerry Stahl, a television writer suffering from drug addiction. **P, serious film**

Pollock
This film, from 2000, provides a fascinating look at the life of abstract expressionist (and substance-abuser) Jackson Pollock (1912–1956). **P, serious film**

Postcards from the Edge
Starring Meryl Streep and Shirley MacLaine, this 1990 film tells the story of Susanne Vale, a struggling Hollywood actress suffering from substance abuse problems. She moves from a stint in rehab to life with an alcoholic mother. **P, comedy/drama**

Requiem for a Dream
From 2000, this film addresses the multiple addictions of a boy, his girlfriend, his buddy, and his mother (including food and diet pills). **P, serious film**

The Rose
This film from 1979 stars Bette Midler as Mary Rose Foster, a character she based on the 1960s singer Janis Joplin who died of a drug overdose. **P, serious film**

Sid & Nancy
This 1986 film is a moving portrayal of the addicted lives and tragic deaths of Sex Pistols bassist, Sid Vicious, and his girlfriend/groupie Nancy Spungen. **P, serious film**

Sideways
This Oscar-winning film from 2004 follows Paul Giamati and Thomas Haden Church on an alcohol-fueled tour through wine country. **P, serious/comedic film**

A Star Is Born
This 1954 remake stars Judy Garland as a starlet whose husband (and manager) is devastated by alcohol abuse. **P, musical/serious film**

Trainspotting
This haunting 1996 film details the heroin culture in a group of Scottish youth. **P, serious film**

Walk the Line
This Academy award–winning film from 2005 stars Joaquin Phoenix as Johnny Cash and Reese Witherspoon as June Carter Cash in a chronicle of the country music singer's life.

When a Man Loves a Woman
This 1994 film stars Meg Ryan as a woman suffering from alcoholism and Andy Garcia as her husband. **P, serious film**

Other Films:

Easy Rider (1969) substance-related disorders. **P, commercial/serious film**
I'm Dancing As Fast As I Can (1982) substance dependence. **P, T, serious film**
Limitless (2011) drug dependence. **P, commercial film**
Lost Weekend (1945) alcohol dependence. **P, serious film**
Love Liza (2002) depression and substance abuse. **P, serious/art film**
Magnolia (1999) substance-related disorders. **P, serious film**
The Man with the Golden Arm (1955) substance dependence. **P, T, serious film**
Naked Lunch (1991) substance-related disorders. **P, hallucinogenic-type film, cult-classic**
Traffic (2000) substance-related disorders. **P, T, commercial/serious film**

Comer Video Segments

Available as a supplement, this revised set of videotapes contains short clips depicting various topics related to abnormal psychology. Please see the accompanying Video Guide for specific clips linked to Chapter 12.

Recommendations for Purchase or Rental

The Comer Video Segments include excerpts from many superb clinical documentaries. While the segments alone are ideal for use in lectures, it often is useful to assign the entire documentary for special class screenings or library use by students. The following videos and other media are available for purchase or rental and appropriate for use in class or for assignment outside of class.

Binge Drinking: The Right to Party?
DUI: Unlicensed to Kill
Eat, Drink, and Be Wary: Women and the Dangers of Alcohol
Getting Help: Drugs: Profiles of Addiction and Recovery
Films for the Humanities & Sciences
Box 2053 Princeton, NJ 08543-2053
1-800-257-5126
ffh.films.com

Influences: Innocence Betrayed
Pyramid Film and Video
2801 Colorado Ave.
Santa Monica, CA 90404
1-213-828-7577

My Friend Jenny: Portrait of an Addict
Filmakers Library
124 East 40th Street
New York, NY 10016
1-212-808-4980

Women: Coming Out of the Shadows
Fanlight Productions
47 Halifax Street
Boston, MA 02130
1-617-524-0980

CLASS DEMONSTRATIONS AND ACTIVITIES

Case Study

Present a case study to the class.

Panel Discussion

Have students volunteer (or assign them) to portray mental health "workers" from different theoretical perspectives in a panel discussion. Each student should present the main explanation and treatment for the substance-related disorders from his or her theoretical perspective. Students in the audience can ask questions of the panelists. Additionally, other students can role-play patients suffering from abuse of or dependence on particular substances. [NOTE: A brief reminder about sensitivity and professionalism is worthwhile here.] Have the panelists attempt to diagnose, based on their theoretical orientation.

"It's Debatable: The Appropriate Role of Cannabis in Society" (see Preface instructions for conducting this activity)

Have students volunteer (or assign them) in teams to opposite sides of the debate topic. Have students present their cases in class, following standard debate guidelines.

Group Work: Drug Searches and Drug Testing

Present yourself as a school district superintendent who must decide whether to allow random drug searches and mandatory drug testing in your schools. Arkansas has used blood tests, Breathalyzer tests, and polygraph tests on high school students. New Jersey conducts spot searches of lockers, gym bags, and purses, even though the Fourth Amendment outlaws "searches and seizures" without a warrant issued upon "probable cause." You are seeking the informed opinion of experts. One side is for such activities, the other is against it. Divide students into groups, then assign each group one of these two positions. Tell students to prepare their arguments.

Group Work: Pregnancy and Drugs

Either lead the class in a discussion or assign groups to discuss whether pregnant women who use drugs should face criminal prosecution. Do students think facing charges would cut down on a pregnant woman's drug abuse, or would it keep such women away from professionals who provide prenatal care because they might get arrested? Is fetal abuse the equivalent of child abuse? Can you think of alternatives to criminal charges? Because parents who smoke increase their young children's risk of asthma, should smokers also be liable? Because a man's sperm count can remain low for more than two years after he stops using cocaine, should a wife who is unable to become pregnant be able to sue her husband if he had used cocaine? This is not just an abstract discussion, as several states have enacted laws that punish the mother for endangering the fetus.

Abuse Versus Dependence

The difference between these diagnoses can be confusing to students. Display the criteria for each side by side, and point out the differences. Abuse involves maladaptive behavior, whereas dependence involves not just maladaptive behavior but also physical symptoms and apparent lack of control. Of course, the former is the precursor of the latter.

Media and Drug Use

Use an overhead transparency to develop a list of the drug behaviors that are currently portrayed in the media, particularly the movies. Ask students for examples from the most current movies. Ask if drug-related behaviors are changing in the movies. If yes, in what manner? Are drugs becoming more accepted in our society?

Presume You Are an Expert . . .

Tell the students that you received a phone call from your senator last night at home. He or she recognized that you are doing a fine job instructing students on the issue of substance abuse. Your senator wants you and several students to come to Washington, D.C., to testify before a Senate subcommittee on a proposed change in drug enforcement laws. Ask students to prepare a five-minute presentation outlining the most important aspects of illegal drug usage. Remind them that their testimony will influence law. Also remind them that their testimony is "expert" and that the validity of their statements may be challenged.

SUGGESTED TOPICS FOR DISCUSSION

Open Discussion: Cannabis and Society

Ask students to discuss the role of cannabis in society (see text pp. 368–369 for some information). Should it be legalized? Is medical use appropriate? What are the risks and benefits of such social change?

Open Discussion: College Binge Drinking

Using PsychWatch (p. 352 in the text) as a platform, have students discuss binge drinking on your campus. Is it a problem? What efforts have been made to address it?

Open Discussion: Alcohol Use or Abuse?

Ask students where they draw the line between the use and abuse of alcohol. Do their answers focus more on the amount or type of alcohol used? Ask for examples of friends' behavior that are clearly abuse.

Open Discussion: Does DARE Work?

Discuss the effectiveness of drug education today. How effective have current efforts, such as DARE (Drug Abuse Resistance and Education), been in preventing children from becoming drug abusers? Recent data indicate that this program is less successful than originally hoped. Ask your students to discuss what they would do to improve the DARE program.

Open Discussion: Alcohol Versus Drugs

Drug use and interdiction is a major focus of activity of the U.S. government, but its effects pale in comparison to the negative effects of alcohol. Ask students which is more of a problem for the country, alcohol or drugs? (Alcohol accounts for 20 percent of all national expenditures on health care; costs the United States $90 billion or more annually; is a factor in one-third to one-half of all suicides, homicides, assaults, rapes, and accidental deaths; and accounts for 40 percent of all fatal car accidents, 50 percent of deaths from falls, 52 percent of deaths from fires, and 38 percent of deaths by drowning.) Lead a discussion of why the country focuses on drugs and generally ignores alcohol.

Open Discussion: BAC Awareness

It is important for those who choose to drink to understand the relationships between amount of consumption, sex, weight, and BAC/BAL. Using Table 12-2 on p. 351 in the text or any of a number of free Internet resources, lead students in a discussion of good decision making around alcohol consumption.

ASSIGNMENTS/EXTRA CREDIT SUGGESTIONS

"Write a Pamphlet"

With the use of a software program like Microsoft Publisher or simply paper and markers, students can create a pamphlet on one or all of the substance-related disorders, specific classifications of substances, or specific treatment models. Students should be encouraged to be as accurate and up-to-date as possible and to present all sides of the issue (e.g., alternate treatment approaches or theories).

Keep a Journal

In addition to helping students synthesize material, this activity is helpful in developing writing skills. Have students keep a journal of their thoughts on course material through the semester. This can be done in the first or last five minutes of class or as an out-of-class assignment. Faculty generally should have students submit their journals for review on an on-going basis, since students can tend to delay writing until the end of the semester. Some suggestions for journal topics include: reactions to the case examples; strengths and weaknesses of prevailing theoretical explanations; hypothetical conversations with sufferers of specific disorders, etc.

Abnormal Psychology Student Tool Kit Video Questions

As a homework assignment, have students watch a video clip and answer the accompanying questions. Students can answer the questions directly into the online assessment feature. The results of these quizzes report to the site's built-in grade book.

Web Site Quiz

For homework or extra credit, have students complete the quiz for Chapter 12 located on the companion Web site. Students can complete an online test of the key chapter material (using questions NOT from the test bank) and have their scores e-mailed directly to the course instructor.

Essay Topics

For homework or extra credit, have students write an essay addressing one (or more) of the following topics:

(1) Discuss your experience with binge drinking on campus. Is it a problem? What do you think the administration should do (if anything) to combat it? Do you think students over- or under-report their drinking?

(2) Discuss the mechanism and risk associated with heroin overdose.

(3) Why do people start smoking and why do they continue to do so? Using PsychWatch, p. 360 in the text as a platform, discuss some of the issues related to nicotine addiction.

(4) Explain the mechanism of action for antagonist therapy for substance dependence.

(5) Discuss the growing use of club drugs [See Psych Watch, text p. 365] and energy drinks [See text p. 383] among college students. Is there a connection? Should anything be done (and, if so, what?) to combat this trend?

Research Topics

For homework or extra credit, have students write a research report addressing one (or more) of the following topics:

(1) Research music lyrics and band names that glamorize, glorify, or seem to combat substance use and abuse. [See "Between the Lines," text p. 371 for a partial list]

(2) Conduct a "Psych Info" search and write an annotated bibliography on treatment outcome studies for various substances. What model is being investigated?

(3) Research and review the literature on Project MATCH, a multisite clinical trial supported by the National Institute of Alcohol Abuse and Alcoholism.

(4) Research and review the literature on methadone maintenance therapy for opiate dependence.

(5) Research and review the literature on narcotic antagonist therapy for alcohol dependence.

Case Study Evaluations

To complement the Comer and Gorenstein supplemental case study text, case study evaluations have been created. Students can be assigned the appropriate case study and evaluation as homework or for class discussion. While case study evaluation questions are listed in their entirety on the companion Web site at www.worthpublishers.com/comer, relevant case studies follow.

Case Study 10: Alcohol Dependence and Marital Distress

Web-Based Case Studies

Nine Web-based case studies have been created and posted on the companion Web site. These cases describe the individual's history and symptoms and are accompanied by a series of guided questions that point to the precise DSM-IV-TR criteria for each disorder. Students can both identify the disorder and suggest a course of treatment. Students can be assigned the appropriate case study and questions as homework or for class discussion. The case relevant to Chapter 12 is referenced below.

The Case of Jerry: Alcohol Dependence

Crossword Puzzles

As a homework assignment or for extra credit, have students complete and submit Crossword Puzzle #12.

Word Searches

As a homework assignment or for extra credit, have students complete and submit Word Search #12.

CHAPTER :13

Sexual Disorders and Gender Identity Disorder

TOPIC OVERVIEW

LECTURE OUTLINE

I. **SEXUAL DISORDERS AND GENDER IDENTITY DISORDER**
   A. Sexual behavior is a major focus of both our private thoughts and public discussions
   B. Experts recognize two general categories of sexual disorders:
      1. Sexual dysfunctions—problems with sexual responses
      2. Paraphilias—repeated and intense sexual urges and fantasies toward socially inappropriate objects or situations
   C. In addition to the sexual disorders, DSM includes a diagnosis called gender identity disorder (GID), a sex-related pattern in which people feel that they have been born to the wrong sex
   D. Relatively little is known about racial and other cultural differences in sexuality
      1. Sex therapists and sex researchers have only recently begun to attend systematically to the importance of culture and race

II. **SEXUAL DYSFUNCTIONS**
   A. Sexual dysfunctions are disorders in which people cannot respond normally in key areas of sexual functioning
      1. As many as 31 percent of men and 43 percent of women in the United States suffer from such a dysfunction during their lives
      2. Sexual dysfunctions typically are very distressing and often lead to sexual frustration, guilt, loss of self-esteem, and interpersonal problems
      3. Often these dysfunctions are interrelated; many patients with one dysfunction experience another as well
   B. The human sexual response can be described as a cycle with four phases: [See Figure 13-1, text p. 388]:
      1. Desire
      2. Excitement
      3. Orgasm
      4. Resolution
   C. Sexual dysfunctions affect one or more of the first three phases
   D. Some people struggle with sexual dysfunction their whole lives (labeled "lifelong" in DSM-IV-TR); others have normal functioning that preceded the disorder (labeled "acquired")
   E. In some cases, the dysfunction is present during all sexual situations (labeled "generalized"); in others, it is tied to particular situations (labeled "situational")

III. **DISORDERS OF DESIRE**
   A. The desire phase of the sexual response cycle consists of an urge to have sex, sexual fantasies, and sexual attraction to others
   B. Two dysfunctions affect this phase:
      1. Hypoactive sexual desire disorder
         a. This disorder is characterized by a lack of interest in sex and little sexual activity
         b. Physical responses may be normal
         c. This disorder may be found in as many as 16 percent of men and 33 percent of women
         d. DSM-IV-TR criteria refers to "deficient" sexual interest/activity but provides no definition of "deficient"
            (a) In reality, this criterion is difficult to define
      2. Sexual aversion disorder
         a. This disorder is characterized by a total aversion to (disgust of) sex
            (a) Sexual advances may sicken, repulse, or frighten
         b. This disorder seems to be rare in men and somewhat more common in women
   C. A person's sex drive is determined by a combination of biological, psychological, and sociocultural factors, and any of them may reduce sexual desire

D. Most cases of low sexual desire or sexual aversion are caused primarily by sociocultural and psychological factors, but biological conditions can also lower sex drive significantly
   1. Biological causes
      a. A number of hormones interact to produce sexual desire and behavior
         (a) Abnormalities in their activity can lower sex drive
         (b) These hormones include prolactin, testosterone, and estrogen for both men and women
      b. Recent investigation has also linked sexual desire disorders to excessive activity of the neurotransmitters (NTs) serotonin and dopamine
      c. Sex drive also can be lowered by chronic illness, some medications (including birth control pills and pain medications), some psychotropic drugs, and a number of illegal drugs
   2. Psychological causes
      a. A general increase in anxiety, depression, or anger may reduce sexual desire in both men and women
      b. Fears, attitudes, and memories also may contribute to sexual dysfunction
      c. Certain psychological disorders also may lead to sexual desire disorders, including depression and obsessive-compulsive disorder
   3. Sociocultural causes
      a. The attitudes, fears, and psychological disorders that contribute to sexual desire disorders occur within a social context
      b. Many sufferers of desire disorders are experiencing situational pressures
         (a) For example: divorce, death, job stress, infertility, and/or relationship difficulties
      c. Cultural standards can set the stage for the development of these disorders
      d. The trauma of sexual molestation or assault also especially likely to produce sexual dysfunction

IV. **DISORDERS OF EXCITEMENT**
  A. The excitement phase of the sexual response cycle is marked by changes in the pelvic region, general physical arousal, and increases in heart rate, muscle tension, blood pressure, and respiration
   1. In men: erection of the penis
   2. In women: swelling of the clitoris and labia and vaginal lubrication
  B. Two dysfunctions affect this phase:
   1. Female sexual arousal disorder (formerly "frigidity")
      a. This disorder is characterized by persistent inability to maintain proper lubrication or genital swelling during sexual activity
      b. Many with this disorder also experience desire or orgasmic disorders
      c. It is estimated that more than 70 percent of women experience this disorder
      d. Because this disorder co-occurs so often with orgasmic disorder, researchers usually study the two together; causes of the two disorders will be examined together
   2. Male erectile disorder (ED) (formerly "impotence")
      a. This disorder is characterized by persistent inability to attain or maintain an adequate erection during sexual activity
      b. This problem occurs in as much as 10 percent of the general male population
      c. According to surveys, half of all adult men experience erectile difficulty during intercourse at least some of the time
  C. Most cases of erectile disorder result from an interaction of biological, psychological, and sociocultural processes
   1. Biological causes
      a. The same hormonal imbalances that can cause hypoactive sexual desire also can produce ED
         (a) Most commonly, vascular problems are involved
      b. ED can be caused by damage to the nervous system from various diseases, disorders, or injuries

        c.   Additionally, the use of certain medications and substances may interfere with erections

        d.   Medical procedures have been developed for diagnosing biological causes of ED

             (a)   One strategy includes measuring nocturnal penile tumescence (NPT)

             (b)   Men typically have erections during REM sleep; abnormal or absent night time erections usually indicate a physical basis for erectile failure

  2.   Psychological causes

        a.   Any of the psychological causes of hypoactive sexual desire also can interfere with arousal and lead to erectile dysfunction

             (a)   For example, as many as 90 percent of men with severe depression experience some degree of ED

        b.   One well-supported cognitive explanation for ED emphasizes performance anxiety and the spectator role

             (a)   Once erectile difficulties have begun, men become fearful and worried during sexual encounters; instead of being a participant, the man becomes a spectator and judge

             (b)   This can create a vicious cycle of sexual dysfunction where the original cause of the erectile failure becomes less important than the fear of failure

  3.   Sociocultural causes

        a.   Each of the sociocultural factors tied to hypoactive sexual desire also have been linked to ED

             (a)   Job and marital distress are particularly relevant

V.   DISORDERS OF ORGASM

  A.   During the orgasm phase of the sexual response cycle, an individual's sexual pleasure peaks and sexual tension is released as the muscles in the pelvic region contract rhythmically

      1.   For men: semen is ejaculated

      2.   For women: the outer third of the vaginal walls contract

  B.   There are three disorders of this phase:

      1.   Rapid, or premature, ejaculation

        a.   This disorder is characterized by persistent reaching of orgasm and ejaculation with little sexual stimulation

             (a)   As many as 30 percent of men experience rapid ejaculation at some time

        b.   Psychological, particularly behavioral, explanations of this disorder have received more research support than other explanations

             (a)   The dysfunction seems to be typical of young, sexually inexperienced men

        c.   It also may be related to anxiety, hurried masturbation experiences, or poor recognition of arousal

        d.   There is a growing belief among many clinical theorists that biological factors may also play a key role in many cases of this disorder

             (a)   One theory states that some men are born with a genetic predisposition

             (b)   A second theory argues that the brains of men with rapid ejaculation contain certain serotonin receptors that are overactive and others that are underactive

             (c)   A third explanation holds that men with this dysfunction experience greater sensitivity or nerve conduction in the area of their penis

      2.   Male orgasmic disorder

        a.   This disorder is characterized by repeated inability to reach or a very delayed orgasm after normal sexual excitement

             (a)   This disorder occurs in 8 percent of the male population

        b.   Biological causes include low testosterone, neurological disease, and head or spinal cord injury

        c.   Medications also can affect ejaculation, including drugs that slow down the sympathetic nervous system and certain antidepressants (especially the SSRIs)

        d.   A leading psychological cause appears to be performance anxiety and the spectator role, the cognitive factors involved in ED

             (a)   Another psychological factor may be past masturbation habits

             (b)   This disorder also may develop out of hypoactive sexual desire disorder

3. Female orgasmic disorder
   a. This disorder is characterized by persistent delay in or absence of orgasm following normal sexual excitement
     (a) Almost 24 percent of women appear to have this problem
     (b) 10 percent or more have never reached orgasm
     (c) An additional 9 percent reach orgasm only rarely
   b. Women who are more sexually assertive and more comfortable with masturbation tend to have orgasms more regularly
   c. Female orgasmic disorder appears more common in single women than in married or cohabiting women
   d. Most clinicians agree that orgasm during intercourse is not mandatory for normal sexual functioning
     (a) Lack of orgasm during intercourse was once considered to be pathological according to psychoanalytic theory—current evidence suggests this is untrue
   e. This disorder typically is linked to female sexual arousal disorder, and the two tend to be studied and treated together
   f. Once again, biological, psychological, and sociocultural factors may combine to produce these disorders
     (a) Biological causes
       (i) A variety of physiological conditions can affect a woman's arousal and orgasm
         1. These conditions include diabetes and multiple sclerosis
       (ii) The same medications and illegal substances that affect erection in men also can affect arousal and orgasm in women
       (iii) Postmenopausal changes also may be responsible
     (b) Psychological causes
       (i) The psychological causes of hypoactive sexual desire and sexual aversion, including depression, also may lead to female arousal and orgasmic disorders
       (ii) In addition, memories of childhood trauma and relationship distress also may be related
     (c) Sociocultural causes
       (i) For years, the leading sociocultural theory of female sexual dysfunction was that it resulted from sexually restrictive cultural messages
         1. This theory has been challenged because:
           a. Sexually restrictive histories are equally common in women with and without disorders
           b. Cultural messages about female sexuality have been changing while the rate of female sexual dysfunction stays constant
       (ii) Researchers suggest that unusually stressful events, traumas, or relationships may produce the fears, memories, and attitudes that characterize these dysfunctions
       (iii) Research also has linked orgasmic behavior to certain qualities in a woman's intimate relationships (such as emotional intimacy)

VI. DISORDERS OF SEXUAL PAIN
  A. Two sexual dysfunctions do not fit neatly into a specific phase of the sexual response cycle
  B. These are the sexual pain disorders:
    1. Vaginismus
     a. This disorder is characterized by involuntary contractions of the muscles of the outer third of the vagina
      (a) Severe cases can prevent a woman from having intercourse
      (b) This problem has received relatively little research, but estimates are that it occurs in fewer than 1 percent of all women
     b. Most clinicians agree with the cognitive-behavioral theory that vaginismus is a learned fear response

      c.   A variety of factors can set the stage for this fear, including anxiety and ignorance about intercourse, exaggerated stories, trauma of an unskilled partner, and the trauma of childhood sexual abuse or adult rape

         (a)   Some women experience painful intercourse because of infection or disease

      d.   Many women with vaginismus also experience other sexual disorders as well

  2. Dyspareunia

      a.   This disorder is characterized by severe pain in the genitals during sexual activity

         (a)   As many as 14 percent of women and about 3 percent of men suffer from this condition

      b.   Dyspareunia in women usually has a physical cause, usually injury sustained in childbirth

      c.   Although psychological factors or relationship problems may contribute, psychosocial factors alone rarely are responsible

VII. TREATMENTS FOR SEXUAL DYSFUNCTIONS

  A.   The last forty years have brought major changes to the treatment of sexual dysfunction

  B.   A brief historical perspective:

    1. Early twentieth century: Psychodynamic approaches

      a.   It was believed that sexual dysfunction was caused by a failure to progress through the stages of psychosexual development

      b.   Therapy focused on gaining insight and making broad personality changes and generally was unhelpful

    2. 1950s and 1960s: Behavior therapy

      a.   Behavior therapists attempted to reduce fear by employing relaxation training and systematic desensitization

      b.   These approaches had some success but failed to work in cases where the key problems included misinformation, negative attitudes, and lack of effective sexual technique

    3. 1970: *Human Sexual Inadequacy*

      a.   This text, published by William Masters and Virginia Johnson, revolutionized treatment of sexual dysfunction

      b.   This original "sex therapy" program has evolved into a complex, multidimensional approach, including techniques from cognitive-behavioral, couples, and family systems therapies along with a number of sex-specific techniques

      c.   More recently, biological interventions also have been incorporated

VIII. WHAT ARE THE GENERAL FEATURES OF SEX THERAPY?

  A.   These are the general features of sex therapy:

    1. Modern sex therapy is short-term and instructive

    2. Therapy typically lasts from 15 to 20 sessions

    3. It is centered on specific sexual problems rather than broad personality issues

    4. Modern sex therapy focuses on:

      a.   Assessment and conceptualization of the problem

      b.   Mutual responsibility

      c.   Education about sexuality

      d.   Emotion identification

      e.   Attitude change

      f.   Elimination of performance anxiety and the "spectator role"

      g.   Increase of sexual and general communication skills

      h.   Changing destructive lifestyles and marital interactions

      i.   Addressing physical and medical factors

IX. WHAT TECHNIQUES ARE APPLIED TO PARTICULAR DYSFUNCTIONS?

  A.   These techniques are applied to particular dysfunctions:

    1. In addition to the general components of sex therapy, specific techniques can help in each of the sexual dysfunctions:

      a.   Hypoactive sexual desire and sexual aversion

(a) These disorders are among the most difficult to treat because of the many issues that feed into them

(b) Therapists typically apply a combination of techniques, which may include:

    (i) Affectual awareness, self-instruction training, behavioral techniques, insight-oriented exercises, and biological interventions, such as hormone treatments

b. Erectile disorder

(a) Treatments for ED focus on reducing a man's performance anxiety and/or increasing his stimulation

    (i) May include sensate-focus exercises such as the "tease technique"

(b) Biological approaches have gained great momentum with the development of sildenafil (Viagra) and other erectile dysfunction drugs

(c) Most other biological approaches have been around for decades and include gels suppositories, penile injections, and a vacuum erection device (VED)

    (i) These procedures are now viewed as "second-line" treatment

c. Male orgasmic disorder

(a) Like treatment for ED, therapies to reduce this disorder include techniques to reduce performance anxiety and increase stimulation

(b) When the cause of the disorder is physical, treatment may include a drug to increase arousal of the sympathetic nervous system

d. Rapid, or premature, ejaculation

(a) Premature ejaculation has been successfully treated for years by behavioral procedures, such as the "start-stop" or "pause" procedure

(b) Some clinicians use SSRIs, the serotonin-enhancing antidepressant drugs

    (i) Because these drugs often reduce sexual arousal or orgasm, they may be helpful in delaying premature ejaculation

    (ii) Many studies have reported positive results with this approach

e. Female arousal and orgasmic disorders

(a) Specific treatments for these disorders include cognitive-behavioral techniques, self-exploration, enhancement of body awareness, and directed masturbation training

    (i) Biological treatments, including hormone therapy or the use of sildenafil (Viagra), have also been tried, but research has not found such interventions to be consistently helpful

(b) Again, a lack of orgasm during intercourse is not necessarily a sexual dysfunction, provided the woman enjoys intercourse and is orgasmic through other means

    (i) For this reason, some therapists believe that the wisest course of action is simply to educate women whose only concern is lack of orgasm through intercourse, informing them that they are quite normal

f. Vaginismus

(a) Specific treatment for vaginismus typically involves two approaches:

    (i) Practice tightening and releasing the muscles of the vagina to gain more voluntary control

    (ii) Overcome fear of penetration through gradual behavioral exposure treatment

(b) Most women treated for vaginismus using these methods eventually report pain-free intercourse

g. Dyspareunia

(a) Determining the specific cause of dyspareunia is the first stage of treatment

(b) Given that most cases are due to physical causes, medical intervention may be necessary

X. WHAT ARE THE CURRENT TRENDS IN SEX THERAPY?

A. These are the current trends in sex therapy

    1. Sex therapists have moved well beyond the approach first developed by Masters and Johnson

        a.   Treatment now includes unmarried couples, those with other psychological disorders, couples with severe marital discord, the elderly, the medically ill, the physically handicapped, gay clients, or clients with no long-term sex partner

    2.   Recently, therapists began paying attention to excessive sexuality, sometimes called hypersexuality or *sexual addiction*

    3.   Finally, the use of medications to treat sexual dysfunction is troubling to many therapists

        a.   There is concern that therapists will choose biological interventions rather than a more integrated approach

XI. PARAPHILIAS

    A.   These disorders are characterized by unusual fantasies and sexual urges or behaviors that are recurrent and sexually arousing

    B.   Paraphilias often involve:

        1.   Nonhuman objects

        2.   Children

        3.   Nonconsenting adults

        4.   Humiliation of self or partner

    C.   According to DSM-IV-TR, paraphilias should be diagnosed only when the urges, fantasies, or behaviors last at least six months

    D.   For most paraphilias, the urges, fantasies, or behaviors must also cause great distress or interfere with one's functioning

        1.   For certain paraphilias, however, performance of the behavior itself is indicative of a disorder even if the individual experiences no distress or impairment

            a.   Example: Sexual contact with children

    E.   Some people with one kind of paraphilia display others as well

        1.   Relatively few people receive a formal diagnosis, but clinicians suspect that the patterns may be quite common

    F.   Some experts argue that, with the exception of nonconsensual paraphilias, paraphilic activities should be considered a disorder only when they are the exclusive or preferred means of achieving sexual excitement and orgasm

    G.   Although theorists have proposed various explanations for paraphilias, there is little formal evidence to support them

    H.   None of the treatments applied to paraphilias has received much research or proved clearly effective

        1.   Psychological and sociocultural treatments have been available the longest, but today's professionals are also using biological interventions

    I.   The eight paraphilias are:

        1.   Fetishism

            a.   The key features of fetishism are recurrent intense sexual urges, sexually arousing fantasies, or behavior that involves the use of a nonliving object, often to the exclusion of all other stimuli

            b.   The disorder, far more common in men than women, usually begins in adolescence

            c.   Almost anything can be a fetish

                (a)   Women's underwear, shoes, and boots are especially common

            d.   Researchers have been unable to pinpoint the causes of fetishism

                (a)   Psychodynamic theorists view fetishes as defense mechanisms, but therapy using this model has been unsuccessful

                (b)   Behaviorists propose that fetishes are learned through classical conditioning

                    (i)   Fetishes are sometimes treated with aversion therapy or covert sensitization

                    (ii)   Another behavioral treatment is masturbatory satiation, where clients are instructed to masturbate to boredom while imagining the fetish object

                    (iii)   A final behavioral approach to fetishes is orgasmic reorientation, a process that teaches individuals to respond to more appropriate sources of sexual stimulation

        2.   Transvestic fetishism (also known as transvestism or cross-dressing)

    a.   This disorder is characterized by fantasies, urges, or behaviors involving dressing in clothes of the opposite sex as a means of sexual arousal

    b.   The typical case is a heterosexual male who began cross-dressing in childhood or adolescence

    c.   This pattern often is confused with gender identity disorder (transsexualism), but the two are separate conditions

    d.   The development of the disorder seems to follow the behavioral principles of operant conditioning

3.   Exhibitionism

    a.   Also known as "flashing," this disorder is characterized by arousal from the exposure of genitals in a public setting

    b.   Sexual contact is rarely initiated nor desired

    c.   Generally, the disorder begins before age 18 and is most common in males

    d.   Treatment generally includes aversion therapy and masturbatory satiation, possibly combined with orgasmic reorientation, social skills training, or cognitive-behavioral therapy

4.   Voyeurism

    a.   This disorder is characterized by fantasies, urges, or behaviors involving the act of observing an unsuspecting person as they undress or to spy on couples having intercourse

    b.   The person may masturbate during the act of observing or while remembering it later

    c.   The risk of discovery often adds to the excitement

    d.   Many psychodynamic theorists propose that voyeurs are seeking power

    e.   Behaviorists explain the disorder as a learned behavior that can be traced to chance

5.   Frotteurism

    a.   A person who develops frotteurism has repeated and intense fantasies, urges, or behaviors involving touching and rubbing against a nonconsenting person

    b.   Almost always male, the person fantasizes during the act that a caring relationship is occurring with the victim

    c.   The disorder usually begins in the teenage years or earlier

    d.   Acts generally decrease and disappear after age 25

6.   Pedophilia

    a.   This disorder is characterized by fantasies, urges, or behaviors involving sexual activity with a prepubescent child, usually 13 years of age or younger

    b.   Some people are satisfied with child pornography; others are driven to watching, fondling, or engaging in sexual intercourse with children

    c.   Victims may be male, but evidence suggests that two-thirds are female

    d.   People with pedophilia develop the disorder in adolescence

        (a)   Some were sexually abused as children

        (b)   Many were neglected, excessively punished, or deprived of close relationships in childhood

    e.   Most are immature, display distorted thinking, and have an additional psychological disorder

    f.   Some theorists have proposed a biochemical or brain structure abnormality, but clear biological factors have yet to emerge in research

    g.   Most people with pedophilia are imprisoned or forced into treatment

    h.   Treatments include aversion therapy, masturbatory satiation, orgasmic reorientation, and treatment with antiandrogen drugs

        (a)   There also is a cognitive-behavioral treatment: relapse prevention training, modeled after programs used for substance dependence

7.   Sexual masochism

    a.   A person with sexual masochism has fantasies, urges, or behaviors involving the act or thought of being humiliated, beaten, bound, or otherwise made to suffer

    b.   Most masochistic fantasies begin in childhood and seem to develop through the behavioral process of classical conditioning

8.   Sexual sadism

a. A person with sexual sadism finds fantasies, urges, or behaviors involving the thought or act of psychological or physical suffering of a victim sexually exciting

b. Named for the infamous Marquis de Sade, people with sexual sadism imagine that they have total control over a sexual victim

c. Fantasies may first appear in childhood or adolescence and the pattern is long-term

d. Sadism appears to be related to classical conditioning and/or modeling

e. Psychodynamic and cognitive theorists view people with sexual sadism as having underlying feelings of sexual inadequacy

f. Biological studies have found signs of possible brain and hormonal abnormalities

g. The primary treatment for this disorder is aversion therapy

J. A word of caution

   1. The definitions of paraphilias, like those of sexual dysfunctions, are strongly influenced by the norms of the particular society in which they occur

   2. Some clinicians argue that, except when people are hurt by them, many paraphilic behaviors should not be considered disorders at all

XII. GENDER IDENTITY DISORDER

A. According to current DSM-IV-TR criteria, people with this disorder persistently feel that they have been assigned to the wrong biological sex and experience gender dysphoria

   1. They would like to remove their primary and secondary sex characteristics and acquire the characteristics of the opposite sex

B. The DSM-IV-TR categorization of this disorder has become controversial in recent years

   1. Many people believe that transgender experiences reflect alternative—not pathological—ways of experiencing one's gender identity

   2. Others argue that gender identity is in fact a medical problem that may produce personal unhappiness

C. Men with GID outnumber women 2 to 1

D. People with this problem often experience anxiety or depression and may have thoughts of suicide

E. The disorder sometimes emerges in childhood and disappears with adolescence

   1. In some cases, it develops into adult gender identity disorder

F. Many clinicians suspect biological—perhaps genetic or prenatal—factors

   a. Abnormalities in the brain, including the hypothalamus (particularly the bed nucleus of stria terminalus [BST]), are a potential link

G. In order to more effectively assess and treat those with the disorder, clinical theorists have tried to distinguish the most common patterns of gender dysphoria:

   1. Female-to-male

   2. Male-to-female: androphilic type

   3. Male-to-female: autogynephilic type

H. Many adults with GID receive psychotherapy

   1. Some adults with this disorder change their sexual characteristics by way of hormones; others opt for sexual reassignment (sex-change) surgery

LEARNING OBJECTIVES

1. Describe each of the four phases of the sexual response cycle: desire, arousal, orgasm, and resolution.

2. Explain the two most common dysfunctions of the desire phase, hypoactive sexual desire and sexual aversion; then describe dysfunctions of the arousal phase, male erectile disorder, and female arousal disorder.

3. Discuss the orgasmic sexual dysfunctions of premature ejaculation, male orgasmic disorder, and female orgasmic disorder.

4.   Discuss the sexual pain disorders of vaginismus and dyspareunia.

5.   Discuss therapy for the sexual dysfunctions.

6.   Define paraphilias and describe behavioral treatment for them.

7.   Define, compare, and contrast the major paraphilic diagnoses.

8.   Define and discuss gender identity disorder.

9.   Discuss the changes for these disorders proposed by the DSM-5 Task Force.

XIII. CALL FOR CHANGE: DSM-5

A.   The DSM-5 Task Force has proposed that the disorder discussed here be separated into three unrelated groupings: Sexual Dysfunctions, Paraphilias, and Gender Dysphoria

B.   Within the Sexual Dysfunctions grouping, the Task Force recommends:

   1.   Two categories be relabeled:

      a   Delayed ejaculation should replace male orgasmic disorder

      b.   Early ejaculation should replace premature ejaculation

   2.   Some categories be combined:

      a.   Female hypoactive sexual desire disorder *and* female sexual arousal disorder become sexual interest/arousal disorder in women

      b.   Dyspareunia *and* vaginismus become gentio-pelvic pain/penetration disorder

C.   Within the Paraphilias grouping, the Task Force recommends that a clear distinction be made between paraphilic disorder and paraphilias

   1.   A disorder is only in order when individuals experience distress or impairment or cause harm

      a.   For example, the Task Force recommends that fetishism *and* sexual masochism be changed to fetishitic disorder *and* sexual masochism disorder

D.   The Task Force also proposes adding "number of victims" as a criterion for those paraphilias that involve victimization

   1.   The Task Force gave particular attention to pedophilia

      a.   It proposed a name change to pedohebephilic disorder

      b.   It also proposed that people should receive this diagnosis if they act on their arousal, are distressed or impaired by the arousal, or repeatedly view child pornography and experience their highest sexual arousal from child pornography

E.   The Task Force proposed that gender dysphoria replace gender identity disorder

   1.   It proposed that gender dysphoria in children and gender dysphoria in adolescents or adults be separate categories

KEY TERMS

aversion therapy
bed nucleus of stria
   terminalis (BST)
cross-dressing
desire phase
directed masturbation training
dyspareunia
erectile disorder
excitement phase
exhibitionism
female orgasmic disorder
female sexual arousal disorder
fetishism
frotteurism
gender dysphoria
gender identity disorder

hypoactive sexual desire
   disorder
male erectile disorder
male orgasmic disorder
masturbatory satiation
nocturnal penile tumescence
   (NPT)
orgasm phase
orgasmic reorientation
paraphilias
pedophilia
performance anxiety
premature ejaculation
rapid ejaculation
relapse-prevention training
sensate focus

sex therapy
sex-change surgery
sexual addiction
sexual aversion disorder
sexual dysfunction
sexual masochism
sexual response cycle
sexual sadism
spectator role
stop-start technique
transsexualism
transvestic fetishism
transvestism
vaginismus
voyeurism

MEDIA RESOURCES

Abnormal Psychology Student Tool Kit

Produced and edited by Ronald J. Comer, Princeton University and Gregory Comer, Princeton Academic Resources. Tied directly to the CyberStudy sections in the text, this Student Tool Kit offers 57 intriguing Video Cases running 3 to 7 minutes each. The Video Cases focus on persons affected by disorders discussed in the text. Students first view the video and then answer a series of thought-provoking questions. Additionally, the Student Tool Kit contains multiple-choice practice test questions with built-in instructional feedback for every option.

PowerPoint Slides

Available at the Instructor's site on the companion Web site are comprehensive PowerPoint slide presentations and supplemental student handouts for Chapter 13. The slide files reflect the main points of the chapter in significant detail. Student handouts were created using the instructor slides as a base, with key points replaced as "fill-in" items. Answer keys and suggestions for use also are provided.

DSM-IV-TR Masters

B-38, DSM-IV-TR Diagnostic Criteria for Hypoactive Sexual Desire Disorder

B-38, DSM-IV-TR Diagnostic Criteria for Sexual Aversion Disorder

B-39, DSM-IV-TR Diagnostic Criteria for Female Sexual Arousal Disorder

B-39, DSM-IV-TR Diagnostic Criteria for Male Erectile Disorder

B-40, DSM-IV-TR Diagnostic Criteria for Female Orgasmic Disorder

B-40, DSM-IV-TR Diagnostic Criteria for Male Orgasmic Disorder

B-41, DSM-IV-TR Diagnostic Criteria for Premature Ejaculation

B-41, DSM-IV-TR Diagnostic Criteria for Dyspareunia

B-41, DSM-IV-TR Diagnostic Criteria for Vaginismus

B-42, DSM-IV-TR Diagnostic Criteria for Exhibitionism

B-42, DSM-IV-TR Diagnostic Criteria for Fetishism

B-42, DSM-IV-TR Diagnostic Criteria for Frotteurism

B-42, DSM-IV-TR Diagnostic Criteria for Pedophilia

B-43, DSM-IV-TR Diagnostic Criteria for Sexual Masochism

B-43, DSM-IV-TR Diagnostic Criteria for Sexual Sadism

B-43, DSM-IV-TR Diagnostic Criteria for Transvestic Fetishism

B-43, DSM-IV-TR Diagnostic Criteria for Voyeurism

B-44, DSM-IV-TR Diagnostic Criteria for Gender Identity Disorder

Internet Sites

Please see Appendix A for full and comprehensive references.

Sites relevant to Chapter 13 material are:

http://www.sca-recovery.org (Sexual Compulsives Anonymous)
SCA is a fellowship of men and women who share their experience, strength, and hope with each other, that they may solve their common problem and help others to recover from sexual compulsion.

http://www.aasect.org/
The American Association of Sex Educators, Counselors, and Therapists (AASECT) is a not-for-profit, interdisciplinary professional organization that promotes understanding of human sexuality and healthy sexual behavior.

http://www.siecus.org/
The Sexuality Information and Education Council of the U.S. (SIECUS) is a national, nonprofit organization that affirms that sexuality is a natural and healthy part of living.

http://www.guttmacher.org/
The Alan Guttmacher Institute (AGI) is a nonprofit organization focused on sexual and reproductive health research, policy analysis, and public education.

Mainstream Films

Films relevant to Chapter 13 material are listed and summarized below.

Key to Film Listings:
P = psychopathology focus
T = treatment focus
E = ethical issues raised

Please note that some of the films suggested may have graphic sexual or violent content due to the nature of certain subject matter.

Adventures of Priscilla, Queen of the Desert
This Australian film from 1994 follows three cabaret drag queens who trek across the outback. **P, comedy**

Belle de Jour
Scandalous when first released in 1965, this film is Luis Bunuel's story of an affluent housewife (Catherine Deneuve) who acts out her sexual fantasies by taking a job at a Paris brothel. **P, serious film**

The Birdcage
A remake of the French *La Cage Aux Folles*, this American film from 1996 stars Robin Williams and Nathan Lane as a gay cabaret owner and his transvestite companion (actually a drag performer) trying to hide their relationship so that their son can introduce them to his fiance's conservative parents. **P, comedy**

Boys Don't Cry
From 1999, this powerful film stars Hilary Swank as Teena Brandon, a young woman who claims a new male identity in the rural town of Falls City, Nebraska. Based on a true story. **P, E, serious film**

A Clockwork Orange
In this 1971 film by Stanley Kubrick, Alex, a member of a brutal teenage gang, is imprisoned and agrees to aversion therapy. **P, T, E, serious film**

The Crying Game
This 1992 film focuses on the relationship between a person with gender identity disorder and his unsuspecting partner. **P, serious film**

Damage
This 1993 film portrays the troubling story of a married and respected middle-aged member of Britain's Parliament who becomes romantically and obsessively involved with his son's fiancée. **P, E, serious film**

Kinsey
From 2004, this biopic stars Liam Neeson as Alfred Kinsey, a man who created a media sensation with his sexuality research and subsequent book *Sexual Behavior in the Human Male*. **P, E, serious film**

Kiss of the Spider Woman
From 1985, this film stars William Hurt and Raul Julia as two cellmates in a South American prison—the first is a man who molested a young boy and the other is a political activist. **P, E, serious film**

Lolita
From 1962, this Stanley Kubrick adaptation of Nabokov's book is set in 1947 and details a troubled man in a troubled relationship with a very young girl. **P, E, comedic/serious film**

Looking for Mr. Goodbar
Starring Diane Keaton, this 1977 film paints an intense portrait of the free-spirited singles scene in New York City and the turmoil of one woman's attempt to find her own sexual identity. **P, serious film**

Ma vie en rose
In this Golden Globe–winning film from 1997, Ludovic is a boy who cross-dresses, acts like a girl, and talks of marrying his neighbor's son. **P, serious film**

My Own Private Idaho
In this moving film from 1991, River Phoenix plays a narcoleptic, psychologically scarred street prostitute, working and traveling with his best friend (Keanu Reeves). **P, serious film**

Normal
This 2003 film provides a relatively realistic portrayal of a married man undergoing gender transition. **P, E, serious film**

Secretary
From 2002, this film depicts Maggie Gyllenhall as a smart, quirky masochistic woman having an unorthodox relationship with her boss. **P, E, serious film**

sex, lies, and videotape
This 1989 film directed by Steven Soderbergh examines the triangle created when an old college friend re-enters the lives of a sexually repressed woman and her husband. They discover their friend has a fetish for videotaping women talking about sex. His appearance forces them to reexamine their marriage. **P, T, E, serious film**

Transamerica
This Oscar-nominated film stars Felicity Huffman as a preoperative male-to-female transsexual trying to forge a relationship with her son. **P, serious film**

The Woodsman
This 2004 film stars Kevin Bacon as a child molester who returns to his hometown after his release from prison. **P, E, serious film**

The World According to Garp
From 1982, this acclaimed adaptation of the John Irving book follows a feminist activist (Glenn Close) who publishes a feminist manifesto that makes her a lightning rod for all manner of victimized women. Among her followers is a transsexual ex-football player (John Lithgow). **P, T, comedy/serious film**

Other Films:

Auto-Focus (2002) exhibitionism and sexual addiction. **P, serious film**
Body Double (1984) voyeurism. **P, commercial/serious film**
Crash (1996) paraphilia. **P, serious film** (Note: Graphic sexual content)
Happiness (1998) paraphilia. **P, T, serious film**
Hedwig and the Angry Inch (2001). **P, independent film**
M (1931) paraphilia. **P, serious film**

Comer Video Segments

Available as a supplement, this revised set of video-tapes contains short clips depicting various topics related to abnormal psychology. Please see the accompanying Video Guide for specific clips linked to Chapter 13.

Recommendations for Purchase or Rental

The Comer Video Segments include excerpts from many superb clinical documentaries. While the segments alone are ideal for use in lectures, it often is useful to assign the entire documentary for special class screenings or library use by students. The following videos and other media are available for purchase or rental and appropriate for use in class or for assignment outside of class.

Phallacies
Bullfrog Films
P.O. Box 149
Oley, PA 19547
Tel: 610/779-8226
Fax: 610/370-1978

Sex: Unknown
WGBH
P.O. Box 200
Boston, MA 02134
Tel: 617-300-5400
http://main.wgbh.org/wgbh/shop/

*Me, My Sex, and I: Disorders of Sexual Development
Portraits in Human Sexuality: Sexual Dysfunction and
Therapy*
Films for the Humanities & Sciences
Box 2053 Princeton, NJ 08543-2053
1-800-257-5126
ffh.films.com

CLASS DEMONSTRATIONS AND ACTIVITIES

Case Study

Present a case study to the class.

Panel Discussion

Have students volunteer (or assign them) to portray mental health "workers" from different theoretical perspectives in a panel discussion. Each student should present the main explanation and treatment for the sexual disorders (or for gender identity disorder) from his or her theoretical background. Students in the audience can ask questions of the panelists. Additionally, other students can role-play patients suffering from particular sexual disorders. [NOTE: A brief reminder about sensitivity and professionalism is useful here.] Have the panelists attempt to diagnose based on their theoretical orientation.

"It's Debatable: Is Sexual Activity in Video Games Appropriate?" (see Preface instructions for conducting this activity)

Have students volunteer (or assign them) in teams to opposite sides of the debate topic—use the textbox on page 422 as a starting point. Have students present their cases in class, following standard debate guidelines.

"It's Debatable: Should Clinical Practitioners and Researchers Consider the Potential Impact of Their Decisions on Society? (see Preface instructions for conducting this activity)

Have students volunteer (or assign them) in teams to opposite sides of the debate topic. [See PsychWatch, text p. 412] Have students present their cases in class, following standard debate guidelines.

The Anonymous Five-Minute Essay

Take five minutes and permit students to write any concerns or questions they might have about sexuality, including variations of sexual behavior. Review the responses and answer them (or as many as you can) in the next class period.

Group Work: Childhood Misconceptions

Have the class form small groups to create lists of sexual messages and misconceptions they were exposed to during childhood. Have each group develop a list and elect a spokesperson to discuss their list. Have class members listen for themes or common misconceptions. Ask them how such misinformation might influence someone's sexual behavior as an adult.

Childhood Sexual Abuse Controversies

Introduce students to some of the controversies surrounding the evaluation of possible victims of sexual abuse of children (some of whom are evaluated as adults). Have the students discuss the controversies and suggest solutions. Some of the difficulties include the following:

A. Discrepancies

Discrepancies are often noted between the stories told by children and those told by their accused offenders. Although denial or minimization can play a role in the offender's account, differences are also found in the types of sexual behavior described in events and their sequences, as well as in timing. One big problem is that young children's sequencing abilities are not adequate to enable them to encode some facts accurately. The feelings they express are likely to reflect their experiences more accurately than the details of the events they describe.

B. Leading Questions

Leading questions, such as "Did he touch your private parts?" can influence what children say and come to believe. Such questions are inadmissible as evidence in the courtroom, and they are ill-advised in therapy, too.

C. Anatomically Correct Dolls

Some clinicians believe that anatomically correct dolls are leading questions in another form. Indeed, they increase the probability of a sexual response, whether or not it is accurate (nonvictimized children also may play at pseudosexual behavior with these dolls). They are more useful as a facilitative tool in therapy than as an investigative tool.

SUGGESTED TOPICS FOR DISCUSSION

Sex-Role Myths

Lead a discussion on the MYTHS of male and female sexuality. Be sure to correct these misconceptions and discuss the realities. A related discussion point is the impact of shows like *Sex and the City* on beliefs and perceptions about sexuality.

Open Discussion: Cultural and Sexual Behavior

Point out how cultural norms, beliefs, and values influence what is considered healthy sexuality. For example, homosexual intercourse is not only permitted but encouraged in some cultures. Discuss how cultural norms change. For example, homosexuality was considered a mental illness in early versions of the DSM (students are fascinated by overheads of these particular pages from the manual). Outmoded terms such as "nymphomania" (which in the Victorian era applied to women who were regularly orgasmic and enjoyed sex) and "masturbatory insanity" (in the 1930s, physicians believed that masturbation could cause fatigue, physical illness, and mental illness) can be used for illustration. Some of these ideas persist today without scientific evidence to support them. For example, many varsity coaches insist that college players not have sex prior to a game because having it will reduce their athletic ability.

Open Discussion: Sexual Fantasies

Ask students to define "sexual fantasy." Ask them to then determine at what point normal fantasy becomes abnormal.

Open Discussion: False Memory Syndrome

Some people believe that therapists have helped clients create false memories of childhood abuse in some patients. Whereas, unfortunately, many people have been sexually abused as children, it is also true that memories can be forgotten, distorted, and created (i.e., generated from nothing).

ASSIGNMENTS/EXTRA CREDIT SUGGESTIONS

"Write a Pamphlet"

With the use of a software program like Microsoft Publisher or simply paper and markers, students can create a pamphlet on one or all of the sexual disorders or general identity disorder. Students should be encouraged to be as accurate and up-to-date as possible and also to present all sides of the disorder (e.g., alternate treatment approaches or theories).

Keep a Journal

In addition to helping students synthesize material, this activity is helpful in developing writing skills. Have students keep a journal of their thoughts on course material throughout the semester. This can be done in the first or last five minutes of class or as an out-of-class assignment. Faculty generally should have students submit their journals for review on an ongoing basis as students can tend to delay writing until the end of the semester. Some suggestions for journal topics include: reactions to the case examples; strengths and weaknesses of prevailing theoretical explanations; hypothetical conversations with sufferers of specific disorders, etc.

Abnormal Psychology Student Tool Kit Video Questions

As a homework assignment, have students watch a video clip and answer the accompanying questions. Students can answer the questions directly into the online assessment feature. The results of these quizzes report to the site's built-in grade book.

Web Site Quiz

For homework or extra credit, have students complete the quiz for Chapter 13 located on the companion Web site. Students can complete an online test of the key chapter material (using questions NOT from the test bank) and have their scores e-mailed directly to the course instructor.

Essay Topics

For homework or extra credit, have students write an essay addressing one (or more) of the following topics:

(1) Where do you stand on the topic of Viagra vs. the Pill [See PsychWatch, text p. 404]? What are the differences between the two medications that support the disparate policies? What are the similarities that refute it?

(2) Discuss the implications of the proposed changes to the DSM-5 criteria for paraphilias versus paraphilic disorders.

(3) Discuss the implications of homosexuality being listed as a DSM disorder and being removed from the DSM in the 1980 edition. What parallels may be drawn to proposed changes in DSM-5?

Research Topics

For homework or extra credit, have students write a research report addressing one (or more) of the following topics:

(1) Conduct a "Psych Info" search and write an annotated bibliography on treatments for three of the sexual dysfunctions described in the text. Which treatments are proving most effective?

(2) Research and review the literature on "cybersex"—what are the research findings on Internet pornography as it relates to sexual dysfunction? Are there any positive findings?

(3) Research and review the literature on Internet chat rooms for children and teens and the link to pedophilia.

Film Review

To earn extra credit, have students watch one (or more) of the mainstream films listed earlier in the chapter and write a brief (3–5 pages) page. Students should summarize the plot of the film in sufficient detail to demonstrate familiarity, but should focus their papers on the depiction of psychological abnormality. What errors or liberties did the filmmaker take? What is the message (implicit or explicit) concerning the mentally ill?

Case Study Evaluations

To complement the Comer and Gorenstein supplemental case study text, case study evaluations have been created. Students can be assigned the appropriate case study and evaluation as homework or for class discussion. While case study evaluation questions are listed in their entirety on the companion Web site at www.worthpublishers.com/comer, the relevant case studies follow.

Case Study 11: Sexual Dysfunction: Male Erectile Disorder

Crossword Puzzles

As a homework assignment or for extra credit, have students complete and submit Crossword Puzzle #13.

Word Searches

As a homework assignment or for extra credit, have students complete and submit Word Search #13.

Schizophrenia

LECTURE OUTLINE

I. **PSYCHOSIS**
   A. Psychosis is a state defined by a loss of contact with reality
      1. The ability to perceive and respond to the environment is significantly disturbed; functioning is impaired
      2. Symptoms may include hallucinations (false sensory perceptions) and/or delusions (false beliefs)
   B. Psychosis may be substance-induced or caused by brain injury, but most appears in the form of schizophrenia

II. **SCHIZOPHRENIA**
   A. Schizophrenia affects approximately 1 in 100 people in the world
      1. Currently, there are about 2.5 million Americans experiencing the disorder
   B. The financial and emotional costs are enormous
      1. Sufferers have an increased risk of suicide and physical—often fatal—illness
   C. The disorder appears in all socioeconomic groups but is found more frequently in lower levels
      1. Leading theorists argue that the stress of poverty causes the disorder

2. Other theorists argue that the disorder causes victims from higher social levels to fall and remain at lower levels
    a. This is called the downward drift theory
D. Equal numbers of men and women are diagnosed
    1. The average age of onset for men is 21 years, compared to 27 years for women
E. Rates of diagnosis differ by marital status
    1. 3 percent of divorced or separated people
    2. 2 percent of single people
    3. 1 percent of married people
    4. It is unclear whether marital problems are a cause or a result

III. THE CLINICAL PICTURE OF SCHIZOPHRENIA
A. This disorder produces many "clinical pictures"
    1. The symptoms, triggers, and course of schizophrenia vary greatly
    2. Some clinicians have argued that schizophrenia is actually a group of distinct disorders that share common features
B. What are the symptoms of schizophrenia?
    1. Symptoms can be grouped into three categories:
        a. Positive symptoms
        b. Negative symptoms
        c. Psychomotor symptoms
C. Positive symptoms
    1. These symptoms are bizarre additions to a person's behavior—"pathological excesses," including:
        a. Delusions—faulty interpretations of reality
            (a) Delusions may have a variety of bizarre content: being controlled by others; persecution; reference; grandeur; control
        b. Disordered thinking and speech
            (a) May include loose associations; neologisms; perseverations; clang:
                (i) Loose associations (derailment):
                    1. "The problem is insects. My brother used to collect insects. He's now a man 5 foot 10 inches. You know, 10 is my favorite number, I also like to dance, draw, and watch tv."
                (ii) Neologisms (made-up words):
                    1. "It is an *amorition* law"
                (iii) Perseveration
                    1. Patients repeat their words and statements again and again
                (iv) Clang (rhyme):
                    1. How are you? "Well, hell, it's well to tell"
                    2. How's the weather? "So hot, you know it runs on a cot"
        c. Heightened perceptions
            (a) Sufferers may feel that their senses are being flooded by sights and sounds, making it impossible to attend to anything important
        d. Hallucinations—sensory perceptions that occur in the absence of external stimuli
            (a) Auditory are most common and seem to be spoken directly to the hallucinator or overheard
            (b) Hallucinations can involve any of the other senses—tactile, somatic, visual, gustatory, or olfactory
        e. Inappropriate affect—emotions that are unsuited to the situation
D. Negative symptoms
    1. These symptoms are characteristics that are lacking in an individual—"pathological deficits." They include:
        a. Poverty of speech (alogia)
            (a) Restriction on quantity of speech or speech content
            (b) Long lapses before responding to questions or failure to answer
        b. Blunted and flat affect—shows less emotion than most people
            (a) Avoidance of eye contact

          (b)   Immobile, expressionless face

          (c)   Monotonous voice, low and difficult to hear

          (d)   Anhedonia—general lack of pleasure or enjoyment

    c.   Loss of volition (motivation or directedness)

          (a)   Feeling drained of energy and interest in normal goals

          (b)   Inability to start or follow through on a course of action

          (c)   Ambivalence—conflicted feelings about most things

    d.   Social withdrawal

          (a)   May withdraw from social environment and attend only to their own ideas and fantasies

          (b)   This seems to lead to a breakdown of social skills, including the ability to recognize other people's needs and emotions accurately

E.   Psychomotor symptoms

    1.   People with schizophrenia sometimes experience psychomotor symptoms, including awkward movements, repeated grimaces, and odd gestures

        a.   These movements seem to have a magical quality

    2.   These symptoms may take extreme forms, collectively called catatonia

        a.   Includes stupor, rigidity, posturing, and excitement

F.   What is the course of schizophrenia?

    1.   Schizophrenia usually first appears in the late teens and mid-30s

    2.   Many sufferers experience three phases:

        a.   Prodromal—Beginning of deterioration with mild symptoms

        b.   Active—Symptoms become apparent

        c.   Residual—A return to prodromal-like levels

    3.   One-quarter recover fully; three-quarters continue to have residual problems

    4.   Each phase of the disorder may last for days or years

    5.   A fuller recovery from the disorder is more likely in subjects:

        a.   With good premorbid (before onset of the disorder) functioning

        b.   With a stress trigger

        c.   With abrupt onset

        d.   With later onset, during middle age

        e.   Who receive early treatment

G.   Diagnosing schizrenia

    1.   DSM-IV-TR calls for a diagnosis only after signs of the disorder continue for six months or more

    2.   In addition, people must show a deterioration in their work, social relations, and ability to care for themselves

    3.   The DSM-IV-TR distinguishes five subtypes:

        a.   Disorganized—Characterized by confusion, incoherence, and flat or inappropriate affect

        b.   Catatonic—Characterized by psychomotor disturbance of some sort

        c.   Paranoid—Characterized by an organized system of delusions and auditory hallucinations

        d.   Undifferentiated—Characterized by symptoms that fit no subtype; vague category

        e.   Residual—Characterized by symptoms that have lessened in strength and number; may continue to display blunted or inappropriate emotions, as well as social withdrawal, eccentric behavior, and some illogical thinking

    4.   Apart from the DSM-IV categories, many researchers believe that a distinction between Type I and Type II schizophrenia helps predict the course of the disorder

        a.   Type I schizophrenia is dominated by positive symptoms

          (a)   People seem to have better adjustment prior to the disorder, late onset of symptoms, and greater likelihood of improvement

          (b)   May be linked more closely to biochemical abnormalities in the brain

        b.   Type II is dominated by negative symptoms

          (a)   May be tied largely to structural abnormalities in the brain

IV. **HOW DO THEORISTS EXPLAIN SCHIZOPHRENIA?**
   A. As with many other disorders, research has focused on biological factors (most promising), psychological factors, and sociocultural factors
       a. Biological explanations have received the most research support
   B. A diathesis-stress relationship may be at work: People with a biological predisposition will develop schizophrenia only if certain kinds of stressors or events also are present
   C. Biological views
       1. Genetic and biological studies of schizophrenia have dominated clinical research in the last several decades
           a. These studies have revealed the key roles of inheritance and brain activity and have opened doors to important changes in treatment
       2. Genetic factors
           a. Following the diathesis-stress approach, genetic researchers believe that some people inherit a biological predisposition to schizophrenia
               (a) This disposition (and disorder) is triggered by later exposure to extreme stress
           b. This theory has been supported by studies of relatives, twins, and adoptees, and by genetic linkage studies and molecular biology
               (a) Family pedigree studies repeatedly have found that schizophrenia is more common among relatives of people with the disorder
                   (i) The more closely related the relatives are to the person with schizophrenia, the greater their likelihood for developing the disorder [See Figure 14-2, text p. 434]
                       1. General population = 1 percent
                       2. Second-degree relatives = 3 percent
                       3. First-degree relatives = 10 percent
                   (ii) Factors other than genetics may explain these findings
               (b) Twins have received particular research study
                   (i) Studies of identical twins have found that if one twin develops the disorder, there is a 48 percent chance that the other twin will do so as well
                   (ii) If the twins are fraternal, the second twin has a 17 percent chance of developing the disorder
                   (iii) Again, factors other than genetics may explain these findings
               (c) Adoption studies have compared adults with schizophrenia who were adopted as infants with both their biological and adoptive relatives
                   (i) Because they were reared apart from their biological relatives, similar symptoms in those relatives would indicate genetic influences; similarities to their adoptive relatives would suggest environmental influences
                   (ii) Researchers have found that the biological relatives of adoptees with schizophrenia are more likely to display schizophrenic symptoms than are their adoptive relatives
           c. Genetic linkage and molecular biology studies indicate that possible gene defects on numerous chromosomes may predispose individuals to develop schizophrenia
               (a) These varied findings may indicate: (1) a case of "mistaken identity"—some of these gene sites do not contribute to the disorder; (2) that different types of schizophrenia are linked to different genes; or (3) that schizophrenia, like many disorders, is a polygenic disorder—caused by a combination of gene defects
           d. Genetic factors may lead to the development of schizophrenia through two kinds of (potentially inherited) biological abnormalities: biochemical abnormalities and abnormal brain structure
       3. Biochemical brain abnormalities
           a. Over the past four decades, researchers have developed a dopamine hypothesis to explain their findings on schizophrenia—certain neurons using dopamine fire too often, producing symptoms of schizophrenia
           b. This theory is based on the effectiveness of antipsychotic medications (dopamine antagonists)

(a) Originally developed for treatment of allergies, antipsychotic drugs were found to cause a Parkinson's disease–like tremor response in patients

(b) Scientists knew that Parkinson's patients had abnormally low levels of dopamine, which caused their shaking

(c) This relationship between symptoms suggested that symptoms of schizophrenia were related to excess dopamine

c. Research since the 1960s has supported and clarified this hypothesis

(a) Example: Patients with Parkinson's disease develop schizophrenic symptoms if they take too much L-dopa, a medication that raises dopamine levels

(b) Example: People who take high doses of amphetamines, which increase dopamine activity in the brain, may develop amphetamine psychosis—a syndrome similar to schizophrenia

d. Investigators also have located the dopamine receptors to which antipsychotic drugs bind

(a) The drugs apparently are dopamine antagonists that bind to the receptors, preventing dopamine binding and neuron firing

(b) These findings suggest that, in schizophrenia, messages traveling from dopamine-sending neurons to dopamine-receptors (particularly D-2) may be transmitted too easily or too often

e. This is an appealing theory because certain dopamine receptors are known to play a key role in guiding attention

(a) Dopamine may be overactive in people with schizophrenia due to a larger-than-usual number of dopamine receptors (particularly D-2) or their dopamine receptors may operate abnormally

(i) Autopsy findings have found an unusually large number of dopamine receptors in people with the disorder

(ii) Imaging studies have revealed particularly high occupancy levels of dopamine at D-2 receptors in patients with schizophrenia

f. Though enlightening, the dopamine hypothesis has certain problems

(a) It has faced some challenge from the discovery of a new type of antipsychotic drugs (called "atypical" antipsychotics), which are more effective than traditional antipsychotics and which also bind to D-1 receptors and to serotonin receptors

(b) Another challenge to the theory is that some theorists claim that excessive dopamine activity contributes only to the positive symptoms of schizophrenia

(i) These symptoms respond particularly well to the conventional antipsychotic drugs that bind to D-2 receptors

(c) Still other studies suggest that negative symptoms may be related to abnormal brain structure, rather than to dopamine overactivity

4. Abnormal brain structure

a. During the past decade, researchers also have linked schizophrenia (particularly cases dominated by negative symptoms) to abnormalities in brain structure

(a) For example, brain scans have found that many people with the disorder have enlarged ventricles—the brain cavities that contain cerebrospinal fluid

(b) This enlargement may be a sign of poor development or damage in related brain regions

b. People with schizophrenia also have been found to have smaller temporal and frontal lobes, smaller amounts of grey matter, and abnormal blood flow to certain brain areas

5. Viral problems

a. A growing number of researchers suggest that the biochemical and structural abnormalities seen in schizophrenia result from exposure to viruses before birth

(a) Some of the evidence comes from animal model investigations and other evidence is circumstantial

(b) Circumstantial evidence for this theory comes from the unusually large numbers of people with schizophrenia born in winter months

        (c)   More direct evidence comes from studies showing that mothers of children with schizophrenia were more often exposed to the influenza virus during pregnancy than mothers of children without schizophrenia

        (d)   Other studies have found a link between schizophrenia and antibodies to a particular group of viruses found in animals, suggesting that people had at some point been exposed to those particular viruses

    6.   While the biochemical, brain structure, and viral findings are beginning to shed much light on the mysteries of schizophrenia, at the same time they offer only a partial explanation

        a.   Some people who have these biological problems never develop schizophrenia

        b.   Why not? Possibly because biology sets the stage for the disorder, but psychological and social/sociocultural factors must be present for it to appear

D.   Psychological views

    1.   When schizophrenia investigators began to identify genetic and biological factors of schizophrenia, clinicians largely abandoned psychological theories

    2.   During the past few decades, however, psychological factors are again being considered important

        a.   Leading psychological explanations come from the psychodynamic, behavioral, and cognitive perspectives

    3.   The psychodynamic explanation

        a.   Freud believed that schizophrenia develops from two processes: (1) regression to a pre-ego stage; and (2) efforts to reestablish ego control

        b.   He proposed that when their world is extremely harsh, people who develop schizophrenia regress to the earliest points in their development (the stage of primary narcissism), in which they recognize and meet only their own needs

        c.   This regression leads to "self-centered" symptoms such as neologisms, loose associations, and delusions of grandeur

        d.   Freud's theory posits that attempts to reestablish ego control from such a state fail and lead to further schizophrenic symptoms

        e.   Years later, another psychodynamic theorist elaborated on Freud's idea of harsh parents

        (a)   The theory of schizophrenegenic mothers proposed that mothers of people with schizophrenia were cold, domineering, and uninterested in their children's needs

        f.   Both of these theories have received little research support and have been rejected by most psychodynamic theorists

    4.   The behavioral view

        a.   Behaviorists cite operant conditioning and principles of reinforcement as the cause of schizophrenia

        b.   They propose that some people are not reinforced for their attention to social cues and, as a result, they stop attending to those cues and focus instead on irrelevant cues (e.g., room lighting)

        (a)   As such, their responses become increasingly bizarre yet are rewarded with attention and, thus, are likely to be repeated

        c.   Support for this model has been circumstantial and the view is considered (at best) a partial explanation

    5.   The cognitive view

        a.   Leading cognitive theorists agree that biological factors are producing symptoms

        b.   They argue, though, that further features of the disorder emerge due to a faulty interpretation and misunderstanding of symptoms

        (a)   Example: A man experiences auditory hallucinations and approaches his friends for help; they deny the reality of his experience; he concludes that they are trying to hide the truth from him; he begins to reject all feedback and starts feeling persecuted

        c.   There is little direct, clear research support for this view

E.   Sociocultural views

1. Sociocultural theorists believe that three main social forces contribute to schizophrenia:
   a. Multicultural factors
   b. Social labeling
   c. Family dysfunction
2. Although these forces are considered important in the development of schizophrenia, research has not yet clarified what the precise causal relationships might be
3. Multicultural factors
   a. Rates of the disorder differ between racial and ethnic groups
      (a) As many as 2.1 percent of African Americans are diagnosed compared with 1.4 percent of Caucasians
      (b) According to the census, however, African Americans are also more likely to be poor and to experience marital separation
      (c) When controlling for these factors, rates of schizophrenia become closer between the two racial groups
      (d) Consistent with the economic explanation, Hispanic Americans who also are, on average, economically disadvantaged, appear to have a much higher likelihood of being diagnosed than white Americans
   b. Rates also differ between countries, as do the course and outcome of the disorder
      (a) Some theorists believe the differences partly reflect genetic differences from population to population
      (b) Others argue that the psychosocial environments of developing countries tend to be more supportive than developed countries, leading to more favorable outcomes for people with schizophrenia
4. Social labeling
   a. Many sociocultural theorists believe that the features of schizophrenia are influenced by the diagnosis itself
      (a) Society labels people who fail to conform to certain norms of behavior
      (b) Once assigned, the label becomes a self-fulfilling prophecy
   b. The dangers of social labeling have been well demonstrated
      (a) Example: Rosenhan's "pseudo-patient" study
5. Family dysfunctioning
   a. One of the best known family theories of schizophrenia focuses on double-bind communication
      (a) This theory says that some parents repeatedly communicate pairs of mutually contradictory messages that place the children in so-called double-binds—the child cannot avoid displeasing the parents because nothing they do is right
         (i) In theory, the symptoms of schizophrenia represent the child's attempt to deal with the double-binds
      (b) Double-bind messages typically consist of a verbal (primary) communication and an accompanying—and contradictory—nonverbal communication (meta communication)
      (c) According to the theory, a child repeatedly exposed to these communications will adopt a special strategy for coping with them—possibly progressing toward paranoid schizophrenia
      (d) This theory is closely related to the psychodynamic notion of a schizophrenegic mother; it has been similarly unsupported by research (but popular in clinical practice)
   b. A number of studies suggest that schizophrenia often is linked to family stress:
      (a) Parents of people with the disorder often (1) display more conflict, (2) have greater difficulty communicating, and (3) are more critical of and overinvolved with their children than other parents
      (b) Family theorists long have recognized that some families are high in "expressed emotion"—family members frequently express criticism and hostility and intrude on each other's privacy
         (i) Individuals who are trying to recover from schizophrenia are almost four times as likely to relapse if they live with such a family

F.   R. D. Laing's View (a sociocultural-existential view)
   1.   This explanation of schizophrenia is the most controversial and argues that the dis-order is actually a *constructive* process in which people try to cure themselves of the confusion and unhappiness caused by their social environments
   2.   Laing believed that, left alone to complete this process, people with schizophrenia would indeed achieve a healthy outcome
   3.   Most theorists reject this notion; research has largely ignored it

V.   **CALL FOR CHANGE: DSM-5**
   A.   The DSM-5 Task Force proposed two key changes for schizophrenia and other psychotic disorders:
      1.   All individuals who fit a clinical picture of schizophrenia receive a straightforward diagnosis, eliminating subtyping, but rating severity of nine specific symptoms
      2.   A new category – *attenuated psychosis syndrome* – to be added to the list of psychotic disorders

LEARNING OBJECTIVES

1.   Describe the positive symptoms of schizophrenia: delusions, disorganized thinking, height-ened perceptions and hallucinations, and inappropriate affect.

2.   Compare and describe delusions of persecution, reference, grandeur, and control.

3.   Discuss the negative symptoms of schizophrenia, that is, poverty of speech, blunted and flat affect, loss of volition, and social withdrawal.

4.   Describe the psychomotor symptoms of schizophrenia.

5.   Summarize the characteristics of the prodromal, active, and residual phases of schizophrenia.

6.   Compare and contrast disorganized, catatonic, paranoid, and undifferentiated schizo-phrenia. Describe residual schizophrenia.

7.   Compare and contrast Type I and Type II schizophrenia.

8.   Summarize evidence from biological studies that supports the genetic view of schizophrenia.

9.   Discuss the dopamine hypothesis and evidence that both supports and fails to support it.

10. Describe the abnormal brain structures of some schizophrenic people.

11. Discuss the psychodynamic, behavioral, existential, and cognitive views of schizophrenia.

12. Discuss the sociocultural view of schizophrenia.

13. Discuss the changes for these disorders proposed by the DSM-5 Task Force.

KEY TERMS

alogia	clang	downward drift theory
amphetamine psychosis	delusion	enlarged ventricle
antipsychotic drugs	derailment	expressed emotion
atypical antipsychotic drugs	diathesis-stress	flat affect
avolition	disorganized	formal thought disorder
blunted and flat affect	dopamine hypothesis	genetic linkage
catatonia	double-bind hypothesis	hallucination

inappropriate affect	positive symptoms	schizophrenogenic mother
loose associations	prodromal	Type I schizophrenia
negative symptoms	psychomotor symptom	Type II schizophrenia
neologism	psychosis	undifferentiated
paranoid	residual	
phenothiazines	schizophrenia	

MEDIA RESOURCES

Abnormal Psychology Student Tool Kit

Produced and edited by Ronald J. Comer, Princeton University and Gregory Comer, Princeton Academic Resources. Tied directly to the CyberStudy sections in the text, this Student Tool Kit offers 57 intriguing Video Cases running 3 to 7 minutes each. The Video Cases focus on persons affected by disorders discussed in the text. Students first view the video and then answer a series of thought-provoking questions. Additionally, the Student Tool Kit contains multiple-choice practice test questions with built-in instructional feedback for every option.

PowerPoint Slides

Available at the Instructor's site on the companion Web site are comprehensive PowerPoint slide presentations and supplemental student handouts for Chapter 14. The slide files reflect the main points of the chapter in significant detail. Student handouts were created using the instructor slides as a base, with key points replaced as "fill-in" items. Answer keys and suggestions for use also are provided.

DSM-IV-TR Masters

B-45, DSM-IV-TR Diagnostic Criteria for Schizophrenia

B-46, DSM-IV-TR Diagnostic Criteria for Paranoid Type Schizophrenia

B-46, DSM-IV-TR Diagnostic Criteria for Disorganized Type Schizophrenia

B-46, DSM-IV-TR Diagnostic Criteria for Catatonic Type Schizophrenia

B-47, DSM-IV-TR Diagnostic Criteria for Undifferentiated Type Schizophrenia

B-47, DSM-IV-TR Diagnostic Criteria for Residual Type Schizophrenia

B-48, DSM-IV-TR Diagnostic Criteria for Schizoaffective Disorder

B-48, DSM-IV-TR Diagnostic Criteria for Schizophreniform Disorder

B-49, DSM-IV-TR Diagnostic Criteria for Delusional Disorder

B-50, DSM-IV-TR Diagnostic Criteria for Brief Psychotic Disorder

B-51, DSM-IV-TR Diagnostic Criteria for Shared Psychotic Disorder (Folie à Deux)

B-51, DSM-IV-TR Diagnostic Criteria for Psychotic Disorder Due to a General Medical Condition

B-52, DSM-IV-TR Diagnostic Criteria for Substance-Induced Psychotic Disorder

Internet Sites

Please see Appendix A for full and comprehensive references.

Sites relevant to Chapter 14 material are:

http://www.nimh.nih.gov/health/topics/schizophrenia/index.shtml

This Web site, provided by the U.S. National Library of Medicine, supplies downloadable links to PDF files and booklets on a variety of mental health topics, including schizophrenia.

http://www.nlm.nih.gov/medlineplus/schizophrenia.html

Medline Plus brings together authoritative information from NLM, NIH, and other government agencies and health-related organizations.

http://www.nami.org

Web site of the National Alliance on Mental Illness (NAMI), which offers excellent resources on mental health issues.

http://www.schizophrenia.com

The Schizophrenia Home Page contains links to chat rooms and to sites for families of affected individuals and individuals with schizophrenia. It also contains suggestions for dealing with this disorder.

http://www.mentalhealth.com/

Basic facts about schizophrenia produced by The British Columbia Friends of Schizophrenia Society.

Mainstream Films

Films relevant to Chapter 14 material are listed and summarized below.

Key to Film Listings:
P = psychopathology focus
T = treatment focus
E = ethical issues raised

Please note that some of the films suggested may have graphic sexual or violent content due to the nature of certain subject matter.

A Beautiful Mind
This Oscar-winning film from 2001 stars Russell Crowe as real-life mathematician John Nash Jr., a Nobel prize-winner who developed a groundbreaking economic theory while struggling with schizophrenic delusions. **P, T, E, serious film**

Benny & Joon
From 1993, this film portrays an artist with psychological dysfunctioning who is finding love. After watching the film, the diagnosis of the main character has been questioned—some argue schizophrenia, some argue schizotypal personality disorder. **P, serious film**

Canvas
From writer-director Joseph Greco, this 2006 drama stars Joe Pantoliano in an outstanding portrayal of mental illness. **P, T, E, serious film**

Clean Shaven
This accurate and graphic 1993 film depicts life through the eyes of an untreated man with paranoid schizophrenia searching for his daughter. **P, serious film**

The Couch Trip
This 1988 comedy stars Charles Grodin as a stressed-out radio shrink, whose producer ends up unwittingly hiring a schizophrenic patient (Dan Aykroyd) to replace him during his hiatus. **P, T, E, comedy**

Don Juan Demarco
In this 1995 comedy, Johnny Depp portrays a patient in a psychiatric hospital who claims to be Don Juan, the world's greatest lover. Marlon Brando plays the psychiatrist who tries to analyze his patient's apparent delusion. **P, T, E comedy/serious film**

Donnie Darko
From 2001, this film stars Jake Gyllenhaal as a disturbed teen who has visions of a human-sized rabbit telling him to do bad things. **P, T, serious film**

The Fisher King
This 1991 film follows Jack Lucas (Jeff Bridges), an irreverent radio talk show host who sinks into alcoholism after a tragedy. He is rescued by a delusional, homeless man (Robin Williams) on a quest for the Holy Grail. **P, serious film**

I Never Promised You a Rose Garden
From 1977, this gripping drama recounts a schizophrenic teenager's struggle to cope with her illness with the help of a caring psychiatrist. **P, T, E, serious film**

Love Actually
In a secondary plotline, this Hugh Grant film from 2003 depicts the impact of schizophrenia on a family. **P, T, comedy**

Pi
From 1998, this thriller follows a paranoid mathematician. **P, commercial film**

Proof
This Gwyneth Paltrow/Anthony Hopkins film shows the work of a psychotic mathematician and his relationship with his possibly psychotic daughter. **P, serious film**

Shutter Island
From 2010 and starring Leo DiCaprio, this film follows a U.S. Marshall on a twisting journey to find a missing murderess. **P, T, serious film**

Other Films:

The Caine Mutiny (1954) psychosis. **P, serious film**
Network (1976) psychosis. **P, serious film**
Shine (1996) psychosis. **P, T, serious film**
Sophie's Choice (1982) psychosis. **P, serious film**
Spider (2002) schizophrenia. **P, serious film**
They Might Be Giants (1971) schizophrenia, treatment. **P, T, E, commercial/serious/comedy film**

Comer Video Segments

Available as a supplement, this revised set of videotapes contains short clips depicting various topics related to abnormal psychology. Please see the accompanying Video Guide for specific clips linked to Chapter 14.

Recommendations for Purchase or Rental

The Comer Video Segments include excerpts from many superb clinical documentaries. While the segments alone are ideal for use in lectures, it often is useful to assign the entire documentary for special class screenings or library use by students. The following videos and other media are available for purchase or rental and appropriate for use in class or for assignment outside of class.

The Brain: Madness
Annenberg/CPB Project
P. O. Box 2345
South Burlington, VT 05407-2345
(800)-LEARNER

Living with Schizophrenia
Guilford Publications, Inc.
72 Spring Street
New York, NY 10012
Phone: (800) 365-7006
or (212) 431-9800
Fax: (212) 966-6708
(800) 365-7006
www.guilford.com

Preventing Relapse in Schizophrenia
P. O. Box 2053
Princeton, NJ 08543-2053
Phone: 800-257-5126
Fax: 609-275-3767
Email to: custserv@films.com

Dark Voices: Schizophrenia
P. O. Box 2053
Princeton, NJ 08543-2053
Phone: 800-257-5126
Fax: 609-275-3767
Email to: custserv@films.com

Schizophrenia
This specially adapted Phil Donahue program is regarded as one of the most helpful programs on schizophrenia addressed to nonspecialist audiences (28 min.)

P. O. Box 2053
Princeton, NJ 08543-2053
Phone: 800-257-5126
Fax: 609-275-3767
Email to: custserv@films.com

Psychiatric Interview #18: Evaluation for Diagnosis
Educational Media Collection
Box 353090
University of Washington
Seattle, WA 98195-3090
Scheduling: (206) 543-9909
Preview: (206) 543-9908
Reference: (206) 543-9907

Full of Sound and Fury: Living with Schizophrenia
Filmakers Library
124 East 40th St. Suite 901
New York, NY 10016
Phone: (212) 808-4980
Fax: (212) 808-4983
Email: info@filmakers.com
Web: http://www.filmakers.com

Dialogues with Madwomen
Women Make Movies
462 Broadway, 5th FL
New York, NY 10013
Phone: (212) 925-0606
Fax: (212) 925-2052
Email: info@wmm.com
Web: http://www.wmm.com/
Various titles also are available through
Films for the Humanities & Sciences
Box 2053 Princeton, NJ 08543-2053
1-800-257-5126
ffh.films.com

CLASS DEMONSTRATIONS AND ACTIVITIES

Case Study

Present a case study to the class.

Guest Speaker

Invite a mental health consumer or consumer advocate into your class to discuss his or her experiences with the mental health care system. NAMI (National Alliance on Mental Illness) sponsors several excellent programs designed to foster understanding and dis-

cussion of the problems impacting those with severe mental illness and their loved ones.

Panel Discussion

Have students volunteer (or assign them) to portray mental health "workers" from different theoretical perspectives in a panel discussion. Each student should present the main explanation and treatment for the schizophrenia from his or her theoretical perspective. Students in the audience can ask questions of the panelists. Additionally, other students can role-play patients suffering from particular subtypes of schizophrenia. [NOTE: A brief reminder about sensitivity and professionalism is useful here.] Have the panelists attempt to diagnose, based on their theoretical orientation.

"It's Debatable: Postpartum Psychosis: The Case of Andrea Yates" (see Preface instructions for conducting this activity)

Have students volunteer (or assign them) in teams to opposite sides of the debate topic using PsychWatch, text p. 436, as a platform. Have students present their cases in class, following standard debate guidelines.

Family Links

Show the class Figure 14-2 (Risk of developing schizophrenia based on familial relationship) and discuss the impact of such data.

"It's Debatable: People with Schizophrenia Should Be Prevented from Having Children" (see Preface instructions for conducting this activity)

Have students volunteer (or assign them) in teams to opposite sides of the debate topic using Figure 14-2 as a platform. Have students present their cases in class, following standard debate guidelines.

"Pretend, for a moment, that you are a . . . "

Ask students to imagine that they are health professionals confronted by a person experiencing paranoid delusions. What questions would they have for the person? Would they want to interview others who know the person? What difficulties might they encounter interviewing this individual?

The Anonymous Five-Minute Essay

Ask students to take five minutes to write down everything they believe about schizophrenia, whether they know it to be true or not. Many students admit that they are under the impression that schizophrenia is impossible to treat, that schizophrenia is a disorder from which no one recovers, and that schizophrenia is associated with severe dangerousness. Subsequent to this, ask students the source of these impressions.

Distinguishing Delusions

Students often have difficulty distinguishing the various types of delusions, and a simple exercise can reinforce the distinctions. Present an overhead with various statements representing different delusions and ask students to identify them (silently, on a sheet of paper). For example, put the following on an overhead: "They are talking about me" (persecution or grandeur, depending on what they are saying), "The radio is sending me a special message" (reference), and "The man who lives above me is stealing my thoughts" (control or thought broadcasting).

SUGGESTED TOPICS FOR DISCUSSION

Family Links

Using Figure 14-2, discuss the implications for individuals diagnosed with schizophrenia and for their family members in terms of future generations and risk of transmission. What do the data NOT mean?

Rosenhan's "On Being Sane in Insane Places"

To discuss the problem of "sticky" diagnostic labels and the manner in which they influence others' per-

ceptions, describe Rosenhan's study, "On Being Sane in Insane Places" (*Science*, 1973, pp. 250–257). In this study, eight mentally healthy people, several of them psychologists and psychiatrists, complained of hearing voices that repeated "Empty," "Dull," and "Thud," and were admitted to mental hospitals. Once inside, they acted normally for the remainder of their stay. One of the pseudopatients was a professional artist, and the staff interpreted her work in terms of her illness and recovery. As the pseudopatients took notes about their experience staff members referred to the note-taking as schizophrenic writing. Ask students for any other types of behavior that they can think of that would be misinterpreted in this situation. Ask students for other examples, which they have encountered or could imagine occurring, where a psychiatric label (such as depression, anxiety, or eating disorder) might "stick" and influence others' perceptions.

When discussing this study and students' reactions to it, it might be worthwhile to discuss criticisms of the study. For example, it will be important to emphasize that auditory hallucinations (such as those supposedly heard by the pseudopatients) are extremely rare and pathognomonic (indicate severe pathology), and that it might have been entirely appropriate for these persons to be hospitalized immediately. Also, the "patients" were discharged with the diagnosis "in remission," which means "without signs of the illness," a very rare diagnosis. Regarding the use of the study to criticize psychiatric diagnoses as unreliable or invalid, one author responded: "If I were to drink a quart of blood and, concealing what I had done, come to the emergency room of any hospital vomiting blood, the behavior of the staff would be quite predictable. If they labeled and treated me as having a bleeding peptic ulcer, I doubt

that I could argue convincingly that medical science does not know how to diagnose that condition" (Kety, 1974, p. 959).

Differential Diagnosis for Schizophrenia

Schizophrenia was once a wastebasket category for many individuals who did not fit the criteria of other disorders. Discuss the sometimes difficult task of differentiating schizophrenia from other disorders. Ask students to generate possible scenarios or situations wherein delusions or even hallucinations might be "normal" even in the absence of a schizophrenic process. Possibilities include posttraumatic stress, borderline personality disorder, and substance effects.

Szasz and Schizophrenia

According to Thomas Szasz, the idea of mental illness, including schizophrenia, is a myth. Szasz believes that schizophrenia should be properly regarded as problems of living in a society that mistreats individuals who are different. Do your students believe this assertion? Have them discuss the pros and cons of this proposition.

ASSIGNMENTS/EXTRA CREDIT SUGGESTIONS

"Write a Pamphlet"

With the use of a software program like Microsoft Publisher or simply paper and markers, students can create a pamphlet on schizophrenia or on one of the other psychotic disorders. Students should be encouraged to be as accurate and up-to-date as possible and to present all sides of the disorder (e.g., alternate treatment approaches or theories).

Keep a Journal

In addition to helping students synthesize material, this activity is helpful in developing writing skills. Have students keep a journal of their thoughts on course material throughout the semester. This can be done in the first or last five minutes of class or as an out-of-class assignment. Faculty generally should have students submit their journals for review on an ongoing basis, since students can tend to delay writing until the end of the semester. Some suggestions for journal topics include: reactions to the case examples; strengths and weaknesses of prevailing theoretical explanations; hypothetical conversations with sufferers of specific disorders, etc.

Abnormal Psychology Student Tool Kit Video Questions

As a homework assignment, have students watch a video clip and answer the accompanying questions. Students can answer the questions directly into the online assessment feature. The results of these quizzes report to the site's built-in grade book.

Web Site Quiz

For homework or extra credit, have students complete the quiz for Chapter 14 located on the companion Web site. Students can complete an online test of the key chapter material (using questions NOT from the test bank) and have their scores e-mailed directly to the course instructor.

Essay Topics

For homework or extra credit, have students write an essay addressing one (or more) of the following topics:

(1) Watch the acclaimed film *A Beautiful Mind* and compare the presentation of Nash's symptoms in

the film to the text's description of schizophrenia. What symptoms did he have? What types of treatment did he experience?

(2) Discuss the topic of postpartum depression/psychosis and the case of Andrea Yates [See Psych-Watch, text p. 436]. Do you agree with the diagnosis? What was the outcome at trial? What conclusions were made about her mental health? Do the proposed changes to the new edition of the *DSM* address this disorder?

Research Topics

For homework or extra credit, have students write a research report addressing one (or more) of the following topics:

(1) Research and review the literature on schizophrenegenic mothers. Is this topic still being examined? Were schizophrenegenic fathers ever examined?

(2) Research and report on other psychotic disorders [See Table 14-2, text p. 435]. How are they different from schizophrenia?

(3) Research and report on the available treatments for Mentally Ill Chemical Abuser. Use the Psych-Watch box on p. 428 of the text as a starting point.

Film Review

To earn extra credit, have students watch one (or more) of the mainstream films listed and write a brief (3–5 pages) report. Students should summarize the plot of the film in sufficient detail to demonstrate familiarity, but should focus their papers on the depiction of psychological abnormality. What errors or liberties did the filmmaker take? What is the message (implicit or explicit) concerning the mentally ill?

Case Study Evaluations

To complement the Comer and Gorenstein supplemental case study text, case study evaluations have been created. Students can be assigned the appropriate case study and evaluation as homework or for class discussion. While case study evaluation questions are listed in their entirety on the companion Web site at www.worthpublishers.com/comer, the relevant case studies follow.

Case Study 12: Schizophrenia

Web-Based Case Studies

Nine Web-based case studies have been created and posted on the companion Web site. These cases describe the individual's history and symptoms and are accompanied by a series of guided questions that point to the precise DSM-IV-TR criteria for each disorder. Students can both identify the disorder and suggest a course of treatment. Students can be assigned the appropriate case study and questions as homework or for class discussion. The case relevant to Chapter 14 is referenced below.

The Case of Randy: Schizophrenia

Crossword Puzzles

As a homework assignment or for extra credit, have students complete and submit Crossword Puzzle #14.

Word Searches

As a homework assignment or for extra credit, have students complete and submit Word Search #14.

CHAPTER :15

Treatments for Schizophrenia and Other Severe Mental Disorders

LECTURE OUTLINE

I. **TREATMENTS FOR SCHIZOPHRENIA**
   A. For much of human history, people with schizophrenia and other severe mental disorders were considered beyond help
   B. While still extremely difficult to treat, with the discovery of antipsychotic drugs, people with the disorder are more able to think clearly and profit from psychotherapies
   C. Each of the models offers treatments for schizophrenia, and all have been influential at one time or another

II. **INSTITUTIONAL CARE IN THE PAST**
   A. For more than half of the twentieth century, people with schizophrenia were institutionalized in public mental hospitals
      1. Because patients failed to respond to traditional therapies, the primary goals of the hospitals were to restrain them and give them food, shelter, and clothing
   B. The move toward institutionalization began in 1793 with the practice of "moral treatment"
      1. Hospitals were located in isolated areas to protect patients from the stresses of daily life and to offer them a healthful psychological environment
      2. States throughout the United States were required by law to establish public mental institutions (state hospitals) for patients who could not afford private care
      3. Unfortunately, problems with overcrowding, understaffing, and poor patient outcomes led to loss of individual care and the creation of "back wards"—human warehouses filled with hopelessness
      4. Many patients not only failed to improve under these conditions but developed additional symptoms, apparently as the result of institutionalization itself
         a. The most common pattern of decline was called the social breakdown syndrome: extreme withdrawal, anger, physical aggressiveness, and loss of interest in personal appearance and functioning

III. **INSTITUTIONAL CARE TAKES A TURN FOR THE BETTER**
   A. In the 1950s, clinicians developed two institutional approaches that brought some hope to chronic patients:
      1. Milieu therapy—based on humanistic principles
         a. The premise behind this type of treatment is that institutions can help patients make clinical progress by creating a social climate ("milieu") that builds productive, meaningful activities, self-respect, and individual responsibility
         b. These types of programs have been set up in institutions throughout the Western world with moderate success
         c. Research has shown that patients with schizophrenia in milieu programs often leave the hospital at higher rates than patients receiving custodial care
      2. Token economies—based on behavioral principles
         a. Based on operant conditioning principles, token economies were employed in institutions to change the behavior of patients with schizophrenia
         b. In token economies, patients are rewarded when they behave in socially acceptable ways and are not rewarded when they behave unacceptably
            (a) Immediate rewards are tokens that can later be exchanged for food, cigarettes, privileges, and other desirable objects
            (b) Acceptable behaviors likely to be targeted include care for oneself and one's possessions, going to a work program, speaking normally, following ward rules, and showing self-control
         c. Researchers have found that token economies do help reduce psychotic and related behavior; however, questions have been raised about such programs:
            (a) Research studies have tended to be uncontrolled—patients often aren't randomly assigned to groups, rather, a whole ward will participate in the system
            (b) Are such programs ethical and legal? Aren't all humans entitled to basic rights, some of which are compromised in a strict token economy system?

(c) Are such programs truly effective? For example, patients may change overt behaviors but not underlying psychotic beliefs

(d) Transition from a token economy system to community living may be difficult for patients

3. Token economies helped improve the personal care and self-image of patients, which were problem areas worsened by institutionalization

a. They are still used in many mental hospitals, usually along with medication

b. These approaches also have been applied to other clinical problems as well

IV. ANTIPSYCHOTIC DRUGS

A. While milieu therapy and token economies improved patients' outcomes, it was the discovery of antipsychotic drugs in the 1950s that revolutionized care for those with schizophrenia

B. The discovery of antipsychotic medications dates back to the 1940s, when researchers developed antihistamine drugs for allergies

1. It was discovered that one group of antihistamines, phenothiazines, could be used to calm patients about to undergo surgery

2. Psychiatrists tested the drug on six patients with psychosis and observed a sharp reduction in their symptoms

3. In 1954, this drug was approved for sale in the United States as an antipsychotic drug under the trade name Thorazine

C. Since the discovery of the phenothiazines, other kinds of psychotic drugs have been developed

1. The ones developed throughout the 1960s, 1970s, and 1980s are now referred to as "conventional" antipsychotic drugs

a. These drugs also are known as neuroleptic drugs because they often produce undesired movement effects similar to symptoms of neurological diseases

2. Drugs developed in recent years are known as the "atypical" or "second generation" antipsychotics

D. How effective are antipsychotic drugs?

1. Research has shown that antipsychotic drugs reduce schizophrenia symptoms in at least 65 percent of patients

2. In direct comparisons, drugs appear to be more effective than any other approach used alone

3. In most cases, the drugs produce the maximum level of improvement within the first six months of treatment

4. Symptoms may return if patients stop taking the drugs too soon

5. Antipsychotic drugs, particularly the conventional ones, reduce the positive symptoms of schizophrenia more completely, or at least more quickly, than the negative symptoms

a. Correspondingly, people who display largely positive symptoms generally have better rates of recovery than those with primarily negative symptoms

6. Although the use of such drugs is now widely accepted, patients often dislike the powerful effects of the drugs, and some refuse to take them

E. The unwanted effects of conventional antipsychotic drugs

1. In addition to reducing psychotic symptoms, the conventional antipsychotic drugs sometimes produce disturbing movement problems

a. The effects are called extrapyramidal effects because they appear to be caused by the drugs' impact on the extrapyramidal areas of the brain

b. These effects are so common that they are listed as a separate category of disorders in the DSM-IV-TR—medication-induced movement disorder

2. The most common of these effects produce Parkinsonian symptoms, reactions that closely resemble the features of the neurological disorder Parkinson's disease, including:

a. Muscle tremor and rigidity

b. Dystonia—bizarre movements of face, neck, tongue, and back

c. Akathisia—great restlessness, agitation, and discomfort in the limbs

3. The Parkinsonian and related symptoms seem to be the result of medication-induced reductions of dopamine activity in the basal ganglia and sustantia nigra, parts of the brain that coordinate movement and posture
    a. In most cases, the symptoms can be reversed if an anti-Parkinsonian drug is taken along with the antipsychotic
        (a) Sometimes the dosage must be decreased or the medication must be halted altogether
4. In as many as 1 percent of patients, particularly elderly ones, conventional antipsychotic drugs produce neuroleptic malignant syndrome, a severe potentially fatal reaction
    a. Symptoms include muscle rigidity, fever, altered consciousness, and improper functioning of the autonomic nervous system
    b. As soon as the syndrome is recognized, drug use is discontinued and each symptom treated medically
    c. Individuals also may be given dopamine-enhancing drugs
5. A more difficult side effect of the conventional antipsychotic drugs appears up to one year after starting the medication
    a. This reaction, called tardive dyskinesia, involves involuntary writhing or tic-like movements, usually of mouth, lips, tongue, legs, or body
        (a) It affects more than 10 percent of those taking these drugs for an extended time
        (b) Tardive dyskinesia can be difficult, sometimes impossible, to eliminate
6. Since learning of the unwanted side effects of the conventional antipsychotic drugs, clinicians have become more careful in their prescription practices:
    a. They try to prescribe the lowest effective dose
    b. They gradually reduce or stop medication weeks or months after the patient is seeing improvement in symptoms
F. Newer antipsychotic drugs
    1. In recent years, new antipsychotic drugs have been developed
        a. Examples: Clozaril, Resperidal, Zyprexa, Seroquel, Geodon, and Abilify
    2. These drugs are called "atypical" because they work using a different mechanism of action than the conventional antipsychotics
    3. They appear more effective than conventional antipsychotic drugs, especially for negative symptoms
        a. They cause few extrapyramidal side effects and seem less likely to cause tardive dyskinesia
        b. They do, however, carry an independent risk of agranulocytosis—a life-threatening drop in white cells
        c. They also may cause weight gain, dizziness, and significant elevations in blood sugar

V. **PSYCHOTHERAPY**
    A. Before the discovery of antipsychotic drugs, psychotherapy was not an option for people with schizophrenia
        1. Most were too far removed from reality to profit from it
    B. Today, psychotherapy is successful in many more cases of schizophrenia
    C. The most helpful forms of psychotherapy include cognitive-behavioral therapy and two broader sociocultural therapies—family therapy and social therapy
        1. Often, these approaches are combined
    D. Cognitive-behavioral therapy
        1. An increasing number of clinicians employ techniques that seek to change how individuals view and react to their hallucinatory experiences, including
            a. Provide education and evidence of the biological causes of hallucinations
            b. Help clients learn about the "comings and goings" of their own hallucinations and delusions
            c. Challenge clients' inaccurate ideas about the power of their hallucinations
            d. Teach clients to reattribute and more accurately interpret their hallucinations
            e. Teach techniques for coping with their unpleasant sensations

      2.   New-wave cognitive-behavioral therapies also help clients to accept their streams of problematic thoughts

      3.   These techniques help patients gain a greater sense of control, become more functional, and move forward in life

      4.   Studies indicate that these various techniques are often very helpful

  E.   Family therapy

      1.   Over 50 percent of persons with schizophrenia and other severe disorders live with family members, a situation that creates significant family stress

          a.   As we observed, those with schizophrenia living with relatives who display high levels of expressed emotion are at greater risk for relapse than those living with more positive or supportive families

          b.   Family therapy attempts to address such issues, as well as creating more realistic expectations and psychoeducation about the disorder

      2.   Families also may turn to family support groups and family psychoeducation programs

          a.   Although research has yet to determine the usefulness of these groups, the approach has become popular

  F.   Social therapy

      1.   Many clinicians believe that the treatment of people with schizophrenia should include techniques that address social and personal difficulties in the clients' lives

          a.   These include: practical advice, problem-solving, decision making, social skills training, medication management, employment counseling, financial assistance, and housing

          b.   Research supports this model in terms of a decrease in the return to hospitalization

VI. THE COMMUNITY APPROACH

  A.   The broadest approach for the treatment of schizophrenia and other severe mental disorders is the community approach

  B.   In 1963, Congress passed the Community Mental Health Act, which provided that patients should be able to receive care within their own communities, rather than being transported to institutions far from home

      1.   This act led to massive deinstitutionalization of patients with schizophrenia—unfortunately, community care was (and is) inadequate for their care

          a.   The result is a "revolving door" syndrome

  C.   What are the features of effective community care?

      1.   People recovering from schizophrenia and other severe disorders need medication, psychotherapy, help in handling daily pressures and responsibilities, guidance in making decisions, training in social skills, residential supervision, and vocational counseling

          a.   This combination of services sometimes is called assertive community treatment

      2.   Other key features of effective community care include:

          a.   Coordinated services

              (a)   Community mental health centers provide medications, psychotherapy, and inpatient emergency care

              (b)   Coordination of services is especially important for mentally ill chemical abusers (MICAs)

          b.   Short-term hospitalization

              (a)   If treatment on an outpatient basis is unsuccessful, patients may be transferred to short-term hospital programs

              (b)   After hospitalization lasting a few weeks, patients are released to aftercare programs for follow-up in the community

          c.   Partial hospitalization

              (a)   If patient needs fall between full hospitalization and outpatient care, day center programs may be effective

              (b)   These programs provide daily supervised activities and programs to improve social skills

              (c)   Another kind of institution that has become popular is the semihospital, or residential crisis center—houses or other structures in the community that provide 24-hour nursing care for those with severe mental disorders

  d. Supervised residences

    (a) Halfway houses (or group homes) provide shelter and supervision for patients unable to live alone or with their families, but who do not require hospitalization

    (b) Staff are usually paraprofessionals, and houses are run with a milieu therapy philosophy

    (c) These programs help those with schizophrenia adjust to community life and avoid rehospitalization

  e. Occupational training

    (a) Paid employment provides income, independence, self-respect, and the stimulation of working with others

    (b) Many people recovering from schizophrenia receive occupational training in a sheltered workshop—a supervised workplace for employees who are not ready for competitive or complicated jobs

    (c) An alternative work opportunity for individuals with severe disorders is supported employment

D. How has community treatment failed?

  1. There is no doubt that effective community programs can help people with schizophrenia and other severe mental disorders recover

    a. However, fewer than half of all people who need them receive appropriate community mental health services

    b. In fact, in any given year, 40 to 60 percent of all people with schizophrenia receive no treatment at all

  2. Two factors primarily are responsible:

    a. Poor coordination of services

      (a) Mental health agencies in a community often fail to communicate with one another

      (b) To combat this problem, a growing number of community therapists have become case managers for people with schizophrenia

        (i) While they offer therapy and advice, teach problem-solving and social skills, and ensure compliance with medications, case managers also try to coordinate available community services for their clients, guide them through the system and protect their legal rights

    b. Shortage of services

      (a) The number of community programs available to people with schizophrenia falls woefully short

      (b) Also, the centers that do exist generally fail to provide adequate services for people with severe disorders

      (c) While there are various reasons for these shortages, the primary one is economic

E. What are the consequences of inadequate community treatment?

  1. When community treatment fails, many people with schizophrenia and other severe mental disorders receive no treatment at all

  2. Many return to their families and receive medication and perhaps emotional and financial support, but little else in the way of treatment

  3. Around 8 percent of patients enter an alternative care facility (e.g., nursing homes), where they receive custodial care and medication

  4. As many as 18% are placed in privately run residences where supervision is provided by untrained individuals

  5. As many as 34 percent of patients are placed in single-room occupancy hotels, generally in run-down environments, where they exist on government disability payments

  6. Finally, a great number of people with schizophrenia become homeless

    a. Approximately one-third of the homeless in America have a severe mental disorder, commonly schizophrenia

F. The promise of community treatment

  1. Despite these very serious problems, proper community care has shown great potential for assisting recovery from schizophrenia

2. In addition, a number of national interest groups, including the National Alliance on Mental Illness (NAMI), have formed to push for better community treatment
3. Today, community care is a major feature of treatment for people recovering from severe mental disorders in countries around the world
   a. Both in the United States and abroad, varied and well-coordinated community treatment is seen as an important part of the solution to the problem of schizophrenia

LEARNING OBJECTIVES

1. Summarize past institutional care and the improved institutional care of the milieu therapy and token economy programs.

2. Discuss the effectiveness of antipsychotic drugs.

3. Discuss the side effects of antipsychotic drugs: Parkinsonian and related symptoms, neuroleptic malignant syndrome, and tardive dyskinesia.

4. Discuss the newer antipsychotic drugs.

5. Discuss the effects of psychotherapy on schizophrenia, including cognitive-behavioral, social, and family therapies.

6. Describe effective community care of patients with schizophrenia.

7. Discuss the problems with community care and potential solutions.

KEY TERMS

aftercare	day center	neuroleptic drugs
agranulocytosis	deinstitutionalization	paraprofessional
antipsychotic drugs	extrapyramidal effects	sheltered workshop
back wards	halfway house	state hospitals
case managers	lobotomy	tardive dyskinesia
community mental health center	milieu therapy	token economy program
	national interest group	

MEDIA RESOURCES

Abnormal Psychology Student Tool Kit

Produced and edited by Ronald J. Comer, Princeton University and Gregory Comer, Princeton Academic Resources. Tied directly to the CyberStudy sections in the text, this Student Tool Kit offers 57 intriguing Video Cases running 3 to 7 minutes each. The Video Cases focus on persons affected by disorders discussed in the text. Students first view the video and then answer a series of thought-provoking questions. Additionally, the Student Tool Kit contains multiple-choice practice test questions with built-in instructional feedback for every option.

PowerPoint Slides

Available at the Instructor's site on the companion Web site are comprehensive PowerPoint slide presentations and supplemental student handouts for Chapter 15. The slide files reflect the main points of the chapter in significant detail. Student handouts were created using the instructor slides as a base, with key points replaced as "fill-in" items. Answer keys and suggestions for use also are provided.

Internet Sites

Please see Appendix A for full and comprehensive references.

Sites relevant to Chapter 15 material are:

http://www.nimh.nih.gov/health/topics/schizophrenia/index.shtml
This Web site, provided by the U.S. National Library of Medicine, supplies downloadable links to PDF files and booklets on a variety of mental health topics, including schizophrenia.

http://www.nlm.nih.gov/medlineplus/schizophrenia.html
Medline Plus brings together authoritative information from NLM, NIH, and other government agencies and health-related organizations.

http://www.nami.org
Web site of the National Alliance on Mental Illness (NAMI), which offers excellent resources on mental health issues.

http://www.schizophrenia.com/
This Web site is from a nonprofit information, support, and education center.

http://www.mentalhealth.com/
Basic facts about mental health issues, including schizophrenia.

Mainstream Films

Films relevant to Chapter 15 material are listed and summarized below.

Key to Film Listings:
P = psychopathology focus
T = treatment focus
E = ethical issues raised

Please note that some of the films suggested may have graphic sexual or violent content due to the nature of certain subject matter.

An Angel at My Table
This 1990 film by Jane Campion recounts the autobiographical tale of New Zealand poet Janet Frame who was misdiagnosed with schizophrenia and spent eight years in a psychiatric hospital. **P, T, E, serious film**

A Beautiful Mind
This Oscar-winning film from 2001 stars Russell Crowe as real-life mathematician John Nash Jr., a Nobel prizewinner who developed a groundbreaking economic theory while struggling with schizophrenic delusions. **P, T, E, serious film**

Don Juan Demarco
In this 1995 comedy, Johnny Depp portrays a patient in a psychiatric hospital who claims to be Don Juan, the world's greatest lover. Marlon Brando plays the psychiatrist who tries to analyze his patient's apparent delusion. **P, T, E comedy/serious film**

I Never Promised You a Rose Garden
From 1977, this gripping drama recounts a schizophrenic teenager's struggle to cope with her illness with the help of a caring psychiatrist. **P, T, E, serious film**

One Flew Over the Cuckoo's Nest
This film tells the story of Randall P. McMurphy (Jack Nicholson), a convict sent to a northwestern psychiatric hospital for evaluation and treatment. While there, McMurphy experiences first-hand the use of electroconvulsive therapy. **P, T, E, serious film**

Shutter Island
From 2010 and starring Leo DiCaprio, this film follows a U.S. Marshall on a twisting journey to find a missing murderess. **P, T, serious film**

Snake Pit
Based on an autobiography, this film, made in 1948, is one of the first and best about mental illness and the treatment of patients in asylums and hospitals. Olivia de Haviland portrays a woman suffering from a nervous breakdown. **P, T, E, serious film**

Other Films:

A Fine Madness (1966) personality disorders, lobotomy. **P, T, serious/comedy film**
Frances (1982) personality disorder. **P, T, E, serious film**
They Might Be Giants (1971) schizophrenia, treatment. **P, T, E, commercial/serious/comedy film**
Tillicut Follies (1967) institutionalization. **P, T, E, serious documentary**

Comer Video Segments

Available as a supplement, this revised set of videotapes contains short clips depicting various topics related to abnormal psychology. Please see the accompanying Video Guide for specific clips linked to Chapter 15.

Recommendations for Purchase or Rental

The Comer Video Segments include excerpts from many superb clinical documentaries. While the segments alone are ideal for use in lectures, it often is useful to assign the entire documentary for special class screenings or library use by students. The following videos and other media are available for purchase or rental and appropriate for use in class or for assignment outside of class.

The Brain: Madness
Annenberg/CPB Project
P. O. Box 2345
South Burlington, VT 05407-2345
(800)-LEARNER

Living with Schizophrenia
Guilford Publications, Inc.
72 Spring Street
New York, NY 10012
Phone: (800) 365-7006
or (212) 431-9800
Fax: (212) 966-6708
(800) 365-7006
www.guilford.com

Preventing Relapse in Schizophrenia
P. O. Box 2053
Princeton, NJ 08543-2053
Phone: 800-257-5126
Fax: 609-275-3767
Email To: custserv@films.com

Dark Voices: Schizophrenia
P. O. Box 2053

Princeton, NJ 08543-2053
Phone: 800-257-5126
Fax: 609-275-3767
Email To: custserv@films.com

Schizophrenia
This specially adapted Phil Donahue program is regarded as one of the most helpful programs on schizophrenia addressed to nonspecialist audiences. (28 min.)
P. O. Box 2053
Princeton, NJ 08543-2053
Phone: 800-257-5126
Fax: 609-275-3767
Email To: custserv@films.com

Psychiatric Interview #18: Evaluation for Diagnosis
Educational Media Collection
Box 353090
University of Washington
Seattle, WA 98195-3090
Scheduling: (206) 543-9909
Preview: (206) 543-9908
Reference: (206) 543-9907

Full of Sound and Fury: Living with Schizophrenia
Filmakers Library
124 East 40th St. Suite 901
New York, NY 10016
Phone: (212) 808-4980
Fax: (212) 808-4983
Email: info@filmakers.com
Web: http://www.filmakers.com

Dialogues with Madwomen
Women Make Movies
462 Broadway, 5th Floor
New York, NY 10013
Phone: (212) 925-0606
Fax: (212) 925-2052
Email: info@wmm.com
Web: http://www.wmm.com/
Various titles also are available through
Films for the Humanities & Sciences
Box 2053 Princeton, NJ 08543-2053
1-800-257-5126
ffh.films.com

CLASS DEMONSTRATIONS AND ACTIVITIES

Case Study

Present a case study to the class.

Guest Speaker

Invite a mental health consumer or consumer advocate into your class to discuss his or her experiences with the mental health care system. NAMI (National Alliance on Mental Illness) sponsors several excellent programs designed to foster understanding and discussion of the problems impacting those with severe mental illness and their loved ones.

Panel Discussion

Have students volunteer (or assign them) to portray mental health "workers" from different theoretical perspectives in a panel discussion. Each student should present the main explanation and treatment for schizophrenia from his or her theoretical perspective. Students in the audience can ask questions of the panelists. Additionally, other students can role-play patients suffering from particular subtypes of schizophrenia. [NOTE: A brief reminder about sensitivity and professionalism is useful here.] Have the panelists attempt to diagnose based on their theoretical orientation.

"It's Debatable: The Ethics of Antipsychotic Drugs" (see Preface instructions for conducting this activity)

Have students volunteer (or assign them) in teams to opposite sides of the debate topic. Have students present their cases in class, following standard debate guidelines.

"Here's $25,000 to be awarded to . . . "

Have groups of students compete for an award to be given to the best token economy.

"Let's Write a Self-Help Bestseller."

Discuss the fact that there are few (if any) self-help books for persons with schizophrenia (there are several for families). Divide students into groups, then ask each group to write an outline for such a manual. The results will be interesting.

SUGGESTED TOPICS FOR DISCUSSION

Neuroleptic Drugs

Discuss some of the controversies that surround neuroleptic drugs. An ongoing controversy involves the control and costs of the blood tests necessary to monitor patients who take Clozaril.

Lobotomy: How Could It Happen?

Using PsychWatch on p. 453 in the text as a platform, lead a class discussion on the use of lobotomy as a treatment for schizophrenia. What are students' reactions to this piece of psychology's history? What are their reactions to the continued use of psychosurgery?

"NIMBY: Not In My Backyard"

Discuss some of the community concerns about the placement of halfway houses and other types of community care services in residential neighborhoods.

ASSIGNMENTS/EXTRA CREDIT SUGGESTIONS

"Write a Pamphlet"

With the use of a software program like Microsoft Publisher or simply paper and markers, students can create a pamphlet on treatment for schizophrenia. Students should be encouraged to be as accurate and up-to-date as possible and to present all sides of the disorder (e.g., alternate treatment approaches or theories).

Keep a Journal

In addition to helping students synthesize material, this activity also is helpful in developing writing skills.

Have students keep a journal of their thoughts on course material through the semester. This can be done in the first or last five minutes of class or as an out-of-class assignment. Faculty generally should have students submit their journals for review on an on-going basis, since students can tend to delay writing until the end of the semester. Some suggestions for journal topics include: reactions to the case examples; strengths and weaknesses of prevailing theoretical explanations; hypothetical conversations with sufferers of specific disorders, etc.

Abnormal Psychology Student Tool Kit Video Questions

As a homework assignment, have students watch a video clip and answer the accompanying questions. Students can answer the questions directly into the online assessment feature. The results of these quizzes report to the site's built-in grade book.

Web Site Quiz

For homework or extra credit, have students complete the quiz for Chapter 15 located on the companion Web site. Students can complete an online test of the key chapter material (using questions NOT from the test bank) and have their scores e-mailed directly to the course instructor.

Essay Topics

For homework or extra credit, have students write an essay addressing one (or more) of the following topics:

(1) Discuss the use of antipsychotic medication to treat schizophrenia. Do you think there are ethical concerns with the use of conventional medications, given their high risk of side effects? Should a person with schizophrenia be "allowed" to refuse to take medications because of the risk of side effects?

(2) Discuss the case of Larry Hogue, the "Wild Man of West 96th Street" described in PsychWatch p. 428 in the text. What are the unique treatment issues affecting MICA clients?

(3) Discuss the NIMBY (Not In My Back Yard) phenomenon that hinders community treatment efforts. What could be done to reduce this?

(4) The Media Speaks on pp. 462–463 in the text discusses a support group for those who hear voices. Discuss the pros and cons of such a group.

Research Topics

For homework or extra credit, have students write a research report addressing one (or more) of the following topics:

(1) Conduct a "Psych Info" search and write an annotated bibliography on community treatments for schizophrenia. What research is being conducted? Which components of treatment are most examined?

(2) Research and review the literature on psychotherapy for schizophrenia. What issues are most raised by clients? What areas are most addressed by researchers?

(3) Research and review the statistics on homelessness, mental illness, and community care programs in your state or county. What efforts are being made to address the problems of the severely mentally ill?

(4) Review one or two of the research studies discussed in PsychWatch on p. 459 in the text. What are the ethical issues under investigation? What are other areas of study on this topic?

Film Review

To earn extra credit, have students watch one (or more) of the mainstream films listed and write a brief (3–5 pages) report. Students should summarize the plot of the film in sufficient detail to demonstrate familiarity, but should focus their papers on the depiction of psychological abnormality. What errors or liberties did the filmmaker take? What is the message (implicit or explicit) concerning the mentally ill?

Case Study Evaluations

To complement the Comer and Gorenstein supplemental case study text, case study evaluations have been created. Students can be assigned the appropriate case study and evaluation as homework or for class discussion. While case study evaluation questions are listed in their entirety on the companion Web site at www.worthpublishers.com/comer, the relevant case studies are referenced next.

Case Study 12: Schizophrenia

Web-Based Case Studies

Nine Web-based case studies have been created and posted on the companion Web site. These cases describe the individual's history and symptoms and are accompanied by a series of guided questions that point to the precise DSM-IV-TR criteria for each disorder. Students can both identify the disorder and suggest a course of treatment. Students can be assigned the appropriate case study and questions as homework or for class discussion. The case relevant to Chapter 15 is referenced below.

The Case of Randy: Schizophrenia

Crossword Puzzles

As a homework assignment or for extra credit, have students complete and submit Crossword Puzzle #15.

Word Searches

As a homework assignment or for extra credit, have students complete and submit Word Search #15.

Personality Disorders

LECTURE OUTLINE

I. **WHAT IS PERSONALITY?**
   A. It is a unique and long-term pattern of inner experience and outward behavior
   B. Personality tends to be consistent and often is described in terms of "traits"
      1. These traits may be inherited, learned, or both
   C. Personality also is flexible, allowing us to learn and adapt to new environments
      1. For those with personality disorders, however, that flexibility usually is missing

II. **WHAT IS A PERSONALITY DISORDER?**
   A. It is an inflexible pattern of inner experience and outward behavior
      1. This pattern is seen in most interactions, differs from the experiences and behaviors usually expected of people, and continues for years
      2. The rigid traits of people with personality disorders often lead to psychological pain for the individual and social or occupational difficulties
      3. The disorder may also bring pain to others
   B. Classifying personality disorders
      1. A personality disorder typically becomes recognizable in adolescence or early adulthood
         a. These are among the most difficult psychological disorders to treat
         b. Many sufferers are not even aware of their personality problems
      2. It has been estimated that between 9 and 13 percent of all adults may have a personality disorder
      3. These disorders are diagnosed on Axis II of DSM-IV
         a. These patterns are not typically marked by changes in intensity or periods of clear improvement
         b. It is common for those diagnosed with personality disorders also to be diagnosed with an Axis I disorder
            (a) This relationship is called "comorbidity"
         c. It may be that Axis II disorders predispose people to also develop an Axis I condition *or* that Axis I disorders set the stage for Axis II disorders *or* that some biological condition sets the stage for both
         d. Whatever the reason, research indicates that the presence of a personality disorder complicates and reduces a person's chances for a successful recovery
      4. DSM-IV-TR identifies 10 personality disorders separated into three categories or "clusters:"
         a. Odd or eccentric behavior
            (a) Paranoid, schizoid, and schizotypal
         b. Dramatic, emotional, or erratic behavior
            (a) Antisocial, borderline, narcissistic, and histrionic
         c. Anxious or fearful behavior
            (a) Avoidant, dependent, and obsessive-compulsive
      5. The various personality disorders overlap each other significantly, so much so that it can be hard to distinguish one from another [See Figure 16-1, text p. 477]
      6. The frequent lack of agreement between clinicians and diagnosticians has raised concerns about the *validity* (accuracy) and *reliability* (consistency) of these categories
      7. It should be clear that diagnoses of such disorders can easily be overdone

III. **"ODD" PERSONALITY DISORDERS**
   A. People with these disorders display behaviors similar to but not as extensive as schizophrenia, including extreme suspiciousness, social withdrawal, and peculiar ways of thinking and perceiving things
      1. Such behaviors leave the person isolated
      2. Some clinicians believe that these disorders are actually related to schizophrenia, and thus call them *schizophrenia-spectrum disorders*

B. Clinicians have learned much of the symptoms but little of their causes or how to treat them
   1. In fact, people with these disorders rarely seek treatment
C. The cluster of "odd" personality disorders includes:
   1. Paranoid personality disorder
      a. This disorder is characterized by deep distrust and suspicion of others
         (a) Although inaccurate, this suspicion usually is not "delusional"—the ideas are not so bizarre or so firmly held as to clearly remove the individuals from reality
      b. As a result of their mistrust, people with paranoid personality disorder often remain cold and distant
      c. They are critical of weakness and fault in others, particularly at work
         (a) They are unable to recognize their own mistakes and are extremely sensitive to criticism
         (b) They often blame others for the things that go wrong in their lives, and they repeatedly bear grudges
      d. Between 0.5 and 3 percent of adults are believed to experience this disorder, apparently more men than women
      e. How do theorists explain paranoid personality disorder?
         (a) The proposed explanations of this disorder, like most of the personality disorders, have received little systematic research
         (b) Psychodynamic theories trace the pattern back to early interactions with demanding parents
         (c) Cognitive theorists suggest that maladaptive assumptions such as "People are evil and will attack you if given the chance" are to blame
         (d) Biological theorists propose genetic causes and have looked at twins studies to support this model
      f. Treatments for paranoid personality disorder
         (a) People with paranoid personality disorder do not typically see themselves as needing help
            (i) Few come to treatment willingly
         (b) Those who are in treatment often distrust and rebel against their therapists
            (i) As a result, therapy for this disorder, as for most of the other personality disorders, has limited effect and moves slowly
         (c) Object relations therapists try to see past patient anger and work on the underlying wish for a satisfying relationship
         (d) Behavioral and cognitive therapists try to help clients control anxiety and improve interpersonal skills
         (e) Cognitive therapists also try to restructure client's maladaptive assumptions and interpretations
         (f) Drug therapy is of limited help
   2. Schizoid personality disorder
      a. This disorder is characterized by persistent avoidance of social relationships and limited emotional expression
      b. Withdrawn and reclusive, people with this disorder do not have close ties with other people; they genuinely prefer to be alone
         (a) People with schizoid personality disorder focus mainly on themselves and often are seen as flat, cold, humorless, and dull
      c. The prevalence of the disorder is not known, but it is estimated to affect fewer than 1 percent of the population
         (a) It is slightly more likely to occur in men than in women
      d. How do theorists explain schizoid personality disorder?
         (a) Many psychodynamic theorists, particularly object relations theorists, link schizoid personality disorder to an unsatisfied need for human contact
            (i) The parents of those with the disorder are believed to have been unaccepting or abusive of their children
         (b) Cognitive theorists propose that people with schizoid personality disorder suffer from deficiencies in their thinking

(i) Their thoughts tend to be vague and empty, and they have trouble scanning the environment for accurate perceptions

e. Treatments for schizoid personality disorder

(a) Their extreme social withdrawal prevents most people with this disorder from entering therapy unless some other disorder makes treatment necessary

(i) Even then, patients are likely to remain emotionally distant from the therapist, seem not to care about treatment, and make limited progress

(b) Cognitive-behavioral therapists have sometimes been able to help people with this disorder experience more positive emotions and more satisfying social interactions

(i) The cognitive end focuses on thinking about emotions

(ii) The behavioral end focuses on the teaching of social skills

(c) Group therapy apparently is useful when it offers a safe environment for social contact

(d) Drug therapy is of little benefit

3. Schizotypal personality disorder

a. This disorder is characterized by a range of interpersonal problems, marked by extreme discomfort in close relationships, odd (even bizarre) ways of thinking, and behavioral eccentricities

(a) These symptoms may include *ideas of reference* and/or *bodily illusions*

b. People with the disorder often have great difficulty keeping their attention focused; conversation is typically digressive and vague, even sprinkled with loose associations

c. They tend to drift aimlessly and lead an idle, unproductive life, choosing undemanding jobs in which they are not required to interact with other people

(a) It has been estimated that 2 to 4 percent of all people (slightly more males than females) may have schizotypal personality disorder

d. How do theorists explain schizotypal personality disorder?

(a) Because the symptoms of this personality disorder so often resemble schizophrenia, researchers have hypothesized that similar factors are at work in both disorders

(i) They often have found that schizotypal symptoms are linked to family conflicts and to psychological disorders in parents

(b) Researchers also have begun to link schizotypal personality disorder to some of the same biological factors found in schizophrenia, such as high dopamine activity

(c) The disorder also has been linked to mood disorders, especially depression

e. Treatments for schizotypal personality disorder

(a) Therapy is as difficult in cases of schizotypal personality disorder as in cases of paranoid and schizoid personality disorders

(b) Most therapists agree on the need to help clients "reconnect" and to recognize the limits of their thinking and powers

(c) Cognitive-behavioral therapists further try to teach clients to objectively evaluate their thoughts and perceptions, and provide speech lessons and social skills training

(d) Antipsychotic drugs also have been given, and they appear to be somewhat helpful in reducing certain thought problems

IV. "DRAMATIC" PERSONALITY DISORDERS

A. The behaviors of people with these problems are so dramatic, emotional, or erratic that it is almost impossible for them to have relationships that are truly giving and satisfying

B. These personality disorders are more commonly diagnosed than the others

1. Only antisocial and borderline personality disorders have received much study

C. The causes of the disorders are not well understood
D. Treatments range from ineffective to moderately effective
E. The cluster of "dramatic" personality disorders includes:
    1. Antisocial personality disorder
        a. Sometimes described as "psychopaths" or "sociopaths," people with antisocial personality disorder persistently disregard and violate others' rights
        b. Aside from substance-related disorders, this is the disorder most linked to adult criminal behavior
        c. The DSM-IV requires that a person must be at least 18 years of age to receive this diagnosis
        d. Most people with the antisocial personality disorder displayed some patterns of misbehavior before they were 15 years old
        e. People with the disorder are likely to lie repeatedly, be reckless, and impulsive
            (a) They have little regard for other individuals, and can be cruel, sadistic, aggressive, and violent
        f. Surveys indicate that 2 to 3.5 percent of people in the United States meet criteria for this disorder
            (a) The disorder is four times more common in men than women
        g. Because people with this disorder are often arrested, researchers frequently look for people with antisocial patterns in prison populations
            (a) Studies indicate higher rates of alcoholism and other substance-related disorders among this group
        h. Children with a conduct disorder and an accompanying attention-deficit/hyperactivity disorder apparently have a heightened risk of developing antisocial personality disorder
        i. How do theorists explain antisocial personality disorder?
            (a) Explanations come from the major models:
                (i) Psychodynamic theorists propose that this disorder begins with an absence of parental love, leading to a lack of basic trust
                (ii) Many behaviorists have suggested that antisocial symptoms may be learned through modeling or unintentional reinforcement
                (iii) The cognitive view states that people with the disorder hold attitudes that trivialize the importance of other people's needs
                (iv) A number of studies suggest that biological factors may play a role:
                    1. Lower levels of serotonin, impacting impulsivity and aggression
                    2. Deficient functioning in the frontal lobes of the brain
                    3. Lower levels of anxiety and arousal, leading them to be more likely than other people to take risks and seek thrills
        j. Treatments for antisocial personality disorder
            (a) Treatments are typically ineffective
            (b) A major obstacle is the individual's lack of conscience or desire to change
                (i) Most have been forced to come to treatment
            (c) Some cognitive therapists try to guide clients to think about moral issues and the needs of other people
            (d) Hospitals and prisons have attempted to create therapeutic communities
            (e) Atypical antipsychotic drugs also have been tried, but systematic studies are still needed
    2. Borderline personality disorder
        a. People with this disorder display great instability, including major shifts in mood, an unstable self-image, and impulsivity
            (a) Interpersonal relationships also are unstable
        b. People with borderline personality disorder are prone to bouts of anger, which sometimes result in physical aggression and violence
            (a) Just as often, however, they direct their impulsive anger inward and harm themselves

c. Many of the patients who come to mental health emergency rooms are individuals with borderline personality disorder who have intentionally hurt themselves
   (a) Their impulsive, self-destructive behavior can include:
      (i) Alcohol and substance abuse
      (ii) Reckless behavior, including driving and unsafe sex
      (iii) Self-injurious or self-mutilation behavior
      (iv) Suicidal actions and threats
d. People with the disorder frequently form intense, conflict-ridden relationships while struggling with recurrent fears of impending abandonment
e. Between 1.5 and 2.5 percent of the general population are thought to suffer from this disorder
   (a) Close to 75 percent of those diagnosed are women
f. The course of the disorder varies
   (a) In the most common pattern, the instability and risk of suicide reach a peak during young adulthood and then gradually wane with advancing age
g. How do theorists explain borderline personality disorder?
   (a) Because a fear of abandonment tortures so many people with the disorder, psychodynamic theorists look to early parental relationships to explain the disorder
   (b) Object-relations theorists propose a lack of early acceptance or abuse/neglect by parents
      (i) Research has found some support for this view, including a link to early sexual abuse
   (c) Some features of the disorder also have been linked to biological abnormalities, such as an overly reactive amygdale and an underactive prefrontal cortex
      (i) In addition, sufferers who are particularly impulsive apparently have lower brain serotonin activity
      (ii) Close relatives of those with borderline personality disorder are five times more likely than the general population to have the disorder
   (d) A number of theorists currently use a biosocial theory, stating that the disorder results from a combination of internal and external forces
   (e) Some sociocultural theorists suggest that cases of borderline personality disorder are particularly likely to emerge in cultures that change rapidly
h. Treatments for borderline personality disorder
   (a) It appears that psychotherapy can eventually lead to some degree of improvement for people with this disorder
   (b) It is extraordinarily difficult, though, for a therapist to strike a balance between empathizing with a patient's dependency and anger and challenging his or her way of thinking
   (c) Contemporary psychodynamic therapy has been somewhat more effective than traditional psychodynamic approaches when it focuses on the patient's central relationship disturbance, poor sense of self, and pervasive loneliness and emptiness
      (i) Over the past two decades, an integrative treatment approach, called dialectical behavior therapy, has received more research support than any other treatment for this disorder
   (d) Antidepressant, antibipolar, antianxiety, and antipsychotic drugs have helped some individuals to calm their emotional and aggressive storms
      (i) Given the numerous suicide attempts by these patients, their use of drugs on an outpatient basis is controversial
   (e) Some patients have benefited from a combination of drug therapy and psychotherapy
3. Histrionic personality disorder
   a. People with histrionic personality disorder are extremely emotional and continually seek to be the center of attention
      (a) They often engage in attention-getting behaviors and are always "on stage"

                (b)   Approval and praise are the lifeblood of these individuals

      b.   People with histrionic personality disorder often are described as vain, self-centered, and demanding

            (a)   Some make suicide attempts, often to manipulate others

      c.   This disorder was once believed to be more common in women than in men

            (a)   However, research has revealed gender bias in past diagnoses

            (b)   The latest statistics suggest that approximately 2 to 3 percent of adults have this personality disorder, with males and females equally affected

      d.   How do theorists explain histrionic personality disorder?

            (a)   The psychodynamic perspective was originally developed to explain hysteria, and theorists have retained their interest in the disorder today

                (i)   Most psychodynamic theorists believe that, as children, people with this disorder experienced unhealthy relationships in which cold parents left them feeling unloved and afraid of abandonment

               (ii)   To defend against deep-seated fears of loss, the individuals learned to behave dramatically, inventing crises that would require people to act protectively

            (b)   Cognitive theorists look at the lack of substance and extreme suggestibility seen in people with the disorder

                (i)   Some argue that people with histrionic personality disorder hold a general assumption that they are helpless to care for themselves, so they seek out others who will meet their needs

            (c)   Sociocultural and multicultural theorists believe the disorder is caused in part by society's norms and expectations

                (i)   The vain, dramatic, and selfish behavior may be an exaggeration of femininity as our culture once defined it

      e.   Treatments for histrionic personality disorder

            (a)   Unlike people with most other personality disorders, those with histrionic personality disorder are more likely to seek treatment on their own

                (i)   Working with them can be difficult because of their demands, tantrums, seductiveness, and attempts to please the therapist

            (b)   Cognitive therapists try to change their patients' belief that they are helpless and to help them develop better, more deliberate ways of thinking and solving problems

            (c)   Psychodynamic therapy and group therapy also have been applied to help clients deal with their dependency

            (d)   Clinical case reports suggest that each of the approaches can be useful

            (e)   Drug therapy is less successful, except as a means of relieving the depression experienced by some patients

4.   Narcissistic personality disorder

      a.   People with narcissistic personality disorder are generally grandiose, need much admiration, and feel no empathy with others

      b.   People with this disorder exaggerate their achievements and talents, and often appear arrogant

      c.   People with this disorder are seldom interested in the feelings of others

            (a)   Many take advantage of others to achieve their own ends

      d.   Approximately 1 percent of adults display narcissistic personality disorder, and up to 75 percent of them are men

            (a)   This type of behavior is common among normal teenagers and does not usually lead to adult narcissism

      e.   How do theorists explain narcissistic personality disorder?

            (a)   Psychodynamic theorists more than others have theorized about this disorder, focusing on cold, rejecting parents

                (i)   Object-relations theorists interpret the grandiose self-presentation seen in people with the disorder as a way to convince themselves that they are self-sufficient and without need of warm relationships

          (ii)   In support of this theory, research has found increased risk for developing the disorder among abused children and those who lost parents through adoption, divorce, or death

    (b)   Cognitive-behavioral theorists propose that the disorder may develop when people are treated *too positively* rather than too negatively in early life

          (i)   Those with the disorder have been taught to "overvalue their self-worth"

    (c)   Finally, many sociocultural theorists see a link between narcissistic personality disorder and "eras of narcissism" in society

    f.   Treatments for narcissistic personality disorder

       (a)   Narcissistic personality disorder is one of the most difficult personality patterns to treat

       (b)   Clients who consult therapists usually do so because of a related disorder, most commonly depression

       (c)   Once in treatment, the individuals may try to manipulate the therapist into supporting their sense of superiority

       (d)   None of the major treatment approaches has had much success

V.   "ANXIOUS" PERSONALITY DISORDERS

A.   People with these disorders typically display anxious and fearful behavior

B.   Although many of the symptoms are similar to those of anxiety and depressive disorders, researchers have found no direct links between those personality disorders and those Axis I patterns

C.   As with most of the personality disorders, research is very limited, but treatments for this cluster appear to be modestly to moderately helpful—considerably better than for other personality disorders

D.   The cluster of "anxious" personality disorders includes:

    1.   Avoidant personality disorder

       a.   People with avoidant personality disorder are very uncomfortable and inhibited in social situations, overwhelmed by feelings of inadequacy, and extremely sensitive to negative evaluation

         (a)   They believe themselves unappealing or inferior and often have few close friends

       b.   The disorder is similar to social phobia, and many people with one disorder experience the other

         (a)   Similarities between the two disorders include a fear of humiliation and low self-confidence

         (b)   A key difference is that people with social phobia mainly fear social *circumstances*, while people with the personality disorder tend to fear close social *relationships*

       c.   As many as 1 and 2 percent of adults have avoidant personality disorder, men as frequently as women

       d.   How do theorists explain avoidant personality disorder?

         (a)   Theorists often assume that avoidant personality disorder has the same causes as anxiety disorders, including:

           (i)   Early trauma

           (ii)   Conditioned fears

           (iii)   Upsetting beliefs

           (iv)   Biochemical abnormalities

         (b)   Research has not directly tied the personality disorder to the anxiety disorders

         (c)   Psychodynamic theorists focus mainly on the general sense of shame felt by people with avoidant personality disorder

           (i)   Some trace the shame back to early toileting experiences

         (d)   Cognitive theorists believe that harsh criticism and rejection in early childhood may lead people to assume that their environment will always judge them negatively

                (i)   In several studies, individuals reported memories that supported both the psychodynamic and cognitive theories

        (e)   Behavioral theorists suggest that people with this disorder typically fail to develop normal social skills

    e.   Treatments for avoidant personality disorder

        (a)   People with avoidant personality disorder come to therapy seeking acceptance and affection

        (b)   Keeping them in therapy can be challenging because they soon begin to avoid sessions

        (c)   A key task of the therapist is to gain the individual's trust

        (d)   Beyond trust building, therapists tend to treat the disorder as they treat social phobia and anxiety

                (i)   These treatments have had modest success

        (e)   Group therapy formats, especially those that follow cognitive-behavioral principles, also help by providing practice in social interactions

        (f)   Antianxiety and antidepressant drugs are also sometimes helpful

2.   Dependent personality disorder

    a.   People with dependent personality disorder have a pervasive, excessive need to be taken care of

        (a)   As a result, they are clinging and obedient, fearing separation from their loved ones

        (b)   They rely on others so much that they cannot make the smallest decision for themselves

    b.   The central feature of the disorder is a difficulty with *separation*

        (a)   Many people with this disorder feel distressed, lonely, and sad

        (b)   Often they dislike themselves

    c.   They are at risk for depression, anxiety, and eating disorders and may be especially prone to suicidal thoughts

    d.   Studies suggest that over 2 percent of the population experience the disorder

        (a)   Research suggests that men and women are affected equally

    e.   How do theorists explain dependent personality disorder?

        (a)   Psychodynamic explanations for this personality disorder are very similar to those for depression

                (i)   Freudian theorists argue that unresolved conflicts during the oral stage of development can give rise to a lifelong need for nurturance

                (ii)   Object-relations theorists say that early parental loss or rejection may prevent normal experiences of attachment and separation, leaving some children with lingering fears of abandonment

                (iii)   Other theorists argue that parents were overinvolved and overprotective, increasing their children's dependency

        (b)   Behaviorists propose that parents of those with dependent personality disorder unintentionally rewarded their children's clinging and "loyal" behavior while punishing acts of independence

                (i)   Alternatively, some dependent behaviors seen in parents may have acted as models

        (c)   Cognitive theorists identify two maladaptive attitudes as helping to produce and maintain this disorder:

                (i)   "I am inadequate and helpless to deal with the world"

                (ii)   "I must find a person to provide protection so I can cope

                (iii)   Such thinking prevents sufferers of the disorder from making efforts to be autonomous

    f.   Treatments for dependent personality disorder

        (a)   In therapy, people with this disorder usually place all responsibility for their treatment and well-being on the clinician

        (b)   A key task is to help patients accept responsibility for themselves

        (c)   Couple or family therapy can be helpful and often is recommended

        (d)   Treatment can be at least modestly helpful

    (i)   Psychodynamic therapists focus on many of the same issues as therapy for people with depression

    (ii)   Cognitive-behavioral therapists try to help clients challenge and change their assumptions of incompetence and helplessness and provide assertiveness training

    (iii)   Antidepressant drug therapy has been helpful for those whose disorder is accompanied by depression

    (iv)   Group therapy also can be helpful because it provides clients an opportunity to receive support from a number of peers, and group members may serve as models for one another

3.   Obsessive-compulsive personality disorder

    a.   People with obsessive-compulsive personality disorder are so preoccupied with order, perfection, and control that they lose all flexibility, openness, and efficiency

    b.   They set unreasonably high standards for themselves and others and, fearing a mistake, may be afraid to make decisions

       (a)   These individuals tend to be rigid and stubborn

       (b)   They may have trouble expressing affection, and their relationships often are stiff and superficial

    c.   As many as 1 and 2 percent of the population has this disorder, with white, educated, married, and employed individuals receiving the diagnosis most often

       (a)   Men are twice as likely as women to display the disorder

    d.   Many clinicians believe that obsessive-compulsive personality disorder and obsessive-compulsive disorder (the anxiety disorder) are closely related

       (a)   While the disorders do share similar symptoms, researchers have not found a specific link between them

    e.   How do theorists explain obsessive-compulsive personality disorder?

       (a)   Most explanations of obsessive-compulsive personality disorder borrow heavily from those of obsessive-compulsive anxiety disorder, despite the doubts concerning a link

       (b)   Psychodynamic explanations dominate and research is limited

          (i)   Freudian theorists suggest that people with obsessive-compulsive personality disorder are *anal regressive*

             1.   Because of overly harsh toilet training, individuals become angry and remain *fixated* at this stage of psychosexual development

             2.   To keep their anger under control, they resist both their anger and their instincts to have bowel movements

             3.   As a result, they become extremely orderly and restrained

          (ii)   Cognitive theorists have little to say about the origins of the disorder, but they do propose that illogical thinking processes help maintain it

    f.   Treatments for obsessive-compulsive personality disorder

       (a)   People with obsessive-compulsive personality disorder do not usually believe there is anything wrong with them

       (b)   They are therefore unlikely to seek treatment unless they also are suffering from another disorder, most frequently anxiety or depression

       (c)   Individuals with this personality disorder often appear to respond well to psychodynamic or cognitive therapy

       (d)   A number of clinicians report success with SSRIs.

VI. MULTICULTURAL FACTORS: RESEARCH NEGLECT

    A.   According to DSM-IV-TR, a pattern diagnosed as a personality disorder must "deviate markedly from the expectations of a person's culture"

       1.   Given the importance of culture in the definition, it is striking how little multicultural research has been conducted

       2.   Clinical theorists have suspicions, but no compelling evidence, that cultural differences exist or that such differences are important to the field's understanding and treatment of personality disorders

B. The lack of multicultural research is of special concern with regard to borderline personality disorder
   1. Theorists are convinced that gender and other cultural differences may be particularly important in both the development and diagnosis of the disorder

VII. WHAT PROBLEMS ARE POSED BY THE DSM-IV-TR CATEGORIES?
   A. Most of today's clinicians believe that personality disorders are important and troubling patterns
      1. Yet, these disorders are particularly hard to diagnose, easy to misdiagnose, and raise serious issues of reliability and validity
      2. Several specific problems have been raised:
         a. Some of the diagnostic criteria cannot be observed directly
         b. The diagnoses often rely heavily on the impressions of the individual clinician
         c. Similarly, clinicians differ widely in their judgments about when a normal personality style crosses the line and deserves to be called a disorder
         d. The similarity of disorders within a cluster or between clusters creates classification difficulties
            (a) Research suggests that people with disorders of personality *typically* meet diagnostic criteria for several personality disorders
            (b) People with quite different personalities may be given the same diagnosis
            (c) Individuals must meet a certain number of criteria to receive a given diagnosis, but no single feature is necessary for any diagnosis

VIII. ARE THERE BETTER WAYS TO CLASSIFY PERSONALITY DISORDERS?
   A. The leading criticism of DSM-IV-TR's approach to personality disorders is that the classification system uses *categories*—rather than *dimensions*—of personality
      1. Like a light switch, DSM-IV-TR's categorical approach assumes that
         a. Problematic personality traits are either present or absent
         b. A personality disorder is either displayed or not displayed
         c. A person who suffers from a personality disorder is not markedly troubled by personality traits outside of that disorder
      2. Many theorists now believe that personality disorders actually differ more in *degree* than in type of dysfunction
         a. They have proposed that the disorders should be organized by the severity of certain key traits, or personality dimensions, rather than the presence or absence of specific traits
   B. The "Big Five" theory of personality and personality disorders
      1. A large body of research conducted with diverse populations consistently suggests that the basic structure of personality may consist of five factors or "supertraits"—neuroticism, extroversion, openness to experiences, agreeableness, and conscientiousness
         a. Each of these factors, collectively referred to as the "Big Five," consists of a number of subfactors
         b. Theoretically, everyone's personality can be summarized by a combination of these supertraits
      2. Many proponents of the five-factor model further argue that it would be more useful to describe all people with personality disorders as either high, low, or in-between on the five supertraits, and to drop the DSM's current use of personality disorder categories altogether
   C. Alternative Dimensional Approaches
      1. Although many clinical theorists now agree that a dimensional approach would more accurately reflect personality pathology than the categorical approach of DSM-IV-TR, not all of them believe that the "Big Five" model is the most useful dimensional approach
      2. Thus, alternative dimensional models have also been proposed

IX. **CALL FOR CHANGE: DSM-5**
A. In response to the problems, criticisms, and suggestions preciously discussed, the DSM-5 Task Force proposed a *hybrid* model for diagnosing these disorders
1. The model retains several of the categories of personality disorders, while, at the same time, requiring diagnosticians to assess the severity of the disorders
2. In addition, the model allows diagnosticians to diagnose other, more idiosyncratic personality patterns as disorders if individuals have trait problems that severely disrupt their functioning
B. According to the proposal, there are two routes for diagnosis:
1. The traditional route—with six categories being retained (paranoid, schizoid, histrionic, and dependent were dropped)—and additional evaluations of *self-functioning* and *interpersonal functioning*
2. The new route — a diagnosis of *personality disorder trait specified (PDTS)* for those cases that don't fit one of the six existing categories
C. These proposals have caused a stir in the clinical community
1. Clinicians in favor of a dimensional approach dislike retaining so many categories
2. Other clinicians believe the proposed changes give too much latitude and too little structure to diagnosticians
3. Still others worry that the proposals are too complicated

LEARNING OBJECTIVES

1. Define and discuss explanations and treatments for the "odd" personality disorders, including paranoid, schizoid, and schizotypal.

2. Define and discuss explanations and treatments for the "dramatic" personality disorders, including antisocial, borderline, histrionic, and narcissistic.

3. Define and discuss explanations and treatments for the "anxious" personality disorders, including avoidant, dependent, and obsessive-compulsive.

4. Discuss the issues related to the neglect of multicultural factors in personality disorders.

5. Discuss difficulties involved in the categorizing of personality disorders and evaluate the possible solutions.

6. Discuss the changes for these disorders proposed by the DSM-5 Task Force.

KEY TERMS

anal regressive
antisocial personality disorder
"anxious" personality disorders
avoidant personality disorder
borderline personality disorder

comorbidity
dependent personality disorder
dialectical behavior therapy (DBT)
"dramatic" personality disorders

histrionic personality disorder
narcissistic personality disorder
obsessive-compulsive personality disorder
"odd" personality disorders

paranoid personality
   disorder
passive-aggressive
   personality disorder
personality

personality disorder
psychopathy
schizoid personality
   disorder

schizotypal personality
   disorder
sociopath

MEDIA RESOURCES

Abnormal Psychology Student Tool Kit

Produced and edited by Ronald J. Comer, Princeton University and Gregory Comer, Princeton Academic Resources. Tied directly to the CyberStudy sections in the text, this Student Tool Kit offers 57 intriguing Video Cases running 3 to 7 minutes each. The Video Cases focus on persons affected by disorders discussed in the text. Students first view the video and then answer a series of thought-provoking questions. Additionally, the Student Tool Kit contains multiple-choice practice test questions with built-in instructional feedback for every option.

PowerPoint Slides

Available at the Instructor's site on the companion Web site are comprehensive PowerPoint slide presentations and supplemental student handouts for Chapter 16. The slide files reflect the main points of the chapter in significant detail. Student handouts were created using the instructor slides as a base, with key points replaced as "fill-in" items. Answer keys and suggestions for use also are provided.

DSM-IV-TR Masters

B-53, DSM-IV-TR General Diagnostic Criteria for a Personality Disorder

B-54, DSM-IV-TR Diagnostic Criteria for Paranoid Personality Disorder

B-54, DSM-IV-TR Diagnostic Criteria for Schizoid Personality Disorder

B-55, DSM-IV-TR Diagnostic Criteria for Schizotypal Personality Disorder

B-56, DSM-IV-TR Diagnostic Criteria for Antisocial Personality Disorder

B-56, DSM-IV-TR Diagnostic Criteria for Borderline Personality Disorder

B-57, DSM-IV-TR Diagnostic Criteria for Histrionic Personality Disorder

B-57, DSM-IV-TR Diagnostic Criteria for Narcissistic Personality Disorder

B-58, DSM-IV-TR Diagnostic Criteria for Avoidant Personality

B-58, DSM-IV-TR Diagnostic Criteria for Dependent Personality Disorder

B-59, DSM-IV-TR Diagnostic Criteria for Obsessive-Compulsive Personality Disorder

Internet Sites

Please see Appendix A for full and comprehensive references.

Sites relevant to Chapter 16 material are:

http://www.isspd.com/
The International Society for the Study of Personality Disorders, ISSPD, stimulates and supports scholarship, clinical experience, international collaboration, and communication of research on all aspects of personality disorders including diagnosis, course, and treatment.

http://www.bpdcentral.com/
BPD Central is a list of resources for people who care about someone with borderline personality disorder (BPD). They are one of the oldest and largest sites about BPD on the Web.

http://www.nmha.org/go/information/get-info/personality-disorders
The National Mental Health Association is the oldest-existing organization dedicated to providing mental health care. This site offers information on the subject of personality and related disorders. It discusses the different forms of personality disorder, symptoms to recognize, causes, and options to treat it.

http://www.ncbi.nlm.nih.gov/pubmedhealth/PMH0001935/
This site, published by the U.S. National Library of Medicine, supplies information on a variety of topics, including personality disorders.

Mainstream Films

Films relevant to Chapter 16 material are listed and summarized below.

Key to Film Listings:
P = psychopathology focus
T = treatment focus
E = ethical issues raised

Please note that some of the films suggested may have graphic sexual or violent content due to the nature of certain subject matters.

Benny & Joon
From 1993, this film portrays an artist with psychological dysfunctioning who is finding love. After watching the film, the diagnosis of the main character has been questioned—some argue schizophrenia, some argue schizotypal personality disorder. **P, serious film**

Cape Fear
While the 1962 version won more acclaim than the 1991 Scorsese remake, both films follow a vengeful ex-convict seeking revenge on the attorney who improperly defended him. **P, thriller/serious film**

A Clockwork Orange
In this 1971 film by Stanley Kubrick, Alex, a member of a brutal teenage gang, is imprisoned and agrees to aversion therapy. **P, T, E, serious film**

Copycat
This 1996 film stars Sigourney Weaver as a forensic psychologist who develops agoraphobia as the result of an assault. Her help is needed to capture a psychopath who is copying the crimes of renowned serial killers. **P, T, serious/commercial film**

The Crush
This 1993 film stars Alicia Silverstone as a teen obsessed with the next-door neighbor. **P, thriller/serious film**

Dead Man Walking
This 1995 critically acclaimed film portrays the true story of spiritual advisor Sister Helen Prejean and her first client—Matthew Poncelet (Sean Penn), a man convicted of rape and murder and awaiting execution. **P, T, E, serious film**

Fatal Attraction
From 1987, this suspenseful film follows a happily married man (Michael Douglas) who engages in a one-night stand with a troubled woman (Glenn Close) who refuses to end the affair. **P, thriller/serious film**

Five Easy Pieces
This 1970 film stars Jack Nicholson as a gifted man struggling to find his place in the world. **P, serious film**

Girl, Interrupted
Based on an autobiographical novel by Susanna Kaysen, this film details the experiences of several women as patients in a psychiatric hospital in the 1960s. The 1999 film challenges the diagnosis of mental illness and the relationship between diagnosis and social norm violations. **P, T, serious film**

The Hand That Rocks the Cradle
This 1992 film stars Rebecca De Mornay as a nanny with borderline personality disorder. **P, thriller**

Kalifornia
From 1993, this dark film follows a liberal journalist (David Duchovny) writing a book on homicidal maniacs with his exhibitionist-photographer lover (Michelle Forbes) while in the company of a sociopath (Brad Pitt) and his girlfriend (Juliette Lewis). **P, serious film**

Misery
This Oscar-wining film from 1990 stars Kathy Bates as a novelist's "number-one fan." **P, dramatic thriller**

Mommie Dearest
Starring Faye Dunaway as Joan Crawford, this 1981 adaptation of Christina Crawford's controversial autobiography details the horror in the movie star's life. **P, serious film**

Monster
This Academy award–winning film from 2003 stars Charlize Theron as Aileen Wuornos, a Daytona Beach prostitute who became a serial killer. Based on a true story. **P, drama**

Natural Born Killers
Acclaimed by some, panned by others, this disturbing 1994 Oliver Stone film follows Mickey Knox (Woody Harrelson) and his wife Mallory (Juliette Lewis) as they take off on a three-week killing spree across the country. **P, T, E, serious/commercial film**

One Hour Photo
From 2002, Robin Williams plays a photo employee obsessed with a suburban family. **P, dramatic thriller**

Seven
This dark film from 1995 examines how a sociopathic serial killer uses the seven deadly sins—gluttony, greed, sloth, envy, wrath, pride, and lust—to punish sinners for their ignorance. **P, E, thriller**

The Silence of the Lambs, and sequels *Hannibal, (2001) and Red Dragon (2002),* as well as *Manhunter (1986)*
This 1991 film of the Thomas Harris book follows an ambitious FBI agent (Jodi Foster) who enlists the aid of a criminally insane ex-psychiatrist (Anthony Hopkins

as Hannibal Lechter) to help track down a serial killer. **P, E, thriller/serious/commercial films**

Single White Female
From 1992, Jennifer Jason Leigh portrays a young woman with borderline personality disorder who tries to eliminate and replace her roommate played by Bridget Fonda. **P, serious film**

Sleeping with the Enemy
Starring Julia Roberts, this 1991 film follows a woman who flees a compulsive, controlling, and violent husband. **P, serious film**

The Talented Mr. Ripley
Matt Damon plays Tom Ripley, a young man desperate to be someone else, in this 1999 film set in 1950s New York. **P, dramatic thriller**

Taxi Driver
This classic 1976 film stars Robert DeNiro as Travis Bickle, an unstable Vietnam veteran, and Jodie Foster as the teen prostitute who befriends him. **P, drama**

Other Films:

American Psycho (2000) antisocial personality. **P, dark comedy film**
Apocalypse Now (1979) antisocial personality disorder. **P, serious film**
Arsenic and Old Lace (1944) antisocial personality. **P, comedy**
The Boston Strangler (1968) antisocial personality disorder. **P, serious film**
The Caine Mutiny personality disorder. **P, serious film**
Catch Me if You Can (2002) antisocial personality disorder. **P, commercial/serious film**
Compulsion (1959) antisocial personality disorder. **P, serious film**
Fight Club (1999) antisocial personality disorder. **P, serious film**
A Fine Madness (1966) personality disorders, lobotomy. **P, T, serious/comedy film**
Frances (1982) personality disorder. **P, T, E, serious film**
Full Metal Jacket (1987) **P, serious film**
Goodfellas (1990) antisocial personality. **P, serious/commercial film**
House of Games (1987) antisocial personality disorder. **P, serious film**
In Cold Blood (1967) antisocial personality disorder. **P, serious film**
Magnolia (1999) narcissistic personality disorder. **P, serious film**
The Royal Tennenbaums (2001) antisocial personality disorder. **P, comedy/serious film**
Shine (1996) psychosis, personality disorder. **P, T, serious film**

Swimfan (2002) borderline personality disorder. **P, commercial film**
Willard (1971, remake 2002) antisocial personality. **P, entertainment horror film**
A Woman under the Influence (1974) institutionalization and ECT. **P, T, E, serious film**

Comer Video Segments

Available as a supplement, this revised set of videotapes contains short clips depicting various topics related to abnormal psychology. Please see the accompanying Video Guide for specific clips linked to Chapter 16.

Recommendations for Purchase or Rental

The Comer Video Segments include excerpts from many superb clinical documentaries. While the segments alone are ideal for use in lectures, it often is useful to assign the entire documentary for special class screenings or library use by students. The following videos and other media are available for purchase or rental and appropriate for use in class or for assignment outside of class.

Understanding Borderline Personality Disorder: The Dialectical Approach
Guilford Publications, Inc.
72 Spring Street
New York, NY 10012
Phone: (800) 365-7006
or (212) 431-9800
Fax: (212) 966-6708
(800) 365-7006
www.guilford.com

Treating Borderline Personality Disorder: The Dialectical Approach
Guilford Publications, Inc.
72 Spring Street
New York, NY 10012
Phone: (800) 365-7006
or (212) 431-9800
Fax: (212) 966-6708
(800) 365-7006
www.guilford.com

The Iceman and the Psychiatrist
Personality Disorders
The Psychopathic Mind
These and other relevant titles are available through Films for the Humanities & Sciences
Box 2053 Princeton, NJ 08543-2053
1-800-257-5126
ffh.films.com

CLASS DEMONSTRATIONS AND ACTIVITIES

Profiles of Personality Disorders

Ask students to form small groups and then assign each group a personality disorder. Give each group a brief description, such as a possible patient profile, for its personality disorder. On an overhead transparency, summarize the diagnostic criteria each group comes up with for its disorder. You can compare the types of behaviors with the DSM-IV-TR masters B–46 through B–52 (in Appendix B), which gives the criteria for different personality disorders. Facilitate a discussion of each disorder.

Reinforcement

Ask the students in small groups to analyze the most typical reinforcement in their lives. What are some examples of reinforcers in their roles as college students? As family members? What patterns are the most common in a small group? In a class? On an overhead transparency, list the types of reinforcers students have generated. Continue the discussion in terms of how personality disorders are reinforced.

Therapy-Resistant Personality Disorders

Personality disorders are resistant to treatment efforts. Individuals with personality disorders rarely volunteer for treatment. Many times, they seek therapy because of external pressure, from the courts, or from demands by friends and family. Ask students if we should invest the effort to "cure" individuals who believe that they do not have any problems. When might forced treatment be appropriate, if ever?

Narcissism in the United States

Ask students if narcissism is becoming more common in the United States. If so, why? What role does narcissism play in the lives of politicians? Rock and movie stars? Business executives? Is there both a narcissistic style and a narcissistic personality disorder? What would the similarities and differences be? Develop a list of student responses on an overhead transparency.

Similarities and Differences in Narcissistic and Histrionic Personality Disorders

Ask students to form small groups and list ways in which they think Nancy the Narcissist and her twin sister, Heloise the Histrionic, would differ from and resemble each other, especially in their interactions with other people. You can make an overhead transparency from the DSM-IV-TR Master B–57 (in Appendix B) and show it for reference to the class. Explore Nancy's and Heloise's behaviors and the students' perceptions and reactions to the transparency.

Role-Playing Personality Disorders

Ask students to form small groups, then ask each group to role-play one of the following personality disorders: (1) narcissistic, (2) obsessive-compulsive, (3) antisocial, or (4) histrionic. Use the criteria from the DSM-IV-TR masters listed for this chapter as the basis of these exercises. Have each group present its examples to the class. [NOTE: A brief reminder about sensitivity and professionalism is worthwhile here.]

Case Study

Present a case study to the class.

Panel Discussion

Have students volunteer (or assign them) to role-play patients suffering from particular personality disorders in a panel discussion. [NOTE: A brief reminder about sensitivity and professionalism is worthwhile here.] Students in the audience can ask questions of the panelists.

"It's Debatable: Categorization or Classification?" (see Preface instructions for conducting this activity)

Have students volunteer (or assign them) in teams to opposite sides of the debate topic. Have students present their cases in class following standard debate guidelines.

SUGGESTED TOPICS FOR DISCUSSION

Personality Disorders and Success

Lead a discussion with the intent of identifying when a specific personality disorder might be an advantage to a person or vocation. Could narcissistic personality be an advantage for a beauty pageant contestant? Could an antisocial personality be helpful to a prizefighter or professional hockey player? Develop a list on an overhead transparency; is there a pattern that is forming?

The Student Personality Disorder

Lead a discussion on the question: Do students see themselves in each of the personality disorders? If so, why does this happen? What criteria should be used to separate the "normal" students from individuals with diagnosable personality disorders?

Personality Disorders and Levels of Maladaptive Behaviors

Start a discussion with the question, Are personality disorders mental disorders? Personality disorders are maladaptive ways of dealing with reality that interfere with functioning. Although they are coded on Axis II of the DSM-IV-TR, are they really mental disorders? Does calling these behaviors mental disorders excuse the individual and allow him or her not to take responsibility for his or her behavior?

New Age/Psychic or Personality Disorder?

Lead a class discussion on schizotypal symptoms that may include magical thinking, such as mind reading and clairvoyance; odd perceptions, such as hallucinations about hearing the voice of a dead friend; and other unusual thoughts. How are New Age/psychic persons similar to schizotypal persons? How do they differ? Do the students think that most psychic experiences are due to schizotypal personality disorder? If not, how could they detect the differences between someone with schizotypal personality disorder and a person with psychic abilities?

Personality Disorders and the Movies

Since Hollywood portrayals of the personality disorders are so common, lead a discussion about some of the more well-known portrayals (e.g., in *Mommie Dearest*; *Taxi Driver*; *Fatal Attraction*; *Girl, Interrupted*). See the Mainstream Film section in this chapter for other suggestions.

Personality and the Brain: The Case of Phineas Gage

Using PsychWatch on p. 478 in the text as a platform, lead a discussion on the fascinating case of Phineas Gage. How does his experience help us understand the basis of personality and personality disorders?

ASSIGNMENTS/EXTRA CREDIT SUGGESTIONS

"Write a Pamphlet"

With the use of a software program like Microsoft Publisher or simply paper and markers, students can create a pamphlet on one or all of the personality disorders. Students should be encouraged to be as accurate and up-to-date as possible and also to present all sides of the disorder (e.g., alternate treatment approaches or theories).

Keep a Journal

In addition to helping students synthesize material, this activity is helpful in the development of writing skills. Have students keep a journal of their thoughts on course material through the semester. This can be done in the first or last five minutes of class or as an out-of-class assignment. Faculty generally should have students submit their journals for review on an ongoing basis, since students can have the tendency to delay writing until the end of the semester. Some suggestions for journal topics include: reactions to the case examples; strengths and weaknesses of prevailing theoretical explanations; hypothetical conversations with sufferers of specific disorders, etc.

Abnormal Psychology Student Tool Kit Video Questions

As a homework assignment, have students watch a video clip and answer the accompanying questions. Students can answer the questions directly into the online assessment feature. The results of these quizzes report to the site's built-in grade book.

Web Site Quiz

For homework or extra credit, have students complete the quiz for Chapter 16 located on the companion Web site. Students can complete an online test of the key chapter material (using questions NOT from the test bank) and have their scores e-mailed directly to the course instructor.

Essay Topics

For homework or extra credit, have students write an essay addressing one (or more) of the following topics:

(1) Discuss the prevalence of Internet videos depicting self-injurious behaviors, as discussed in the MediaSpeak box on p. 492 of the text. What are the implications of these videos getting such widespread attention? What, if anything, can and should be done to combat them?

(2) Make an argument for including (or against including) such diagnoses as "cell phone addiction" or "Internet addiction" as legitimate psychological disorders.

(3) Discuss media representations of the personality disorders discussed in the chapter. Why are some disorders more common in the media than oth-

ers? Does the media do a fair job characterizing the symptoms and the sufferers?

(4) Read The Media Speaks on p. 494 in the text and write a reaction paper. What do you think about Dr. Linehan's self-disclosure? Do you think her personal experience is helpful or harmful to her work? Mark an argument for EACH side.

Research Topics

For homework or extra credit, have students write a research report addressing one (or more) of the following topics:

(1) Conduct a "Psych Info" search and write a brief literature review on the classification of personality disorders. What various models currently are being investigated?

(2) Conduct a "Psych Info" search and write an annotated bibliography on the impulse disorders discussed in PsychWatch on p. 487 in the text: pyromania, kleptomania, intermittent explosive disorder, trichotillomania, and pathological gambling. What research is being done on these disorders? In what ways do they differ from the disorders covered in the chapter?

(3) Research and review the literature on one of the personality disorders discussed in the chapter. What research is being conducted currently? What model is being examined? What techniques have been found to be effective?

Film Review

To earn extra credit, have students watch one (or more) of the mainstream films listed and write a brief (3–5 pages) report. Students should summarize the plot of the film in sufficient detail to demonstrate familiarity, but should focus their papers on the depiction of psychological abnormality. What errors or liberties did the filmmaker take? What is the message (implicit or explicit) concerning the mentally ill?

Case Study Evaluations

To complement the Comer and Gorenstein supplemental case study text, case study evaluations have been created. Students can be assigned the appropriate case study and evaluation as homework or for class discussion. While case study evaluation questions are listed in their entirety on the companion Web site at www.worthpublishers.com/comer, the following relevant case studies are referenced.

Case Study 13: Borderline Personality Disorder

Case Study 14: Antisocial Personality Disorder

Case Study—You Decide

The Comer and Gorenstein supplemental case study text offers three cases in which patients are neither diagnosed nor treated. These cases provide students with the opportunity to identify disorders and suggest appropriate therapies. Throughout each case, students are asked to consider a number of issues and to arrive at various decisions, including diagnostic and treatment decisions. Each case can be assigned as homework or for class discussion. The case study relevant to Chapter 16 is referenced below.

You Decide: The Case of Suzanne, Hair Pulling

Crossword Puzzles

As a homework assignment or for extra credit, have students complete and submit Crossword Puzzle #16.

Word Searches

As a homework assignment or for extra credit, have students complete and submit Word Search #16.

Disorders of Childhood and Adolescence

LECTURE OUTLINE

I. **DISORDERS OF CHILDHOOD AND ADOLESCENCE**
    A. Abnormal functioning can occur at any time in life
    B. Some patterns of abnormality, however, are more likely to emerge during particular periods

II. **CHILDHOOD AND ADOLESCENCE**
    A. People often think of childhood as a carefree and happy time—yet it also can be frightening and upsetting
        1. Children of all cultures typically experience at least some emotional and behavioral problems as they encounter new people and situations
        2. Surveys indicate that *worry* is a common experience:
            a. Bedwetting, nightmares, temper tantrums, and restlessness are other problems experienced by many children
    B. Adolescence also can be a difficult period
        1. Physical and sexual changes, social and academic pressures, personal doubts, and temptation cause many teenagers to feel anxious, confused, and depressed
        2. A particular concern among children and adolescents is that of being bullied
            a. Over one-quarter of students report being bullied frequently, and more than 70 percent report having been a victim at least once
    C. Beyond these common concerns and psychological difficulties, at least one-fifth of all children and adolescents in North America also experience a diagnosable psychological disorder
            a. Boys with disorders outnumber girls, even though most of the adult psychological disorders are more common in women
    D. Some disorders of children—childhood anxiety disorders and childhood depression—have adult counterparts
        1. Other childhood disorders—elimination disorders, for example—usually disappear or radically change form by adulthood
        2. There also are disorders that begin in birth or childhood and persist in stable forms into adult life
            a. These include autistic disorder and mental retardation

III. **CHILDHOOD ANXIETY DISORDERS**
    A. Anxiety is, to a degree, a normal and common part of childhood
        1. Since children have had fewer experiences than adults, their world is often new and scary
        2. Children also may be affected greatly by parental problems or inadequacies
        3. Beyond such environmental problems, there also is genetic evidence that some children are prone to an anxious temperament
    B. Childhood Anxiety Disorders
        1. For some children, such anxieties become chronic and debilitating, interfering with their daily lives and their ability to function appropriately; they may be suffering from an anxiety disorder
        2. Surveys indicate that between 8 and 29 percent of all children and adolescents display an anxiety disorder
        3. Some of these disorders are similar to their adult counterparts, but more often they take on a somewhat different character due to cognitive and other limitations
            a. Typically, anxiety disorders of young children are dominated by behavioral and somatic symptoms
            b. They tend to center on specific, sometimes imaginary, objects and events
        4. Separation anxiety disorder, one of the most common childhood anxiety disorders, follows this profile and is displayed by 4 to 10 percent of all children
            a. Sufferers feel extreme anxiety, often panic, whenever they are separated from home or a parent

      b.   A separation anxiety disorder may further take the form of a school phobia or school refusal—a common problem in which children fear going to school and often stay home for a long period

  C.   Treatments for Childhood Anxiety Disorders

      1.   Despite the high prevalence of these disorders, approximately two-thirds of anxious children go untreated

      2.   Among the children who do receive treatment, psychodynamic, behavioral, cognitive, cognitive-behavioral, family, and group therapies, separately or in combination, have been applied most often—each with some degree of success

      3.   Clinicians have also used drug therapy in some cases, often in combination with psychotherapy, but it has begun only recently to receive much research attention

      4.   Because children typically have difficulty recognizing and understanding their feelings and motives, many therapists, particularly psychodynamic therapists, use play therapy as part of treatment

IV. CHILDHOOD MOOD PROBLEMS

  A.   Approximately 2 percent of children and 9 percent of adolescents currently experience major depressive disorder; as many as 20 percent of adolescents experience at least one depressive episode

  B.   Major Depressive Disorder

      1.   As with anxiety disorders, very young children lack some of the cognitive skills that help produce clinical depression, thus accounting for the low rate of depression among the very young

      2.   Depression in the young may be triggered by negative life events (particularly losses), major changes, rejection, or ongoing abuse

      3.   Childhood depression is commonly characterized by such symptoms as headaches, stomach pain, irritability, and a disinterest in toys and games

      4.   Clinical depression is much more common among teenagers than among young children

          a.   Suicidal thoughts and attempts are particularly common

      5.   While there is no difference between rates of depression in boys and girls before the age of 13, girls are twice as likely as boys to be depressed by the age of 16

          a.   Several factors have been suggested, including hormonal changes, increased stressors, and increased emotional investment in social and intimate relationships

          b.   Another factor that has received attention is teenage girls' growing dissatisfaction with their bodies

      6.   For years, it was generally believed that childhood and teenage depression would respond well to the same treatments that have been of help to depressed adults—cognitive-behavioral therapy, interpersonal approaches, and antidepressant drugs—and many studies indicated the effectiveness of such approaches

          a.   However, some recent studies and events have raised questions about these approaches and findings, especially in relation to the use of antidepressant drugs, highlighting again the importance of research, particularly in the treatment realm

  C.   Bipolar Disorder

      1.   For decades, conventional clinical wisdom held that bipolar disorder is exclusively an *adult* mood disorder, where the earliest age of onset is the late teens

      2.   However, since the mid-1990s, clinical theorists have begun to believe that many children display bipolar disorder

      3.   Most theorists believe that the growing numbers of children diagnosed with this disorder reflect not an increase in prevalence but a new diagnostic trend

      4.   Other theorists believe the diagnosis is currently being overapplied to children and adolescents

          a.   They suggest the label has become a clinical "catchall" that is being applied to almost every explosive, aggressive child

      5.   The outcome of the debate is important, particularly because the current shift in diagnoses has been accompanied by an increase in the number of children who receive adult medications

          a.   Few of these drugs have been tested on and approved specifically for use in children

V. OPPOSITIONAL DEFIANT DISORDER AND CONDUCT DISORDER
   A.   Children consistently displaying extreme hostility and defiance may qualify for a diagnosis of *oppositional defiant disorder* or *conduct disorder*
       1.   This disorder is characterized by repeated arguments with adults, loss of temper, anger, and resentment
       2.   Children with this disorder ignore adult requests and rules, try to annoy people, and blame others for their mistakes and problems
       3.   As many as 10 percent of children qualify for this diagnosis
       4.   The disorder is more common in boys than girls before puberty but equal in both sexes after puberty
   B.   Children with *conduct disorder,* a more severe problem, repeatedly violate the basic rights of others
       1.   They often are aggressive and may be physically cruel to people and animals
       2.   Many steal from, threaten, or harm their victims, committing such crimes as shoplifting, forgery, mugging, and armed robbery
       3.   Conduct disorder usually begins between 7 and 15 years of age
       4.   As many as 10 percent of children, three-quarters of them boys, qualify for this diagnosis
       5.   Children with a mild conduct disorder may improve over time, but severe cases frequently continue into adulthood and develop into antisocial personality disorder or other psychological problems
   C.   Many clinical theorists believe that there are actually several kinds of conduct disorder
       1.   One team distinguishes four patterns:
           a.   Overt-destructive
           b.   Overt-nondestructive
           c.   Covert-destructive
           d.   Covert-nondestructive
       2.   It may be that the different patterns have different causes
   D.   Other researchers distinguish yet another pattern of aggression found in certain cases of conduct disorder—*relational aggression*—in which individuals are socially isolated and primarily display social misdeeds
       1.   Relational aggression is more common among girls than boys
   E.   Many children with conduct disorder are suspended from school, placed in foster homes, or incarcerated
       1.   When children between the ages of 8 and 18 break the law, the legal system often labels them *juvenile delinquents*
       2.   More than half of the juveniles who are arrested each year are *recidivists*, meaning they have records of previous arrests
           a.   Boys are much more involved in juvenile crime than are girls, although rates for girls are on the increase
   F.   What are the causes of conduct disorder?
       1.   Many cases of conduct disorder have been linked to genetic and biological factors, drug abuse, poverty, traumatic events, and exposure to violent peers or community violence
       2.   They have most often been tied to troubled parent-child relationships, inadequate parenting, family conflict, marital conflict, and family hostility
   G.   How do clinicians treat conduct disorder?
       1.   Because aggressive behaviors become more locked in with age, treatments for conduct disorder are generally most effective with children younger than 13
       2.   A number of interventions have been developed, but none of them alone is the answer for this difficult problem
           a.   Today's clinicians are increasingly combining several approaches into a wide-ranging treatment program
       3.   Given the importance of family factors in conduct disorder, therapists often use family interventions
           a.   One such approach is called *parent-child interaction therapy*
           b.   A related family intervention is *video modeling*

c. When children reach school age, therapists often use a family intervention called *parent management training*

d. These treatments often have achieved a measure of success

4. Other sociocultural approaches, such as community residential treatment programs and programs at school, have also helped some children improve

a. One such approach is *treatment foster care*

5. In contrast to these other approaches, institutionalization in *juvenile training centers* has not met with much success and may, in fact, strengthen delinquent behavior

6. Treatments that focus primarily on the child with conduct disorder, particularly cognitive-behavioral interventions, have achieved some success in recent years

a. In *problem-solving skills training*, therapists combine modeling, practice, role-playing, and systematic rewards

b. Another child-focused approach, *The Anger Coping and Coping Power Program*, has children participate in group sessions that teach them to manage anger more effectively

c. Studies indicate that these approaches do reduce aggressive behaviors and prevent substance use in adolescence

7. Recently, drug therapy also has been used

8. It may be that the greatest hope for reducing the problem of conduct disorder lies in *prevention* programs that begin in early childhood

a. These programs try to change unfavorable social conditions before a conduct disorder develops

b. All such approaches work best when they educate and involve the family

VI. ATTENTION-DEFICIT/HYPERACTIVITY DISORDER

A. Children who display attention-deficit/hyperactivity disorder (ADHD) have great difficulty attending to tasks or behave overactively and impulsively, or both

1. The primary symptoms of ADHD may feed into one another, but in many cases one of the symptoms stands out more than the other

B. About half the children with ADHD also have:

1. Learning or communication problems

2. Poor school performance

3. Difficulty interacting with other children

4. Misbehavior, often serious

5. Mood or anxiety problems

C. Approximately 4-9 percent of schoolchildren display ADHD, as many as 70 percent of them boys

1. Those whose parents have had ADHD are more likely than others to develop it

2. This disorder usually persists through childhood, but many children show a lessening of symptoms as they move into mid-adolescence

3. Between 35 and 60 percent continue to have ADHD as adults

D. How do clinicians assess ADHD?

1. ADHD is a difficult disorder to assess

a. Ideally, the child's behavior should be observed in several environmental settings because symptoms must be present across multiple settings to meet DSM-IV-TR's criteria

b. It also is important to obtain reports of the child's symptoms from their parents and teachers

c. Clinicians also commonly employ diagnostic interviews, rating scales, and psychological tests

E. What are the causes of ADHD?

1. Clinicians generally consider ADHD to have several interacting causes including:

a. Biological causes, particularly abnormal dopamine activity and abnormalities in the frontal-striatal regions of the brain

b. High levels of stress

c. Family dysfunctioning

2. Sociocultural theorists also point out that ADHD symptoms and a diagnosis of ADHD may actually create interpersonal problems and produce additional symptoms in the child

F. How is ADHD treated?
1. About 80 percent of all children and adolescents with ADHD receive treatment
2. There is, however, heated disagreement about the most effective treatment for the disorder
3. The most commonly applied approaches are drug therapy, behavioral therapy, or a combination
4. Millions of children and adults with ADHD are currently treated with methylphenidate (Ritalin), a stimulant drug that has been available for decades, or with certain other stimulants
   a. It is estimated that 2.2 million children in the United States, 3 percent of all school children, take Ritalin or other stimulant drugs for ADHD
   b. However, many clinicians worry about the possible long-term effects of the drugs and others question the applicability of study findings to minority children
   c. Extensive investigations indicate that ADHD is overdiagnosed in the United States, so many children who are receiving Ritalin may, in fact, have been inaccurately diagnosed
   d. On the positive side, Ritalin is apparently very helpful for those who do have the disorder, and most studies indicate its safety
5. Behavioral therapy has been applied in many cases of ADHD
   a. Parents and teachers learn how to apply operant conditioning techniques to change behavior
   b. These treatments often have been helpful, especially when combined with drug therapy

G. Multicultural factors and ADHD
1. Race seems to come into play with regard to ADHD
   a. A number of studies indicate that African American and Hispanic American children with significant attention and activity problems are less likely than white American children to be assessed for ADHD, receive an ADHD diagnosis, or undergo treatment for the disorder
   b. Children from racial minorities who do receive a diagnosis are less likely than white children to be treated with interventions that seem to be the most helpful, including the promising (but more expensive) *long-acting* stimulant drugs
2. In part, racial differences in diagnosis and treatment are tied to economic factors
3. Some clinical theorists further believe that social bias and stereotyping may contribute to the racial differences seen in the diagnosis and treatment of ADHD
4. While many of today's clinical theorists correctly alert us that ADHD may be generally overdiagnosed and overtreated, it is important that they also recognize that children from certain segments of society may actually be underdiagnosed and undertreated

VII. ELIMINATION DISORDERS
A. Children with elimination disorders repeatedly urinate or pass feces in their clothes, in bed, or on the floor
1. They already have reached an age at which they are expected to control these bodily functions
2. These symptoms are not caused by physical illness
B. Enuresis
1. Enuresis is repeated involuntary (or in some cases intentional) bedwetting or wetting of one's clothes
   a. It typically occurs at night during sleep but may also occur during the day
2. Children must be at least 5 years of age to receive this diagnosis
3. The problem may be triggered by a stressful event
4. The prevalence of the disorder decreases with age

5. Those with enuresis typically have a close relative who has had or will have the same disorder
6. Research has not favored one explanation for the disorder over others
    a. Psychodynamic theorists explain it as a symptom of broader anxiety and underlying conflicts
    b. Family theorists point to disturbed family interactions
    c. Behaviorists often view it as the result of improper, unrealistic, or coercive toilet training
    d. Biological theorists suspect the physical structure of the urinary system develops more slowly in some children
7. Most cases of enuresis correct themselves without treatment
    a. Therapy, particularly behavior therapy, can speed up the process

C. Encopresis
1. Encopresis, repeatedly defecating in one's clothing, is less common than enuresis and less well researched
2. The problem:
    a. Is usually involuntary
    b. Seldom occurs during sleep
    c. Starts after the age of 4
    d. Is more common in boys than girls
3. Encopresis causes intense social problems, shame, and embarrassment
4. Cases may stem from stress, constipation, improper toilet training, or a combination
5. The most common treatments are behavioral and medical approaches, or combinations of the two
    a. Family therapy also has been helpful

VIII. LONG-TERM DISORDERS THAT BEGIN IN CHILDHOOD
A. Two groups of disorders that emerge during childhood are likely to continue unchanged throughout a person's life:
1. Pervasive Developmental Disorders
2. Mental retardation
B. Clinicians have developed a range of treatment approaches that can make a major difference in the lives of people with these problems
C. Pervasive Developmental Disorders
1. Pervasive developmental disorders are a group of disorders marked by impaired social interactions, unusual communications, and inappropriate responses to stimuli in the environment
2. The group includes *autistic disorder, Asperger's disorder, Rett's disorder,* and *childhood disintegrative disorder*
    a. Because autistic disorder initially received so much more attention than the others, these disorders are often referred to as *autism-spectrum disorders*
3. Although the patterns are similar in many ways, they do differ in the degree of social impairment that sufferers experience
4. Just a decade ago, the autism spectrum disorders seemed to affect approximately 1 out of every 2000 children; it now appears that at least 1 in 600 and perhaps as many as 1 in 150 children display one of these disorders
D. Autistic Disorders
1. Autistic disorder, or autism, was first identified in 1943
2. Children with this disorder are extremely unresponsive to others, uncommunicative, repetitive, and rigid
3. Symptoms appear early in life, before age 3
4. Approximately 80 percent of all cases appear in boys
5. As many as 90 percent of children with autism remain severely disabled into adulthood and are unable to lead independent lives
    a. Even the highest-functioning adults with autism typically have problems in social interactions and communication and have restricted interests and activities

E. What are the features of autism?
1. The central feature of autism is the *individual's lack of responsiveness*, including extreme aloofness and lack of interest in people
2. *Language and communication problems* take various forms
   a. One common speech peculiarity is *echolalia*, the exact phrasing spoken by others
   b. Another is *pronominal reversal*, or confusion of pronouns
3. Autism also is marked by *limited imaginative play* and *very repetitive and rigid behavior*
   a. This has been termed a *"perseveration of sameness"*
   b. Many sufferers become strongly attached to particular objects—plastic lids, rubber bands, buttons, water—and may collect, carry, or play with them constantly
4. The *motor movements* of people with autism may be unusual
   a. Often called *"self-stimulatory"* behaviors, some children jump, flap their arms, and make faces
   b. Children with autism also may engage in *self-injurious* behaviors
   c. Children may at times seem *overstimulated* and/or *understimulated* by their environments
F. Asperger's Disorder
1. Children with Asperger's disorder (or syndrome) experience the kinds of social deficits, impairments in expressiveness, idiosyncratic interests, and restricted and repetitive behaviors that characterize children with autism, but, in contrast, children with Asperger's disorder often have normal intellectual, adaptive, and language skills
2. Clinical research suggests that there may be several subtypes of Asperger's disorder, each having a particular set of symptoms, including
   a. Rule boys
   b. Logic boys
   c. Emotion boys
3. If treatment begins early in life, the individual has a better chance of being successful at school and living independently
G. What are the causes of pervasive developmental disorders?
1. Much more research has been conducted on autism than on Asperger's disorder or other pervasive developmental disorders
2. Currently, many clinicians and researchers believe that other disorders are caused by factors similar to those responsible for autism
3. A variety of explanations for autism have been offered
   a. Sociocultural explanations are now seen as having been overemphasized
   b. More recent work in the psychological and biological spheres has persuaded clinical theorists that cognitive limitations and brain abnormalities are the primary causes of the disorder
4. Sociocultural causes
   a. Theorists initially thought that family dysfunction and social stress were the primary causes of autism
      (a) Kanner argued that particular personality characteristics of parents created an unfavorable climate for development—"Refrigerator parents"
      (b) These claims had enormous influence on the public and the self-image of parents, but research totally failed to support this model
   b. Some clinicians proposed a high degree of *social and environmental stress*, a theory also unsupported by research
5. Psychological causes
   a. According to certain theorists, people with autism have a central perceptual or cognitive disturbance
      (a) One theory holds that individuals fail to develop a theory of mind—an awareness that other people base their behaviors on their own beliefs, intentions, and other mental states, not on information they have no way of knowing

          (b)   Repeated studies have shown that people with autism have this kind of "mindblindness"

      b.   It has been theorized that early biological problems prevented proper cognitive development

    6.   Cognitive-Biological causes

      a.   While a detailed biological explanation for autism has not yet been developed, promising leads have been uncovered

          (a)   Examinations of relatives keeps suggesting a *genetic factor* in the disorder

             (i)   Prevalence rates are higher among siblings and highest among identical twins

          (b)   Some studies have linked autism to *prenatal difficulties* or *birth complications*

          (c)   Researchers also have identified specific *biological abnormalities* that may contribute to the disorder, particularly in the cerebellum

      b.   Many researchers believe that autism may have multiple biological causes

      c.   Perhaps all relevant biological factors lead to a common problem in the brain—a "final common pathway"—that produces the features of the disorder

      d.   Finally, because it has received so much attention over the past 15 years, it is worth examining a biological explanation that has NOT been borne out

          (a)   In 1998, some investigators proposed that a postnatal event—the MMR vaccine—might produce autism in some children, thus alarming many parents

          (b)   Virtually all research conducted since then has argued against this theory and, in fact, the original study was found to be flawed and had been retracted

H.   How do clinicians and educators treat pervasive developmental disorders?

    1.   Treatment can help people with autism adapt better to their environments, although no treatment yet known totally reverses the autistic pattern

    2.   Treatments of particular help are *cognitive-behavioral therapy, communication training, parent training,* and *community integration.*

    3.   In addition, psychotropic drugs and certain vitamins have sometimes helped when combined with other approaches

      a.   Cognitive-Behavioral therapy

          (a)   Behavioral approaches have been used in cases of autism to teach new, appropriate behaviors, including speech, social skills, classroom skills, and self-help skills, while reducing negative ones

             (i)   Most often, therapists use modeling and operant conditioning

          (b)   Therapies ideally are applied when they are started early in the children's lives

          (c)   Given the recent increases in the prevalence of autism, many school districts are now trying to provide education and training for autistic children in special classes; most school districts, however, remain ill equipped to meet the profound needs of these students

          (d)   Although significantly impaired, children with Asperger's disorder have less profound educational and treatment needs

      b.   Communication training

          (a)   Even when given intensive behavioral treatment, half of the people with autism remain speechless

          (b)   They are often taught other forms of communication, including sign language and simultaneous communication—a method of combining sign language and speech

          (c)   They also may use augmentative communication systems, such as "communication boards" or computers that use pictures, symbols, or written words to represent objects or needs

          (d)   Such programs also now use *child-initiated interactions* to help improve communication skills

      c.   Parent training

          (a)   Today's treatment programs involve parents in a variety of ways

                (i)   For example, behavioral programs train parents so they can apply behavioral techniques at home

           (b)   In addition, individual therapy and support groups are becoming more available to help parents deal with their own emotions and needs

       d.   Community integration

           (a)   Many of today's school-based and home-based programs for autism teach self-help; self-management; and living, social, and work skills

           (b)   In addition, greater numbers of *group homes* and *sheltered workshops* are available for teens and young adults with autism

                (i)   These programs help individuals become a part of their community and also reduce the concerns of aging parents

IX.   MENTAL RETARDATION

    A.   The term "mental retardation" has been applied to a varied population

       1.   In recent years, the less stigmatizing term *"intellectual disability"* has become synonymous with mental retardation in many clinical settings

       2.   As many as 3 of every 100 persons meets the criteria for this diagnosis

          a.   Approximately three-fifths of them are male, and the vast majority are considered *mildly* retarded

    B.   According to DSM-IV-TR, people should receive a diagnosis of mental retardation when they display general intellectual functioning that is well below average, in combination with poor adaptive behavior

       1.   IQ must be 70 or below

       2.   The person must have difficulty in such areas as communication, home living, self-direction, work, or safety

       3.   Symptoms must appear before age 18

    C.   Assessing intelligence

       1.   Educators and clinicians administer intelligence tests to measure intellectual functioning

       2.   These tests consist of a variety of questions and tasks that rely on different aspects of intelligence

          a.   Having difficulty in one or two of these subtests or areas of functioning does not necessarily reflect low intelligence

          b.   An individual's overall test score, or intelligence quotient (IQ), is thought to indicate general intellectual ability

       3.   Many theorists have questioned whether IQ tests are indeed valid

          a.   Intelligence tests also appear to be socioculturally biased

       4.   If IQ tests do not always measure intelligence accurately and objectively, then the diagnosis of mental retardation also may be biased

          a.   That is, some people may receive the diagnosis partly because of test inadequacies, cultural difference, discomfort with the testing situation, or the bias of a tester

    D.   Assessing adaptive functioning

       1.   Diagnosticians cannot rely solely on a cutoff IQ score of 70 to determine whether a person suffers from mental retardation

          a.   Several scales, such as the *Vineland* and *AAMR Adaptive Behavior Scales*, have been developed to assess adaptive behavior

          b.   For proper diagnosis, clinicians should observe the functioning of each individual in his or her everyday environment, taking both the person's background and the community standards into account

    E.   What are the features of mental retardation?

       1.   The most consistent sign of mental retardation is that the person learns very slowly

          a.   Other areas of difficulty are attention, short-term memory, planning, and language

          b.   Those who are institutionalized with mental retardation are particularly likely to have these limitations

       2.   DSM-IV-TR describes four levels of mental retardation:

          a.   *Mild* (IQ 50–70)

        b.   *Moderate* (IQ 35–49)

        c.   *Severe* (IQ 20–34)

        d.   *Profound* (IQ below 20)

    3.   In contrast, the American Association of Mental Retardation prefers to distinguish different kinds of mental retardation according to the level of support the person needs in various aspects of his or her life—*intermittent, limited, extensive,* or *pervasive*

F.   Mild retardation

    1.   Some 80–85 percent of all people with mental retardation fall into the category of mild retardation (IQ 50–70)

    2.   They sometimes are called "educably retarded" because they can benefit from schooling

    3.   Their jobs tend to be unskilled or semiskilled

    4.   Intellectual performance seems to improve with age

    5.   Research has linked mild mental retardation mainly to sociocultural and psychological causes, particularly:

        a.   Poor and unstimulating environments

        b.   Inadequate parent-child interactions

        c.   Insufficient early learning experiences

    6.   Although these factors seem to be the leading causes of mild mental retardation, at least some biological factors also may be operating

        a.   Studies have implicated mother's moderate drinking, drug use, or malnutrition during pregnancy in cases of mild retardation

G.   Moderate, severe, and profound retardation

    1.   Approximately 10 percent of persons with mental retardation function at a level of moderate retardation (IQ 35–49)

        a.   They can care for themselves, benefit from vocational training, and can work in unskilled or semiskilled jobs

    2.   Approximately 3–4 percent of persons with mental retardation function at a level of severe retardation (IQ 20–34)

        a.   They usually require careful supervision and can perform only basic work tasks

        b.   They are rarely able to live independently

    3.   About 1 percent of persons with mental retardation function at a level of profound retardation (IQ below 20)

        a.   With training, they may learn or improve basic skills but require a very structured environment

    4.   Severe and profound levels of mental retardation often appear as part of larger syndromes that include severe physical handicaps

H.   What are the causes of mental retardation?

    1.   The primary causes of moderate, severe, and profound retardation are biological, although people who function at these levels are also greatly affected by their family and social environment

        a.   Sometimes genetic factors are the roots of these biological problems

        b.   Other biological causes come from unfavorable conditions that occur before, during, or after birth

    2.   Chromosomal causes

        a.   The most common chromosomal disorder leading to mental retardation is Down syndrome

        b.   Fewer than one of every 1,000 live births result in Down Syndrome, but this rate increases greatly when the mother's age is over 35

        c.   Several types of chromosomal abnormalities may cause Down syndrome, but the most common is *trisomy 21*

        d.   *Fragile X syndrome* is the second most common chromosomal cause of mental retardation

    3.   Metabolic causes

        a.   In metabolic disorders, the body's breakdown or production of chemicals is disturbed

        b.   The metabolic disorders that affect intelligence and development typically are caused by the pairing of two defective *recessive* genes, one from each parent

          (a)   Examples include:
          (i)   *Phenylketonuria (PKU)*
          (ii)   *Tay-Sachs disease*

4. Prenatal and birth-related causes
   a. As a fetus develops, major physical problems in the pregnant mother can threaten the child's healthy development
      (a) Low iodine = *cretinism*
      (b) Alcohol use = *fetal alcohol syndrome (FAS)*
      (c) Certain maternal infections during pregnancy (e.g., *rubella, syphilis*)
   b. Birth complications also can lead to mental retardation, particularly a prolonged period without oxygen (*anoxia*)

5. Childhood problems
   a. After birth, particularly up to age 6, certain injuries and accidents can affect intellectual functioning
      (a) Examples include poisoning, serious head injury, excessive exposure to x-rays, and excessive use of certain chemicals, minerals, and/or drugs (e.g., lead paint)
      (b) In addition, certain infections, such as *meningitis* and *encephalitis*, can lead to mental retardation if they are not diagnosed and treated in time

I. Interventions for people with mental retardation

1. The quality of life attained by people with mental retardation depends largely on sociocultural factors
   a. Thus, intervention programs try to provide comfortable and stimulating residences, social and economic opportunities, and a proper education

2. What is the proper residence?
   a. Until recently, parents of children with mental retardation would send them to live in public institutions—state schools—as early as possible
      (a) These overcrowded institutions provided basic care, but residents were neglected, often abused, and isolated from society
      (b) During the 1960s and 1970s, the public became more aware of these sorry conditions, and, as part of the broader *deinstitutionalization* movement, demanded that many people be released from these schools
   b. People with mental retardation faced similar challenges by deinstitutionalization as people with schizophrenia
   c. Since deinstitutionalization, reforms have led to the creation of *small institutions* and other *community residences* (group homes, halfway houses, local branches of larger institutions, and independent residences) that teach self-sufficiency, devote more time to patient care, and offer education and medical services
      (a) These programs follow the principle of normalization—they try to provide living conditions similar to those enjoyed by the rest of society
   d. Today, the vast majority of children with mental retardation live at home rather than in an institution
      (a) Most people with mental retardation, including almost all with mild mental retardation, now spend their adult lives either in the family home or in a community residence

3. Which educational programs work best?
   a. Because early intervention seems to offer such great promise, educational programs for individuals with mental retardation may begin during the earliest years
   b. At issue are special education vs. mainstream classrooms
      (a) In special education, children with mental retardation are grouped together in a separate, specially designed educational program
      (b) Mainstreaming places them in regular classes with nonretarded students
      (c) Neither approach seems consistently superior
      (d) Teacher preparedness is a factor that plays into decisions about mainstreaming

        c.   Many teachers use operant conditioning principles to improve the self-help, communication, social, and academic skills of individuals with mental retardation
           (a)   Many schools also employ token economy programs

    4.   When is therapy needed?
        a.   People with mental retardation sometimes experience emotional and behavioral problems
        b.   Approximately 30 percent or more have a diagnosable psychological disorder other than mental retardation
        c.   Furthermore, some suffer from low self-esteem, interpersonal problems, and adjustment difficulties
        d.   These problems are helped to some degree with individual or group therapy, and psychotropic medication sometimes is prescribed

    5.   How can opportunities for personal, social, and occupational growth be increased?
        a.   People need to feel effective and competent in order to move forward in life
           (a)   Those with mental retardation are most likely to achieve these feelings if their communities allow them to grow and make many of their own choices
        b.   Socializing, sex, and marriage are difficult issues for people with mental retardation and their families
           (a)   With proper training and practice, the individuals can learn to use contraceptives and carry out responsible family planning
           (b)   The National Association for Retarded Citizens offers guidance in these matters
           (c)   Some clinicians have developed *dating skills programs*
        c.   Some states restrict marriage for people with mental retardation
           (a)   These laws rarely are enforced
        d.   Finally, adults with mental retardation need the financial security and personal satisfaction that come from holding a job
           (a)   Many can work in sheltered workshops but there are too few training programs available
           (b)   Additional programs are needed so that more people with mental retardation may achieve their full potential, as workers and as human beings

X.   CALL FOR CHANGE: DSM-5
   A.   The DSM-5 Task Force proposed a number of key changes for the disorders discussed here:
       1.   Eliminate the overall grouping "Disorders Usually First Diagnosed in Infancy, Childhood, or Adolescence" and, instead, list these disorders under different categories
        a.   One new grouping is "Neurodevelopmental Disorders" and would include mental retardation, ADHD, and the learning, communication, and coordination disorders described in PsychWatch (p. 549)
       2.   Change the name of the mental retardation category to *intellectual developmental disorder*
       3.   Within the "Neurodevelopmental Disorders" grouping, combine *autistic disorder*, *Asperger's disorder*, and *childhood disintegrative disorder* into a single category called *autism spectrum disorder*
       4.   List the remaining childhood and adolescent disorders under other groupings
        a.   List *separation anxiety disorder* in the "Anxiety Disorders" grouping
        b.   List *oppositional defiant disorder* and *conduct disorder* in a new grouping called "Disruptive, Impulse Control, and Conduct Disorders"
        c.   List *enuresis* and *encopresis* in a grouping called "Elimination Disorders"
       5.   Add several new categories, including *disruptive mood dysregulation disorder* and *nonsuicidal self-injury*

LEARNING OBJECTIVES

1. Describe childhood anxiety disorders and their treatment.

2. Describe the childhood mood problems of major depressive disorder and bipolar disorder.

3. Describe the prevalence, symptoms, causes, and treatments of oppositional defiant disorder and conduct disorder.

4. Describe the prevalence, symptoms, causes, and treatments of attention-deficit/hyperactivity disorder (ADHD).

5. Name and describe the elimination disorders. Discuss possible causes and treatments.

6. Describe the types and symptoms of pervasive developmental disorders. Discuss the various etiologies and treatments that have been proposed.

7. Describe the prevalence of the various types of mental retardation, and discuss the environmental, genetic, and biological factors that contribute to mental retardation. Describe and evaluate treatments and therapies for individuals with mental retardation, including normalization programs and behavioral techniques.

8. Discuss the changes for these disorders proposed by the DSM-5 Task Force.

KEY TERMS

amniocentesis
Asperger's disorder
attention-deficit/
   hyperactivity disorder
   (ADHD)
augmentative communication
   system
autistic disorder, or autism
cerebellum
conduct disorder
cyberbullying
dating skills program
deinstitutionalization
Down syndrome
echolalia
encopresis

enuresis
fetal alcohol syndrome
fragile X syndrome
intelligence quotient (IQ)
mainstreaming
mental retardation
methylphenidate (Ritalin)
mild retardation
moderate retardation
normalization
oppositional defiant disorder
perseveration of sameness
pervasive developmental
   disorder
phenylketonuria (PKU)
play therapy

profound retardation
recessive genes
self-injurious behavior
self-stimulatory behavior
separation anxiety disorder
severe retardation
sheltered workshop
simultaneous communication
special education
state school
Tay-Sachs disease
theory of mind
token economy program
trisomy 21

MEDIA RESOURCES

Abnormal Psychology Student Tool Kit

Produced and edited by Ronald J. Comer, Princeton University and Gregory Comer, Princeton Academic Resources. Tied directly to the CyberStudy sections in the text, this Student Tool Kit offers 57 intriguing Video Cases running 3 to 7 minutes each. The Video Cases focus on persons affected by disorders discussed in the text. Students first view the video and then answer a series of thought-provoking questions. Additionally, the Student Tool Kit contains multiple-choice practice test questions with built-in instructional feedback for every option.

PowerPoint Slides

Available at the Instructor's site on the companion Web site are comprehensive PowerPoint slide presentations and supplemental student handouts for Chapter 17. The slide files reflect the main points of the chapter in significant detail. Student handouts were created using the instructor slides as a base, with key points replaced as "fill-in" items. Answer keys and suggestions for use also are provided.

DSM-IV-TR Masters

B-60, DSM-IV-TR Diagnostic Criteria for Separation Anxiety Disorder

B-61, DSM-IV-TR Diagnostic Criteria for Oppositional Defiant Disorder

B-62–B-63, DSM-IV-TR Diagnostic Criteria for Conduct Disorder

B-64–B-65, DSM-IV-TR Diagnostic Criteria for Attention-Deficit/Hyperactivity Disorder

B-66, DSM-IV-TR Diagnostic Criteria for Enuresis

B-66, DSM-IV-TR Diagnostic Criteria for Encopresis

B-67, DSM-IV-TR Diagnostic Criteria for Autistic Disorder

B-68, DSM-IV-TR Diagnostic Criteria for Asperger's Disorder

B-69, DSM-IV-TR Diagnostic Criteria for Mental Retardation

B-70, DSM-IV-TR Diagnostic Criteria for Mathematics Disorder

B-70, DSM-IV-TR Diagnostic Criteria for Disorder of Written Expression

B-70, DSM-IV-TR Diagnostic Criteria for Reading Disorder

B-71, DSM-IV-TR Diagnostic Criteria for Phonological Disorder

B-71, DSM-IV-TR Diagnostic Criteria for Expressive Language Disorder

B-72, DSM-IV-TR Diagnostic Criteria for Mixed Receptive/Expressive Language Disorder

B-73, DSM-IV-TR Diagnostic Criteria for Stuttering

B-74, DSM-IV-TR Diagnostic Criteria for Developmental Coordination Disorder

Internet Sites

Please see Appendix A for full and comprehensive references.

Sites relevant to Chapter 17 material are:

http://www.thearc.org

This site includes information on the Arc, an organization of and for people with intellectual and developmental disabilities, chapter locations, and links to additional resources.

http://www.conductdisorders.com/

This site is maintained by a "group of parents raising challenging children."

http://members.tripod.com/~tourette13/

This site discusses how Tourette's syndrome (TS) is a neurological disorder characterized by tics or involuntary, rapid, sudden movements or vocalizations that occur repeatedly in the same way.

http://www.nimh.nih.gov/health/publications

This Web site, provided by the National Institute of Mental Health, supplies downloadable links to PDF files and booklets on a variety of mental health topics, including ADHD and conduct disorders.

http://www.chadd.org

Run by children and adults with ADHD, this site offers support for individuals, parents, teaches, professionals, and others.

Mainstream Films

Films relevant to Chapter 17 material are listed and summarized below.

Key to Film Listings:
P = psychopathology focus
T = treatment focus
E = ethical issues raised

Please note that some of the films suggested may have graphic sexual or violent content due to the nature of certain subject matters.

The Breakfast Club
From 1985, this John Hughes classic follows five high school students from different social groups spending a Saturday together in detention. **P, comedy/serious film**

Charly
From the award-winning book *Flowers for Algernon*, this 1968 film portrays Charly, an adult suffering from mental retardation. The film details Charly's experiences with doctors attempting to "cure" him, leading up to his participation in an experimental treatment that raises his IQ to genius levels but not his emotional maturity. Issues of informed consent and the responsibilities that accompany science are handled well. **P, T, E, serious film**

Crazy/Beautiful
This 2001 film stars Kirsten Dunst as a troubled, rebellious rich girl who abuses drugs and alcohol and is medicated for depression. Her romance with a boy from the wrong side of the tracks helps her put her life back together. **P, serious film**

Dead Poet's Society
This 1989 film stars Robin Williams as an unconventional teacher in a strict prep school. The suicide of one of his students is explored. **P, E, serious film**

Dominick and Eugene
From 1988, this touching film follows fraternal twins—one (Ray Liotta) is an ambitious medical student, the other (Tom Hulce) is a "slow" trash collector. **P, serious film**

Equus
In this 1977 film, psychiatrist Richard Burton treats a young boy (Peter Firth) who has blinded horses, seemingly for no reason. **P, T, E serious film**

I Am Sam
From 2001, this Sean Penn film follows Sam Dawson, a father with the mental capacity of a 7-year-old. **P, E, serious/commercial film**

Mad Love
This 1995 stars Chris O'Donnell as a teen "saving" Drew Barrymore after her family puts her in a psychiatric hospital. **P, serious film**

The Other Sister
From 1999, this film stars Juliette Lewis as a young woman with mental retardation striving for independence from her (overly) protective mother (Diane Keaton). **P, commercial/serious film**

Pretty in Pink
This 1986 story of teen angst stars Molly Ringwald as a quirky girl from the bad side of town and Andrew McCarthy as her rich kid crush. **P, commercial comedy/serious film**

Prince of Tides
In this 1991 film, an adaptation of a Pat Conroy novel, Nick Nolte plays a football coach who is estranged from his wife and who enters into an affair with the psychiatrist (Barbra Streisand) of his suicidal sister. **P, T, E, serious/commercial film**

Rain Man
This 1988 film stars Dustin Hoffman as a man with autism and savant syndrome who is forced to travel cross-country with his self-centered, greedy younger brother (Tom Cruise). **P, T, serious film**

Thirteen
This disturbing film from 2003 follows two girls on the edge of adolescence and identity development. **P, serious film**

What's Eating Gilbert Grape
This 1994 film stars Johnny Depp as Gilbert, the eldest brother in a family with a very large mother (Darlene Cates) who hasn't left the house since her husband committed suicide years before. Leonardo DiCaprio plays Arnie, Gilbert's teenage brother who suffers from mental retardation and needs constant supervision. **P, serious film**

William Shakespeare's Romeo & Juliet
This 1996 Baz Luhrmann adaptation of the Shakespeare classic stars Leonardo DiCaprio and Claire Danes as star-crossed, teen-aged lovers whose ill-fated relationship ultimately ends in both their deaths. **P, serious film**

Other Films:

Igby Goes Down (2002) problems of childhood and adolescence. **P, serious film**
Silent Fall (1994) autism. **P, commercial/serious film**
Spellbound (1945) **P, T, E, commercial thriller/romance**

Comer Video Segments

Available as a supplement, this revised set of videotapes contains short clips depicting various topics related to abnormal psychology. Please see the accompanying Video Guide for specific clips linked to Chapter 17.

Recommendations for Purchase or Rental

The Comer Video Segments include excerpts from many superb clinical documentaries. While the segments alone are ideal for use in lectures, it often is useful to assign the entire documentary for special class screenings or library use by students. The following videos and other media are available for purchase or rental and appropriate for use in class or for assignment outside of class.

Behavioral Treatment of Autistic Children
Focus International
1160 E. Jericho Turnpike
Huntington, NY 11743
(516) 549-5320

Hills and Valleys: Teen Depression
Autism
Films for the Humanities and Sciences
P.O. Box 2053
Princeton, NJ 08543-2053
Phone: 800-257-5126
Fax: 609-275-3767
Email To: custserv@films.com

ADHD—What Can We Do?
ADHD—What Do We Know?
Understanding the Defiant Child
Techniques of Play Therapy: A Clinical Demonstration
Guilford Publications, Inc.
72 Spring Street

New York, NY 10012
Phone: (800) 365-7006
or (212) 431-9800
Fax: (212) 966-6708
(800) 365-7006
www.guilford.com

CLASS DEMONSTRATIONS AND ACTIVITIES

Case Study

Present a case study to the class.

Panel Discussion

Have students volunteer to discuss their own experiences with childhood disorders. [NOTE: A brief reminder about sensitivity and professionalism is worthwhile here.]

"It's Debatable: Ritalin: Straightjacket or Miracle Drug?" (see Preface instructions for conducting this activity)

Using the text as a platform, have students volunteer (or assign them) in teams to opposite sides of the debate topic. Have students present their case in class following standard debate guidelines.

"It's Debatable: The rise of social networking and online friendships is causing more harm than good" (see Preface instructions for conducting this activity)

Have students volunteer (or assign them) in teams to opposite sides of the debate topic. Use MediaSpeak on p. 523 of the text as a starting point. Have students present their cases in class following standard debate guidelines.

Ritalin

The use of stimulant medications such as Ritalin has led to one of the more effective treatments for attention-deficit/hyperactivity disorder. The drugs reduce the activity-level problems, thereby making the child more manageable at home and in the classroom. Ask your students to put themselves in the roles of parents, teachers, and children and to discuss the implications, both pro and con, of using stimulant medications to control children's behavior.

SUGGESTED TOPICS FOR DISCUSSION

Bullying

Using Psych Watch on p. 529 in the text as a platform, lead a discussion on bullying in schools. Do students think it is a serious problem? What are their suggestions for reducing it?

Children's Problems

Lead a discussion about ways to help children deal with such family adjustments as divorce, financial changes, and death. Ask for student input into the types of problems these children can be expected to encounter.

Learning Disabilities

Using PsychWatch on p. 549 of the text, lead a discussion on how students feel about labeling learning disabilities (LDs) as mental illness. Learning disabled students show few, if any, signs of emotional disturbance, and some authorities question classifying learning disabilities as psychological disorders. Inform the class that several students in your class will fit into this classification. Use an overhead projector to list the advantages and disadvantages of calling LDs mental illness.

Presume You Are a Teacher . . .

Johnny is 7 years old and in the first grade. He has trouble sitting still, often loses things, is very loud, and acts very impulsively. He is disruptive to your classroom. You are fairly certain he has ADHD. You are meeting with his parents tomorrow night during Parent-Teacher Night. As typically happens at these events, you and the child's parents will have 10 minutes together. You want to convince them to seek an evaluation. What do you say? Do you recommend a formal evaluation by a mental health professional? Why or why not?

Presume You Are a Mental Health Professional . . .

Johnny is 7 years old and in the first grade. He has trouble sitting still, often lose things, is very loud, and acts very impulsively. Your evaluation has determined that he meets criteria for ADHD. His parents are coming to your office tomorrow to discuss the results. How do you tell them? What if they feel that they've done something wrong? Do you recommend psychotherapy? Do you recommend medication?

Presume You Are a Therapist . . .

Lead a discussion on the ethical issues of counseling with children and adolescents. As minors, their parents have a legal right to information about their treatment. How would students—acting as therapist—deal with confidentiality issues? What do they think a parent should have the right to know? How would they explain the various aspects of confidentiality to an elementary school child? To an adolescent?

Mainstreaming

Lead a discussion on the topic of mainstreaming mentally retarded students. What are the pros and cons of this issue? Does mainstreaming risk setting up the retarded child for social rejection? Many students will have been exposed to this practice in the K–12 schooling.

ASSIGNMENTS/EXTRA CREDIT SUGGESTIONS

"Write a Pamphlet"

With the use of a software program like Microsoft Publisher or simply paper and markers, students can create a pamphlet on one or all of the disorders of childhood and adolescence. Students should be encouraged to be as accurate and up-to-date as possible and also to present all sides of the disorder (e.g., alternate treatment approaches or theories).

Keep a Journal

In addition to helping students synthesize material, this activity is helpful in developing writing skills. Have students keep a journal of their thoughts on course material through the semester. This can be done in the first or last five minutes of class or as an out-of-class assignment. Faculty generally should have students submit their journals for review on an on-going basis, since students can have the tendency to delay writing until the end of the semester. Some suggestions for journal topics include: reactions to the case examples; strengths and weaknesses of prevailing theoretical explanations; hypothetical conversations with sufferers of specific disorders, etc.

Presume You Are an Expert . . .

Tell the students that you received a phone call from your senator last night at home. He or she recognized that you are doing a fine job instructing students on the issue of childhood abuse. Your senator wants you and several students to come to Washington, D.C., to testify before a Senate subcommittee on a new law intended

to prevent the abuse of children. Ask students to prepare a five-minute presentation outlining a recommendation for a law that might reduce child abuse. Remind them that their testimony will influence law. Also remind them that their testimony is "expert" and that they may be challenged about the validity of what they are saying.

Abnormal Psychology Student Tool Kit Video Questions

As a homework assignment, have students watch a video clip and answer the accompanying questions. Students can answer the questions directly into the online assessment feature. The results of these quizzes report to the site's built-in grade book.

Web Site Quiz

For homework or extra credit, have students complete the quiz for Chapter 17 located on the companion Web site. Students can complete an online test of the key chapter material (using questions NOT from the test bank) and have their scores e-mailed directly to the course instructor.

Essay Topics

For homework or extra credit, have students write an essay addressing one (or more) of the following topics:

(1) Discuss the issue of bullying [See PsychWatch, text p. 529]. From your experience, is bullying really problematic? What interventions do you

think should be researched and implemented to stem this (growing) problem?

(2) Using Media Speaks (p. 523 in the text) as a platform, discuss the impact of increased Internet use on social and emotional development

(3) Discuss the use of Ritalin as treatment for ADHD.

Research Topics

For homework or extra credit, have students write a research report addressing one (or more) of the following topics:

(1) Conduct a "Psych Info" search and write an annotated bibliography on Ritalin as a treatment for ADHD. What types of symptoms are best treated by this medication? What studies are examining the risks? Have validity studies been conducted to examine the criteria used for diagnosis?

(2) Research and review the literature on child abuse [See PsychWatch, text p. 537]. What are the predictors of child abuse? What are the long-term problems victims have? What treatments are successful for abusers? For victims?

(3) Research and review the literature on ADHD and race. What conclusions are being drawn?

(4) Research and review the literature on learning, communication, and/or developmental coordination disorders [See PsychWatch, text p. 549]. What are the symptoms, treatments, and prognoses for these disorders? What interventions are being investigated?

Film Review

To earn extra credit, have students watch one (or more) of the mainstream films listed in this chapter and write a brief (3–5 pages) report. Students should summarize the plot of the film in sufficient detail to demonstrate familiarity, but should focus their papers on the depic-

tion of psychological abnormality. What errors or liberties did the filmmaker take? What is the message (implicit or explicit) concerning the mentally ill?

Case Study Evaluations

To complement the Comer and Gorenstein supplemental case study text, case study evaluations have been created. Students can be assigned the appropriate case study and evaluation as homework or for class discussion. While case study evaluation questions are listed in their entirety on the companion Web site at www.worthpublishers.com/comer, the relevant case studies follow.

Case Study 15: Autism

Case Study 16: Attention-Deficit/Hyperactivity Disorder

Case Study 17: Conduct Disorder

Web-Based Case Studies

Nine Web-based case studies have been created and posted on the companion Web site. These cases describe the individual's history and symptoms and are accompanied by a series of guided questions which point to the precise DSM-IV-TR criteria for each disorder. Students can both identify the disorder and suggest a course of treatment. Students can be assigned the appropriate case study and questions as homework or for class discussion. The case relevant to Chapter 17 is referenced below.

The Case of Eric: Disorders of Childhood

Crossword Puzzles

As a homework assignment or for extra credit, have students complete and submit Crossword Puzzle #17.

Word Searches

As a homework assignment or for extra credit, have students complete and submit Word Search #17.

Disorders of Aging and Cognition

LECTURE OUTLINE

I.   **DISORDERS OF AGING AND COGNITION**
    A.   Dementia—deterioration of one's memory and related cognitive faculties—is currently the most publicized and feared psychological problem among the elderly
        1.   It is, however, hardly the only one
    B.   A variety of psychological disorders are tied closely to later life

C.   As with childhood disorders, some of the disorders of old age are caused primarily by pressures that are particularly likely to appear at that time of life, others by unique traumatic experiences, and still others—like dementia—by biological abnormalities

II.   OLD AGE AND STRESS
A.   Old age is usually defined in our society as the years past age 65
   1.   There are more than 36 million "old" people in the United States—12 percent of the population and growing
   2.   Older women outnumber older men by 3 to 2
B.   Like childhood, old age brings special pressures, unique upsets, and profound biological changes
   1.   The stresses of elderly people need not result in psychological disorders; however, studies indicate that as many as 50 percent of elderly people would benefit from mental health services
      a.   Yet, fewer than 20 percent actually receive them
   2.   Geropsychology is the field of psychology dedicated to the mental health of elderly people
C.   The psychological problems of elderly persons may be divided into two groups:
   1.   Disorders that are found in people of all ages but are connected to the process of aging
      a.   Depressive, anxiety, and substance-related disorders
   2.   Disorders of cognition that result from brain abnormalities
      a.   Delirium, dementia

III.   DEPRESSION IN LATER LIFE
A.   Depression is one of the most common mental health problem of older adults
B.   The features of depression are the same for elderly people as for younger people
C.   Overall, as many as 20 percent of the elderly experience this disorder
   1.   The rate is highest in older women
D.   Several studies suggest that depression among older people raises their chances of developing significant medical problems
E.   Elderly persons are also more likely to commit suicide than younger ones, and often their suicides are related to depression
F.   Like younger adults, older people who are depressed may be helped by cognitive-behavioral therapy, interpersonal therapy, antidepressant medications, or a combination of these approaches
   1.   More than half of older patients with depression improve with these treatments
G.   It sometimes is difficult to use antidepressant drugs effectively and safely because the body's metabolism works differently in later life
   1.   Moreover, among elderly people, antidepressant drugs have a higher risk of causing some cognitive impairment

IV.   ANXIETY DISORDERS IN LATER LIFE
A.   Anxiety also is common among the elderly
   1.   At any given time, around 6 percent of elderly men and 11 percent of elderly women in the United States experience at least one of the anxiety disorders
   2.   GAD is particularly common, experienced by up to 7 percent of all elderly persons
B.   The prevalence of anxiety increases throughout old age and anxiety in the elderly may be underreported
C.   There are many things about aging that may heighten anxiety levels, including declining health
   1.   Researchers have not, however, systematically tied anxiety disorders among the elderly to specific events or losses
D.   Older adults with anxiety disorders often are treated with psychotherapy of various kinds, particularly cognitive-behavioral therapy
   1.   Many also receive antianxiety medications
   2.   Again, all such drugs must be used cautiously with older people

V.   SUBSTANCE ABUSE IN LATER LIFE
   A.   Although alcohol abuse and other forms of substance abuse are significant problems for many older persons, the prevalence of such patterns actually appears to decline after age 60
      1.   It is important to note, though, that accurate data about the rate of substance abuse among older adults is difficult to obtain because many elderly persons do not suspect or admit they have such a problem
   B.   Surveys find that 4 to 7 percent of older people, particularly men, display alcohol-related disorders in a given year
   C.   Researchers often distinguish between older problem drinkers who have experienced significant alcohol-related problems for many years and those who do not start the pattern until their 50s and 60s
      1.   The latter group typically begins abusive drinking as a reaction to the negative events and pressures of growing older
   D.   Alcohol abuse and dependence in elderly people are treated much as in younger adults
      1.   Approaches include detoxification, Antabuse, Alcoholics Anonymous (AA), and cognitive-behavioral therapy
   E.   A leading kind of substance abuse in this population is the misuse of prescription drugs
      1.   Most often it is unintentional
      2.   Yet another drug-related problem is the misuse of powerful medications at nursing homes

VI.   PSYCHOTIC DISORDERS IN LATER LIFE
   A.   Elderly people have a higher rate of psychotic symptoms than younger persons
      1.   Among aged people, these symptoms are usually due to underlying medical conditions such as delirium and dementia
      2.   However, some elderly persons suffer from schizophrenia or delusional disorder
   B.   Schizophrenia is less common in older persons than in younger ones
      1.   Many people with schizophrenia find their symptoms lessen in later life
      2.   It is uncommon for new cases of schizophrenia to emerge in later life
   C.   Another kind of psychotic disorder found among the elderly is delusional disorder, in which individuals develop beliefs that are false but not bizarre
      1.   This disorder is rare in most age groups but its prevalence appears to increase in the elderly population
      2.   Some clinicians suggest that the rise is related to the deficiencies in hearing, social isolation, greater stress, or heightened poverty experienced by many elderly persons

VII.   DISORDERS OF COGNITION
   A.   Cognitive "mishaps" (e.g., leaving without keys, forgetting someone's name) are a common and quite normal feature of stress or of aging
      1.   As people move through middle age, these memory difficulties and lapses of attention increase, and they may occur regularly by age 60 or 70
      2.   Sometimes, however, people experience memory and other cognitive changes that are far more extensive and problematic
   B.   While problems in memory and related cognitive processes can occur without organic causes (in the form of dissociative disorders), cognitive problems do have organic roots, particularly when they appear in later life
   C.   The leading cognitive disorders among elderly persons are delirium and dementia
   D.   Delirium
      1.   Delirium is a clouding of consciousness
      2.   As a person's awareness of the environment becomes less clear, he or she has great difficulty concentrating, focusing attention, and thinking sequentially
         a.   This leads to misinterpretations, illusions, and, on occasion, hallucinations
         b.   This state of massive confusion typically occurs over a short period of time, usually hours or days
      3.   Delirium may occur in any age group, including children, but it is most common in elderly persons

a. It affects fewer than 0.5% of the nonelderly population, 1% of people over 55, and 14% of those over 85 years of age

4. Fever, certain diseases and infections, poor nutrition, head injuries, strokes, stress (including the trauma of surgery), and intoxication by certain substances may all cause delirium

E. Dementia

1. People with dementia experience significant memory losses along with losses in other cognitive functions such as abstract thinking or language

2. People with this syndrome also may experience changes in personality and behavior

3. At any given time, around 3 to 9 percent of the world's adult population are suffering from dementia

4. The experience of dementia is closely related to age

a. Among people 65 years of age, the prevalence is around 1 to 2%, increasing to as much as 50% among those over the age of 85

5. Like delirium, some forms of dementia result from nutritional or other problems that can be corrected

a. Most forms, however, are caused by brain diseases or injuries, such as Alzheimer's disease or stroke, which are currently difficult or impossible to correct

6. Alzheimer's disease

a. This disease, identified in 1907, is the most common form of dementia, accounting for as many as two-thirds of all cases

b. Around 5 million people in the United States currently have this disease

c. This gradually progressive disease sometimes appears in middle age (early onset), but most often occurs after the age of 65 (late onset)

d. Its prevalence increases markedly among people in their late 70s and early 80s

e. The time between onset and death typically is about 8 to 10 years, although some people may survive for as many as 20 years

(a) It usually begins with mild memory problems, lapses of attention, and difficulties in language and communication

(b) As symptoms worsen, the person has trouble completing complicated tasks and remembering important appointments

(c) Eventually sufferers also have difficulty with simple tasks, distant memories are forgotten, and changes in personality often become very noticeable

(d) As the symptoms of dementia intensify, people show less and less awareness of their limitations

(e) Eventually they become fully dependent on other people; they lose almost all knowledge of the past and fail to recognize the faces of even close relatives

f. Alzheimer's victims usually remain in good health until the later stages of the disease

g. In most cases, the disease can be diagnosed with certainty only after death, when structural changes in the brain can be fully examined

(a) Senile plaques are sphere-shaped deposits of a small molecule known as the beta-amyloid protein that form in the spaces *between* cells in the hippocampus, cerebral cortex, and certain other brain regions and blood vessels

(b) Neurofibrillary tangles are twisted protein fibers found *within* the cells of the hippocampus

(c) Research has suggested several possible causes for the development of the disease, including genetic factors and abnormalities in brain structure and brain chemistry

7. What are the genetic causes of Alzheimer's disease?

a. It appears that Alzheimer's disease often has a genetic basis

(a) Clinicians now distinguish between early-onset/familial Alzheimer's disease and late-onset/sporadic Alzheimer's disease

(i) Early-Onset

1. Studies have found that mutations in particular genes increase the likelihood of plaque and tangle formations and, in turn, of Alzheimer's disease

          2.   Apparently some families transmit these mutations and the onset of the disease is set into motion

    (ii) Late-Onset

        1.   This form of the disease appears to result from a combination of genetic, environmental, and lifestyle factors

        2.   The genetic factor at play in sporadic Alzheimer's disease is different from the ones involved in familial Alzheimer's disease

8.   How does brain structure relate to Alzheimer's disease?

    a.   Researchers have identified a number of biological factors related to the brain abnormalities seen in Alzheimer's disease

    b.   To understand the role of these factors, an understanding of the operation and biology of memory is necessary:

      (a) Human memory

        (i)   The human brain has two memory systems that work together to help us learn and recall

            1.   Short-term memory, or working memory, gathers new information

                a.   Information held in short-term memory must be transformed, or consolidated, into long-term memory if we are to hold on to it

            2.   Long-term memory is the accumulation of information that we have stored over the years

                a.   Remembering information stored in long-term memory is called retrieval

        (ii) Certain brain structures seem to be especially important in memory, including (see Figure 18-3 in the text):

            1.   The prefrontal lobes, which appear to hold information temporarily and to continue working with it as long as it is needed

            2.   The temporal lobes and the diencephalon, which seem to help transform short-term into long-term memory

            3.   Research indicates that cases of dementia involve damage to or improper functioning of one or more of these areas

        (iii) Memory researchers also have identified biochemical changes that occur in cells as memories form

            1.   For example, several chemicals are responsible for the production of proteins produced in key cells when new information is acquired and stored

            2.   If the activity of these chemicals is disturbed, the proper production of proteins may be prevented and the formation of memories interrupted

            3.   Some research suggests that abnormal activity by these chemicals may contribute to the symptoms of Alzheimer's disease

    c.   In addition to these two explanations, researchers offer additional possibilities:

      (a) Several lines of research suggest that certain substances found in nature, including zinc, may produce brain toxicity, which may contribute to the development of the disease

      (b) Another line of research suggests that the environmental toxin lead may contribute to the development of Alzheimer's disease

      (c) Another explanation is the autoimmune theory:

        (i)   Several researchers have speculated that the changes in aging brain cells may trigger an autoimmune response, leading to the disease

      (d) A final explanation is a viral theory

        (i)   Because Alzheimer's disease resembles Creutzfeldt-Jakob disease (a form of dementia caused by a virus), some researchers propose that a similar virus may cause Alzheimer's disease

        (ii) To date, no such virus has been detected in the brains of Alzheimer's victims

9. Other forms of dementia
    a. A number of other disorders may also lead to dementia, including:
        (a) Vascular dementia (multi-infarct dementia)—May follow a cerebrovascular accident, or stroke, during which blood flow to specific areas of the brain was cut off, with resultant damage
            (i) This dementia is progressive but its symptoms begin suddenly, rather than gradually
            (ii) Cognitive functioning may continue to be normal in the areas of the brain not affected by the stroke
        (b) Pick's disease—a rare disorder that affects the frontal and temporal lobes and is clinically similar to Alzheimer's disease
        (c) Creutzfeldt-Jakob disease—caused by a slow-acting virus, this disease has symptoms that include spasms of the body
        (d) Huntington's disease—an inherited progressive disease in which memory problems worsen over time, along with personality changes, mood difficulties, and movement problems
        (e) Parkinson's disease—a slowly progressive neurological disorder marked by tremors, rigidity, and unsteadiness can cause dementia
        (f) Viral and bacterial infectious disorders—such as HIV and AIDS, meningitis, and advanced syphilis
        (g) Brain seizure disorder
        (h) Drug abuse
10. Assessing and predicting dementia
    a. Most cases of Alzheimer's disease can be diagnosed with certainty only after death, when autopsy is performed
    b. However, brain scans, which reveal structural abnormalities in the brain, now are commonly used as assessment tools
    c. Several research teams are currently trying to develop tools that can identify persons likely to develop dementia
        (a) One research team is using PET scans
    d. Because the most effective interventions for dementia are those that help prevent problems or, at the very least, are applied early, it is essential to have tools that identify the disorders as early as possible
    e. Treatments for the cognitive features of Alzheimer's have been at best modestly helpful
    f. A number of approaches have been applied, including drug therapy, cognitive techniques, behavioral interventions, support for caregivers, and sociocultural approaches
    g. The drugs currently prescribed affect acetylcholine and glutamate, the neurotransmitters known to play an important role in memory
        (a) Although the benefits of the drugs are limited and the risk for harmful side effects sometimes high, the drugs have been approved by the FDA
    h. Alternative drug treatments currently are being investigated
    i. A number of studies also seem to suggest that certain substances (e.g., estrogen, ibuprofen) may reduce the risk of Alzheimer's disease
    j. Cognitive treatments have been applied with some *temporary* success
    k. Behavioral interventions have been tried with modest success
    l. Caregiving can take a heavy toll on the close relatives of people with dementia
        (a) Almost 90 percent of all people with dementia are cared for by their relatives
        (b) One of the most frequent reasons for the institutionalization of Alzheimer's victims is that overwhelmed caregivers can no longer cope with the difficulties of keeping them at home
    m. In recent years, sociocultural approaches have begun to play an important role in treatment
        (a) A number of day-care facilities and assisted-living facilities have been opened to provide care to those with dementia

(b) Studies suggest that such facilities often help slow the cognitive decline of residents and enhance their enjoyment of life

VIII. ISSUES AFFECTING THE MENTAL HEALTH OF THE ELDERLY

A. As the study and treatment of elderly people have progressed, three issues have raised concern among clinicians:
  1. The problems faced by elderly members of racial and ethnic minority groups
     a. Discrimination due to race and ethnicity has long been a problem in the United States, particularly for those who are old
     b. To be both old and a member of a minority group is to be considered in "double jeopardy" by many observers
        (a) Older women in minority groups are considered in "triple jeopardy"
     c. Due to language barriers and cultural issues, it is common for elderly members of ethnic minority groups to rely solely on family members or friends for remedies or health care
  2. The inadequacies of long-term care
     a. Many older people require long-term care outside the family
        (a) This term may refer variously to the services offered in a partially supervised apartment, in a senior housing complex, or in a nursing home
            (i) The quality of care at such residences varies widely
     b. Many worry about being "put away" and the costs of long-term care
        (a) Worry over these issues can greatly harm the mental health of older adults, perhaps leading to depression and anxiety as well as family conflict
  3. The need for a health-maintenance approach to medical care in an aging world
     a. Finally, medical scientists suggest that the current generation of young adults should take a health-maintenance, or wellness, approach to their own aging process
     b. There is a growing belief that older adults will adapt more readily to changes and negative events if their physical and psychological health is good

IX. CALL FOR CHANGE: DSM-5

A. The DSM-5 Task Force proposed that the disorders of cognition be placed in a grouping called "Neurocognitive Disorders"
  1. This clarifies that some kind of brain dysfunction underlies these disorders
B. They suggested only minimal changes for the category of delirium
C. The Task Force made two key proposals regarding the categories characterized by dementia:
  1. Eliminate the term "dementia" as it has become stigmatizing and demeaning
     a. New term: "*major* neurocognitive disorder" (e.g., *major neurocognitive disorder associated with Alzheimer's disease*)
  2. Add a new category: "*mild neurocognitive disorder*" to aid with early diagnosis and treatment

LEARNING OBJECTIVES

1. Discuss the issues of old age and stress.

2. Describe the disorders of depression, anxiety, substance abuse, and psychotic disorders in later life.

3. Describe the disorders of cognition.

4. Distinguish between short-term memory and long-term memory. Summarize the anatomy and biochemistry of memory.

5. Describe the dementias, including Alzheimer's disease, Pick's disease, Huntington's disease, Creutzfeldt-Jakob disease, and Parkinson's disease.

6. Describe the genetic, structural, and biochemical causes of Alzheimer's disease.

7. Discuss treatments for dementias.

8. Describe the issues affecting the mental health of the elderly.

9. Discuss the changes for these disorders proposed by the DSM-5 Task Force.

KEY TERMS

acetylcholine
Alzheimer's disease
amnestic disorders
anterograde amnesia
beta-amyloid protein
Creutzfeldt-Jakob disease
delirium
dementia

geropsychology
Huntington's disease
Korsakoff's syndrome
long-term memory
memory
neurofibrillary tangles
Parkinson's disease
Pick's disease

retrograde amnesia
senile plaques
short-term memory, or
    working memory
stroke
vascular dementia, or multi-
    infarct dementia

MEDIA RESOURCES

Abnormal Psychology Student Tool Kit

Produced and edited by Ronald J. Comer, Princeton University and Gregory Comer, Princeton Academic Resources. Tied directly to the CyberStudy sections in the text, this Student Tool Kit offers 57 intriguing Video Cases running three to seven minutes each. The Video Cases focus on persons affected by disorders discussed in the text. Students first view the video and then answer a series of thought-provoking questions. Additionally, the Student Tool Kit contains multiple-choice practice test questions with built-in instructional feedback for every option.

PowerPoint Slides

Available at the Instructor's site on the companion Web site are comprehensive PowerPoint slide presentations and supplemental student handouts for Chapter 18. The slide files reflect the main points of the chapter in significant detail. Student handouts were created using the instructor slides as a base, with key points replaced as "fill-in" items. Answer keys and suggestions for use also are provided.

DSM-IV-TR Masters

B-75, DSM-IV-TR Diagnostic Criteria for Dementia of the Alzheimer's Type

B-76, DSM-IV-TR Diagnostic Criteria for Dementia Due to Other General Medical Conditions

Internet Sites

Please see Appendix A for full and comprehensive references.

Sites relevant to Chapter 18 material are:

http://alzheimer.wustl.edu/
This is the site of the Charles K. and Joanne Knight Alzheimer's Disease Research Center of Washington University School of Medicine in St. Louis. It offers links to resources, research articles, and clinical studies. In addition it supplies possible outreach programs and education opportunities.

http://aging.med.nyu.edu/
This site is part of the Center for Excellence on Brain Aging of NYU Langone Medical Center. It supplies links to research and programs that the institute offers on related aging disorders. The Center is "devoted to research and clinical advances toward the

treatment and cure of neurodegenerative diseases affecting cognition."

http://www.nimh.nih.gov/topics/topic-page-alzheimers-disease.shtml

This Web site, provided by the National Institute of Mental Health, supplies downloadable links to PDF files and booklets on a variety of mental health topics, including Alzheimer's disease.

http://www.alz.org (The Alzheimer's Association)

The Alzheimer's Association is the national voluntary health agency dedicated to researching the prevention, cure, and treatment of Alzheimer's disease and related disorders, and providing support and assistance to afflicted patients and their families.

http://www.ilcusa.org

The ILC-USA is the first private, nonpartisan international center devoted to science-based policy development on aging populations.

http://www.aging-institute.org

Alzheimer's Drug Discovery Foundation is a public charity dedicated to discovery and development of drugs to prevent, treat, and cure Alzheimer's disease.

Mainstream Films

Films relevant to Chapter 18 material are listed and summarized below.

Key to Film Listings:
P = psychopathology focus
T = treatment focus
E = ethical issues raised

Please note that some of the films suggested may have graphic sexual or violent content due to the nature of certain subject matters.

Awakenings
This 1991 film is based on the true story of research physician Oliver Sacks (played by Robin Williams) who uses an experimental drug to "awaken" the catatonic victims (including Robert DeNiro) of a rare sleeping sickness. **P, T, E, serious film**

Away from Her
Starring Julie Christie, this 2006 film chronicles a woman's descent into alzheimer's disease and her husband's decision to institutionalize her. **P, T, E serious film**

Eternal Sunshine of the Spotless Mind
From 2003, this quirky film follows a couple (Jim Carrey and Kate Winslet) as they have their memories erased in an effort to forget each other. **P, E, comedy/romance, independent film**

Fifty First Dates
This Adam Sandler/Drew Barrymore film from 2004 follows the couple as they comedically cope with her memory impairment. **P, comedy/commercial film**

Memento
This artful thriller from 2000 follows Guy Pearce, a man with no short-term memory, on a confusing journey to find his wife's killer. **P, commercial/serious film**

On Golden Pond
From 1981, this film tells the story of Norman, a retired professor (Henry Fonda) and Ethel, his wife (Katharine Hepburn) who visit their summer cottage for Norman's birthday. Over the course of their trip, Ethel comes to realize Norman is in the early stages of Alzheimer's disease. **P, serious film**

Regarding Henry
From 1991, this film stars Harrison Ford as a ruthless attorney who loses his memory (dramatically changing his personality) after being shot by a robber. **P, serious film**

Tuesdays with Morrie
Morrie (played by Jack Lemmon) is an elderly man slowly dying of a terminal illness. He is a retired teacher who, although he's sick, dying, and often in pain, is not afraid of death. Rather, he is more interested in getting as much as possible out of the life he has left. **P, serious film**

Other Films:

About Schmidt (2002) issues of aging. **P, serious film**
Driving Miss Daisy (1991) issues of aging. **P, serious film**
Iris (2001) Alzheimer's disease. **P, T, serious film**

Comer Video Segments

Available as a supplement, this revised set of videotapes contains short clips depicting various topics related to abnormal psychology. Please see the accompanying Video Guide for specific clips linked to Chapter 18.

Recommendations for Purchase or Rental

The Comer Video Segments include excerpts from many superb clinical documentaries. While the segments alone are ideal for use in lectures, it often is useful to assign the entire documentary for special class screenings or library use by students. The following videos and other media are available for purchase or rental and appropriate for use in class or for assignment outside of class.

Alzheimer's: Coping with Catastrophic Reaction
Health Sciences Consortium
201 Silver Cedar Court
Chapel Hill, NC 27514-1517
(919) 942-8731

Elderly Suicide
Films for the Humanities and Sciences
P.O. Box 2053
Princeton, NJ 08543-2053
Phone: 800-257-5126

Fax: 609-275-3767
Email To: custserv@films.com

Facing Death
Films for the Humanities and Sciences
P.O. Box 2053
Princeton, NJ 08543-2053
Phone: 800-257-5126
Fax: 609-275-3767
Email To: custserv@films.com
Various titles also are available through
Films for the Humanities & Sciences
Box 2053, Princeton, NJ 08543-2053
1-800-257-5126
ffh.films.com

CLASS DEMONSTRATIONS AND ACTIVITIES

Case Study

Present a case study to the class.

Guest Speaker

Invite a mental health consumer or consumer advocate into your class to discuss his or her experiences with the elderly and the mental health care system. NAMI (National Alliance on Mental Illness) sponsors several excellent programs designed to foster understanding and discussion of the problems impacting those with severe mental illness and their loved ones.

The Genetics of Alzheimer's Disease

Lead a discussion of whether students would want to know if they were at high risk for developing Alzheimer's disease, now that a new test is available. Even though there has been a test for Huntington's disease, a disease with a genetic basis, many individuals at risk prefer not to know. Use an overhead projector or white board to list the pros and cons of knowing or not knowing.

"Here's $25,000 to be awarded to . . ."

Given the common awareness and sometimes erroneous information about memory disorders, many

elderly persons often worry about their memory. Some elderly worry that their memory is worsening, perhaps due to a degenerative disorder. Announce that the local chapter of the AARP (formerly the American Association of Retired Persons) will be giving a $25,000 award to help alleviate these worries by assisting the elderly in performing simple, at-home evaluations to determine whether their memory is indeed deteriorating (and, therefore, that a professional referral should be considered). Ask groups to create criteria or guidelines for distinguishing normal forgetfulness and a memory problem due to brain pathology. Point out that forgetfulness can also be due to undiagnosed depression, alcohol misuse, or drug interactions.

The Anonymous Five-Minute Essay

Ask students to write what they believe or know about getting old. Compare what is commonly "known," which is rife with misinformation and myths (e.g., "You forget things," "You lose interest in sex," "You're in pain all the time"), to the actual facts about later life.

SUGGESTED TOPICS FOR DISCUSSION

Open Discussion or Group Work: The Genetics of Alzheimer's Disease

Present recent advances in genetic testing, which enable doctors and their patients to determine whether a person

is at risk for developing particular disorders or illnesses. Either lead a discussion or divide students into groups to discuss advantages and disadvantages of knowing such information. To focus the discussion, you can let students know that there is a new test that can determine whether a person is at high risk for developing Alzheimer's disease.

Open Discussion of Alzheimer's and Caregivers

Ask students to volunteer personal information of their family's experience of taking care of a person with Alzheimer's. Is the person in a nursing home or at home? Was the person at home during the early stages of the illness? Would the caregiver or family prefer to have them at home?

Group Work: Special Problems of the Elderly

Divide students into groups. Ask each group to create a list of problems or difficulties (vulnerabilities) that the elderly in particular face. These would include declining health, decreasing support system (e.g., widowhood, loss of friends), unintentional medication overuse, and abuse. Alternatively, give each group one of the vulnerabilities and ask it to come up with a creative solution to it.

ASSIGNMENTS/EXTRA CREDIT SUGGESTIONS

"Write a Pamphlet"

With the use of a software program like Microsoft Publisher or simply paper and markers, students can create a pamphlet on one or all of the disorders of aging and/or cognition. Students should be encouraged to be as accurate and up-to-date as possible and also to present all sides of the disorder (e.g., alternate treatment approaches or theories).

Keep a Journal

In addition to helping students synthesize material, this activity is helpful in developing writing skills. Have students keep a journal of their thoughts on course material through the semester. This can be done in the first or last five minutes of class or as an out-of-class assignment. Faculty generally should have students submit their journals for review on an on-going basis, since students can have the tendency to delay writing until the end of the semester. Some suggestions for journal topics include: reactions to the case examples; strengths and weaknesses of prevailing theoretical explanations; hypothetical conversations with those sufferering from specific disorders, etc.

Group Work: Alzheimer's and Suicide

Inform the class that you and they have been hired by an attorney working on the following case: a doctor helped a woman with Alzheimer's disease commit suicide. The woman was in the early stages of the disease and had not lost any physical or mental abilities, but was quite despondent over the diagnosis and wanted to spare her family from having to deal with her suffering. The two sides of the debate are that (1) this was acceptable and allowable, versus (2) it was not acceptable and should not be allowed. Divide stu-

dents into groups, then assign each group one of these two positions. Have the groups prepare and present their argument.

Abnormal Psychology Student Tool Kit Video Questions

As a homework assignment, have students watch a video clip and answer the accompanying questions. Students can answer the questions directly into the online assessment feature. The results of these quizzes report to the site's built-in grade book.

Web Site Quiz

For homework or extra credit, have students complete the quiz for Chapter 18 located on the companion Web site. Students can complete an on-line test of the key chapter material (using questions NOT from the test bank) and have their scores e-mailed directly to the course instructor.

Essay Topics

For homework or extra credit, have students write an essay addressing one of the following topics:

(1) Discuss the issue of overmedicating the elderly, as discussed in MediaSpeak on p. 568 of the text. How widespread do you think this problem is? What is the solution?

(2) Discuss the social fear of aging. You can interview some elderly members of your community for personal insight and examples.

Research Topics

For homework or extra credit, have students write a research report addressing one (or more) of the following topics:

(1) Conduct a "Psych Info" search and write an annotated bibliography on one of the "other forms of dementia" discussed on p. 575 in the text. What interventions are currently being studied?

(2) Research and review the literature on amnestic disorders (see PsychWatch on pp. 576-577 in the text). How are these disorders similar and different from the more commonly researched disorders of cognition (especially Alzheimer's disease)?

Film Review

To earn extra credit, have students watch one (or more) of the mainstream films listed in the chapter and write a brief (3 to 5) page report. Students should summarize the plot of the film in sufficient detail to demonstrate familiarity, but should focus their papers on the depiction of psychological abnormality. What errors or liberties did the filmmaker take? What is the message (implicit or explicit) concerning the mentally ill?

Case Study—You Decide

The Comer and Gorenstein supplemental case study text offers three cases in which patients are neither diagnosed nor treated. These cases provide students with the opportunity to identify disorders and suggest appropriate therapies. Throughout each case, students are asked to consider a number of issues and to arrive at various decisions, including diagnostic and treatment decisions. Each case can be assigned as homework or for class discussion. The case study relevant to Chapter 18 is referenced below.

You Decide: The Case of Fred, Memory Problems

Crossword Puzzles

As a homework assignment or for extra credit, have students complete and submit Crossword Puzzle #18.

Word Searches

As a homework assignment or for extra credit, have students complete and submit Word Search #18.

Society and the Mental Health Profession

LECTURE OUTLINE

I. **SOCIETY AND THE MENTAL HEALTH PROFESSION**
    A. Psychological dysfunctioning of an individual does not occur in isolation
        1. It is influenced—sometimes caused—by societal and social factors
        2. It affects the lives of relatives, friends, and acquaintances
    B. Clinical scientists and practitioners do not conduct their work in isolation
        1. They are affecting and being affected by other institutions of society
    C. Two social institutions have a particularly strong impact—the legislative and judicial systems—collectively called "the legal field"
        1. This relationship has two distinct aspects:
            a. Mental health professionals often play a role in the criminal justice system—"Psychology in law"

b.   The legislative and judicial systems act upon the clinical field, regulating certain aspects of mental health care—"Law in psychology"

2.   The intersection between the mental health field and the legal and judicial systems are collectively referred to as forensic psychology

II. PSYCHOLOGY IN LAW: HOW DO CLINICIANS INFLUENCE THE CRIMINAL JUSTICE SYSTEM?

A.   To arrive at just and appropriate punishments, the courts need to know whether defendants are *responsible* for committing crimes and capable of *defending* themselves in court

    1.   For example, people who suffer from "severe mental instability" may not be responsible for their actions or able to aid in their defense in court

    2.   These determinations are guided by the opinions of mental health professionals

B.   When people accused of crimes are judged to be mentally unstable, they are usually sent to a mental institution for treatment

    1.   This process is called criminal commitment

        a.   Several forms:

            (a)   Mentally unstable *at the time of the crime* = NGRI: If found not guilty by reason of insanity, committed until improved enough to be released

            (b)   Mentally unstable *at the time of trial:* Committed until competent to stand trial

C.   These judgements of mental instability have stirred many arguments

    1.   Some consider the judgments "loopholes"

    2.   Others argue that a legal system cannot be just unless it allows for extenuating circumstances, such as mental instability

    3.   The practice of criminal commitment differs from country to country

D.   Criminal commitment and insanity during commission of a crime

    1.   "Insanity" is a *legal* term

        a.   Defendant may have a mental disorder but not qualify for a legal definition of insanity

    2.   The original definition can be traced to the murder case of Daniel M'Naghten in England in 1843:

        a.   The M'Naghten test/rule states that experiencing a mental disorder at the time of a crime does not by itself mean that the person was insane; the defendant also had to be *unable to know right from wrong*

    3.   In the late 19th century, some U.S. courts adopted a different standard of insanity:

        a.   The irresistible impulse test

            (a)   This test emphasizes the inability to control one's actions ("fit of passion" defense)

    4.   A third test also briefly became popular:

        a.   The Durham test

            (a)   People are not criminally responsible if their "unlawful act was the product of mental disease or defect"

    5.   In 1955, the American Law Institute (ALI) developed a test that combined aspects of the M'Naghten, irresistible impulse, and Durham tests

        a.   The American Law Institute test held that people are not criminally responsible if at the time of the crime they had a mental disorder or defect that prevented them from knowing right or wrong *or* from being able to control themselves and to follow the law

        b.   The test was adopted but criticized for being too "liberal"

    6.   In 1983, the American Psychiatric Association recommended a return to M'Naghten

        a.   This test now is used in all cases tried in federal courts and about half of state courts

        b.   The more liberal ALI standard is still used in the remaining state courts, save 4, which have essentially eliminated the insanity plea altogether

        c.   Under this standard, about two-thirds of defendants acquitted by reason of insanity qualify for a diagnosis of schizophrenia

            (a)   The vast majority have a history of past hospitalization, arrest, or both

            (b)   About 50 percent are Caucasian

            (c)   About 86 percent are male

(d) About 65 percent of cases involve violent crime of some sort

    (i) Close to 15 percent of those acquitted are accused specifically of murder

E. What concerns are raised by the insanity defense?

    1. Despite changes in the insanity standard, criticism of the defense continues

        a. One concern is the fundamental difference between the law and the science of human behavior

            (a) The law assumes that individuals have free will and are generally responsible for their actions

            (b) In contrast, several models of human behavior assume that physical or psychological forces act to determine the individual's behavior

        b. A second criticism points to the uncertainty of scientific knowledge about abnormal behavior

        c. The largest criticism is that the defense allows dangerous criminals to escape punishment

            (a) In reality, the number of such cases is small (less than 1 in 400)

    2. During most of U.S. history, successful insanity pleas equaled long-term prison sentences

        a. Today, offenders are being released earlier and earlier as the result of the increasing effectiveness of drug therapy and other treatments in institutions, the growing reaction against extended institutionalization, and a greater emphasis on patients' rights

F. What other verdicts are available?

    1. Over the past few decades, another verdict has been added—guilty but mentally ill

        a. Defendants receiving this verdict are found mentally ill at the time of their crimes, but their illness was not fully related to or responsible for the crime

    2. Some states allow for another defense—guilty with diminished capacity

        a. A defendant's mental dysfunction is viewed as an extenuating circumstance which should be considered

G. What are sex offender statutes?

    1. Since 1937 when Michigan passed the first "sex psychopath" law, many states have placed sex offenders in a special category—mentally disordered sex offenders

        a. People categorized this way are found guilty of a crime and judged to be responsible but are committed to a mental health facility instead of prison

        b. Over the past two decades, most states have changed or abolished these laws

        c. States are now less concerned about the rights and needs of sex offenders, given the growing number of sex crimes taking place; some have passed *sexually violent predator laws,* which require prison and, *in addition,* involuntary treatment

H. Criminal commitment and incompetence to stand trial

    1. Regardless of their state of mind at the time of a crime, defendants may be judged to be mentally incompetent to stand trial

    2. This requirement is meant to ensure that defendants understand the charges they are facing and can work with their lawyers to present an adequate defense

        a. This standard of competence was specified by the U.S. Supreme Court in 1960

    3. If the court decides that the defendant is incompetent, the person is assigned to a mental health facility until competent to stand trial

        a. Many more cases of criminal commitment result from decisions of mental incompetence than from verdicts of NGRI

    4. The majority of criminals currently institutionalized are convicted inmates whose psychological problems have led prison officials to decide they need treatment

    5. Until the early 1970s, most states required that mentally incompetent defendants be committed to maximum-security institutions

        a. Under current law, they have greater flexibility and some defendants are treated on an outpatient basis

III. **LAW IN PSYCHOLOGY: HOW DO THE LEGISLATIVE AND JUDICIAL SYSTEMS INFLUENCE MENTAL HEALTH CARE?**

A. Just as clinical science and practice have influenced the legal system, so has the legal system impacted clinical practice

B. Courts have developed the process of civil commitment, which allows certain people to be forced into mental health treatment

C. Also, the legal system, on behalf of the state, has taken on the responsibility for protecting patients' rights during treatment
   1. This protection extends to patients who have been involuntarily committed and to those who have sought treatment voluntarily

D. Civil commitment
   1. Every year in the United States, large numbers of people with mental disorders are involuntarily committed to treatment
      a. Typically they are committed to mental institutions but most states also have some form of outpatient civil commitment
      b. These laws have long caused controversy and debate
   2. Generally our legal system permits involuntary commitment of individuals who are considered to be *in need of treatment* and *dangerous to themselves or others*
      a. May include suicidal or reckless patients
      b. May include patients who put others at risk intentionally or unintentionally
   3. The state's authority rests on its duties to protect the interests of the individual and of society:
      a. Principle of *parens patriae* ("parent of the country")
      b. Principle of police power

E. What are the procedures for civil commitment?
   1. Civil commitment laws vary from state to state
   2. Family members often begin the proceedings
   3. Few guidelines have been offered by the Supreme Court
      a. 1979: *Minimum standard of proof* required:
         (a) Must be "clear and convincing" proof of illness and of meeting the state's criteria for commitment

F. Emergency commitment
   1. Many states give clinicians the right to certify certain patients as needing temporary commitment and medication
      a. Requires the agreement of two physicians and/or mental health professionals
      b. By tradition, these certifications often are referred to as "2PCs"—two-physician certificates
      c. The length of stay is often limited to three days

G. Who is dangerous?
   1. Historically, people with mental illnesses were less likely than others to commit violent or dangerous acts due to mass hospitalizations
   2. Due to deinstitutionalization, however, this is no longer true
      a. Although approximately 90% of people with mental disorders are in no way violent or dangerous, studies now suggest at least a small relationship between severe mental disorders and violent behavior
   3. A judgment of "dangerousness" often is required for involuntary civil commitment
   4. Research suggests that while mental health professionals very often are wrong in making long-term predictions of violence, short-term predictions—predictions of imminent violence—can be accurate

H. What are the problems with civil commitment?
   1. Civil commitment has been criticized on several grounds:
      a. It is difficult to assess dangerousness
      b. The legal definitions of "mental illness" and "dangerousness" are vague
      c. Civil commitment has questionable therapeutic value
   2. On the basis of these and other arguments, some clinicians argue that involuntary commitment should be abolished
      a. Others advocate finding a more systematic way to evaluate dangerousness

I. Trends in civil commitment
   1. The flexibility of involuntary commitment laws peaked in 1962
   2. Supreme Court ruled that imprisoning people who suffered from drug addictions might violate the constitutional ban on cruel and unusual punishment

3.   As the public became aware of these issues, states passed stricter standards for commitment

4.   Today, fewer people are institutionalized through civil commitment proceedings than in the past

J.   Protecting patients' rights

    1.   Over the past two decades, court decisions and state and federal laws have greatly expanded the rights of patients with mental disorders, in particular the right to treatment and the right to refuse treatment

K.   How is the right to treatment protected?

    1.   When people are committed to mental institutions and do not receive treatment, the institutions become prisons for the unconvicted

        a.   In the late 1960s and 1970s, large mental institutions were just that

    2.   Some patients and their attorneys began to demand that the state honor their right to treatment.

    3.   Several court rulings addressed this issue:

        a.   1972—A federal court ruled that the state was constitutionally obligated to provide "adequate treatment" to all people who had been committed involuntarily

        b.   1975—The Supreme Court ruled that institutions must review case files periodically and that the state cannot continue to institutionalize against their will people who are not dangerous and who can survive on their own or with willing help from responsible family members or friends

        c.   1982—The Supreme Court ruled that people committed involuntarily have a right to "reasonable nonrestrictive confinement conditions" and "reasonable care and safety"

        d.   In 1986, Congress passed the Protection and Advocacy for Mentally Ill Individuals Act

            (a)   This act set up protection and advocacy systems in all states and U.S. territories

        e.   A number of advocates are now suing federal and state agencies, demanding that they fulfill the promises of the community mental health movement

L.   How is the right to refuse treatment protected?

    1.   During the past two decades, the courts also have decided that patients, particularly those in institutions, have the right to refuse treatment

        a.   Most rulings center on biological treatments, including psychosurgery

    2.   In addition, some states have acknowledged a patient's right to refuse ECT and/or psychotropic medications

    3.   In the past, patients did not have the right to refuse psychotropic medications

        a.   As the possible harmful effects of these drugs have become known, some states have granted patients permission to refuse them

M.   What other rights do patients have?

    1.   Court decisions also have protected other patient rights:

        a.   Patients who perform work in mental institutions are now guaranteed at least a minimum wage

        b.   Patients released from state mental hospitals have a right to aftercare and appropriate community residence

        c.   People with mental disorders have a right to receive treatment in the least restrictive facility available

    2.   While people with psychological disorders have civil rights that must be protected at all times, many clinicians express concern that patients' rights rulings may unintentionally deprive these patients of opportunities for recovery

    3.   While these are legitimate concerns, it is important to remember that the clinical field has not always been effective in protecting patients' rights

    4.   Since clinicians themselves often disagree, it seems appropriate for patients, their advocates, and outside evaluators to play key roles in decision making

IV.   IN WHAT OTHER WAYS DO THE CLINICAL AND LEGAL FIELDS INTERACT?

A.   Mental health and legal professionals also may influence each other's work in other ways

B.   During the past twenty-five years, their paths have crossed in four key areas:
1.   Malpractice suits
2.   Professional boundaries
3.   Jury selection
4.   Psychological research of legal topics

C.   Law in psychology: Malpractice suits
1.   The number of malpractice suits against therapists has risen sharply in recent years
2.   These claims have addressed a number of different issues, including patient suicide, sexual activity with a patient, failure to obtain informed consent, negligent drug therapy, omission of drug therapy, improper termination of treatment, and wrongful commitment
3.   A malpractice suit, or fear of one can have major effects on clinical decisions and practice, for better or for worse

D.   Law in psychology: Professional boundaries
1.   During the last several years the legislative and judicial systems have helped to change the boundaries that separate one clinical profession from another
2.   These bodies have given more authority to psychologists and have blurred the lines between psychiatry and psychology
   a.   1991—The Department of Defense set up a training program for Army psychologists to gain prescription writing privileges (previously the domain of psychiatrists only)
   b.   The success of the program prompted the APA to recommend that all psychologists be granted permission to take such training courses and two states now grant such privileges

E.   Psychology in law: Jury selection
1.   During the past 25 years, more and more lawyers have turned to clinicians for advice in conducting trials
2.   A new breed of clinical specialist—"jury specialists"—has evolved
   a.   They advise lawyers about which jury candidates are likely to favor their side and which strategies are likely to win jurors' support during trials

F.   Psychology in law: Psychological research of legal topics
1.   Psychologists have sometimes conducted studies and developed expertise on topics of great importance to the criminal justice system
2.   Two areas have gained particular attention:
   a.   Eyewitness testimony
      (a)   In criminal cases testimony by eyewitnesses is extremely influential
      (b)   Research indicates that eyewitness testimony can be highly unreliable
         (i)   The events usually are unexpected and fleeting
      (c)   Laboratory subjects can be fooled into misremembering information
      (d)   Research also has found that accuracy in identifying perpetrators is influenced by the method used in identification
   b.   Patterns of criminality
      (a)   The study of criminal behavior patterns and the practice of "profiling" has increased in recent years and has been the topic of an increasing number of media programs
      (b)   However, it is not as revealing or influential as the media and the arts would have us believe!

V.   **WHAT ETHICAL PRINCIPLES GUIDE MENTAL HEALTH PROFESSIONALS?**
A.   Each profession within the mental health field has its own code of ethics
B.   The code of the American Psychological Association (APA) is typical:
1.   Psychologists are permitted to offer advice
2.   Psychologists may not conduct fraudulent research, plagiarize the work of others, or publish false data
3.   Psychologists must acknowledge their limitations
4.   Psychologists who make evaluations and testify in legal cases must base their assessments on sufficient information and substantiate their findings appropriately
5.   Psychologists may not take advantage of clients and students, sexually or otherwise

6.   Psychologists must follow the principle of confidentiality
      a.   Exceptions: a therapist in training to a supervisor, Tarasoff's "duty to protect"

VI. MENTAL HEALTH, BUSINESS, AND ECONOMICS

A.   The legislative and judicial systems are not the only social institutions with which mental health professionals interact
    1.   The business and economic fields are two other sectors that influence and are influenced by clinical practice and study

B.   Bringing mental health services to the workplace
    1.   Collectively, psychological disorders are among the 10 leading categories of work-related disorders and injuries in the United States
    2.   The business world often has turned to clinical professionals to help prevent and correct such problems
    3.   Two common means of providing mental health care in the workplace are employee assistance programs and problem-solving seminars
       a.   Employee assistance programs (EAPs) are mental health services made available by a place of business, and run either by mental health professionals who work directly for a company or by outside mental health agencies
       b.   Stress-reduction and problem-solving seminars are workshops or group sessions in which mental health professionals teach employees techniques for coping, solving problems, and handling and reducing stress

C.   The economics of mental health
    1.   Economic decisions by the government may influence the clinical care of people with psychological disorders
       a.   For example, financial concerns were of primary consideration in the deinstitutionalization movement
    2.   Although government funding has risen for people with psychological disorders over the past five decades however, that funding is insufficient
    3.   The large economic role of private insurance companies has had a significant effect in the way clinicians go about their work
    4.   Managed care programs and peer review systems have been implemented and criticized by many mental health professionals

VII. TECHNOLOGY AND MENTAL HEALTH

A.   Today's ever-changing technology has begun to have significant effects – both positive and negative – on the mental health field
    1.   Examples: the Internet, cell phones, video games, and social networking

B.   New triggers and vehicles for psychopathology
    1.   Our digital world provides new triggers and vehicles for the expression of abnormal behavior
       a.   Example: individuals who grapple with impulse-control problems and/or paraphilias
    2.   Some clinicians believe that violent video games may contribute to the development of antisocial behavior, and perhaps to the onset of conduct disorder
       a.   A number of clinicians also worry that social networking can contribute to psychological dysfunction in certain cases

C.   New forms of psychopathology
    1.   Research also indicates that today's technology also is helping to produce new psychological disorders
       a.   *Internet addiction* is marked by excessive and dysfunctional levels of texting, tweeting, networking, Internet browsing, etc.
    2.   Similarly, the Internet has brought a new exhibitionistic feature to certain kinds of abnormal behavior, for example, posting videos of self-cutting

C.   Cybertherapy
    1.   Cybertherapy as a treatment option is growing by leaps and bounds

        a.   Examples include: long-distance therapy using Skype, therapy offered by computer programs, treatment enhanced by video game-like avatars, and Internet-based support groups

    2.   Unfortunately, this movement is not without its problems, including a wealth of misinformation and a lack of quality control

VIII. THE PERSON WITHIN THE PROFESSION

    A.   The actions of clinical researchers and practitioners not only influence and are influenced by other institutions, they are closely tied to their personal needs and goals

    B.   Surveys found that as many as 84 percent of therapists have reported being in therapy themselves at least once

        1.   Their reasons are largely the same as those of other clients, with emotional problems, depression, and anxiety topping the list

        2.   It is not clear why so many therapists report having psychological problems

        3.   Possible theories include: job stress, increased awareness of negative feelings, biased entry into the field itself

    C.   The science and profession of abnormal psychology seeks to understand, predict, and change abnormal functioning, but we must not lose sight of the fact that mental health researchers and clinicians are human beings, living within a society of human beings, working to serve human beings

LEARNING OBJECTIVES

1.   Define and discuss criminal commitment and insanity during the commission of a crime.

2.   Discuss criticisms of the insanity defense.

3.   Define and discuss criminal commitment and incompetence to stand trial.

4.   Compare and contrast the M'Naghten test, the irresistible impulse test, the Durham test and the ALI test.

5.   Define civil commitment and include the topics of why one ought to consider commitment, current procedures, emergency commitments, who is dangerous, and criticisms of civil commitment.

6.   Define and discuss the concept of protecting patients' rights. Include the topic of the right to treatment, the right to refuse treatment, and other patients' rights.

7.   Discuss the concepts of business and mental health and economics and mental health.

8.   Discuss the positive and negative impacts of technology on the mental health field.

9.   Discuss the concept of the "person within the profession."

KEY TERMS

American Law Institute test	dangerousness	guilty with diminished
civil commitment	Durham test	capacity
code of ethics	duty to protect	irresistible impulse test
confidentiality	employee assistance program	jury selection
criminal commitment	forensic psychology	malpractice suit
cybertherapy	guilty but mentally ill	managed care program

mental incompetence
minimum standard of proof
M'Naghten test
not guilty by reason of insanity
(NGRI)

parens patriae
peer review system
police power
right to refuse treatment
right to treatment

stress-reduction and problem-
solving seminar
two-physician certificate
(2 PC)

MEDIA RESOURCES

Abnormal Psychology Student Tool Kit

Produced and edited by Ronald J. Comer, Princeton University and Gregory Comer, Princeton Academic Resources. Tied directly to the CyberStudy sections in the text, this Student Tool Kit offers 57 intriguing Video Cases running three to seven minutes each. The Video Cases focus on persons affected by disorders discussed in the text. Students first view the video and then answer a series of thought-provoking questions. Additionally, the Student Tool Kit contains multiple-choice practice test questions with built-in instructional feedback for every option.

PowerPoint Slides

Available at the Instructor's site on the companion Web site are comprehensive PowerPoint slide presentations and supplemental student handouts for Chapter 19. The slide files reflect the main points of the chapter in significant detail. Student handouts were created using the instructor slides as a base, with key points replaced as "fill-in" items. Answer keys and suggestions for use also are provided.

Internet Sites

Please see Appendix A for full and comprehensive references.
    Sites relevant to Chapter 19 material are:

http://bama.ua.edu/~jhooper
This is the Forensic Psychiatry Resource Page, from the University of Alabama, Department of Psychiatry and Neurology, created by James F. Hooper, MD, DFA PA.

http://bama.ua.edu/~jhooper/law-psy.html
This Law for Psychiatrists page discusses how most psychiatrists have to deal with the law since there are many legal issues related to mental illness, such as civil commitment, informed consent, and competency.

http://bama.ua.edu/~jhooper/ psy-law.html
This site defines mental illness specifically for attorneys.

http://bama.ua.edu/~jhooper/insanity.html
This site is a brief summary of the insanity defense.

http://www.aapl.org
American Academy of Psychiatry and the Law is an organization of psychiatrists dedicated to excellence in practice, teaching, and research in forensic psychiatry.

http://www.bazelon.org/
The Judge David L. Bazelon Center for Mental Health Law contains issues related to mental health law.

http://www. psychlaws.org
This is the site of the Treatment Advocacy Center, a nonprofit organization dedicated to eliminating legal and clinical barriers for Americans with severe brain disorders who are not receiving appropriate medical care.

Mainstream Films

Films relevant to Chapter 19 material are listed and summarized below.

Key to Film Listings:
P = psychopathology focus
T = treatment focus
E = ethical issues raised

Please note that some of the films suggested may have graphic sexual or violent content due to the nature of certain subject matters.

Copycat
This 1996 film stars Sigourney Weaver as a forensic psychologist who develops agoraphobia as the result of an assault. Her help is needed to capture a psychopath who is copying the crimes of renowned serial killers. **P, T, serious/commercial film**

Murder in the First
This 1995 drama centers on an ambitious young public defender who takes on the case of a man (Kevin Bacon) whose cruel treatment at Alcatraz turned him into a killer. **P, serious film**

Nuts
From 1987, this film stars Barbra Streisand as a prostitute who kills a customer in self-defense. To avoid scandal, her parents try to have her declared mentally incompetent. **P, E, drama/commercial film**

One Flew Over the Cuckoo's Nest
Award-winning 1975 film about a convict who feigns mental dysfunction in order to gain admission to a psychiatric hospital rather than spend time in prison. **P, T, E, serious film**

Primal Fear
From 1996, this film stars Edward Norton as an accused killer claiming DID and Richard Gere as his attorney. The film is full of plot twists and turns. **P, T, E, commercial/thriller/serious film**

Prince of Tides
In this 1991 film, an adaptation of a Pat Conroy novel, Nick Nolte plays a football coach who is estranged from his wife and who enters into an affair with the psychiatrist (Barbra Streisand) of his suicidal sister. **P, T, E, serious/commercial film**

Seven
This dark film from 1995 examines how a sociopathic serial killer uses the seven deadly sins—gluttony, greed, sloth, envy, wrath, pride, and lust—to punish sinners for their ignorance. **P, E, thriller**

Silence of the Lambs, (1999) and sequels *Hannibal,* (2001), *Red Dragon* (2002), *Manhunter* (1986)
This 1991 film of the Thomas Harris book follows an ambitious FBI agent (Jodi Foster) who enlists the aid of a criminally insane ex-psychiatrist (Anthony Hopkins as Hannibal Lechter) to help track down a serial killer. **P, E, thriller/serious/commercial films**

Snake Pit
Based on an autobiography, this film, made in 1948, is one of the first and best about mental illness and the treatment of patients in asylums and hospitals. Olivia de Haviland portrays a woman suffering from a nervous breakdown. **P, T, E, serious film**

Other Films:

Sleeping with the Enemy (1991) **P, serious film**
Titicut Follies (1967) institutionalization. **P, T, E, serious documentary**
What About Bob? (1991) **P, T, E, comedy/commercial film**
A Woman under the Influence (1974) institutionalization and ECT. **P, T, E, serious film**

Comer Video Segments

Available as a supplement, this revised set of videotapes contains short clips depicting various topics related to abnormal psychology. Please see the accompanying Video Guide for specific clips linked to Chapter 19.

Recommendations for Purchase or Rental

The Comer Video Segments include excerpts from many superb clinical documentaries. While the segments alone are ideal for use in lectures, it often is useful to assign the entire documentary for special class screenings or library use by students. The following videos and other media are available for purchase or rental and appropriate for use in class or for assignment outside of class.

The Iceman and the Psychiatrist
False Memories
Inside the Criminal Mind
Films for the Humanities and Sciences
P.O. Box 2053
Princeton, NJ 08543-2053
Phone: 800-257-5126
Fax: 609-275-3767
Email To: custserv@films.com
ffh.films.com

CLASS DEMONSTRATIONS AND ACTIVITIES

Case Study
Present a case study to the class.

Guest Speaker
Invite a mental health consumer, consumer advocate, or attorney into your class to discuss his or her experiences with the legal profession and the mental health care system. NAMI (National Alliance on the Mental Illness) sponsors several excellent programs designed to foster understanding and discussion of the problems impacting those with severe mental illness and their loved ones.

"It's Debatable: Sex Offender Statutes Are Ethical" (see Preface instructions for conducting this activity)

Have students volunteer (or assign them) in teams to opposite sides of the debate topic. Have students present their case in class following standard debate guidelines.

"It's Debatable: Deinstitutionalization Was/Is Ethical" (see Preface instructions for conducting this activity)

Have students volunteer (or assign them) in teams to opposite sides of the debate topic. Have students present their case in class following standard debate guidelines.

"Presume you are a therapist . . .": Duty to Protect

Present the following case to the class: you are a therapist, and your client tells you that he intends to kill a woman he was having obsessional thoughts about, a woman he met once at a party. What do you do?

In August 1969, Prosenjit Poddar was in treatment and told his therapist that he intended to kill Tatiana Tarasoff, a woman he was having obsessional thoughts about, a woman he met once at a party. The therapist notified the police, who arrested Poddar and held him briefly. (Neither Tarasoff nor her family was informed of the threat.) Two months later, Poddar killed Tarasoff. The young woman's parents sued the therapist and his employer, the University of California, charging that they should have been warned of the man's intention. The California Supreme Court ruled in favor of the Tarasoffs, saying that "when a therapist determines . . . that a patient presents a serious danger of violence to another, he incurs an ob-

ligation to use reasonable care to protect the intended victim."

The Insanity Defense

The insanity plea is grossly misunderstood in our society. On March 30, 1981, John Hinckley aimed and fired six hollow-tipped, exploding bullets from a .22-caliber revolver at President Ronald Reagan. One of the bullets ricocheted off the presidential limousine and entered Reagan's chest. Another hit a police officer, another a secret service agent, and another James Brady, the president's press secretary, who was paralyzed as a result. The act was caught on film. In June 1982, Hinckley stood trial and was found not guilty by reason of insanity. He was committed to Saint Elizabeth's Hospital in Washington, D.C., to stay there until he is viewed by the hospital as no longer dangerous as a result of his mental illness.

Discuss the differences between descriptive responsibility (Did the person do the action?) and ascriptive responsibility (Is the person responsible for behaving in this fashion?). The following arguments can be presented: Thomas S. Szasz argues that "[b]y codifying acts of violence as expressions of mental illness, we neatly rid ourselves of the task of dealing with criminal offenses as more or less rational, goal-directed acts, no different in principle from other forms of conduct" (1963, p. 141). In other words, the insanity defense is a way for society to avoid taking responsibility. It has also been argued that the insanity defense actually does the exact opposite. Alan A. Stone argues that "[t]he insanity defense is in every sense the exception that proves the rule. It allows the courts to treat every other defendant as someone who chose between good and evil" (Stone, 1975). By not pleading insanity, everyone who stands before a court is saying, "I was responsible for what I am found guilty of doing."

SUGGESTED TOPICS FOR DISCUSSION

Group Work: "Presume you are a therapist . . . "

Divide students into groups, then present them with the following issue: You are a therapist seeing a 16-year-old female patient. She discloses to you that she is sexually active with multiple partners, and that she occasionally (once a month) gets drunk and then drives. You are seriously concerned about her safety. Do you have an obligation to inform the parents, even over the objections of the patient (i.e., are you obliged to break confidentiality)? Assign these two positions: one is that confidentiality should not be broken, the other is that

it should be. Alternatively, have groups argue from the perspective of the adolescent versus the perspective of the parents.

Group Work: The Defendant's Mental State

Divide students into small groups. The issue is whether juries should take information about the defendant's mental state into account in their deliberations about guilt (i.e., whether a defendant's mental state should affect a verdict). Present a specific example from national headlines in which an insanity plea was successful (e.g., Lorena Bobbitt or Theodore Kaczyinski). One side should be assigned the task of working for the prosecuting attorney (i.e., arguing that mental state does not influence culpability). The other side, working for the defense attorney, should argue that mental state is relevant and should result in a verdict of not guilty by reason of insanity. Ask each group to present its argument to the class. Point out at the end of the discussion that such an arrangement is almost always present in such cases: the two sides will hire their own advisors, who will argue their particular position (resulting in somewhat embarrassing contradictions being presented by two different "mental health experts").

Open Discussion: Homelessness and Mental Health

Lead a discussion on the issue of homeless people. How much has the revolving-door syndrome of mental hospitals contributed to this problem? Should selected patients be kept in a hospital setting for longer periods of time? What about the problem of individuals who do not seek or want treatment for their disorders? Should they be forced into treatment?

Open Discussion: Therapist Abuse

Lead a discussion on the consequences that should be imposed on therapists who seduce their clients. Should they lose their licenses? Should they be prosecuted for sexual abuse or rape? When would it be acceptable for a therapist to develop a relationship with a former client?

Open Discussion: Who Is Responsible?

Present a hypothetical example of a severely mentally ill person committing murder. Ask the class to discuss the culpability of the person's parents in the behavior. Ask some to take the role of advising the plaintiff's attorney (i.e., take the perspective that the parents are responsible), and ask others to adopt the role of advisor to the defense attorney (i.e., take the perspective that the parents are not responsible).

Open Discussion: Technology and Mental Health

Using the information from the text, lead a discussion on the various positive and negative effects of our current technology on mental health. What concerns do students have (if any) about social networking in particular?

ASSIGNMENTS/EXTRA CREDIT SUGGESTIONS

"Write a Pamphlet"

With the use of a software program like Microsoft Publisher or simply paper and markers, students can create a pamphlet on one or all the ethical principles that guide mental health professionals. Students should be encouraged to be as accurate and up-to-date as possible and also to present all sides of the disorder (e.g., alternate treatment approaches or theories).

Abnormal Psychology Student Tool Kit Video Questions

As a homework assignment, have students watch a video clip and answer the accompanying questions. Students can answer the questions directly into the online assessment feature. The results of these quizzes report to the site's built-in grade book.

Web Site Quiz

For homework or extra credit, have students complete the quiz for Chapter 19 located on the companion Web site. Students can complete an online test of the key chapter material (using questions NOT from the test

bank) and have their scores e-mailed directly to the course instructor.

Essay Topics

For homework or extra credit, have students write an essay addressing one (or more) of the following topics:

(1) Discuss some of the famous "insanity defense" cases listed in PsychWatch on p. 608 in the text as they relate to your understanding of the M'Naughten rule and the primary symptoms of the presenting disorder. For example, is it possible that Andrea Yates knew "right from wrong" if she was experiencing postpartum psychosis? What are the issues for the mental health profession? For the legal profession?

(2) Table 19-1 addresses some multicultural issues in forensic psychology. Discuss some of the findings reported here, especially in light of other multicultural findings discussed throughout the text.

(3) Discuss the issues of "Serial Killers: Madness or Badness" in Psych Watch (pp. 640–641 in the text). How can we understand this behavior?

(4) Discuss the APA's Code of Ethics. Is it sufficient? Are there areas you think should be strengthened? Weakened? Eliminated? Added?

Research Topics

For homework or extra credit, have students write a research report addressing one (or more) of the following topics:

(1) Conduct a "Psych Info" search and write an annotated bibliography on forensic psychology and the area of criminal profiling. What empirical research is being done in this area?

(2) Research and review the literature on managed care and psychological treatment. What changes have been suggested? Implemented? What are the primary complaints of practicing clinicians and their patients?

(3) Research and review the literature on employee assistance programs. What are the main areas of focus of these programs? How common and effective are they?

(4) Research and review the growing field of cybertherapy. What kinds of research is being conducted? Do the data support or not support the use of these kinds of therapies?

Film Review

To earn extra credit, have students watch one (or more) of the mainstream films listed in this chapter and write a brief (3 to 5) page report. Students should summarize the plot of the film in sufficient detail to demonstrate familiarity but should focus their papers on the depiction of psychological abnormality. What errors or liberties did the filmmaker take? What is the message (implicit or explicit) concerning the mentally ill?

Crossword Puzzles

As a homework assignment or for extra credit, have students complete and submit Crossword Puzzle #19.

Word Searches

As a homework assignment or for extra credit, have students complete and submit Word Search #19.

APPENDIX :**A**

Internet Sites

Listed here are a variety of sites about mental illness description, causes, and treatment, psychopharmacology, neuroscience, and other topics related directly or indirectly to abnormal psychology. Students can be encouraged or instructed to visit these sites for either class activities or assignments. Several sites have links to electronic journals and other resources that students may use to research a writing assignment.

These pages can be photocopied and distributed to students at the beginning of the course. This list comprises primarily general sites that are excellent starting points for an Internet search on a specific topic. A brief list of recommended specific sites with information about particular disorders or topics also is provided.

Many of these links are very dense with information and will require substantial "loading time" unless the user has a high-speed Internet connection. At the time of publication of this IRM, all these sites were "alive."

General Psychology Sites

http://www.apa.org
American Psychological Association
The APA's home page contains a wealth of information about the APA, the largest scientific and professional organization representing psychology in the United States, and includes numerous links to information about mental illness and its treatment. A page on the site gives the basics of library research for psychology studies (www.apa.org/science/lib.html).

http://www.psycport.com/
PsycPORT was developed by the American Psychological Association (APA) and is intended to provide quality psychological and mental health information and resources on the Web.

http://www.psychologicalscience.org
Association for Psychological Science
The APS's home page. This site contains a wealth of information on this organization, including schedules for conventions, and teaching, research, and other psychological society information.

http://www.nmha.org
Mental Health America
Through its national office and more than 300 affiliates nationwide, Mental Health America is dedicated to improving the mental health of all individuals and achieving victory over mental illnesses.

http://www.nih.gov
National Institutes of Health—NIH
The major government funding agency for the study of health issues, including mental health, addictions, and aging. NIH comprises several institutes, including the National Institute of Mental Health, the National Institute of Alcoholism and Alcohol Abuse, and the National Institute on Drug Abuse, which deal with particular mental health issues.

http://www.nimh.nih.gov
National Institute of Mental Health—NIMH
The home page of NIMH, a component of NIH. NIMH is the federal agency that conducts and supports (funds) research on mental illness and mental health.

http://www.nimh.nih.gov/health/publications
NIMH Publications
This Web site, provided by the National Institute of Mental Health, supplies downloadable links to PDF files and booklets on a variety of mental health topics.

http://www.nami.org
National Alliance on Mental Illness—NAMI
The home page of NAMI has links to other sites and searchable indexes of mental disorders.

http://www.mentalhealth.com
Internet Mental Health
Internet Mental Health is an extensive and fairly comprehensive site full of mental health information. It includes a glossary of terms used in pharmacology, descriptions of all the disorders, and a long list of links to other English-language Internet sites. This site provides extensive information about all of the DSM disorders and is a very useful starting page for Internet searches.

http://psychcentral.com
Psych Central
Psych Central is Dr. John Grohol's Mental Health Page, "the Internet's largest and oldest independent mental health social network." The resources page has an extensive listing of sites related to abnormal psychology.

http://www.realtime.net/~mmjw
A listing of specific mental health resources, in particular, of self-help sites and links.

http://www.apa.org/education/undergrad/library-research.aspx
Created by the American Psychological Association (APA) Science Directorate, this online pamphlet was designed to help students and nonpsychologists find relevant research on psychological topics of interest.

http://www.psichi.org
This is the Web site for Psi Chi, the national honor society for psychology undergraduates.

http://psibeta.org/site/
This is the Web site for Psi Beta, the national honor society in psychology for community and junior colleges

http://www.alleydog.com
"The Psychology Student's Best Friend," this site provides glossaries, forums, and "class help."

http://www.ship.edu/~cgboeree/genpsy.html
This site was developed by Dr. C. George Boeree, a professor at Shippensburg University. It provides a brief introduction to general psychology with links to major themes and aspects in psychology that are often dealt with in textbooks.

Abnormal Psychology: Past and Present

http://www3.niu.edu/acad/psych/Millis/History/2002/mainsheet.htm
Abnormal Psychology Time Machine—this site details various theories to explain psychological disturbances over time.

http://elvers.us/hop/welcome.asp
The History of Psychology Web site, provided as a "gateway for teachers and students to over 1000 World Wide Web resources related to the history of psychology."

Research in Abnormal Psychology

http://www.psy.pdx.edu/~nicole/psytutor/index.htm
The Psychology Tutor, this site provides great information on research method and design.

http://www.med.nyu.edu/bhp/
This Web site provides an overview of the behavioral health programs offered at NYU Medical Center, including clinical research and current studies. It also provides links to general psychological research, hospital and patient care information, and education.

http://www.nimh.nih.gov
National Institute of Mental Health–NIMH
The homepage of NIMH, a component of NIH. NIMH is the federal agency that conducts and supports (funds) research on mental illness and mental health.

Models of Abnormality

http://www.med.harvard.edu/AANLIB/home.html
The Whole Brain Atlas—information, images, and QuickTime movies all related to the brain. Included is a discussion on the pathology of Alzheimer's disease. A complete reference to the brain.

http://www.nlm.nih.gov/research/visible/visible_human.html
The Visible Human Project is creating a complete, anatomically detailed, three-dimensional representation of both the male and female human bodies.

http://faculty.washington.edu/chudler/ehceduc.html
Extremely detailed site that consists of links for neuroscience education. This site is large enough to spend several days exploring.

http://www.4therapy.com/
A general therapy site, this listing is full of good information on many types of psychological models and associated therapies but is geared toward provider referral.

http://easyweb.easynet.co.uk/simplepsych/204.html
This site offers general information on psychodynamic therapy—what it is, duration of treatment, training, etc.

http://www.abct.org

This site is the home page for the Association for Behavioral and Cognitive Therapies, a "professional, interdisciplinary organization committed to the advancement of a scientific approach to the understanding and amelioration of problems of the human condition. "

http://www.rebt.org

A form of cognitive-behavior therapy created in 1955 by Dr. Albert Ellis, rational emotive behavior therapy (REBT) is an action-oriented approach that stimulates emotional growth by teaching people to replace their self-defeating thoughts, feelings, and actions with new and effective thoughts.

http://www.ahpweb.org

The Association for Humanistic Psychology is "the voice of ordinary people with an extraordinary vision for a more conscious and humane global society."

Clinical Assessment, Diagnosis, and Treatment

http://www.apa.org/science/programs/testing/index .aspx

Created by the American Psychological Association's Science Directorate, this site offers information on the process of psychological testing and assessment.

http://www.guidetopsychology.com/testing.htm
http://www.guidetopsychology.com/diagnos.htm

These web sites, part of the main site—A Guide to Psychology and Its Practice—are maintained by Dr. Raymond Lloyd Richmond and covers the process of psychological testing and diagnosis clearly.

http://www.queendom.com
http://www.psychtests.com

These two sites, run by the same parent company, offer many versions of different psychological tests. Some tests mirror more famous (and expensive) assessments and tout solid psychometrics while others are strictly for fun. There is a fee to use some of the more detailed measures.

Anxiety Disorders

http://www.ocfoundation.org

This comprehensive site, the home page of the obsessive compulsive foundation, details both research and treatment of obsessive-compulsive disorder.

http://www.anxietynetwork.com/gahome.html

This site is the Anxiety Network International's Generalized Anxiety Home Page, filled with information about the disorder.

http://www.socialphobia.org/

This site is the home page of the Social Phobia/Social Anxiety Association.

http://www.mentalhealth.com/dis/p20-an03.html

This is the "Internet Mental Health Site" page for Social Phobia and includes an assessment measure.

http://www.apa.org/topics/anxiety/panic-disorder.aspx

Created by the APA, this Fact Sheet is home to very good information on panic disorder and its treatments.

http://www.geonius.com/ocd

This site provides links to various sites on obsessive-compulsive disorder.

http://www.nimh.nih.gov/health/topics/anxiety-disorders/index.shtml

This Web site, provided by the National Institute of Mental Health, supplies downloadable links to PDF files and booklets on a variety of mental health topics, including anxiety disorders.

http://www.adaa.org/

Homepage of the Anxiety Disorders Association of America, this site is dedicated to the research, education, and treatment of anxiety disorders. It includes helpful links to finding a therapist, the different types of anxiety disorders, support groups, and other resources.

http://www.npadnews.com/

This site is concerned with anxiety, panic attacks, and other phobias. It offers links to different forms of anxiety disorders, including social anxiety disorder, posttraumatic stress disorder, and obsessive-compulsive disorder. It also has current articles on the topic.

Stress Disorders

http://www.ptsd.va.gov/

This Web site of the National Center for PTSD is provided as an educational resource concerning PTSD and other enduring consequences of traumatic stress.

http://www.npadnews.com/

This site is concerned with anxiety, panic attacks, and other phobias. It offers links to different forms of anxiety disorders, including posttraumatic stress disorder. It also has current articles on the topic.

http://www.nimh.nih.gov/health/topics/post-traumatic-stress-disorder-ptsd/index.shtml
This Web site, provided by the National Institute of Mental Health, supplies downloadable links to PDF files and booklets on a variety of mental health topics, including stress disorders.

http://www.ncbi.nlm.nih.gov/pubmedhealth/PMH0001923/
This Web site, provided by the U.S. National Library of Medicine provides solid information on PTSD, among other disorders.

Somatoform and Dissociative Disorders

http://www.cdc.gov/cfs
A comprehensive page from the CDC that discusses the many factors associated with chronic fatigue syndrome.

http://allpsych.com/disorders/somatoform/
This site includes characteristics, etiology, symptoms, and treatment of somatoform disorders.

http://www.isst-d.org
This Web site of the International Society for the Study of Trauma and Dissociation supplies copyrighted Guidelines for Treating Dissociative Identity Disorder in Adults, with links to each section of the guidelines. There are also links specified for general information, assisting professionals, and finding a therapist.

Mood Disorders

http://bipolar.mentalhelp.net/
A site that includes the symptoms, treatments, and online support groups for bipolar disorder.

http://www.nimh.nih.gov/health/topics/depression/index.shtml
http://www.nimh.nih.gov/health/topics/bipolar-disorder/index.shtml
These Web sites, provided by the National Institute of Mental Health, supplies downloadable links to PDF files and booklets on depression and bipolar disorder but information on other disorders is available as well.

http://www.adolescent-mood-disorders.com/
This site reviews the difficulties in recognizing depression and other mood disorders among teenagers.

http://www.canmat.org
This Canadian site endeavors to provide "information about anxiety, depression and bipolar disorders for the health professional and the general public."

http://www.depression.com/
This site, developed and funded by GlaxoSmithKline, focuses on the understanding and treatment of depression. It also has information on coping with depression on a daily basis.

Suicide

http://www.save.org/
Suicide Awareness/Voices of Education Web site includes links and other information on suicide.

http://www.nimh.nih.gov/health/topics/suicide-prevention/index.shtml
This Web site, provided by the National Institute of Mental Health, supplies downloadable links to PDF files and booklets on a variety of mental health topics, including suicide prevention.

http://www.hopeline.com
The Kristin Brooks Hope Center offers crisis support and information on suicide.

http://www.suicidology.org/
The Web site for the American Association of Suicidology which is dedicated to the understanding and prevention of suicide.

http://www.suicideinfo.ca
The Canadian site, the Centre for Suicide Prevention, is a library and resource center providing information on suicide and suicidal behavior.

http://www.cdc.gov/ViolencePrevention/suicide/index.htm
This site is maintained by the Centers for Disease Control and Prevention. It includes a suicide fact sheet, prevention strategies, and publications focused on the topic of suicide.

http://www.afsp.org
This site is the home of the American Foundation for Suicide Prevention. It includes fundraisers and supports for people suffering from suicidal thoughts or who have been affected by someone's death. There is also supporting research and education for professionals and suicide survivors.

Eating Disorders

http://www.eating-disorder.com/
This site contains discussion of symptoms, support groups, and links to other sites to explore the eating disorders.

http://www.something-fishy.org
A major site on all eating disorders including descriptions, diagnosis, and treatments.

http://www.nimh.nih.gov/topics/topic-page-eating-disorders.shtml
This Web site, provided by the National Institute of Mental Health, supplies downloadable links to PDF files and booklets on a variety of mental health topics, including eating disorders..

http://www.nationaleatingdisorders.org
This Web site for the National Eating Disorders Association is an excellent source of resources and support.

http://www.nedic.ca/
This is the site of the Canadian National Eating Disorder Information Centre. It provides information relevant to eating disorders, body image, and self-esteem, including definitions, treatment, prevention, and statistics. It also includes a resource library with a variety of information related to the topic.

Substance-Related Disorders

http://www.aa.org
A large site containing the history of Alcoholics Anonymous (AA), meeting sites and regional meetings, online meetings, and other resources.

http://www.ccsa.ca/
(Canadian Centre on Substance Abuse)
The Canadian Centre on Substance Abuse is a nonprofit organization working to minimize the harm associated with the use of alcohol, tobacco, and other drugs.

http://www.higheredcenter.org/
The National Clearinghouse for Alcohol and Drug Information (NCADI) is the information service of the Center for Substance Abuse Prevention of the U.S. Department of Health & Human Services. NCADI is the world's largest resource for current information and materials concerning substance-abuse prevention.

http://www.nida.nih.gov/nidahome.html
The National Institute on Drug Abuse Web site features informational links for students, young adults, parents, teachers, researchers, and health professionals.

http://www.abovetheinfluence.com/
Informational resource from the National Youth Anti-Drug Media Campaign on illegal substances includes club drugs, hallucinogens, heroin, rohypnol, and methamphetamines geared toward writers and feature journalists.

http://www.nimh.nih.gov/health/publications
This Web site, provided by the National Institute of Mental Health, supplies downloadable links to PDF files and booklets on a variety of mental health topics, including substance abuse.

http://www.al-anon.alateen.org
AL-ANON (and ALATEEN for younger members) is a worldwide organization that offers a self-help recovery program for families and friends, of alcoholics, whether or not the alcoholic seeks help or even recognizes the existence of a drinking problem.

Sexual Disorders and Gender Identity Disorder

http://www.sca-recovery.org
(Sexual Compulsives Anonymous)
SCA is a fellowship of men and women who share their experience, strength, and hope with each other, that they may solve their common problem and help others to recover from sexual compulsion.

http://www.aasect.org/
The American Association of Sex Educators, Counselors, and Therapists (AASECT) is a not-for-profit, interdisciplinary professional organization that promotes understanding of human sexuality and healthy sexual behavior.

http://www.siecus.org/
The Sexuality Information and Education Council of the U.S. (SIECUS) is a national, nonprofit organization that affirms that sexuality is a natural and healthy part of living.

http://www.guttmacher.org/
The Alan Guttmacher Institute (AGI) is a nonprofit organization focused on sexual and reproductive health research, policy analysis, and public education.

Schizophrenia

http://www.schizophrenia.com/
The Schizophrenia home page contains links to chat rooms and to sites for individuals with schizophrenia and their families. It also contains suggestions for dealing with this disorder.

http://www.mentalhealth.com/
Basic facts about mental health issues, including schizophrenia.

http://www.nimh.nih.gov/health/topics/schizophreni a/index.shtml

This Web site, provided by the U.S. National Library of Medicine, supplies downloadable links to PDF files and booklets on a variety of mental health topics, including schizophrenia.

http://www.nlm.nih.gov/medlineplus/schizophrenia. html

Medline Plus brings together authoritative information from NLM, NIH, and other government agencies and health-related organizations.

http://www.nami.org

Web site of the National Alliance on Mental Illness (NAMI), which offers excellent resources on mental health issues.

Personality Disorders

http://www.isspd.com/

The International Society for the Study of Personality Disorders, ISSPD, stimulates and supports scholarship, clinical experience, international collaboration, and communication of research on all aspects of personality disorders including diagnosis, course, and treatment.

http://www.bpdcentral.com/

BPD Central is a list of resources for people who care about someone with borderline personality disorder (BPD). It is one of the oldest and largest sites about BPD on the Web.

http://www.nmha.org/go/information/get-info/personality-disorders

The National Mental Health Association is the oldest active organization dedicated to providing mental health care. This site offers information on the subject of personality-related disorders. It discusses the different forms of personality disorder, symptoms to recognize, causes, and treatment options.

http://www.ncbi.nlm.nih.gov/pubmedhealth/PMH00 01935/

This site, published by the U.S. National Library of Medicine, supplies information on a variety of topics, including personality disorders.

Disorders of Childhood and Adolescence

http://members.tripod.com/~tourette13/

This site discusses how Tourette's syndrome (TS) is a neurological disorder characterized by tics or involuntary, rapid, sudden movements or vocalizations that occur repeatedly in the same way.

http://www.thearc.org

This site includes information on the Arc, an organization of and for people with intellectual and developmental disabilities, chapter locations, and links to additional resources.

http://www.conductdisorders.com/

This site is maintained by a "group of parents raising challenging children."

http://www.nimh.nih.gov/health/publications

This site, provided by the National Institute of Mental Health, supplies downloadable links to PDF files and booklets on a variety of mental health topics, including ADHD and conduct disorder.

http://www.chadd.org

Run by Children and Adults with AD/HD, this site offers support for individuals, parents, teachers, professionals, and others.

Disorders of Aging and Cognition

http://www.alz.org (The Alzheimer's Association)

The Alzheimer's Association is the national voluntary health agency dedicated to researching the prevention, cure, and treatment of Alzheimer's disease and related disorders, and providing support and assistance to afflicted patients and their families.

http://www.ilcusa.org

The ILC-USA is the first private, nonpartisan international center devoted to science-based policy development on aging populations.

http://www.alzdiscovery.org

The Alzheimer's Drug Discovery Foundation is a public charity dedicated to discovery and development of drugs to prevent, treat, and cure Alzheimer's disease.

http://www.nimh.nih.gov/topics/topic-page-alzheimers-disease.shtml

This Web site, provided by the National Institute of Mental Health, supplies downloadable links to PDF files and booklets on a variety of mental health topics, including Alzheimer's Disease.

http://alzheimer.wustl.edu/

This is the site of the Charles K. and Joanne Knight Alzheimer's Disease Research Center of Washington University School of Medicine in St. Louis. It offers links to resources, research articles, and clinical studies. In addition, it supplies outreach programs and education opportunities.

http://aging.med.nyu.edu/

This site is part of the Center for Excellence on Brain Aging of NYU Langone Medical Center. The Center is "devoted to research and clinical advances toward the treatment and cure of neurodegenerative diseases affecting cognition."

http://bama.ua.edu/~jhooper

This is the Forensic Psychiatry Resource Page, from the University of Alabama, Department of Psychiatry and Neurology, created by James F. Hooper, MD, DFA PA.

http://bama.ua.edu/~jhooper/law-psy.html

This Law for Psychiatrists page discusses how most psychiatrists have to deal with the law since there are many legal issues related to mental illness, such as civil commitment, informed consent, and competency.

http://bama.ua.edu/~jhooper/psy-law.html

This site defines mental illness specifically for attorneys.

http://bama.ua.edu/~jhooper/insanity.html

This site is a brief summary of the insanity defense.

http://www.psychlaws.org/

This is the site of the Treatment Advocacy Center, a nonprofit organization dedicated to eliminating legal and clinical barriers for Americans with severe brain disorders who are not receiving appropriate medical care. The focus is on schizophrenia and manic-depressive illness (bipolar disorder).

http://www.aapl.org

American Academy of Psychiatry and the Law is an organization of psychiatrists dedicated to excellence in practice, teaching, and research in forensic psychiatry.

http://www.bazelon.org/

The Judge David L. Bazelon Center for Mental Health Law contains issues related to mental health law.

DSM-IV-TR Masters

Contents	Description

Changes in DSM-IV-TR from DSM-IV

The *DSM-IV Text Revision* (APA, 2000) changed the diagnostic criteria for a number of disorders in DSM-IV.

Disorder	DSM-IV (APA, 1994)	DSM-IV Text Revision (APA, 2000)
Tourette's Disorder	Symptoms must cause marked distress or significant impairment in order to warrant diagnosis.	Diagnosis is warranted even if symptoms do not cause marked distress or significant impairment.
Chronic Motor or Vocal Tic Disorder	Symptoms must cause marked distress or significant impairment in order to warrant diagnosis.	Diagnosis is warranted even if symptoms do not cause marked distress or significant impairment.
Transient Tic Disorder	Symptoms must cause marked distress or significant impairment in order to warrant diagnosis.	Diagnosis is warranted even if symptoms do not cause marked distress or significant impairment.
Dementia Due to Other General Medical Conditions	Lists as Distinct Axis I disorders: *Dementia due to HIV disease* *Dementia due to head trauma* *Dementia due to Parkinson's disease* *Dementia due to Huntington's disease* *Dementia due to Pick's disease* *Dementia due to Creutzfeldt-Jakob disease*	These are no longer listed as distinct Axis I disorders. Instead, they are grouped together as *Dementia due to other general medical conditions*, with the particular medical condition coded on Axis III.
Personality Change Due to a General Medical Condition	Diagnosis is not warranted if the personality change occurs as part of dementia.	A diagnosis is warranted even in cases of dementia when the personality change is prominent.
Exhibitionism	Sexually arousing fantasies, sexual urges, or behaviors must cause significant distress or impairment in order to warrant diagnosis.	Diagnosis is warranted if person acts on sexual urges, even if such actions do not cause marked distress, impairment, or interpersonal difficulty. If person manifests only sexual urges or fantasies (not actions), these must cause marked distress or interpersonal difficulty to warrant diagnosis.
Frotteurism	Sexually arousing fantasies, sexual urges, or behaviors must cause significant distress or impairment in order to warrant diagnosis.	Diagnosis is warranted if person acts on sexual urges, even if such actions do not cause marked distress, impairment, or interpersonal difficulty. If person manifests only sexual urges or fantasies (not actions), these must cause marked distress or interpersonal difficulty to warrant diagnosis.

Source: APA, 2000, 1994

Changes in DSM-IV-TR from DSM-IV

The *DSM-IV Text Revision* (APA, 2000) has changed the diagnostic criteria for a number of disorders in DSM-IV.

Disorder	DSM-IV (APA, 1994)	DSM-IV Text Revision (APA, 2000)
Pedophilia	Sexually arousing fantasies, sexual urges, or behaviors must cause significant distress or impairment in order to warrant diagnosis.	Diagnosis is warranted if person acts on sexual urges, even if such actions do not cause marked distress, impairment, or interpersonal difficulty. If person manifests only sexual urges or fantasies (not actions), these must cause marked distress or interpersonal difficulty to warrant diagnosis.
Sexual Sadism	Sexually arousing fantasies, sexual urges, or behaviors must cause significant distress or impairment in order to warrant diagnosis.	Diagnosis is warranted if person acts on sexual urges with a non-consenting person, even if such actions do not cause the patient marked distress, impairment, or interpersonal difficulty. If the individual manifests only sexual urges or fantasies (not actions), these must cause marked distress or interpersonal difficulty to warrant diagnosis.
Voyeurism	Sexually arousing fantasies, sexual urges, or behaviors must cause significant distress or impairment in order to warrant diagnosis.	Diagnosis is warranted if person acts on sexual urges, even if such actions do not cause marked distress, impairment, or interpersonal difficulty. If person manifests only sexual urges or fantasies (not actions), these must cause marked distress or interpersonal difficulty to warrant diagnosis.

Source: APA, 2000, 1994

Axis I Disorders in DSM-IV-TR

Disorders Usually First Diagnosed in Infancy, Childhood, and Adolescence
Disorders in this group tend to emerge and sometimes dissipate before adult life. They include pervasive developmental disorders (such as autism); learning disorders; attention-deficit hyperactivity disorder; conduct disorders; and separation anxiety disorder.

Delirium, Dementia, Amnestic, and Other Cognitive Disorders
These disorders are dominated by impairment in cognitive functioning. They include Alzheimer's disease and Huntington's disease.

Mental Disorders Due to a General Medical Condition
These are mental disorders that are caused primarily by a general medical disorder. They include mood disorder due to a general medical condition.

Substance-Related Disorders
These disorders are brought about by the use of substances that affect the central nervous system, such as alcohol use disorders, opioid use disorders, amphetamine use disorders, cocaine use disorders, and hallucinogen use disorders.

Schizophrenia and Other Psychotic Disorders
In this group of disorders, functioning deteriorates until the patient reaches a state of psychosis or loss of contact with reality.

Mood Disorders
Disorders in this group are marked by severe disturbances of mood that cause people to feel extremely and inappropriately sad or elated for extended periods of time. They include major depressive disorder and bipolar disorder.

Anxiety Disorders
Anxiety is the predominant disturbance in this group of disorders. They include generalized anxiety disorder, phobic disorders, panic disorder, obsessive-compulsive disorder, acute stress disorder, and posttraumatic stress disorder.

Somatoform Disorders
These disorders, marked by physical symptoms that apparently are caused primarily by psychological rather than physiological factors, include pain disorders, conversion disorders, somatization disorder, and hypochondriasis.

Factitious Disorders
People with these disorders intentionally produce or feign psychological or physical symptoms.

Source: APA, 2000, 1994
© 2013 by Worth Publishers

Axis I Disorders in DSM-IV-TR (Continued)

Dissociative Disorders
These disorders are characterized by a change in the usually integrated functions of memory and identity. They include dissociative amnesia; dissociative fugue, and dissociative identity disorder (multiple personality disorder).

Eating Disorders
People with these disorders display abnormal patterns of eating that significantly impair their functioning. The disorders include anorexia nervosa and bulimia nervosa.

Sexual Disorders and Gender Identity Disorders
These disorders in sexual functioning, behavior, or preferences include paraphilias, sexual dysfunctions, and gender identity disorder.

Sleep Disorders
People with these disorders display chronic sleep problems. The disorders include primary insomnia, primary hypersomnia, sleep terror disorder, and sleepwalking disorder.

Impulse-Control Disorders
People with these disorders are chronically unable to resist impulses, drives, or temptations to perform certain acts that are harmful to them or to others. The disorders include pathological gambling, kleptomania, pyromania, and intermittent explosive disorders.

Adjustment Disorder
The primary feature of these disorders is a maladaptive reaction to a clear stressor such as divorce or business difficulties that occur within three months after the onset of the stressor.

Other Conditions That May Be a Focus of Clinical Attention
This category consists of certain conditions or problems that are worth noting because they cause significant impairment, such as relational problems, problems related to abuse or neglect, medication-induced movement disorders, and psychophysiological disorders.

Source: APA, 2000, 1994

Global Assessment of Functioning (GAF) Scale

Consider psychological, social, and occupational functioning on a hypothetical continuum of mental health–illness. Do not include impairment in functioning due to physical (or environmental) limitations.

Code   [Note: Use intermediate codes when appropriate (e.g., 45, 68, 72).]

91–100   Superior functioning in a wide range of activities. Life's problems never seem to get out of hand, is sought out by others because of his or her many positive qualities. No symptoms.

81–90   Absent or minimal symptoms (e.g., mild anxiety before an exam), good functioning in all areas, interested and involved in a wide range of activities, socially effective, generally satisfied with life, no more than everyday problems or concerns (e.g., an occasional argument with family members).

71–80   If symptoms are present, they are transient and expectable reactions to psychosocial stressors (e.g., difficulty concentrating after family argument); no more than slight impairment in social, occupational, or school functioning (e.g., temporarily falling behind in schoolwork).

61–70   Some mild symptoms (e.g., depressed mood and mild insomnia) or some difficulty in social, occupational, or school functioning (e.g., occasional truancy, or theft within the household), but generally functioning pretty well; has some meaningful interpersonal relationships.

51–60   Moderate symptoms (e.g., flat affect and circumstantial speech, occasional panic attacks) or moderate difficulty in social, occupational, or school functioning (e.g., new friends, conflicts with peers or co-workers).

41–50   Serious symptoms (e.g., suicidal ideation, severe obsessional rituals, frequent shoplifting) or any serious impairment in social, occupational, or school functioning (e.g., no friends, unable to keep a job).

Source: APA, 2000, 1994

Global Assessment of Functioning (GAF) Scale (Continued)

31–40   Some impairment in reality testing or communication (e.g., speech is at times illogical, obscure, or irrelevant) or major impairment in several areas, such as work or school, family relations, judgment, thinking, or mood (e.g., depressed man avoids friends, neglects family, and is unable to work; child frequently beats up younger children, is defiant at home, and is failing at school).

21–30   Behavior is considerably influenced by delusions or hallucinations or serious impairment in communication or judgment (e.g., sometimes incoherent, acts grossly inappropriately, suicidal preoccupation) or inability to function in almost all areas (e.g., stays in bed all day; no job, home, or friends).

11–20   Some danger of hurting self or others (e.g., suicide attempts without clear expectation of death; frequently violent; manic excitement) or occasionally fails to maintain minimal personal hygiene (e.g., smears feces) or gross impairment in communication (e.g., largely incoherent or mute).

1–10   Persistent danger of severely hurting self or others (e.g., recurrent violence) or persistent inability to maintain minimal personal hygiene or serious suicidal act with clear expectation of death.

0   Inadequate information.

Source: APA, 2000, 1994

Diagnostic Criteria for Generalized Anxiety Disorder

A. Excessive anxiety and worry (apprehensive expectation), occurring more days than not for at least 6 months, about a number of events or activities (such as work or school performance).

B. The person finds it difficult to control the worry.

C. The anxiety and worry are associated with three (or more) of the following six symptoms (with at least some symptoms present for more days than not for the past 6 months). Note: Only one item is required in children.
    (1) restlessness or feeling keyed up or on edge
    (2) being easily fatigued
    (3) difficulty concentrating or mind going blank
    (4) irritability
    (5) muscle tension
    (6) sleep disturbance (difficulty falling or staying asleep, or restless unsatisfying sleep)

D. The focus of the anxiety and worry is not confined to features of an Axis I disorder, e.g., the anxiety or worry is not about having a Panic Attack (as in Panic Disorder), being embarrassed in public (as in Social Phobia), being contaminated (as in Obsessive-Compulsive Disorder), being away from home or close relatives (as in Separation Anxiety Disorder), gaining weight (as in Anorexia Nervosa), having multiple physical complaints (as in Hypochondriasis); and the anxiety and worry do not occur exclusively during Posttraumatic Stress Disorder.

E. The anxiety, worry, or physical symptoms cause clinically significant distress or impairment in social, occupational, or other important areas of functioning.

F. The disturbance is not due to the direct physiological effects of a substance (e.g., a drug of abuse, a medication) or a general medical condition (e.g., hyperthyroidism) and does not exclusively occur during a Mood Disorder, a Psychotic Disorder, or a Pervasive Developmental Disorder.

Source: APA, 2000, 1994

Diagnostic Criteria for Specific Phobia

A. Marked and persistent fear that is excessive or unreasonable, cued by the presence or anticipation of a specific object or situation (e.g., flying, heights, animals, receiving an injection, seeing blood).

B. Exposure to the phobic stimulus almost invariably provokes an immediate anxiety response, which may take the form of a situationally bound or situationally predisposed Panic Attack. Note: In children, the anxiety may be expressed by crying, tantrums, freezing, or clinging.

C. The person recognizes that the fear is excessive or unreasonable. Note: In children, this feature may be absent.

D. The phobic situation(s) is(are) avoided or else enured with intense anxiety or distress.

E. The avoidance, anxious anticipation, or distress in the feared situation(s) interferes significantly with the person's normal routine, occupational (academic) functioning, or social activities or relationships, or there is a marked distress about having the phobia.

F. In individuals under 18 years, the duration is at least 6 months.

G. The anxiety, Panic Attacks, or phobic avoidance associated with the specific object or situation is not better accounted for by another mental disorder, such as Obsessive-Compulsive Disorder (e.g., fear of dirt in someone with an obsession about contamination), Posttraumatic Stress Disorder (e.g., avoidance of stimuli associated with a severe stressor), Separation Anxiety Disorder (e.g., avoidance of school), Social Phobia (e.g., avoidance of social situations because of fear of embarrassment), Panic Disorder With Agoraphobia, or Agoraphobia Without History of Panic Disorder.

Specify type:

Animal Type

Natural Environment Type (e.g., heights, storms, water)

Blood-Injection-Injury Type

Situational Type (e.g., airplanes, elevators, enclosed places)

Other Type (e.g., phobic avoidance of situations that may lead to choking, vomiting, or contracting an illness; in children, avoidance of loud sounds or costumed characters)

Source: APA, 2000, 1994

Diagnostic Criteria for Social Phobia

A. A marked and persistent fear of one or more social or performance situations in which the person is exposed to unfamiliar people or to possible scrutiny by others. The individual fears that he or she will act in a way (or show anxiety symptoms) that will be humiliating or embarrassing. Note: In children, there must be evidence of the capacity for age-appropriate social relationships with familiar people and the anxiety must occur in peer settings, not just in interactions with adults.

B. Exposure to the feared social situation almost invariably provokes anxiety, which may take the form of a situationally bound or situationally predisposed Panic Attack. Note: In children, the anxiety may be expressed by crying, tantrums, freezing, or shrinking from social situations with unfamiliar people.

C. The person recognizes that the fear is excessive or unreasonable. Note: In children, this feature may be absent.

D. The feared social or performance situations are avoided or else are endured with intense anxiety or distress.

E. The avoidance, anxious anticipation, or distress in the feared social or performance situation(s) interferes significantly with the person's normal routine, occupational (academic) functioning, or social activities or relationships, or there is a marked distress about having the phobia.

F. In individuals under 18 years, the duration is at least 6 months.

G. The fear of avoidance is not due to the direct physiological effects of a substance (e.g., a drug of abuse, a medication) or a general medical condition and is not better accounted for by another mental disorder (e.g., Panic Disorder With or Without Agoraphobia, Separation Anxiety Disorder, Body Dysmorphic Disorder, a Pervasive Developmental Disorder, or Schizoid Personality Disorder).

H. If a general medical condition or another mental disorder is present, the fear in Criterion A is unrelated to it, e.g., the fear is not of Stuttering, trembling in Parkinson's disease, or exhibiting abnormal eating behavior in Anorexia or Bulimia Nervosa.

Source: APA, 2000, 1994

Criteria for Panic Attack

Note: A Panic Attack is not a codable disorder. Code the specific diagnosis in which the Panic Attack occurs (e.g., 300.21 Panic Attack with Agoraphobia).

A discrete period of intense fear or discomfort, in which four (or more) of the following symptoms developed abruptly and reached a peak within 10 minutes:

(1)   palpitations, pounding heart, or accelerated heart rate
(2)   sweating
(3)   trembling or shaking
(4)   sensations of shortness of breath or smothering
(5)   feeling of choking
(6)   chest pain or discomfort
(7)   nausea or abdominal distress
(8)   feeling dizzy, unsteady, lightheaded, or faint
(9)   derealization (feelings of unreality) or depersonalization (being detached from oneself)
(10)   fear of losing control or going crazy
(11)   fear of dying
(12)   paresthesias (numbness or tingling sensations)
(13)   chills or hot flushes

Source: APA, 2000, 1994
© 2013 by Worth Publishers

Criteria for Agoraphobia

Note: Agoraphobia is not a codable disorder. Code the specific disorder in which the Agoraphobia occurs (e.g., 300.21 Panic Attack with Agoraphobia or 300.22 Agoraphobia Without History of Panic Disorder).

A.   Anxiety about being in places or situations from which escape might be difficult (or embarrassing) or in which help may not be available in the event of having an unexpected or situationally predisposed Panic Attack or panic-like symptoms. Agoraphobic fears typically involve characteristic clusters of situations that include being outside the home alone; being in a crowd or standing in a line; being on a bridge; and traveling in a bus, train, or automobile.

   Note: Consider the diagnosis of Specific Phobia if the avoidance is limited to one or only a few specific situations, or Social Phobia if the avoidance is limited to social situations.

B.   The situations are avoided (e.g., travel is restricted) or else are endured with marked distress or with anxiety about having a Panic Attack or panic-like symptoms, or require the presence of a companion.

C.   The anxiety of phobic avoidance is not better accounted for by another mental disorder, such as Social Phobia (e.g., avoidance limited to social situations because of fear of embarrassment), Specific Phobia (e.g., avoidance limited to a single situation like elevators), Obsessive-Compulsive Disorder (e.g., avoidance of dirt in someone with an obsession about contamination), Posttraumatic Stress Disorder (e.g., avoidance of stimuli associated with a severe stressor), or Separation Anxiety Disorder (e.g., avoidance of leaving home or relatives).

Source: APA, 2000, 1994

Diagnostic Criteria for Panic Disorder Without Agoraphobia

A. Both (1) and (2):
  (1) recurrent unexpected Panic Attacks
  (2) at least one of the attacks has been followed by 1 month (or more) of one (or more) of the following:
    (a) persistent concern about having additional attacks
    (b) worry about the implications of the attack or its consequences (e.g., losing control, having a heart attack, "going crazy")
    (c) a significant change in behavior related to the attacks

B. Absence of Agoraphobia.

C. The Panic Attacks are not due to the direct physiological effects of a substance (e.g., a drug of abuse, a medication) or a general medication condition (e.g., hyperthyroidism).

D. The Panic Attacks are not better accounted for by another mental disorder, such as Social Phobia (e.g., on exposure to feared social situations), Specific Phobia (e.g., on exposure to a specific phobic situation), Obsessive-Compulsive Disorder (e.g., on exposure to dirt by someone with an obsession about contamination), Posttraumatic Stress Disorder (e.g., in response to stimuli associated with a severe stressor), or Separation Anxiety Disorder (e.g., in response to being away from home or close relatives).

Source: APA, 2000, 1994

Diagnostic Criteria for Obsessive-Compulsive Disorder

A. Either obsessions or compulsions:

Obsessions as defined by (1), (2), (3), and (4):

(1) recurrent and persistent thoughts, impulses, or images that are experienced, at some time during the disturbance, as intrusive and inappropriate and that cause marked anxiety or distress

(2) the thoughts, impulses, or images are not simply excessive worries about real-life problems

(3) the person attempts to ignore or suppress such thoughts, impulses, or images, or to neutralize them with some other thought or action

(4) the person recognizes that the obsessional thoughts, impulses, or images are a product of his or her own mind (not imposed from without as in thought insertion)

Compulsions are defined by (1) and (2):

(1) repetitive behaviors (e.g., hand washing, ordering, checking) or mental acts (e.g., praying, counting, repeating words silently) that the person feels driven to perform in response to an obsession, or according to rules that must be applied rigidly

(2) the behaviors or mental acts are aimed at preventing or reducing distress or preventing some dreaded event or situation; however, these behaviors or mental acts either are not connected in a realistic way with what they are designed to neutralize or prevent or are clearly excessive

B. At some point during the course of the disorder, the person has recognized that the obsessions or compulsions are excessive or unreasonable. Note: This does not apply to children.

C. The obsessions or compulsions cause marked distress, are time consuming (take more than 1 hour a day), or significantly interfere with the person's normal routine, occupational (or academic) functioning, or usual social activities or relationships.

D. If another Axis I disorder is present, the content of the obsessions or compulsions is not restricted to it (e.g., preoccupation with food in the presence of an Eating Disorder; hair pulling in the presence of Trichotillomania; concern with appearance in the presence of Body Dysmorphic Disorder; preoccupation with having a serious illness in the presence of Hypochondriasis; preoccupation with sexual urges or fantasies in the presence of a Paraphilia; or guilty ruminations in the presence of a Major Depressive Disorder).

E. The disturbance is not due to the direct physiological effects of a substance (e.g., a drug of abuse, a medication) or a general medical condition.

Source: APA, 2000, 1994

Diagnostic Criteria for Posttraumatic Stress Disorder

A. The person has been exposed to a traumatic event in which both of the following were present:
   (1) The person experienced, witnessed, or was confronted with an event or events that involved actual or threatened death or serious injury, or a threat to the physical integrity of self or others
   (2) The person's response involved intense fear, helplessness, or horror. Note: In children, this may be expressed instead by disorganized or agitated behavior.

B. The traumatic event is persistently reexperienced in one or more of the following ways:
   (1) recurrent and intrusive distressing recollections of the event, including images, thoughts, or perceptions. Note: In young children, repetitive play may occur in which themes or aspects of the trauma are expressed.
   (2) recurrent distressing dreams of the event. Note: In children, there may be frightening dreams without recognizable content.
   (3) acting or feeling as if the traumatic event were recurring (includes a sense of reliving the experience, illusions, hallucinations, and dissociative flashback episodes, including those that occur on awakening or when intoxicated). In young children, trauma-specific reenactment may occur.
   (4) intense psychological distress at exposure to internal or external cues that symbolize or resemble an aspect of the traumatic event
   (5) physiological reactivity on exposure to internal or external cues that symbolize or resemble an aspect of the traumatic event

C. Persistent avoidance of stimuli associated with the trauma and numbing of general responsiveness (not present before the trauma), as indicated by three (or more) of the following:
   (1) efforts to avoid thoughts, feelings, or conversations associated with the trauma
   (2) efforts to avoid activities, places, or people that arouse recollections of the trauma
   (3) inability to recall an important aspect of the trauma
   (4) markedly diminished interest or participation in significant activities
   (5) feeling of detachment or estrangement from others
   (6) restricted range of affect (e.g., unable to have loving feelings)
   (7) sense of a foreshortened future (e.g., does not expect to have a career, marriage, children, or a normal life span)

D. Persistent symptoms of increased arousal (not present before the trauma), as indicated by two (or more) of the following:
   (1) difficulty falling or staying asleep
   (2) irritability or outbursts of anger
   (3) difficulty concentrating
   (4) hypervigilance
   (5) exaggerated startle response

Source: APA, 2000, 1994

Diagnostic Criteria for Posttraumatic Stress Disorder
(Continued)

E. Duration of the disturbance (symptoms in criteria B, C, D) is more than 1 month.

F. The disturbance causes clinically significant distress or impairment in social, occupational, or other important areas of functioning.

Specify if:

Acute: if duration of symptoms is less than 3 months

Chronic: if duration of symptoms is 3 months or more

Specify if:

With Delayed Onset: if onset of symptoms is at least 6 months after the stressor

Source: APA, 2000, 1994
© 2013 by Worth Publishers

Diagnostic Criteria for Acute Stress Disorder

A. The person has been exposed to a traumatic event in which both of the following were present:
(1) the person experienced, witnessed, or was confronted with an event or events that involved actual or threatened death or serious injury, or a threat to the physical integrity of self or others.
(2) the person's response involved intense fear, helplessness, or horror

B. Either while experiencing or after experiencing the distressing event, the individual has three (or more) of the following Dissociative symptoms:
(1) a subjective sense of numbing, detachment, or absence of emotional responsiveness
(2) a reduction in awareness of his or her surroundings
(3) derealization
(4) depersonalization
(5) Dissociative amnesia

C. The traumatic event is persistently reexperienced in at least one of the following ways: recurrent images, thoughts, dreams, illusions, flashback episodes, or a sense of reliving the experience; or distress on exposure to reminders of the traumatic event.

D. Marked avoidance of stimuli that arouse recollections of the trauma (e.g., thoughts, feelings, conversations, activities, places, people).

E. Marked symptoms of anxiety or increased arousal (e.g., difficulty sleeping, irritability, poor concentration, hypervigilance, exaggerated startle response, motor restlessness).

F. The disturbance causes clinically significant distress or impairment in social, occupational, or other important areas of functioning or impairs the individual's ability to pursue some necessary task, such as obtaining necessary assistance or mobilizing personal resources by telling family members about the traumatic experience.

G. The disturbance lasts for a minimum of 2 days and a maximum of 4 weeks and occurs within 4 weeks of the traumatic event.

H. The disturbance is not due to the direct physiological effects of a substance or general medical condition, is not better accounted for by Brief Psychotic Disorder, and is not merely an exacerbation of a preexisting Axis I or Axis II disorder.

Source: APA, 2000, 1994

Diagnostic Criteria for Psychological Factors
Affecting General Medical Condition

A. A general medical condition (coded on Axis III) is present.

B. Psychological factors adversely affect the general medical condition in one of the following ways:
   (1) the factors have influenced the course of the general medical condition as shown by a close temporal association between the psychological factors and the development or exacerbation of, or delayed recovery from, the general medical condition
   (2) the factors interfere with the treatment of the general medical condition
   (3) the factors constitute additional health risks for the individual
   (4) stress-related physiological responses precipitate or exacerbate symptoms of the general medical condition

Choose name based on the nature of the psychological factors (if more than one factor is present, indicate the most prominent):

Mental Disorder Affecting... *[Indicate the General Medical Condition]* (e.g., an Axis I disorder such as Major Depressive Disorders delaying recovery from a myocardial infarction)

Psychological Symptoms Affecting... *[Indicate the General Medical Condition]* (e.g., depressive symptoms delaying recovery from surgery; anxiety exacerbating asthma)

Personality Traits or Coping Style Affecting... *[Indicate the General Medical Condition]* (e.g., pathological denial of the need for surgery in a patient with cancer; hostile, pressured behavior contributing to cardiovascular disease)

Maladaptive Health Behaviors Affecting... *[Indicate the General Medical Condition]* (e.g., overeating; lack of exercise; unsafe sex)

Stress-Related Physiological Response Affecting... *[Indicate the General Medical Condition]* (e.g., stress-related exacerbations of ulcer, hypertension, arrhythmia, or tension headache)

Other of Unspecified Psychological Factors Affecting... *[Indicate the General Medical Condition]* (e.g., interpersonal, cultural, or religious factors)

Source: APA, 2000, 1994

Diagnostic Criteria for Somatization Disorder

A. A history of many physical complaints beginning before age 30 years that occur over a period of several years and result in treatment being sought or significant impairment in social, occupational, or other important areas of functioning.

B. Each of the following criteria must have been met, with individual symptoms occurring at any time during the course of the disturbance.
(1) Four pain symptoms: a history of pain related to at least four different sites or functions (e.g., head, abdomen, back, joints, extremities, chest, rectum, during menstruation, during sexual intercourse, or during urination)
(2) Two gastrointestinal symptoms: a history of at least two gastrointestinal symptoms other than pain (e.g., nausea, bloating, vomiting other than during pregnancy, diarrhea, or intolerance of several different foods)
(3) One sexual symptom: a history of at least one sexual or reproductive symptom other than pain (e.g., sexual indifference, erectile or ejaculatory dysfunction, irregular menses, excessive menstrual bleeding, vomiting throughout pregnancy)
(4) One pseudoneurological symptom: a history of at least one symptom or deficit suggesting a neurological condition not limited to pain (conversion symptoms such as impaired coordination or balance, paralysis or localized weakness, difficulty swallowing or lump in throat, aphonia, urinary retention, hallucinations, loss of touch or pain, double vision, blindness, deafness, seizures; dissociative symptoms such as amnesia; or loss of consciousness other than fainting)

C. Either (1) or (2):
(1) After appropriate investigation, each of the symptoms in Criterion B cannot be fully explained by a known general medical condition or the direct effects of a substance (e.g., a drug of abuse, a medication)
(2) When there is a related general medical condition, the physical complaints or resulting social or occupational impairment are in excess of what would be expected from the history, physical examination, or laboratory findings

D. The symptoms are not intentionally produced or feigned (as in Factitious Disorder or Malingering).

Source: APA, 2000, 1994

Diagnostic Criteria for Conversion Disorder

A. One or more symptoms or deficits affecting voluntary motor or sensory function that suggest a neurological or other general medical condition.

B. Psychological factors are judged to be associated with the symptom or deficit because the initiation or exacerbation of the symptom or deficit is preceded by conflicts or other stressors.

C. The symptom or deficit is not intentionally produced or feigned (as in Factitious Disorder or Malingering).

D. The symptom or deficit cannot, after appropriate investigation, be fully explained by a general medical condition, or by the direct effects of a substance, or as a culturally sanctioned behavior or experience.

E. The symptom or deficit causes clinically significant distress or impairment in social, occupational, or other important areas of functioning or warrants medical evaluation.

F. The symptom or deficit is not limited to pain or sexual dysfunction, does not occur exclusively during the course of the Somatization Disorder, and is not better accounted for by another mental disorder.

Source: APA, 2000, 1994
© 2013 by Worth Publishers

Diagnostic Criteria for Pain Disorder

A. Pain in one or more anatomical sites is the predominant focus of the clinical presentation and is of sufficient severity to warrant clinical attention.

B. The pain causes clinically significant distress or impairment in social, occupational, or other important areas of functioning.

C. Psychological factors are judged to have an important role in the onset, severity, exacerbation, or maintenance of the pain.

D. The symptom or deficit is not intentionally produced or feigned (as in Factitious Disorder or Malingering).

E. The pain is not better accounted for by a Mood, Anxiety, or Psychotic Disorder and does not meet criteria for Dyspareunia.

Diagnostic Criteria for Hypochondriasis

A. Preoccupation with fears of having, or the idea that one has, a serious disease based on the person's misinterpretation of bodily symptoms.

B. The preoccupation persists despite appropriate medical evaluation and reassurance.

C. The belief in Criterion A is not of delusional intensity (as in Delusional Disorder, Somatic Type) and is not restricted to a circumscribed concern about appearance (as in Body Dysmorphic Disorder).

D. The preoccupation causes clinically significant distress or impairment in social, occupational, or other important areas of functioning.

E. The duration of the disturbance is at least 6 months.

F. The preoccupation is not better accounted for by Generalized Anxiety Disorder, Obsessive-Compulsive Disorder, Panic Disorder, a Major Depressive Episode, Separation Anxiety, or another Somatoform Disorder.

Source: APA, 2000, 1994

Diagnostic Criteria for Body Dysmorphic Disorder

A. Preoccupation with an imagined defect in appearance. If a slight physical anomaly is present, the person's concern is markedly excessive.

B. The preoccupation causes clinically significant distress or impairment in social, occupational, or other important areas of functioning.

C. The preoccupation is not better accounted for by another mental disorder (e.g., dissatisfaction with body shape and size in Anorexia Nervosa).

Diagnostic Criteria for Factitious Disorder

A. Intentional production or feigning of physical or psychological signs or symptoms.

B. The motivation for the behavior is to assume a sick role.

C. External incentives for the behavior (such as economic gain, avoiding legal responsibility, or improving physical well-being, as in Malingering) are absent.

Code based on type:
  With Predominantly Psychological Signs and Symptoms
  With Predominantly Physical Signs and Symptoms
  With Combined Psychological and Physical Signs and Symptoms

Source: APA, 2000, 1994

Diagnostic Criteria for Dissociative Amnesia

A. The predominant disturbance is one or more episodes of inability to recall important personal information, usually of a traumatic or stressful nature, that is too extensive to be explained by ordinary forgetfulness.

B. The disturbance does not occur exclusively during the course of Dissociative Identity Disorder, Dissociative Fugue, Posttraumatic Stress Disorder, Acute Stress Disorder, or Somatization Disorder and is not due to the direct physiological effects of a substance (e.g., a drug of abuse, a medication) or a neurological or other general medical condition (e.g., Amnestic Disorder Due to Head Trauma).

C. The symptoms cause clinically significant distress or impairment in social, occupational, or other important areas of functioning.

Diagnostic Criteria for Dissociative Fugue

A. The predominant disturbance is sudden, unexpected travel away from home or one's customary place of work, with inability to recall one's past.

B. Confusion about personal identity or assumption of a new identity (partial or complete).

C. The disturbance does not occur exclusively during the course of Dissociative Identity Disorder and is not due to the direct physiological effects of a substance (e.g., a drug of abuse, a medication) or a general medical condition (e.g., temporal lobe epilepsy).

D. The symptoms cause clinically significant distress or impairment in social, occupational, or other important areas of functioning.

Source: APA, 2000, 1994

Diagnostic Criteria for Dissociative Identity Disorder

A. The presence of two or more distinct identities or personality states (each with its own relatively enduring pattern of perceiving, relating to, and thinking about the environment and self).

B. At least two of these identities or personality states recurrently take control of the person's behavior.

C. Inability to recall important personal information that is too extensive to be explained by ordinary forgetfulness.

D. The disturbance is not due to the direct physiological effects of a substance (e.g., blackouts or chaotic behavior during Alcohol Intoxication) or a general medical condition (e.g., complex partial seizures).

Diagnostic Criteria for Depersonalization Disorder

A. Persistent or recurrent experiences of feeling detached from, and as if one is an outside observer of, one's mental processes or body (e.g., feeling like one is in a dream).

B. During the depersonalization experience, reality testing remains intact.

C. The depersonalization causes clinically significant distress or impairment in social, occupational, or other important areas of functioning.

D. The depersonalization experience does not occur exclusively during the course of another mental disorder, such as Schizophrenia, Panic Disorder, Acute Stress Disorder, or another Dissociative Disorder, and is not due to the direct physiological effects of a substance (e.g., a drug of abuse, a medication) or a general medical condition (e.g., temporal lobe epilepsy).

Source: APA, 2000, 1994

Criteria for Major Depressive Episode

A. Five (or more) of the following symptoms have been present during the same 2-week period and represent a change from the previous functioning; at least one of the symptoms is either (1) depressed mood or (2) loss of interest or pleasure.

Note: Do not include symptoms that are clearly due to a general medical condition, or mood-incongruent delusions or hallucinations.
  (1) depressed mood most of the day, nearly every day, as indicated by either subjective report (e.g., feels sad or empty) or observation made by others (e.g., appears tearful).
  (2) markedly diminished interest or pleasure in all, or almost all, activities most of the day, nearly every day (as indicated by either subjective account or observations made by others)
  (3) significant weight loss when not dieting or weight gain (e.g., a change of more than 5% of body weight in a month), a decrease or increase in appetite nearly every day. Note: In children, consider failure to make expected weight gains.
  (4) insomnia or hypersomnia nearly every day
  (5) psychomotor agitation or retardation nearly every day (observable by others)
  (6) fatigue or loss of energy nearly every day
  (7) feelings of worthlessness or excessive or inappropriate guilt (which may be delusional) nearly every day
  (8) diminished ability to think or concentrate, or indecisiveness, nearly every day (either by subjective account or observed by others)
  (9) recurrent thoughts of death (not just fear of dying), recurrent suicidal ideation without a specific plan, or a suicide attempt or a specific plan for committing suicide

B. The symptoms do not meet criteria for a Mixed Episode.

C. The symptoms cause clinically significant distress or impairment in social, occupational, or other important areas of functioning.

D. The symptoms are not due to the direct physiological effects of a substance (e.g., a drug of abuse, a medication) or a general medical condition (e.g., hypothyroidism).

E. The symptoms are not better accounted for by Bereavement, i.e., after the loss of a loved one, the symptoms persist for longer than 2 months or are characterized by marked functional impairment, morbid preoccupation with worthlessness, suicidal ideation, psychotic symptoms, or psychomotor retardation.

Source: APA, 2000, 1994
© 2013 by Worth Publishers

Criteria for Manic Episode

A. A distinct period of abnormally and persistently elevated, expansive, or irritable mood lasting at least 1 week (or any duration if hospitalization is necessary).

B. During the period of mood disturbance, three (or more) of the following symptoms have persisted (four if the mood is only irritable) and have been present to a significant degree:
   (1) inflated self-esteem or grandiosity
   (2) decreased need for sleep (e.g., feels rested after only 3 hours of sleep)
   (3) more talkative than usual or pressure to keep talking
   (4) flight of ideas or subjective experience that thoughts are racing
   (5) distractibility (i.e., attention too easily drawn to unimportant or irrelevant external stimuli)
   (6) increase in goal-directed activity (either socially, at work or school, or sexually) or psychomotor agitation
   (7) excessive involvement in pleasurable activities that have a high potential for painful consequences (e.g., engaging in unrestrained buying sprees, sexual indiscretions, or foolish business investments)

C. The symptoms do not meet the criteria for a Mixed Episode.

D. The mood disturbance is sufficiently severe to cause marked impairment in occupational functioning or in usual social activities or relationships with others, or to necessitate hospitalization to prevent harm to self or others, or there are psychotic features.

E. The symptoms are not due to the direct physiological effects of a substance (e.g., a drug of abuse, a medication, or other treatment) or a general medical condition (e.g., hyperthyroidism).

Criteria for Mixed Episode

A. The criteria are met both for a Manic Episode and for a Major Depressive Episode (except for duration) nearly every day during at least a 1-week period.

B. The mood disturbance is sufficiently severe to cause marked impairment in occupational functioning or in usual social activities or relationships with others, or to necessitate hospitalization to prevent harm to self or others, or there are psychotic features.

C. The symptoms are not due to the direct physiological effects of a substance (e.g., a drug of abuse, a medication, or other treatment) or a general medical condition (e.g., hyperthyroidism).

Source: APA, 2000, 1994

Criteria for Hypomanic Episode

A. A distinct period of persistently elevated, expansive, or irritable mood, lasting throughout at least 4 days, that is clearly different from the usual nondepressed mood.

B. During the period of mood disturbance, three (or more) of the following symptoms have persisted (four, if the mood is only irritable) and have been present to a significant degree:
    (1) inflated self-esteem or grandiosity
    (2) decreased need for sleep (e.g., feels rested after only 3 hours of sleep)
    (3) more talkative than usual or pressure to keep talking
    (4) flight of ideas or subjective experience that thoughts are racing
    (5) distractibility (i.e., attention too easily drawn to unimportant or irrelevant external stimuli)
    (6) increase in goal-directed activity (either socially, at work or school, or sexually) or psychomotor agitation
    (7) excessive involvement in pleasurable activities that have a high potential for painful consequences

C. The episode is associated with an unequivocal change in functioning that is uncharacteristic of the person when not symptomatic.

D. The disturbance in mood and the change in functioning are observable by others.

E. The episode is not severe enough to cause marked impairment in social or occupational functioning, or to necessitate hospitalization, and there are no psychotic features.

F. The symptoms are not due to the direct physiological effects of a substance (e.g., a drug of abuse, a medication, or other treatment) or a general medical condition (e.g., hypothyroidism).

Note: Hypomanic-like episodes that are clearly caused by somatic antidepressant treatment should not count toward a diagnosis of Bipolar II disorder.

Source: APA, 2000, 1994

Diagnostic Criteria for Major Depressive Disorder, Single Episode

A. Presence of a single Major Depressive Episode

B. The Major Depressive Episode is not better accounted for by Schizoaffective Disorder and is not superimposed on Schizophrenia, Schizophreniform Disorder, Delusional Disorder, or Psychotic Disorder Not Otherwise Specified.

C. There has never been a Manic Episode, a Mixed Episode, or a Hypomanic Episode. Note: This exclusion does not apply if all the manic-like, mixed-like, or hypomanic-like episodes are substance or treatment induced or are due to the direct physiological effects of a general medical condition.

Diagnostic Criteria for Major Depressive Disorder, Recurrent

A. A presence of two or more Major Depressive Episodes.

Note: To be considered separate episodes, there must be an interval of at least 2 consecutive months in which criteria are not met for a Major Depressive Episode.

B. The Major Depressive Episodes are not better accounted for by Schizoaffective Disorder and are not superimposed on Schizophrenia, Schizophreniform Disorder, Delusional Disorder, or Psychotic Disorder Not Otherwise Specified.

C. There has never been a Manic Episode, a Mixed Episode, or a Hypomanic Episode.

Note: This exclusion does not apply if all the manic-like, mixed-like, or hypomanic-like episodes are substance or treatment induced or are due to the direct physiological effects of a general medical condition.

Source: APA, 2000, 1994
© 2013 by Worth Publishers

Diagnostic Criteria for Dysthymic Disorder

A.   Depressed mood for most of the day, for more days than not, as indicated either by subjective account or observation by others, for at least 2 years. Note: In children and adolescents, mood can be irritable and duration must be at least 1 year.

B.   Presence, while depressed, of two (or more) of the following:
(1)   poor appetite or overeating
(2)   insomnia or hypersomnia
(3)   low energy or fatigue
(4)   low self-esteem
(5)   poor concentration or difficulty making decisions
(6)   feelings of hopelessness

C.   During the 2-year period (1 year for children or adolescents) of the disturbance, the person has never been without the symptoms in Criteria A and B for more than 2 months at a time.

D.   No Major Depressive Episode has been present during the first 2 years of the disturbance (1 year for children and adolescents); i.e., the disturbance is not better accounted for by chronic Major Depressive Disorder, or Major Depressive Disorder, In Partial Remission.

Note: There may have been a previous Major Depressive Episode provided there was a full remission (no significant signs or symptoms for 2 months) before development of the Dysthymic Disorder. In addition, after the initial 2 years (1 year in children or adolescents) of Dysthymic Disorder, there may be superimposed episodes of Major Depressive Disorder, in which case both diagnoses may be given when the criteria are met for a Major Depressive Episode.

E.   There has never been a Manic Episode, a Mixed Episode, or a Hypomanic Episode, and criteria have never been met for Cyclothymic Disorder.

F.   The disturbance does not occur exclusively during the course of a chronic Psychotic Disorder, such as Schizophrenia or Delusional Disorder.

G.   The symptoms are not due to the direct physiological effects of a substance (e.g., a drug of abuse, a medication) or a general medical condition (e.g., hypothyroidism).

H.   The symptoms cause clinically significant distress or impairment in social, occupational, or other important areas of functioning.

Specify if:

Early Onset: if onset is before age 21 years

Late Onset: if onset is age 21 or older

Source: APA, 2000, 1994

Diagnostic Criteria for Bipolar I Disorder, Single Manic Episode

A.   Presence of only one Manic Episode and no past major Depressive Episodes.

   Note: Recurrence is defined as either a change in polarity from depression or an interval of at least 2 months without manic symptoms.

B.   The Manic Episode is not better accounted for by Schizoaffective Disorder and is not superimposed on Schizophrenia, Schizophreniform Disorder, Delusional Disorder, or Psychotic Disorder Not Otherwise Specified.

Diagnostic Criteria for Bipolar II Disorder

A.   Presence (or history) of one or more Major Depressive Episodes.

B.   Presence (or history) of at least one Hypomanic Episode.

C.   There has never been a Manic Episode or a Mixed Episode.

D.   The mood symptoms in criteria A and B are not better accounted for by Schizoaffective Disorder and are not superimposed on Schizophrenia, Schizophreniform Disorder, Delusional Disorder, or Psychotic Disorder Not Otherwise Specified.

E.   The symptoms cause clinically significant distress or impairment in social, occupational, or other important areas of functioning.

Source: APA, 2000, 1994

Diagnostic Criteria for Cyclothymic Disorder

A. For at least 2 years, the presence of numerous periods with hypomanic symptoms and numerous periods with depressive symptoms that do not meet criteria for a Major Depressive Episode. Note: In children and adolescents, the duration must be at least 1 year.

B. During the above 2-year period (1 year in children and adolescents), the person has not been without the symptoms in Criterion A for more than 2 months at a time.

C. No Major Depressive Episode, Manic Episode, or Mixed Episode has been present during the first 2 years of the disturbance.

D. The symptoms in Criterion A are not better accounted for by Schizoaffective Disorder and are not superimposed on Schizophrenia, Schizophreniform Disorder, or Psychotic Disorder Not Otherwise Specified.

E. The symptoms are not due to the direct physiological effects of a substance (e.g., a drug of abuse, a medication) or a general medical condition (e.g., hyperthyroidism).

F. The symptoms cause clinically significant distress or impairment in social, occupational, or other important areas of functioning.

Source: APA, 2000, 1994

Diagnostic Criteria for Anorexia Nervosa

A. Refusal to maintain body weight at or above a minimally normal weight for age and height (e.g., weight loss leading to maintenance of body weight less than 85% of that expected; or failure to make expected weight gain during period of growth, leading to body weight less than 85% of that expected).

B. Intense fear of gaining weight or becoming fat, even though underweight.

C. Disturbance in the way in which one's body weight or shape is experienced, undue influence of body weight or shape on self-evaluation, or denial of the seriousness of the current low body weight.

D. In postmenarcheal females, amenorrhea, i.e., the absence of at least three consecutive menstrual cycles. (A woman is considered to have amenorrhea if her periods occur only following hormone administration, e.g., estrogen.)

Specify type:

Restricting Type: during the current episode of Anorexia Nervosa, the person has not regularly engaged in binge-eating or purging behavior (i.e., self-induced vomiting or the misuse of laxatives, diuretics, or enemas)

Binge-Eating/Purging Type: during the current episode of Anorexia Nervosa, the person has regularly engaged in binge-eating or purging behavior (i.e., self-induced vomiting or the misuse of laxatives, diuretics, or enemas)

Source: APA, 2000, 1994
© 2013 by Worth Publishers

Diagnostic Criteria for Bulimia Nervosa

A. Recurrent episodes of binge-eating. An episode of binge eating is characterized by both of the following:
   (1) Eating, in a discrete period of time (e.g., within any 2-hour period), an amount of food that is definitely larger than most people would eat during that similar period of time under similar circumstances
   (2) A sense of lack of control over eating during the episode (e.g., a feeling that one cannot stop eating or control what or how much one is eating)

B. Recurrent inappropriate compensatory behavior in order to prevent weight gain, such as self-induced vomiting; misuse of laxatives, diuretics, enemas, or other medications; fasting; or excessive exercise.

C. The binge eating and inappropriate compensatory behavior both occur, on average, at least twice a week for 3 months.

D. Self-evaluation is unduly influenced by body shape and weight.

E. The disturbance does not occur exclusively during episodes of Anorexia Nervosa.

Specify type:

   Purging Type: during the current episode of Bulimia Nervosa, the person has regularly engaged in self-induced vomiting or the misuse of laxatives, diuretics, or enemas.

   Nonpurging Type: during the current episode of Bulimia Nervosa, the person has used other inappropriate compensatory behaviors, such as fasting or excessive exercise, but has not regularly engaged in self-induced vomiting or the misuse of laxatives, diuretics, or enemas.

Source: APA, 2000, 1994

Diagnostic Criteria for Substance Intoxication

A. The development of a reversible substance-specific syndrome due to recent ingestion of (or exposure to) a substance. Note: Different substances may produce similar or identical syndromes.

B. Clinically significant maladaptive behavioral or psychological changes that are due to the effect of the substance on the central nervous system (e.g., belligerence, mood lability, cognitive impairment, impaired judgment, impaired social or occupational functioning) and develop during or shortly after use of the substance.

C. The symptoms are not due to a general medical condition and are not better accounted for by another mental disorder.

Diagnostic Criteria for Substance Withdrawal

A. The development of a substance-specific syndrome due to the cessation of (or reduction in) substance use that has been heavy and prolonged.

B. The substance-specific syndrome causes clinically significant distress or impairment in social, occupational, or other important areas of functioning.

C. The symptoms are not due to a general medical condition and are not better accounted for by another mental disorder.

Source: APA, 2000, 1994

Diagnostic Criteria for Substance Abuse

A. A maladaptive pattern of substance use leading to clinically significant impairment or distress, as manifested by one (or more) of the following, occurring within a 12-month period:

   (1) recurring substance use resulting in failure to fulfill major role obligations at work, school, or home (e.g., repeated absences or poor work performance related to substance use; substance-related absences, suspensions, or expulsions from school; neglect of children or household

   (2) recurrent substance use in situations in which it is physically hazardous (e.g., driving an automobile or operating a machine when impaired by substance use)

   (3) recurrent substance-related legal problems (e.g., arrests for substance-related disorderly conduct)

   (4) continued substance use despite having persistent or recurrent social or interpersonal problems caused or exacerbated by the effects of the substance (e.g., arguments with spouse about consequences of intoxication, physical fights)

B. The symptoms have never met the criteria for Substance Dependence for this class of substance.

Source: APA, 2000, 1994

Diagnostic Criteria for Substance Dependence

A maladaptive pattern of substance use, leading to clinically significant impairment or distress, as manifested by three (or more) of the following, occurring at any time in the same 12-month period:

(1) tolerance as defined by either of the following:
    (a) a need for markedly increased amounts of the substance to achieve intoxication or desired effect
    (b) markedly diminished effect with continued use of the same amount of the substance

(2) withdrawal, as manifested by either of the following:
    (a) the characteristic withdrawal syndrome for the substance (refer to Criteria A and B of the criteria sets for Withdrawal from the specific substances)
    (b) the same (or a closely related) substance is taken to relieve or avoid withdrawal symptoms

(3) the substance is often taken in larger amounts or over a longer period than was intended

(4) there is a persistent desire or unsuccessful effort to cut down or control substance use

(5) a great deal of time is spent in activities necessary to obtain the substance (e.g., visiting multiple doctors or driving long distances), use the substance (e.g., chainsmoking), or recover from its effects

(6) important social, occupational, or recreational activities are given up or reduced because of substance use

(7) the substance use is continued despite knowledge of having a persistent or recurrent physical or psychological problem that is likely to be exacerbated by the substance (e.g., current cocaine use despite recognition of cocaine-induced depression, or continued drinking despite recognition that an ulcer was made worse by alcohol consumption)

Source: APA, 2000, 1994

Diagnostic Criteria for Hypoactive Sexual Desire Disorder

A. Persistently or recurrently deficient (or absent) sexual fantasies and desire for sexual activity. The judgment of deficiency or absence is made by the clinician, taking into account the factors that affect sexual functioning, such as age and the context of the person's life.

B. The disturbance causes marked distress or interpersonal difficulty.

C. The sexual dysfunction is not better accounted for by another Axis I disorder (except another Sexual Dysfunction) and is not due exclusively to the direct physiological effects of a substance (e.g., a drug of abuse, a medication) or a general medical condition.

Diagnostic Criteria for Sexual Aversion Disorder

A. Persistent or recurrent extreme aversion to, and avoidance of, all (or almost all) genital sexual contact with a sexual partner.

B. The disturbance causes marked distress or interpersonal difficulty.

C. The sexual dysfunction is not better accounted for by another Axis I disorder (except another Sexual Dysfunction).

Source: APA, 2000, 1994

Diagnostic Criteria for Female Sexual Arousal Disorder

A. Persistent or recurrent inability to attain, or to maintain until completion of the sexual activity, an adequate lubrication-swelling response to sexual excitement.

B. The disturbance causes marked distress or interpersonal difficulty.

C. The sexual dysfunction is not better accounted for by another Axis I disorder (except another Sexual Dysfunction) and is not due exclusively to the direct physiological effects of a substance (e.g., a drug of abuse, a medication) or a general medical condition.

Diagnostic Criteria for Male Erectile Disorder

A. Persistent or recurrent inability to attain, or to maintain until completion of the sexual activity, an adequate erection.

B. The disturbance causes marked distress or interpersonal difficulty.

C. The erectile dysfunction is not better accounted for by another Axis I disorder (other than a Sexual Dysfunction) and is not due exclusively to the direct physiological effects of a substance (e.g., a drug of abuse, a medication) or a general medical condition.

Diagnostic Criteria for Female Orgasmic Disorder

A. The persistent or recurrent delay in, or absence of, orgasm following a normal sexual excitement phase. Women exhibit wide variability in the type or intensity of stimulation that triggers orgasm. The diagnosis of Female Orgasmic Disorder should be based on the clinician's judgment that the woman's orgasmic capacity is less than would be reasonable for her age, sexual experience, and the adequacy of stimulation she receives.

B. The disturbance causes marked distress or interpersonal difficulty.

C. The orgasmic dysfunction is not better accounted for by another Axis I disorder (except another Sexual Dysfunction) and is not due exclusively to the direct physiological effects of a substance (e.g., a drug of abuse, a medication) or a general medical condition.

Diagnostic Criteria for Male Orgasmic Disorder

A. Persistent or recurrent delay in, or absence of, orgasm following a normal sexual excitement phase during sexual activity that the clinician, taking into account the person's age, judges to be adequate in focus, intensity, and duration.

B. The disturbance causes marked distress or interpersonal difficulty.

C. The orgasmic dysfunction is not better accounted for by another Axis I disorder (except another Sexual Dysfunction) and is not due exclusively to the direct physiological effects of a substance (e.g., a drug of abuse, a medication) or a general medical condition.

Source: APA, 2000, 1994

Diagnostic Criteria for Premature Ejaculation

A. Persistent or recurrent ejaculation with minimal sexual stimulation before, on, or shortly after penetration and before the person wishes it. The clinician must take into account factors that affect duration of the excitement phase, such as age, novelty of sexual partner or situation, and recent frequency of sexual activity.

B. The disturbance causes marked distress or interpersonal difficulty.

C. The premature ejaculation is not due exclusively to the direct effects of a substance (e.g., withdrawal from opioids).

Diagnostic Criteria for Dyspareunia

A. Recurrent or persistent genital pain associated with sexual intercourse in either a male or a female.

B. The disturbance causes marked distress or interpersonal difficulty.

C. The disturbance is not caused exclusively by Vaginismus or lack of lubrication, is not better accounted for by another Axis I disorder (except another Sexual Dysfunction), and is not due exclusively to the direct physiological effects of a substance (e.g., a drug of abuse, a medication) or a general medical condition.

Diagnostic Criteria for Vaginismus

A. Recurrent or persistent involuntary spasm of the musculature of the outer third of the vagina that interferes with sexual intercourse.

B. The disturbance causes marked distress or interpersonal difficulty.

C. The disturbance is not better accounted for by another Axis I disorder (e.g., Somatization Disorder) and is not due exclusively to the direct physiological effects of a general medical condition.

Source: APA, 2000, 1994
© 2013 by Worth Publishers

Diagnostic Criteria for Exhibitionism

A.   Over a period of at least 6 months, recurrent, intense sexually arousing fantasies, sexual urges, or behaviors involving the exposure of one's genitals to an unsuspecting stranger.

B.   The person has acted on these sexual urges, or the sexual urges or fantasies cause marked distress or interpersonal difficulty.

Diagnostic Criteria for Fetishism

A.   Over a period of at least 6 months, recurrent, intense sexually arousing fantasies, sexual urges, or behaviors involving the use of nonliving objects (e.g., female undergarments).

B.   The fantasies, sexual urges, or behaviors cause clinically significant distress or impairment in social, occupational, or other important areas of functioning.

C.   The fetish objects are not limited to articles of female clothing used in cross-dressing (as in Transvestic Fetishism) or devices designed for the purpose of tactile genital stimulation (e.g., a vibrator).

Diagnostic Criteria for Frotteurism

A.   Over a period of at least 6 months, recurrent, intense sexually arousing fantasies, sexual urges, or behaviors involving touching and rubbing against a nonconsenting person.

B.   The person has acted on these sexual urges, or the sexual urges or fantasies cause marked distress or interpersonal difficulty.

Diagnostic Criteria for Pedophilia

A.   Over a period of at least 6 months, recurrent, intense sexually arousing fantasies, sexual urges, or behaviors involving sexual activity with a prepubescent child or children (generally age 13 years or younger).

B.   The person has acted on these sexual urges, or the sexual urges or fantasies cause marked distress or interpersonal difficulty.

C.   The person is at least 16 years old and at least 5 years older than the child or children in Criterion A.

Note: Do not include an individual in late adolescence involved in an ongoing sexual relationship with a 12- or 13-year-old.

Source: APA, 2000, 1994
© 2013 by Worth Publishers

Diagnostic Criteria for Sexual Masochism

A. Over a period of at least 6 months, recurrent, intense sexually arousing fantasies, sexual urges, or behaviors involving the act (real, not simulated) of being humiliated, beaten, bound, or otherwise made to suffer.

B. The fantasies, sexual urges, or behaviors cause clinically significant distress or impairment in social, occupational, or other important areas of functioning.

Diagnostic Criteria for Sexual Sadism

A. Over a period of at least 6 months, recurrent, intense sexually arousing fantasies, sexual urges, or behaviors involving acts (real, not simulated) in which the psychological or physical suffering (including humiliation) of the victim is sexually exciting to the person.

B. The person has acted on these sexual urges with a nonconsenting person, or the sexual urges or fantasies cause marked distress or interpersonal difficulty.

Diagnostic Criteria for Transvestic Fetishism

A. Over a period of at least 6 months, in a heterosexual male, recurrent, intense sexually arousing fantasies, sexual urges, or behaviors involving cross-dressing.

B. The fantasies, sexual urges, or behaviors cause clinically significant distress or impairment in social, occupational, or other important areas of functioning.

Diagnostic Criteria for Voyeurism

A. Over a period of at least 6 months, recurrent, intense sexually arousing fantasies, sexual urges, or behaviors involving the act of observing an unsuspecting person who is naked, in the process of disrobing, or engaging in sexual activity.

B. The person has acted on these sexual urges, or the sexual urges or fantasies cause marked distress or interpersonal difficulty.

Source: APA, 2000, 1994

Diagnostic Criteria for Gender Identity Disorder

A. A strong and persistent cross-gender identification (not merely a desire for any perceived cultural advantages of being the other sex).

In children, the disturbance is manifested by four (or more) of the following:
(1) repeatedly stated desire to be, or insistence that he or she is, the other sex
(2) in boys, preference for cross-dressing or simulating female attire; in girls, insistence on wearing only stereotypical masculine clothing
(3) strong and persistent preferences for cross-sex roles in make-believe play or persistent fantasies about being the other sex
(4) intense desire to participate in the stereotypical games and pastimes of the other sex
(5) strong preference for playmates of other sex

In adolescents and adults, the disturbance is manifested by symptoms such as a stated desire to be the other sex, frequent passing as the other sex, desire to live and be treated as the other sex, or the conviction that he or she has the typical feelings and reactions of the other sex.

B. Persistent discomfort with his or her sex or sense of inappropriateness in the gender role of that sex.

In children, the disturbance is manifested by any of the following: in boys, assertion that his penis or testes are disgusting or will disappear or assertion that it would be better not to have a penis, or aversion toward rough-and-tumble play and rejection of male stereotypical toys, games, and activities; in girls, rejection of urinating in a sitting position, assertion that she has or will grow a penis, or assertion that she does not want to grow breasts or menstruate, or marked aversion toward normative feminine clothing.

In adolescents and adults, the disturbance is manifested by symptoms such as preoccupation with getting rid of primary and secondary sex characteristics (e.g., request for hormones, surgery, or other procedures to physically alter sexual characteristics that simulate the other sex), or belief that he or she was born the wrong sex.

C. The disturbance is not concurrent with a physical intersex condition.

D. The disturbance causes clinically significant distress or impairment in social, occupational, or other important areas of functioning.

Source: APA, 2000, 1994

Diagnostic Criteria for Schizophrenia

A. Characteristic symptoms: Two (or more) of the following, each present for a significant portion of time during a 1-month period (or less if successfully treated):
   (1) delusions
   (2) hallucinations
   (3) disorganized speech (e.g., frequent derailment or incoherence)
   (4) grossly disorganized or catatonic behavior
   (5) negative symptoms, i.e., affective flattening, alogia, or avolition

   Note: Only one Criterion A symptom is required if delusions are bizarre or hallucinations consist of a voice keeping up a running commentary on the person's behavior or thoughts, or two or more voices conversing with each other.

B. Social/occupational dysfunction: For a significant portion of the time since the onset of the disturbance, one or more major areas of functioning such as work, interpersonal relations, or self-care are markedly below the level achieved prior to the onset (or when the onset is in childhood or adolescence, failure to achieve expected level of interpersonal, academic, or occupational achievement).

C. Duration: Continuous signs of the disturbance persist for at least 6 months. This 6-month period must include at least 1 month of symptoms (or less if successfully treated) that meet Criterion A (i.e., active-phase symptoms) and may include periods of prodromal or residual symptoms. During these prodromal or residual periods, the signs of the disturbance may be manifested by only negative symptoms or two or more symptoms listed in Criterion A present in an attenuated form (e.g., odd beliefs, unusual perceptual experiences).

D. Schizoaffective and Mood Disorder exclusion: Schizoaffective Disorder and Mood Disorder With Psychotic Features have been ruled out because either (1) no Major Depressive, Manic, or Mixed Episodes have occurred concurrently with active-phase symptoms; or (2) if mood episodes have occurred during active-phase symptoms, their total duration has been brief relative to the duration of the active and residual periods.

E. Substance/general medical condition exclusion: The disturbance is not due to the direct physiological effects of a substance (e.g., a drug of abuse, a medication) or a general medical condition.

F. Relationship to a Pervasive Developmental Disorder: If there is history of Autistic Disorder or another Pervasive Developmental Disorder, the additional diagnosis of Schizophrenia is made only if prominent delusions or hallucinations are also present for at least a month (or less if successfully treated).

Source: APA, 2000, 1994
© 2013 by Worth Publishers

Diagnostic Criteria for Paranoid Type

A type of Schizophrenia in which the following criteria are met:

A.   Preoccupation with one or more delusions or frequent auditory hallucinations.

B.   None of the following is prominent: disorganized speech, disorganized or catatonic behavior, or flat or inappropriate affect.

Diagnostic Criteria for Disorganized Type

A type of Schizophrenia in which the following criteria are met:

A.   All of the following are prominent:
   (1)   disorganized speech
   (2)   disorganized behavior
   (3)   flat or inappropriate affect

B.   The criteria are not met for Catatonic Type.

Diagnostic Criteria for Catatonic Type

A type of Schizophrenia in which the following criteria are met:

   (1)   motoric immobility as evidenced by catalepsy (including waxy flexibility) or stupor
   (2)   excessive motor activity (that is apparently purposeless and not influenced by external stimuli)
   (3)   extreme negativism (an apparently motiveless resistance to all instructions, or maintenance of a rigid posture against attempts to be moved) or mutism
   (4)   peculiarities of voluntary movement as evidenced by posturing (voluntary assumption of inappropriate or bizarre postures), stereotyped movements, prominent mannerisms, or prominent grimacing
   (5)   echolalia or echopraxia

Source: APA, 2000, 1994

Diagnostic Criteria for Undifferentiated Type

A type of Schizophrenia in which symptoms that meet Criterion A are present, but the criteria are not met for the Paranoid, Disorganized, or Catatonic Type.

Diagnostic Criteria for Residual Type

A type of Schizophrenia in which the following criteria are met:

A. Absence of prominent delusions, hallucinations, disorganized speech, and grossly disorganized or catatonic behavior.

B. There is continuing evidence of the disturbance, as indicated by the presence of negative symptoms or two or more symptoms listed in Criterion A for Schizophrenia, present in an attenuated form (e.g., odd beliefs, unusual perceptual experiences).

Source: APA, 2000, 1994

Diagnostic Criteria for Schizoaffective Disorder

A. An uninterrupted period of illness during which, at some time, there is either a Major Depressive Episode, a Manic Episode, or a Mixed Episode concurrent with symptoms that meet Criterion A for Schizophrenia.

Note: The Major Depressive Episode must include Criterion A1: depressed mood.

B. During the same period of illness, there have been delusions or hallucinations for at least two weeks in the absence of prominent mood symptoms.

C. Symptoms that meet criteria for a mood episode are present for a substantial portion of the total duration of the active and residual periods of the illness.

D. The disturbance is not due to the direct physiological effects of a substance (e.g., a drug of abuse, a medication) or a general medical condition.

Specify type:
Bipolar Type: if the disturbance includes Manic or a Mixed Episode (or a Manic or Mixed Episode and Major Depressive Episodes).

Depressive Type: if the disturbance only includes Major Depressive Episode.

Diagnostic Criteria for Schizophreniform Disorder

A. Criteria A, D, and E of Schizophrenia are met.

B. An episode of the disorder (including prodromal, active, and residual phases) lasts at least 1 month but less than 6 months. (When the diagnosis must be made without waiting for recovery, it should be qualified as "Provisional.")

Specify if:

Without Good Prognostic Features

With Good Prognostic Features: as evidenced by two (or more) of the following:
(1) onset of prominent psychotic symptoms within 4 weeks of the first noticeable change in usual behavior or functioning
(2) confusion or perplexity at the height of the psychotic episode
(3) good premorbid social and occupational functioning
(4) absence of blunted or flat affect

Source: APA, 2000, 1994

Diagnostic Criteria for Delusional Disorder

A. Nonbizarre delusions (i.e., involving situations that occur in real life, such as being followed, poisoned, infected, loved at a distance, or deceived by spouse or lover, or having a disease) of at least 1 month's duration.

B. Criterion A for Schizophrenia has never been met. Note: Tactile and olfactory hallucinations may be present in Delusional Disorder if they are related to the delusional theme.

C. Apart from the impact of the delusion(s) or its ramifications, functioning is not markedly impaired and behavior is not obviously odd or bizarre.

D. If mood episodes have occurred concurrently with delusions, their total duration has been brief relative to the duration of the delusional periods.

E. The disturbance is not due to the direct physiological effects of a substance (e.g., a drug of abuse, a medication) or a general medical condition.

Specify type (the following types are assigned based on the predominant delusional theme):

Erotomanic Type: delusions that another person, usually of higher status, is in love with the individual.

Grandiose Type: delusions of inflated worth, power, knowledge, identity, or special relationship to a deity or famous person.

Jealous Type: delusions that the individual's sexual partner is unfaithful

Persecutory Type: delusions that the person (or someone to whom the person is close) is being malevolently treated in some way.

Somatic Type: delusions that the person has some physical defect or general medical condition

Mixed Type: delusions characteristic of more than one of the above types but no one theme predominates

Unspecified Type

Source: APA, 2000, 1994

Diagnostic Criteria for Brief Psychotic Disorder

A.   Presence of one (or more) of the following symptoms:
(1)   delusions
(2)   hallucinations
(3)   disorganized speech (e.g., frequent derailment or incoherence)
(4)   grossly disorganized or catatonic behavior

Note: Do not include a symptom if it is a culturally sanctioned response pattern.

B.   Duration of an episode of the disturbance is at least 1 day but less than 1 month, with eventual full return to premorbid level of functioning.

C.   The disturbance is not better accounted for by a Mood Disorder with Psychotic Features, Schizoaffective Disorder, or Schizophrenia and is not due to the direct physiological effects of a substance (e.g., a drug of abuse, a medication) or a general medical condition.

Specify if:

With Marked Stressor(s) (brief reactive psychosis): if symptoms occur shortly after and apparently in response to events that, singly or together, would be markedly stressful to almost anyone in similar circumstances in the person's culture

Without Marked Stressor(s): if symptoms do *not* occur shortly after, or are not apparently in response to events that, singly or together, would be markedly stressful to almost anyone in similar circumstances in the person's culture

With Postpartum Onset: if onset is within 4 weeks postpartum

Diagnostic Criteria for Shared Psychotic Disorder
(Folie à Deux)

A. A delusion develops in an individual in the context of a close relationship with another person(s), who has an already established delusion.

B. The delusion is similar in content to that of the person who already has the established delusion.

C. The disturbance is not better accounted for by another Psychotic Disorder (e.g., Schizophrenia) or a Mood Disorder with Psychotic Features and is not due to the direct physiological effects of a substance (e.g., a drug of abuse, a medication) or a general medical condition.

Diagnostic Criteria for Psychotic Disorder due to
a General Medical Condition

A. Prominent hallucinations or delusions.

B. There is evidence from the history, physical examination, or laboratory findings that the disturbance is the direct physiological consequence of a general medical condition.

C. The disturbance is not better accounted for by another mental disorder.

D. The disturbance does not occur exclusively during the course of a delirium.

Source: APA, 2000, 1994
© 2013 by Worth Publishers

Diagnostic Criteria for Substance-Induced Psychotic Disorder

A. Prominent hallucinations or delusions. Note: Do not include hallucinations if the person has insight that they are substance induced.

B. There is evidence from the history, physical examination, or laboratory findings of either (1) or (2):

    (1)   the symptoms in Criterion A developed during, or within a month of, Substance Intoxication or Withdrawal

    (2)   medication use is etiologically related to the disturbance

C. The disturbance is not better accounted for by a Psychotic Disorder that is not substance induced. Evidence that the symptoms are better accounted for by a Psychotic Disorder that is not substance induced might include the following: the symptoms precede the onset of the substance use (or medication use); the symptoms persist for a substantial period of time (e.g., about a month) after the cessation of acute withdrawal or severe intoxication, or are substantially in excess of what would be expected given the type or amount of the substance used or the duration of use; or there is other evidence that suggests the existence of an independent non-substance-induced Psychotic Disorder (e.g., a history of recurrent non-substance-related episodes).

D. The disturbance does not occur exclusively during the course of a delirium.

Note: This diagnosis should be made instead of a diagnosis of Substance Intoxication or Substance Withdrawal only when symptoms are in excess of those usually associated with the intoxication or withdrawal syndrome and when the symptoms are sufficiently severe to warrant independent clinical attention.

Specify if:

    With Onset During Intoxication: if criteria are met for Intoxication with the substance and the symptoms develop during the intoxication syndrome

    With Onset During Withdrawal: if criteria are met for Withdrawal from the substance and the symptoms develop during, or shortly after, a withdrawal syndrome

Source: APA, 2000, 1994

General Diagnostic Criteria for a Personality Disorder

A. An enduring pattern of inner experience and behavior that deviates markedly from the expectations of the individual's culture. This pattern is manifested in two (or more) of the following areas:

   (1) cognition (i.e., ways of perceiving and interpreting self, other people, and events)
   (2) affectivity (i.e., the range, intensity, ability, and appropriateness of emotional response)
   (3) interpersonal functioning
   (4) impulse control

B. The enduring pattern is inflexible and pervasive across a broad range of personal and social situations.

C. The enduring pattern leads to clinically significant distress or impairment in social, occupational, or other important areas of functioning.

D. The pattern is stable and of long duration and its onset can be traced back at least to adolescence or early childhood.

E. The enduring pattern is not better accounted for as a manifestation or consequence of another mental disorder.

F. The enduring pattern is not due to the direct physiological effects of a substance (e.g., a drug of abuse, a medication) or a general medical condition (e.g., head trauma).

Source: APA, 2000, 1994

Diagnostic Criteria for Paranoid Personality Disorder

A.   A pervasive distrust and suspiciousness of others such that their motives are interpreted as malevolent, beginning by early adulthood and present in a variety of contexts, as indicated by four (or more) of the following:

   (1)   suspects, without sufficient basis, that others are exploiting, harming, or deceiving him or her

   (2)   is preoccupied with unjustified doubts about the loyalty or trustworthiness of friends or associates

   (3)   is reluctant to confide in others because of unwarranted fear that the information will be used maliciously against him or her

   (4)   reads hidden, demeaning, or threatening meanings into benign remarks or events

   (5)   persistently bears grudges, i.e., is unforgiving of insults, injuries, or slights

   (6)   perceives attacks on his or her character or reputation that are not apparent to others and is quick to react angrily or to counterattack

   (7)   has recurrent suspicions, without justification, regarding fidelity of spouse or sexual partner

B.   Does not occur exclusively during the course of Schizophrenia, a Mood Disorder With Psychotic Features, or another Psychotic Disorder and is not due to the direct physiological effects of a general medical condition.

Diagnostic Criteria for Schizoid Personality Disorder

A.   A pervasive pattern of detachment from social relationships and a restricted range of expression of emotions in interpersonal settings, beginning in early adulthood and present in a variety of contexts, as indicated by four (or more) of the following:

   (1)   neither desires nor enjoys close relationships, including being part of a family

   (2)   almost always chooses solitary activities

   (3)   has little, if any, interest in having sexual experiences with another person

   (4)   takes pleasure in few, if any, activities

   (5)   lacks close friends or confidants other than first-degree relatives

   (6)   appears indifferent to the praise or criticism of others

   (7)   shows emotional coldness, detachment, or flattened affectivity

B.   Does not occur exclusively during the course of Schizophrenia, a Mood Disorder With Psychotic Features, another Psychotic Disorder, or a Pervasive Developmental Disorder and is not due to the direct physiological effects of a general medical condition.

Source: APA, 2000, 1994

Diagnostic Criteria for Schizotypal Personality Disorder

A. A pervasive pattern of social and interpersonal deficits marked by acute discomfort with, and reduced capacity for, close relationships as well as by cognitive or perceptual distortions and eccentricities of behavior, beginning by early adulthood and present in a variety of contexts, as indicated by five (or more) of the following:

   (1) ideas of reference (excluding delusions of reference)
   (2) odd beliefs or magical thinking that influences behavior and is inconsistent with subcultural norms (e.g., superstitiousness, belief in clairvoyance, telepathy, or "sixth sense"; in children and adolescents, bizarre fantasies or preoccupations)
   (3) unusual perceptual experiences, including bodily illusions
   (4) odd thinking and speech (e.g., vague, circumstantial, metaphorical, overelaborate, or stereotyped)
   (5) suspiciousness or paranoid ideation
   (6) inappropriate or constricted affect
   (7) behavior or appearance that is odd, eccentric, or peculiar
   (8) lack of close friends or confidants other than first-degree relatives
   (9) excessive social anxiety that does not diminish with familiarity and tends to be associated with paranoid fears rather than negative judgments about self

B. Does not occur exclusively during the course of Schizophrenia, a Mood Disorder With Psychotic Features, another Psychotic Disorder, or a Pervasive Developmental Disorder.

Source: APA, 2000, 1994

Diagnostic Criteria for Antisocial Personality Disorder

A. There is a pervasive pattern of disregard for and violation of the rights of others occurring since age 15 years, as indicated by three (or more) of the following:
   (1) failure to conform to social norms with respect to lawful behaviors as indicated by repeatedly performing acts that are grounds for arrest
   (2) deceitfulness, as indicated by repeated lying, use of aliases, or conning others for personal profit or pleasure
   (3) impulsivity or failure to plan ahead
   (4) irritability and aggressiveness, as indicated by repeated physical fights or assaults
   (5) reckless disregard for safety of self or others
   (6) consistent irresponsibility, as indicated by repeated failure to sustain consistent work behavior or honor financial obligations
   (7) lack of remorse, as indicated by being indifferent to or rationalizing having hurt, mistreated, or stolen from another

B. The individual is at least age 18 years.

C. There is evidence of Conduct Disorder with onset before age 15 years.

D. The occurrence of antisocial behavior is not exclusively during the course of Schizophrenia or a Manic Episode.

Diagnostic Criteria for Borderline Personality Disorder

A pervasive pattern of instability of interpersonal relationships, self-image, and affects, and marked impulsivity beginning by early adulthood and present in a variety of contexts, as indicated by five (or more) of the following:

(1) frantic efforts to avoid real or imagined abandonment. Note: Do not include suicidal or self-mutilating behavior covered in Criterion 5.
(2) a pattern of unstable and intense interpersonal relationships characterized by alternating between extremes of idealization and devaluation
(3) identity disturbance: markedly and persistently unstable self-image or sense of self
(4) impulsivity in at least two areas that are potentially self-damaging (e.g., spending, sex, substance abuse, reckless driving, binge eating). Note: Do not include suicidal or self-mutilating behavior covered in Criterion 5.
(5) recurrent suicidal behavior, gestures, or threats, or self-mutilating behavior
(6) affective instability due to a marked reactivity of mood (e.g., intense episodic dysphoria, irritability, or anxiety usually lasting a few hours and only rarely more than a few days)
(7) chronic feelings of emptiness
(8) inappropriate, intense anger or difficulty controlling anger (e.g., frequent displays of temper, constant anger, recurrent physical fights)
(9) transient, stress-related paranoid ideation or severe dissociative symptoms

Source: APA, 2000, 1994
© 2013 by Worth Publishers

Diagnostic Criteria for Histrionic Personality Disorder

A pervasive pattern of excessive emotionality and attention seeking, beginning by early adulthood and present in a variety of contexts, as indicated by five (or more) of the following:

(1) is uncomfortable in situations in which he or she is not the center of attention
(2) interaction with others often characterized by inappropriate sexually seductive or provocative behavior
(3) displays rapidly shifting and shallow expression of emotions
(4) consistently uses physical appearance to draw attention to self
(5) has a style of speech that is excessively impressionistic and lacking in detail
(6) shows self-dramatization, theatricality, and exaggerated expression of emotion
(7) is suggestible, i.e., easily influenced by others or circumstances
(8) considers relationships to be more intimate than they actually are

Diagnostic Criteria for Narcissistic Personality Disorder

A pervasive pattern of grandiosity (in fantasy or behavior), need for admiration, and lack of empathy, beginning by early adulthood and present in a variety of contexts, as indicated by five (or more) of the following:

(1) has a grandiose sense of self-importance (e.g., exaggerates achievements and talents, expects to be recognized as superior without commensurate achievements)
(2) is preoccupied with fantasies of unlimited success, power, brilliance, beauty, or ideal love
(3) believes that he or she is "special" and unique and can only be understood by, or should associate with, other special or high-status people (or institutions)
(4) requires excessive admiration
(5) has a sense of entitlement, i.e., unreasonable expectations of especially favorable treatment or automatic compliance with his or her expectations
(6) is interpersonally exploitative, i.e., takes advantage of others to achieve his or her own ends
(7) lacks empathy: is unwilling to recognize or identify with the feelings and needs of others
(8) is often envious of others or believes that others are envious of him or her
(9) shows arrogant, haughty behaviors or attitudes

Source: APA, 2000, 1994
© 2013 by Worth Publishers

Diagnostic Criteria for Avoidant Personality Disorder

A pervasive pattern of social inhibition, feelings of inadequacy, and hypersensitivity to negative evaluation, beginning by early adulthood and present in a variety of contexts, as indicated by four (or more) of the following:

(1) avoids occupational activities that involve significant interpersonal contact, because of fears of criticism, disapproval, or rejection
(2) is unwilling to get involved with people unless certain of being liked
(3) shows restraint within intimate relationships because of the fear of being shamed or ridiculed
(4) is preoccupied with being criticized or rejected in social situations
(5) is inhibited in new interpersonal situations because of feelings of inadequacy
(6) views self as socially inept, personally unappealing, or inferior to others
(7) is unusually reluctant to take personal risks or to engage in any new activities because they may prove embarrassing

Diagnostic Criteria for Dependent Personality Disorder

A pervasive and excessive need to be taken care of that leads to submissive and clinging behavior and fears of separation, beginning by early adulthood and present in a variety of contexts, as indicated by five (or more) of the following:

(1) has difficulty making everyday decisions without an excessive amount of advice and reassurance from others
(2) needs others to assume responsibility for most major areas of his or her life
(3) has difficulty expressing disagreement with others because of fear of loss of support or approval. Note: Do not include realistic fears of retribution.
(4) has difficulty initiating projects or doing things on his or her own (because of lack of self-confidence in judgment or abilities rather than a lack of motivation or energy)
(5) goes to excessive lengths to obtain nurturance and support from others, to the point of volunteering to do things that are unpleasant
(6) feels uncomfortable or helpless when alone because of exaggerated fears of being unable to care for himself or herself
(7) urgently seeks another relationship as a source of care and support when a close relationship ends
(8) is unrealistically preoccupied with fears of being left to take care of himself or herself

Source: APA, 2000, 1994

Diagnostic Criteria for Obsessive-Compulsive Personality Disorder

A pervasive pattern of preoccupation with orderliness, perfectionism, and mental and interpersonal control, at the expense of flexibility, openness, and efficiency, beginning by early adulthood and present in a variety of contexts, as indicated by four (or more) of the following:

(1) is preoccupied with details, rules, lists, order, organization, or schedules to the extent that the major point of the activity is lost

(2) shows perfectionism that interferes with task completion (e.g., is unable to complete a project because his or her own overly strict standards are not met)

(3) is excessively devoted to work and productivity to the exclusion of leisure activities and friendships (not accounted for by obvious economic necessity)

(4) is overly conscientious, scrupulous, and inflexible about matters of morality, ethics, or values (not accounted for by cultural or religious identification)

(5) is unable to discard worn-out or worthless objects even when they have no sentimental value

(6) is reluctant to delegate tasks or to work with others unless they submit to exactly his or her way of doing things

(7) adopts a miserly spending style toward both self and others; money is viewed as something to be hoarded for future catastrophes

(8) shows rigidity and stubbornness

Source: APA, 2000, 1994

Diagnostic Criteria for Separation Anxiety Disorder

A. Developmentally inappropriate and excessive anxiety concerning separation from home or from those to whom the individual is attached, as evidenced by three (or more) of the following:
   (1) recurrent excessive distress when separation from home or major attachment figures occurs or is anticipated
   (2) persistent and excessive worry about losing, or about possible harm befalling, major attachment figures
   (3) persistent and excessive worry that an untoward event will lead to separation from a major attachment figure (e.g., getting lost or being kidnapped)
   (4) persistent reluctance or refusal to go to school or elsewhere because of fear of separation
   (5) persistently and excessively fearful or reluctant to be alone or without major attachment figures at home or without significant adults in other settings
   (6) persistent reluctance or refusal to go to sleep without being near a major attachment figure or to sleep away from home
   (7) repeated nightmares involving the theme of separation
   (8) repeated complaints of physical symptoms (such as headaches, stomachaches, nausea, or vomiting) when separation from major attachment figures occurs or is anticipated

B. The duration of the disturbance is at least 4 weeks.

C. The onset is before age 18 years.

D. The disturbance causes clinically significant distress or impairment in social, academic (occupational), or other important areas of functioning.

E. The disturbance does not occur exclusively during the courses of a Pervasive Developmental Disorder, Schizophrenia, or other Psychotic Disorder and, in adolescents and adults, is not better accounted for by Panic Disorder With Agoraphobia.

Early Onset: if onset occurs before age 6 years

Source: APA, 2000, 1994

Diagnostic Criteria for Oppositional Defiant Disorder

A. A pattern of negativistic, hostile, and defiant behavior lasting at least 6 months, during which four (or more) of the following are present:
(1) often loses temper
(2) often argues with adults
(3) often actively defies or refuses to comply with adults' requests or rules
(4) often deliberately annoys people
(5) often blames others for his or her mistakes or misbehavior
(6) is often touchy or easily annoyed by others
(7) is often angry or resentful
(8) is often spiteful or vindictive

Note: Consider a criterion met only if the behavior occurs more frequently than is typically observed in individuals of comparable age and developmental level.

B. The disturbance in behavior causes clinically significant impairment in social, academic, or occupational functioning.

C. The behaviors do not occur exclusively during the course of a Psychotic or Mood Disorder.

D. Criteria are not met for Conduct Disorder, and, if the individual is age 18 years or older, criteria are not met for Antisocial Personality Disorder.

Diagnostic Criteria for Conduct Disorder

A.   A repetitive and persistent pattern of behavior in which the basic rights of others or major age-appropriate societal norms or rules are violated, as manifested by the presence of three (or more) of the following criteria in the past 12 months, with at least one criterion present in the past 6 months:

Aggression to people and animals
(1)   often bullies, threatens, or intimidates others
(2)   often initiates physical fights
(3)   has used a weapon that can cause serious physical harm to others (e.g., a bat, brick, broken bottle, knife, gun)
(4)   has been physically cruel to people
(5)   has been physically cruel to animals
(6)   has stolen while confronting a victim (e.g., mugging, purse snatching, extortion, armed robbery)
(7)   has forced someone into sexual activity

Destruction of property
(8)   has deliberately engaged in fire setting with the intention of causing serious damage
(9)   has deliberately destroyed others' property (other than by fire setting)

Deceitfulness or theft
(10) has broken into someone else's house, building, or car
(11) often lies to obtain goods or favors or to avoid obligations (i.e., "cons" others)
(12) has stolen items of nontrivial value without confronting a victim (e.g., shoplifting, but without breaking and entering; forgery)

Serious violations of rules
(13) often stays out at night despite parental prohibitions, beginning before age 13 years
(14) has run away from home overnight at least twice while living in parental or parental surrogate home (or once without returning for a lengthy period)
(15) is often truant from school, beginning before age 13 years

B.   The disturbance in behavior causes clinically significant impairment in social, academic, or occupational functioning.

C.   If the individual is age 18 years or older, criteria are not met for Antisocial Personality Disorder.

Source: APA, 2000, 1994

Diagnostic Criteria for Conduct Disorder (Continued)

Specify type based on age at onset:

> Childhood-Onset Type: onset of at least one criterion characteristic of Conduct Disorder prior to age 10 years

> Adolescent-Onset Type: absence of any criteria characteristic of Conduct Disorder prior to age 10 years

Specify severity:

> Mild: few if any conduct problems in excess of those required to make the diagnosis and conduct problems cause only minor harm to others

> Moderate: number of conduct problems and effect on others intermediate between "mild" and "severe"

> Severe: many conduct problems in excess of those required to make the diagnosis or conduct problems cause considerable harm to others

Source: APA, 2000, 1994

Diagnostic Criteria for Attention-Deficit/ Hyperactivity Disorder

A. Either (1) or (2):

  (1) six (or more) of the following symptoms of inattention have persisted for at least 6 months to a degree that is maladaptive and inconsistent with developmental level:

  Inattention

  (a) often fails to give close attention to details or makes careless mistakes in schoolwork, work, or other activities
  (b) often has difficulty sustaining attention in tasks or play
  (c) often does not seem to listen when spoken to directly
  (d) often does not follow through on instructions and fails to finish schoolwork, chores, or duties in the workplace (not due to oppositional behavior or failure to understand instructions)
  (e) often has difficulty organizing tasks and activities
  (f) often avoids, dislikes, or is reluctant to engage in tasks that require sustained mental effort (such as schoolwork or homework)
  (g) often loses things necessary for tasks or activities (e.g., toys, school assignments, pencils, books, or tools)
  (h) is often easily distracted by extraneous stimuli
  (i) is often forgetful in daily activities

  (2) six (or more) of the following symptoms of hyperactivity-impulsivity have persisted for at least 6 months to a degree that is maladaptive and inconsistent with developmental level:

  Hyperactivity
  (a) often fidgets with hands or feet or squirms in seat
  (b) often leaves seat in classroom or in other situations in which remaining seated is expected
  (c) often runs about or climbs excessively in situations in which it is inappropriate (in adolescents or adults, may be limited to subjective feelings of restlessness)
  (d) often has difficulty playing or engaging in leisure activities quietly
  (e) is often "on the go" or often acts as if "driven by a motor"
  (f) often talks excessively

  Impulsivity
  (g) often blurts out answers before questions have been completed
  (h) often has difficulty awaiting turn
  (i) often interrupts or intrudes on others (e.g., butts into conversations or games)

B. Some hyperactive-impulsivity or inattentive symptoms that caused impairment were present before age 7 years.

Source: APA, 2000, 1994
© 2013 by Worth Publishers

Diagnostic Criteria for Attention-Deficit/ Hyperactivity Disorder (Continued)

C. Some impairment from the symptoms is present in two or more settings (e.g., at school [or work] and at home).

D. There must be clear evidence of clinically significant impairment in social, academic, or occupational functioning.

E. The symptoms do not occur exclusively during the course of a Pervasive Developmental Disorder, Schizophrenia, or other Psychotic Disorder and are not better accounted for by another mental disorder (e.g., Mood Disorder, Anxiety Disorder, Dissociative Disorder, or a Personality Disorder).

Attention-Deficit/Hyperactivity Disorder, Combined Type: if both Criteria A1 and A2 are met for the past 6 months

Attention-Deficit/Hyperactivity Disorder, Predominantly Inattentive Type: if Criterion A1 is met but Criterion A2 is not met for the past 6 months

Attention-Deficit/Hyperactivity Disorder, Predominantly Hyperactive-Impulsive Type: if Criterion A2 is met but Criterion A1 is not met for the past 6 months

Source: APA, 2000, 1994

Diagnostic Criteria for Enuresis

A. Repeated voiding of urine into bed or clothes (whether involuntary or intentional).

B. The behavior is clinically significant as manifested by either a frequency of twice a week for at least 3 consecutive months or the presence of clinically significant distress or impairment in social, academic (occupational), or other important areas of functioning.

C. Chronological age is at least 5 years (or equivalent developmental level).

D. The behavior is not due exclusively to the direct physiological effect of a substance (e.g., a diuretic) or a general medical condition (e.g., diabetes, spina bifida, a seizure disorder).

Diagnostic Criteria for Encopresis

A. Repeated passage of feces into inappropriate places (e.g., clothing or floor) whether involuntary or intentional.

B. At least one such event per month for at least 3 months.

C. Chronological age is at least 4 years (or equivalent developmental level).

D. The behavior is not due exclusively to the direct physiological effects of a substance (e.g., laxatives) or a general medical condition except through a mechanism involving constipation.

Source: APA, 2000, 1994

Diagnostic Criteria for Autistic Disorder

A.   A total of six (or more) items from (1), (2), and (3), with at least two from (1), and one each from (2) and (3):

(1)   qualitative impairment in social interaction, as manifested by at least two of the following:

(a)   marked impairment in the use of multiple nonverbal behaviors such as eye-to-eye gaze, facial expression, body postures, and gestures to regulate social interaction

(b)   failure to develop peer relationships appropriate to developmental level

(c)   a lack of spontaneous seeking to share enjoyment, interests, or achievements with other people (e.g., by a lack of showing, bringing, or pointing out objects of interest)

(d)   lack of social or emotional reciprocity

(2)   qualitative impairments in communication, as manifested by at least one of the following:

(a)   delay in, or total lack of, the development of spoken language (not accompanied by an attempt to compensate through alternative modes of communication such as gesture or mime)

(b)   in individuals with adequate speech, marked impairment in the ability to initiate or sustain a conversation with others

(c)   stereotyped or repetitive use of language or idiosyncratic language

(d)   lack of varied, spontaneous make-believe play or social imitative play appropriate to developmental level

(3)   restricted repetitive and stereotyped patterns of behavior, interests, and activities, as manifested by at least one of the following:

(a)   encompassing preoccupation with one or more stereotyped and restricted patterns of interest that is abnormal either in intensity or focus

(b)   apparently inflexible adherence to specific, nonfunctional routines or rituals

(c)   stereotyped and repetitive motor mannerisms (e.g., hand or finger flapping or twisting, or complex whole-body movements)

(d)   persistent preoccupation with parts of objects

B.   Delays or abnormal functioning in at least one of the following areas, with onset prior to age 3 years: (1) social interaction, (2) language as used in social communication, or (3) symbolic or imaginative play.

C.   The disturbance is not better accounted for by Rett's Disorder or Childhood Disintegrative Disorder.

Source: APA, 2000, 1994

Diagnostic Criteria for Asperger's Disorder

A. Qualitative impairment in social interaction, as manifested by at least two of the following:
    (1) marked impairment in the use of multiple nonverbal behaviors such as eye-to-eye gaze, facial expression, body postures, and gestures to regulate social interaction
    (2) failure to develop peer relationships appropriate to developmental level
    (3) a lack of spontaneous seeking to share enjoyment, interests, or achievements with other people (e.g., by a lack of showing, bringing, or pointing out objects of interest to other people)
    (4) lack of social or emotional reciprocity

B. Restricted repetitive and stereotyped patterns of behavior, interests, and activities, as manifested by at least one of the following.
    (1) encompassing preoccupation with one or more stereotyped and restricted patterns of interest that is abnormal either in intensity or focus
    (2) apparently inflexible adherence to specific, nonfunctional routines or rituals
    (3) stereotyped and repetitive motor mannerisms (e.g., hand or finger flapping or twisting, or complex whole-body movements)
    (4) persistent preoccupation with parts of objects

C. The disturbance causes clinically significant impairment in social, occupational, or other important areas of functioning.

D. There is no clinically significant general delay in language (e.g., single words used by age 2 years, communicative phrases used by age 3 years).

Source: APA, 2000, 1994

Diagnostic Criteria for Mental Retardation

A. Significantly subaverage intellectual functioning: an IQ of approximately 70 or below on an individually administered IQ test (for infants, a clinical judgment of significantly subaverage intellectual functioning).

B. Concurrent deficits or impairments in present adaptive functioning (i.e., the person's effectiveness in meeting the standards expected for his or her age by his or her cultural group) in at least two of the following areas: communication, self-care, home living, social/interpersonal skills, use of community resources, self-direction, functional academic skills, work, leisure, health, and safety.

C. The onset is before age 18 years.

Code based on degree of severity reflecting level of intellectual impairment:

Mild Mental Retardation:	IQ level 50–55 to approximately 70
Moderate Mental Retardation:	IQ level 35–40 to 50–55
Severe Mental Retardation:	IQ level 20–25 to 35–40
Profound Mental Retardation:	IQ level below 20 or 25

Source: APA, 2000, 1994

Diagnostic Criteria for Mathematics Disorder

A. Mathematical ability, as measured by individually administered standardized tests, is substantially below that expected given the person's chronological age, measured intelligence, and age-appropriate education.

B. The disturbance in Criterion A significantly interferes with academic achievement or activities of daily living that require mathematical ability.

C. If a sensory deficit is present, the difficulties in mathematical ability are in excess of those usually associated with it.

Diagnostic Criteria for Disorder of Written Expression

A. Writing skills, as measured by individually administered standardized tests (or functional assessments of writing skills), are substantially below those expected given the person's chronological age, measured intelligence, and age-appropriate education.

B. The disturbance in Criterion A significantly interferes with academic achievement or activities of daily living that require the composition of written texts (e.g., writing grammatically correct sentences and organized paragraphs).

C. If a sensory deficit is present, the difficulties with writing skills are in excess of those usually associated with it.

Diagnostic Criteria for Reading Disorder

A. Reading achievement, as measured by individually administered standardized tests of reading accuracy or comprehension, is substantially below that expected given the person's chronological age, measured intelligence, and age-appropriate education.

B. The disturbance in Criterion A significantly interferes with academic achievement or activities of daily living that require reading skills.

C. If a sensory deficit is present, the reading difficulties are in excess of those usually associated with it.

Source: APA, 2000, 1994

Diagnostic Criteria for Phonological Disorder

A.   Failure to use developmentally expected speech sounds that are appropriate for age and dialect (e.g., errors in sound production, use, representation, or organization, such as, but not limited to, substitutions of one sound for another [use of /t/ for target /k/ sound] or omissions of sounds such as final consonants).

B.   The difficulties in speech sound production interfere with academic or occupational achievement or with social communication.

C.   If Mental Retardation, a speech-motor or sensory deficit, or environmental deprivation is present, the speech difficulties are in excess of those usually associated with these problems.

Diagnostic Criteria for Expressive Language Disorder

A.   The scores obtained from standardized individually administered measures of expressive language development are substantially below those obtained from standardized measures of both nonverbal intellectual capacity and receptive language development. The disturbance may be manifest clinically by symptoms that include having a markedly limited vocabulary, making errors in tense, or having difficulty in recalling words or producing sentences with developmentally appropriate length or complexity.

B.   The difficulties with expressive language interfere with academic or occupational achievement or with social communication.

C.   Criteria are not met for Mixed-Receptive-Expressive Language Disorder or a Pervasive Developmental Disorder.

D.   If Mental Retardation, a speech-motor or sensory deficit, or environmental deprivation is present, the language difficulties are in excess of those usually associated with these problems.

Coding note: If a speech-motor or sensory deficit or a neurological condition is present, code the condition on Axis III.

Diagnostic Criteria for Mixed Receptive/Expressive Language Disorder

A. The scores obtained from a battery of standardized individually administered measures of both receptive and expressive language development are substantially below those obtained from standardized measures of nonverbal intellectual capacity. Symptoms include those for Expressive Language Disorder as well as difficulty understanding words, sentences, or specific types of words, such as spatial terms.

B. The difficulties with receptive and expressive language significantly interfere with academic or occupational achievement or with social communication.

C. Criteria are not met for a Pervasive Developmental Disorder.

D. If Mental Retardation, a speech-motor or sensory deficit, or environmental deprivation is present, the language difficulties are in excess of those usually associated with these problems.

Coding note: If a speech-motor or sensory deficit or a neurological condition is present, code the condition on Axis III.

Source: APA, 2000, 1994

Diagnostic Criteria for Stuttering

A. Disturbance in the normal fluency and time patterning of speech (inappropriate for the individual's age), characterized by frequent occurrences of one or more of the following:

   (1) sound and syllable repetitions
   (2) sound prolongations
   (3) interjections
   (4) broken words (e.g., pauses within a word)
   (5) audible or silent blocking (filled or unfilled pauses in speech)
   (6) circumlocutions (word substitutions to avoid problematic words)
   (7) words produced with an excess of physical tension
   (8) monosyllabic whole-word repetitions (e.g., "I-I-I-I see him")

B. The disturbance in fluency interferes with academic or occupational achievement or with social communication.

C. If a speech-motor or sensory deficit is present, the speech difficulties are in excess of those usually associated with these problems.

Coding note: If a speech-motor or sensory deficit or a neurological condition is present, code the condition on Axis III.

Source: APA, 2000, 1994

Diagnostic Criteria for Developmental Coordination Disorder

A. Performance in daily activities that require motor coordination is substantially below that expected given the person's chronological age and measured intelligence. This may be manifested by marked delays in achieving motor milestones (e.g., walking, crawling, sitting), dropping things, "clumsiness," poor performances in sports, or poor handwriting.

B. The disturbance in Criterion A significantly interferes with academic achievement or activities of daily living.

C. The disturbance is not due to a general medical condition (e.g., cerebral palsy, hemiplegia, or muscular dystrophy) and does not meet criteria for a Pervasive Developmental Disorder.

D. If Mental Retardation is present, the motor difficulties are in excess of those usually associated with it.

Coding note: If general medical condition or sensory deficit is present, code the condition on Axis III.

Source: APA, 2000, 1994

Diagnostic Criteria for Dementia of the Alzheimer's Type

A. The development of multiple cognitive deficits manifested by both
   (1) memory impairment (impaired ability to learn new information or to recall previously learned information)
   (2) one (or more) of the following cognitive disturbances:
      (a) aphasia (language disturbance)
      (b) apraxia (impaired ability to carry out motor activities despite intact motor function)
      (c) agnosia (failure to recognize or identify objects despite intact sensory function)
      (d) disturbance in executive functioning (i.e., planning, organizing, sequencing, abstracting)

B. The cognitive deficits in Criteria A1 and A2 each cause significant impairment in social or occupational functioning and represent a significant decline from a previous level of functioning.

C. The course is characterized by gradual onset and continuing cognitive decline.

D. The cognitive deficits in Criteria A1 and A2 are not due to any of the following:
   (1) other central nervous system conditions that cause progressive deficits in memory and cognition (e.g., cerebrovascular disease, Parkinson's disease, Huntington's disease, subdural hematoma, normal-pressure hydrocephalus, brain tumor)
   (2) systemic conditions that are known to cause dementia (e.g., hypothyroidism, vitamin B12 or folic acid deficiency, niacin deficiency, hypercalcemia, neurosyphilis, HIV infection)
   (3) substance-induced conditions

E. The deficits do not occur exclusively during the course of a delirium.

F. The disturbance is not better accounted for by another Axis I disorder (e.g., Major Depressive Disorder, Schizophrenia).

Code based on presence or absence of a clinically significant behavioral disturbance:

   Without Behavioral Disturbance: if the cognitive disturbance is not accompanied by any clinically significant behavioral disturbance.

   With Behavioral Disturbance: if the cognitive disturbance is accompanied by a clinically significant behavioral disturbance (e.g., wandering, agitation).

Specify subtype:

   With Early Onset: if onset is age 65 years or below

   With Late Onset: if onset is after age 65 years

Source: APA, 2000, 1994

Diagnostic Criteria for Dementia Due to Other General Medical Conditions

A. The development of multiple cognitive deficits manifested by both
   (1) memory impairment (impaired ability to learn new information or to recall previously learned information)
   (2) one (or more) of the following cognitive disturbances:
       (a) aphasia (language disturbance)
       (b) apraxia (impaired ability to carry out motor activities despite intact motor function)
       (c) agnosia (failure to recognize or identify objects despite intact sensory function)
       (d) disturbance in executive functioning (i.e., planning, organizing, sequencing, abstracting)

B. The cognitive deficits in Criteria A1 and A2 each cause significant impairment in social or occupational functioning and represent a significant decline from a previous level of functioning.

C. There is evidence from the history, physical examination, or laboratory findings that the disturbance is the direct physiological consequence of one of the general medical conditions listed below.

D. The deficits do not occur exclusively during the course of a delirium.

Code based on presence or absence of a clinically significant behavioral disturbance:

   Without Behavioral Disturbance: if the cognitive disturbance is not accompanied by any clinically significant behavioral disturbance.

   With Behavioral Disturbance: if the cognitive disturbance is accompanied by a clinically significant behavioral disturbance (e.g., wandering, agitation).

Also code the general medical condition on Axis III (e.g., HIV infection, head injury, Parkinson's disease, Huntington's disease, Pick's disease, Creutzfeldt-Jakob disease)

DSM-IV-TR Classification

From the American Psychiatric Association: Diagnostic and Statistical Manual of Mental Disorders, Fourth Edition, Washington, DC, American Psychiatric Association, 1994, Revised, 2000. Reprinted by permission.

(All categories are on Axis I except those indicated otherwise.)

Disorders Usually First Diagnosed in Infancy, Childhood, or Adolescence

Mental Retardation

Note: These are coded on Axis II.
Mild mental retardation
Moderate mental retardation
Severe mental retardation
Profound mental retardation
Mental retardation, severity unspecified

Learning Disorders

Reading disorder
Mathematics disorder
Disorder of written expression
Learning disorder NOS*

Motor Skills Disorder

Developmental coordination disorder

Communication Disorders

Expressive language disorder
Mixed receptive-expressive language
    disorder
Phonological disorder
Stuttering
Communication disorder NOS*

Pervasive Developmental Disorders

Autistic disorder
Rett's disorder
Childhood disintegrative disorder
Asperger's disorder
Pervasive development disorder NOS*

Attention-Deficit and Disruptive Behavior Disorders

Attention-deficit/hyperactivity disorder
    Combined type
    Predominantly inattentive type
    Predominantly hyperactive-impulsive type

Attention-deficit/hyperactivity disorder
    NOS*
Conduct disorder
Oppositional defiant disorder
Disruptive behavior disorder NOS*

Feeding and Eating Disorders of Infancy or Early Childhood

Pica
Rumination disorder
Feeding disorder of infancy or early
    childhood

Tic Disorders

Tourette's disorder
Chronic motor or vocal tic disorder
Transient tic disorder
Tic disorder NOS*

Elimination Disorders

Encopresis
    With constipation and overflow
        incontinence
    Without constipation and overflow
        incontinence
Enuresis (not due to a general medical
    condition)

Other Disorders of Infancy, Childhood, or Adolescence

Separation anxiety disorder
Selective mutism
Reactive attachment disorder of infancy or
    early childhood
Stereotypic movement disorder
Disorder of infancy, childhood, or
    adolescence NOS*

*NOS = Not otherwise specified

DSM-IV-TR Classification (Continued)

From the American Psychiatric Association: Diagnostic and Statistical Manual of Mental Disorders, Fourth Edition, Washington, DC, American Psychiatric Association, 1994, Revised, 2000. Reprinted by permission.

(All categories are on Axis I except those indicated otherwise.)

Delirium, Dementia, and Amnestic and Other Cognitive Disorders

Delirium

Delirium due to . . . *(indicate the general medical condition)*
Substance intoxication delirium
Substance withdrawal delirium
Delirium due to multiple etiologies
Delirium NOS*

Dementia

Dementia of the Alzheimer's type, with early onset
Dementia of the Alzheimer's type, with late onset
Vascular dementia

Dementia Due to Other General Medical Conditions

Dementia due to HIV disease
Dementia due to head trauma

Dementia due to Parkinson's disease
Dementia due to Huntington's disease
Dementia due to Pick's disease
Dementia due to Creutzfeldt-Jakob disease
Dementia due to . . . *(indicate the general medical condition not listed above)*
Substance-induced persisting dementia
Dementia due to multiple etiologies
Dementia NOS*

Amnestic Disorders

Amnestic disorders due to . . . *(indicate the general medical condition)*
Substance-induced persisting amnestic disorder
Amnestic disorder NOS*

Other Cognitive Disorders

Cognitive disorder NOS*

Mental Disorders Due to a General Medical Condition Not Elsewhere Classified

Catatonic disorder due to . . . *(indicate the general medical condition)*
Personality change due to . . . *(indicate the general medical condition)*

Mental disorder NOS* due to . . . *(indicate the general medical condition)*

DSM-IV-TR Classification (Continued)

From the American Psychiatric Association: Diagnostic and Statistical Manual of Mental Disorders, Fourth Edition, Washington, DC, American Psychiatric Association, 1994, Revised, 2000. Reprinted by permission.

(All categories are on Axis I except those indicated otherwise.)

Substance-Related Disorders

[Specific substance categories: Alcohol; Amphetamine; Caffeine; Cannabis; Cocaine; Hallucinogen; Inhalant; Nicotine; Opioid; Phencyclidine; Sedative, Hypnotic, or Anxiolytic; Polysubstance; Other or unknown]

Substance Use Disorders

Substance dependence
Substance abuse

Substance-Induced Disorders

Substance intoxication
Substance withdrawal

Substance intoxication delirium
Substance withdrawal delirium
Substance-induced persisting dementia
Substance-induced persisting amnestic
    disorder
Substance-induced psychotic disorder
Substance-induced mood disorder
Substance-induced anxiety disorder
Substance-induced sexual dysfunction
Substance-induced sleep disorder
Substance-related disorder NOS*

Schizophrenia and Other Psychotic Disorders

Schizophrenia
    Paranoid type
    Disorganized type
    Catatonic type
    Undifferentiated type
    Residual type
Schizophreniform disorder
Schizoaffective disorder

Delusional disorder
Brief psychotic disorder
Shared psychotic disorder
Psychotic disorder due to . . . (indicate the
    general medical condition)
Substance-induced psychotic disorder
Psychotic disorder NOS*

Mood Disorders

Depressive Disorders

Major depressive disorder
Dysthymic disorder
Depressive disorder NOS*

Bipolar Disorders

Bipolar I disorder

Bipolar II disorder
Cyclothymic disorder
Bipolar disorder NOS*
Mood disorder due to . . . (indicate the general
    medical condition)
Substance-induced mood disorder
Mood disorder NOS*

Source: APA, 2000, 1994

DSM-IV-TR Classification (Continued)

From the American Psychiatric Association: Diagnostic and Statistical Manual of Mental Disorders, Fourth Edition, Washington, DC, American Psychiatric Association, 1994, Revised, 2000. Reprinted by permission.

(All categories are on Axis I except those indicated otherwise.)

Anxiety Disorders

Panic disorder without agoraphobia
Panic disorder with agoraphobia
Agoraphobia without history of panic
    disorder
Specific phobia
Social phobia
Obsessive-compulsive disorder

Posttraumatic stress disorder
Acute stress disorder
Generalized anxiety disorder
Anxiety disorder due to . . . (*indicate the*
    general medical condition)
Substance-induced anxiety disorder
Anxiety disorder NOS*

Somatoform Disorders

Somatization disorder
Undifferentiated somatoform disorder
Conversion disorder
Pain disorder
Associated with psychological factors

Associated with both psychological factors
    and a general medical condition
Hypochondriasis
Body dysmorphic disorder
Somatoform disorder NOS*

Factitious Disorders

Factitious disorder
With predominantly psychological signs and
    symptoms
With predominantly physical signs and
    symptoms

With combined psychological and physical
    signs and symptoms
Factitious disorder NOS*

Dissociative Disorders

Dissociative amnesia
Dissociative fugue
Dissociative identity disorder

Depersonalization disorder
Dissociative disorder NOS*

Source: APA, 2000, 1994

DSM-IV-TR Classification (Continued)

From the American Psychiatric Association: Diagnostic and Statistical Manual of Mental Disorders, Fourth Edition, Washington, DC, American Psychiatric Association, 1994, Revised, 2000. Reprinted by permission.

(All categories are on Axis I except those indicated otherwise.)

Sexual and Gender Identity Disorders

Sexual Dysfunctions

Sexual Desire Disorders
Hypoactive sexual desire disorder
Sexual aversion disorder

Sexual Arousal Disorders
Female sexual arousal disorder
Male erectile disorder

Orgasmic Disorders
Female orgasmic disorder
Male orgasmic disorder
Premature ejaculation

Sexual Pain Disorders
Dyspareunia (not due to a general medical condition)
Vaginismus (not due to a general medical condition)

Sexual Dysfunction Due to a General Medical Condition

Substance-induced Sexual Dysfunction
Sexual Dysfunction NOS*

Paraphilias
Exhibitionism
Fetishism
Frotteurism
Pedophilia
Sexual Masochism
Sexual Sadism
Transvestic Fetishism
Voyeurism
Paraphilia NOS*

Gender Identity Disorders
Gender identity disorder
  In children
  In adolescents or adults
Gender identity disorder NOS*
Sexual disorder NOS*

Eating Disorders

Anorexia nervosa
Bulimia nervosa

Eating disorder NOS*

Sleep Disorders

Primary Sleep Disorders

Dyssomnias
Primary insomnia
Primary hypersomnia
Narcolepsy
Breathing-related sleep disorder
Circadian rhythm sleep disorder
Dyssomnia NOS*

Parasomnias
Nightmare disorder

Sleep terror disorder
Sleepwalking disorder
Parasomnia NOS*

Sleep Disorders Related to Another Mental Disorder

Other Sleep Disorders
Sleep disorder due to . . . (indicate the general medical condition)
Substance-induced sleep disorder

Source: APA, 2000, 1994
© 2013 by Worth Publishers

DSM-IV-TR Classification (Continued)

From the American Psychiatric Association: Diagnostic and Statistical Manual of Mental Disorders, Fourth Edition, Washington, DC, American Psychiatric Association, 1994, Revised, 2000. Reprinted by permission.

(All categories are on Axis I except those indicated otherwise.)

Impulse-Control Disorders Not Elsewhere Classified

Intermittent explosive disorder
Kleptomania
Pyromania

Pathological gambling
Trichotillomania
Impulse-control disorder NOS*

Adjustment Disorders

Adjustment disorder
  With depressed mood
  With anxiety
  With mixed anxiety and depressed mood

With disturbance of conduct
With mixed disturbance of emotions and
  conduct
Unspecified

Personality Disorders

Note: These are coded on Axis II.

Paranoid personality disorder
Schizoid personality disorder
Schizotypal personality disorder
Antisocial personality disorder
Borderline personality disorder

Histrionic personality disorder
Narcissistic personality disorder
Avoidant personality disorder
Dependent personality disorder
Obsessive-compulsive personality disorder
Personality disorder NOS*

DSM-IV-TR Classification (Continued)

From the American Psychiatric Association: Diagnostic and Statistical Manual of Mental Disorders, Fourth Edition, Washington, DC, American Psychiatric Association, 1994, Revised, 2000. Reprinted by permission.

(All categories are on Axis I except those indicated otherwise.)

Other Conditions That May Be a Focus of Clinical Attention

Psychological Factors Affecting Medical Condition

Mental disorder affecting medical condition

Psychological symptoms affecting medical condition

Personality traits or coping style affecting medical condition

Maladaptive health behaviors affecting medical condition

Stress-related physiological response affecting medical condition

Other or unspecified psychological factors affecting medical condition

Medication-Induced Movement Disorders

Neuroleptic-induced Parkinsonism

Neuroleptic malignant syndrome

Neuroleptic-induced acute dystonia

Neuroleptic-induced acute akathisia

Neuroleptic-induced tardive dyskinesia

Medication-induced postural tremor

Medication-induced movement disorder NOS*

Other Medication-Induced Disorder

Adverse effects of medication NOS*

Relational Problems

Relational problem related to a mental disorder or general medical condition

Parent-child relational problem

Partner relational problem

Sibling relational problem

Relational problem NOS*

Problems Related to Abuse or Neglect

Physical abuse of child

Sexual abuse of child

Neglect of child

Physical abuse of adult

Sexual abuse of adult

Additional Conditions That May Be a Focus of Clinical Attention

Noncompliance with treatment

Malingering

Adult antisocial behavior

Child or adolescent antisocial behavior

Borderline intellectual functioning

Age-related cognitive decline

Bereavement

Academic problem

Occupational problem

Identity problem

Religious or spiritual problem

Acculturation problem

Phase of life problem

Source: APA, 2000, 1994
© 2013 by Worth Publishers

APPENDIX **C**

Crossword Puzzles

*Answers follow starting on page C-40.

CROSSWORD PUZZLE—CHAPTER I

Across

3. Clinical theorist Thomas _____ has asserted that the entire concept of mental illness is an invalid myth that is forwarded by societies that wish to control the actions of people who behave in unusual ways. (p. 5) (5)

5. A _____ was a specially trained priest whose job was to perform rituals designed to drive evil spirits from the

body of a person suffering from a mental illness. (p. 9) (6)

7. When emotional, cognitive, and behavioral processes become psychologically abnormal, one might be described as suffering from a mental _____, which is sometimes referred to as psychopathology or maladjustment. (p. 1) (7)

8. The methods of Philippe Pinel in France and William Tuke in England led to the beginning of spread of _____ treat-

ment of those with mental illnesses, because they emphasized humane and respectful techniques. (p. 12) (5)

9. The techniques of psychoanalysis, developed by _____, involved getting insight into a client's unconscious processes. (p. 15) (5)

12. _____ is a criterion of abnormality that refers to a subjective state of discomfort. Though often present in those with mental illnesses, it is not always seen, and thus is an important but not failsafe predictor of psychopathology. (p. 4) (8)

14. The dominant form of health coverage is the managed _____ program, in which insurance companies determine key issues about the nature of therapy for those in need of such services. (p. 19) (4)

17. The explicit and implicit rules for proper conduct that are established by a particular culture or society are referred to as _____. (p. 3) (5)

19. During the Renaissance, several hospitals and monasteries were converted into _____, which were places whose primary purpose was to care for people with mental illnesses. (p. 12) (7)

20. Glamorized by a 1973 movie, one early treatment for abnormality was to perform a(n) _____, during which a specially trained priest would recite prayers and incantations to bless the body of one suffering from a mental illness. (p. 9) (8)

22. Thomas is regarded by his neighbors as being very strange and unusual, although he never bothers them or does things to disrupt their lives. Thomas's unique individuality might be best described as an _____ and not an abnormality that requires an intervention (p. 5) (12)

23. Hippocrates, often referred to as the father of modern medicine, believed that mental illnesses were caused by an imbalance of the four _____, or fluids that flowed through the body. They included blood, phlegm, and yellow and black bile. (p. 9) (6)

24. Many of today's community mental health programs focus on _____, which refers to targeting and addressing the various social conditions that underlie psychological problems and helping individuals who are at risk for developing emotional difficulties. (p. 17) (10)

26. Despite popular misconception, most people struggling with anxiety, depression, and even bizarre thinking pose no immediate _____ to themselves or to anyone else, (p. 5) (6)

27. The theory of _____, first posited by Sigmund Freud, held that many forms of abnormal and normal psychological functioning are caused by unconscious processes. (p. 15) (14)

28. All forms of therapy require three essential features, one of which is the presence of a series of _____ between a properly trained expert and an individual who is seeking relief from pathological symptoms (p. 7) (8)

32. All forms of therapy require three essential features, one of which is the presence of a _____, who is a trained expert whose qualifications are accepted by the person who is experiencing the pathological symptoms. (p. 7) (6)

33. The ancient practice of using a sharp stone to cut holes in the skull, thereby creating a path for evil spirits to escape, is called _____. (p. 9) (12)

35. Mysterious bodily ailments that have no apparent physical cause or basis are referred to as _____ disorders. (p. 15) (10)

36. Jamal's job description includes the detection, assessment, and treatment of abnormal patterns of functioning. Such professionals are referred to as clinical _____. (p. 2) (13)

Down

1. In one form of mass madness that has been seen in history, people believed that they were possessed by _____, and imagined that they were growing fur all over their bodies. (p. 10) (6)

2. Katrina is interested in studying _____ psychology, which focuses on the scientific study of unusual or pathological behaviors in order to describe, predict, explain, and change unhealthy or maladaptive ways of functioning. (p. 2) (8)

4. Clinical _____ gather information in a systematic manner so that they can describe, predict, and explain the phenomena that they study. (p. 2) (10)

5. The work of a Boston schoolteacher campaigning for the moral and kind treatment of those with mental illnesses led to the opening of many _____ hospitals in the United States. Eventually, this pattern spread throughout Europe as well. (p. 13) (5)

6. Antidepressant, antipsychotic, and antianxiety drugs are all forms of _____ medications, which are drugs that primarily affect the brain and alleviate many symptoms of mental dysfunctioning. (p. 16) (12)

8. An Austrian physician, Dr. _____. had a practice in Paris where he placed clients in a trancelike state. These techniques were the precursors of the current practice of hypnosis. (p. 15) (6)

10. Dorothea _____, a schoolteacher from Boston, took up the cause of moral treatment of those with mental illnesses, and campaigned for such reform across the United States. (p. 12) (3)

11. The word _____ comes from the chaotic and disorganized conditions that existed at the Bethlehem Hospital which was an asylum that was founded in London in 1547. (p. 12) (6)

12. As a result of medications used to treat psychological illnesses, a policy of _____, or releasing hundreds of thousands of patients from public mental hospitals, has been adopted by many of the developed nations of the world. (p. 16) (22)

13. All forms of therapy require three essential features, one of which is the presence of a _____ who is seeking relief from another, a properly trained expert. (p. 7) (8)

15. The _____ perspective, suggesting that the chief causes of abnormal functioning are psychological, was championed by such theorists as Friedrich Anton Mesmer, Josef Breuer, and Sigmund Freud. (p. 13) (11)

16. Lizette is quite convinced that mental illnesses are caused by disruptions in a person's physical functioning. This approach to pathology is known as the _____ perspective. (p. 13) (11)

18. Juanita really enjoys wearing freshly sliced onions around her neck when she goes into town to do her marketing. Because this is such an unusual behavior, Juanita's behaviors are a prime example of the _____ criterion of abnormality. (p. 3) (8)

21. As societies have become more and more diverse, the area of study called _____ psychology has emerged, with the goal of understanding the psychological differences of individuals from various races, cultures, and genders. (p. 19) (13)

25. _____ psychology is the study and enhancement of feelings such as optimism and happiness and traits such as perseverance and wisdom. By promoting these attributes, it is believed that psychological wellness can be enhanced and sustained. (p. 18) (8)

26. When an individual's abnormal behaviors interfere with their daily responsibilities (e.g., social interactions, work responsibilities, self-care), they are experiencing the _____ criterion of abnormality. (p. 4) (11)

29. _____, often called therapy, is a procedure designed to change abnormal behavior into more normal behavior. (p. 6) (9)

30. A society's norms grow from its particular _____, which refers to its history, values, institutions, habits, skills, technology, and arts. (p. 3) (7)

31. Benjamin _____, a physician from Pennsylvania, was most responsible for the early spread of moral treatment in the United States. One of his suggestions was that physicians should occasionally give small gifts to their patients. (p. 12) (4)

34. An arrangement where an individual pays a therapist directly for their services is called _____ psychotherapy. (p. 17) (7)

CROSSWORD PUZZLE—CHAPTER 2

Across

1. The difference between experiments and _____-experiments is that in the latter, subjects are not randomly assigned to the various participant groups. (p. 39) (5)
3. Marquisha wants to know how many new cases of rubella have occurred during the past six months. Her desire to study the number of cases appearing in a given time period is referred to as the study of _____. (p. 35) (9)
7. Chaim is interested in knowing how many cases of schizophrenia have appeared in the entire country of Israel over the past three decades. Because his research includes both current and past cases appearing in a particular time period, Chaim is studying the _____ of schizophrenia. (p. 35) (10)
9. Because some research participants might expect to have certain effects if they find out that they are in a particular subject group, researchers have to take steps to prevent this sort of bias. One method is to use a(n) _____ design, which prevents participants from knowing which group they have been assigned to. (p. 38) (5)
11. When variables move in opposition to each other—when one variable increases as the other variable decreases—those two conditions are demonstrating a(n) _____ correlation. (p. 32) (8)
14. Clinical practitioners seek to understand the unique and individual situations that their clients face when dealing with psychological difficulties. This type of comprehension is referred to as _____ understanding. (p. 26) (11)
15. Because clinical scientists look for universal or general laws or principles of abnormal psychology rather than studying individual clients, we say that they are searching for _____, or general, understanding of psychopathology. (p. 26) (10)
19. Sigmund Freud's in-depth study of the patient called "Little Hans" is a classic example of a _____ study, which is a detailed description of one person's life and psychological problems. (p. 27) (4)
20. _____ validity refers to the accuracy with which a study can pinpoint one of various possible factors as the cause of a phenomenon. (p. 30) (8)
23. Imitation, or _____, therapy is often used to test the effectiveness of various sorts of therapeutic interventions by giving some research participants something that looks or tastes like real therapy but has none of its key ingredients. (p. 38) (7)
24. When the results of a study can be generalized to cases beyond that single study, the research can be described as having high _____ validity. (p. 30) (8)
25. Liam decides that the best way to conduct his research is to use the _____ method, which determines

the extent to which events or characteristics vary along with each other. (p. 30) (13)

Down

2. When one research participant is studied before and after some sort of experimental manipulation of an independent variable, this is called a(n) _____-subject experimental design. (p. 41) (6)
4. A statistical term called the correlation _____ is a number that describes the relationship between two variables, and it must always fall somewhere between −1.00 and +1.00. (p. 33) (11)
5. Dr. Zarkiah is doing an experiment to determine whether a new headache medication effectively treats migraines. So that he can know for sure if his new medicine is effective, he must try to eliminate all _____ from his study, which are factors other than the independent variable (medicine) that may impact his dependent variable (migraine pain). (p. 36) (9)
6. Jordan is interested in answering questions related to the appearance of symptoms in schizophrenic individuals. She follows a very specific process of posing questions, speculating on the answers, gathering data, and evaluating different conclusions. This formal process is called the _____ method. (p. 26) (10)
7. When there is a _____ correlation between two variables, the variables change in the same direction; that is, when one of the variables increases, the other increases with it. (p. 32) (8)
8. An _____ is a research procedure in which one variable is manipulated to see if it causes a change in another variable. (p. 36) (10)
10. Research that uses animals as substitute participants for human beings is referred to as a(n) _____ experiment. (p. 40) (8)
12. Darnelle is involved in an experiment designed to pinpoint the relationship between acetylcholine levels in the brain and the loss of memory functions in patients with Alzheimer's disease. He speculates that a loss of this neurotransmitter directly causes memory skills to diminish. This educated guess that comes before any data is collected is referred to as a(n) _____. (p. 27) (10)
13. Dr. Wash is studying the relationship between growing up in poverty and developing behavioral disorders in childhood and adolescence. He follows the same 500 children over the course of several years, which is a research approach called a(n) _____ study. It is also referred to as a high-risk or developmental study. (p. 35) (12)
16. In experimental research, the variable that is manipulated by the researcher is referred to as the _____ variable. (p. 36) (11)

17. When participants are studied before an independent variable is given and then after, and then again when it is removed and reintroduced, this is referred to as an ABAB, or _____, design. (p. 41) (8)
18. One limitation of case studies is that that they are reported by _____ observers, which refers to therapists who have a personal stake in seeing their treatments succeed. This calls into question the objectivity of such case reports. (p. 30) (6)
21. _____ experiments, which are actually a type of quasi-experiment, are so named because the independent variables are manipulated by nature, and not by the researcher. (p. 39) (7)
22. In an experiment the _____ group is a group of research participants who are not exposed to the dependent variable under investigation. This group provides an important baseline to which the experimental group can be compared. (p. 37) (7)

CROSSWORD PUZZLE—CHAPTER 3

Across

1. _____ therapy is a type of counseling where several individuals, all of whom are related to each other, meet with a single clinician to work on the problems of both individuals as well as the group. Even if only one member of the group has a specific diagnosis, the entire group is seen as a cohesive unit that needs to address change. (p. 73) (6)

7. The _____ principle, which guides the functions of the ego, is the recognition that while pleasure needs are important, we cannot always gratify our id impulses, especially when those desires conflict with the demands of social rules and mores. (p. 54) (7)

8. According to the psychodynamic perspective, the conflict that is caused by the clashing of our id and superego impulses is kept in our unconscious by ego _____ mechanisms. (p. 54) (7)

11. Each cell in the normal human body contains 23 pairs of chromosomes, each of which is made up of numerous _____. These individual units of heredity determine a person's traits and physical characteristics. (p. 50) (5)

13. Ivan Pavlov first demonstrated the basic principles of _____ conditioning with dogs and meat powder. (p. 60) (9)

14. The basic premises of _____ therapy are that self-recognition and self-acceptance are the goal, but that they can only be accomplished by challenging and even frustrating a client. (p. 67) (7)

16. In _____ conditioning, human beings and animals learn to behave in certain ways as a result of receiving rewards whenever they do so. (p. 59) (7)

20. The _____ model, which is based on the original work of Sigmund Freud, holds that psychological functioning, whether healthy or pathological, is determined by unconscious mechanisms over which we have little control. (p. 53) (13)

21. In the therapy approach of Aaron Beck, called simply _____ therapy, therapists help clients recognize negative thoughts and biased interpretations, and then help them replace maladaptive thoughts with positive, realistic messages. (p. 63) (9)

23. When a gene that ordinarily appears in appropriate form changes shape and emerges by accident, it is known as a genetic _____. (p. 50) (8)

24. Tens of thousands of patients suffering from depression turn to ECT, or electro_____ therapy, when other treatments have failed to provide relief from symptoms. The technique is relatively effective, though some research suggests that some memory impairment might be a side effect. (p. 52) (10)

26. Leslie believes that the root of psychological pathologies is maladaptive learning, and that the best way to treat these problems is to use learning theory to replace inappropriate behaviors with adaptive ones. Leslie is clearly a believer in the _____ model of abnormal psychology. (p. 58) (10)

30. Therapies that are geared toward the unique and specific challenges and struggles that are faced by women are called gender-sensitive, or _____, therapies. (p. 77) (8)

33. A popular format of psychological counseling is _____ therapy, in which several clients who share common concerns or issues meet with a therapist at the same time. While each client may get less individual attention compared to one-on-one therapy, this format is often less expensive and has the advantage of developing social support and skills. (p. 72) (5)

36. When electrical impulses reach the end of a neuron, they cause the release of a chemical, called a _____ , and that chemical is responsible for taking a message to the post-synaptic neuron. (p. 49) (16)

39. Proponents of the _____ model believe that in order to understand a human being's thoughts, emotions, and behaviors, we must understand the various intricacies of their physical make-up, including genetic influences. (p. 49) (10)

40. When a Gestalt therapist refuses to meet the demands of her client, she is practicing a technique called skillful _____. (p. 67) (11)

42. One of the most effective treatments for those suffering from a phobia is _____ desensitization, a form of exposure therapy where the patient learns to replace an anxious response with one of calm and relaxation. (p. 60) (10)

43. _____ mental health treatment programs allow clients, particularly those with severe forms of psychopathology, to receive treatment in familiar social surroundings as opposed to inpatient psychiatric institutions. (p. 75) (9)

45. In _____ therapy, people are encouraged to accept responsibility for their lives and their problems. Addi-

tionally, the counseling focuses on the concept of individual freedom to choose different paths in life. (p. 68) (11)

46. The tiny space that separates one neuron from another is called a _____ and can only be traversed by specific chemical substances. (p. 49) (7)

48. According to Rogers's humanistic therapy, some children require conditions of _____ when their parents or caregivers fail to provide unconditional positive regard during childhood. (p. 65) (5)

49. Possibly the greatest advancement in the treatment of psychological disorders since the 1950s has been the development of _____ medications. (p. 51) (12)

51. Kara suffers from _____ disease, which is a disorder that is marked by emotional outbursts, memory loss, suicidality, involuntary body movements, and absurd beliefs. This illness has been traced to a loss of basal ganglia cells in the brain. (p. 49) (11)

Down

2. _____, or couple, therapy is a form of counseling in which the therapist works with two individuals who are in a long-term relationship. As the clients are often husband and wife (though not necessarily so), the therapy frequently focuses on forms of communication and improving interactions for both members of the relationship. (p. 74) (7)

3. A format of counseling that is similar to group therapy is the self-help group (or _____ help group). People in such groups come together to discuss a specific shared problem, but do not have the benefit of the direct leadership of a trained professional clinician. (p. 73) (6)

4. "I'd like you to lie back on the couch and talk about anything that comes to mind. Don't try to talk about things that you think are necessarily important, but instead just say anything that you think of, even if it doesn't seem to be terribly useful." This is a statement that might come from a psychodynamic therapist who is using the technique of free _____. (p. 55) (11)

5. Babies tend to demonstrate a remarkable lack of concern for the needs, schedules, or desires of anyone but themselves. They are only interested in having their own needs gratified, and thus are a pure demonstration of Freud's concept of the id, which operates on the _____ principle. (p. 54) (8)

6. When patients unconsciously take steps to halt the forward progress of their own counseling, they are showing _____ to the therapy. (p. 56) (10)

9. Antianxiety drugs, which are also called minor tranquilizers or _____, help reduce tension and anxiety (p. 52) (11)

10. To become _____ means to get stuck at one of the early stages of personality development. This psychody-

namic term suggests that failure to resolve the conflicts of each developmental stage can have influences on later life functioning. (p. 55) (7)

12. When an individual is going through systematic desensitization, the second step is to construct a fear _____, which is a list of feared objects or situations starting with those that are less feared and ending with those that are most dreaded. (p. 61) (9)

15. According to family _____ theory, individual members of a family represent a system of interacting parts who interact with one another in consistent ways and follow rules that are unique to that specific family. (p. 72) (7)

17. The multi-_____ perspective seeks to understand how such factors as race, ethnicity, gender, and other demographic factors affect behavior and thought and how people of diverse backgrounds are psychologically different. (p. 76) (8)

18. _____ positive regard, which refers to nonjudgmental love that we receive from others, primarily our parents during childhood, can set up a very positive self-image later in life. This allows a person to see him or herself as being a valuable, good person, even in spite of faults and flaws.(p. 65) (13)

19. In 2000, scientists completed the mapping, or sequencing, of all of the genes in the human body. This enormous undertaking was called the Human _____ Project. (p. 50) (6)

22. Tiny spaces on the surface of a neuron's dendrites that are designed to receive neurotransmitters from presynaptic neurons are called _____. (p. 49) (9)

25. Psychodynamic therapists believe that patients must experience _____, or a reliving of past repressed feelings, if they are to settle unconscious conflicts and overcome their problems. (p. 57) (9)

27. Humanists believe that people are driven to self-_____; that is, they are internally motivated to reach their full potential for goodness and growth. This goal, however, requires a strong sense of honesty and open acceptance of one's weaknesses. (p. 65) (9)

28. According to Freud, _____ are the "royal road to the unconscious." (p. 57) (6)

29. Some biologists have suggested that certain abnormal brain structures or biochemical dysfunctions are actually caused by _____ infections. For example, some research has suggested that schizophrenia may be caused by exposure to these infections before birth. (p. 51) (5)

31. The brain is made up of about 100 billion individual nerve cells, are called _____, which are supported by thousands of billions of glia cells. (p. 49) (7)

32. The belief that all actions happen for a reason—that no behaviors are "acciden-

tal"—is consistent with the _____ assumption of the psychodynamic paradigm. (p. 53) (13)

34. In science the perspectives used to explain events are known as models, or _____. (p. 48) (9)

35. When Tiger Woods steps up to the tee in a championship round of golf, he has a very strong sense of his ability to hit the golf ball exactly where he wants it to go. This positive feeling is called self-_____. (p. 61) (8)

37. According to psychodynamic theorists, some clients might demonstrate _____ during therapy. This occurs when a client acts and/or feels toward the therapist as they did or do toward important persons in their lives, especially their parents, siblings, or spouses. (p. 56) (12)

38. Chemicals that are released into the bloodstream by glands—the endocrine, pituitary, and adrenal glands, for instance—are called _____. (p. 50) (8)

41. Carl Rogers's humanistic therapy is sometimes referred to as _____-centered therapy, as the goal is to create a supportive climate that fosters honesty and acceptance. (p. 65) (6)

44. _____ relations theorists propose that people are motivated by a need to have relationships with others, and that problems in the relationships between children and their parents or caregivers lead to abnormal development of the personality. (p. 55) (6)

47. While many people incorrectly use this term as meaning "pride," the _____ is in fact one of Freud's three components of personality. Its main responsibility is to balance the pleasure needs of the id with the moral needs of the superego. (p. 54) (3)

50. The _____ is the most primitive and instinctual of the three components of the human personality. Constantly seeking gratification, Freud believed that it operates on the pleasure principle. (p. 53) (2)

CROSSWORD PUZZLE—CHAPTER 4

Across

1. The Rorschach test, the thematic apperception test, and the sentence-completion test are all examples of _____ tests. (p. 88) (10)
2. The _____ of an assessment instrument refers to its accuracy; that is, the extent to which the tool measures what it is supposed to measure. (p. 84) (8)
4. Josue goes into a psychologists office to take a test where he looks at cards with inkblots on them, and then talks about what he sees in each picture. This type of projective assessment is called a _____ test. (p. 88) (9)
8. Clinical practitioners seek to understand the unique and individual challenges and facets of each client with whom they work. This _____ understanding allows them to fully empathize with the difficulties of each client. (p. 83) (11)
10. There are three different categories of _____ inventories—affective, social skills, and cognitive inventories. (p. 92) (8)
12. The *Diagnostic and _____ Manual of Mental Disorders (DSM)* is a classification system that was developed by the American Psychiatric Association. It has been revised several times since its first publication. (p. 99) (11)
16. A personality _____ asks respondents a wide range of questions about their behavior, beliefs, and feelings. (p. 90) (9)
17. The most widely used personality assessment tool is called the _____ Multiphasic Personality Inventory, and it consists of over 500 statements that a respondent must describe as "true," "false," or "cannot say." (p. 90) (9)
18. When certain symptoms appear to regularly occur together in a cluster, they are called a _____. (p. 99) (8)
19. Measures that assess physical responses as possible indicators of psychological problems are called psycho_____ tests. (p. 93) (13)
21. To _____ an assessment tool means that a specific set of instructions for how that tool is administered and scored is created. In order for the tool to be valid, these instructions must be followed. (p. 84) (11)
25. The DSM-IV-TR requires a clinician to evaluation a client's condition on five separate _____, or branches of information, when making a diagnosis. Each of these areas provides important data that may help inform the best treatment approach. (p. 100) (4)
26. Dr. Crenshaw is working with an 8-year-old boy named Lewis. To assess the extent to which Lewis has difficulties staying on task and remaining quiet and focused in his school classroom, Dr. Crenshaw goes to Lewis's class, sits quietly in the back for a while, and makes observations about Lewis's actions. This form of assessment is an example of _____ observation. (p. 96) (12)
27. Therapy _____ studies are designed to measure the effects of various types of treatment. (p. 107) (7)
28. Computerized axial tomography (CAT or CT scan), positron emission tomography (PET scan), magnetic resonance imaging (MRI) and functional magnetic resonance imaging (fMRI) are all _____ techniques, designed to take "pictures" of the brain. (p. 94) (12)
29. The fifth Axis of a complete DSM-IV-TR diagnosis requires the clinician to assign a number on a 100-point scale that represents the client's overall level of functioning. This scale is called the _____ assessment of functioning. (p. 100) (6)
30. When an assessment tool appears to be valid just because it makes sense and seems reasonable, this is called _____ validity. Researchers have to be careful, however, because some measures that appear to be valid are, in fact, not! (p. 84) (4)
31. Therese decides to weigh herself on her bathroom scale three times in a row. She gets on the sale, gets off for fifteen seconds, and then gets on again. Each time, the scale tells her that she weighs 138 pounds. Because this assessment instrument is giving Therese consistent results, we can say that it has high _____. (p. 90) (11)

Down

1. _____ validity refers to a tool's ability to anticipate future characteristics or behaviors. (p. 85) (10)
3. The term _____ refers to making a determination that a person's psychological difficulties constitute a particular mental disorder. (p. 99) (9)
5. Recent research has attempted to identify a set of common strategies that may run through the work of all effective therapists, regardless of their clinical or theoretical orientation. This trend is called a _____ movement. (p. 109) (13)
6. _____ tests are designed to directly measure brain structures or activities. (p. 94) (12)
7. Javier is given an intelligence test when he is 21 years old, and again when he is 31 years old. The scores he receives are virtually identical. Because this measure produces the same results each time it is given to the same person, it would be described as having high test-_____ reliability. (p. 84) (6)
9. The ratio of a person's "mental" age to his or her "chronological" age multiplied by 100 is a measure called the intelligence _____. (p. 96) (8)
11. Jenny, Larika, and Ashley are out at a nightclub together. They all see the same man standing at the bar, but they have very different reactions. Jenny thinks that he is "sooooo cute," and Larika says, "he's okay, but he's not really my type." Ashley, on the other hand, says "You guys are crazy. I think he's ugly!" The fact that three different people came up with three very different assessments of the same person suggests that they are low in _____ (or *interjudge*) reliability. (p. 84) (5)
13. A list of disorders, along with descriptions of symptoms and guidelines for making appropriate diagnoses, is called a(n) _____ system. (p. 99) (14)
14. In 1905, French psychologist Alfred Binet and his colleague Theodore Simon produced the first widely used _____ test that assessed verbal and nonverbal skills. (p. 96) (12)
15. The process of collecting and interpreting relevant information about a client or research participant is called _____. It is a crucial step in the process of getting to know the unique challenges faced by clinical patients. (p. 83) (10)
19. A psycho_____ is a psychiatrist whose primary responsibility is to provide prescriptions for psychotropic medication. (p. 109) (14)
20. After he had an accident at work in which he was struck on the head with a large box, Thomas was taken to the hospital where a physician conducted a mental _____ exam by asking a set of questions that evaluated his overall awareness, consciousness, and general orientation. (p. 86) (6)
22. Mitzi has decided to seek out therapy for a particular mental disorder from which she suffers. She wants to make sure she is seeing a therapist who uses techniques that are supported by solid research that has scientific merit. Mitzi is seeking out someone who uses _____ supported, or evidence-based, treatment techniques. (p. 107) (11)
23. If one assessment tool produces results that agree with the results of a second assessment tool, they would be described as being high in _____ validity. (p. 85) (10)
24. _____ assessment is used to determine how and why a person is behaving in an abnormal or pathological manner, as well as what the best method is to help that individual. (p. 83) (8)

CROSSWORD PUZZLE—CHAPTER 5

Across

1. Derived from the Greek word for "fear", a _____ is a persistent and unreasonable fear of a particular object, activity, or situation. (p. 126) (6)

6. The central nervous system's physiological and emotional response to a vague sense of threat or danger is known as _____, and can result in a number of different psychological disorders when it interferes with one's well-being and daily functioning. (p. 114) (7)

10. Systematic desensitization, flooding, and modeling are all approaches that are forms of _____ treatments, because in all of them individuals are encouraged to face the objects or situations that cause them anxiety. (p. 130) (8)

11. A practitioner of Albert Ellis's technique of _____-emotive therapy points out the irrational assumptions held by clients, suggests more appropriate assumptions, and assigns homework that helps the client practice this "assumption substitution" on his or her own. (p. 121) (8)

12. Little Eli is only two years old, but already his father has started giving him light spankings whenever he raises his voice or does not obey when he is told to do something. The fear and worry that Eli develops would be categorized as _____ anxiety according to the psychodynamic perspective. (p. 116) (5)

14. One of the earliest discovered classes of antianxiety medications was the group called _____, chemicals that worked on the receptors of certain neurotransmitters. Commonly prescribed medications that belong to this group include Xanax, Ativan, and Valium. (p. 123) (15)

15. Giselle often experiences periodic, short bursts of anxiety that occur suddenly, peak within ten minutes, and then gradually pass. Her attacks are often accompanied by physical symptoms that are similar to a heart attack, and she sometimes thinks she is about to die during these attacks. Giselle would best be diagnosed with _____ disorder. (p. 135) (5)

16. The fear of snakes, heights, water, blood, spiders, thunderstorms, or enclosed spaces are all examples of a(n) _____ phobia. (p. 126) (8)

17. Binal is seeing a behavioral therapist to overcome her fear of dogs. The therapist engages a method called _____ in which Binal observes him with dogs. As she sees the dog act in friendly and nonthreatening ways, and also observes the therapist responding to the dogs in a calm and relaxed manner, she feels her own fear slowly diminishing. (p. 128) (8)

19. Dr. Werthol observes that in many of his clients with anxiety problems, there seems to be a very serious intolerance of _____, which means that the clients believe that any possibility of a negative event occurring, no matter how slim, means that the event is likely to occur. (p. 120) (11)

21. Client-centered therapy is an approach that was developed by Carl _____, and it focuses on showing unconditional positive regard for a client and empathizing with their unique challenges. (p. 118) (6)

23. The neurotransmitter GABA, or *gamma-_____ acid*, has been found to be very important in the development of anxiety disorders. This neurotransmitter serves as a neural inhibitor; that is, when GABA is received by a neuron it causes that neuron to stop firing. (p. 123) (12)

24. The constant and nonspecific worry that people with generalized anxiety disorder experience is something described as free-_____ anxiety because it seems like a cloud of worry is always hovering over the sufferer. (p. 114) (8)

26. Though the exact cause of panic disorder is not fully understood, many researchers believe that panic-prone individuals have a high degree of anxiety _____; that is they focus on their bodily sensations much of the time and are unable to process them logically. (p. 139) (11)

27. In biological _____ tests, researchers intentionally produce hyperventilation or other biological sensations by administering drugs or by instructing participants to breathe, exercise, or simply think in certain ways. (p. 139) (9)

30. The small, almond-shaped part of the brain that interprets emotional information and stimulates other brain areas to activate an "alarm-and-escape" response is called the _____. (pp. 124, 138) (8)

31. The most widely applied method of biofeedback for the treatment of anxiety uses a device called a(n) _____ (EMG), which provides information about the level of muscular tension in the body. (p. 125) (15)

32. According to Freud, children who face actual danger experience _____ anxiety. (p. 116) (9)

34. The locus _____ is an area in the midbrain that is rich with neurons that use norepinephrine, and overstimulation of this area is directly related to anxiety symptoms and panic-like reactions. (p. 136) (8)

35. Some evidence of the involvement of the neurotransmitter norepinephrine in panic disorder comes from the fact that certain _____ drugs were effective at preventing or at least reducing the frequency of panic attacks. (p. 136) (14)

36. Some behaviorists suggest that specific phobias can lead to more widespread anxiety through a process called stimulus _____, where responses to one stimulus are also elicited by similar stimuli. (p. 128) (14)

Down

1. One behavioral-evolutionary explanation of phobias suggests that human beings are biologically wired to be afraid of certain things, particularly stimuli that can be hazardous or even life-threatening. This concept is known as _____. (p. 130) (12)

2. In _____ a client is given information about electrical signals in the body so (s)he can learn to control these physiological responses voluntarily. (p. 125) (11)

3. _____ are persistent thoughts, ideas, impulses, or images that seem to invade a person's consciousness. (p. 140) (10)

4. When a person engages in repetitive and rigid behaviors or mental acts because they feel they must perform them in order to prevent or reduce anxiety, they are engaging in _____. (p. 140) (11)

5. In a family _____ study, researchers determine how many and which relatives of a person with a mental disorder have that same illness. (p. 122) (8)

7. The basic premise behind _____ training, a nonchemical biological technique used to treat generalized anxiety disorder is that physical tranquility and calmness can induce a state of psychological calmness. (p. 125) (10)

8. People who engage in _____ perform acts that are meant to erase or "cancel out" their unacceptable or undesirable wishes or impulses. (p. 143) (7)

9. _____ is a Freudian ego defense mechanism in which a person suppresses an unacceptable desire or impulse by taking on a lifestyle that expresses the opposite desire. (p. 152) (17)

13. One of the new wave cognitive explanations of generalized anxiety disorder, the _____ theory, holds that people with this problem implicitly hold both positive *and* negative beliefs about worrying. (p. 120) (13)

15. In a behavioral treatment called exposure and response (or ritual) _____, clients are exposed to objects or situations that would ordinarily produce anxiety, fear or compulsive behaviors. They are then instructed to resist performing any behaviors that they feel bound to perform. (p. 144) (10)

18. Norma's mother and father constantly forbid her from doing things that give her pleasure. She is not allowed to run around, make noise, play with toys the way she wants to, and generally indulge her id impulses. According to the psychodynamic perspective, Norma is likely to develop _____ anxiety. (p. 116) (8)

20. _____ kyofusho is a culture-bound disorder that is particularly common in Asian countries such as Japan and Korea. It bears strong similarity to a social phobia, as many experts suspect that its central feature is the fear of negative evaluation by others. (p. 132) (5)

22. Vanna has difficulty leaving her house, because she has a terrible fear that she may do something stupid in public that will cause her intense embarrassment. Because these symptoms interfere significantly with Vanna's life, she might be diagnosed as suffering from a(n) _____ phobia. (p. 132) (24)

24. Alex's father, Mauricio, is tired of the fact that his son is afraid of water. Every time they go to the beach either he or his wife has to sit with Alex on the sand while the rest of the family enjoys the water. On their latest trip to the beach, Mauricio picked up Alex, carried him into the water, and put him down where he could stand with the water up to his waist. This variation of exposure therapy is known as _____. (p. 131) (8)

25. In cognitive therapy for obsessive-compulsive disorder, clients are instructed to try to _____ unwanted thoughts by thinking or behaving in ways that create an internal sense that things are okay, or right. This is a method of offsetting unacceptable thoughts. (p. 145) (10)

26. According to _____ theorists, generalized anxiety disorder is more likely to develop in people who are faced with conditions that are truly dangerous. In fact, research has found that those who live in highly threatening environments are more likely to develop feelings of tension, anxiety, fatigue, and increased startle response. (p. 115) (13)

28. Katarina has noticed lately that she seems to be anxious and uptight no matter where she is. When she is at home, she worries about things at work. When she is at work, she worries about things at school. When she is in class, she worries about things at home. If she visits a therapist, she might be diagnosed with _____ anxiety disorder. (p. 114) (11)

29. In the 1950s, a new group of benzodiazepines was marketed as sedative-_____ drugs because they induced relaxation at lower doses and caused people to fall asleep in higher doses. (p. 124) (8)

33. A state of immediate alarm that is experienced when a person is faced with a serious threat to their well-being is called _____. (p. 114) (4)

CROSSWORD PUZZLE—CHAPTER 6

(crossword grid)

Across

1. Cortisol is one of many hormones, called cortico_____, which are released by the body in response to stress. (p. 156) (8)

4. The body's immune system is a network of activities and cells that identify and destroy _____, including foreign invaders (bacteria, viruses, fungi, and parasites) and cancer cells. (p. 179) (8)

7. Julia is going to a stress clinic, where she will be hooked up to different machines and instruments to get information about how her body's involuntary functions are working. Her hope is that this form of therapy, called _____ training, will help her reduce her stress-related symptoms. (p. 182) (11)

11. _____ is a condition where one has difficulty falling or staying asleep, and it affects approximately 25 percent of the population each year. (p. 171) (8)

13. According to the Social Adjustment Rating Scale, the most stressful life event for an adult is the death of a _____. (pp. 178–179) (6)

14. Many veterans of combat experience flashbacks of their time in battle, avoid thoughts or conversations that remind them of those events, have problems sleeping, are irritable, and have difficulty concentrating years after returning from war. Taken together, these symptoms might indicate post_____ stress disorder. (p. 157) (9)

17. Muscle _____ headaches are typically marked by pain at the back or front of the head, or the back of the neck. Sometimes called tension

headaches, they affect around 40 million Americans each year. (p. 171) (11)

18. _____ anxiety is the general level of arousal and anxiety that each person brings to different events in their lives. (p. 156) (5)

19. A very severe type of headache that is marked by extreme and often near-paralyzing pain on one side of the head is called a(n) _____. (p. 171) (8)

22. The interaction of biological, psychological, and sociocultural factors can lead to a group of physical illnesses. Formerly referred to as psychophysiological or psychosomatic disorders, the DSM-IV-TR now refers to these illnesses as "psychological factors affecting _____ condition." (p. 169) (7)

23. Jamilla was driving down the street when a small dog suddenly ran out in front of her. Her body immediately responded by releasing adrenaline, increasing her pulse and respiratory rates, and causing the pupils of her eyes to dilate. These involuntary processes are controlled by the _____ nervous system. (p. 155) (11)

24. When you encounter a stressful situation, your hypothalamus sends messages to the pituitary gland, which in turn stimulates the _____ gland, which is located just above your kidneys. This process is called the "HPA pathway." (p. 156) (7)

26. The individual reactions a person has to demands or opportunities that require the person to change are referred to as his/her stress _____. (p. 153) (8)

28. The _____ is the part of the brain that deals with arousal and fear, releasing neurotransmitters, triggering the firing of neurons throughout the brain, and stimulating the release of chemicals throughout the body. (p. 154) (12)

30. Debra was in a very serious car accident last week, and is now suffering from nightmares, flashbacks, and other stress-related symptoms. Because her condition has lasted less than one month, the best diagnosis for her problem would be _____ stress disorder (p. 157) (5)

31. White blood cells that are triggered into action by the presence of a foreign invader are called _____. (p. 179) (11)

32. The _____ personality style is characterized by hostility, cynicism, drivenness, impatience, competitiveness, and ambition. (p. 174) (5)

33. _____ is the use of brutal, degrading, and disorienting strategies in order to reduce victims to a state of utter helplessness, and is often done to force an individual to reveal information or make a confession. (p. 162) (7)

34. PTSD, a serious stress-related disorder often experienced by combat veterans, has been referred to by many names in the past. It was called "_____" during World War I, and "combat fatigue" during World War II and the Korean War. (p. 158) (10)

35. _____ heart disease is a very serious predictor of a blockage of blood vessels that supply blood to the heart and myocardial infarction (a heart attack). (p. 172) (10)

36. Psychoneuro_____ is the scientific study of the relationship between stress, the body's immune system, and health. (p. 179) (10)

37. A technique where a person turns their concentration inward to attain a slightly changed state of consciousness is called _____. By helping an individual to temporarily ignore all external stressors, this technique has been shown to be effective in reducing physical distress. (p. 183) (10)

Down

2. Immediately after the attacks in New York on September 11, 2001, teams of clinicians and counselors were on hand to conduct critical incident stress _____, which is a form of crisis intervention that has victims talk extensively about their feelings and reactions to highly traumatic and stressful events. (p. 168) (10)

3. The field of treatment that combines psychological and physical approaches to treat or prevent medical problems is known as _____ medicine. (p. 182) (10)

5. Marquisha goes to an expert to be guided into a sleeplike, suggestible state. This form of therapy is called _____, and is often used to aid psychotherapy and help treat certain physical conditions. (p. 183) (8)

6. State, or _____, anxiety is the experience of getting tense or uptight in very specific circumstances, and each person differs in their individual perceptions of how stressful various events are. (p. 156) (9)

8. The _____ system is a group of many glands, all of which are responsible for the release of hormones throughout the body. (p. 155) (9)

9. Rahab has been experiencing severe PTSD for over a year, and has decided to try a form of exposure therapy called eye movement _____ and reprocessing (EMDR). (p. 166) (15)

10. Approximately 90 percent of all cases of high blood pressure are called _____ hypertension, and are the result of a combination of psychosocial and physiological factors. These can include constant stress, environmental danger, and feelings of anger or depression, as well as obesity, smoking, poor kidney functioning, and excess collagen in the blood vessels. (p. 171). (9)

12. The neurotransmitter/hormone _____ has been found in higher levels in the urine, blood, and saliva of people who have encountered severe stressors such as combat, rape, or living in a concentration camp. This finding suggests that these chemicals are partially responsible for psychological stress disorders. (p. 162) (14)

15. Lewis works in a very high-stress occupation, and has regular problems with _____, which are lesions or holes in the stomach that can lead to gastrointestinal symptoms, such as vomiting, stomach pain, or stomach bleeding. (p. 170) (6)

16. The complimentary workings of the sympathetic and parasympathetic divisions of the autonomic nervous system are collectively called the "fight-or-_____" response. (p. 156) (6)

20. _____ is one form of victimization that can lead to stress disorders. It involves forced sexual intercourse or another sexual act committed against a nonconsenting person. It also refers to having sexual intercourse with an underage person. (p. 160) (4)

21. Eric suffers from _____, which causes his airway to occasionally narrow and interfere with breathing. His doctor has advised him to reduce stress in his life, so that his attacks will be less severe and less frequent. (p. 170) (6)

25. Due to its success in the treatment of anxiety, _____ training is believed to help prevent or treat medical illnesses that are related to stress. (p. 182) (10)

26. The behavioral exposure technique of EMDR involves moving the eyes in a _____, or rhythmic, pattern from side to side while flooding their minds with images of objects and situations they would ordinarily avoid. (p. 166) (8)

27. Any event that creates demands or opportunities that require us to change in some manner is referred to as a _____. (p. 153) (8)

28. _____ is a general term that refers to a chronic state of high blood pressure, and can be extremely serious, leading to other conditions such as stroke, kidney problems, and coronary heart disease. (p. 171) (12)

29. Two parts of the brain—the amygdala and the _____—appear to be affected by the ongoing anxiety and tension of a psychological stress disorder. (pp. 162–163) (11)

30. The _____ nervous system is an extensive network of nerves and fibers that connect the brain and spinal cord to all other organs in the body. (p. 155) (9)

CROSSWORD PUZZLE—CHAPTER 7

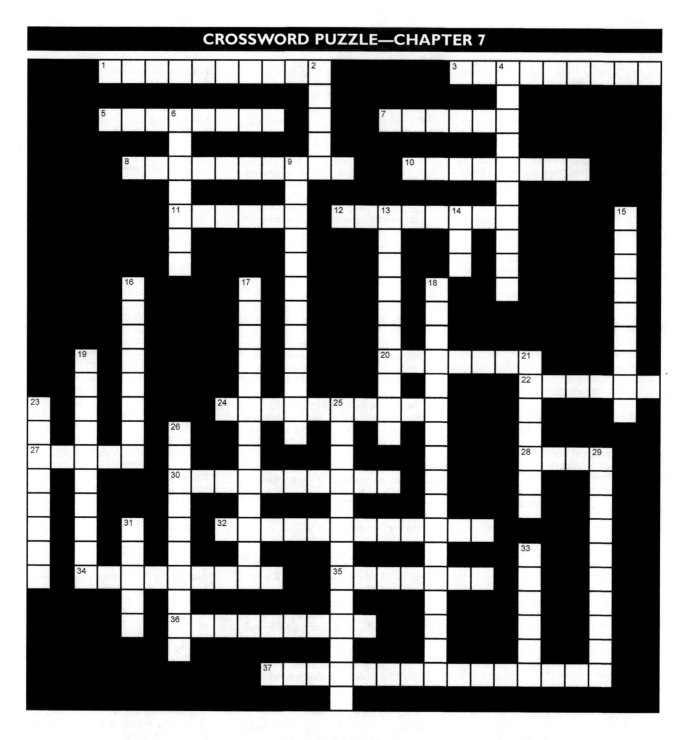

Across

1. The one form of amnesia that involves an inability to accurately encode new memories is called _____ amnesia. (p. 204) (10)

3. Also called circumscribed amnesia, _____ amnesia occurs when a person loses all memory of events that took place within a specific time period. (p. 204) (9)

5. When you get the sensation that you are experiencing for the first time something that should be familiar to you, you are experiencing the memory error called _____. (p. 213) (8)

7. The ultimate goal of hypnotherapy with people suffering from dissociative identity disorder is a state of _____, in which there is a final merging of two or more subpersonalities. (p. 215) (6)

8. A severe and chronic form of factitious disorder is called _____ syndrome after an 18th century Baron who went from town to town in Europe making up fantastic tales about his various adventures. (p. 194) (10)

10. Sometimes the belief that one is receiving treatment is enough to bring about a reduction in symptoms. This finding is the basis for the use of _____, which are basically pretend, or sham, treatments. (p. 200) (8)

11. _____ amobarbital and _____ pentobarbital are two barbiturates, commonly referred to as truth serums, that help people with dissociative amnesia and fugue to recover lost memories. (p. 214) (Hint: The answer to both blanks is the same word.) (6)

12. Somatization disorder is also known as _____ syndrome, after the French physician who first described the symptom pattern in 1859. (p. 192) (8)

20. According to Freud, young girls (between the ages of 3 and 5 years) experience the _____ complex, during which they develop sexual feelings for their fathers and resentment toward their mothers. (p. 197) (7)

22. They key to our sense of identity—our very basic knowledge of who we are, where we've been, and where we come from—is _____. This link to our past, present, and future is often compromised in dissociative disorders. (p. 202) (6)

24. _____ are naturally produced opioid substances in the human body and help to reduce pain sensations. (p. 200) (10)

27. Louisa went to great lengths to hide the fact that she was intentionally making her son, Jordan, ill. She would put tasteless chemicals into his food so that he would have severe gastrointestinal symptoms, and then went to different hospitals and doctors to get Jordan treated. Her actions, which some consider a form of child abuse rather than an illness, describe the diagnosis of factitious disorder by _____. (p. 194) (5)

28. Some theorists believe that dissociative disorders are the result of a process called _____-hypnosis, in which one alters their consciousness in order to block the memory of unpleasant events. (p. 212) (4)

30. When a physical ailment has no apparent medical cause, doctors may suspect a _____ disorder, which is a pattern of physical complaints with largely psychosocial causes. (p. 190) (10)

32. When an individual experiences a major disruption of memory, identity, or consciousness that has no identifiable physical explanation, they are suffering from a(n) _____ disorder. (p. 202) (12)

34. When the various identities that exist in a person with dissociative identity disorder are well aware of each other, this is called a mutually _____ pattern. (p. 208) (9)

35. Psychodynamic theorists suggest that people achieve _____ gain when their hysterical symptoms keep their internal conflicts out of awareness. (p. 198) (7)

36. Sufferers of dissociative identity disorder experience the emergence of one or more _____ personalities, or subpersonalities, that coexist with the primary, or host, personality. (p. 208) (9)

37. LaJuan has exhausted his physician's patience! He goes to his doctor for emergency appointments whenever he experiences the slightest physical complaint. His latest visit was for "terrible sinus congestion" which his doctor diagnosed as a "slight" case of the common cold. LaJuan's exaggerated interpretation of minor physical symptoms indicates that he may suffer from _____. (p. 194) (15)

Down

2. _____-dependent learning suggests that if a person learns something when they are in a particular situation or frame of mind that they will be more likely to remember it accurately when they are in the same situation or frame of mind. (p. 211) (5)

4. Paralysis, blindness, or anesthesia (loss of feeling) are three commonly experienced symptoms of _____ disorder, which is so named because the sufferer's mind transforms psychosocial conflicts into dramatic physical symptoms. (p. 190) (10)

6. People who suffer from dissociative _____ are unable to recall important information, usually of an upsetting nature, about their lives. The memory loss is much more extensive than normal forgetting, and has no physical or organic cause. (p. 204) (7)

9. Sheila has been complaining for months about a wide variety of physical ailments. Some of her many symptoms include migraines, irregular menstrual periods, constipation, dizziness, and double vision. Because physical examination reveals no organic cause for these symptoms, the most appropriate psychiatric diagnosis would be _____ disorder. (p. 192) (12)

13. Many people believe that dissociative identity disorder does not truly exist, and argue that these cases are _____; that is, unintentionally produced by practitioners. (p. 209) (10)

14. *Sybil* and *The Three Faces of* _____ are two of the best known accounts of individuals who have suffered from multiple personality disorder. (p. 202) (3)

15. Joella is set to give a presentation in front of 450 people at work this afternoon, but when she wakes up her voice has mysteriously disappeared. Her symptom of laryngitis has no physical cause, but because it allows her to avoid an unpleasant activity, psychodynamic theorists would suggest that she is achieving a(n) _____ gain from her lost voice. (p. 198) (9)

16. In the movie *Me, Myself, and Irene*, Jim Carrey portrayed an individual who had several personalities in him at the same time. Though many incorrectly believe that his character suffered from schizophrenia, in fact he would be correctly diagnosed with dissociative _____ disorder. (p. 208) (8)

17. Some cognitive theorists suggest that hysterical disorders are forms of _____, providing a means to express emotions that might otherwise be difficult to convey. (p. 199) (13)

18. People who suffer from _____ often feel as though they have become separated from their body and are observing themselves from outside. (p. 215) (17)

19. Owen spends hours each day staring in the mirror at the tiny freckle on his left cheek. Although his friends have assured him that the freckle is barely visible, Owen convinces himself that it is all people look at when they see him. Owen's misinterpretation of this minor skin feature suggests that he suffers from body _____ disorder. (p. 195) (10)

21. One pattern of multiple personalities disorder is called a mutually _____ relationship, in which different personalities have no awareness of each other. (p. 208) (7)

23. Research in the late nineteenth century at the Nancy School in Paris, France, suggested that the symptoms of hysterical somatoform disorders could be both produced *and* eliminated by _____ suggestion. (p. 196) (8)

25. People who suffer from _____ somatoform disorders misinterpret and overreact to bodily symptoms and sensations, no matter what friends, relatives, and physicians may say. (p. 194) (13)

26. The DSM-IV-TR lists three _____ somatoform diagnoses: conversion disorder, somatization disorder, and pain disorder associated with psychological factors. The shared feature of these three illnesses is that the sufferer experiences actual changes in their physical functioning. (p. 190) (10)

29. Marita is a 32-year-old single woman who often pretends to be sick so that others will pay attention to her. She enjoys the fact that playing the "patient role" gets people to visit her, shower her with kindness, and be more sociable. Because she has no real physical symptoms, Marita might be diagnosed with _____ disorder. (p. 194) (10)

31. Anwar recently left his home town and traveled across the country. Once he got to a place that felt comfortable, he began calling himself Edward, got a new job and a new home, and started a new life for himself. Anwar/Edward's memory loss was not caused by any physical event, so he might be diagnosed as suffering from a dissociative _____. (p. 205) (5)

33. Body dysmorphic disorder is sometimes referred to as dysmorpho_____. (p. 195) (6)

CROSSWORD PUZZLE—CHAPTER 8

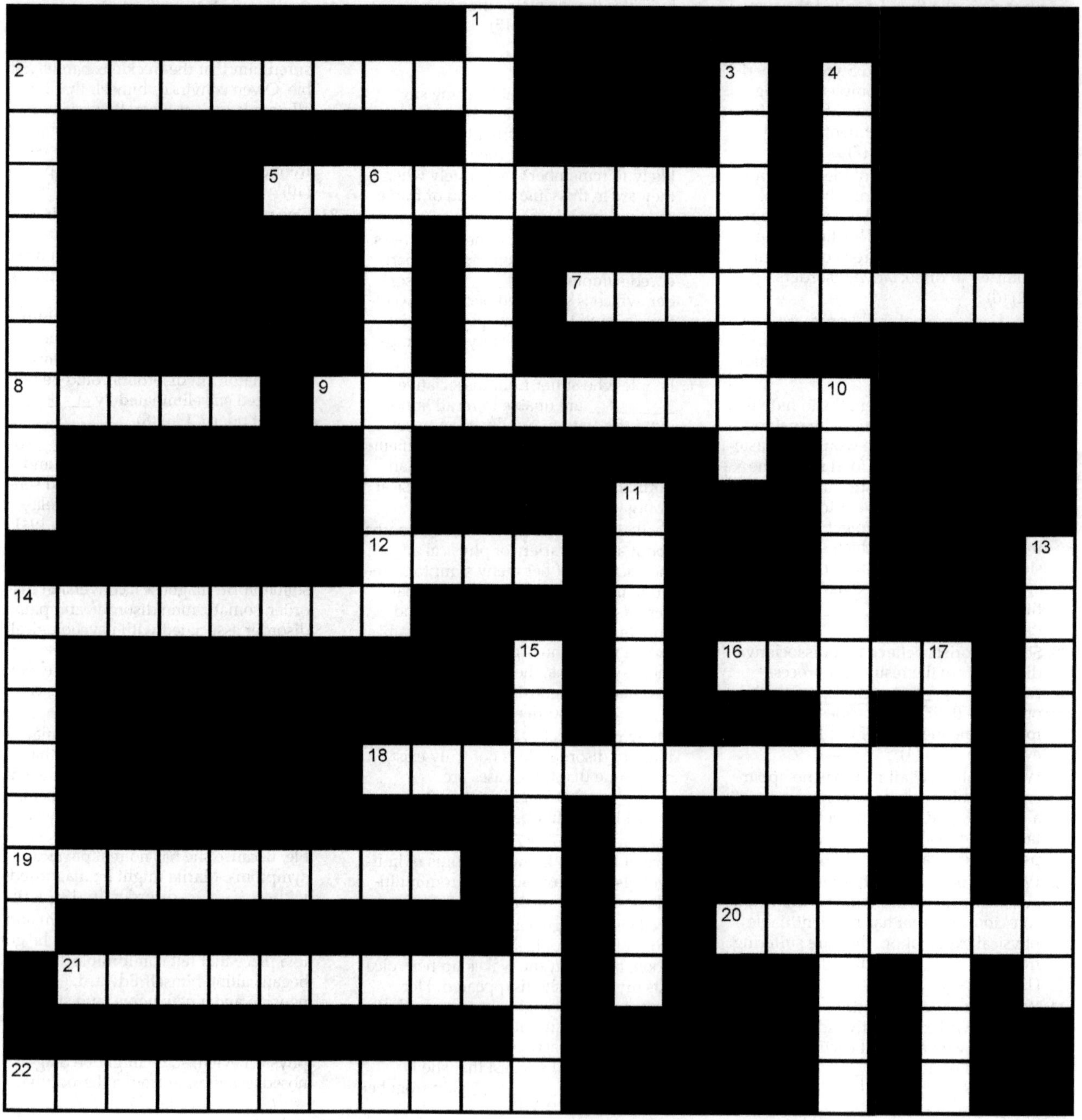

Across

2. _____ is a low, sad state in which life seems dark and its challenges overwhelming. (p. 223) (10)

5. Larika and her husband Spence welcomed a new son into their family just two weeks ago, but rather than enjoy and celebrate this happy event, Larika has been sad, exhausted, and has not been able to get out of bed for more than an hour a day. The best diagnosis for Larika would be _____ depression. (pp. 228–229) (10)

7. One of the primary components of the cognitive theory of depression is that individuals suffering from depressive symptoms experience _____ thoughts, a steady train of unpleasant thoughts that cause them to feel ineffective and worthless. (p. 237) (9)

8. _____ depressive disorder refers to a severe pattern of depression that is disabling and is not caused by such factors as drugs or a general medical condition. (p. 228) (5)

9. In an updated version of Seligman's theory on what causes depression symptoms, the _____-helplessness theory suggests that people experience such symptoms when they make attributions to events that are internal, global, and stable. (p. 240) (11)

12. Investigators have found neuronal deficits in people who suffer from bipolar disorder, wherein there is abnormal functioning in the proteins that help transport _____ across a neuron's cellular membrane. (p. 251) (4)

14. The fourth part of the "depression brain circuit," known as _____ Area 25, tends to be smaller in depressed people than in nondepressed people. (p. 233) (8)

16. Aaron Beck, a noted theorist in the area of depression, suggested that people suffering from depressive symptoms often think negatively in three specific areas, what he called the cognitive _____. (p. 237) (5)

18. Martin Seligman performed experiments using laboratory dogs to demonstrate that the concept of learned _____ is very salient in cases of depression. He suggested that depression often occurs when people believe that they are incapable of changing or controlling their surroundings. (p. 239) (12)

19. _____ depression is a pattern of depressed behavior found among very young children that is caused by separation from one's mother. (p. 235) (9)

20. The _____ explanation of depression holds that specific chemical changes in women make them more susceptible to depression when compared to men. (p. 242) (7)

21. _____ is the tendency to keep focusing on one's feelings when depressed and to repeatedly consider the causes and consequences of that depression. (p. 243) (10)

22. When a person experiences numerous periods of hypomanic symptoms and mild depressive symptoms, the DSM-IV-TR assigns a diagnosis of _____ disorder. (p. 249) (11)

Down

1. Of the two major categories of mood disorders, _____ is the more common, and includes only low, sad states without vacillating moods. (p. 223) (8)

2. Vo has been mildly depressed for the past two years, but has still been able to take care of his daily responsibilities, including going to school, showing up for his part-time job, and spending time with friends. This chronic but less disabling set of depressive symptoms is called _____ disorder. (p. 228) (9)

3. As an explanation for depressive symptoms, Freud proposed the concept of _____, or imagined, loss, in which people equate other kinds of events with the loss of a loved one. (p. 235) (8)

4. Barbara has been experiencing a state of breathless euphoria and frenzied energy, and has had thoughts that she is much more skilled, talented, and capable than she actually is. This state, called _____, is the opposite of a depressive episode. (p. 223) (5)

6. While several different neurotransmitters may be responsible for the symptoms of depression, some research suggests that one, _____, acts as a neuromodulator. This means that this single neurotransmitter affects the activities of others. (p. 232) (9)

10. For years it was thought that one of two neurotransmitters, serotonin or _____, was responsible for producing depression, but more recent studies suggest that it may be a combined rather than individual effect. (p. 232) (14)

11. Translated as "internally generated," the type of depression whose symptoms seem to be a response to internal factors rather than external stressors is called a(n) _____ depression. (p. 228) (10)

13. The "_____" are so common in new mothers that approximately 80% of women experience them after giving birth. Most researchers, in fact, consider them to be normal. (p. 229) (Hint: The answer includes two words.) (9)

14. The mood disorder that is marked by alternating periods of mania and depression is called _____ disorder. (pp. 223–224, 244) (7)

15. While sufferers of bipolar I disorder experience moods swings that range from full depression to full mania, bipolar II disorder is marked by shifts from full depression to _____ episodes. (p. 246) (9)

17. Proposed for inclusion in the upcoming DSM-5, premenstrual _____ disorder is marked by the repeated onset of depression and related symptoms during the week prior to menses. (p. 252) (9)

CROSSWORD PUZZLE—CHAPTER 9

Across

1. In _____ ECT, one electrode is applied to each side of the forehead and a current passes through both sides of the brain. (pp. 267–268) (9)

4. Wilhelm has suffered from extreme shyness and social awkwardness for as long as he can remember. Though he likes other people and wants to be friends with several of his classmates, his interpersonal _____ lead to depression symptoms. IPT therapists would focus on teaching him appropriate social skills to overcome his problems. (p. 265) (8)

7. When a neurotransmitter binds to the receptors of a receiving neuron, a series of changes occur within the receiving neuron to set the stage for firing. These substances in the neuron that carry out those changes are often called _____ messengers, because they rely on the original message from the receptor site to the firing mechanism of the neuron. (p. 281) (6)

8. Treatment for those suffering from bipolar disorder got a real boost in 1970, when the Food and Drug Administration approved the use of _____, a naturally occurring silvery-white element, as a psychotropic drug. (p. 278) (7)

9. A key to behavior therapies for depression is the training of effective _____ skills, including eye contact, facial expression, posture, and other behaviors that send messages to other people. (p. 261) (6)

13. Loss, role dispute, role transition, and deficits are four different types of problems that may lead to depression, according to the founders of _____ psychotherapy, Gerald Klerman and Myrna Weissman. (p. 265) (13)

15. _____ inhibitors are antidepressant drugs that work to stop the enzyme monoamine oxidase from degrading the neurotransmitter norepinephrine. Because of potentially serious side effects, however, patients on these medications have to stick to a rigid diet that reduces their intake of the chemical tyramine. (p. 269) (3)

16. While colleges and universities recognize the importance of having psychological counseling available for students, nearly half of all college counseling offices lack a full-fledged staff _____ , which means that students would not be likely to receive prescriptions for important psychotropic medications at these offices. (p. 260) (12)

18. Since the discovery of lithium for the treatment of bipolar disorder, other mood _____, or antibipolar, drugs have been developed and are now used extensively due to the fact that they produce fewer side effects and better clinical outcomes. (p. 278) (11)

20. The main purpose of ECT is to induce a brain _____ that lasts from 25 seconds to a few minutes. (p. 267) (7)

21. One of the most controversial forms of treatment for depression is electro_____ therapy, or ECT. Though it is often misperceived as a barbaric and ineffective treatment approach, it has actually been found to be quite effective and fast-acting for the treatment of unipolar depression symptoms. (pp. 266–269) (10)

23. _____ therapy is an approach to counseling in which a therapist works with two people who share a long-term relationship. (p. 266) (6)

24. One experimental treatment for depression that was developed after similar techniques were successfully applied to patients suffering from seizure disorders or Parkinson's disease is _____ brain stimulation (DBS). (p. 274) (4)

25. An herbal treatment for cases of mild depression includes taking Saint _____ Wort, a common flower that produces few side effects. This supplement is not effective, however, for cases of severe depression. (p. 267) (5)

Down

2. The first stage of Albert Ellis's therapy approach to addressing depression involves increasing _____ and elevating moods. This includes preparing detailed hourly schedules for the upcoming week, schedules which are co-constructed by the therapist and client. (p. 262) (10)

3. The discovery of _____ drugs, so named because of their three-ring chemical structure, was accidental. Researchers were looking for a new drug to treat schizophrenia, and instead created an antidepressant medication. (p. 270) (9)

5. The _____ management approach to treating depression involves ignoring a client's depressive behaviors and/or statements while praising or otherwise rewarding constructive statements and behaviors. (p. 261) (11)

6. In _____ magnetic stimulation (TMS) clinicians pass an electromagnetic coil on or above the patient's head in order to increase neuron activity in the prefrontal cortex of the brain. (p. 274) (12)

7. The natural supplement s-adenosylmethionine, also referred to as _____, has been used for more than 20 years in Italy and 13 other countries to treat depression. It is fast acting and produces relatively few undesired side effects. Its main limitation, however, is that it is relatively expensive. (p. 267) (4)

10. Some people who take antidepressant medications choose to continue taking them even after their symptoms have been eliminated. People who take the drugs for three or more years after their initial improvement—a practice called _____ therapy—may significantly reduce their risk of relapse. (p. 270) (11)

11. While Aaron Beck is most noted for his work developing the cognitive approach to treating depression, Albert _____ developed a four-stage model of cognitive therapy called rational-emotive therapy. (p. 262) (5)

12. Learning to recognize and change negative thought processes and irrational maladaptive assumptions is the focus of _____ therapy. (pp. 262–263) (9)

14. Some of the most widely recognized and prescribed medications in the world belong to the category known as selective serotonin _____ inhibitors (SSRIs), and include Zoloft, Prozac, and Lexapro. (p. 271) (8)

17. In order to maximize the likelihood of minority clients overcoming the symptoms of depression, _____-sensitive approaches are being increasingly combined with traditional forms of psychotherapy. (p. 264) (7)

19. When major life changes such as marriage, divorce, or the birth of a child occur, these experiences of interpersonal _____ transition may lead to depressed symptoms. (p. 265) (4)

22. Theresa is undergoing a surgical procedure in which a surgeon implants a small device called a pulse generator under the skin of her chest, and then guides a wire up the neck to a major nerve. This form of treatment, _____ nerve stimulation, is used to send messages to the brain every five minutes. (p. 273) (5)

CROSSWORD PUZZLE—CHAPTER 10

Across

1. Studies suggest that as many as 70 percent of those who commit suicide consume _____ before the act. (p. 295) (7)

5. Taking its name from the French word that means "without law," this type of suicide occurs when an individual's social environment fails to provide stable structure in their life. As a result, this person may feel a deep lack of belonging in society. (p. 299) (6)

6. According to Freud, suicide occurs when individuals direct their "death instinct," or _____, at themselves instead of at others. (p. 298) (8)

9. When an individual plays an overt, indirect, partial, or unconscious role in their own demise, this is referred to by Shneidman as _____ death. (p. 288) (14)

11. The death _____ is a person who is ambivalent about their wish to die even as (s)he attempts suicide. (p. 288) (5)

14. A suicide attempt that does not result in death is called a(n) _____. It is difficult to know the exact number of such attempts, given the challenges in collecting data from individuals who have tried but failed to kill themselves. (p. 286) (11)

18. _____ is a pessimistic belief that one's present circumstances, problems, or mood will not change, and it is highly correlated with suicidal feelings. (p. 293) (12)

19. The controversy over "Black Box" warnings surrounds the issue of increased risk of suicidal thoughts and actions among children and teenagers who take _____ medications. (p. 304) (14)

20. In studies of the relationship between age, ethnicity, and suicide, researchers have consistently found that the highest teenage suicide rate is displayed by American _____. (p. 291) (7)

21. _____ intervention refers to a treatment approach that tries to help people experiencing psychological turmoil to view their situation more accurately, make better decisions, and act more constructively until the difficulties subside or at least are reduced. (p. 310) (6)

22. One alarming research finding regarding suicidal behaviors among teenagers suggests that for every completed suicide in this age group, 200 other individuals _____ to kill themselves. (p. 303) (7)

Down

2. Highlighting the possibility for suicide by one person to set up a family pattern of such behavior, famous novelist Ernest _____ killed himself approximately 35 years before his granddaughter Margaux, a model and actress, committed suicide by taking an overdose of barbiturates. This family had five instances of suicide in only four generations. (p. 286) (9)

3. _____ environments, such as being a prisoner of war, living in a concentration camp, or being a victim of domestic violence, can lead people to try to "escape" their situation through suicide. (p. 293) (7)

4. Demonstrating the problem of suicide contagion, the national suicide rate rose 12 percent after the suicide of Marilyn _____ in 1963. (p. 297) (6)

5. When his father's store was robbed, Buck chased the thieves into the street and jumped on their getaway car to prevent them from taking his father's money. Buck was unfortunately killed during this event, and thus Durkheim would label this as a(n) _____ suicide. (p. 299) (10)

7. Individuals who engage in _____ thinking (i.e., seeing the world in either/or terms) tend to experience greater levels of suicidality. (p. 293) (11)

8. Certain that God is waiting for him and that he will receive the joys and treasures of heaven, Kevin kills himself so that he can move on from his earthly existence to this new plane of being. Kevin is an example of a death _____. (p. 288) (7)

10. After a suicide, clinicians and researchers may gather information about the deceased individual in an attempt to determine the reasons behind the suicide. This "psychological autopsy" is sometimes referred to as a(n) _____ analysis, since it involves looking back at the individual's life. (p. 289) (13)

11. This psychiatric illness has the greatest relationship with suicide. Research suggests that half of all suicide victims had suffered from this problem before their deaths. (p. 308) (10)

12. Research into the relationship between religion and suicidal feelings has found that merely having religion in one's life is not enough to prevent suicidal actions; rather, it is the level of _____ that seems to have an insulating effect against suicidality. (p. 291) (10)

13. The first suicide _____ program in the United States was founded in Los Angeles in 1955. The goal of this program was to identify people at risk of killing themselves and to offer them support and crisis intervention. (p. 309) (10)

15. Ophelia decided that she wanted to die. She was quite certain that this was the right choice for her, right up until the moment when she pulled the trigger of the gun that killed her. According to Shneidman, Ophelia would be classified as a death _____. (p. 288) (6)

16. Sherilyn suffers from amyotrophic lateral sclerosis (ALS), more commonly known as Lou Gehrig's disease. As the illness has robbed her of control of her body and will surely cause her death within several months, she has decided to take an overdose of sleeping pills so that she can die quietly and with dignity. Sherilyn is an example of a death _____, according to Edwin Shneidman's labels. (p. 288) (9)

17. _____ suicides are committed by people over whom society has little or no control. Those likely to engage in this form of suicide are often isolated, alienated, and nonreligious. (p. 299) (8)

CROSSWORD PUZZLE—CHAPTER 11

Across

1. Influential family theorist Salvador Minuchin coined the phrase _____ family pattern. This refers to a family system in which members are over-involved with each other's affairs and individuality and healthy separation from other family members are lacking. (p. 331) (8)

6. The _____ hypothalamus (LH) is a region of the brain that, when stimulated, produces hunger and motivates eating behaviors. (p. 327) (7)

8. A behavioral intervention used to interrupt the binge-purge cycle is _____ and response prevention, which is a technique also used to treat obsessive-compulsive disorder. For those suffering from bulimia, they are encouraged to eat particular kinds and amounts of food _without_ engaging in self-induced vomiting or other purging behaviors. (p. 340) (8)

10. Another name for bulimia nervosa is _____-purge syndrome. (p. 320) (5)

11. Biological researchers have suggested that each person has their own weight _____ point, which is the weight level that a person is predisposed to maintain. Many factors contribute to this unique feature of each individual, including various brain areas and chemicals. (p. 329) (3)

12. Sadly, research suggests that between 2 and 6 percent of those with anorexia will die from their illness. Death can come by one of two mechanisms—from the medical complications related to starvation or from _____. (p. 319) (7)

15. Stimulation of the _____ hypothalamus (VMH) is associated with the depression of hunger and the cessation of eating behaviors. (p. 328) (12)

19. Hilda Bruch forwarded a psychodynamic explanation of the origin of eating disorders suggesting that disturbed mother-child interactions lead to serious _____ deficiencies and perceptual disturbances in a child that jointly help produce disordered eating patterns. (p. 324) (3)

21. An individual's body _____ index is a formula used to indicate whether a person's weight is appropriate for his or her height. It is calculated as the person's weight (in kilograms) divided by the square of his or her height (in meters). (p. 328) (4)

22. While many people believe that those who engage in self-induced vomiting should be diagnosed with bulimia nervosa, this is not always true. Those who engage in such behaviors might also be diagnosed with binge-eating/ _____-type anorexia nervosa. (p. 318) (7)

23. Just as it is in women, body _____ seems to be a key factor in the development of eating disorders for men. (p. 335) (5)

25. _____ environment has been found to play an important role in the development of eating disorders, as many people suffering from these diagnoses live in homes where weight, thinness, and body image are emphasized. (p. 331) (6)

26. Jennifer Ringer, a dancer in the New York City Ballet's production of "The _____," was criticized for looking like she was overweight during the production. This highlights the pressure that is put on ballerinas to be thin, perhaps dangerously thin, to get and keep their jobs as performers. (p. 342) (10)

Down

2. _____ account for only 5 to 10 percent of all cases of eating disorders, and many experts blame Western society's double standards for attractiveness as one of the key reasons for this gender-related trend. (p. 334) (5)

3. A theory that identifies several kinds of risk factors that are combined to help cause a disorder is called a multi_____ risk perspective. It basically states that the more risk factors present, the greater the risk of developing the disorder. (p. 324) (11)

4. Research has found that dieting to lose weight does not tend to meet with long-term success. In fact, long-term studies have revealed that obese people who lose weight on low-calorie diets often end up with a net weight _gain_. This is referred to as a _____ effect. (p. 328) (7)

5. Anti_____ medications have been used to help treat bulimia nervosa. Research suggests that these drugs can reduce binges by as much as 67 percent and vomiting by 56 percent. (p. 341) (10)

7. Lynette is 17 years old, and has recently experienced a lot of weight loss. Though she is not sexually active, she has noticed that her menstrual cycles have recently stopped. First they became irregular, then they disappeared entirely. This symptom, called _____, is seen in women with anorexia nervosa. (p. 320) (10)

9. Malaika seeks to lose weight by gradually reducing the variety of foods she allows herself to eat. After some time, her "permitted" foods have been reduced to only bananas, non-fat yogurt, and rice cakes. Clearly Malaika is suffering from _____-type anorexia nervosa. (p. 318) (11)

13. Examples of _____ behaviors include all of the following—misusing laxatives, diuretics, or enemas; fasting; exercising excessively; and engaging in self-induced vomiting. (p. 320) (12)

14. Jared goes through the same behavior cycle several times per week. First he will consume massive quantities of food—much more than he would normally eat—and then he will starve himself for two days to make up for the calories he ingested. This pattern of behavior is indicative nonpurging-type bulimia of _____. (p. 320) (7)

16. Many people with eating disorders, particularly those with bulimia nervosa, experience symptoms of _____, leading some theorists to suggest that this mood disorder sets the stage for the development of eating disorders. (p. 327) (10)

17. _____ nervosa is a serious illness that is marked by extreme thinness, an intense fear of gaining weight, and disturbed body perception. (p. 318) (8)

18. A new kind of eating disorder that primarily affects men is called muscle dysmorphobia, or _____ anorexia nervosa. It is seen in men who are quite muscular but who see themselves as scrawny and small. (p. 335) (7)

20. _____ nervosa is an eating disorder marked by frequent eating binges that are followed by self-induced vomiting or other extreme behaviors used to avoid gaining weight. (p. 320) (7)

24. In the soon-to-be-published DSM-5, three childhood eating disorders will be added to the category currently called "eating disorders." They include one diagnosis, _____, which involves the eating of non-food substances. (p. 343) (4)

CROSSWORD PUZZLE—CHAPTER 12

Across

2. When David first came to college, he would get very tipsy after drinking only one beer. Three years later, he is known as the "best drinker" in his fraternity, because he can put away a 12-pack without getting very drunk. This ability to ingest more of the substance with a reduced effect is called _____. (p. 348) (9)

5. A synthetically created substitute for heroin is called _____, and it was developed in the 1960s to reduce the amount of heroin usage in the United States. Some have argued that it should no longer be used because it simply substitutes one addiction for another. (p. 379) (9)

7. Free-_____ is a technique for ingesting cocaine in which the pure cocaine basic alkaloid is chemically separated from processed cocaine and is then inhaled with a pipe after being vaporized by a flame. (p. 361) (6)

8. Many self-help programs have expanded into _____ treatment cen-

ters, also called therapeutic communities. In such environments, people formerly addicted to drugs live, work, and socialize in a drug-free environment while promoting healthy choices, therapy, and making the transition back to community life. (p. 381) (11)

9. Some experts believe that all drugs eventually work in the same fashion; that is, by stimulating the _____ center, or "pleasure pathway" of the brain. (p. 374) (6)

10. _____-prevention training is an approach to treating alcoholism that focuses on planning ahead for risky situations where the overuse of alcohol will be particularly tempting and/or likely. (p. 377) (7)

12. Some theorists believe that people who abuse drugs do not receive enough reward experiences through normal activities, a process called reward-_____ syndrome. The use of drugs is therefore intended to artificially stimulate their pleasure pathway. (p. 374) (10)

13. Neurotransmitters that are effective at relieving pain and reducing emotional tension are called _____. Opioids are able to produce pain relief by mimicking the chemical action of these neurotransmitters. (p. 357) (10)

17. The most powerful stimulant currently known is _____, which is the central active ingredient of a South American plant. Though it is most frequently snorted, some users prefer injecting or smoking it. (p. 358) (7)

21. _____ are substances that increase the activity of the central nervous system. (p. 358) (10)

23. Ecstasy is the common street name of the popular party drug _____, whose chemical formula is *3,4-methyl-enedioxymethamphetamine*. (p. 365) (4)

25. The most common group of antianxiety drugs are the _____, which include Valium and Xanax. They are able to provide enhanced calm and relaxation without the hypnotic and sedative effects of barbiturates. (p. 355) (15)

27. When a sufferer of extreme alcohol dependence discontinues the use of the drug, (s)he may experience a very severe withdrawal reaction called delirium _____ (the "DTs") which include very frightening visual hallucinations, confusion, and clouded consciousness. (p. 353) (7)

30. One dangerous long-term effect of LSD is the experience of _____, or recurrences of sensory and emotional changes that are experienced after the LSD has left the body. Some people report having these experiences months or even years after using LSD. (p. 366) (10)

32. _____ are a category of substances that slow the activity of the central nervous system, and include alcohol, sedative-hypnotics, and opioids. (p. 349) (11)

34. When one ingests an excessive amount of alcohol in a short period of time, one may suffer from a state called _____, which literally means "poisoning." This can lead to poor judgment, mood changes, irritability, slurred speech, and poor coordination. (p. 348) (12)

35. _____ is a highly addictive drug that is made from the sap of the poppy. It was used for quite a few years for the reduction of both physical and emotional pain before its dangerous addictive properties were fully recognized. (p. 356) (5)

36. One type of sedative-hypnotic drugs includes _____, which are very addictive and can reduce anxiety and produce sleep. (p. 355) (12)

37. _____-hypnotic drugs, also known as *anxiolytics*, produce feelings of drowsiness and relaxation. At low doses they can have a calming effect, but at high doses they can serve as sleep inducers, or *hypnotics*. (p. 355) (8)

38. Marvin is undergoing aversion therapy for his addiction to cigarettes. He is left in a small, closed room and instructed to puff on a cigarette every few seconds until he begins to feel sick and cannot smoke any further. This approach, known as _____ smoking, is designed to create a distaste for cigarettes. (p. 360) (5)

40. While cocaine is a derivative of a naturally occurring substance, _____ are stimulant drugs that are 100 percent synthetic; that is, they are made entirely in a laboratory. (p. 361) (12)

42. Readily available in a number of different forms, including coffee, tea, chocolate, energy drinks, and sodas, _____ is easily the world's most widely used stimulant. (p. 362) (8)

43. The single most widely used depressant drug in the world is _____, with the World Health Organization estimating that it is consumed by over 2 billion people around the globe. (p. 349) (7)

44. A third attempt to create an opium derivative that was both effective and safe produced the drug _____, which was first created in 1898. Though extremely powerful as a pain reliever, it was even more addictive than the morphine from which it was created. As a result, in 1917 the U.S. Congress determined that all opium derivatives ("opioids") were addictive and restricted their use to medical settings. (p. 356) (6)

45. Because two different drugs may act in a similar fashion on the brain, people can display a condition called _____-tolerance, where symptoms of withdrawal from one drug can be reduced by taking another drug. (p. 369) (5)

Down

1. *Disulfram* (commonly known as Antabuse) is a(n) _____ drug that counteracts the chemical effects of alcohol. (p. 378) (10)

3. According to a recent survey of tenth-grade students, alcohol is the easiest drug to get. _____ are the second easiest! (Hint: See Figure 12-3.) (p. 367) (10)

4. Derived from opium, _____ was and still is used for the relief of pain. Though more potent than opium, it is also extremely addictive. (Hint: This drug gets its name from the Greek god of sleep.) (p. 356) (8)

6. The systematic and medically supervised withdrawal from a drug is known as _____, and it can be performed on an inpatient or outpatient basis. (p. 378) (14)

11. Hallucinogens, also known as _____ drugs, cause powerful changes in sensory perception, occasionally creating extremely powerful and unusual experiences known as "trips." (p. 364) (11)

14. The single greatest risk of cocaine use is an _____, which can lead to a heart arrhythmia that results in cardiac arrest and, in many cases, death. (p. 361) (8)

15. A _____-related disorder refers to a long-term pattern of maladaptive behaviors centered on the abuse of or dependence on a combination of drugs. (p. 369) (13)

16. _____ syndrome is an alcohol-related disorder marked by extreme confusion, memory impairment, and other neurological symptoms. To make up for the lost memories, people suffering from this condition may "confabulate," or make up memories to fill in holes in their own memory. (pp. 354-355) (10)

18. _____ drugs are produced from the varieties of a hemp plant. They cause a mixture of hallucinogenic, depressant, and stimulant effects. (p. 366) (8)

19. One of the best-known and yet weakest forms of cannabis is _____, which produces different types of effects when ingested at different dosages. (p. 366) (9)

20. _____ drinking has become a very serious problem on college campuses, and is generally defined as the consumption of five or more drinks on a single occasion. Sadly, this practice can easily lead to death. (p. 352) (5)

22. _____, a powerful hallucinogenic drug that was first derived from ergot alkaloids in 1938, can cause hallucinosis (p. 364) (3)

24. When a woman consumes alcohol during pregnancy, it may lead to a condition called _____ alcohol syndrome in her baby. Symptoms of this condition include mental retardation, hyperactivity, physical deformities, and heart defects. (p. 355) (5)

26. If a user takes more than one drug at a time, it is possible that the individual effects of each substance may be significantly increased, or "potentiated." This is known as a(n) _____ effect. (p. 369) (11)

28. _____ is a term frequently commonly used to refer to substance dependence. The term is generally associated with a loss of control over drug usage habits. (p. 348) (9)

29. Bettina has recently decided to stop smoking, and has opted to quit all at once, or "cold turkey." For several days after quitting, she experienced headaches, irritability, physical cravings, and some nausea from the lack of nicotine. These symptoms are called _____, and often occur when an individual suddenly reduces or discontinues the use of a drug. (p. 348) (10)

31. One form of behavioral therapy for treating substance-related problems uses _____ management, which makes incentives dependent on the submission of drug-free urine samples. (p. 377) (11)

33. A very serious pattern of drug use is called substance _____, and it includes indications of both physical addiction (tolerance and withdrawal) as well as psychological addiction (a loss of control over the usage habits). (p. 348) (10)

34. When a person ingests a drug by _____ it, they may experience the effects on the brain in as few as 7 seconds. (Hint: See Table 12-4.) (p. 372) (8)

39. A very powerful and addictive ready-to-smoke form of freebase cocaine is called _____. It gets its name from the distinctive sound that it makes when it is inhaled. (p. 361) (5)

40. Kendra has recently been using cocaine with great regularity. She occasionally shows up late to work because of her habit, she has started neglecting her relationships, and she was arrested twice for trying to buy the drug from an undercover police office. The best diagnosis for Kendra's situation would be substance _____. (p. 348) (5)

41. The specific chemical that is contained in all alcoholic beverages is _____ alcohol, a substance that is quickly absorbed into the blood through the stomach and intestines. (p. 349) (5)

CROSSWORD PUZZLE—CHAPTER 13

Across

1. Some people who may suffer from sexual masochism enjoy being strangled or smothered during sexual activities. Tragically, some people who attempt to do this to themselves while masturbating die from a reduction of oxygen. This is called autoerotic _____. (p. 413) (8)

4. _____ is the abbreviation for the stage of sleep when men typically experience erections due to changes in the electrical activity of the brain. (p. 393) (3)

7. The _____ are disorders in which individuals repeatedly have intense sexual urges or fantasies that focus around nonhuman objects, children, nonconsenting adults, or the experience of suffering or humiliation. (p. 406) (11)

10. Gender _____ refers to the experience of being unhappy with one's given gender. (p. 415) (9)

13. One basic premise of sex therapy is providing clients with _____ about sexuality, since many people know very little about the physiology

and techniques of sexual activity. (p. 401) (9)

15. The first step in the human sexual response cycle is the _____ phase, which is marked by the urge to have sex, sexual fantasies, and sexual attraction to others. (p. 388) (6)

17. Carla has recently experienced a sharp decline in her sexual appetite. She rarely fantasizes about sex, has little interest in having sex, and rarely engages in sexual activities. On the infrequent occasions when she does choose to

have sex, there are no problems with her physical functioning. Carla would best be diagnosed with _____ sexual desire disorder. (p. 389) (10)

18. Male _____ disorder refers to a persistent inability to achieve or maintain adequate penile rigidity during sexual activities. (p. 392) (8)

19. A major tenet of sex therapy is increasing sexual and general _____ skills, so that partners can express their feelings, needs, and desires in a mutually supportive and nonthreatening manner. (p. 402) (13)

20. People who fantasize about sexual _____ typically imagine that they have total control over their partner, and then engage in humiliating and/or torturing their victim. (p. 414) (6)

22. The need or desire to dress in the clothing of the opposite sex in order to achieve sexual arousal is a paraphilia known as _____ fetishism, and is sometimes referred to as cross-dressing. (p. 408) (11)

24. Erik finds the thought of sexual activities absolutely repulsive. He is nearly sickened by the sexual activities that many people enjoy, and though he has a girlfriend the only "sexual" activity between them is kissing. In fact, Erik's disdain for sexual behaviors is threatening to end his relationship. Erik is likely suffering from sexual _____ disorder. (p. 389) (8)

26. Gender _____ disorder is a disorder in which a person persistently feels that a mistake was made and that they were born into the wrong sex. (p. 415) (8)

30. _____ focus, or *nondemand pleasuring*, is a sexual therapy technique that stresses caresses, touching, and physical pleasure that is not focused on orgasm or intercourse. The goal is to increase the overall experience of sex and reduce the exclusive focus on achieving an orgasm. (p. 401) (7)

33. Though research is far from certain, there have been findings that the bed nucleus of _____ terminalis (BST) is a part of the brain that is related to gender identity disorder and appears to be of different sizes in those suffering from this diagnosis. (p. 416) (5)

34. The third state of the human sexual response cycle is the _____ phase, which is marked by a peak of sexual pleasure, muscular contractions in the pelvic and genital areas, and a release of sexual tension. (p. 395) (6)

35. Researchers have found that certain hormones play a large role in an individual's sex drive. High levels of prolactin and/or low levels of testosterone can diminish sex drive, while high *or* low levels of _____ can have the same effect. (p. 390) (8)

36. Virgil enjoys going to the local wave pool, because in the chaos of the swirling water he can physically rub up against other people without them real-

izing that he is getting sexually aroused by the contact. He also enjoys crowded places like elevators or subway cars where such physical contact can occur. Virgil is experiencing a paraphilia known as _____. (p. 410) (11)

Down

2. Women who suffer from female sexual _____ disorder may become psychological excited by sexual thoughts or activities, but lack the vaginal swelling and/or lubrication needed to facilitate sexual penetration. (p. 392) (7)

3. A person who engages in _____ has repeated and intense sexual desires to observe unsuspecting and nonconsenting individuals as they undress or engage in sexual activities. (p. 410) (9)

5. A nocturnal penile _____ (NPT) test measures erections during sleep and is particularly useful at helping to diagnose the cause of male erectile disorder. (p. 393) (10)

6. Beth very much wants to have sex with her boyfriend, but whenever they attempt intercourse she experiences involuntary contractions of the outer one-third of her vaginal muscles, which makes intercourse very painful. Beth's symptoms are consistent with a diagnosis of _____. (p. 399) (10)

8. Sexual gratification that comes from watching, touching, or engaging in sexual acts with prepubescent children (usually under the age of 13) is called _____. (p. 411) (10)

9. Once a man begins to experience difficulties with achieving erections, he may become fearful about the problem repeating itself in the future. This worry, called _____ anxiety, can actually cause the problem to reoccur even though it may not have happened again on its own. (p. 394) (11)

11. _____ (trade name *Viagra*) was developed in 1998 and has been shown to increase blood flow to the penis and thus help men with erectile difficulties. While effective in 75% of men who use it, the drug does carry some dangerous side effects for men with certain heart conditions. (p. 403) (10)

12. Orgasmic _____ is a behavioral approach to treating various paraphilias. It is designed to substitute conventional sexual stimuli for objects that are considered inappropriate. (p. 408) (13)

13. The second stage of the human sexual response cycle is the _____ phase, which is marked by changes in the pelvic region (erection in men and vaginal lubrication in women), physical arousal, and increases in pulse, muscle tension, blood pressure, and respiratory rate. (p. 392) (10)

14. Before the development of medications used to help stimulate erections, many men used a _____ erection device (VED) which drew blood into the penis to produce an erection. (p. 403) (6)

16. Masturbatory _____ is a technique used to treat fetishism that is designed to reduce the sexual response to the target of the fetish by creating a sense of boredom that is connected to the inappropriate object. (p. 408) (9)

21. Therapists conducting sex therapy stress the concept of _____ responsibility, which means that the problem "belongs" to both of them, regardless of who actually experiences the dysfunction. This approach leads to greater teamwork when addressing the problem. (p. 401) (6)

23. The _____ role refers to a state of mind that some people experience during sex, focusing on their performance so much that their performance and enjoyment are reduced. (p. 394) (9)

25. While some people with gender identity disorder undergo sexual _____ surgery, others find a satisfactory existence through the use of hormone therapy and psychological counseling. (p. 418) (12)

27. While a reduction in this hormone can lower sexual desire, it has also been found to interfere with ejaculation. (p. 397) (12)

28. Oscar has become very distressed about his problem. You see, he regularly experiences sharp and severe pains in his genitals during sex, and he worries so much about the pain coming back that he has begun making excuses to his partner in order to avoid sex. Oscar is suffering from _____. (p. 399) (11)

29. Research suggests that women who suffer from an absence of orgasms may benefit from _____ masturbation training, during which she is taught step by step how to masturbate to achieve an orgasm on her own. After this is accomplished, orgasm during intercourse becomes possible in approximately 30 percent of those who use the technique. (p. 405) (8)

31. One study into the cause of gender identity disorder found that those with the disorder demonstrated heightened blood flow to two different parts of the brain, the insula and the anterior _____ cortex. (p. 416) (9)

32. Dominic finds that he cannot get sexually excited unless he is very close to, preferably holding, a pair of women's leather knee-length boots. He constantly asks his girlfriend to wear them before and during sex. Because this obsession is causing problems in his relationship. Dominic is suffering from _____. (p. 407) (9)

CROSSWORD PUZZLE—CHAPTER 14

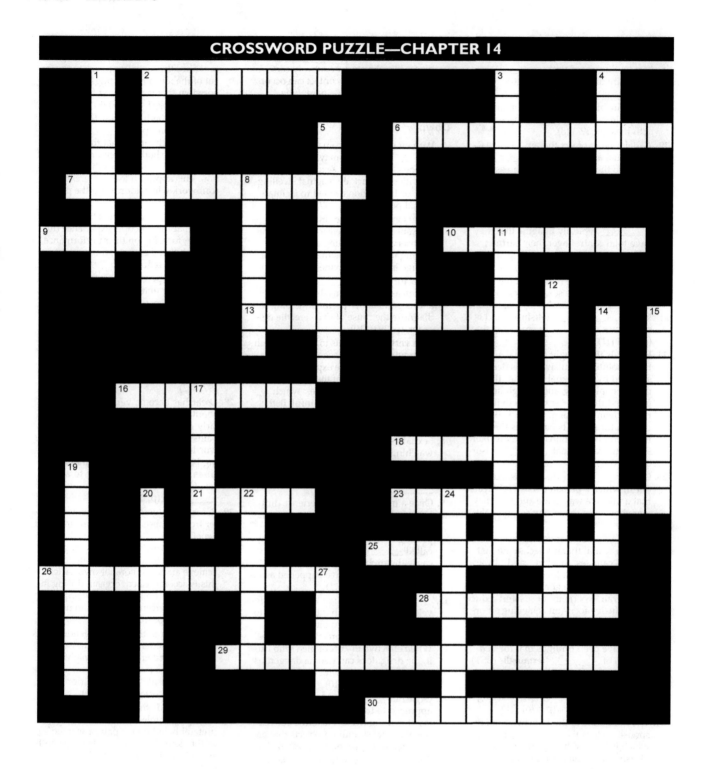

Across

2. _____ symptoms of schizophrenia are marked by a deficit of a particular behavior or skill, and are sometimes referred to as pathological absences. (p. 431) (8)

6. According to one psychodynamic theorist, Frieda Fromm-Reichmann, those suffering from schizophrenia were raised by mothers who were simultaneously overprotective and rejecting. She referred to these women as schizo_____ mothers. This theory has generally been dismissed in the years since it was first forwarded. (p. 440) (11)

7. A common thinking disturbance in schizophrenia is the experience of loose _____, also called derailment, which is characterized by rapid shifts from one topic of conversation to another. (p. 429) (12)

9. Poverty of speech, or _____, is a negative symptom of schizophrenia that is marked by a decrease in speech or speech content. (p. 431) (6)

10. _____ symptoms of schizophrenia are marked by pathological excesses of certain conditions, behaviors, thoughts, or emotions. They are sometimes described as "bizarre additions" to a person's behavior profile. (p. 427) (8)

13. A(n) _____ is defined as having a sensory and/or perceptual experience in the absence of an associated stimulus. In other words, it is when a person sees, hears, smells, tastes, or feels things that are not really there. (p. 430) (13)

16. There are several different types of schizophrenia. The most common type, _____ schizophrenia, is marked by an organized system of delusions and hallucinations that may guide the sufferer's life. (p. 433) (8)

18. When people from different economic statuses are compared, the highest rate of schizophrenia is seen among those from the _____ socioeconomic classes. (p. 426) (5)

21. "Hi there, Marty! You sure are a smarty. I don't know about you, but I'm going to the party." This sentence demonstrates the use of _____, which refers to the tendency of a schizophrenic individual to rhyme his or her sentences for no apparent reason. (p. 429) (5)

23. The delusion that one is truly an animal is called _____, and it originally referred to the belief that people who demonstrated the symptoms of a mental illness were, indeed, werewolves! (p. 429) (11)

25. _____ psychosis affects 1 to 2 of every 1,000 mothers who have recently given birth, and the symptoms of this illness are thought to be triggered by the massive hormone shifts that occur after pregnancy. (p. 436) (10)

26. The central symptoms of _____ type of schizophrenia include confusion, incoherence, and flat or inappropriate affect. These individuals may have significant disturbances in their ability to communicate, and may come across as being silly or childish at times. (p. 433) (12)

28. _____ antipsychotic drugs refers to a relatively new group of antipsychotic drugs whose biological action is different from the previous generation of medications used to treat these individuals. (p. 438) (8)

29. When no one clear pattern of symptoms dominates a schizophrenic individual's clinical presentation, (s)he may be diagnosed with schizophrenia of the _____ type. (p. 433) (16)

30. The belief that the activity of a specific neurotransmitter is found to be excessive in the brain of those suffering from schizophrenia is called the _____ hypothesis. (p. 437) (8)

Down

1. A(n) _____ is a strange or unusual false belief that an individual clings firmly to despite either (1) evidence that the belief is incorrect or (2) an absence of evidence to support that belief structure. (p. 427) (8)

2. When asked how his day was going, Terrell replied, "Well, I'll tell you. It has been a very schmorpish morning. How about you. Are you having a schmorpish day?" The fact that Terrell has made up a new word and inserted it into his vocabulary demonstrates the use of a(n) _____, a symptom often seen in those suffering from schizophrenia. (p. 429) (9)

3. A very well-known theory of schizophrenia suggests that parents repeatedly and unintentionally communicate opposing messages to their children, messages that put their kids in a no-win situation. This is called the double-_____ hypothesis, and is believed to plant the seeds of schizophrenia from a very early age. (p. 444) (4)

4. The term "schizophrenia" comes from the Greek words that mean "split _____." (p. 426) (4)

5. Small areas in the brain where cerebrospinal fluid collects called _____ are believed to be enlarged in those suffering from schizophrenia, suggesting a physiological cause for this illness. (p. 439) (10)

6. People who experience a loss of contact with reality in key areas of functioning are experiencing a state of _____. (p. 426) (9)

8. Formal _____ disorders occur when people with schizophrenia experience an interruption in their ability to think logically, speak in a coherent manner, and experience great confusion. (p. 429) (7)

11. _____ is a psychotic disorder in which strange perceptions, unusual emotions, and motor abnormalities interfere with personal, social, and occupational functioning. (p. 426) (13)

12. _____ drugs are those medications that are designed to reduce the grossly confused or distorted thinking of those suffering from schizophrenia. They are generally effective, but also carry the risk of different types of troubling side effects. (p. 437) (13)

14. The psychotic disorder that shows many of the symptoms of schizophrenia and lasts between one and six months in duration is called schizo_____ disorder. (p. 435) (10)

15. By far, the most common type of hallucination is a(n) _____ hallucination. (p. 430) (8)

17. Flat _____ refers to a marked lack of expressed or even experienced emotions, and is a common symptom of schizophrenia. (p. 432) (6)

19. A symptom of schizophrenia that involves a loss of will or ability to start or complete a course of action is called _____. (p. 432) (9)

20. _____ emotion is the general level of criticism, disapproval, and hostility that is communicated in a family. (p. 444) (9)

22. When the rates of schizophrenia are compared across racial and ethnic groups, _____ Americans seem to have a higher likelihood of receiving this diagnosis. This may reflect a reality that the illness is more prevalent among this population, or it may indicate a bias on the part of those who diagnose illnesses in the first place. (p. 442) (7)

24. A pattern of extreme psychomotor disturbance sometimes seen by those suffering from a rare form of schizophrenia is called _____. (p. 432) (9)

27. The fact that people of lower socioeconomic backgrounds seem more vulnerable to developing schizophrenia has a lot of explanations; however, this tendency is generally known as the downward _____ theory. (p. 426) (5)

CROSSWORD PUZZLE—CHAPTER 15

Across

6. Crisis or group homes, also known as _____ houses, are residences for those with schizophrenia or other severe problems that are staffed by paraprofessionals. They are for those who do not need constant supervision but who are also not able to live independently. (p. 467) (7)

9. A _____ center (or hospital) is a facility where patients can get outpatient help and treatment, but still return to their homes at night. (p. 466) (3)

10. _____ therapy is a humanistic approach to institutional treatment based on the belief that institutions can help patients' recovery by creating a climate that promotes self-respect, responsible behavior, and meaningful activity. (p. 452) (6)

12. The discharge of hundreds of thousands of patients with schizophrenia and other chronic mental illnesses from long-term treatment facilities in the mid-1960s was called _____. (p. 465) (22)

15. While antipsychotic drugs are currently used to treat the symptoms of schizophrenia, they were first discovered when a particular class of antihistamines called _____ were discovered to have a calming effect for patients about to undergo surgery. (p. 455) (14)

17. Thanks to the work of Philippe Pinel in 1793, a movement toward _____ treatment of those with mental disorders became a trend that grew across Europe and then the United States. (p. 451) (5)

18. Follow-up monitoring and treatment in the community is provided for those who are released from mental health hospitals after they have shown improvement. This monitoring is called _____ and helps facilitate ongoing recovery. (p. 466) (9)

20. Mental health patients who suffer from a _____ abuse or dependence problem in addition to another diagnosis are known as *mentally ill abusers*. (p. 466) (8)

21. A sheltered _____ is a supervised workplace for people who are not yet ready for competitive jobs. It provides some income, the chance to develop job skills, and the self-esteem that comes with having a job that one can successfully complete, even with help. (p. 467) (8)

23. _____ and commitment therapy is used to help people with schizophrenia become detached and comfortable observers of their symptoms. It helps teach patients to work with their symptoms instead of constantly struggling and fighting against them. (p. 461) (10)

Down

1. _____ therapy conceptualizes the recovery from schizophrenia as being greatly influenced by the behavior and reactions of a person's relatives at home, and seeks to improve those relationships to support better psychological functioning. (pp. 462–463) (6)

2. A case _____ is a community therapist who offers a full range of services for people with schizophrenia and/or other severe psychiatric disorders. They may provide therapy, advice, medication, guidance, and protection of a patient's rights. (p. 468) (7)

3. Unwanted movements, such as severe shaking, strange grimaces, twisting of the body, and extreme restlessness are examples of extra_____ effects that are sometimes produced by conventional antipsychotic drugs. (p. 457) (9)

4. The *National _____ on Mental Illness* (NAMI) began in 1979 and now, with over 220,000 members is made up largely of relatives of those suffering from mental disorders. They provide a number of services, including education and information, as well as political lobbying for the rights of the mentally ill. (p. 470) (8)

5. A _____ mental health center is a treatment facility that provides medication, psychotherapy, and emergency care for psychological problems and coordinates treatment in a person's own neighborhood. (p. 466) (9)

7. _____ is a life-threatening reduction in white blood cells that is sometimes produced by the atypical antipsychotic drug *clozapine*. This drug can still be effectively used, but patients must undergo regular blood tests so that this side effect, if emerging, can be detected early. (p. 458) (15)

8. While initially believed to be a "miracle cure" for those suffering from schizophrenia and other serious mental illnesses, we now know that the _____ is actually a rather brutal surgical procedure. (p. 453) (8)

9. Patients taking antipsychotic medications must be monitored for the appearance of tardive _____, a side effect that can lead to tics or tremors primarily seen in the face or head. (p. 457) (10)

11. A behavioral approach to treating schizophrenia is the use of a _____ economy, in which a person's desirable behaviors are reinforced throughout the day by providing rewards that can be exchanged for goods or privileges. (p. 453) (5)

13. The drugs that eliminate, or at least reduce, many of the symptoms of schizophrenia are called _____, and were discovered in the 1950s. (p. 455) (13)

14. The Community _____ Act of 1963 was a governmental initiative designed to promote a wide range of services to patients with psychological disorders, including outpatient therapy, inpatient treatment, emergency and preventative care, and aftercare. (Hint: The answer is two words.) (p. 465) (6,6)

16. Mellaril, Prolixin, Stelazine, and Haldol are all examples of _____ drugs, so named because they often produce undesired side effects that resemble the symptoms of various neurological disorders. (p. 456) (11)

19. One problem that was encountered by the state hospital system was overcrowding. This led to patients being transferred to _____ wards, or chronic wards, if they did not make rapid progress. These chronic wards provided little treatment and resembled the asylum conditions of the previous centuries. (p. 451) (4)

22. _____ hospitals are public mental hospitals in the United States that were established to provide care for patients who could not afford private hospital care. (p. 451) (5)

CROSSWORD PUZZLE—CHAPTER 16

Across

3. According to a 1995 survey, teenagers who were asked to write stories describing how fictional characters would respond to various conflicts were very likely to include violence in their responses. In fact, the country whose teenagers gave the highest frequency of violent responses was _____. (Hint: The United States came in fourth place.) (p. 489) (10)

7. _____ is described as the consistent tendency to steal items, even those of trivial value, despite having adequate money to pay for the products. It is described as an impulse-control disorder because the goal is not the possession of the stolen good, but rather the "rush" of getting away with the act of stealing. (p. 487) (11)

8. One of the personality groupings is the _____ personality disorders, which consist of paranoid, schizoid, and schizotypal personality disorders. (p. 479) (3)

10. On his first date with Lorene, James quickly becomes irritated with her inability to make a decision. She asks him to decide where they will go for dinner, what movie they will see, what time he will pick her up at, and what she should wear. At the restaurant, he is very put off by her insistence that he order a meal for her instead of choosing for herself. Clearly, Lorene is suffering from _____ personality disorder. (p. 504) (9)

11. Around 75% of people who receive a diagnosis of borderline personality disorder are _____. (p. 508) (6)

13. Those with _____ personality disorder are often perceived as being very odd and unusual. They may have noticeably disturbed thoughts and behaviors, but will not have symptoms that are extreme enough to be diagnosed with a psychotic disorder. (p. 482) (11)

14. In the movie *Backdraft*, Donald Sutherland played a character who delighted in setting fires without regard to the damage or injury that they might cause. Because he did not set the fires for revenge or financial gain (a pattern called *arson*), this pattern of firesetting would be diagnosed as _____. (p. 487) (9)

15. One of the most famous cases of personality disturbance was that of Phineas _____, a railroad worker who was the victim of a serious brain injury that left him with severe personality changes for the remainder of his life. (p. 478) (4)

17. A _____ disorder is an inflexible pattern of inner experience and outward behavior that is seen in most of a person's interactions, continues for years, and produces actions that are significantly different than would be expected by society. (p. 475) (11)

20. The popular television show *Monk* is about a detective who has an extreme need for things to be orderly, clean, and perfect. This character's Axis II diagnosis would be _____-compulsive personality disorder, an illness that does share some features with the Axis I disorder that shares its name. (p. 506) (9)

21. While many professional athletes display colorful and entertaining personalities, some seem endlessly fixated on how wonderful, special, and talented they are. In fact, they talk about themselves so much that they often become annoying. Further, when they make a mistake, they always seem to have a reason why it was someone else's fault. This pattern of behaviors might remind you of _____ personality disorder. (p. 499) (12)

22. The ten personality disorders that can be diagnosed according to the current edition of the DSM are often combined into three different groups, or _____. (p. 476) (8)

23. A new diagnosis that has been called for in the upcoming DSM-5 is called *personality disorder _____ specified (PDTS)*, which would occur if a person does not fit into the diagnostic category of a full personality disorder but has personality characteristics that significantly impair their functioning. (p. 512) (5)

24. Remus has worked for years as a long-distance truck driver. He generally prefers to be left alone, and when he is around others he acts and feels very awkward. He has never had a romantic relationship worth mentioning, and others describe him as being "emotionless." Remus probably suffers from _____ personality disorder. (p. 481) (8)

25. Among the many professions that are likely to foster mistrust among citizens, this group of professionals seems to elicit the greatest amount of mistrust. (p. 480) (7)

Down

1. Individuals with intermittent _____ disorder have periodic aggressive outbursts during which they may become violent, destroying property or hurting other people. The level of intensity of their outbursts is far beyond the level of any provocation they may have experienced. (p. 487) (9)

2. Those who suffer from schizotypal personality disorder may experience ideas of _____, which are beliefs that unrelated events pertain to them in some important way. While technically not delusions, these idea patterns highlight the relationship between this Axis II disorder and schizophrenia-related Axis I problems. (p. 483) (9)

4. One treatment technique that has shown promise for those with borderline personality disorder is _____ behavior therapy (DBT). It is an eclectic therapy approach borrowing from cognitive, behavioral, humanistic, and contemporary psychodynamic models. (p. 494) (11)

5. Those who are constantly seeking attention and acting out in emotional and dramatic ways might be suffering from _____ personality disorder. They tend to be very uncomfortable in situations where they are not the center of attention. (p. 496) (10)

6. The main characteristics of _____ personality disorder are unstable relationships, a shifting and changing self-image, dramatic changes in mood, and impulsive, often dangerous behaviors. (p. 489) (10)

9. The _____ grouping of personality disorders includes antisocial, borderline, histrionic, and narcissistic personality disorders, and is often marked by emotional and/or erratic behaviors that severely interfere with relationships. (p. 484) (8)

12. Those who suffer from _____ personality disorder can be very difficult to treat because they do not accept that they have a problem. Their behaviors that persistently disregard and violate the rights of others often serve their own purposes, and thus they don't see a need to change. (p. 485) (10)

13. Neurological studies have found that those persons with borderline personality disorder who are particularly impulsive—attempting suicide or aggressing against others—may have lower activity of the hormone _____. (p. 493) (9)

16. The _____ group of personality disorders includes dependent, avoidant, and obsessive-compulsive personality disorders. Sufferers are often fearful and worried about various things in their surroundings, and their symptoms often resemble different Axis I disorders. (p. 501) (7)

17. The central characteristic of _____ personality disorder is a deep-seated mistrust of others and a constant air of suspicion regarding the motives of other people. (p. 479) (8)

18. Janine is very uncomfortable and inhibited in social situations. She convinces herself that she is not as good or "cool" as others, and she is intensely afraid of rejection. Given that this pattern of behavior has been going on for the better part of her life, she might be diagnosed as suffering from _____ personality disorder. (p. 501) (8)

19. Freudian theorists suggest that people with obsessive-compulsive personality disorder have a fixation of one of the basic psychosexual stages of development, leaving them with an anal-_____ personality. (p. 507) (10)

CROSSWORD PUZZLE—CHAPTER 17

Across

3. In addition to findings that indicate abnormal neurotransmitter activity, research also indicates that abnormalities in the _____-striatal regions of the brain may explain some of the symptoms of ADHD. (p. 532) (7)

5. Millions of children and adults alike have been treated for their symptoms of ADHD with _____, which is the trade name for the stimulant drug methyphenidate. (p. 532) (7)

11. Communication boards, sign language, and computers that use pictures, symbols, or written words to replace spoken language are collectively called _____ communication systems, and are used to help those suffering from autistic disorder. (p. 546) (12)

12. One disorder that is related to autism is _____ syndrome, which is marked by significant social impairments. People who suffer from this problem do not have the cognitive and language deficits of autistic disorder, but may appear awkward to others and therefore become socially isolated. (p. 541) (9)

14. Approximately 3 to 4 percent of mentally retarded individuals display _____ retardation, which is marked by a very low IQ (20-34) and significant deficits of cognitive, motor, social, and neurological functions.

While they may be able to function with the assistance of group homes, they are rarely able to live independently. (p. 551) (6)

16. Children with _____ defiant disorder show a repetitive pattern of arguing with adults, losing their tempers, swearing, and feeling anger and resentment. (p. 525) (12)

18. Extreme cases of separation anxiety disorder can lead to _____ phobia, a problem in which children fear academic settings and end up staying at home for long periods of time. Though often related to fear of separation, this condition can also be related to depression or social fears. (p. 521) (6)

19. Many schools have begun implementing a policy called _____, also known as *inclusion*, wherein children with mental retardation are put into regular classrooms instead of being separated from nonretarded students. There are varying opinions about the benefits and risks of such policies. (p. 554) (13)

21. _____ aggression, which is more common among girls than boys, involves social misdeeds such as slandering others, spreading rumors, and manipulating friendships. (p. 527) (10)

22. One child-focused treatment for conduct disorder is called the _____ *Coping and Coping Power Program*, the purpose of which is to teach the client how to handle his or her own aggressive emotions, solve problems, build social skills, and handle peer pressure. (p. 530) (5)

23. The most common chromosomal cause of mental retardation is _____ syndrome, which is caused by the presence of three of the twenty-first chromosomes instead of two. It is also known as *trisomy-21*, and occurs in fewer than 1 out of every 1000 live births. (p. 552) (4)

24. Marta is six years old, and regularly urinates in her clothes. Though she knows how to use the toilet and can do so when instructed to, she continues to have this problem and it has caused a great deal of embarrassment for her. Marta is suffering from _____. (p. 535) (8)

25. The word _____ is French for "learned" or "clever," and refers to an individual who has some major mental disorder or handicap, yet also has a spectacular ability or area of particular brilliance. (p. 542) (6)

27. Those with _____ mental retardation have an IQ between 35 and 49, and often demonstrate clear deficits in language development and play during their early (preschool) years. (p. 551) (8)

28. Children who display attention-deficit/_____ disorder (ADHD) have great difficulty attending to tasks, or behave overactively and impulsively, or both. (p. 530) (13)

31. When a child has the _____-destructive pattern of conduct disorder, (s)he displays openly aggressive and confrontational behaviors. (p. 526) (5)

32. _____ is the principle that those with mental retardation should be exposed to living conditions and opportunities that are similar to those found in the rest of society. (p. 554) (13)

34. An individual with an intelligence _____, or IQ, below 70 may qualify for a diagnosis of mental retardation; however, several other symptoms must be present for this diagnosis to be made. (p. 548) (8)

35. Anna has been pregnant for 4 months, and despite knowing that she is expecting a child she still regularly enjoys a few cocktails after work. Her colleagues are all uncomfortable seeing her drink, because they know that it increases the chance of the baby being born with _____ alcohol syndrome. (p. 553) (5)

Down

1. Recent neuropsychological research suggests that the neurotransmitter _____ shows abnormal activity in children with ADHD. (p. 532) (8)

2. The skill in arithmetic, written expression, or reading exhibited by children with _____ disorders is well below their intellectual capacity, and causes academic and personal dysfunctioning. (p. 549) (8)

4. A 6-year study of depression in young persons called the *Treatments for _____ with Depression Study (TADS)* gave some very surprising findings that helped clarify the best practices (and ineffective treatments) for addressing teenage depression. (p. 522) (11)

5. Mental _____ is a diagnosis that describes a person who has a significant deficit of both intellectual and adaptive skills (home living, communication, self-care, self-direction, work, or safety). (p. 547) (11)

6. One possible risk of using antidepressant medication with children and adolescents is the potential increased risk of _____. The FDA now mandates that these medications carry a warning of this problem so that parents can be fully informed of the medicine's risks. (p. 524) (7)

7. The use of toys, dolls, drawing, and making up stories as an intervention for childhood anxiety disorders is called _____ therapy, and has been found to be effective at helping children face their feelings and/or fears. (p. 521) (4)

8. One of the most common childhood anxiety disorders is _____ anxiety disorder, which is marked by excessive anxiety, even panic, whenever the child is parted from home or parent. (p. 520) (10)

9. In order to help their son overcome his nighttime bedwetting, Roger and Elise are using a technique called _____ training, in which their son is regularly awakened through the night and encouraged to use the toilet before he wets the bed. By learning to control his nighttime urinating and learning to respond to the signals of his body, his problem should begin to decline quickly. (p. 536) (Hint: This is a two-word answer with a dash in the middle. For this clue, remove the dash to get the right answer.) (6)

10. The _____, a part of the brain that controls functions including the coordination of movement and the shifting of attention, has been found to develop abnormally in people suffering from autistic disorder. (p. 543) (10)

13. A _____ workshop is a protected and supervised workplace that offers job opportunities and training at a pace and level tailored to people with various psychological disabilities. Such work environments promote understanding and success, rather than frustration and discouragement. (p. 555) (9)

15. _____ is a childhood disorder that involves repeated defecating in inappropriate places, such as one's clothing. It is more common in boys than in girls. (p. 536) (10)

17. _____ retardation is the most serious degree of mental retardation, and is marked by an IQ below 20, very early presentation of symptoms (at birth or in infancy), and a lack of basic self-care skills. While these individuals may learn to feed themselves, walk, or communicate in basic forms, they need structure, close supervision, and a one-on-one relationship with a caregiver to reach their maximum potential. (p. 551) (8)

19. Ahmad has an IQ of 62. His parents have noticed that he is sometimes slower than his classmates and friends to catch on to things, but with enough help he usually grasps concepts at an acceptable level. He tends to need the most help when he is anxious and under stress. Based on his symptoms, Ahmad might be diagnosed as suffering from _____ mental retardation. (p. 550) (4)

20. One form of sociocultural treatment designed to reduce the symptoms of conduct disorder is called parent-child _____ therapy. In such interventions, parents are taught to respond to their children positively, setting appropriate limits, acting consistently, and setting fair and reasonable expectations for the child's behavior. (p. 527) (11)

26. The _____ developmental disorders include autism, Asperger's disorder, Rett's disorder, and childhood disintegrative disorder. They are also known as the autism-spectrum disorders. (p. 538) (9)

29. _____ disorder, masterfully depicted by Dustin Hoffman in the movie *Rain Man*, involves several different categories of symptoms, including (1) lack of responsiveness, (2) language and communication problems, (3) disturbed motor movements, (4) limited imaginative or abstract play, and (5) repetitive and rigid behaviors. (p. 539) (8)

30. A very serious childhood problem that is marked by repeated violations of the basic rights of others, aggression, cruelty to people and/or animals, destruction of property, and running away from home or school is called _____ disorder. (p. 526) (7)

33. The nonaccidental use of excessive physical or psychological force by an adult on a child with the intent of hurting that child is referred to as child _____. Clearly this event can have a disastrous effect on that child's future psychological and physical health. (p. 537) (5)

CROSSWORD PUZZLE—CHAPTER 18

Across

3. Most forms of _____ are caused by brain diseases or injuries, such as Alzheimer's disease or stroke. The symptoms include significant memory losses along with losses of other cognitive functions. (p. 570) (8)

5. Vascular dementia is also known as multi-_____ dementia because it is caused by repeated occurrences of an interruption of oxygenated blood getting to the brain. (p. 575) (7)

8. _____ disorder occurs when there is a significant memory loss that is caused by brain disease or injuries. (p. 576) (8)

11. When one experiences _____, they experience a clouding of consciousness that involves a loss of concentration, difficulty focusing attention, and trouble following an orderly sequence of thought. It is treated by addressing the underlying medical cause. (p. 569) (8)

12. Although brain scans can give a physician significant confidence in the diagnosis of Alzheimer's disease, the only certain way of making this assessment happens when a(n) _____ is performed. (p. 576) (7)

14. Public figures such as actor Michael J. Fox and former boxing champion Muhammad Ali have brought greater awareness of _____ disease to the public. (p. 575) (10)

16. Current medical science has focused on helping young adults to take a health-maintenance, or _____ promotion, approach to their own aging, so that the diseases of old age can be reduced through proper health decisions earlier in life. (p. 583) (8)

17. A leading kind of substance problem in the elderly, one that often occurs unintentionally, is the misuse of _____ drugs. (p. 567) (12)

19. The drugs that are currently prescribed for patients with Alzheimer's disease affect glutamate and _____, the neurotransmitters that play important roles in memory. (p. 578) (13)

Down

1. The human memory system that contains all of the information that we have accrued over the years is called _____-term memory. (p. 573) (4)

2. A combination of alcohol abuse and an improper diet can lead to a deficiency of vitamin B, which in turn can lead to _____ syndrome. The primary symptom is the inability to remember newly encoded information. (p. 576) (10)

4. Named after a German physician in 1907, _____ disease is the most common form of dementia, accounting for nearly two-thirds of all cases. (p. 570) (10)

6. Neurofibrillary _____ are twisted protein fibers that form within certain brain cells as people age, and they are directly implicated in Alzheimer's disease. (p. 572) (7)

7. Because Alzheimer's disease resembles Creutzfeldt-Jakob disease, some researchers have proposed a _____ theory to explain the origins of Alzheimer's disease. This theory has not found support to date, however. (p. 757) (5)

9. The field of psychology dedicated to the mental health of elderly people is called _____. (p. 563) (14)

10. One form of dementia that is caused by a slow-acting virus in the body is Creutzfeldt-_____ disease. People with this illness experience muscular spasms in addition to the cognitive symptoms of dementia. (p. 575) (5)

11. _____ is a very common experience for the elderly, occurring in as many as 20 percent of individuals in old age. The rate is highest for older women. (p. 564) (10)

13. _____ dementia occurs when a series of strokes, sometimes too small to be recognized by the patient, add up to significant brain injury and a loss of cognitive functions. (p. 575) (8)

15. People with Alzheimer's disease have an excessive number of senile _____, which are sphere-shaped deposits of beta-amyloid proteins that form between certain brain cells and in certain blood vessels. (p. 572) (7)

18. The human memory system that collects and processes new information is called _____-term memory, and is also known as *working* memory. (p. 573) (5)

CROSSWORD PUZZLE—CHAPTER 19

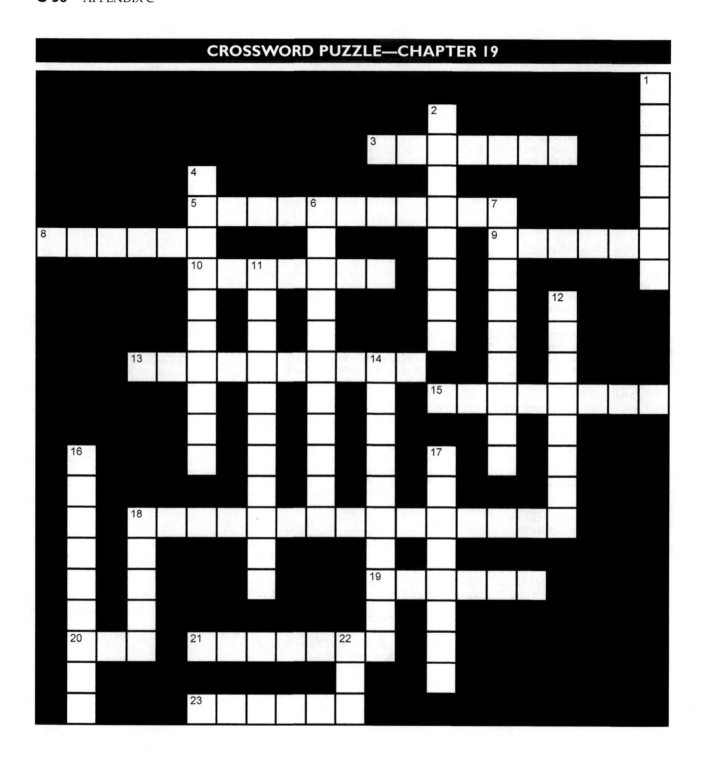

Across

3. The influential 1976 case of *Tarasoff v. Regents of the University of California* gave rise to a new ethical code that therapists have a duty to _____ a person who is the proposed victim of a client's criminal intent. (p. 610) (7)

5. When an individual is (1) unable to understand the charges against them, and/or (2) unable to aid their attorney in their own defense, they may be found mentally _____ to stand trial. In such a case, that individual would be kept in a mental health facility until their mental status improved. (p. 597) (11)

8. The criterion of insanity that states that a person is not criminally responsible for an act if that act was the result of a mental disorder or defect is known as the _____ test. (p. 591) (6)

9. Justin was civilly committed to a psychiatric hospital, and while there the staff forced him to undergo electroconvulsive therapy despite his attempt to decline the treatments. In this case, the treating facility has violated Justin's right to _____ treatment. (p. 603) (6)

10. After coming home from work to find his wife having a sexual affair with another man, Bernard took a gun and killed his wife and her lover. When he was tried for murder, he claimed that he was not guilty of the crime under the terms of the irresistible _____ test, because he acted in an uncontrollable fit of passion. (p. 591) (7)

13. Many companies have started providing employee _____ programs that offer psychological counseling to their workers through contracted mental health providers. (p. 611) (10)

15. Because there has been such public outcry over recent increases in sex crimes, 21 states have passed *sexually violent* _____ laws that require psychiatric treatment for sex offenders after their jail term has been served. This differs from past statutes where treatment was offered *instead* of jail time. (p. 597) (8)

18. The principle that certain professionals will not divulge the information they obtain from a client is known as _____; however, this code does have exceptions. In those exceptional cases, a therapist may be legally and ethically required to reveal to authorities secrets that a client has shared. (p. 610) (15)

19. Each profession within the mental health field has its own code of _____, which is a body of principles and rules for ethical behavior designed to guide decisions and actions by members of that profession. (p. 609) (6)

20. One verdict option that jurors can consider in addition to NGRI is *guilty but mentally* _____, which gives them the ability to convict a person whom they perceive as being dangerous but also recommend psychiatric treatment in addition to jail time. Some experts believe that this verdict serves no useful purpose. (p. 594) (3)

21. Of all persons who are found NGRI after committing a crime, physical _____ makes up the largest percentage of their crimes at 38%. (Hint: See figure 19-1.) (p. 592) (7)

23. Sometimes clinicians actually go to work for an insurance company, examining the treatment records of other professionals to make sure that money is being properly spent for the most effective treatments. This is called a peer _____ system. (p. 612) (6)

Down

1. An insurance program in which the insurance company decides the cost, method, provider, and length of psychological treatment is called a _____ care program. (p. 612) (7)

2. _____ psychology is the field of study that refers to the intersection of the mental health and legal/judicial fields. (p. 590) (8)

4. When a defendant's mental dysfunctioning is viewed as an extenuating circumstance in consideration of their guilt for committing a crime, they may be found *guilty with* _____ *capacity.* This finding can open the door for a reduced sentence in specific circumstances. (p. 595) (10)

6. A _____ suit is a legal suit charging a therapist with improper conduct in the course of treatment. (p. 605) (11)

7. When an individual is committed, either civilly or criminally, they have the legal right to _____. Such interventions are legally required to be adequate to give the individual an opportunity to improve their psychological functioning. (p. 603) (9)

11. Of all prison inmates who displayed the symptoms of a psychiatric disorder, a majority of them (52 percent) met the diagnostic requirements for a _____ disorder, with antisocial being the most common type. (p. 598) (11)

12. One form of criminal commitment occurs when a person accused of a crime pleads not guilty by reason of _____, or NGRI. By making this claim, the defendant is stating that they were mentally unstable *at the time of the crime*, and therefore not guilty of wrongdoing. (p. 590) (8)

14. When an individual is judged to be mentally unstable at the time a criminal act occurred, they may be sent to a mental institution instead of prison. This process is called criminal _____. (p. 590) (10)

16. A 2-PC, also known as a two-_____ certificate, refers to the fact that in many states the assent of two specific mental health or medical professionals is necessary in order to commit a person for psychiatric treatment against his or her will. (pp. 600–601) (9)

17. An attempt to assassinate the Prime Minister of England in 1843 gave rise to the _____ test (or rule), that states a person is not guilty of a crime if they did not know right from wrong or if they did not know the nature of the act they were committing. (p. 591) (8)

18. _____ commitment is a legal process by which an individual can be forced to undergo mental health treatment even when they have committed no crime or illegal act. (p. 598) (5)

22. The American _____ Institute Test, formulated in 1955, combined aspects of the M'Naghten, irresistible impulse, and Durham tests. (p. 592) (3)

Answers to Crossword Puzzle 1—Chapter 1

The completed crossword grid contains the following answers:

- Across: ILLNESS, SHAMAN, MORAL, FREUD, DISTRESS, CARE, NORMS, ASYLUMS, EXORCISM, ECCENTRICITY, HUMORS, PREVENTION, DANGER, PSYCHOANALYSIS, CONTACTS, HEALER, TREPHINATION, HYSTERICAL, PRACTITIONERS, SZASZ
- Down: WOLVERSMSBEDLAM, ABNORMALITY, STITUTE, PSYCHOTHROTR, PREFERRED, CICINTISTS, DINDIX, SOMEMARVAPOAC, SUFFOCATION, DEPRIVATION, CRIMINAL, MOLESTATIONNT, MULTICULTURAL, PITYPSYCHOYU, TREATMENT, PRACTICE

Page References Answers to Crossword Puzzle 1—Chapter 1

Clue Numbers Across	Textbook Pages	Clue Numbers Down	Textbook Pages
3	5	1	10
5	9	4	2
7	1	5	13
8	12	6	16
9	15	8	15
12	4	10	12
14	19	11	12
17	3	12	16
19	12	13	7
20	9	15	13
22	13	16	13
23	9	18	3
24	17	21	19
26	5	25	18
27	15	26	18
28	7	29	6
32	7	30	3
33	9	31	12
35	15	34	17
36	2		

Answers to Crossword Puzzle 2—Chapter 2

Page References Answers to Crossword Puzzle 2—Chapter 2

Clue Numbers	Textbook Pages	Clue Numbers	Textbook Pages
Across		**Down**	
1	39	2	41
3	35	4	33
7	35	5	36
9	38	6	26
11	32	7	32
14	26	8	36
15	26	10	40
19	27	12	27
20	30	13	35
23	38	16	36
24	30	17	41
25	30	18	30
		21	39
		22	37

Answers to Crossword Puzzle 3—Chapter 3

FAMILY
REALITY
DEFENSE
GENES
CLASSICAL
GESTALT
OPERANT
PSYCHODYNAMIC
COGNITIVE
MUTATION
CONVULSIVE
BEHAVIORAL
FEMINIST
GROUP
NEUROTRANSMITTER
BIOLOGICAL
FRUSTRATION
SYSTEMATIC
COMMUNITY
EXISTENTIAL
SYNAPSE
WORTH
PSYCHOTROPIC
HUNTINGTONS

Page References Answers to Crossword Puzzle 3—Chapter 3

Clue Numbers	Textbook Pages	Clue Numbers	Textbook Pages
Across		Down	
1	73	2	74
7	54	3	73
8	54	4	55
11	50	5	54
13	60	6	56
14	67	9	52
16	59	10	55
20	53	12	61
21	63	15	72
23	50	17	76
24	52	18	65
26	58	19	50
30	77	22	49
33	72	25	57
36	49	27	65
39	49	28	57
40	67	29	51
42	60	31	49
43	75	32	53
45	68	34	48
46	49	35	61
48	65	37	56
49	51	38	50
51	49	41	65
		44	55
		47	54
		50	53

Answers to Crossword Puzzle 4—Chapter 4

Page References Answers to Crossword Puzzle 4—Chapter 4

Clue Numbers	Textbook Pages	Clue Numbers	Textbook Pages
Across		**Down**	
1	88	1	85
2	84	3	99
4	88	5	109
6	90	6	94
8	83	7	84
10	92	9	96
12	99	11	84
16	90	13	99
17	90	14	96
18	99	15	83
19	93	19	109
21	84	20	86
25	100	22	107
26	96	23	85
27	107	24	83
28	94		
29	100		
30	84		
31	90		

Answers to Crossword Puzzle 5—Chapter 5

Page References Answers to Crossword Puzzle 5—Chapter 5

Clue Numbers	Textbook Pages	Clue Numbers	Textbook Pages
Across		**Down**	
1	126	1	130
6	114	2	125
10	130	3	140
11	121	4	140
12	116	5	122
14	123	7	125
15	135	9	152
16	126	13	120
17	128	15	144
19	120	18	116
21	118	20	132
23	123	22	132
24	117	24	131
26	139	25	145
27	139	26	115
30	124, 138	28	114
31	125	29	124
32	116	33	114
34	136		
35	136		
36	128		

Answers to Crossword Puzzle 6—Chapter 6

Page References Answers to Crossword Puzzle 6—Chapter 6

Clue Numbers	Textbook Pages	Clue Numbers	Textbook Pages
Across		**Down**	
1	156	2	168
4	179	3	182
7	182	5	183
11	171	6	156
13	178–179	8	155
14	157	9	166
17	171	10	171
18	156	12	162
19	171	15	170
22	169	16	156
23	155	20	160
24	156	21	170
26	153	25	182
28	154	26	166
30	157	27	153
31	179	28	171
32	174	29	162–163
33	162	30	155
34	158		
35	172		
36	179		
37	183		

Answers to Crossword Puzzle 7—Chapter 7

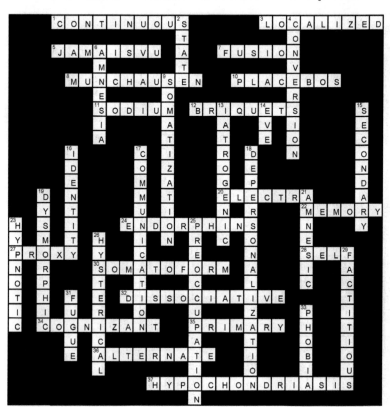

Page References Answers to Crossword Puzzle 7—Chapter 7

Clue Numbers	Textbook Pages	Clue Numbers	Textbook Pages
Across		**Down**	
1	204	2	211
3	204	4	190
5	213	6	204
7	215	9	192
8	194	13	209
10	200	14	202
11	214	15	198
12	192	16	208
20	197	17	199
22	202	18	215
24	200	19	195
27	194	21	208
28	212	23	196
30	190	25	194
32	202	26	190
34	208	29	194
35	198	31	205
36	208	33	195
37	194		

Answers to Crossword Puzzle 8—Chapter 8

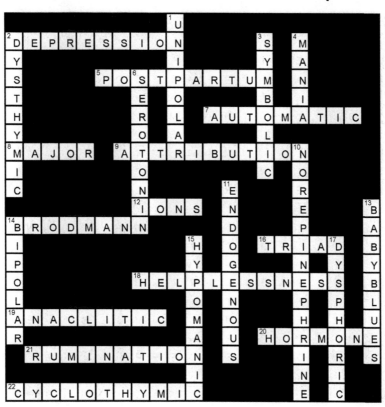

Page References Answers to Crossword Puzzle 8—Chapter 8

Clue Numbers	Textbook Pages	Clue Numbers	Textbook Pages
Across		**Down**	
2	223	1	223
5	228–229	2	228
7	237	3	235
8	228	4	223
9	240	6	232
12	251	10	232
14	233	11	228
16	237	13	229
18	239	14	223–224, 244
19	235	15	246
20	242	17	252
21	243		
22	249		

Answers to Crossword Puzzle 9—Chapter 9

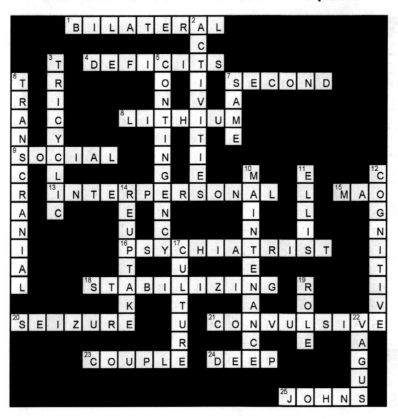

Page References Answers to Crossword Puzzle 9—Chapter 9

Clue Numbers	Textbook Pages	Clue Numbers	Textbook Pages
Across		**Down**	
1	267–268	2	262
4	265	5	261
7	281	6	274
8	278	7	267
9	261	10	270
13	265	11	262
15	269	12	262–263
16	260	14	271
18	278	17	264
20	267	19	265
21	266–269	22	273
23	266		
24	274		
25	267		

Answers to Crossword Puzzle 10—Chapter 10

Page References Answers to Crossword Puzzle 10—Chapter 10

Clue Numbers	Textbook Pages	Clue Numbers	Textbook Pages
Across		**Down**	
1	295	2	286
5	299	3	293
6	298	4	297
9	288	5	299
11	288	7	293
14	286	8	288
18	293	10	289
19	304	11	308
20	291	12	291
21	310	13	309
22	303	15	288
		16	288
		17	299

Answers to Crossword Puzzle 11—Chapter 11

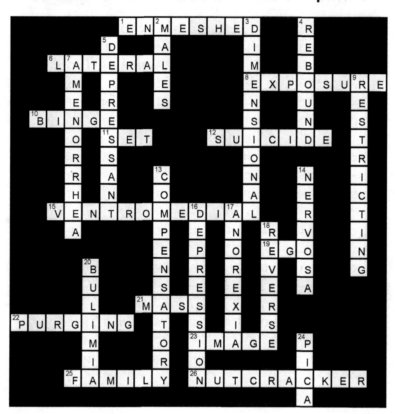

Page References Answers to Crossword Puzzle 11—Chapter 11

Clue Numbers	Textbook Pages	Clue Numbers	Textbook Pages
Across		**Down**	
1	331	2	334
6	327	3	324
8	340	4	328
10	320	5	341
11	324	7	320
12	319	9	318
15	328	13	320
19	324	14	320
21	328	16	327
22	318	18	335
23	335	20	320
25	331	24	343
26	342		

Answers to Crossword Puzzle 12—Chapter 12

Page References Answers to Crossword Puzzle 12—Chapter 12

Clue Numbers	Textbook Pages	Clue Numbers	Textbook Pages
Across		**Down**	
2	348	1	378
5	379	3	367
7	361	4	356
8	381	6	378
9	374	11	364
10	377	14	361
12	374	15	369
13	357	16	354–355
17	358	18	366
21	358	19	366
23	365	20	352
25	355	22	364
27	353	24	355
30	366	26	369
32	349	28	348
34	348	29	348
35	356	31	377
36	355	33	348
37	355	34	372
38	360	39	361
40	361	40	348
42	362	41	349
44	356		
45	369		

Answers to Crossword Puzzle 13—Chapter 13

Page References Answers to Crossword Puzzle 13—Chapter 13

Clue Numbers	Textbook Pages	Clue Numbers	Textbook Pages
Across		**Down**	
1	413	2	392
4	393	3	410
7	406	5	393
10	415	6	399
13	401	8	411
15	388	9	394
17	389	11	403
18	392	13	392
19	402	14	403
20	414	16	408
22	408	21	401
24	389	23	394
26	415	25	418
30	401	27	397
33	416	28	399
34	395	29	405
35	390	31	416
36	410	32	407

Answers to Crossword Puzzle 14—Chapter 14

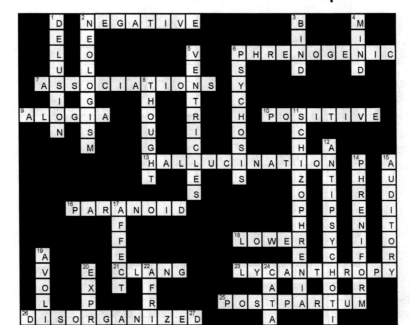

Page References Answers to Crossword Puzzle 14—Chapter 14

Clue Numbers	Textbook Pages	Clue Numbers	Textbook Pages
Across		**Down**	
2	431	1	427
6	440	2	429
7	429	3	444
9	431	4	426
10	427	5	439
13	430	6	426
16	433	8	429
18	426	11	426
21	429	12	437
23	429	14	435
26	433	17	432
28	438	19	432
29	433	20	444
30	437	22	442
		24	432
		27	426

Answers to Crossword Puzzle 15—Chapter 15

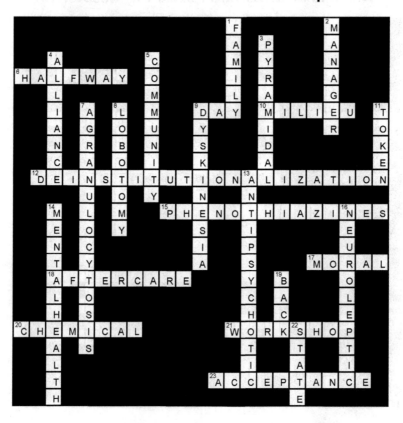

Page References Answers to Crossword Puzzle 15—Chapter 15

Clue Numbers	Textbook Pages	Clue Numbers	Textbook Pages
Across		**Down**	
6	467	1	462–463
9	466	2	468
10	452	3	468
12	465	4	470
15	455	5	466
17	451	7	458
18	466	8	453
20	466	9	457
21	467	11	453
23	461	13	455
		14	465
		16	456
		19	451
		22	451

Answers to Crossword Puzzle 16—Chapter 16

Page References Answers to Crossword Puzzle 16—Chapter 16

Clue Numbers	Textbook Pages	Clue Numbers	Textbook Pages
Across		**Down**	
3	489	1	487
7	487	2	483
8	479	4	494
10	504	5	496
11	508	6	489
13	482	9	484
14	487	12	485
17	475	13	493
20	506	16	501
22	476	17	479
23	512	18	501
24	481	19	507
25	480		

Answers to Crossword Puzzle 17—Chapter 17

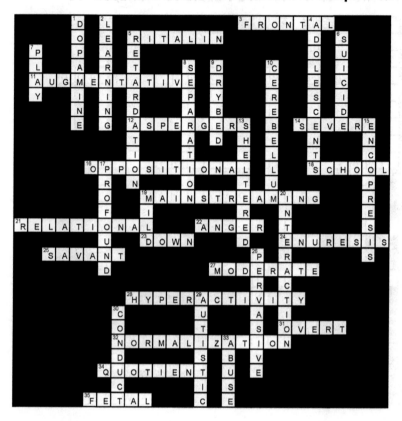

Page References Answers to Crossword Puzzle 17—Chapter 17

Clue Numbers	Textbook Pages	Clue Numbers	Textbook Pages
Across		**Down**	
3	532	1	532
5	532	2	549
11	546	4	522
12	541	6	524
14	551	8	520
16	525	9	536
18	521	10	543
19	554	13	555
21	527	15	555
22	530	17	551
23	552	19	550
24	535	20	527
25	542	26	538
27	551	29	539
28	530	30	526
31	526	33	537
32	554		
34	548		
35	553		

Answers to Crossword Puzzle 18—Chapter 18

Completed crossword grid with answers: LOG, KOS, DEMENTIA, ALZHEIMER, INFARCT, AMNESTIC, VRAE, GENE, JAKAKB, DELIRIUM, AUTOPSY, PARKINSONS, VASCULAR, PLAQUE, WELLNESS, PRESCRIPTION, ACETYLCHOLINE, PSYCHOLOGY, etc.

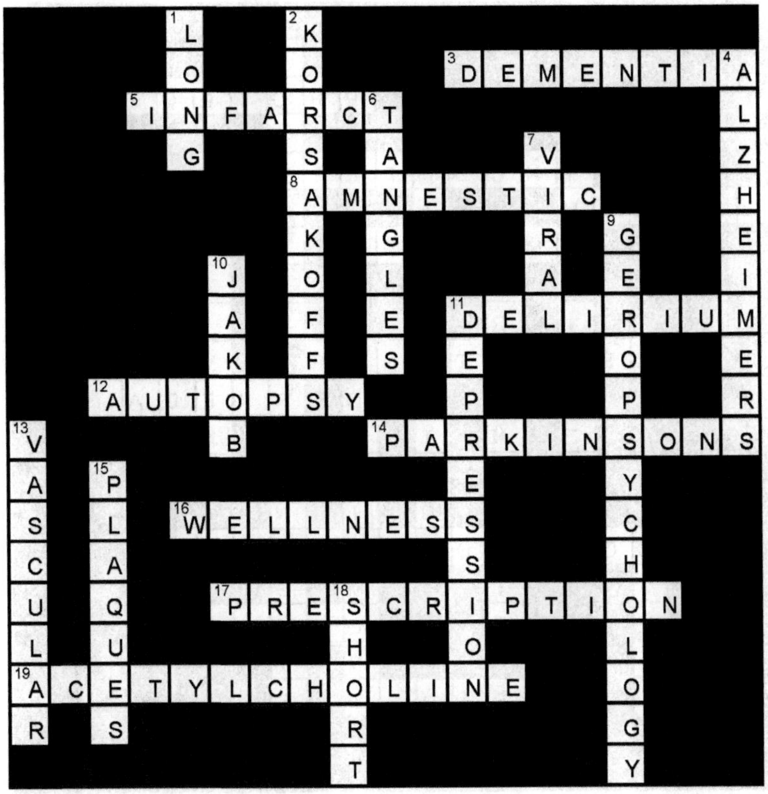

Page References Answers to Crossword Puzzle 18—Chapter 18

Clue Numbers Across	Textbook Pages	Clue Numbers Down	Textbook Pages
3	570	1	573
5	575	2	576
8	576	4	570
11	569	6	572
12	576	7	757
16	583	9	563
17	567	10	575
19	578	11	564
		13	575
		15	572
		18	573

Answers to Crossword Puzzle 19—Chapter 19

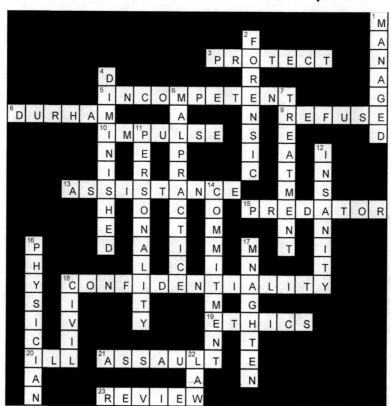

Page References Answers to Crossword Puzzle 19—Chapter 19

Clue Numbers	Textbook Pages	Clue Numbers	Textbook Pages
Across		**Down**	
3	610	1	612
5	597	2	590
8	591	4	595
9	603	6	605
13	591	7	603
15	597	11	598
18	610	12	590
19	609	16	600–601
20	594	17	591
21	592	18	598
23	612	22	592

Word Searches

*Answers follow starting on page D-40.

CHAPTER I WORD SEARCH

```
A S L A V W B Q A U V H P F W K W O B J D V J H B
L T J Y B Q E U T K N W X R T U S G K X E E X Z X
I V T T Z V F I V V W M L Q I B M U M V I G J B P
A M O R A L T R E A T M E N T V B E V Q N Y Z V D
P H G A L P P T G T L Y J Y L F A M Q N S N Y F O
S G A U E N S Q O R J U A Q L I G T P E T N G E H
Y R I S A E Y Y E E J J J L G E Z B E R I I N Q T
C M L V S T C X C P J S Q Q S X P X X S T E C Q R
H Z T H S R H F B H Z W K K K O O B V T U M W K Q
O F L A U E O Q H I O P H Y R R S I Z A T D Q P Z
G I B V G A T E Z N W A E I J C I U M T I D I R E
E L V B J T R X F A C V N R T I T K W E O H G E S
N N F W H M O I L T H S C A T S I F D H N U Y V O
I Q J V B E P A M I C O G I L M V Q S O A M Z E M
C Q C Z Y N I Q G O X L G P Z Y E X M S L O W N A
W I C U U T C W O N F E K U W X S D H P I R B T T
X S M E O A S Z D C L J U O M T K I E I Z S V I O
C X F H V D F I Q H K F X W C Z U Q S T A J N O G
R A B N O R M A L P S Y C H O L O G Y A T A T N E
O J P C X E B T V U M Y B M G J T H D L I G W N N
R Q T O M U L T I C U L T U R A L F K S O P N M I
I X G T K K T J L T X F A S I H F Y Q T N P L O C
M E U I A Y R A S Y L U M U M L W T N O R M S P F
C U L T U R E G M I E C C E N T R I C M R F S W S
C M A B J N X F C I T V P P W W F O R Q Q Z N R N
```

Chapter I CLUES

1. _____ A procedure designed to help change abnormal behavior into more normal behavior. Also called *therapy*.

2. _____ A society's stated and unstated rules for proper conduct.

3. _____ Classification of medications that primarily affect the brain and reduce various symptoms of mental dysfunctioning.

4. _____ The discharge of large numbers of patients from long-term institutional care so that they might be treated in community programs.

5. _____ A psychotherapy arrangement in which a person directly pays a therapist or counseling service.

6. _____ A subfield of psychology that focuses on study and enhancement of positive feelings, traits, and abilities.

7. _____ The perspective that abnormal psychological functioning has physical causes.

8. _____ According to Greek and Roman physicians, bodily chemicals that influence mental and physical functioning.

9. _____ A nineteenth-century approach to treating people with mental dysfunction that emphasized moral guidance and humane and respectful treatment. [two words]

10. _____ The scientific study of abnormal behavior in an effort to describe, predict, explain, and change abnormal patterns of functioning. [two words]

11. _____ A type of institution that first became popular in the sixteenth century to provide care for persons with mental disorders. Most became virtual prisons.

12. _____ Person who deviates from conventional norms in odd, irregular, or even bizarre ways, but is not displaying a psychological disorder.

13. _____ The perspective that the chief causes of abnormal functioning are psychological.

14. _____ A key feature of community mental health programs that seek to prevent or minimize psychological disorders.

15. _____ An ancient operation in which a stone instrument was used to cut away a circular section of the skull, perhaps to treat abnormal behavior.

16. _____ Either the theory or the treatment of abnormal mental functioning that emphasizes unconscious psychological forces as the cause of psychopathology.

17. _____ The practice in early societies of treating abnormality by coaxing evil spirits to leave the person's body.

18. _____ The field of psychology that examines the impact of culture, race, ethnicity, gender, and similar factors on our behaviors and thoughts, and also focuses on how such factors may influence the origin, nature, and treatment of abnormal behavior.

19. _____ State-run public mental institutions in the United States. [two words]

20. _____ A people's common history, values, institutions, habits, skills, technology, and arts.

CHAPTER 2 WORD SEARCH

```
U M Y M C C I N T E R N A L V A L I D I T Y G H R
B S V H E P I D E M I O L O G I C A L G N M Y B W
S C I E N T I F I C M E T H O D L P Z J Q M S T J
J X C O R R E L A T I O N G E F T F U I K R J U Y
B X D Q Q U A S I - E X P E R I M E N T L K N T U
L E I J N K X D B M T M F J S P C N M Z O O I L T
I H P E Z F H N V X X X F B V E I P V A K O N S D
N R S O B T J E X P E R I M E N T L C N O T C C W
D A A M X X H N L I E P M Y Z Z J A H A B E I O H
D K J N D L O N G I T U D I N A L C W L L X D N K
E P S Q D E S S C C H R G K X D P E C O K T E T E
S P R U C O P X S A O C E Z N I J B M G V E N R E
I M V E F V M E Q T S N W R L G L O X U P R C O J
G Z B C V H A A N H H E F F L M B T Y E I N E L B
N J C A C A Z R S D S T S O V V P H C E I A Y G K
Q H D U Z J L A T S E L Y T U E X E C X N L C R G
C U B R F U V E U N I N I X U N F R A P D V Z O M
V H V J K I G I N W G G T D O D D A A E E A E U B
K G K O H J S H Q C W V N K I O Y P Z R P L R P D
T O Y F V M S G D W E L Q M T T E Y E I E I W A B
C S P F T X E B O V N L T M E Q K G N M N D Q B E
L Z D V X N O M O T H E T I C N O U B E D I J T O
W T M G S M V V Z V U N A G Y E T R N N E T X K J
H U M T O K K N U F U M H A T D Z T K T N Y Z O E
C W D T Z H Q Q V A G H M B F X M K K W T J O K F
```

Chapter 2 CLUES

1. _____ A research procedure in which a variable is manipulated and the effect of the manipulation is observed.

2. _____ A type of study that observes the same subjects on many occasions over a long period of time.

3. _____ The variable in an experiment that is expected to change as the independent variable is manipulated.

4. _____ The accuracy with which a study can pinpoint one of various possible factors as the cause of a phenomenon. [two words]

5. _____ In an experiment, a group of subjects who are not exposed to the independent variable. [two words]

6. _____ A detailed account of a person's life and psychological problems. [two words]

7. _____ The number of new cases of a disorder occurring in a population over a specific period of time.

8. _____ An experiment in which investigators make use of control and experimental groups that already exist in the world at large. Also called a *mixed design.* [two words, hyphenated]

9. _____ A research method in which the experimenter produces abnormal-like behavior in laboratory subjects and then conducts experiments on the subjects. [two words]

10. _____ A general understanding of the nature, causes, and treatments of abnormal psychological functioning in the form of laws or principles.

11. _____ A type of study that measures the incidence and prevalence of a disorder in a given population.

12. _____ An experiment in which subjects do not know whether they are in the experimental or the control condition. [two words]

13. _____ The process of systematically gathering and evaluating information through careful observations to gain an understanding of a phenomenon. [two words]

14. _____ The degree to which events or characteristics vary along with each other.

15. _____ A sham treatment that the subject in an experiment believes to be genuine. [two words]

16. _____ The variable in an experiment that is manipulated to determine whether it has an effect on another variable.

17. _____ The degree to which the results of a study may be generalized beyond that study. [two words]

18. _____ A selection procedure that ensures that participants are randomly placed either in the control group or in the experimental group. [two words]

19. _____ In an experiment, a variable other than the independent variable that may also be acting on the dependent variable.

20. _____ The total number of cases of a disorder occurring in a population over a specific period of time.

CHAPTER 3 WORD SEARCH

```
O D W M N C B B I O P S Y C H O S O C I A L U P X
O B J E C T R E L A T I O N S D L H J O L T U L Z
J K E H E D I A T H E S I S - S T R E S S W N P N
E W O L M I P O P M N O P S R R Z W Z Y S D O E X
O V H O O B S P S Q P J Q B R P P D T T A P U R Q
X Z K J D M Y E Y R Q O D M L J V N B D H R R M F
V D G A E E C R C J P K X B M V T G I W V H C T F
Q R S C L L H A H H J V M B M V F I X A T I O N J
O O V M I E O N O W M B J N B Y Q S P M Z C B X M
Y N O L N C S T T Q T H M S E R K S E A W S F I T
X K Y O G T U C R A B A X D F U W C Z N Q E V P S
C P N P J R R O O X I R S K E M R A A T R Z Y Y W
O V K O O O G N P K U L P E A W N O K I E X T J H
G S M W U C E D I Y W P P G X C D P N D C I I O W
N K T H Z O R I C D J X W O J C E U V E E S K J B
I O Q H T N Y T W C T S S G U Z A Y L P P S Q U Y
T C T D R V Q I E E G Y M O D E L X B R T U K M U
I R M X H U H O B H Q N H Q O O E K D E O P N Z Q
V H P I N S K N C T K A G R O U P L L S R E W P V
E V F D D I A I H I A P D M Y N N V B S Z R Z F L
U F Y H R V J N K E P S L X J X I N V A U E X U T
F P U D Q E F G R J I E Y Y X J P H K N Z G N E T
Q I N E U R O T R A N S M I T T E R A T T O W B W
S Q K U R K Y N A C K S W G U T I B D S S L J Z Y
O W C L I E N T - C E N T E R E D T H E R A P Y R
```

Chapter 3 CLUES

1. _____ Psychotropic drugs that improve the mood of people with depression.

2. _____ A set of assumptions and concepts that help scientists explain and interpret observations. Also called a *paradigm*.

3. _____ According to Freud, the psychological force that employs reason and operates in accordance with the reality principle.

4. _____ A nerve cell. The brain contains billions of them.

5. _____ A chemical that, released by one neuron, crosses the synaptic space to be received at receptors on the dendrites of neighboring neurons.

6. _____ A type of therapy developed by Aaron Beck that helps people identify and change the maladaptive assumptions and ways of thinking that help cause their psychological disorders.

7. _____ According to Freud, a condition in which the id, ego, and superego do not mature properly, causing the person to become entrapped at an early stage of development.

8. _____ A process of learning in which behavior that leads to satisfying consequences, or rewards, is likely to be repeated. [two words]

9. _____ Drugs that primarily affect the brain and reduce various symptoms of mental dysfunction.

10. _____ The humanistic therapy developed by Carl Rogers in which clinicians try to help clients by being accepting,

empathizing accurately and conveying genuineness [three words; hyphenated]

11. _____ A form of treatment, used primarily in cases of unipolar depression, in which electrodes attached to a person's head send an electric current through the brain, causing a brain seizure.

12. _____ The tiny space between the nerve ending of one neuron and the dendrite of another.

13. _____ A therapy format in which a group of people with similar problems meet together with a therapist to work on their problems.

14. _____ The view that a person must first have a predisposition to a disorder and then be subjected to immediate psychosocial stress in order to develop the disorder. [two words; hyphenated]

15. _____ A site on a neuron that receives a neurotransmitter.

16. _____ Brain surgery for mental disorders. Also called neurosurgery.

17. _____ A process of learning in which an individual acquires responses by observing and imitating others. Also, a therapy approach based on the same principle.

18. _____ According to Freud, the psychological force that emphasizes one's conscience, values, and ideals.

19. _____ Explanations that attribute the cause of abnormality to an interaction of genetic, biological, developmental, emotional, behavioral, cognitive, social, and societal influences.

20. _____ The psychodynamic theory that views the desire for relationships as the key motivating force in human behavior. [two words]

CHAPTER 4 WORD SEARCH

```
I  N  T  E  L  L  I  G  E  N  C  E  Q  U  O  T  I  E  N  T  S  L  V  O  Q
M  F  T  W  S  E  L  F  -  M  O  N  I  T  O  R  I  N  G  V  X  M  L  P  F
L  C  O  S  K  F  B  O  O  O  Y  D  I  N  S  M  H  U  A  A  E  K  R  S  Y
A  Y  L  P  O  E  D  P  X  O  K  I  X  A  Y  W  L  D  S  L  L  J  U  Y  H
V  N  O  A  V  T  R  V  N  J  I  A  E  T  N  B  K  M  S  I  S  A  D  C  V
W  N  A  L  S  I  P  Q  K  Y  W  G  P  U  D  Y  U  M  E  D  T  G  V  H  A
I  B  F  L  Y  S  A  N  D  P  G  N  D  R  R  X  Q  T  S  I  A  U  U  O  J
D  C  K  C  O  B  I  G  L  Z  D  O  M  A  O  J  S  T  S  T  N  Y  B  P  Q
I  K  L  L  G  G  B  F  G  F  Z  S  J  L  M  F  U  E  M  Y  D  J  Q  H  Z
O  E  E  I  R  G  F  S  I  H  R  I  W  I  E  C  U  S  E  L  A  L  M  Y  H
G  C  V  N  E  E  F  N  D  C  H  S  K  S  K  N  W  T  N  Y  R  R  E  S  Y
R  B  Q  I  L  A  S  G  X  M  A  S  I  T  I  Y  I  Z  T  U  D  A  N  I  I
A  E  O  C  I  X  N  M  E  A  D  T  T  I  P  W  C  M  R  X  I  P  T  O  Z
P  Q  A  A  A  A  E  C  H  P  R  Q  I  C  T  K  I  Y  K  O  Z  P  A  L  G
H  N  G  L  B  I  U  C  C  O  R  E  V  O  X  S  I  J  E  V  A  R  L  O  T
I  E  Z  I  I  E  R  T  A  Z  Z  O  J  B  N  Z  X  W  W  M  T  O  S  G  T
C  D  N  N  L  R  O  O  P  Z  O  P  J  S  Z  S  S  W  C  P  I  C  T  I  X
O  F  X  T  I  C  L  Z  H  L  B  L  K  E  F  Q  Y  U  F  X  O  H  A  C  S
L  P  D  E  T  C  O  P  B  X  X  G  P  R  C  Q  C  S  U  N  N  E  T  A  E
D  E  C  R  Y  O  G  P  B  Q  F  H  V  V  O  T  D  G  T  S  H  M  U  L  S
F  A  U  V  Y  L  I  N  H  A  O  B  D  A  A  L  I  P  Z  E  F  E  S  G  W
N  A  X  I  Z  L  C  D  R  Y  K  X  U  T  I  J  N  V  L  G  M  N  E  Q  O
R  Z  O  E  F  B  A  T  T  E  R  Y  J  I  E  X  F  B  E  D  W  T  X  X  G
C  G  W  W  F  K  L  M  E  S  O  D  Q  O  M  Y  M  P  T  B  X  D  A  R  Q
D  R  V  R  H  R  M  F  I  Q  U  A  S  N  I  E  I  U  J  B  G  F  M  Z  R
```

Chapter 4 CLUES

1. _____ Clients' observation of their own behavior. [two words; hyphenated]

2. _____ The process of collecting and interpreting relevant information about a client or subject.

3. _____ A cluster of symptoms that usually occur together.

4. _____ A set of interview questions and observations designed to reveal the degree and nature of a client's abnormal functioning. [three words]

5. _____ A test that consists of vague material that people interpret or respond to.

6. _____ The process of administering a test to a large group of persons whose performance then serves as a common standard or norm against which any individual's score can be measured.

7. _____ A method for observing behavior in which people are observed in artificial settings such as clinicians' offices or laboratories.

8. _____ A measure of the consistency of test or research results.

9. _____ A determination that a person's problems reflect a particular disorder.

10. _____ A device for gathering information about a few aspects of a person's psychological functioning from which broader information about the person can be inferred.

11. _____ A test that measures physical responses (such as heart rate and muscle tension) as possible indicators of psychological problems.

12. _____ The accuracy of a test's or study's results; that is, the extent to which the test or study actually measures or shows what it claims to.

13. _____ A series of tests, each of which each measures a specific skill area.

14. _____ An understanding of the behavior of a particular individual.

15. _____ A general score derived from an intelligence test that theoretically represents a person's overall intellectual capacity. [two words]

16. _____ A list of disorders, along with descriptions of symptoms and guidelines for making appropriate diagnoses. [two words]

17. _____ An effort to identify a set of common strategies that characterize the work of all effective therapists.

18. _____ A test that directly measures brain structure or activity.

19. _____ A face-to-face encounter in which clinicians ask questions of clients, weigh their responses and reactions, and learn about them and their psychological problems. [two words]

20. _____ A method of observing behavior in which clinicians or researchers observe people in their everyday environments. [two words]

CHAPTER 5 WORD SEARCH

```
O B S E S S I O N Z D Z S E R O T O N I N I W O M
R F L O R W Q M K V R U N D O I N G Y E C E R C C
O E S E W W E D E M H C A U D A T E N U C L E I L
A A L P M Z N A J P R E P A R E D N E S S B M T X
T R R V M F I U W O G H R Y N M W Z M G E E X R W
Z H G A B A F P K T I Y G I L U G U P X O N B E T
K I A X Q V Q A N B D V X N K D I G B I M Z F C Q
U E G N H R B N M B Q N E K T T E C I W R O S O Z
P R O F E U K Q W I O V P A N I C L D J G D T M Q
H A R M S P P E R W L E T X I N N G B I K I B P U
O R A P O P S M L Q R Y K X E M R J K A H A I U R
B C P N B M J Z I D W K P A W Y Q P Y Z N Z O L A
I H H Y P C L I E N T - C E N T E R E D X E F S M
A Y O Z U A N X I E T Y W M D D K D W C P P E I R
G L B N P P C B W P X M J C Q I U N W N F I E O E
D Z I C B I D T L V M U U I C F G M M W Z N D N S
K I A R X A K H Q X A N I T C V V R W C J E B J P
S H D H K S Y B S A O D M E U J M P E N C S A S O
D K E P Q I Y V L X C D A R W C D J Z E V J C H N
S E D A T I V E - H Y P N O T I C L E J T N K T S
C U X J W O L Z S O K R Y F E S P U X O M E D D E
S L U E G C Q X G D S I N T E E Q A A E N B G S M
A H G C Z Y Y X L T Z I S T A A T V Z R S D S X U
N B H Z X F Y S B Y R A K T I R R Y I Z R F X N E
I Z P Q Q T P N O R E P I N E P H R I N E B K D L
```

Chapter 5 CLUES

1. _____ A persistent and unreasonable fear of a particular object, activity, or situation.

2. _____ A neurotransmitter whose abnormal activity is linked to depression and panic disorder.

3. _____ The central nervous system's physiological and emotional response to a vague sense of threat or danger.

4. _____ An anxiety disorder in which a person is afraid to be in places or situations from which escape might be difficult (or embarrassing) or help unavailable if panic-like symptoms were to occur.

5. _____ The humanistic therapy developed by Carl Rogers in which clinicians try to help clients by being accepting, empathizing accurately, and conveying genuineness. [two words; hyphenated]

6. _____A drug used in low doses to reduce anxiety and in higher doses to help people sleep. Also called *anxiolytic drug.* [two words; hypenanted]

7. _____ An anxiety disorder marked by recurrent and unpredictable panic attacks.

8. _____ The neurotransmitter gamma-aminobutyric acid, whose low activity has been linked to generalized anxiety disorder.

9. _____ A list of objects or situations that frighten a person, starting with those that are slightly feared and ending with those that are feared greatly. [two words]

10. _____ A repetitive and rigid behavior or mental act that a person feels driven to perform in order to prevent or reduce anxiety.

11. _____ A neurotransmitter whose abnormal activity is linked to depression, obsessive-compulsive disorder, and eating disorders.

12. _____ A technique in which a client is given information about physiological reactions as they occur and learns to control the reactions voluntarily.

13. _____ An ego defense mechanism whereby a person unconsciously cancels out an unacceptable desire or act by performing another act.

14. _____ The most common group of antianxiety drugs, which includes Valium and Xanax.

15. _____ Structures in the brain, within the region known as the basal ganglia, that help convert sensory information into thoughts and actions. [two words]

16. _____ The central nervous system's physiological and emotional response to a serious threat to one's well-being.

17. Exposure and _____ prevention. A behavioral treatment for obsessive-compulsive disorder that exposes a client to anxiety-arousing thoughts or situations and then prevents the client from performing his or her compulsive acts. Also called *exposure and ritual prevention.*

18. _____ A persistent thought, idea, impulse, or image that is experienced repeatedly, feels intrusive, and causes anxiety.

19. _____ A research design in which investigators determine how many and which relatives of a person with a disorder have the same disorder. [two words]

20. _____ A predisposition to develop certain fears.

CHAPTER 6 WORD SEARCH

```
S T B U N U F A U N I D K T B B G C T Z N J U K P
Z X J X A M Y U R A C C O O J F A A F E U L C E R
U U M E D I T A T I O N X V G L M L J X J I X M C
A N N I M M U N E S Y S T E M R J U G H H G I R X
V E I M H O U V J B F E E U Z Y R C C K U W O Q X
Q A Y B M R P J M P O S T T R A U M A T I C F F P
V H N D M A A Q I E H C V J L V O S U L P H B D S
C Y N T D A S E N N O Z Q W J Y K F R A U P W Y
H P A E I K G K D D V R H F J X R W V P R O F B C
A E L X M G N N - O R T A U I I A X B D A Z O T H
A R Z P Q V E D B C E I D K Y G P N A S S Q U R O
A T F V C L J N O R V C E G W M G L V T Y R J A P
Y E R T Q D Z N D I J O T N G R R F M W M E F I H
C N Y A U C J J Y N O S Y A D C O R N J P A G T Y
N S R Q E M N Q D E Z T P V G D U Y R T A R A D S
Y I R O D Y S A U W V E E O S Q P X E O T Z T L I
I O V H G T R M A F Q R A Q D P W U T R H N G G O
C N F C Y P A H L B R O H X K L F X Q Y E D A M L
K A I F T P O J I P K I D R D W H G G N T O Y Z O
X O P Y E F N F S S V D H F H M I G R A I N E H G
Y R F C O P P O M Y X S S T R E S S O R C L H O I
M L U P P M L U S T V T M I U I N S O M N I A M C
Q V V A S T H M A I F I J B N J O F J Y O Y M D A
Z I Q F S O R C Z H S Y M P A T H E T I C Q H E L
U A F N F L S B F W Z B H U F V N Q S J I W N O G
```

Chapter 6 CLUES

1. _____ A group of hormones released by the adrenal glands at times of stress.

2. _____ An event that creates a sense of threat by confronting a person with a demand or opportunity for change of some kind.

3. _____ A medical problem marked by narrowing of the trachea and bronchi, which results in shortness of breath, wheezing, coughing, and a choking sensation.

4. _____ A sleeplike suggestible state during which a person can be directed to act in unusual ways, to experience unusual sensations, to remember seemingly forgotten events, or to forget remembered events.

5. _____ The nerve fibers of the autonomic nervous system that quicken the heartbeat and produce other changes experienced as fear or anxiety.

6. _____ The body's network of activities and cells that identify and destroy antigens and cancer cells. [two words]

7. _____ René Descartes's position that the mind is separate from the body. [three words; hyphenated]

8. _____ The system of glands located throughout the body that helps control important activities such as growth and sexual activity.

9. _____ A technique of turning one's concentration inward and achieving a slightly changed state of consciousness.

10. _____ The general level of anxiety that a person brings to the various events in his or her life.

11. _____ A foreign invader of the body, such as a bacterium or virus.

12. _____ The nerve fibers of the autonomic nervous system that help maintain normal organ functioning. They slow organ functioning after stimulation and return other bodily processes to normal.

13. _____ The most common dyssomnia, characterized by difficulties initiating and maintaining sleep.

14. _____ An extremely severe headache that occurs on one side of the head, often preceded by a warning sensation and sometimes accompanied by dizziness, nausea, or vomiting.

15. _____ Illnesses that result from an interaction of both psychosocial and physical factors. DSMIV-TR labels these illnesses *psychological factors affecting medical condition*. Also known as *psychosomatic disorders*.

16. _____ A personality pattern characterized by hostility, cynicism, drivenness, impatience, competitiveness, and ambition. [two words]

17. _____ An anxiety disorder in which fear and related symptoms continue to be experienced long after a traumatic event.

18. _____ Chronic high blood pressure.

19. _____ A lesion that forms in the wall of the stomach or of the duodenum.

20. _____ A group that meets to talk about and explore problems in an atmosphere of mutual support.

CHAPTER 7 WORD SEARCH

```
C H P U S Y V K M J O C E W R Y L N T Y P G Z B S
B Q F E O F A W S K K H U K F W G S M P L I R T X
F I N K W T J V V G A M C M E Y B E U J A S P U V
N D S S E M S N V D U K O S J E W L N B C T K L P
C P M O E M E R I E H E Q T M H Y F C N E L U C R
D Y B M S N R M X P S S L D R H O - H F B P M R I
E A F A V A M Q O E P W X M K L M H A X O N G L M
I C U T H C V Z Q R P A X A Z I W Y U I W F S Q A
W X K I Y V W R I S Y S R H B A I P S S J A U B R
A K Q Z S D N Z Z O F E G Y E T H N E V R C B O Y
X O I A T T S W W N L C G P H R G O N Y J T P D U
I E E T E Z T Y X A Z O E O R O G S O H Z I E Y D
E S E I R V C V T L R N T C F G B I B Q K T R D G
D S P O I I Z C I I G D E H G E Z S J G L I S Y Z
I D L N C Z Y O V Z S A V O I N U A D Q N O O S T
S X O I A J O N F A M R N N U I S L W Y S U N M A
S A N G L X Z V U T B Y K D S C U I S V U S A O M
O J T Z I F V E G I Z R E R U Y T D A A W F L R N
C N Q U O S U R U O J J D I J P W A T Z Y G I P E
I V Z U M G J S E N K J F A H W K H Q L D Z T H S
A C S R T O Q I I C W X T S X A H V M U D Y I I I
T G C R U A B O C O Q B V I J Y L T N Q J F E C A
I K L D M K W N S D N G B S G D J Q O I X S S E B
V G A S T A T E - D E P E N D E N T E L S B G Z Z
E I E G C Q N F O C Q E A U E A M S S Y W C D X Q
```

Chapter 7 CLUES

1. _____ A somatoform disorder marked by numerous recurring physical ailments without an organic basis. Also known as *Briquet's syndrome.*

2. _____ An extreme and long-term form of factitious disorder in which a person produces symptoms, gains admission to a hospital, and receives treatment.

3. _____ A sham treatment that a subject believes to be genuine.

4. _____ An illness with no identifiable physical cause in which the patient is believed to be intentionally producing or faking symptoms in order to assume a sick role.

5. _____ The final merging of two or more subpersonalities in multiple personality disorder.

6. _____ The faculty for recalling past events and past learning.

7. _____ Loss of memory.

8. _____ A dissociative disorder in which a person travels to a new location and may assume a new identity, simultaneously forgetting his or her past.

9. _____ Type of learning that becomes associated with the conditions under which it occurred so that what is learned is best remembered under the same conditions. [two words; hyphenated]

10. _____ The distinct personalities found in individuals suffering from multiple personality disorder. Also known as *alternate personalities.*

11. _____ A disorder marked by a persistent and recurrent feeling of being detached from one's own mental processes or body; that is, one feels unreal and alien.

12. _____ Class of disorders marked by major changes in memory that are not due to clear physical causes.

13. _____ In psychodynamic theory, the gain achieved when hysterical symptoms elicit kindness from others or provide an excuse to avoid unpleasant activities.

14. _____ A disorder marked by excessive worry that some aspect of one's physical appearance is defective. Also known as *dysmorphophobia.* [two words]

15. _____ A somatoform disorder in which people mistakenly fear that minor changes in their physical functioning indicate a serious disease.

16. _____ The process of hypnotizing oneself—for example, to forget unpleasant events. [two words; hyphenated]

17. _____ In psychodynamic theory, the gain achieved when hysterical symptoms keep internal conflicts out of awareness.

18. _____ Produced or caused inadvertently by a clinician.

19. _____ Class of somatoform disorders in which people experience actual changes in their physical functioning.

20. _____ A somatoform disorder in which a psychosocial need or conflict is converted into dramatic physical symptoms that affect voluntary motor or sensory function.

CHAPTER 8 WORD SEARCH

```
P N X G C L D T K K N A M W V L P P H N L P E O B
M G U H S T P O S T P A R T U M F T Q G I M M J N
I L E A R N E D H E L P L E S S N E S S Y S B V M
L H H Z L O U N I P O L A R N V D R E A C T I V E
P A O U T A O N H O P E L E S S N E S S A V M V C
J L C Y C L O T H Y M I C V P E C N O C M A N I A
V L U F R G H C D F O M F E M J P H N X A L A Y X
Z U J X D D G V O A L Y A C Z W T U I Q C I G X Q
Z C Z M C K U C U M I N B B R D Y T W C Z F S G L
Y I C N L I A K B I I N S L I T P M V D Y D H N I
R N O D O G N S L L V W K N H P U S J R J E T A K
D A G Y M S A E E Y C X J O S E O N P H B P W F A
L T N L E Q C F B P E D B R Y O S L V F T R M V V
F I I L Q U L P I E X C T E M H E V A Q Y E V I P
O O T L Y J I V P D V H O P B Y R Y P R J S W P Z
R N I U H C T I Y I I K N I O P O N M Q E S T P W
F U V X F K I E X G R F I N L O T H H G F I V A C
Q E E P S W C H M R M B C E I M O M B D V O O H O
C C T I W X H F F E E Q A P C A N C A N P N U D R
Z H R J G Q Q D S E V G E H W N I Z X I D S P T T
D L I G K K L L U A T A T R E I N I Y P Z X G G I
G N A M I F U E M F Q M P I J C Q Q U H C H Q A S
C Z D M K Y A I H E D J Z N Z G W Z I L A A I O O
T O K W Z L T Q T Q I I O E S F P R X B N A Q W L
M E D Y S T H Y M I C I M B K D J R S W R M K J Z
```

Chapter 8 CLUES

1. _____ A pattern of depressed behavior among very young children that is caused by separation from the mother.

2. _____ A disorder marked by alternating or intermixed periods of mania and depression.

3. _____ According to Freudian theory, the loss of a valued object (for example, a loss of employment) that is unconsciously interpreted as the loss of a loved one. Also called *imagined loss*.

4. _____ A low state marked by significant levels of sadness, lack of energy, low self-worth, guilt, or related symptoms.

5. _____ A disorder marked by numerous periods of hypomanic symptoms and mild depressive symptoms.

6. _____ A neurotransmitter whose abnormal activity is linked to depression and panic disorder.

7. _____ The perception, based on past experiences, that one has no control over one's reinforcements. [two words]

8. _____ A neurotransmitter whose abnormal activity is linked to depression, obsessive-compulsive disorder, and eating disorders.

9. _____ A state or episode of euphoria or frenzied activity in which people may have an exaggerated belief that the world is theirs for the taking.

10. _____ The experiencing of imagined sights, sounds, or other sensory experiences as if they were real.

11. _____ A mood disorder that is similar to but longer-lasting and less disabling than a major depressive disorder.

12. _____ A sequence in which dysthymic disorder leads to a major depressive disorder; termed "_____ depression."

13. _____ A research design in which investigators determine how many and which relatives of a person with a disorder have the same disorder. [two words]

14. _____ An episode of depression experienced by some new mothers that begins within four weeks after giving birth.

15. _____ A pattern in which a person displays symptoms of mania, but the symptoms are less severe and cause less impairment than a manic episode.

16. _____ A hormone released by the adrenal glands when a person is under stress.

17. _____ A pessimistic belief that one's present circumstances, problems, or mood will not change.

18. _____ A depression that appears to be triggered by clear events. Also known as *exogenous depression*.

19. _____ Depression without a history of mania.

20. _____ The three forms of negative thinking that Aaron Beck theorizes lead people to feel depressed. It consists of a negative view of one's experiences, oneself, and the future. [two words]

CHAPTER 9 WORD SEARCH

```
V T B W V Z R Z Q M F N G E Y M H F I L J N I X W
R C W G V Q V M H N Z I N I S C T R E U P T A K E
Z X M E A N A O E L U F A S A T I E D Z Y H F V H
X O S S P M G O O S O P B W Z K U J T O L Z L V W
U Y H O B J U D X Y J Y Q L X T X K R A Q K U K P
V O W C D A S S J J K A C P V K A S A Z P J O E H
G E B I F G S T S B L F D C G L E A N Y N J X Z Y
C T G O S G E A X C I E A J O G J P S Z U J E X L
N Z M C I U R B Q I T L B Q U N Y P C B Q U T S X
X F S U N H O I C A H E Y X B N T K R N V F I C J
P V P L T H T L I U I C T I U O C I A H T G N R N
J W G T E Y O I U W U T Y Z X R O T N T L Y E I H
O X W U R A N Z O Q M R R Y N E P Z I U B N J O K
W F M R P M I I B E E O A S K P S P A D A L R V B
T A B A E P N N D P V C M W C I Y M L N L T R Q B
C G M L R V P G O J T O I K R N C D M A T X I M Y
R R U D S M Z T D F R N N A I E H S A E E U I O Q
B I O L O G I C A L S V E N Y P O X G G G N N O N
R N G D N Y K W C W W U M B A H L B N V W Y H V H
B H D J A K W D P S F L M O K R O Y E S L C I F O
F U P T L L G A M Y R S B P C I G N T F C P B Z A
J D S K Z V U A K K R I Q E B N I M I Z Y D I B P
P T R I C Y C L I C H V Y V C E C F C G K W T E P
K X Z F C M V K H H L E L F A K A V Q X U R O I G
J M Z Z C O U P L E K X G E K Y L Y C N K I R Y O
```

Chapter 9 CLUES

1. _____ A metallic element that occurs in nature as a mineral salt and is an effective treatment for bipolar disorders.

2. _____ A form of treatment, used primarily in cases of unipolar depression, in which electrodes attached to a person's head send an electric current through the brain, causing a brain seizure.

3. _____ A treatment procedure for depression in which an electromagnetic coil, which is placed on or above a person's head, sends a current into the individual's brain —_____ _____ stimulation. [two words]

4. _____ This treatment approach includes psychodynamic, behavioral, and cognitive models.

5. _____ The neurotransmitter affected by MAO.

6. _____ A therapy format in which the therapist works with two people who share a long-term relationship.

7. _____ Taking antidepressant medications for five months after the relief of symptoms is called "_____" therapy.

8. _____ This treatment approach traces the cause of unipolar depression to the broader social structure in which people live.

9. _____ Tricylic antidepressants are believed to reduce depression by affecting neurotransmitter "_____."

10. _____ An antidepressant drug such as imipramine that has three rings in its molecular structure.

11. _____ MAOs can cause a potentially fatal rise in blood pressure if one eats foods containing _____.

12. _____ The generic name for Prozac.

13. _____ Psychotropic drugs that help stabilize the moods of people suffering from bipolar mood disorder. Also known as *antibipolar drugs*. [two words]

14. _____ An antidepressant drug that prevents the action of the enzyme monoamine oxidase – MAO _____.

15. _____ Many clinicians now use individual, group, or family therapy as an _____ to mood stabilizing drugs

16. _____ This treatment approach includes electroconvulsive therapy and antidepressant drugs.

17. _____ A psychotherapy for unipolar depression that is based on the belief that clarifying and changing one's interpersonal problems will help lead to recovery.

18. _____ The originator of the leading cognitive treatment for unipolar depression, Aaron _____.

19. _____ The neurotransmitter targeted by SSRIs.

20. _____ In a newer treatment procedure for depression, an implanted pulse generator sends regular electrical stimulation to the _____ nerve; the nerve, in turn, stimulates the brain.

CHAPTER 10 WORD SEARCH

```
K Y Q E G O I S T I C S N C A N K Z R K I T F I P
T H A N A T O S I P C M R M N F P W M R K Y G Y C
Z O Z X C N N G D C D Q E V C S U I C I D E O W K
O A N O M I C W Q E T D T K O Z D Y I L S C G B S
F D Y B Q P Y E S X H K R O N D Y V N I Q Y N Y G
G P R E V E N T I O N A O K T H L T I G V T P C B
G S F Y M K A B R N E Z S Z A D V A T N K G A R G
H C U S U W C Z W L V L P S G J T X I O P P R I P
B O N B O W C H V U H Y E E I A E S A R P A A S F
G C K R I C N J Y K Z Y C U O U L T T E I R P I A
Y U Q D R N I T V H V C T G N N D W O R O A R S L
K T Z I A F T A S V O I I N H H E C R C H S O I D
T C Z C P E N E L F M P V X L M R V Q Q Z U F N Z
Z Q S H V Z J H N V S E E K E R L W D N U I E T G
P E Z O H Q V Y P T K T I L V J Y W A G N C S E L
C N P T R A L G R G I N H G E I R M R C R I S R D
N P X O G G G V Y A M O H W G S L F E S N D I V L
E F M M N Y Q P M R E M N R I M S A R I X E O E H
X X V O L P L B I K U Z K A U G L N G S U H N N L
Y I M U Z V O K M P Z L U L L R E C E Q L I A T Q
W J Y S L S D G A M X U Y D G H Q O S S P S L I J
Q H G H V I A L T R U I S T I C A E Y O S N S O R
S T I Q W E R B W S O V O K I Z M B V P Z S U N R
N L V Z D Y Q T W F K Z Y K G O Y K U Z Z G D Q W
V U O L T C T F F O P Z B Q F P T D Y L U M W L E
```

Chapter 10 CLUES

1. _____ A pessimistic belief that one's present circumstances, problems, or mood will not change.

2. _____ A person who clearly intends to end his or her life at the time of a suicide attempt; death _____

3. _____ Type of thinking characterized by viewing problems and solutions in rigid either/or terms.

4. _____ A psychological autopsy in which clinicians and researchers piece together information about a person's suicide from the person's past; _____ analysis.

5. _____ A suicide attempt that does not result in death.

6. _____ Suicide committed by people who intentionally sacrifice their lives for the well-being of society.

7. _____ A person who is ambivalent about the wish to die even as he or she attempts suicide; death _____

8. _____ A self-inflicted death in which the person acts intentionally, directly, and consciously.

9. _____ A type of program that tries to identify people who are at risk killing themselves and to offer them crisis intervention – suicide _____.

10. _____ A death in which the victim plays an indirect, hidden, partial, or unconscious role.

11. _____ Suicide committed by individuals whose social environment fails to provide stability, thus leaving them without a sense of belonging.

12. _____ Suicide committed by people over whom society has little or no control, people who are not inhibited by the norms or rules of society.

13. _____ Suicide is related to marital status and level of _____ support.

14. _____ A person who attempts suicide without recognizing the finality of death; death _____

15. _____ According to the Freudian view, the basic death instinct that functions in opposition to the life instinct.

16. _____ Modeling is referred to as the "_____" of suicide.

17. _____ A treatment approach that tries to help people in a psychological crisis view their situation more accurately, make better decisions, act more constructively, and overcome the crisis. [two words]

18. _____ A person who attempts suicide believing that the process of death is already under way and that he or she is simply hastening the process; death _____.

19. _____ In Western society, this age group is more likely to commit suicide than any other age group.

20. _____ A person without previous professional training who provides services under the supervision of a mental health professional.

CHAPTER 11 WORD SEARCH

```
O I U E G O D E F I C I E N C I E S R Z V S V F L
M W R H S T B D M A E F E M M E R Y L Y C X D P O
O M B U L I M I A N E R V O S A Y N Y A S T I K J
T D K K R U J N Q O C O U T P A T I E N T I P F O
F O W B J H U T J R T Z B E I Y V W Z T A Y T Z G
S W J I E A Z H B E R R P X M J L A X A T I V E S
P T M N B W S G G X F E M A L E S Y R T O D M Y Z
B Q U G S K K N Y I W X K Q L A T E R A L Y R M K
M O L E E W L U M A X C Q Q Z O Z P O S T Q I R E
E T T - T B S H N N S L A N U G O T V M K O D W X
A A I E P I C P A E G X V H Y P O T H A L A M U S
Q O D A O N N C S R S U E E U O M V A Z C S Z X G
U T I T I G X R T V K E D F N R X D Q J U I F L O
U A M I N E F L S O X O T G P T Q O Q N Q R G Y I
W K E N T P C J R S Q B M T F S R V I A F A T T Y
B N N G D M D T Z A W Z M Y H K C O O Y V X W S K
Z R S D H H H N M S H P E I M E H U M N O R I Q R
S J I N S V A R O I S O Y S V E S C G E B C J H L
F U O G F V G X S A H Y V H K N B T E Z D M Z G J
M Q N P G A M E N O R R H E A M V D A K T I P G X
N T A J A D I E T I N G L L L E X H O G D L A I N
E P L N B T W A G M I B T J J S E R G Y E Q L L Q
H S Z J K B T N K T O F I Z M H I X K J D J S F M
D Z S T A R V A T I O N V O Y E C Z R O E C I X N
G W M T U Y H J N K Y O H R B D I I V E R N O W V
```

Chapter 11 CLUES

1. _____ An episode of uncontrollable eating during which a person ingests a very large quantity of food.

2. _____ A part of the brain that helps maintain various bodily functions, including eating and hunger.

3. _____ About 90 to 95 percent of anorexia cases occur in _____.

4. _____ The absence of menstrual cycles.

5. _____ The famous 1940s _____ study used conscientious objectors to the war as subjects.

6. _____ A family pattern in which members are overinvolved with each other's affairs and overconcerned about each other's welfare.

7. _____ Downy, white hair that grows on the bodies of those with severe anorexia.

8. _____ A type of eating disorder in which a person displays a pattern of binge eating without any accompanying compensatory behaviors. [two words; hyphenated]

9. _____ The region of the hypothalamus that, when activated, produces hunger.

10. _____ The region of the hypothalamus that, when activated, depresses hunger.

11. _____ The weight level that a person is predisposed to maintain, controlled in part by the hypothalamus. [two words]

12. _____ Compensatory behaviors for those with bulimia often include vomiting, _____, and diuretics.

13. _____ A disorder marked by frequent eating binges that are followed by forced vomiting or other extreme compensatory behaviors to avoid gaining weight. Also known as *binge-purge syndrome.* [two words]

14. _____ The onset of both anorexia and bulimia typically follows a period of _____.

15. _____ A theory that identifies several different kinds of risk factors that may combine to help cause a disorder. The more such factors present, the greater the risk of developing the disorder.

16. _____ Twenty percent of these female athletes met the full criteria for an eating disorder when surveyed.

17. _____ A disorder marked by the pursuit of extreme thinness and by extreme loss of weight. [two words]

18. _____ Bruch argues that disturbed mother-child interactions lead to serious _____ in the child and to severe cognitive disturbances. [two words]

19. _____ Theorists believe that mood disorders may "_____" for eating disorders. [three words]

20. _____ A person who receives diagnosis or treatment in a clinic, hospital, or therapist's office but is not hospitalized overnight.

CHAPTER 12 WORD SEARCH

```
I C B J P I C O C A I N E A A J P Y R N T F T Q Y
H B A E K L D Q N W D S K W T B U I L Y C G T A I
M Q R S E D A T I V E - H Y P N O T I C Q F W X X
F F B A W Z O H E N D O R P H I N S Y P G R W M T
A J I S Y N E R G I S T I C F O R S S B K H A Z O
D I T W C S Y R E W A R D - D E F I C I E N C Y L
N P U B N I F L A S H B A C K N T U X P N F K D E
Z T R B E T X M Q M C P O Z U U V K P K A W O E R
P L A T C N O V R T V R O Y I S G P R S U Y R L A
I Z T M S K Z J A N T A G O N I S T M M M K S I N
T G E X S O M O M J O Z Y A A G B Z S O W W A R C
K X S S K T Q Y D P V D D O O Y X J B R T N K I E
K D Z N A R C O T I C S J H Q Z I Q N K I X O U W
Q W N R F O D J D A A M R N P B D O R N P F F M A
N C L C H V M J E Y I Z B R A V E R S I O N F T X
J C R E L A P S E - P R E V E N T I O N R L ' R N
E E R I P D A B U S E K D P E H W I Q G Q Y S E H
M C X E Y U Q D E T O X I F I C A T I O N R W M Y
M W I T H D R A W A L A Z V B N Y U A U O T B E H
C H O N L D B N H E T Z X G T A E O A G T C W N S
Q O N T I R G E P Z F Z S N F P Q S M C M Q P S U
E C X C B D Z N I J T U U E N S O Z L V M B S Y M
D E P E N D E N C E D R Q F U T Q N P H M U V T U
X L I T I X E M B L E E J D L W Y J P E C G R P J
I R I H A L L U C I N O G E N E T H H E K Q E K E
```

Chapter 12 CLUES

1. _____ The class of drugs including opium or any of the drugs derived from opium, including morphine, heroin, and codeine are known collectively as _____.

2. _____ Upon regular use of a drug, the need of the brain and the body for ever larger doses in order to achieve the drug's earlier effects.

3. _____ The most common group of antianxiety drugs, which includes Valium and Xanax.

4. _____ Such excessive and repeated reliance on a drug that the behavior disrupts the person's life; substance _____.

5. _____ An addictive stimulant obtained from the coca plant; the most powerful natural stimulant known.

6. _____ Systematic and medically supervised withdrawal from a drug.

7. _____ Neurotransmitters that help relieve pain and reduce emotional tension; sometimes referred to as the body's own opioids.

8. _____ A dramatic withdrawal reaction experienced by some people who are alcohol-dependent; consists of mental confusion, clouded consciousness, and terrifying visual hallucinations. Also called *alcohol withdrawal delirium.* [two words]

9. _____ Such excessive reliance on a drug that one makes it the center of one's life and perhaps builds a tolerance to it, experiences withdrawal symptoms when one stops taking it, or both; substance _____.

10. _____ The recurrence of LSD-induced sensory and emotional changes long after the drug has left the body. Or, in post-traumatic stress disorder, the reexperiencing of past traumatic events.

11. _____ Unpleasant, sometimes dangerous reactions that may occur when people who use a drug regularly stop taking or reduce their dosage of the drug.

12. _____ A treatment based on the principles of classical conditioning in which people are repeatedly presented with shocks or another unpleasant stimuli while they are performing undesirable behaviors such as taking a drug.

13. _____ A syndrome, suspected to be present in some individuals, in which the brain's reward center is not readily activated by the usual events in their lives. [two words; hyphenated]

14. _____ A drug used in low doses to reduce anxiety and in higher doses to help people sleep. Also called *anxiolytic drug.* [two words; hyphenated]

15. _____ A training approach to treating alcohol abuse that is similar to BSCT and also has clients plan ahead for risky situations and reactions. [two words; hyphenated]

16. _____ Drugs derived from barbituric acid, used to help people relax or sleep.

17. _____ In pharmacology, an increase of effects that occurs when more than one substance is acting on the body at the same time.

18. _____An amnestic disorder marked by extreme confusion, memory impairment, and other neurological symptoms; caused by long-term alcoholism, an accompanying poor diet, and, in turn, a deficiency of vitamin B (thiamine).

19. _____ Substances that cause powerful changes in sensory perception, including strengthening perceptions and producing illusions and hallucinations. Also called *psychedelic drug.*

20. _____ Drugs that block or change the effects of an addictive drug.

CHAPTER 13 WORD SEARCH

```
J E T M J F S J N K R F U S E X - C H A N G E G D
I S A P S M P T V I N X E G V O Y E U R I S M V P
Y V G R A X I I Z I H Y P O A C T I V E S R I C P
U R D E D G W A U C S M J B Z A E C S H P R R O E
V A B M I V U Y D I P P H W T C Y E Y F E O I H X
V E M A S M V P E Q Y U V X N X N D P Y C R B A H
P P K T M J V N E O R G A S M F D P A U T E E P I
M X A U D Y S P A R E U N I A P V M V Q A V O L B
B F U R O Q U V P M F O N D E S I R E Z T F K R I
T M P E A I V V W B A O U O B O G L R P O E G Z T
W C C E F P K W W Z P S R Z J K L B S F R T H C I
E P W J F E H I Z Q H G O M Y K S W I C R I A H O
C A Z A R X P I U O T I E C A G T O O P O S O I N
Y D S C F C Q C L Z M W H N H N G E N J L H G L I
F O S U H I H E L I N J Z A D I C T D S E I R B S
Q V W L K T F P W O A S B S I E S E H G M S D V M
A A I A X E D N Z Y F S B F R B R M A V Y M I V V
P G S T G M C G L C L Z F X B C T I F N M P T B O
V I N I O E D I K F M U J R N U T L D W X C J X C
K N C O T N G L P M L K D S B K G T Q E N I Y N R
X I B N T T U Z P E D O P H I L I A I C N Q E R T
N S R X G W N W W L B R C N O K R D I A J T L T O
E M A L K L D K T K G G B T O U O W V W E I I B Y
C U L R R K F D K C J E F R O T T E U R I S M T W
G S L W R S E A M J H N S K E Y O C K N A O O V Y
```

Chapter 13 CLUES

1. _____ A paraphilia consisting of recurrent and intense sexual urges, fantasies, or behaviors that involve the use of a nonliving object, often to the exclusion of all other stimuli.

2. _____ The disorder marked by a lack of interest in sex and hence a low level of sexual activity.

3. _____ A disorder in which a person experiences severe pain in the genitals during sexual activity.

4. _____ A dysfunction in which a man reaches orgasm and ejaculates before, on, or shortly after penetration and before he wishes to. [two words]

5. _____ A state of mind that some people experience during sex in which they focus on their sexual performance to such an extent that their performance and their enjoyment are reduced. [two words]

6. _____ A paraphilia consisting of repeated and intense sexual urges, fantasies, or behaviors that involve touching and rubbing against a nonconsenting person.

7. _____ The phase of the sexual response cycle consisting of an urge to have sex, sexual fantasies, and sexual attraction to others.

8. _____ A paraphilia in which a person has repeated and intense sexual urges or fantasies about watching, touching, or engaging in sexual acts with prepubescent children, and may carry out these urges or fantasies.

9. _____ A paraphilia in which persons have repeated sexually arousing urges or fantasies about exposing their genitals to another person, and may act upon those urges.

10. _____ A paraphilia characterized by repeated and intense sexual urges, fantasies, or behaviors that involve being humiliated, beaten, bound, or otherwise made to suffer.

11. _____ A sexual disorder characterized by an avoidance of genital sexual interplay.

12. _____ The fear of performing inadequately and a related tension experienced during sex. [two words]

13. _____ The phase of the sexual response cycle during which an individual's sexual pleasure peaks and sexual tension is released as muscles in the pelvic region contract rhythmically.

14. _____ A surgical procedure that changes a person's sex organs and features, and, in turn, sexual identity. [two words; hyphenated]

15. _____ A condition marked by involuntary contractions of the muscles around the outer third of the vagina, preventing entry of the penis.

16. _____ Disorders characterized by recurrent and intense sexual urges, fantasies, or behaviors involving nonhuman objects, children, nonconsenting adults, or experiences of suffering or humiliation.

17. _____ A paraphilia characterized by repeated and intense sexual urges, fantasies, or behaviors that involve inflicting suffering on others.

18. _____ The phase of the sexual response cycle marked by changes in the pelvic region, general physical arousal, and increases in heart rate, muscle tension, blood pressure, and rate of breathing.

19. _____ A paraphilia in which a person has repeated and intense sexual desires to observe unsuspecting people in secret as they undress or to spy on couples having intercourse. The person may also act upon these desires.

20. _____ The disorder in which a person persistently feels extremely uncomfortable about his or her assigned sex and strongly wishes to be a member of the opposite sex. [two words]

CHAPTER 14 WORD SEARCH

```
E P E L H D A T P G S D L B N F W C N X S S Q V R
V Y Y W W B P R T L A V O L I T I O N J L E G Z A
V I E L O O S E A S S O C I A T I O N S W G Q S H
J Y A N T I P S Y C H O T I C Q D F E A K Q C D F
R I Z C D G E H C H A A W W L A K H H L M F E F L
C U N D A P S C H I Z O P H R E N O G E N I C E A
J N U A H Q M K K C S J S R B D R L V J W M S P T
S P N C P A X I A T Y P I C A L P T L B V F Q Z A
C X D S Z P Q Z J O K K M V U F U J M K F C Q M F
H Q I R E N R O F R L Q R P S Y C H O S I S J Y F
I X F N E O L O G I S M D Y Y Q S X V Y O C O C E
Z N F V P V K R P H E N O T H I A Z I N E S C B C
O D E W U J I U L R P J Q R R I G T D K K X A G T
P J R V Z O T Q H K I R K D N H R G S E A H T Y D
H F E P O S I T I V E A Q X K X U U W S A X A O E
R T N K V O L V Z A E Y T W P U S S T J B B T J L
E F T G D U Y J V Y M H P E P R U R R V B H O Y U
N A I C W C O Y I Q Q X M Q A U C U V C L N N D S
I G A D W L Z X E X X P Q F F F E R P A Y W I F I
A N T E Y U W F A T F V G K T N F F R Y Y P A D O
M H E Y F F X T E X P R E S S E D E M O T I O N N
M J D A Q Z C E I H G G Z T E X H S C A R H C E E
L K D X W Q B A O Q N E G A T I V E K T E B H P T
P L Q S D O U B L E - B I N D Y J S A L O G I A Y
A Y A V T D O T A H A L L U C I N A T I O N T K F
```

Chapter 14 CLUES

1. _____ A decrease in speech or speech content; a symptom of schizophrenia. Also known as *poverty of speech*.

2. _____ A state in which a person loses contact with reality in key ways.

3. _____ A symptom of schizophrenia marked by apathy and an inability to start or complete a course of action.

4. _____ A group of antihistamine drugs that became the first group of effective antipsychotic medications.

5. _____ Symptoms of schizophrenia that seem to be excesses of or bizarre additions to normal thoughts, emotions, or behaviors.

6. _____ A new group of antipsychotic drugs whose biological action is different from that of the traditional antipsychotic drugs.

7. _____A symptom of schizophrenia in which a person displays emotions that are unsuited to the situation. [two words]

8. _____ A strange false belief firmly held despite evidence to the contrary.

9. _____ A type of mother—supposedly cold, domineering, and uninterested in the needs of others—who was once thought to cause schizophrenia in the child.

10. _____ The experiencing of imagined sights, sounds, or other sensory experiences as if they were real.

11. _____ A common thinking disturbance in schizophrenia, characterized by rapid shifts from one topic of conversation to another. Also known as *derailment*. [two words]

12. _____ Symptoms of schizophrenia that seem to be deficits in normal thought, emotions, or behaviors.

13. _____ A theory that some parents repeatedly communicate pairs of messages that are mutually contradictory, helping to produce schizophrenia in their children. [two words; hyphenated]

14. _____ Drugs that help correct grossly confused or distorted thinking.

15. _____ A psychotic disorder in which personal, social, and occupational functioning deteriorate as a result of strange perceptions, disturbed thought processes, unusual emotions, and motor abnormalities.

16. _____ The general level of criticism, disapproval, and hostility expressed in a family. [two words]

17. _____ A symptom of schizophrenia in which the person shows almost no emotion at all. [two words]

18. _____ A made-up word that has meaning only to the person using it.

19. _____ A pattern of extreme psychomotor symptoms, found in some forms of schizophrenia, that may include catatonic stupor, rigidity, or posturing.

20. _____ A type of schizophrenia in which no single set of psychotic symptoms (incoherence, psychomotor disturbances, delusions, or hallucinations) dominates.

CHAPTER 15 WORD SEARCH

```
V W X Z L E K B E A I P N C U M V I Y V I S M V N
C F P U A E R U U C R L O B O T O M Y N F V M W U
R P C N Q B A G R D A Y C E N T E R O Z G B Y S B
A D E I N S T I T U T I O N A L I Z A T I O N U V
G H H O O K R M W B F J V M E Z Z Y D A Q Z L B M
R Y C O N V E N T I O N A L X F Z Q J H Z X D S L
A W E R H Z Y N Z W R H Y Y T P P J U J E K R T A
N G E V L C O A F T E R C A R E Y H H D T E G A N
U I H D S T Q M Y J J V Y X A O M O A K A O S N T
L D D P H A Y K W G V F Y K P V Y R L S R Y B T I
O F I A E I N S Y F M Z W V Y N C U F M D O I I P
C V G N L Z Z M U Z S M T W R F C J W P I V F A S
Y U A S T O M I B S C M O Z A J E Z A V V T M N Y
T X N D E E O L T X A I K L M Z W K Y E E I R I C
O N T Z R K R I E D S C E R I E V J H P D G J G H
S E I B E R A E B J E Z N E D Z L A O X Y H N R O
I U H A D F L U S U M A E R A K E E U V S H T A T
S R I C W B O T Z T A O C E L X W H S Y K A N X I
P O S K O R B H K T N R O N E R W H E M I K R K C
V L T W R X B E Z T A L N A F T V F Y Z N Y G X D
U E A A K A B R E R G X O S F Y E Y B G E O T I W
Y P M R S R T A D K E H M H E X Z I Q Z S V R L W
K T I D H G O P H Z R N Y X C T T M T A I S R C F
S I N S O F O Y Q G A J N B T M B Q Z R A D F B G
X C E Z P N F K K Q Y U P P S Y U W V G P F J D F
```

Chapter 15 CLUES

1. _____ A nineteenth-century approach to treating people with mental dysfunction that emphasized moral guidance and humane and respectful treatment.

2. _____ A term used for the traditional antipsychotic drugs because they often produce undesired effects similar to the symptoms of neurological disorders.

3. _____ A condition characterized by extrapyramidal effects that appear in some patients after they have taken traditional antipsychotic drugs for an extended time. [two words]

4. _____ Problems with overcrowding and understaffing at psychiatric institutions led to the creation of "_____"—human warehouses filled with hopelessness. [two words]

5. _____ A behavioral program in which a person's desirable behaviors are reinforced systematically throughout the day by the awarding of tokens that can be exchanged for goods or privileges. [two words]

6. _____ The discovery of antipsychotic medications dates back to the 1940s, when researchers developed this type of drug for allergies.

7. _____ A program of posthospitalization care and treatment out in the community.

8. _____ Unwanted movements, such as severe shaking, bizarre-looking grimaces, twisting of the body, and extreme restlessness, sometimes produced by conventional antipsychotic drugs. [two words]

9. _____ Psychosurgery in which a surgeon cuts the connections between the brain's frontal lobes and the lower centers of the brain.

10. _____ A life-threatening reduction in white blood cells. This condition is sometimes produced by the atypical antipsychotic drug *clozapine.*

11. _____ A protected and supervised workplace that offers job opportunities and training at a pace and level tailored to people with various disabilities. [two words]

12. _____ A program that offers hospitallike treatment during the day only. Also called *day hospital.* [two words]

13. _____ A community therapist who offers a full range of services for people with schizophrenia or other severe disorders, including therapy, advice, medication, guidance, and protection of patients' rights. [two words]

14. _____ NAMI—the National Alliance on Mental Illness—is one example of a national _____ group formed to push for better community mental health treatment.

15. _____ Humanistic approach to institutional treatment based on the belief that institutions can help patients recover by creating a climate that promotes self-respect, responsible behavior, and meaningful activity. [two words]

16. _____ Antipsychotic drugs developed throughout the 1960s, 1970s, and 1980s are now referred to as "_____" antipsychotics.

17. _____ Drugs that help correct grossly confused or distorted thinking.

18. _____ A residence for people with psychological problems who cannot live alone or with their families, often staffed by paraprofessionals. Also known as a *group home.* [two words]

19. _____ The discharge of large numbers of patients from long-term institutional care so that they might be treated in community programs.

20. _____ The Parkinsonian symptoms seen with some antipsychotic drugs seem to be the result of reductions of dopamine in this specific brain region, responsible for movement coordination and posture. [two words]

CHAPTER 16 WORD SEARCH

```
P U A C N J U U Y K D S C J J Q W V H W E G R X Q
Q P W O W Q F T D T R A D R S J J A I L S J A H G
M T L N S U Y B D Q L L J G Y S P G S L N B I L T
J W B A I E S I F E S B E O I D A L T Z C S J J V
O J S R M C C N U M P E X D Z T G X R D S D C U G
B W P C B D H N G D E E D H T R K W I R P R G C P
S U A I Y S I G D Q C C N Y P I C C O L S A S V E
E D S S Y O Z R F P T D A D R E P Q N J C M C W B
S F S S S V O I C A R P I J E M F V I B O A H W S
S S I I X D T G I R U A V Y L N B I C Z M T I N X
I Y V S M H Y I R A M H Z N N A T X E X O I Z I J
V S E T K O P D B N N U G F H Q U I P E R C O S B
E T - I T S A H O O E Q Z I W X Y I E C B L I T L
- E A C H J L S W I Q G Q B T L V Y R K I U D H P
C M G E V R T B I D Q P S L V P K X S M D S U W B
O A G J I X R H O D V G S A Y G K C O K I T X U L
M T R M Z F B N V R V Q S N T Z M B N Q T E A C K
P I E H B A D H L R D X Q L T Z V Z A G Y R Z A K
U C S J P U V T X N H E Z U T F I F L T D S O T C
L N S C G U N O I L S T R G F A N T I S O C I A L
S D I N R B H W I J W C L L P R G H T L E R F L G
I J V U M Q G B G D A L J O I W J O Y Q F K Q O F
V E E V A O B W K I A A W M Y N L V A K O F P L L
E J C U X L Z M G M W N P R C Q E H M P Q M B O G
Y S V J R B N T L V O C T P H I N E A S G A G E W
```

Chapter 16 CLUES

1. _____ A personality disorder in which an individual is so focused on orderliness, perfectionism, and control that he or she loses flexibility, openness, and efficiency. [two words; hyphenated]

2. _____ A personality disorder in which a person persistently avoids social relationships and shows little expression of emotion.

3. _____ DSM-IV-TR classifies personality disorders into three different categories or "_____."

4. _____ A personality disorder marked by a general pattern of disregard for and violation of other people's rights.

5. _____ A unique and long-term pattern of inner experience and outward behavior that leads to consistent reactions across various situations.

6. _____ DSM-IV-TR axis on which personality disorders are coded. [Roman numeral]

7. _____ The occurrence of two or more disorders in the same person.

8. _____ A personality disorder in which an individual displays repeated instability in interpersonal relationships, self-image, and mood, as well as extremely impulsive behavior.

9. _____ Some clinicians believe that the "odd" personality disorders are actually related to schizophrenia, and thus call them schizophrenia-_____ disorders.

10. _____ A personality disorder is defined as a very _____ pattern of inner experience and outward behavior that differs from the expectations of one's culture and leads to dysfunctioning.

11. _____ Most of the personality disorders have received little _____ research.

12. _____ A personality disorder in which a person displays a pattern of excessive emotionality and attention seeking. Once called *hysterical personality disorder.*

13. _____ A personality disorder in which an individual is consistently uncomfortable and restrained in social situations, overwhelmed by feelings of inadequacy, and extremely sensitive to negative evaluation.

14. _____ A personality disorder characterized by a pattern of clinging and obedience, fear of separation, and a persistent, excessive need to be taken care of.

15. _____ A personality disorder marked by a broad pattern of grandiosity, need for admiration, and lack of empathy.

16. _____ A category of personality disorder listed in past versions of DSM, marked by a pattern of negative attitudes and resistance to the demands of others. [two words; hyphenated]

17. _____ A personality disorder marked by a pattern of extreme distrust and suspiciousness of others.

18. _____ This category of personality disorders includes both antisocial and borderline personality disorders.

19. _____ Full name of the railroad worker who experienced brain trauma and a complete change in personaality. [two words]

20. _____ A personality disorder in which a person displays a pattern of interpersonal problems marked by extreme discomfort in close relationships, odd forms of thinking and perceiving, and behavioral eccentricities.

CHAPTER 17 WORD SEARCH

```
B P Z H Q C W A E N O R M A L I Z A T I O N X A B
P M A I N S T R E A M I N G N I Y B F H I O E O F
P M C J J K L V O T H E O R Y O F M I N D T E N N
E W Y A E W E I F T P E C Y C D C D G G W F F C W
W C L J H F K F B E H T K U S A C O N D U C T T D
T E B O O E D W L T M J I I E S A X V D J N B E
S R L P E M N O H P R A K G N T V N E O Z Z T B N
W E I P S G U U A P D K L B H N Q E W J T V T F C
L B Z O Y O R J O H B N K A Y M P M R E W Q D S O
J E J S F P E B W N B U D S L C O Z A E N I H X P
I L E I T Z S A O N D Y S Z O C N D V W O N G L R
G L H T L Z I A S P E R G E R S O G E F I B J A E
D U C I D Y S G K C Q B D C O X P H W R G Y F J S
S M J O S P E C I A L E D U C A T I O N A J T B I
P H Z N R D G N X R F Q R H J C L E Y L V T U I S
Q U J A P K G C M Z A U T I S T I C S D I B E S R
X S E L D J S H R Q D U Y H W N M I L D C L N X D
K H U D K C Q G J B Y J O X B K M T C F B I L Z E
A T T E N T I O N - D E F I C I T P R O F O U N D
Y U L F F J A I U U V J J I K L Z A Y J K E E G B
Z J H I F C M E N T A L R E T A R D A T I O N Y B
H J A A A T D O W N S Y N D R O M E W O C C K Q W
F N G N K T L X D V R R F E W A H X A A U Z I H G
O M K T N L Z N B X A W Y H L E I N N W M U Q E T
I S V M E T H Y L P H E N I D A T E C T V A K K Z
```

Chapter 17 CLUES

1. _____ A disorder in which people display general intellectual functioning and adaptive behavior that are well below average. Also known as *intellectual disability* or *intellectual developmental disorder*. [two words]

2. _____ A stimulant drug, known better by the trade name *Ritalin*, commonly used to treat ADHD.

3. _____ Awareness that other people base their behaviors on their own beliefs, intentions, and other mental states, not on information they have no way of knowing. [three words]

4. _____ A childhood disorder in which the child repeatedly violates the basic rights of others, displaying aggression and sometimes destroying others' property, stealing, or running away from home.

5. _____ A pervasive developmental disorder/syndrome in which individuals display profound social impairment yet maintain a relatively high level of cognitive functioning and language skills.

6. _____ A level of mental retardation (IQ between 50 and 70) at which people can benefit from education and can support themselves as adults.

7. _____ A childhood disorder marked by repeated bed-wetting or wetting of one's clothes.

8. _____ In which persons are unable to focus their attention, behave overactively and impulsively, or both— _____ hyperactivity disorder. [two words; hyphenated]

9. _____ A pervasive developmental disorder marked by extreme unresponsiveness to others, poor communication skills, and highly repetitive and rigid behavior.

10. _____ An area of the brain that coordinates movement in the body and perhaps helps control a person's rapid attention to things..

11. _____ A childhood disorder characterized by repeated defecating in inappropriate places, such as one's clothing.

12. _____ A level of mental retardation (IQ between 35 and 49) in which persons can learn to care for themselves and can benefit from vocational training.

13. _____ A level of mental retardation (IQ below 20) at which individuals need a very structured environment with constant aid and supervision.

14. _____ An approach to educating children with mental retardation in which they are grouped together and given a separate, specially designed education. [two words]

15. _____ The principle that institutions and community residences should expose people with mental retardation to living conditions and opportunities similar to those found in the rest of society.

16. _____ A childhood disorder in which children argue repeatedly with adults, lose their temper, and feel great resentment. [two words]

17. _____ An approach to educating children with mental retardation in which they are placed in regular classes with children who are not mentally retarded. Also called *inclusion*.

18. _____ A group of problems in a child, including lower intellectual functioning, low birth weight, and irregularities in the hands and face, that result from excessive alcohol intake by the mother during pregnancy. [two words]

19. _____ A form of mental retardation caused by an abnormality in the twenty-first chromosome. [two words]

20. _____ A level of mental retardation (IQ between 20 and 34) in which individuals require careful supervision and can learn to perform basic work in structured and sheltered settings.

CHAPTER 18 WORD SEARCH

```
K O E C O N F A B U L A T I O N Q Q P I C K S P E
B B V R V H B T M R L Z I K D V D Q T C N Y Q D H
T L R F N C R E U T Z F E L D T - J A K O B H V E
E P P N U T X M A I T D Q V D U T Q T K R N L P Y
O D O R E F N I P C M B Z D I E N C E P H A L O N
Z V S U E U I N Q U Q C D T W I R E A M G A N U J
M K S T L F R Z K N E A P L V D F M T E J C Z W X
X T D B W T R O H H W W X N A E U G F T L E R L D
M M P V W Y B O F Z A E T O S M O T G A D T S R G
K A P R H I G E N I U S R L C E F J L B G Y E C G
P P A P L G H E T T B W J Y U N M O D O K L N V Z
R C R B G Q U J E A A R K F L T J F D L V C I T U
E B K K E N N B U F - L I H A I F O S I O H L K Q
S T I A R Q T C F J P A L L R A I U Q S I O E K T
C U N L O K I B H D C N M O L M J Z O M U L P D M
R Z S Z P T N G Y W E J U Y B A F D I W J I L E Y
I W O H S D G K M X S O I F L E R C Y A W N A L H
P J N E Y X T Z Q Y U S M N T O S Y K R K E Q I T
T T S I C Q O U Y C S Z Q L M X I Q T B W F U R Y
I E H M H B N W L O N G - T E R M D Z A Z Y E I Y
O U B E O C S I O U S H O R T - T E R M N J S U M
N W J R L Z F N E L Y D C A J W N C J K Z G X M I
Y X F S O Y F H M Y J I H I E N V E A D X S L D K
R S F X G G Y Q I D C C U Y X N S S E X S J K E X
Q P M D Y L Q V V P I N U G D S J N O C O N N F S
```

Chapter 18 CLUES

1. _____ A brain area (consisting of the mammillary bodies, thalamus, and hypothalamus) that plays a key role in transforming short-term to long-term memory, among other functions.

2. _____ The memory system that contains all the information that we have stored over the years. [two words; hyphenated]

3. _____ The most common disease of dementia, usually occurring after the age of 65.

4. _____ The field of psychology concerned with the mental health of elderly people.

5. _____ A neurotransmitter that has been linked to depression and dementia.

6. _____ Type of dementia caused by a cerebrovascular accident, or stroke, which restricts blood flow to certain areas of the brain. Also known as *multi-infarct dementia.*

7. _____ A syndrome marked by severe problems in memory and in at least one other cognitive function.

8. _____ Sphere-shaped deposits of beta-amyloid protein that form in the spaces between certain brain cells and in certain blood vessels as people age. [two words]

9. _____ An inherited disease characterized by progressive problems in cognition, emotion, and movement, which results in dementia.

10. _____ Regions of the brain that play a key role in short-term memory, among other functions. [two words]

11. _____ A form of dementia caused by a slow-acting virus that may live in the body for years before the disease unfolds. [two words; hyphenated]

12. _____ It sometimes is difficult to use antidepressant drugs effectively and safely with the elderly because the body's _____ works differently in later life.

13. _____ A rapidly developing clouding of consciousness; the person has great difficulty concentrating, focusing attention, and keeping a straight-forward stream of thought.

14. _____ A neurological disease that affects the frontal and temporal lobes, causing dementia.

15. _____ The memory system that collects new information. Also known as *working memory.* [two words; hyphenated]

16. _____ A leading kind of substance abuse in the elderly is the misuse of _____ drugs.

17. _____ A slowly progressive neurological disease, marked by tremors and rigidity, that may also cause dementia.

18. _____ A small protein molecule that forms sphere-shaped deposits called senile plaques, linked to aging and to Alzheimer's disease. [two words; hyphenated]

19. _____ Twisted protein fibers that form within certain brain cells as people age. [two words]

20. _____ A made-up description of one's experience to fill in a gap in one's memory.

CHAPTER 19 WORD SEARCH

```
L H C N G R I G H T T O T R E A T M E N T E V F C
E Z H G V U M E K U L L L W T K T A Y C U M M J R
W M L Q I U I D U T Y T O P R O T E C T J Q H F I
B L P I N J U L W Z U M ' N A U G H T E N A L K M
I N N L C C L E T F K O H A K V B N G R I L I Y I
R C O J O K I G C Y E U O Z Q N P L F E R C D R N
R Y M O M Y R C U E B O J S Y G U U S E G O K E A
E J A H P D E H S B K U Y U K F W O M O T D E S L
S S L C E I J E M N B K T Y H O R L Z J C E G P C
I C P E T N W F A G W A B M T C T Q K C R O H O O
S O R E E J E X B S U K Z G E B C J X Q L F E N M
T N A B N H E J Q H S X S S O N K U H X Y E S S M
I F C D C N H T J I B I F D A A T X A E D T V I I
B I T M E E L W N T Y R S O J Z P A B J J H H B T
L D I C I V I L C O M M I T M E N T L U D I O I M
E E C F W M G A J Z C C Q N A U O S X L G C W L E
I N E O K U G Q X P Y B L Y M N J A F D Y S T I N
M T B X F H I E G W Z H A Q D S C E G T T I P T T
P I T L R U S D U R H A M A O O S E A Q C T L Y Q
U A T H R E E D A Y S I Q R Y B F E T H F D Z L W
L L S W F F F Y E W V R N K X P H O P S L H Q X C
S I R R I G H T T O R E F U S E T R E A T M E N T
E T I D Q O I G J Y M A N A G E D C A R E L J V O
I Y D G B F A H P H D B K N F O R E N S I C A W D
X Z Q P X P A R E N S P A T R I A E A Z U D E R Z
```

Chapter 19 CLUES

1. _____ The principle that therapists must break confidentiality in order to protect a person who may be the intended victim of a client. [three words]

2. _____ A legal process by which certain individuals can be forced to undergo mental health treatment. [two words]

3. _____ The legal right of patients, particularly those who are involuntarily committed, to receive adequate treatment. [three words]

4. _____ A legal process by which persons accused of a crime are instead judged mentally unstable and sent to a mental health facility for treatment. [two words]

5. _____ A mental health program that some businesses offer to their employees. [two words]

6. _____ A system of health care coverage in which the insurance company largely controls the cost, method, provider, and length of treatment. [two words]

7. _____ A legal test for insanity that holds people to be insane at the time of committing a crime if they were driven to do so by an uncontrollable "fit of passion." [two words]

8. _____ The legal right of patients to refuse certain forms of treatment. [four words]

9. _____ A state of mental instability that leaves defendants unable to understand the legal charges and proceedings they are facing and unable to prepare an adequate defense with their attorney.

10. _____ A legal test for insanity that holds people to be insane at the time they committed a crime if their act was the result of a mental disorder or defect.

11. _____ A verdict stating that defendants are guilty of committing a crime but are also suffering from a mental illness that should be treated during their imprisonment. [four words]

12. _____ The principle by which the state can make decisions to promote the individual's best interests and protect him or her from self-harm or neglect. [two words]

13. _____ To arrive at just and appropriate punishments, the courts need to assess a defendant's _____ for committing a crime and his or her capacity to contribute toward a defense.

14. _____ The length of stay granted for emergency commitment is often limited to _____. [two words]

15. _____ The branch of psychology concerned with intersections between psychological practice and research and the judicial system.

16. _____ The four-letter abbreviation for a verdict stating that defendants are not guilty of committing a crime because they were insane at the time of the crime.

17. _____ A widely used legal test for insanity that holds people to be insane at the time of committing a crime if, because of a mental disorder, they did not know the nature of the act or did not know right from wrong.

18. _____ The principle that certain professionals will not divulge the information they obtain from a client.

19. _____ A body of principles and rules for ethical behavior, designed to guide decisions and actions by members of a profession. [three words]

20. _____ A lawsuit charging a therapist with improper conduct or decision-making in the course of treatment.

Chapter 1 ANSWERS

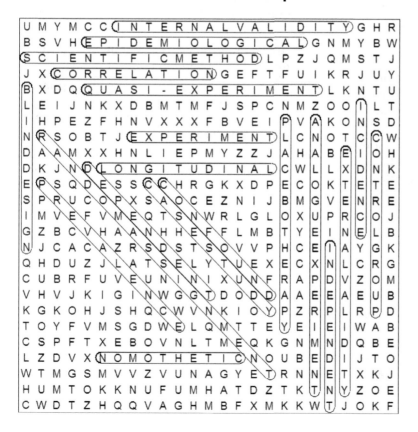

1. treatment
2. norms
3. psychotropic
4. deinstitutionalization
5. eccentric
6. managed care
7. somatogenic
8. humors
9. moral treatment
10. abnormal psychology
11. asylum
12. eccentric
13. psychogenic
14. prevention
15. trephination
16. psychoanalysis
17. exorcism
18. multicultural
19. state hospitals
20. culture

Chapter 2 ANSWERS

1. experiment
2. longitudinal
3. dependent
4. internal validity
5. control group
6. case study
7. incidence
8. quasi-experiment
9. analogue experiment
10. nomothetic
11. epidemiological
12. blind design
13. scientific method
14. correlation
15. placebo therapy
16. independent
17. external validity
18. random assignment
19. confound
20. prevalence

Chapter 3 ANSWERS

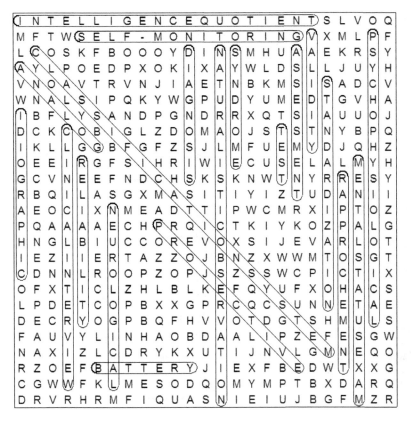

```
O D W M N C B (B I O P S Y C H O S O C I A L) U P X
(O B J E C T R E L A T I O N S) D L H J O L T U L Z
J K E H E (D I A T H E S I S - S T R E S S) W N P N
E W O L (M I P O P) M N O P S R R Z W Z Y S D O E X
O V H O O B S P S Q P J Q B R P P D T T A P U R Q
X Z K J D M Y E Y R Q O D M L J V N B D H R R M F
V D G A E E C R C J P K X B M V T G I W V H C T F
Q R S C L L H A H H J V M B M V (F I X A T I O N) J
O O V M I E O N O W M B J N B Y Q S P M Z C B X M
Y N O L N C S T T Q T H M S E R K S E A W S F I T
X K Y O G T U C R A B A X D F U W C Z N Q E V P S
(C P N P J R R O O X I R S K E M R A A T R Z Y Y W
O V K O O G N P K U L P E A W N O K I E X T J H
G S M W U C E D I Y W P P G X C D P N D C I I O W
N K T H Z O R I C D J X W O J C E U V E E S K J B
I O Q H T N Y T W C T S S G U Z A Y L P P S Q U Y
T C T D R V Q I E E G Y (M O D E L) X B R T U K M U
I R M X H U H O B H Q N H Q O O E K D E O P N Z Q
V H P I N S K N C T K A (G R O U P) L L S R E W P V
E V F D D I A I H I A P D M Y N N V B S Z R Z F L
U F Y H R V J N K E P S L X J X I N V A U E X U T
F P U D Q E F G R J I E Y Y X J P H K N Z G N E T
Q I (N E U R O T R A N S M I T T E R) A T T O W B W
S Q K U R K Y N A C K S W G U T I B D S S L J Z Y
O W (C L I E N T - C E N T E R E D T H E R A P Y) R
```

1. antidepressants
2. model
3. ego
4. neuron
5. neurotransmitter
6. cognitive
7. fixation
8. operant conditioning
9. psychotropic
10. client-centered therapy
11. electroconvulsive
12. synapse
13. group
14. diathesis-stress
15. receptor
16. psychosurgery
17. modeling
18. superego
19. biopsychosocial
20. object relations

Chapter 4 ANSWERS

```
(I N T E L L I G E N C E Q U O T I E N T) S L V O Q
M F T W (S E L F - M O N I T O R I N G) V X M L P F
L C O S K F B O O O Y D I N S M H U A A E K R S Y
A Y L P O E D P X O K I X A Y W L D S L L J U Y H
V N O A V T R V N J I A E T N B K M S I S A D C V
W N A L S I P Q K Y W G P U D Y U M E D T G V H A
I B F L Y S A N D P G N D R X Q T S I A U U O J
D C K C O B I G L Z D O M A O J S T S T N Y B P Q
I K L L G G B F G F Z S J L M F U E M Y D J Q H Z
O E E I R G F S H R I W I E C U S E L A L M H Y H
G C V N E E F N D C H S K S K N W T N Y R R E S Y
R B Q I L A S G X M A S I T I Y I Z T U D A N I Z
A E O C I X N M E A D T T I P W C M R X I P T O Z
P Q A A A E C H P R Q I C T K I Y K O Z P A L O T
H N G L B I U C C O R E V O X S I J E V A R L O G
I E Z I I E R T A Z Z O J B N Z X W W M T O S G T
C D N N L R O O P Z O P J S Z S S W C P I C I I X
O F X T I C L Z H L B L K E F Q Y U F X O H T A C
L P D E T C O P B X X G P R C Q C S U N N E T A E
D E C R Y O G P B Q F H V O T D G T S H M U L S G
F A U V Y L I N H A O B D A A L I P Z E F E S U W
N A X I Z L C D R Y K X U T I J N V L G M N I N G
R Z O E F (B A T T E R Y) J I E X F B E D W T X G
C G W W F K L M E S O D Q O M Y M P T B X D A R Q
D R V R H R M F I Q U A S N I E I U J B G F M Z R
```

1. self-monitoring
2. assessment
3. syndrome
4. mental status exam
5. projective
6. standardization
7. analog
8. reliability
9. diagnosis
10. test
11. psychophysiological
12. validity
13. battery
14. idiographic
15. intelligence quotient
16. classification system
17. rapprochement
18. neurological
19. clinical interview
20. naturalistic observation

Chapter 5 ANSWERS

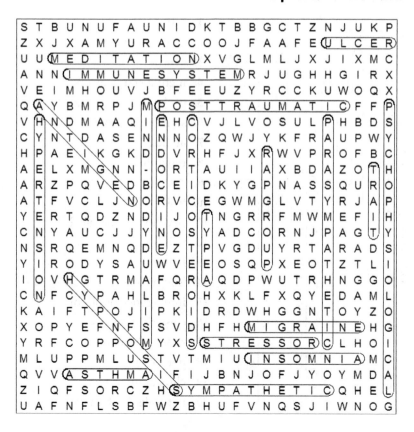

```
O B S E S S I O N Z D Z S E R O T O N I N I W O M
R F L O R W Q M K V R U N D O I N G Y E C E R C C
O E S E W W E D E M H C A U D A T E N U C L E I L
A A L P M Z N A J P R E P A R E D N E S S B M T X
T R R V M F I U W O G H R Y N M W Z M G E E X R W
Z H G A B A F P K T I Y G I L U G U P X O N B E T
K I A X Q V Q A N B D V X N K D I G B I M Z F C Q
U E G N H R B N M B Q N E K T T E C I W R O S O Z
P R O F E U K Q W I O V P A N I C L D J G D T M Q
H A R M S P P E R W L E T X I N N G B I K I B P U
O R A P O P S M L Q R Y K X E M R J K A H A I U R
B C P N B M J Z I D W K P A W Y Q P Y Z N Z O L A
I H H Y P C L I E N T - C E N T E R E D X E F S M
A Y O Z U A N X I E T Y W M D K D W C P P E I R E
G L B N P P C B W P X M J C Q U N W N F I E O E S
D Z I C B I D T L V M U U I C F G M M W Z N D N S
K I A R X A K H Q X A N I T C V V R W C J E B J P
S H D H K S Y B S A O D M E U J P E N C S A S O N
D K E P Q I Y V L X C D A R W C D J Z E V J C H N
S E D A T I V E - H Y P N O T I C L E J T N K T S
C U X J W O L Z S O K R Y F E S P U X O M E D D E
S L U E G C Q X G D S I N T E E Q A A E N B G S M
A H G C Z Y Y X L T Z I S T A A T V Z R S D S X U
N B H Z X F Y S B Y R A K T I R R Y I Z R F X N E
I Z P Q Q T P N O R E P I N E P H R I N E B K D L
```

1. phobia
2. norepinephrine
3. anxiety
4. agoraphobia
5. client-centered
6. sedative-hypnotic
7. panic
8. GABA
9. fear hierarchy
10. compulsion
11. serotonin
12. biofeedback
13. undoing
14. benzodiazepines
15. caudate nuclei
16. fear
17. response
18. obsession
19. family pedigree
20. preparedness

Chapter 6 ANSWERS

```
S T B U N U F A U N I D K T B B G C T Z N J U K P
Z X J X A M Y U R A C C O O J F A A F E U L C E R
U U M E D I T A T I O N X V G L M L J X J I X M C
A N N I M M U N E S Y S T E M R J U G H H G I R X
V E I M H O U V J B F E E U Z Y R C C K U W O Q X
Q A Y B M R P J M P O S T T R A U M A T I C F F P
V H N D M A A Q I E H C V J L V O S U L P H B D S
C Y N T D A S E N N N O Z Q W J Y K F R A U P W Y
H P A E I K G K D D V R H F J X R W V P R O F B C
A E L X M G N N - O R T A U I I A X B D A Z O T H
A R Z P Q V E D B C E I D K Y G P N A S S Q U R O
A T F V C L J N O R V C E G W M G L V T Y R J A P
Y E R T Q D Z N D I J O T N G R R F M W M E F I H
C N Y A U C J J Y N O S Y A D C O R N J P A G T Y
N S R Q E M N Q D E Z T P V G D U Y R T A R A D S
Y I R O D Y S A U W V E E O S Q P X E O T Z T L I
I O V H G T R M A F Q R A Q D P W U T R H N G G O
C N F C Y P A H L B R O H X K L F X Q Y E D A M L
K A I F T P O J I P K I D R D W H G G N T O Y Z O
X O P Y E F N F S S V D H F H M I G R A I N E H G
Y R F C O P P O M Y X S S T R E S S O R C L H O I
M L U P P M L U S T V T M I U I N S O M N I A M C
Q V V A S T H M A F I J B N J O F J Y O Y M D A
Z I Q F S O R C Z H S Y M P A T H E T I C Q H E L
U A F N F L S B F W Z B H U F V N Q S J I W N O G
```

1. corticosteroids
2. stressor
3. asthma
4. hypnosis
5. sympathetic
6. immune system
7. mind-body dualism
8. endocrine
9. meditation
10. trait
11. antigen
12. parasympathetic
13. insomnia
14. migraine
15. psychophysiological
16. Type A
17. posttraumatic
18. hypertension
19. ulcer
20. rap group

Chapter 7 ANSWERS

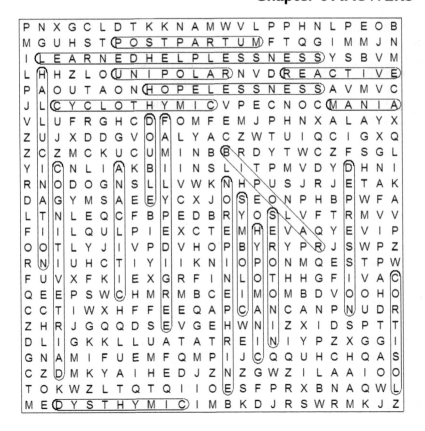

1. somatization
2. Munchausen
3. placebo
4. factitious
5. fusion
6. memory
7. amnesia
8. fugue
9. state-dependent
10. subpersonalities
11. depersonalization
12. dissociative
13. secondary
14. body dysmorphic
15. hypochondriasis
16. self-hypnosis
17. primary
18. iatrogenic
19. hysterical
20. conversion

Chapter 8 ANSWERS

1. anaclitic
2. bipolar
3. symbolic
4. depression
5. cyclothymic
6. norepinephrine
7. learned helplessness
8. serotonin
9. mania
10. hallucination
11. dysthymic
12. double
13. family pedigree
14. postpartum
15. hypomanic
16. cortisol
17. hopelessness
18. reactive
19. unipolar
20. cognitive triad

Chapter 9 ANSWERS

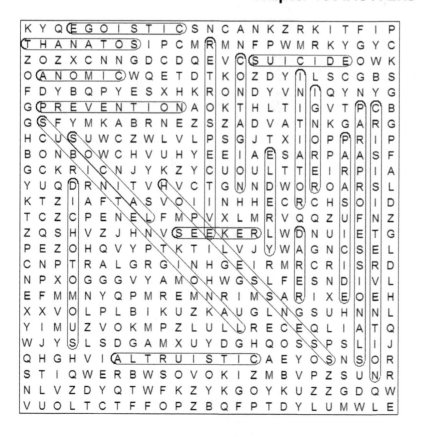

1. lithium
2. electroconvulsive
3. transcranial magnetic
4. psychological
5. norepinephrine
6. couple
7. continuation
8. sociocultural
9. reuptake
10. tricyclic
11. tyramine
12. fluoxetine
13. mood stabilizing
14. inhibitor
15. adjunct
16. biological
17. interpersonal
18. Beck
19. serotonin
20. vagus

Chapter 10 ANSWERS

1. hopelessness
2. seeker
3. dichotomous
4. retrospective
5. parasuicide
6. altruistic
7. darer
8. suicide
9. prevention
10. subintentional
11. anomic
12. egoistic
13. social
14. ignorer
15. Thanatos
16. contagion
17. crisis intervention
18. initiator
19. elderly
20. paraprofessionals

Chapter 11 ANSWERS

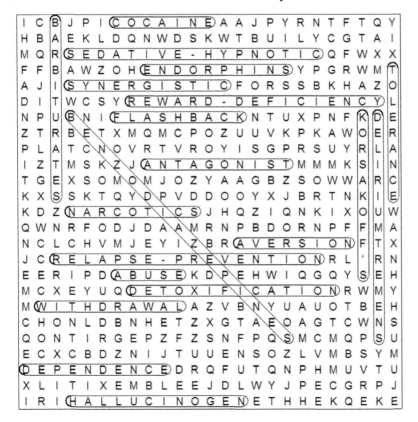

1. binge
2. hypothalamus
3. females
4. amenorrhea
5. starvation
6. enmeshed
7. lanugo
8. binge-eating
9. lateral
10. ventromedial
11. set point
12. laxatives
13. bulimia nervosa
14. dieting
15. multidimensional
16. gymnasts
17. anorexia nervosa
18. ego deficiencies
19. set the stage
20. outpatient

Chapter 12 ANSWERS

1. narcotics
2. tolerance
3. benzodiazepines
4. abuse
5. cocaine
6. detoxification
7. endorphins
8. delirium tremens
9. dependence
10. flashback
11. withdrawal
12. aversion
13. reward-deficiency
14. sedative-hypnotic
15. relapse-prevention
16. barbiturates
17. synergistic
18. Korsakoff's
19. hallucinogen
20. antagonist

Chapter 13 ANSWERS

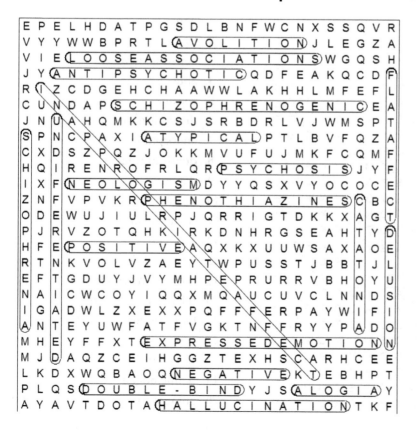

1. fetishism
2. hypoactive
3. dyspareunia
4. premature ejaculation
5. spectator role
6. frotteurism
7. desire
8. pedophilia
9. exhibitionism
10. masochism
11. aversion
12. performance anxiety
13. orgasm
14. sex-change
15. vaginismus
16. paraphilias
17. sadism
18. excitement
19. voyeurism
20. gender identity

Chapter 14 ANSWERS

1. alogia
2. psychosis
3. avolition
4. phenothiazines
5. positive
6. atypical
7. inappropriate affect
8. delusion
9. schizophrenogenic
10. hallucination
11. loose associations
12. negative
13. double-bind
14. antipsychotic
15. schizophrenia
16. expressed emotion
17. flat affect
18. neologism
19. catatonia
20. undifferentiated

Chapter 15 ANSWERS

1. moral
2. neuroleptic
3. tardive dyskinesia
4. back wards
5. token economy
6. antihistamine
7. aftercare
8. extrapyramidal effects
9. lobotomy
10. agranulocytosis
11. sheltered workshop
12. day center
13. case manager
14. interest
15. milieu therapy
16. conventional
17. antipsychotic
18. halfway house
19. deinstitutionalization
20. substantia nigra

Chapter 16 ANSWERS

1. obsessive-compulsive
2. schizoid
3. clusters
4. antisocial
5. personality
6. II
7. comorbidity
8. borderline
9. spectrum
10. rigid
11. systematic
12. histrionic
13. avoidant
14. dependent
15. narcissistic
16. passive-aggressive
17. paranoid
18. dramatic
19. Phineas Gage
20. schizotypal

Chapter 17 ANSWERS

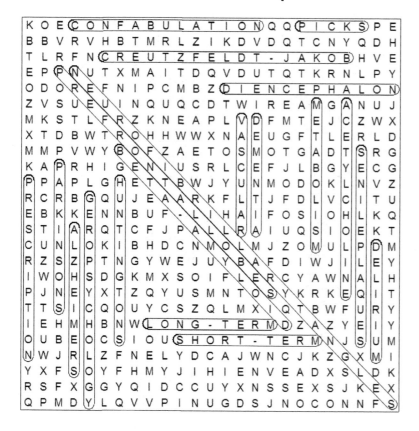

1. mental retardation
2. methylphenidate
3. theory of mind
4. conduct
5. Asperger's
6. mild
7. enuresis
8. attention-deficit
9. autistic
10. cerebellum
11. encopresis
12. moderate
13. profound
14. special education
15. normalization
16. oppositional defiant
17. mainstreaming
18. fetal alcohol
19. Down syndrome
20. severe

Chapter 18 ANSWERS

1. diencephalon
2. long-term
3. Alzheimer's
4. geropsychology
5. acetylcholine
6. vascular
7. dementia
8. senile plaques
9. Huntington's
10. prefrontal lobes
11. Creutzfeldt-Jakob
12. metabolism
13. delirium
14. Pick's
15. short-term
16. prescription
17. Parkinson's
18. beta-amyloid
19. neurofibrillary tangles
20. confabulation

Chapter 19 ANSWERS

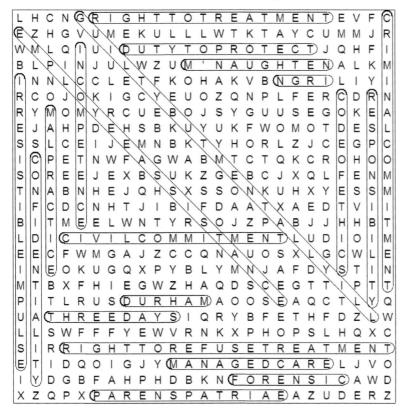

1. duty to protect
2. civil commitment
3. right to treatment
4. criminal commitment
5. employee assistance
6. managed care
7. irresistible impulse
8. right to refuse treatment
9. incompetence
10. Durham
11. guilty but mentally ill
12. parens patriae
13. responsibility
14. three days
15. forensic
16. NGRI
17. M'Naghten
18. confidentiality
19. code of ethics
20. malpractice

Video Faculty Guide

for use with

Video Segments for *Abnormal Psychology* Third Edition

by
Ronald J. Comer,
Princeton University

and

Gregory P. Comer,
Princeton Academic Resources

Critical Thinking Questions

by Nicolas Greco,
College of Lake County

Video Segments for *Abnormal Psychology*, Third Edition

ABNORMAL PSYCHOLOGY: PAST AND PRESENT
1. Benjamin Rush's "Restraint Chair"
2. Carl Jung Talks About Freud, Life, and the Collective Unconscious
3. Medical Procedures Used in Mental Hospitals in the First Half of the Twentieth Century
4. Prefrontal Lobotomy Procedure, 1942
5. Locking Away the "Feebleminded": A Shameful History

RESEARCH IN ABNORMAL PSYCHOLOGY
6. Ethics in Human Research: Violating Ones Privacy?
7. Death of a Subject: The Ethics of Mental Health Research
8. A Laboratory Study: Linking Placebo Effects to Endorphins
9. A Survey Study: Dieting and Body Image Among 33,000 Women

MODELS OF ABNORMALITY
10. Identical Twins: Growing Up Apart
11. Tasting Food: "Learned" Likes and Dislikes
12. Bandura's Bobo Doll Experiment: Modeling of Aggression
13. Gestalt Therapy's "Empty Chair Technique"
14. John and Julie Gottman Examine Marital and Family Stress
15. City of Gheel: Community Mental Health at Its Best
16. Avatars Online: A New Direction in Psychotherapy?

CLINICAL ASSESSMENT, DIAGNOSIS, AND TREATMENT
17. Sibling Wars: Assessment by Observation
18. Bias in Diagnosis: Is Premenstrual Dysphoric Disorder a Mental Disorder?
19. Assessment of Psychopathy
20. Brain Fingerprinting: Memory, Recognition, and Lie Detection

ANXIETY DISORDERS
21. Emotion = Arousal Plus Interpretation
22. Multiple Fears: Two Case Presentations
23. Watson's Famous Study: Little Albert
24. Airplane Phobia: Fear of Flying
25. Exposure Treatment for an Elevator Phobia
26. Obsessive-Compulsive Disorder: A Young Mother's Struggle
27. Treatment of OCD: Exposure and Response Prevention

STRESS DISORDERS
28. The Stress Response
29. Measuring Stress While Running with the Bulls
30. Stress Disorders: How Traumatic Were the 9/11/01 Terrorist Attacks for Americans?
31. Posttraumatic Stress Disorder: A Vietnam Combat Veteran
32. Fear, PTSD and the Brain
33. Stress and the Immune System: Caretakers at Risk
34. Hypnosis: Medical and Psychological Applications
35. Fighting Cancer: Mobilizing the Immune System

SOMATOFORM AND DISSOCIATIVE DISORDERS
36. At Risk for Body Dysmorphic Disorder: Does Society Encourage Physical Perfection in Teenage Girls?
37. Beyond Perfection: Female Body Dysmorphic Disorder
38. Munchausen Syndrome by Proxy: Why Would a Parent Make a Child Sick?

SEGMENT 1   # *BENJAMIN RUSH'S "RESTRAINT CHAIR" (2:25)

Description: Although Benjamin Rush, widely considered the father of American Psychiatry, came to believe in and practice *moral treatment* in the early 1800s, many of his prior treatments reflected contemporary medical thought and would be judged quite harsh by today's standards. A case in point was his famous "restraint chair," presented in this segment.
Source: *Madness: Brainwaves*, 1991 (BBC Worldwide Americas Inc.)

Critical Thinking Questions:

1. Although this chair may seem barbaric, restraints are still used today to calm patients. So what is the difference between the past and the present methods?
2. Why is discussing this chair significant?

*Version available on the **STUDENT TOOL KIT** under the title: *Benjamin Rush's Moral Treatments*

SEGMENT 2   # CARL JUNG TALKS ABOUT FREUD, LIFE, AND THE COLLECTIVE UNCONSCIOUS (4:45)

Description: This module presents a rare and frank interview with Carl Jung, the founder of analytical psychology. Jung reflects on his long-time friendship with Sigmund Freud. He offers a frank assessment of Freud's stubbornness and the two men's significant philosophical differences, which ultimately led to a professional and personal split between them. Jung also addresses the interaction of his spiritual and scientific beliefs, offering his views on the psyche as an entity existing beyond life and death, beyond time and space.
Source: "Professor Jung" *Face to Face* (BBC Motion Gallery)

Critical Thinking Questions:

1. Why did Jung and Freud go their separate ways?
2. Carl Jung believed that death was _____.
3. What did Jung believe about history?

SEGMENT 3   # *MEDICAL PROCEDURES USED IN MENTAL HOSPITALS IN THE FIRST HALF OF THE TWENTIETH CENTURY (4:38)

Description: The medical treatments used in mental hospitals during the first half of this century were crude, largely ineffective, and often unintentionally cruel. Some of the leading approaches are shown in this segment, including the wet pack, insulin therapy, metrazol therapy, and the lobotomy.
Sources: *Treatment in Mental Disorders*, 1949 (James D. Page); *Prefrontal Lobotomy in the Treatment of Mental Disorders*, 1942 (Walter Freeman and James Watts). Courtesy: History of Medicine Division, National Library of Medicine.

Critical Thinking Questions:

1. Why are these treatments now seen as useless and unintentionally cruel?

2. How can we view hot boxes, lamps, wet packs, and so forth?

*Version available on the **STUDENT TOOL KIT** under the title: *Early Hospital Treatments for Severe Mental Disorders*

SEGMENT 4   # PREFRONTAL LOBOTOMY PROCEDURE, 1942 (2:50)

Description: In the late 1930s, the neuropsychiatrist Egas Moniz developed the lobotomy, a brain operation in which a surgeon would cut the connections between the cortex of the brain's frontal lobes and the lower centers of the brain. This segment from 1942 shows graphic excerpts from a lobotomy procedure, done by the American neuropsychiatrist Walter Freeman. Parts of the segment are unpleasant to view.

Source: *"Prefrontal Lobotomy in the Treatment of Mental Disorders"* 1942 (Producers: Walter Freeman and James Watts). Courtesy: History of Medicine Division, National Library of Medicine.

Critical Thinking Questions:

1. Why was lobotomy so popular?

2. Why are lobotomies no longer used?

3. Is it possible to justify the number of lobotomies performed?

SEGMENT 5   # *LOCKING AWAY THE "FEEBLEMINDED": A SHAMEFUL HISTORY (7:55)

Description: This segment depicts the Fernald School, an institution for "feeble-minded" boys that existed in the 1920s, and which was in fact part of the American eugenics movement. It also shows interviews with former residents who recall severe abuse and mistreatment and discuss the lasting impact of an incorrect diagnosis of "moron." The video further explores evidence that involuntary experiments were conducted on the boys in past decades.

Source: "Deep Dark Secret" *60 Minutes* (CBS News)

Critical Thinking Questions:

1. What was the significance of the eugenics movement?

2. Were the radiation experiments conducted at Fernald State School justified?

3. The Fernald State School was nothing more than _____.

*Version available on the **STUDENT TOOL KIT** under the title: *Shameful Past Institutions for Persons with Developmental Disabilities*

SEGMENT 6

*ETHICS IN HUMAN RESEARCH: VIOLATING ONE'S PRIVACY? (7:00)

Description: This segment explores a genetic research project conducted in Iceland that attempts to identify genes that may predispose individuals for certain disorders. The researcher in charge was given the right to collect and analyze the private medical records of all Icelandic citizens. The clip explores the ethical concerns and potential misuses of such information, while also considering the benefits that genetic research may provide.
Source: "Genes" *60 Minutes* (CBS News)

Critical Thinking Questions:

1. What is the concern with allowing 12 years of exclusive rights to decode and potentially market genetic data to HMO's?

2. Does this 12-year collection of genetic data violate privacy?

3. Would you participate in a 12-year collection of your genetic data?

4. Do the potential benefits outweigh the risks of this database?

*Version available on the **STUDENT TOOL KIT** under the title:
Genetic Research: Violating One's Privacy

SEGMENT 7

*DEATH OF A SUBJECT: THE ETHICS OF MENTAL HEALTH RESEARCH (4:00)

Description: This segment focuses on the case of a man with schizophrenia who died after participating in an experimental drug trial at an inpatient treatment facility. The man's background is examined, and his ability to make decisions relating to his own treatment is examined. The video raises questions about the ethics of research using patients with severe mental disorders for experimental drug trials and explores the implications of such practices for the patients and their families.
Source: "Ultimate Risk: Here to Help" *48 Hours* (CBS News)

Critical Thinking Questions:

1. Can patients with schizophrenia truly consent to a clinical research study?

2. The fact that Joseph Santana was on Clozapine tells us what?

3. Is it ethical to remove a subject from a treatment that is working in order to place them in a clinical trial?

*Version available on the **STUDENT TOOL KIT** under the title:
A Tragic Consequence of Research Misconduct

SEGMENT 8

*A LABORATORY STUDY: LINKING PLACEBO EFFECTS TO ENDORPHINS (3:15)

Description: This segment illustrates how *experimental designs* (and their causal conclusions) are conducted by showing a laboratory experiment with human participants. The findings of this study suggest that the effectiveness of placebo drugs is partly a result of the patients' release of endorphins, their natural opioids. The implication is that, for some people, the expectation that a given treatment will soon be helpful causes them, without awareness, to

release endorphins throughout their brain and body. In turn, the endorphins reduce their pain or help them to feel better in other ways.
Source: *The Keys to Paradise*, 1979 (BBC Worldwide Americas Inc.)

Critical Thinking Questions:

1. Should placebo pills be considered as a treatment for people without their knowledge?
2. How can the placebo effect ruin the performance of the study drug in a clinical research study?
3. Are you surprised by Fred's response to the placebo?

*Version available on the **STUDENT TOOL KIT** under the title: *Experimental Design in Action*

SEGMENT 9   # A SURVEY STUDY: DIETING AND BODY IMAGE AMONG 33,000 WOMEN (2:06)

Description: This segment illustrates the nature and design of survey studies by bringing to life the well-known 1984 *Glamour Magazine* survey of 33,000 women, conducted by Drs. Susan Wooley and Wayne Wooley. This survey study suggested that most women in our society, even underweight women, consider themselves overweight, particularly in body parts from the waist down, and diet regularly.
Source: *The Waist Land: Eating Disorders in America*, 1985 (Coronet/MTI).

Critical Thinking Questions:

1. How important is the media in the female body image?
2. If people know that models in magazines are airbrushed, why do they still aspire to that look?
3. Are women objectifying certain parts of their body by conforming to cultural norms?

SEGMENT 10   # *IDENTICAL TWINS: GROWING UP APART (1:48)

Description: This clip shows two identical twins who were separated at birth, each unaware of the other's existence until adulthood. The two exhibit very similar personalities, mannerisms, interests, hobbies, and physical appearance (though one is much heavier than the other). Also, both twins independently went into the same profession, firefighting. The clip surmises that genes play a significant role in people's physical, emotional, social, and mental development.
Source: "In the Genes" *48 Hours* (CBS News)

Critical Thinking Questions:

1. Are you surprised by the similarities of these separated twins?
2. Do you think there may be some underlying psychological issues related to their separation?
3. If you suddenly found out you had a twin, what would your reaction be?
4. Are their similarities over-exaggerated?

*Version available on the **STUDENT TOOL KIT** under the title: *Separated at Birth: Nature versus Nurture*

SEGMENT 11

TASTING FOOD: "LEARNED" LIKES AND DISLIKES (2:50)

Description: This segment illustrates that children try new foods as they develop and learn to enjoy foods they once disliked intensely. Through first-hand accounts, the video also shows how people sometimes acquire food aversions, negative responses to certain foods, through *classical conditioning*. Consistent with the behavioral model, individuals describe the unpleasant experiences and events that first led to current food aversions.

Source: "Taste" *Human Senses* (BBC Motion Gallery)

Critical Thinking Questions:

1. Why do our taste buds change over time?

2. Taste aversion can be caused by _____?

3. Have you ever stopped eating something after a negative experience?

SEGMENT 12

*BANDURA'S BOBO DOLL EXPERIMENT: MODELING OF AGGRESSION (5:00)

Description: Does an individual's observation of aggressive or violent models lead, in turn, to aggressive or violent behavior by the individual? Yes, according to this famous study by Albert Bandura, which helped Bandura develop his behavioral theory of *modeling*. This segment, which is narrated by Bandura himself, shows how children in his study attack a Bobo doll after observing an adult model do the same.

Source: Albert Bandura, Stanford University, and Worth Publishers

Critical Thinking Questions:

1. Can media, such as television and video games, cause modeling behavior in children?

2. What does this video say about the importance of parenting?

3. Does exposure to violence predispose a person to commit violent acts?

4. Do we see a gender difference in modeling behavior in this film?

*Version available on the **STUDENT TOOL KIT** under the title: *Bandura's Bobo Doll: Is Aggressive Behavior Learned?*

SEGMENT 13

GESTALT THERAPY'S "EMPTY CHAIR TECHNIQUE" (5:25)

Description: One of Gestalt therapy's best known techniques is the *empty chair technique*, in which the client is instructed to talk to an empty chair as if it contains a person with whom the client has certain difficulties. The client expresses candid feelings or thoughts toward the chair, then switches chairs and talks back to himself or herself from the perspective of the other person. Today, the empty chair technique is often used by therapists of various orientations, and in this segment it is employed by the eclectic therapist Arnold Lazarus, as he works with a client (played by an actress) who is burdened by unexpressed anger toward her mother.

Source: *The Assessment/Therapy Connection* (Arnold Lazarus, Research Press)

Critical Thinking Questions:

1. What role does the therapist play in this treatment?

2. The woman's anger is directed toward whom?

3. When would the empty chair technique be used?

SEGMENT 14 # JOHN AND JULIE GOTTMAN EXAMINE MARITAL AND FAMILY STRESS (7:15)

Description: In this segment, psychologists John Gottman and Julie Schwartz Gottman demonstrate their research on relationships, and also discuss how couples can maintain romance in their relationship after having children. The Gottman's illustrate the pitfalls many couples fall into, and clarify the pressures that growing families can place on couple relationships. Finally, the researchers show "the Love Lab," a research facility they have set up to look like a typical house or apartment. Couples participating in a research are monitored while fighting or relating to each other, and corresponding brain scans are examined.
Source: *CBS Early Show, CBS Sunday Morning* (CBS News)

Critical Thinking Questions:

1. What causes couples to become unhappy after having children?

2. Couples need to eliminate or lessen what in their lives?

3. How can couples stay intimate after having a baby?

SEGMENT 15 # *CITY OF GHEEL: COMMUNITY MENTAL HEALTH AT ITS BEST (7:15)

Description: This segment focuses on the community of Gheel, Belgium in which over 650 psychiatric patients live with and are cared for by local families. The progress of the patients is examined, and it is noted that many patients require lower levels of medication as a result of participation in family-care. The video also explores how the family-care system impacts the rest of the community.
Source: "All in the Family" *60 Minutes* (CBS News)

Critical Thinking Questions:

1. Is responsibility important for the mentally ill person?

2. Why is family support essential for the mentally ill person?

3. Do you think that extended family placement for the mentally ill could work in the United States?

*Version available on the **STUDENT TOOL KIT** under the title:
City of Gheel: Community Mental Health in Action

SEGMENT 16   # AVATARS ONLINE: A NEW DIRECTION IN PSYCHOTHERAPY? (3:20)

Description: This segment explores an Internet-based treatment approach that is helping to change the outlook for people with agoraphobia and social phobias. Focusing on the case of Patricia, an agoraphobic woman who was once fearful of leaving her house, the segment shows how developing an "avatar" on an online virtual world enabled her to expose herself to activities she had feared previously. Patricia's agoraphobia has improved greatly with this approach. The segment also shows a psychotherapist who interacts online with patients via his own avatar.
Source: *CBS Evening News* (CBS News)

Critical Thinking Questions:

1. How does the avatar allow Patti to deal with her phobias?
2. What are the consequences of seeking help online?
3. Would you ever seek treatment online?

SEGMENT 17   # SIBLING WARS: ASSESSMENT BY OBSERVATION (2:50)

Description: This segment demonstrates the assessment technique of *observation*. It shows a study in which mothers of two children are instructed to ignore their younger child. At first, the younger siblings try to disrupt the older siblings and their mothers. Eventually, the younger siblings even display anger tantrums. Older siblings, on the other hand, when subjected to the same disinterest from their mothers, try to gain their parent's attention through sweet rather than disruptive behavior. The observations suggest that older siblings tend to play by social rules, while younger siblings behave in a rebellious manner, in the face of such family stress.
Source: "Will to Win" *Human Instinct* (BBC Motion Gallery)

Critical Thinking Questions:

1. What happens when the younger children do not receive attention from their mother?
2. What are the consequences of the mother consistently ignoring the younger child?
3. Unlike the younger child, the older child will do what when trying to get his mother's attention?

SEGMENT 18 ## *BIAS IN DIAGNOSIS: IS PREMENSTRUAL DYSPHORIC DISORDER A MENTAL DISORDER? (5:24)

Description: In 1994, after a long and heated debate among task force members, the framers of DSM-IV decided to include *Premenstrual Dysphoric Disorder* in the DSM as a category in need of further study. Some clinicians believe that this pattern should in fact become a formal diagnostic category, while others charge that sexism rather than clinical research is behind the clinical labeling of people with this pattern. This issue comes to life during a spirited debate in 1993 between leading clinicians Robert Spitzer and Paula Caplan.
Source: *Today Show*, 7/12/93 (NBC News)

Critical Thinking Questions:

1. Is PMDD just a milder form of depression that is exacerbated during the premenstrual cycle?

2. Should PMDD be listed as a diagnostic category in the DSM-IV-TR?

3. Is the debate between clinicians unfair considering one is a psychiatrist and the other is a psychologist?

4. Sarafem is an approved medication for PMDD and contains the same ingredient as Prozac (fluoxetine). What does this tell us about the disorder?

*Version available on the **STUDENT TOOL KIT** under the title:
DSM-IV-TR Categories: Bias against Females?

SEGMENT 19 ## *ASSESSMENT OF PSYCHOPATHY (3:55)

Description: This segment offers a clinical picture of psychopathy (sociopathy) and demonstrates a leading tool for assessing this antisocial pattern. The segment focuses on the work of Robert Hare and on the "Hare Psychopathy Checklist," and further considers how well clinicians can predict criminal behavior or violent behavior.
Source: *The Mind*, Second Edition, 1999 (Thirteen, WNET and Worth Publishers)

Critical Thinking Questions:

1. Are psychopathic individuals able to be rehabilitated?

2. Are there treatments available?

3. How does the Hare Psychopathy Checklist aid the clinician?

4. How can predicting psychopathic behavior in adolescents help society?

*Version available on the **STUDENT TOOL KIT** under the title:
Assessing Psychopathy

SEGMENT 20

*BRAIN FINGERPRINTING: MEMORY, RECOGNITION, AND LIE DETECTION (5:00)

Description: This segment examines the technique of brain fingerprinting, which measures brain waves to determine whether or not information is, in fact, stored in the brain. Researchers in the video believe that brain waves can reveal whether information is present even when an individual may want to keep it hidden. A case is explored in which brain fingerprinting was used to determine whether an accused man did, in fact, have information about the details of a past crime.

Source: "Brain Fingerprinting" *60 Minutes* (CBS News)

Critical Thinking Questions:

1. What is the difference between an innocent person versus a guilty person?

2. When the brain recognizes important information, what happens?

3. Do you believe that this technology can truly be used in interrogation?

*Version available on the **STUDENT TOOL KIT** under the title: *"Brain Fingerprinting:" Detecting Hidden Thoughts*

SEGMENT 21

EMOTION = AROUSAL PLUS INTERPRETATION (3:45)

Description: This segment helps address the question of what is anxiety, and distinguishes arousal from emotions such as anxiety. It focuses on the variables previously explored in Schachter and Singer's famous study on emotion, arousal, and context. The video features a study in which all the participants were administered a stimulant drug—amphetamine—but only half were told that the drug was a stimulant, while the other half were told that it was a placebo. The individuals who believed they had been given a placebo interpreted their physical arousal in a negative way, while those who were expecting the arousal effects of the stimulant drug were able to enjoy their arousal and reported feeling energized and focused. The findings suggest that emotions such as anxiety are not only influenced by physiological responses but also by a person's interpretation of their arousal and of the situation.

Source: "In the Heat of the Moment" *Brain Story* (BBC Motion Gallery)

Critical Thinking Questions:

1. Was there a difference between those who were told they received a placebo versus those who knew they received the drug?

2. What does this study tell us about drug therapy?

SEGMENT 22
*MULTIPLE FEARS: TWO CASE PRESENTATIONS (2:07)

Description: In this segment, two individuals describe in powerful terms the symptoms, origins, and effects of their multiple fears.
Source: *Phobias...Overcoming the Fear*, 1991 (Producer, Lalia Gilmore-Madriguera; Connecticut Public Television)

Critical Thinking Questions:

1. What are the effects of phobia on Julio's life?

2. How does Jeanne's social phobia limit her functioning?

*Version available on the **STUDENT TOOL KIT** under the title:
Worrying: Key to Generalized Anxiety

SEGMENT 23
WATSON'S FAMOUS STUDY: LITTLE ALBERT (3:00)

Description: This segment contains footage of the famous 1920 study involving Little Albert, in which behaviorists John Watson and Rosalie Rayner taught a baby boy to fear white rats. The segment has three parts: (1) the baby reacts comfortably prior to the study when confronted by animals, including a rat; (2) the baby reacts fearfully to a white rat after undergoing classical conditioning; (3) the baby's conditioned fear of rats generalizes to similar objects such as other animals, a fur coat, and a mask.
Source: Distributed exclusively by Penn State Media Sales on behalf of the Archives of the History of American Psychology.

Critical Thinking Questions:

1. What are the ethical implications of this study today?

2. What is the significance of not filming the conditioning process (seeing the acquisition)?

SEGMENT 24
*AIRPLANE PHOBIA: FEAR OF FLYING (6:10)

Description: This segment focuses on a woman with a phobic fear of airplane travel. It reveals various aspects of her phobia, including its origins, and observes her participation in a special behavioral exposure treatment program for this problem.
Source: *Phobias...Overcoming the Fear*, 1991 (Producer, Lalia Gilmore-Madriguera; Connecticut Public Television)

Critical Thinking Questions:

1. What role does visual imagery play?

2. Why is it so important that the therapist continues to assess the fearful flyer during the flight?

*Version available on the **STUDENT TOOL KIT** under the title:
Overcoming a Fear of Flying

SEGMENT 25 | **EXPOSURE TREATMENT FOR AN ELEVATOR PHOBIA (2:15)**

Description: This segment features a man who has an intense fear of elevators. We see him attempt to overcome his phobia with behavioral exposure therapy, by confronting the situation (elevator riding) that he dreads. A therapist treats the man with a combination of exposure, group support, and relaxation techniques, and ultimately the man successfully rides an elevator and displays significant improvement.
Source: "Phobias" *48 Hours* (CBS News)

Critical Thinking Questions:

1. What is the importance of the group in treatment?
2. In group treatment, the therapist needs to maintain what kind of structure?

SEGMENT 26 | ***OBSESSIVE-COMPULSIVE DISORDER: A YOUNG MOTHER'S STRUGGLE (7:15)**

Description: This segment focuses on the numerous and intense symptoms of a woman with obsessive-compulsive disorder. Her obsessive fears and compulsive behaviors are tied in particular to her young son and to her concerns for his safety from contamination. The video shows the woman carrying out extreme, ritualized behavior, and it demonstrates the negative impact her compulsions have had on her life and on her ability to parent her child.
Source: "Who's Normal Anyway?" *Obsessions* (BBC Motion Gallery)

Critical Thinking Questions:

1. How does her OCD affect her life?
2. If his mother's OCD is left untreated, how would Jake's development be affected by it?
3. Does she have insight into her condition?

*Version available on the **STUDENT TOOL KIT** under the title:
The Impact of Obsessions and Compulsions

SEGMENT 27 | **TREATMENT OF OCD: EXPOSURE AND RESPONSE PREVENTION (7:15)**

Description: Following up on the previous segment *(Segment 26)*, this module features the treatment intervention for the woman with obsessive-compulsive disorder. Her obsessive fears and compulsive behaviors are tied in particular to her young son and to her concerns for his safety from contamination. The video shows a powerful session of *exposure and response prevention* treatment. By the end of treatment the woman displays significant improvement.
Source: "Who's Normal Anyway?" *Obsessions* (BBC Motion Gallery)

Critical Thinking Questions:

1. How does Stephanie's doctor help her to contaminate the couch?
2. Do individuals with OCD show improvement with cognitive-behavioral therapy?

SEGMENT 28   **THE STRESS RESPONSE (2:45)**

Description: This video looks at the stress ordinary people undergo in today's world. Focusing on one woman who balances a successful law career and family, the video examines hormones, like cortisol, that are related to stress and shows how overproduction of these hormones can lead to mental and physical distress. It also highlights ongoing research into stress and stress management.
Source: *CBS Evening News* (CBS News)

Critical Thinking Questions:

1. Do we have more stress in our lives today?

2. Chronic stress has been found to cause what changes?

SEGMENT 29   ***MEASURING STRESS WHILE RUNNING WITH THE BULLS (4:20)**

Description: This segment features the running of the bulls in Pamplona, Spain, which continues to be a popular event despite the fact that many persons have been gored or even killed since its inception. In particular, the clip focuses on one man who is running with the bulls. His physiological reactions—including heart rate and cortisol levels—are monitored before, during, and after his participation. The nature of the body's fight-or-flight response to danger is also featured.
Source: "Born to Survive" *Human Instinct* (BBC Motion Gallery)

Critical Thinking Questions:

1. Would you ever consider running with the bulls?

2. How does this example relate to other life- threatening events?

*Version available on the **STUDENT TOOL KIT** under the title:
Fight-or-Flight: How Stress Affects Psychological and Bodily Functioning

SEGMENT 30   **STRESS DISORDERS: HOW TRAUMATIC WERE THE 9/11/01 TERRORIST ATTACKS FOR AMERICANS? (1:36)**

Description: This segment examines the lingering psychological impact of the 9/11 terrorist attacks. People describe how memories of the attacks continue to upset and affect them long after the traumatic event. Similarly, a widespread study reveals a striking increase in the prevalence of posttraumatic stress disorder among victims of the attacks.
Source: *NBC News*, 8/06/02

Critical Thinking Questions:

1. Why are people in Washington, DC, less susceptible to PTSD than those in New York City?

2. What feelings would we expect from those who suffered a trauma?

3. Those with PTSD benefit from what type of treatment?

4. Prognosis for those with PTSD is best when _____.

SEGMENT 31

*POSTTRAUMATIC STRESS DISORDER: A VIETNAM COMBAT VETERAN (3:55)

Description: This segment focuses on a Vietnam veteran who suffers from posttraumatic stress disorder, which affects his family, personal, and professional life. We see footage that conveys the intensity and anxiety-arousing nature of his combat experience. The video also features specific symptoms of the disorder and details how flashbacks and persistent watchfulness impede daily functioning. The segment includes the work of the PTSD researcher Douglas Bremner.
Source: "In the Heat of the Moment" *Brain Story* (BBC Motion Gallery)

Critical Thinking Questions:

1. What role does helplessness play in PTSD?
2. Why was the Vietnam War important for the DSM?
3. PTSD is typically comorbid with _____
4. How does Dennis's fear affect his life?

*Version available on the **STUDENT TOOL KIT** under the title:
One Man's Return from Combat

SEGMENT 32

FEAR, PTSD, AND THE BRAIN (4:00)

Description: Focusing on Vietnam combat veterans with PTSD, this segment features research into the physiological causes of the disorder. Brain scans of a PTSD sufferer as he is exposed to images of war reveal that the hippocampus, a brain region implicated in the function of memory, operates abnormally in individuals with PTSD, suggesting that this brain area may be partly responsible for the unusual patterns of anxiety and fear on display in PTSD. The work of PTSD researcher Douglas Bremner is featured in this video module.
Source: "In the Heat of the Moment" *Brain Story* (BBC Motion Gallery)

Critical Thinking Questions:

1. While many veterans remember Vietnam as if it occurred yesterday, they have difficulties with memory for recent events. This type of memory loss is known as_____.
2. Which part of the brain plays a vital role in memory?

SEGMENT 33

*STRESS AND THE IMMUNE SYSTEM: CARETAKERS AT RISK (3:15)

Description: This segment examines the relationship between caretaking (specifically, caring for family members with dementia), stress, and health. The video focuses on a man who cares for his wife with Alzheimer's disease and presents the emotional and physical toll that chronic stress takes on him and on other such individuals. Finally, a study by Janice Kiecolt Glaser and Ronald Glaser is presented, providing evidence that long-term stress can lower the human body's immune response.
Source: "Mind Over Body" *Horizon* (BBC Motion Gallery)

Critical Thinking Questions:

1. Caregivers are at increased risk for_____.

2. While the death of a loved one results in bereavement, chronic, long-term conditions such as Alzheimer's may result in _____.

3. The wound study demonstrated that increased stress results in _____.

*Version available on the **STUDENT TOOL KIT** under the title: *Caretaking: The Physical Toll*

SEGMENT 34 HYPNOSIS: MEDICAL AND PSYCHOLOGICAL APPLICATIONS (5:20)

Description: This segment examines the use and effectiveness of hypnosis in medical settings. It explores the use of hypnosis as a relaxation treatment technique. Research shown in the video demonstrates that medical procedures in which hypnosis is applied often work faster, are more comfortable for patients, and result in fewer side-effects. New hypnosis methods such as virtual reality hypnosis also are explored.
Source: "Hypnosis" *Sunday Morning* (CBS News)

Critical Thinking Questions:

1. Why is hypnosis beneficial for localized surgery?

2. Do you think this present use may give hypnosis more credibility?

3. Is hypnosis in medical applications just a placebo effect?

SEGMENT 35 FIGHTING CANCER: MOBILIZING THE IMMUNE SYSTEM (6:35)

Description: This segment focuses on the use of behavioral therapy, including relaxation techniques and support groups, to help cancer patients cope with the physical and psychological impact of their illness and of their chemotherapy. The video also features research on such interventions, including findings that cancer patients who receive the interventions tend to survive longer. The video includes a focus on the operation of the immune system.
Source: "Mind Over Body" *Horizon* (BBC Motion Gallery)

Critical Thinking Questions:

1. Does a positive attitude benefit a person with a life threatening/terminal condition?

2. How does classical conditioning play a role in fighting cancer?

3. How did relaxation benefit the patients with cancer?

SEGMENT 36   **AT RISK FOR BODY DYSMORPHIC DISORDER: DOES SOCIETY ENCOURAGE PHYSICAL PERFECTION IN TEENAGE GIRLS? (3:20)**

Description: This segment looks at society's endorsement and encouragement of physical perfection, particularly in teenage girls, and the growing trend toward cosmetic surgery by female adolescents. The video follows one individual in particular as she undergoes breast augmentation to overcome what she considers to be her physical "deformity."
Source: "Skin Deep" *48 Hours*, 5/27/99 (CBS News)

Critical Thinking Questions:

1. Is cosmetic or plastic surgery acceptable and ethical for teenage girls and why?
2. Should parents pay for cosmetic surgery and why?
3. Can physical perfection truly be achieved?
4. Haley is at risk for _____.
5. Why do these teenagers ignore the risks of these major surgeries?

SEGMENT 37   **BEYOND PERFECTION: FEMALE BODY DYSMORPHIC DISORDER (4:35)**

Description: This segment focuses on a woman who suffers from body dysmorphic disorder. She perceives her normal facial skin as horribly disfigured. This distorted body image severely impairs her personal and professional life. The video focuses on how her concerns have unfolded since adolescence.
Source: "Seeking Perfection" *Obsessions* (BBC Motion Gallery)

Critical Thinking Questions:

1. In what ways does BDD mimic OCD?
2. How similar is BDD to the eating disorders?
3. The therapist stated her client had OCD, borderline personality disorder, PTSD, major depressive disorder, and BDD. Do you believe that the therapist is correct in her evaluation of comorbidity?
4. Will the patient ever reach her goal of perfection?

*Version available on the **STUDENT TOOL KIT** under the title:
Beyond Perfection: Female Body Dysmorphic Disorder

SEGMENT 38   **MUNCHAUSEN SYNDROME BY PROXY: WHY WOULD A PARENT MAKE A CHILD SICK? (4:09)**

Description: Over the past decade, the public and the clinical field have become increasingly aware of the pattern called *Munchausen syndrome by proxy,*

in which parents secretly make their children sick in order to fulfill some inner psychological needs. This segment follows one such case — a mother who initially received enormous acclaim for her devoted service to her sick daughter, but was later convicted of aggravated child abuse. A jury decided that she had secretly been making her child sick all along.
Source: "A Mother Accused" *48 Hours,* 11/04/99 (CBS News)

Critical Thinking Questions:

1. Why would a parent deliberately make their child ill?

2. Is it easy to prove Munchausen syndrome by proxy?

3. When a child is separated from a parent accused of Munchausen syndrome by proxy what typically occurs?

SEGMENT 39   PHANTOM LIMB SENSATION (3:20)

Description: This segment explores the phenomenon of "phantom limb" sensation. It presents a female patient who experiences pain and other sensations in the hand of her amputated arm. Examining research into this phenomenon, the video concludes that the sensation is the result of activity in areas of the brain that lie near the brain area previously stimulated by the limb, prior to its amputation.
Source: "All in the Mind" *Brain Story* (BBC Motion Gallery)

Critical Thinking Questions:

1. What causes Phantom limb pain?

2. Would a person experiencing phantom limb pain benefit from psychotherapy?

SEGMENT 40   PICKPOCKETS, PLACEBOS, AND PAIN: THE ROLE OF EXPECTATIONS (4:20)

Description: In order to explore the role that expectations may play in the perception of pain and other sensations, this segment first features a man (pickpocket) who is able to remove watches undetected, and then moves on to a research study of the role that expectations may play in the experience of pain. In the study, all participants are given shocks, but half are told that a placebo sugar pill they have taken is a pain killer while the other half are told that it is a pain enhancer. Results show that those expecting the pain to be less intense are in fact able to tolerate higher shock levels. The video illustrates that the perception of sensations can be influenced by factors such as expectations and attention.
Source: "Touch" *Human Senses* (BBC Motion Gallery)

Critical Thinking Questions:

1. If we expect something to hurt, will it be more painful?

2. By giving a placebo painkiller, do you believe subjects feel less pain?

3. To what degree can research on preconceived beliefs positively affect the outcomes in other areas of medicine?

SEGMENT 41

*CREATING FALSE MEMORIES: A LABORATORY STUDY (4:45)

Description: This segment features an experiment into the nature of memory, and shows that "false memories" can be introduced into a person's recollection. In the study, participants are shown and questioned about photographs from their childhood, including one photograph doctored to show an event (a hot air balloon ride) that the participants never really experienced. After a week, half of the participants actually believe that they can recall the experience of the hot air balloon ride. This video shows how subjective and unreliable memory sometimes can be, and how it can be manipulated.
Source: "False Memories" *Tomorrow's World* (BBC Motion Gallery)

Critical Thinking Questions:

1. Why do you believe it is easy to create false memories?
2. What are the implications of false memories for the general public as evidenced by this study?
3. At the end of this laboratory study, what do you believe is the most important thing psychologists have an obligation to do?

*Version available on the **STUDENT TOOL KIT** under the title:
Repressed Memories or False Memories?

SEGMENT 42

DISSOCIATIVE AMNESIA: ARE REPRESSED CHILDHOOD MEMORIES FACT OR FICTION? (3:20)

Description: This segment brings to life the controversial issue of recovered memories of childhood abuse, including both psychological and legal aspects of the issue. It features persons who later came to conclude that their recovered memories of childhood abuse had in fact been false memories. And it considers the impact of "memory retrieval techniques." The segment also follows one of the cases that first helped bring the issue of repressed memories of childhood abuse to the public's attention.
Source: NBC News, 3/10/94; NBC News, 7/3/96

Critical Thinking Questions:

1. How can false memories destroy a family?
2. Are repressed memories truly possible?
3. Are therapists who use memory retrieval techniques—such as hypnosis—reliable?

SEGMENT 43

*THREE FACES OF EVE: THE REAL PERSON (10:00)

Description: Most people have read the book or seen the feature film *The Three Faces of Eve*, or at least heard about this famous case. However, few have actually observed the woman who suffered from this disorder. In this segment — a filmed interview conducted by her therapist a half century ago

— we see Eve's three subpersonalities discussing their views and behaviors and displaying different patterns of speech, gestures, body language, and experiences. It is worth noting that, as it turned out, this woman also experienced many other personalities beyond those on display in this interview or in the case study. Moreover, she later recovered fully.

Source: *"The Real Three Faces of Eve,"* 1957 (Chris Sizemore and the Jerry Naylor Co. LLC)

Critical Thinking Questions:

1. Is the ability to switch personalities on demand suspicious?

2. Who is the host personality?

*Version available on the **STUDENT TOOL KIT** under the title:
Three Faces of Eve: The Real Person

SEGMENT 44   DAYDREAMS (2:05)

Description: This segment explores the nature, themes, and causes of daydreams. It focuses on brain scan findings that auditory pathways are active during daydreams, just as they are when persons are hearing actual sounds and voices.

Source: NBC News Archives

Critical Thinking Questions:

1. What do daydreams mean to you?

2. What is the most common daydream?

SEGMENT 45   *PARENTAL ATTACHMENT IN INFANCY: HARRY HARLOW AND THE "WIRE MOTHER" (7:00)

Description: In this classic 1960 footage, famous researcher Harry Harlow demonstrates his work with rhesus monkeys and considers how this work may help explain the development of attachment and of depression and anxiety. Harlow conducts experiments in which monkeys who have been raised by an artificial mother made out of wire nevertheless turn to artificial mothers made of cloth in times of distress or in unfamiliar surroundings. Harlow also exposes the young monkeys to frightening artificial robot threats, and finds that there is an innate craving by the monkeys for soft tactile comforting touch—touch that cannot be provided by a "wire mother," even one that has been solely responsible for the nursing of the monkeys.

Source: *Conquest: Mother Love* (CBS News)

Critical Thinking Questions:

1. Would Harlow's experiment be considered unethical in the present day?

2. What is the importance of the wire mother?

3. What is the importance of the cloth mother?

*Version available on the **STUDENT TOOL KIT** under the title:
"Wire Mothers" and Attachment: Harlow's Monkeys

SEGMENT 46   ***THE SEARCH FOR HAPPINESS (6:15)**

Description: This segment explores the concept of happiness and the human perception of it. It considers how the definition of happiness has changed over the years, from religious devotion to suffering to the current American emphasis on "the pursuit of happiness." The video further looks at an elderly couple who find happiness in devoting their lives to caring for animals. The segment also focuses on research into how people can learn to accept the happiness that is available in their own lives rather than yearn for a level of happiness that is unrealistic.
Source: "The Pursuit of Happiness" *CBS Sunday Morning* (CBS News)

Critical Thinking Questions:

1. Do we all have the ability to achieve happiness?

2. Do you believe that more money does not bring happiness if you are not secure?

3. What does this video say about the effects of animals on mood?

*Version available on the **STUDENT TOOL KIT** under the title: *Seeking Happiness: To Each His Own*

SEGMENT 47   **A HAPPINESS TRAIT? (2:00)**

Description: This segment focuses on happiness and its stability as a personality trait. It highlights the discovery of a gene that seems to play a key role in the formation of mood and personality. This gene has been linked to general feelings of well-being (or lack of well-being), and it appears to play an especially important role in shaping the behavior of individuals with the "neurotic" personality type. The video explores the implications of this finding for the study of personality development and the use of genetic engineering. The module also clarifies that many genes and environmental factors are likely to contribute to the complex experience of happiness.
Source: "Designer Babies" *Horizon* (BBC Motion Gallery)

Critical Thinking Questions:

1. Do you believe there is a happiness trait?

2. How can this research effect one's health insurance?

3. Would it be ethical to produce a child genetically altered to be happy?

SEGMENT 48   **MANIA (1:38)**

Description: In this segment a woman is interviewed during a severe manic episode. Her symptoms include rushed speech and grandiosity.
Source: *The Mind: Depression*, 1988 (Thirteen, WNET) (New York Educational Broadcasting Corporation)

Critical Thinking Questions:

1. If an antidepressant (like Prozac) is given to a person with bipolar affective disorder, what could happen?

2. This patient's speech and thought pattern is an example of what?

3. When interviewing a person with bipolar affective disorder, which of the following is one thing you may need to do?

SEGMENT 49 | **POSTPARTUM DEPRESSION (6:00)**

Description: This segment explores postpartum depression. Women who previously suffered from postpartum depression and their husbands discuss the feelings they experienced following the birth of their children. The segment also profiles one woman who experienced severe postpartum depression, showing how she was helped by new assessment tools and treatment techniques.

Source: *CBS Weekend Early News; CBS Early Show* (CBS News)

Critical Thinking Questions:

1. What are the risks associated with postpartum depression?

2. Is a brief period of baby blues quite common?

3. Do societal expectations increase the risk of postpartum depression?

SEGMENT 50 | ***DR. AARON BECK INTERVIEWS A DEPRESSED WOMAN (4:00)**

Description: In this segment Aaron Beck, originator of cognitive therapy, conducts an interview with a depressed woman (played by an actress). During the interview, Dr. Beck discusses the woman's current situation with her, points out her cognitive reactions to it, and helps her begin to examine her thinking.

Source: *Cognitive Therapy of Depression*, 1977 (Dr. Aaron Beck, The Beck Institute for Cognitive Therapy and Research)

Critical Thinking Questions:

1. Does Dr. Beck demonstrate a high degree of empathy with the patient?

2. Given this patient's current emotional state, is cognitive therapy the best treatment?

*Version available on the **STUDENT TOOL KIT** under the title: *Depression: A Pervasive Disorder*

SEGMENT 51 | ***DR. AARON BECK CONDUCTS COGNITIVE THERAPY FOR DEPRESSION (6:00)**

Description: In this segment Aaron Beck treats the depressed woman (played by an actress) that he interviewed in Segment 50. Demonstrating cognitive therapy, Dr. Beck helps the client identify the precise thoughts, illogical thinking processes, and maladaptive attitudes that are helping to cause her depression, and he helps her challenge these thoughts and interpretations.

Source: *Cognitive Therapy of Depression*, 1977 (Dr. Aaron Beck, The Beck Institute for Cognitive Therapy and Research)

Critical Thinking Questions:

1. Why is cognitive behavioral therapy so popular?

2. What is most effective for the treatment of depression?

3. Dr. Beck's therapeutic stance is best described as _____?

*Version available on the **STUDENT TOOL KIT** under the title: *Cognitive Therapy in Action*

SEGMENT 52   **EARLY ELECTROCONVULSIVE THERAPIES (4:00)**

Description: In the 1930's, electroconvulsive therapy was developed in the belief that inducing a seizure in patients with severe mental disorders would bring improvement. The graphic footage in this segment shows the early versions of this therapy.

Sources: *Recent Modifications of Convulsive Shock Therapy*, 1941 (A. E. Bennett. Bishop Clarkson Memorial Hospital. Psychiatric Department); *Metrazol, Electric, and Insulin Treatment of the Functional Psychoses*, 1934 (James G. Sheedy). Courtesy: History of Medicine Division. National Library of Medicine

Critical Thinking Questions:

1. What is the difference between past and present ECT?
2. Why is ECT used?
3. Movies such as *One Flew Over the Cuckoo's Nest* portray ECT as a form of restraint and punishment. Is this an accurate view?

SEGMENT 53   ***MODERN ELECTROCONVULSIVE THERAPY (1:40)**

Description: This segment illustrates what ECT is like today, including the use of medication to help persons sleep through the procedure, muscle relaxants to reduce bodily thrashing, and oxygen, and the consequent reduction of the overt symptoms of the seizure produced by ECT.

Source: *The Mind*, Second Edition, 1999 (Thirteen, WNET and Worth Publishers)

Critical Thinking Questions:

1. Which is a side effect of ECT?
2. How many times a week would a person receive ECT?
3. Is modern ECT commonly practiced?

*Version available on the **STUDENT TOOL KIT** under the title: *ECT: Effective and Frightening*

SEGMENT 54   **MAJOR DEPRESSIVE DISORDER WITH PSYCHOTIC SYMPTOMS, AND THE EFFECT OF ECT (3:52)**

Description: In this segment a woman with major depressive disorder also displays psychotic symptoms as part of her depressive episode. In the initial excerpts she is interviewed during the height of her depressive episode, and she displays strong suicidal ideation, among other symptoms. In the final excerpt, she is interviewed after her recovery as a result of electroconvulsive therapy. The contrast is striking.

Source: *The Mind: Depression*, 1988 (Thirteen, WNET, New York Educational Broadcasting Corporation)

Critical Thinking Questions:

1. What are the symptoms of depression she is presenting with?

2. Who is more likely to commit suicide (actually die)?

3. Given Mary's presenting symptoms, why was ECT used?

SEGMENT 55 ANTIDEPRESSANTS AND THE "BLACK BOX" DECISION: BEFORE AND AFTER (3:15)

Description: This segment looks at the controversy concerning the risk of suicide in young people who take antidepressants drugs. First, the segment features a 2004 television news report announcing the U.S. Food and Drug Administration's decision to add "black box" warnings to antidepressant medications—warnings that alert users to a small link between antidepressant use by children and suicide. Next the segment features a 2007 report of a new study that suggests that the benefits of antidepressants for children outweigh their risks.
Source: *CBS Evening News; CBS Early Show* (CBS News)

Critical Thinking Questions:

1. Which antidepressants are the riskiest in terms of suicide?

2. Which antidepressants are less risky in terms of suicide?

3. Do the benefits of antidepressant treatment outweigh the risks of suicide?

SEGMENT 56 QUESTIONING THE EFFECTIVENESS OF ANTIDEPRESSANT DRUGS (1:30)

Description: This segment explores the question of just how effective and necessary antidepressant medications actually are. The segment features a study conducted by Dr. Irving Kirsch, which concludes that antidepressants are not more effective than other approaches in any but the most severe cases of depression, and it suggests that for most cases of depression other forms of treatment are indicated. Other clinical theorists take issue with the study's conclusions.
Source: *CBS Evening News* (CBS News)

Critical Thinking Questions:

1. Would you consider taking an antidepressant if you had depression?

2. Are there too many people who are just the "worried well"?

3. Why do people prefer a pill to therapy?

SEGMENT 57   ***LIGHT THERAPY FOR DEPRESSION: MIMICKING NATURE (3:00)**

Description: Clinicians have become aware that many people suffer from *seasonal affective disorder (SAD)*. They become clinically depressed each winter due apparently to the decreases in light that occur during winter months and to corresponding increases in their body's secretions of the hormone *melatonin*. One helpful treatment for this kind of depression is *light therapy*, treatment that provides SAD sufferers with extra doses of light in winter. This segment focuses on light therapy and its dramatic impact on some persons with S.A.D.
Source: "Desperate for Light" 20-20, 12/30/88 (ABC News)

Critical Thinking Questions:

1. What does light therapy tell us about seasonal affective disorder?
2. Can persons with depression and seasonal affective disorder be treated the same way?
3. Is light therapy still popular for seasonal affective disorder?

*Version available on the **STUDENT TOOL KIT** under the title:
Light Therapy: Treating Seasonal Affective Disorder

SEGMENT 58   **BRAIN AREA 25, DEPRESSION, AND DEEP BRAIN STIMULATION (7:30)**

Description: This segment presents a potential breakthrough in the understanding of depression, and offers a look at the intervention called *deep brain stimulation*. Following the case of a severely depressed woman, the video focuses on the brain area known as Area 25 that is believed by some clinical researchers to be closely linked to depression. The woman receives deep brain stimulation as part of a study led by neurologist Helen Mayberg and neurosurgeon Andreas Lozano in Toronto. The treatment procedure and initial follow-up do not produce immediate improvements, but after several months and treatment adjustments, the woman does improve significantly.
Source: "Area 25" 60 Minutes (CBS News)

Critical Thinking Questions:

1. Is Deborah's depression treatment-resistant?
2. What does deep brain stimulation seem to be driven by?

SEGMENT 59   ***SUICIDE: CASE OF THE "3-STAR" CHEF (4:40)**

Description: This segment focuses on a famous chef, Chef Bernard Loiseau, who committed suicide when he failed to meet his own rigid standards of professional achievement. His depression, fears, and perfectionism were tied in particular to critical reviews of his restaurant. When he believed (incorrectly) that the restaurant was about to lose its 3-star rating, the highest rating in France, his self-esteem plummeted and he ended his life. The video also focuses on his wife, how she had interpreted his preoccupations, and how she is now affected by the suicide.
Source: "The People's Chef" 60 Minutes (CBS News)

Critical Thinking Questions:

1. Was Bernard too self-critical of himself?

2. Did Bernard provide any warning signs of his impending suicide?

3. Why did Bernard choose not get to treatment?

*Version available on the **STUDENT TOOL KIT** under the title: *Case of the "3-Star" Chef: Fame is No Protection*

SEGMENT 60 ***SUICIDE AND ITS IMPACT ON FAMILY MEMBERS (5:50)**

Description: Eight months after a woman committed suicide, her family members discuss their view of the suicide, their attitudes toward their lost relative, their grief and sense of loss, and the suicide's effect on family dynamics.
Source: *Suicides*, 1987 (University of California Regents, Behavioral Sciences Media Laboratory, Neuropsychiatric Institute and Hospital, UCLA)

Critical Thinking Questions:

1. What family dynamic is operating here?

2. The three family members who did not attend may be experiencing what kinds of feelings?

3. Why doesn't anyone comfort the father?

4. Could anything have been done to prevent this?

*Version available on the **STUDENT TOOL KIT** under the title: *Inside the Suicidal Mind*

SEGMENT 61 ***SUICIDE: SHOULD THE GOVERNMENT PREVENT TERMINALLY ILL PEOPLE FROM TAKING THEIR OWN LIVES? (1:23)**

Description: In this segment, a terminally ill person asserts her right to take her own life if her pain becomes unbearable, and she decries efforts by the government to interfere with this personal decision. In addition, interviewed persons state their opinions — pro and con — about the issue of physician-assisted suicide.
Source: NBC News, 10/1/96

Critical Thinking Questions:

1. Does the government have a right to interfere with your decision to live or die?

2. Does physician-assisted suicide contradict the duty of physicians to do no harm?

3. Should a person who requests euthanasia be given a full psychiatric workup?

*Version available on the **STUDENT TOOL KIT** under the title:

An Ethical Dilemma: Do People Have the Right to Take Their Own Lives?

SEGMENT 62   **WOMAN WITH ANOREXIA NERVOSA (3:08)**

Description: This segment focuses on a young woman with anorexia nervosa, including the issues of control and power in her disorder, origins of the disorder, cognitive and other features, and the impact of the disorder.
Source: *The Waist Land: Eating Disorders in America*, 1985 (Coronet/MTI)

Critical Thinking Questions:

1. Are people with eating disorders truly in control?
2. What are some other psychological problems of anorexia?
3. Anorexia involves what type of thinking?

SEGMENT 63   ***OVERCOMING ANOREXIA NERVOSA (3:20)**

Description: This segment focuses on the symptoms of a man with anorexia nervosa, including his distorted cognitions, need for control, perfectionism, and physical changes. The video also shows a comprehensive inpatient treatment program for persons with eating disorders, where multiple interventions are combined.
Source: "Slim Chance" *48 Hours* (CBS News)

Critical Thinking Questions:

1. Does Dave have body image issues?
2. What will the affect be on Dave's children, especially on his daughter towards dieting and exercise?

*Version available on the **STUDENT TOOL KIT** under the title:
Anorexia Nervosa: Not for Women Only

SEGMENT 64   ***WOMAN WITH BULIMIA NERVOSA (3:03)**

Description: This segment focuses on a young woman with bulimia nervosa, including her binge and purge behaviors, origins of her disorder, cognitive and other features, and impact of the disorder.
Source: *The Waist Land: Eating Disorders in America*, 1985 (Coronet/MTI)

Critical Thinking Questions:

1. What are some of the other psychological problems of bulimia?
2. What are some of the common themes of eating disorders?

*Version available on the **STUDENT TOOL KIT** under the title:
Imprisoned by an Eating Disorder

SEGMENT 65   **MAN WITH BULIMIA NERVOSA (4:08)**

Description: This segment focuses on the psychological issues, symptoms, and treatment of a man with bulimia nervosa. His obsession with weight is tied to having been the victim of traumatic teasing (earlier in his life) and his intense desire to fit in. The challenges for men with eating disorders are also examined, particularly the social stigma of having a disorder that is typically

associated with females and the resulting reluctance to admit a need for treatment.
Source: "Slim Chance" *48 Hours* (CBS News)

Critical Thinking Questions:

1. What does bulimia hide?
2. Why are men less likely to admit they have an eating disorder?

SEGMENT 66   # PRO-ANOREXIA WEB SITES (3:45)

Description: This segment looks at the controversial subject of websites that are believed to condone and promote eating disorders. In particular, the video profiles a woman with anorexia nervosa who describes her struggle against the disorder. The woman helps run a Web site for people with anorexia nervosa that she argues provides a supportive community and helps people overcome their disorders. However, critics of this and similar Internet sites argue that users of such Web sites often exchange information about how to maintain and expand their eating disorders—thus promoting rather than combating their dysfunctional eating patterns.
Source: *CBS Early Show* (CBS News)

Critical Thinking Questions:

1. Does Stephanie seem to have Body Dysmorphic Disorder as well?
2. As a single mom, what are the risks if Stephanie continues untreated?
3. Are Pro-Ana sites supportive or detrimental?
4. Is Stephanie lying to herself about her recovery?

SEGMENT 67   # *EATING AND WEIGHT GAIN: A ROLE FOR FIDGETING (3:35)

Description: This segment highlights various factors that may affect eating and weight gain (or loss), from heightened activity to conditioning to genetics. The video features a study conducted at the Mayo Clinic in which participants were subjected to a "slob regime," in which they spent two months overindulging in food and engaging in no exercise. The results revealed that some of the participants gained much less weight than others even though all of the participants had similar metabolic rates. Beyond genetic factors, the researchers discovered that the thinner individuals generally fidget, or move unconsciously, much more than most other people of their age and background.
Source: "Fatbusters" *Horizon* (BBC Motion Gallery)

Critical Thinking Questions:

1. Given Jeff's constant psychomotor activity, does he seem to possibly have ADHD?
2. Jeff's fidgeting has been advantageous to him. Why?

*Version available on the **STUDENT TOOL KIT** under the title: *Weight Gain: A Surprise Factor*

SEGMENT 68

COLLEGE BINGE DRINKING (4:35)

Description: This segment looks at the issue of college binge drinking, which is alarmingly widespread. Various college students are interviewed about their binge drinking habits, and they weigh in on why they regularly drink to excess. The segment also profiles the case of a college student who died following a drinking binge to celebrate his twenty-first birthday. The video further examines the dangers of binge drinking and the misguided thinking found among binge drinkers.

Source: "Binge College Daze" *48 Hours* (CBS News)

Critical Thinking Questions:

1. Do you believe that binge drinking is problematic?

2. What seems to drive binge drinking in college students?

3. Why do college students believe binge drinking won't harm them?

SEGMENT 69

*COCAINE ABUSE AND TREATMENT: SINKING AND RECOVERING (3:24)

Description: In this segment, a man describes his history of cocaine abuse and dependence, which ruined his personal life and professional career. Now no longer addicted, he also describes his treatment, recovery, and successful climb back. It is worth noting that one feature of his recovery is *implicit* aversion therapy, in which he keeps recalling and picturing the life of ruin associated with drug abuse whenever he feels desires or cravings for a drug.

Source: *The Mind,* Second Edition, 1999 (Thirteen, WNET and Worth Publishers)

Critical Thinking Questions:

1. How does implicit aversion therapy help Greg to stay clean?

2. What effects does drug abuse have?

3. Four and a half years of sobriety tells us what about Greg?

4. Is cocaine addiction easier to overcome than heroin addiction?

*Version available on the **STUDENT TOOL KIT** under the title: *Craving for Cocaine*

SEGMENT 70

METHAMPHETAMINE: A POWERFUL DEPENDENCE (4:35)

Description: This segment explores methamphetamine abuse and dependence—a rising epidemic in the United States. The video explores how methamphetamine use affects brain activity and the nature and severity of methamphetamine dependence. It features both law enforcement officials and a former methamphetamine addict discussing the drug's effects. The segment also describes the ease with which methamphetamine can be manufactured from over-the-counter medications, particularly those containing pseudoephedrine (the key ingredient in methamphetamine).

Source: "Epidemic in the Heartland" *60 Minutes* (CBS News)

Critical Thinking Questions:

1. Why is meth so difficult to control?
2. Are you surprised that Missouri had the most meth labs?
3. Which neurotransmitter floods the brain for 12 hours after meth use?

SEGMENT 71 — *THE MEDICAL USE OF MARIJUANA (3:00)

Description: In this segment, we are introduced to a woman who uses legalized marijuana to treat chronic pain after an accident has left her partially paralyzed. Focusing on her case, the video explores the debate concerning the use of marijuana for medical purposes. Some argue that marijuana is an addictive and dangerous substance and that if it is legalized for certain purposes, it will be easier to abuse, especially among young persons. The social and legal implications of regulation of the substance are also examined.
Source: "Legalizing Marijuana" *Sunday Morning* (CBS News)

Critical Thinking Questions:

1. Why hasn't anyone conducted a clinical research study on the medical uses of marijuana?
2. In essence, medicinal use of marijuana affects the war on drugs how?
3. As rational autonomous persons, don't we all have a right to choose what drugs and treatment can help us?

*Version available on the **STUDENT TOOL KIT** under the title:
The Medical Use of Marijuana

SEGMENT 72 — *CHEMICALLY INDUCED HALLUCINATIONS: STUDIES OF ANESTHETIC DRUGS (3:40)

Description: In this segment, a researcher examines how a low dose of the anesthetic ketamine affects brain activity and, in turn, produces hallucinations. It is hypothesized that the drug may weaken or modify communication between neurons, resulting in hallucinations and mood enhancement.
Source: "The Final Mystery" *Brain Story* (BBS Motion Gallery)

Critical Thinking Questions:

1. Do you think that ketamine would be a safe anesthetic?
2. Are studies like the one you just watched important?

*Version available on the **STUDENT TOOL KIT** under the title:
Hallucinogens and the Brain

SEGMENT 73   # THE NATURE AND ABUSE OF ECSTASY (MDMA) (2:50)

Description: This segment explores the biological and psychological effects of the drug *Ecstasy* (MDMA). It features young adults who use the drug in social settings and includes their discussions of why they use Ecstasy. The biological mechanisms affected by Ecstasy are also examined, along with the drug's dangers and possible long-term effects on brain development.
Source: "Ecstasy" *48 Hours* (CBS News)

Critical Thinking Questions:

1. Why are these young people drinking water, sucking on lollipops, and sucking on pacifiers?
2. Do you believe that Ecstasy has long-term negative effects?

SEGMENT 74   # *SEXUAL DYSFUNCTIONS AND THEIR TREATMENTS (6:05)

Description: In this segment, researchers conduct studies on treatments for erectile dysfunction. The video highlights five men who have been treated for erectile dysfunction with drug therapy, to varying degrees of success. Concerns are raised about the promotion and use of such drugs for sexual enhancement rather than for treating sexual dysfunction as originally intended.
Source: "It's Just Sex" *48 Hours* (CBS News)

Critical Thinking Questions:

1. Is sexual dysfunction in men more physically or psychologically based?
2. Is sexual dysfunction better explained by male menopause?
3. Is sexual function important to men's self-esteem?
4. Are the erectile dysfunction commercials more informational, detrimental, taboo, or downright tasteless?

*Version available on the **STUDENT TOOL KIT** under the title: *Viagra: Pathway to Sexual Happiness?*

SEGMENT 75   # *SEXUAL VIOLENCE: SHOULD DANGEROUS SEX OFFENDERS BE COMMITTED TO MENTAL HOSPITALS AFTER SERVING THEIR PRISON TERMS? (1:46)

Description: In the 1997 case of *Kansas vs. Hendricks*, the Supreme Court ruled that convicted sex offenders may be removed from prison prior to release and committed to a mental hospital if they are considered likely to again commit sexually violent acts. This segment is a news piece on this complex legal issue, televised while the court was deliberating the case.
Source: NBC News, 12/10/96

Critical Thinking Questions:

1. Would committing sex offenders to a mental institution be a violation of their rights?

2. What is the difference between mentally ill and mentally abnormal?

*Version available on the **STUDENT TOOL KIT** under the title:
Sex Offenders: Criminals or Patients?

SEGMENT 76   **GENDER IDENTITY DISORDER (4:00)**

Description: In this segment an individual who has undergone sex-change surgery to become a man recalls his past life as a woman with gender identity disorder (including past feelings, body-image, and interactions). He also discusses the changes in his outlook brought about by the surgery. In addition, a specialist in gender identity disorder highlights individuals' expectations regarding sex change surgery, the pros and cons of such surgery, and alternative forms of treatment.
Source: *The World of Abnormal Psychology,* 1992 (The Annenberg/CPB Projects)

Critical Thinking Questions:

1. What types of difficulties do you think Brad has?
2. Will a gender change solve a person's problems?
3. Why is it so important to confront psychological problems before surgery?

SEGMENT 77   ***THE BOY WHO WAS TURNED INTO A GIRL (8:20)**

Description: This segment considers whether sexual reassignment in a "normal" child is appropriate or even possible. It tells the tragic story of the Reimer family, a Canadian family who in the 1960s had twin boys. When one of the boys was being circumcised, a hospital mishap resulted in the destruction of most of his penis. His parents eventually sought the council of psychologist John Money, a sexual reassignment specialist, who believed through his previous work that gender identity is primarily learned. Money advised the family to have their son undergo a sex change operation and to then rear him as a girl (and to keep the child unaware that she had been born male). The segment features interviews with the Reimer family (including David Reimer, the boy himself, interviewed as an adult) after he had chosen to return to his original male sexual identity. The family describes the terribly unhappy childhood and adolescence suffered by "Brenda" Reimer, as the child was called after his surgical sex change. Unhappy through most of his life, David Reimer eventually committed suicide, following a series of unfortunate circumstances.
Source: "Dr. Money and The Boy with No Penis" *Horizon;* "The Boy Who Was Turned into a Girl" *Horizon* (BBC Motion Gallery)

Critical Thinking Questions:

1. How would you react if your sex had been changed without your consent?
2. Was John Money ethical?
3. Since only David's penis was destroyed, why would Dr. Money believe this would work?
4. Why did David choose not to live?

*Version available on the **STUDENT TOOL KIT** under the title:
The Boy Who Was Turned Into a Girl

SEGMENT 78 | # *WOMAN WITH HALLUCINATIONS (3:10)

Description: In this segment, a woman with schizophrenia experiences hallucinations, describes them in detail, and describes their powerful impact upon her life.

Source: *Madness: In Two Minds,* 1991 (BBC Worldwide Americas, Inc.)

Critical Thinking Questions:

1. What is the significance of the doctor holding the patient's hand?

2. Is it appropriate to hold or touch a patient?

3. Does this patient display more negative or positive symptoms of schizophrenia?

*Version available on the **STUDENT TOOL KIT** under the title: *Hallucinations: "The Voices Won't Leave Me Alone"*

SEGMENT 79 | # *YOUNG MAN WITH SCHIZOPHRENIA (4:31)

Description: This segment focuses on a young man with schizophrenia. First, the man, a former policeman, is interviewed in the hospital. Later, he is seen sitting down and talking to his father during a home visit. The man displays delusions of persecution and grandiosity, disorganized thinking, loose associations (derailment), motor symptoms, and inappropriate affect.

Source: *The Brain: Madness,* 1984; *The Brain,* Second Edition, 1997 (The Annenberg/CPB Projects)

Critical Thinking Questions:

1. Why do schizophrenics smoke so much?

2. What subtype of schizophrenia is this patient suffering from?

3. What is the prognosis for those with schizophrenia?

*Version available on the **STUDENT TOOL KIT** under the title: *A Clinical Picture of Schizophrenia*

SEGMENT 80 | # MRI SCAN: COMPARISON OF SCHIZOPHRENIC AND NON-SCHIZOPHRENIC TWINS (1:00)

Description: In this segment, Daniel Weinberger compares the MRI scan of a person with schizophrenia to that of his nonschizophrenic identical twin and points out that the ventricles of the twin with schizophrenia are bigger than those of the nonschizophrenic twin.

Source: *Madness: In Two Minds,* 1991 (BBC Worldwide Americas Inc.)

Critical Thinking Questions:

1. What information can an MRI reveal about schizophrenia?

2. What else can mimic the symptoms of schizophrenia?

3. What can the signs of greater spinal fluid and loss of brain tissue in schizophrenia tell us?

SEGMENT 81   ***POSTPARTUM PSYCHOSIS: WHY DID ANDREA YATES KILL HER FIVE CHILDREN? (7:03)**

Description: On the morning of June 20, 2001, Andrea Yates drowned her five small children in the bathtub. This powerful segment examines this tragic case. It demonstrates her previous loving devotion to her children, documents her past history of postpartum depression and postpartum psychosis, looks at the failures of the medical and mental health fields, and raises questions about the decision made by Mrs. Yates and her husband to have a fifth child. Professors should emphasize the important distinction between *postpartum psychosis* and *postpartum depression* (the latter being more common). Although Mrs. Yates suffered from each syndrome, it was the postpartum psychosis that apparently triggered this tragedy.
Source: "Why Did She Do It?" *60 Minutes*, 12/09/01 (CBS News)

Critical Thinking Questions:

1. Why would Andrea Yates's husband still be supportive of her?
2. By dialing 911 and phoning her husband, did Andrea Yates demonstrate knowledge of right and wrong?
3. Should Mr. and Mrs. Yates have had more children after two prior suicide attempts and a history of depression?
4. Was the murder of her children premeditated?

*Version available on the **STUDENT TOOL KIT** under the title: *Postpartum Psychosis: Why Did Andrea Yates Kill Her Five Children?*

SEGMENT 82   **PATIENTS BEFORE AND AFTER PREFRONTAL LOBOTOMY, 1944 (5:50)**

Description: This segment shows historical footage of patients before and shortly after their lobotomies. Although each case was pointed to as a success at the time, it is obvious, looking back, that the postoperative behavior and functioning of the patients were hardly ideal or problem-free.
Source: *Prefrontal Lobotomy in Chronic Schizophrenia*, 1944 (A. E. Bennett, Bishop Clarkson Memorial Hospital, Psychiatric Department). Courtesy: History of Medicine Division, National Library of Medicine.

Critical Thinking Questions:

1. Is this patient exhibiting aggressive and impulsive behavior?
2. Is his attitude really resistive and antagonistic?
3. This patient appears to be suffering from _____?
4. How would we describe the postoperative functioning of these two men?

SEGMENT 83   ***THE THERAPEUTIC EFFECT OF ANTIPSYCHOTIC DRUGS (2:10)**

Description: This segment demonstrates the near-miraculous turnaround that occurs for some persons with schizophrenia when they take antipsychotic medications. The man featured in the video is extremely confused and unable to verbalize effectively prior to taking a new antipsychotic drug. A month later, after the introduction of the drug, he is clear, coherent, and planning for a return to work.

Source: *The Brain: Madness*, 1984 (Thirteen, WNET, New York Educational Broadcasting Corporation)

Critical Thinking Questions:

1. Why do some schizophrenics stop taking their medications?
2. If Augustine stays on his medications, how would you describe his prognosis?
3. What do schizophrenics need to maintain their wellness?

*Version available on the **STUDENT TOOL KIT** under the title: *Antipsychotic Drugs: Before and After*

SEGMENT 84   **UNDESIRED EFFECTS OF CONVENTIONAL ANTIPSYCHOTIC DRUGS (0:55)**

Description: This segment reveals the undesired effects of conventional antipsychotic drugs, including extrapyramidal effects.

Source: *Madness: Brainwaves*, 1991 (BBC Worldwide Americas, Inc.)

Critical Thinking Questions:

1. Is Thorazine the only drug choice for schizophrenia?
2. What symptoms remain even after treatment with antipsychotics?
3. What symptoms are the most difficult to treat?
4. Is this film a modern view of psychopharmacology?

SEGMENT 85   ***SEVERE MENTAL DISORDERS AND DRUG ABUSE: THE SO-CALLED "WILD MAN OF WEST 96TH STREET" (5:18)**

Description: During the early 1990s, Larry Hogue, nicknamed the "Wild Man of West 96th Street" by his neighbors, was the best known *mentally ill chemical abuser (MICA)* in the United States. This segment, filmed in 1992, focuses on Hogue and his struggles with both psychosis and substance abuse, his impact upon community residents, and the failures of the mental health system and the criminal justice system to address his severe problem.

Source: "Wild Man of West 96th Street" *60 Minutes*, 12/13/92 (CBS News)

Critical Thinking Questions:

1. Is Larry to blame for his actions?

2. Compare and contrast Larry Hogue and John Nash?

3. Do you think it's acceptable to wait for Larry to harm someone before something is done?

*Version available on the **STUDENT TOOL KIT** under the title:
Treating MICAs: "Wild Man of West 96th Street"

SEGMENT 86   *OVERCOMING SCHIZOPHRENIA: JOHN NASH'S BEAUTIFUL MIND (4:50)

Description: Perhaps the most celebrated case of schizophrenia in recent years is that of John Nash, the brilliant mathematician who struggled with this disorder for 35 years, and then was awarded the Nobel Prize for work he had done as a doctoral student back in 1951 at Princeton University. This segment follows Nash's ordeal and triumph, which inspired the award-winning 2001 movie *A Beautiful Mind*. Perhaps the most powerful part of this segment is Nash's interaction with his adult son, also a mathematician, who also suffers from schizophrenia.
Source: "John Nash's Beautiful Mind" *60 Minutes*, 3/17/02 (CBS News)

Critical Thinking Questions:

1. Is John Nash a representative example of most schizophrenics?

2. What could we say about the impact of nature and genetics considering that John Nash's son is also schizophrenic?

3. Why is John Nash so much more functional than other schizophrenics?

*Version available on the **STUDENT TOOL KIT** under the title:
Overcoming Schizophrenia: John Nash's Beautiful Mind

SEGMENT 87   PERSONALITY AND THE BRAIN (5:30)

Description: This segment explores creativity and personality, including their neural links, by focusing on the case of a man who has a degenerative brain disorder. The video describes the changes in his personality, such as a decreased level of empathy and increased artistic ability, and ties those behaviors to changes in his frontal lobe. Various explanations for personality changes as a result of brain disorders are explored.
Source: "All in the Mind" *Brain Story* (BBC Motion Gallery)

Critical Thinking Questions:

1. The loss of brain function has lead Dick to _____.

2. How difficult is Dick's condition for his wife?

SEGMENT 88 ## *PSYCHOPATHY AND CRIMINAL BEHAVIOR (2:59)

Description: This segment focuses on people with psychopathy (sociopathy) who commit criminal behavior. One such individual discusses his behavior and the changes he has experienced. In addition, Robert Hare, an expert on this pattern, discusses the issue of whether psychopathy can be changed or treated. He argues that most of the treatments available for prisoners do not address the key symptoms of psychopathy.

Source: *The Mind,* Second Edition, 1999 (Thirteen, WNET and Worth Publishers)

Critical Thinking Questions:

1. Are our prisons able to provide criminals with gainful rehabilitation?

2. Why are psychopaths less likely to commit crimes as they get older?

*Version available on the **STUDENT TOOL KIT** under the title: *Antisocial Personality Disorder: A Treatable Pattern?*

SEGMENT 89 ## CHILDHOOD VIOLENCE: NATURE VERSUS NURTURE (2:50)

Description: This segment explores whether violent behavior by children is the result of environmental factors, brain abnormalities, or both. It notes that brain scans of children who repeatedly display violence often reveal abnormal activity in areas of the brain relating to impulsivity, empathy, and emotionality. Includes the work of Nora Volkow.

Source: NBC News Archives

Critical Thinking Questions:

1. Is early identification of violence and aggression important?

2. Is there a mental disorder going on here or is this more environmentally based?

3. How is modeling violent behavior detrimental for development?

SEGMENT 90 ## *DO VIDEO GAMES TEACH PEOPLE TO BE VIOLENT? (4:30)

Description: This segment looks at the controversial question of whether video games help produce violent and aggressive behavior in teens. It focuses on the highly publicized case of an 18-year-old, who killed three police officers in an Alabama police station, reportedly after having been influenced by the violent video game Grand Theft Auto. The segment explores a lawsuit that followed the shootings against the makers of the video game, which alleged that the game conditioned the teenager to react violently in real life. The segment considers the theory that because teenage brains are not fully developed and impulse control is not yet available to teens, a game such as this can influence violent behavior if other risk factors are also present.

Source: "Grand Theft Auto" *60 Minutes* (CBS News)

Critical Thinking Questions:

1. Do you believe that children and adolescents lack the ability to separate out violent acts from video games and reality?

2. Are video games a violence simulator?

3. Do you believe that Moore lacked the ability to separate out violent acts from video games and reality?

4. Is Moore mentally ill or a product of the juvenile system?

*Version available on the **STUDENT TOOL KIT** under the title: *Do Video Games Teach People to Be Violent?*

SEGMENT 91 RAGE: ONE MAN'S STORY AND TREATMENT (10:05)

Description: This segment focuses on the symptoms of and treatment for a man with intense and distressing anger. His angry outbursts, which typically occur when he is driving, are often followed by feelings of shame and regret. The video shows two sessions of anger management therapy. At the end of the segment, the patient's stress reactions are measured while he is driving, and he displays significant improvement.
Source: "Personality" *Human Mind* (BBC Motion Gallery)

Critical Thinking Questions:

1. Is Sean's anger better explained by intermittent explosive disorder?

2. What are the potential risks of Sean's anger?

3. Was anger management truly effective for Sean?

SEGMENT 92 INTERNET ADDICTION: A CROSS-CULTURAL PHENOMENON (4:20)

Description: This segment looks at the issue of "Internet addiction," and the effect of excessive computer use in countries across the world. The video first spotlights the United States, where college students describe how much time they spend on social networking Web sites and how their Internet use often distracts their attention from their studies. The segment then shows a controversial "boot camp" in China where children and young adults are sent to be treated for Internet addiction, with a combination of military-style discipline, medication, and, in some cases, even electroconvulsive therapy.
Source: *CBS Early Show; CBS Evening News* (CBS News)

Critical Thinking Questions:

1. Are you addicted to the internet?

2. How many hours a day do you spend on the internet for non-school related work?

3. Do you believe that the internet is an addiction?

4. Is the internet limiting our face-to-face social interactions?

SEGMENT 93

COMPULSIVE GAMBLING AND THE BRAIN'S PLEASURE CENTER (5:20)

Description: This segment highlights research at the University of Minnesota on the causes and treatment of pathological gambling. It looks in particular at the role of the brain's pleasure center. The video features a man who takes a new drug to help treat his gambling pattern, a drug that helps dampen the pleasure associated with his pathological gambling behavior.
Source: "Seeking Perfection" *Obsessions* (BBC Motion Gallery)

Critical Thinking Questions:

1. Should medication only be used to treat Theodore's gambling addiction?
2. Has the Internet caused an increase in gambling?
3. Do you believe there are risks with substituting one addiction for another?

*Version available on the **STUDENT TOOL KIT** under the title: *Compulsive Gambling, the Brain, and Poor Impulse Control*

SEGMENT 94

CHILDHOOD ANXIETY: HOW DID THE 9/11/01 TERRORIST ATTACKS AFFECT CHILDREN? (2:20)

Description: This segment explores the lingering psychological impact of the 9/11/01 terrorist attacks upon children, particularly those living in New York City. It reveals effects such as anxiety, insecurity, poor concentration, and nightmares, and a rise in the prevalence of psychological disorders. It also reports on relevant research findings.
Source: NBC News, 5/22/02

Critical Thinking Questions:

1. Why is it so important to talk with children about horrific acts that have occurred?
2. What are the possible treatments for this young child?
3. If left untreated, children with PTSD can be expected to _____.

*Version available on the **STUDENT TOOL KIT** under the title: *Childhood Anxiety: How Did the 9/11/01 Terrorist Attacks Affect Children?*

SEGMENT 95

CAN CHILDHOOD PSYCHOPATHOLOGY BE CAUSED BY INFECTIONS? (5:45)

Description: This segment looks at the possible impact of physical illness and infections on the development of childhood mental disorders. It focuses on the powerful case of an 8-year-old girl with severe obsessive-compulsive disorder. The footage in this video demonstrates the girl's compulsive rituals and the impact her disorder has on her emotional life. The segment clarifies that a severe throat infection at an early age coincided with the start of

this OCD pattern and that subsequent infections have often signaled additional flare-ups. The video also examines relevant research into this issue.
Source: "Who's Normal Anyway?" *Obsessions* (BBC Motion Gallery)

Critical Thinking Questions:

1. Does Taylor really understand her OCD?
2. Could her OCD be an expression of modeling behavior?
3. Does Taylor truly have an opinion about her condition, or is she parroting her parent's opinions?

SEGMENT 96   SLEEP TERROR DISORDER (4:20)

Description: This segment features a child with sleep terror disorder. We see a series of instances in which the young girl awakens extremely frightened. Although she may walk around and talk to her parents upon such awakenings, she is not fully coherent and indeed not fully awake. The video also explores the effects that the child's irregular sleep patterns have had on her parents' own sleep patterns and marital relationship.
Source: "Night, Night" *The Trouble with Sleep* (BBC Motion Gallery)

Critical Thinking Questions:

1. If Holly were your child, would you seek a sleep study?
2. Do you believe Holly's sleep terrors are real?
3. How would you react to having a child with sleep terrors?
4. By putting Holly in their bed, what are her parents potentially doing?

SEGMENT 97   *ADHD: A FAMILY PROBLEM (6:10)

Description: This segment presents a case in which a young boy's ADHD places a severe strain on his family. The child's impulsive behaviors repeatedly expose him to danger, and he also is unable to obey instructions. A simple shopping trip becomes a nightmare for his weary and, at times, frightened parents. The video examines the theory that oppositional behavior in ADHD children develops as a response to repeated reprimands for behavior they cannot control.
Source: "Living with ADHD" *Horizon* (BBC Motion Gallery)

Critical Thinking Questions:

1. Should Liam be on ADHD medication?
2. How can Liam's behavior affect his other sibling's development?
3. What other comorbid diagnoses would you consider for Liam?

*Version available on the **STUDENT TOOL KIT** under the title:
ADHD: A Family Problem

SEGMENT 98 **READING AND READING DISORDERS (4:20)**

Description: This segment showcases research into the process of learning to read, and offers insight into why some children have trouble learning this important skill. The video shows a poor reader learning to read with the aid of a computer program. Because the child has trouble associating letters with sounds—a critical part of learning to read—the program uses repetition to help him associate sounds with letters. According to the segment, brain scans of people who are reading indicate that a particular area of the brain is responsible for associating letters with sounds. Brain scans of a child in the segment before and after he learns to read effectively seem to support this theory.

Source: "Growing the Mind" *Brain Story* (BBC Motion Gallery)

Critical Thinking Questions:

1. Are reading disorders more common in boys or girls?

2. If reading disorders are not dealt with early on, what are the potential long-term effects?

SEGMENT 99 ***TWO FACES OF AUTISM (4:20)**

Description: This segment focuses on two eleven-year-old boys who have autism. Their behavioral differences and similarities illustrate that autism is characterized by a spectrum of dysfunctioning. Three common features of the disorder are focused on: decreased capacity for social engagements, communication deficits, and lack of imagination.

Source: "Does the MMR Jab Cause Autism?" *Horizon* (BBC Motion Gallery)

Critical Thinking Questions:

1. In comparison to normal children, children with autism lack what specifically?

2. If your child had autism, how would this affect you life?

*Version available on the **STUDENT TOOL KIT** under the title: *Two Faces of Autism*

SEGMENT 100 **THEORY OF MIND: TAKING THE PERSPECTIVE OF OTHERS (1:40)**

Description: This video focuses on the *theory of mind* principle. It features a research study in which children are asked to hide candy from an adult. Older children can do the task, but children under the age of three years are completely unable to do so. This research indicates that at the younger age, the children's brains have not yet developed to the point where they can understand what another person can or cannot see.

Source: "Will to Win" *Human Instinct* (BBC Motion Gallery)

Critical Thinking Questions:

1. Which children's disorder lacks a theory of mind?

2. Children lack a theory of mind before what age?

SEGMENT 101   **DR. IVAR LOVAAS TREATS A YOUNG AUTISTIC CHILD WITH BEHAVIORAL INTERVENTION (3:20)**

Description: In this segment, Ivar Lovaas, a leader in the development of behavioral treatments and programs for people with autism, treats a young child with the disorder. Using behavioral techniques, he is able to change some of the child's dysfunctional behaviors relatively quickly.
Source: *Behavioral Treatment of Autistic Children*, 1988 (Focus International, Inc.)

Critical Thinking Questions:

1. The behavioral treatment displayed best resembles what?
2. Is his hugging and kissing inappropriate?
3. What do we notice about the teacher?

SEGMENT 102   **ADULT WITH AUTISM (2:19)**

Description: This segment first shows Ricky, as a child with autism, learning to communicate in a behavioral treatment program 20 years ago. It then shows Ricky today. During the intervening years, his treatment program, in which he had been making considerable progress initially, was stopped due to a lack of funding, leading to a regression in his functioning.
Source: *Behavioral Treatment of Autistic Children*, 1988 (Focus International, Inc.)

Critical Thinking Questions:

1. What is the importance of early training?
2. What is so unfortunate about cases such as Ricky's?
3. How would you rate Ricky's overall ability to sustain himself in society?

SEGMENT 103   **DOES THE MMR VACCINE CAUSE AUTISM? (6:40)**

Description: One of the field's most heated controversies in recent years has centered on whether MMR vaccines cause autism. This segment presents the case of a young child who had been developing normally but whose language and learning skills then *appeared* to deteriorate following an MMR vaccination. The video presents his mother's observations and her belief that her son's autism is indeed linked to the vaccination he had received. The segment then goes on to present studies that have challenged the theory that MMR vaccinations have a link to the development of autism, a theory first proposed by Andrew Wakefield and his colleagues.
Source: "Does the MMR Jab Cause Autism?" *Horizon* (BBC Motion Gallery)

Critical Thinking Questions:

1. Do you believe the MMR vaccine causes autism?
2. Is there a possibility that the MMR vaccine batches may have been tainted?
3. Is Wakefield's theory too simplistic?

SEGMENT 104 | # SAVANT ART SKILLS: IN AUTISM AND DEMENTIA (5:55)

Description: This segment shows (1) a teenage boy with autism who has advanced artistic abilities, and (2) an elderly woman who developed remarkable painting skills after the onset of dementia. Brain scans of individuals with dementia are examined, and possible explanations for savant skills are offered.

Source: "It's All in Your Head" *48 Hours* (CBS News)

Critical Thinking Questions:

1. Are you surprised by Jonathan's talent?

2. Is Jonathan's talent at risk of being exploited?

3. Given Jonathan's social interactions, is he a high-functioning autistic or does he have Asperger's?

SEGMENT 105 | # DOWN SYNDROME: A SPECIAL FAMILY (6:00)

Description: This segment focuses on individuals with Down Syndrome, profiling in particular a woman who has adopted four children with this disorder. The video addresses the challenges of living with individuals who have special needs, and shows both the problems and positive emotions of persons with Down Syndrome.

Source: *Children with a Difference* (BBC Motion Gallery)

Critical Thinking Questions:

1. Would you ever consider adopting a special needs child?

2. Does Otto seem to be less mentally retarded than the other boys?

3. Is Down Syndrome still considered a socially unacceptable disorder?

SEGMENT 106 | # *COMPANIONSHIP AND SUPPORT: PETS FILL THE VOID (4:35)

Description: This segment focuses on the psychological and physical benefits of providing animal companions for elderly persons in a nursing facility. Similarly, interactions with children and a warm and stimulating environment help nursing home residents achieve greater psychological and physical health. We see in this video that such residents often develop a greater sense of purpose in life and that the rates of illness and mortality at the facility go down significantly.

Source: "Garden of Eden" *48 Hours* (CBS News)

Critical Thinking Questions:

1. Why isn't this positive approach to nursing home care more common?

2. When you grow old, would this be a place you would like to be in?

3. What are the benefits to this type of care?

*Version available on the **STUDENT TOOL KIT** under the title: *Pets and the Elderly: The Impact of Companionship*

SEGMENT 107 **HEALTHY AGING: THE POWER OF POSITIVE THINKING (7:35)**

Description: This segment highlights the effects of positive attitudes on the quality of life in an elderly population. The video examines the roles of increased activity, positive attitudes, and medical advances in helping individuals to age better. The importance of strong interpersonal relationships, self-esteem, positive thinking, and exercise are also examined.
Source: "70 Is the New 50" *Sunday Morning* (CBS News)

Critical Thinking Questions:

1. Why is exercise important for the elderly?
2. Is age just a number?

SEGMENT 108 **OLD AGE: LEARNING AND MOVING AT THE SAME TIME (2:40)**

Description: This segment examines how mental resources are allotted differently in the young and the elderly. A study conducted in Belgium reveals that older individuals have difficulty memorizing words while they are walking, whereas younger adults can easily do both at the same time. Researchers conclude that bodily movements do not typically require much mental attention, but when we become older they require more of our mental resources.
Source: "Growing the Mind" *Brain Story* (BBC Motion Gallery)

Critical Thinking Questions:

1. Does this study seem to have any validity?
2. What does this study say about multitasking?

SEGMENT 109 ***LIVING WITHOUT MEMORY (5:21)**

Description: This segment features an in-depth profile of a man who has lost both his short-term and long-term memory. The module reveals the difficulties and emotional pain of living without memory. It also focuses on the experiences of family members who are caregivers. Alternative techniques for coping with and working around memory loss are presented as well.
Source: *Living Without a Memory* (BBC Motion Gallery)

Critical Thinking Questions:

1. George's memory disappeared overnight. Is this harder for his wife to deal with than if George had Alzheimer's?
2. Does George's condition put more of an emotional or physical strain on his wife?
3. Is George's condition similar to having anterograde amnesia?

*Version available on the **STUDENT TOOL KIT** under the title: *Living Without Memory*

SEGMENT 110 ***ALZHEIMER'S DISEASE: A CASE, RESEARCH, AND NEW DIRECTIONS (8:40)**

Description: This segment explores current research on the symptoms and treatment of Alzheimer's disease and also focuses on a man with early-onset Alzheimer's disease. The video explores features of the disease that distinguish it from general aging, such as tangles and plaques in the brain. It also examines environmental and psychological factors that may play roles in the development and progression of the disease.
Source: "A New Day" *Sunday Morning* (CBS News)

Critical Thinking Questions:

1. Is being diagnosed with Alzheimer's at age 54 worse than at age 65?

2. When do you believe we will find a cure for Alzheimer's?

*Version available on the **STUDENT TOOL KIT** under the title: *Suffering from Alzheimer's Disease*

SEGMENT 111 **ALZHEIMER'S DISEASE: A CLINICAL PICTURE (4:30)**

Description: This segment explores the cognitive, physical, and behavioral progression of Alzheimer's disease, and the impact the disease has on families. It focuses on the deterioration of a woman with Alzheimer's disease. Her family is shown caring for her, while she herself is barely able to respond.
Source: Worth Publishers

Critical Thinking Questions:

1. What do people with Alzheimer's die from?

2. Is it common for a significant physical or psychological loss to exacerbate Alzheimer's?

SEGMENT 112 **STROKE, COGNITION, AND LANGUAGE: A CASE STUDY (4:00)**

Description: This segment focuses on language problems, such as aphasia, that may develop after stroke-induced damage to the left hemisphere of the brain. The video features a male stroke victim whose language and grammar skills declined severely following a stroke, and his rehabilitation efforts. It also examines areas of the brain that are related to language ability.
Source: *First Among Equals* (BBC Motion Gallery)

Critical Thinking Questions:

1. Is plasticity better in childhood or adulthood?

2. Is stroke truly a recoverable condition?

SEGMENT 113 **PARKINSON'S DISEASE: A CASE STUDY (4:10)**

Description: This segment focuses on a man with Parkinson's disease whose medication relieved certain symptoms of the disease but also created undesired effects that were difficult to live with. The video examines his physical and psychological functioning before and after a treatment procedure known as deep brain electrode stimulation.

Source: "Unlocking Parkinson's" *60 Minutes* (CBS News)

Critical Thinking Questions:

1. What would be worse to be diagnosed with—Alzheimer's or Parkinson's?

2. Were there significant changes in his quality of life after the procedure?

SEGMENT 114 **SLEEP AND SLEEPLESSNESS: THE CURRENT SCENE (5:45)**

Description: This segment explores research into the sleep patterns and problems of people today and examines the question of how much sleep people need. Research presented in the video suggests that sleep disorders affect the body as well as the mind. The segment also highlights a study of sleep patterns in killer whales and discusses the study's usefulness for understanding disorders of sleep control in humans.

Source: "Sleepless in America" *Sunday Morning* (CBS News)

Critical Thinking Questions:

1. How much sleep to you get per night?

2. Do you believe we need 8 hours of sleep per night?

3. Is sleep for the mind, body, or both?

SEGMENT 115   ***LAW, DANGEROUSNESS, AND MENTAL DYSFUNCTION: WAS JEFFREY DAHMER NOT GUILTY BY REASON OF INSANITY? (5:28)**

Description: In 1992, the notorious serial murderer Jeffrey Dahmer was found guilty of murdering 15 young men, despite his claim that he should be found not guilty by reason of insanity. This segment consists of direct footage from his trial in which psychologist Judith Becker, a leading expert on sexual disorders, testifies that Dahmer was indeed suffering from "mental disease," making it impossible for him to conform to the law. In graphic testimony, Dr. Beck also describes some of Dahmer's murders, his dismembering of the victim's bodies, and his performance of sexual acts with the dead bodies (a paraphilia known as *necrophilia*).
Source: CNN, 2/4/92

Critical Thinking Questions:

1. The expert witness states that Jeffrey Dahmer suffers from necrophilia, which is categorized under the paraphilias. Are his horrific acts of violence better explained by another disorder?

2. Dahmer propositioned and lured more than 15 victims to his apartment, eluded the police on at least one occasion, and committed premeditated murder for his own sexual pleasure. Was Jeffrey Dahmer truly insane or an intelligent serial killer—and why?

*Version available on the **STUDENT TOOL KIT** under the title:
Jeffrey Dahmer: Not Guilty By Reason of Insanity?

SEGMENT 116   **LAW AND MENTAL DYSFUNCTION: WHAT DID THE HINCKLEY JURORS REALLY BELIEVE? (1:58)**

Description: When a jury pronounced would-be presidential assassin John Hinckley *not guilty by reason of insanity* in 1982, millions of people decried the verdict. As it turned out, some of the jurors themselves had mixed feelings about the verdict and about their judicial options. Several of them express their concerns and their views in this news piece made within hours of the 1982 verdict.
Source: NBC News, 6/22/82

Critical Thinking Questions:

1. What percentage of "not guilty by reason of insanity" is common?

2. Should persons found "not guilty by reason of insanity" be sentenced to jail if they are later deemed sane?

3. Should John Hinckley be let out if ever deemed sane?

4. Do most jurors understand the legal and psychological issues well enough to deliver a verdict?

SEGMENT 117 **LEGAL ISSUES: HOW ARE PERSONS PREPARED FOR COMMITMENT HEARINGS? (2:33)**

Description: A patients' rights advocate at a mental hospital prepares a patient for the next day's commitment hearing, to help ensure that the individual's legal and civil rights are upheld and that his perspective and concerns are considered carefully in the upcoming decision.
Source: *Madness: In Two Minds*, 1991 (BBC Worldwide Americas Inc.)

Critical Thinking Questions:

1. What is the importance of preparing the patient for the commitment hearing?
2. Does this patient seem well enough to be released from the hospital?
3. During commitment proceedings, do most persons get committed?

SEGMENT 118 ***OUTPATIENT COMMITMENT: FORCING PERSONS INTO MENTAL HEALTH TREATMENT (6:10)**

Description: This segment focuses on the development of a legal procedure, known as "Kendra's Law" in New York, for forcing certain individuals with mental disorders into *outpatient* treatment. The effectiveness and implications of such outpatient commitment procedures are examined. The video also features input from an individual with a severe mental disorder who menaced passengers on a busy commuter train with a sword, and from his family, who discuss their experiences with mental disorders and their opinions of the outpatient commitment procedure.
Source: "A Right That Could Be Wrong" *60 Minutes* (CBS News)

Critical Thinking Questions:

1. Should mentally ill patients be forced to take medication?
2. Do police need better training for dealing with the mentally ill?
3. Are we failing persons with mental illness?

*Version available on the **STUDENT TOOL KIT** under the title:
Forcing People Into Mental Health Treatment

SEGMENT 119 **STALKING: OBSESSION OR PSYCHOSIS? (2:49)**

Description: Stalking is a major problem in our society, but as this segment clarifies, there are a variety of reasons that persons may stalk others. With the use of video examples, a psychiatrist in the video suggests that some people stalk because they cannot give up control over a person with whom they have been in a relationship, others stalk attractive or successful strangers because it makes them feel special, and still others stalk because they experience erotomanic delusions. The potential for violence by stalkers can be unpredictable, and treatment has been of limited success.
Source: "To Stop a Stalker" *48 Hours*, 1/31/99 (CBS News)

Critical Thinking Questions:

1. Is there a profile for stalkers?
2. Why do people stalk?

SEGMENT 120 ***WHEN TREATMENT LEADS TO EXECUTION: MENTAL HEALTH AND THE LAW (7:05)**

Description: This segment examines the controversy over whether a convicted murderer with paranoid schizophrenia is competent enough for execution. If his symptoms are reduced through drug treatment and he becomes clearer cognitively, he will become eligible for execution. The ethical and legal dilemmas that this poses for clinicians are explored.
Source: "Doctor's Dilemma" *60 Minutes* (CBS News)

Critical Thinking Questions:

1. Should mentally ill patients be treated with medication only to be executed?
2. If you were a clinician, would you feel any moral dilemmas by treating someone only to have them executed?
3. Was the out-of-state physician paid to render a competency decision?
4. Does this case set a dangerous precedent for other mentally ill persons on death row?

*Version available on the **STUDENT TOOL KIT** under the title:
When Treatment Leads To Execution: Mental Health And The Law